Men of Character
by Douglas William Jerrold

Copyright © 2019 by HardPress

Address:
HardPress
8345 NW 66TH ST #2561
MIAMI FL 33166-2626
USA
Email: info@hardpress.net

Men of Character

Douglas William Jerrold, William Makepeace Thackeray

3 8.

407.

3 5.

407.

MEN OF CHARACTER.

BY

DOUGLAS JERROLD.

"We must admonish thee, my worthy friend (for, perhaps, thy heart may be better than thy head), not to condemn a character as a bad one, because it is not perfectly a good one. If thou dost delight in these models of perfection, there are books enow written to gratify thy taste; but as we have not in the course of our conversation, ever happened to meet with any such person, we have not chosen to introduce any such here."

FIELDING.

IN THREE VOLUMES.

VOL. I.

LONDON:
HENRY COLBURN, PUBLISHER,
GREAT MARLBOROUGH STREET.

MDCCCXXXVIII.

407.

CONTENTS

OF

THE FIRST VOLUME.

JOHN BRITISH, in the bigness of his heart, sat with his doors open to all comers: though we will not deny, that the welcome bestowed upon his guests, depended not always so much upon their deserving merits, as upon their readiness to flatter their host in any of the thousand whims, to which, since truth should be said, JOHN was given. Hence, a bold, empty-headed talker would sometimes be placed on the right hand of JOHN—would be helped to the choicest morsels, and would drink from out the golden goblet of the host,—whilst the meek, wise man might be suffered to stare hungrily from a corner, or at best, pick bits and scraps off a wooden trencher. With all this, JOHN was a generous fellow: for no sooner was he convinced of the true value of his guest, than he would hasten to make profuse amends for past neglect, setting the worthy in the seat of honour, and doing him all graceful reverence. In his time, JOHN had assuredly made grievous blunders: now, twitting him as a zany or a lunatic, who, in after years was JOHN's best councillor—his blithe companion: now, stopping his ears at what in his rash ignorance he called a silly goose, that in later days, became to JOHN the sweetest nightingale.

John has blundered, it is true. It is as true that he has rewarded those he has wronged : and if—for it *has* happened —the injured have been far removed from the want of cakes and ale, has not John put his hand into his pocket, and with a conciliatory, penitent air, promised a tomb-stone ? To our matter :—

Once upon a time, two or three fellows—" Men of Character," as they afterwards dubbed themselves—ventured into the presence of John British. Of the merits of these worthies it is not for us to speak, being, unhappily, related to them. That their reception was very far beyond their deserts, or that their effrontery is of the choicest order, may be gathered from this circumstance : they now bring new comers—other " Men," never before presented, to the house of John, and pray of him to listen to the histories of the strangers, and at his own " sweet will," to bid them pack, or to entertain them.

Masters Pippins, Cheek, Clear, and Palms, most humbly beg places for their anxious worships,—Buff, Runnymede, Quattrino, Applejohn, and Trumps.

D. J.

Haverstock Hill,
     January, 1838.

ADAM BUFF:

THE MAN "WITHOUT A SHIRT."

CHAPTER I.

ADAM lay in bed, and with his heart in his ears, listened—listened, but heard nothing. A shadow fell upon his face; and, uttering an impatient groan or grunt, and hugging the blanket close around his neck, he swung himself, like a resolute pig, upon his side, and then sent forth a long-drawn sigh. Hapless Adam Buff!

Inexorable time, that cruel sandman, goes onward, and Adam sleeps. Oh, ye gentle ministers, who tune our dreaming brains with happy music—who feed the snoring hungry with apples fresh from Paradise—who take the fetters from the slave, and send him free as the wild antelope, bounding to his hut—who make the henpecked spouse, though sleeping near his gentle tyrant, a lordly Turk—who write on the prison walls of the poor debtor, " received in full of all demands"—whatever ye may be, wherever ye reside, we pray ye, for one hour at least, cheat poor Adam Buff! Bear him on your rainbow wings from an attic, once white-washed, in Seven Dials, to the verdant slope of the Cerra Duida; for there, saith the veracious Baron Humboldt, "shirt trees grow fifty feet high!" There, lay him down, under that most household blossom, that "hangs on the bough," and there, let him cast his gladdened eyes upwards, and see shirts, ready made, advertised on every spray. And there, to the sound of the Indian drum, let him see disporting on the grass, men and maidens clothed—for in the Cerra Duida the shirt hath no sex—in newly gathered garments, "the upper opening of which admits the head, and two lateral holes cut admit the arms!" *

(The site of the garden of Eden hath been a favourite dispute with very many theologians, all equally well informed on the subject. Dutchmen have protested that it was somewhere near Amsterdam—and Russians have been found to give their votes for the neighbourhood of Moscow: Humboldt, in his shirt tree, hath satisfactorily proved it not to be the Cerra Duida. Eden, however, brings us back to Buff.)

"Are you up, Mr. Buff?" said a voice on the outside of the door.

* See Humboldt's " Personal Narrative."

" Come in," said Adam, awakened by the querist.
The door opened, and a dry, yellowish matron
of some threescore, entered the room. From her
perfect self-possession, it was evident that she was
landlady of the domain. " Did you see the fire,
last night, Mr. Buff?" asked Mrs. Nox, the widow
of a respectable baker.

" I heard the engines," replied the philosopher.

" The sky was like the last day," said the landlady.

" It *was* red," remarked Adam.

" Poor souls !" and Mrs. Nox stood at the foot
of the bed, rubbing her hands, and looking piteously
at the nose and cheeks of Buff, as they came out in
ruby relief from a halo of blanket.

" Many burned?" asked Adam, with a slight
cough.

" It is n't known yet—but such a loss of property !
Two sugar bake-houses, a distiller's, besides the
house of a pawnbroker. Lost every thing—for I
do hear there was nothing insured," said Mrs. Nox.

" Very sad, indeed ; but this is human life, Mrs.
Nox," observed Adam, with commendable composure.

" It is indeed, Mr. Buff," and the landlady
sighed.

" Yes, this is life ! We rise early, and go to
bed late—we toil and we sweat—we scrape up and

we lay by—we trick and we cheat—we use light weights and short measures"—

"It's as true as the Bible," said the baker's widow.

"We harass our reason to its utmost to arrive at wealth—and then, when we think we have built our nest for life, when we have lined it with wool, and gilded the outside, and taxed our fancy for our best ease—why, what comes of it?—Molly, the housemaid, drops a lighted candle-snuff among the shavings—a cat carries a live coal from under the fire among the linen—the watchman springs his rattle—and, after a considerable time, engines play upon our ruin. Yes, Mrs. Nox, this is life; and as all of us who live must put up with life, grieving's a folly, Mrs. Nox." Thus spoke Adam.

"It's true—it's true, Mr. Buff—but yet to have a great deal, and to lose it all," said the landlady.

"We should always keep philosophy," said Adam Buff.

"A fire-escape?" asked Mrs. Nox doubtingly; and then, with sudden illumination—"Oh, I see—religion."

"The religion of the heathens. For my part, I feel if the warehouses had been my own, I could have looked at the devouring element, without ever forgetting myself."

"You may call it devouring, Mr. Buff,—nothing came amiss to it. Poor Mrs. Savon!"—

" My laundress !" exclaimed Adam, his feet plunging spasmodically under the blanket.

" She lived at the back — all her linen destroyed," said Mrs. Nox.

" *Her* linen !" echoed Adam Buff, turning very white. " What ! all ? — everything ?"

" Every rag," replied Mrs. Nox, with peculiar emphasis.

Adam stretched his legs, and his jaw fell. Poor plaything of malevolent fortune! Adam was precisely in the strait of an author, whose original manuscript is accidentally given to the flames, no other copy being extant. Plainly, Mrs. Savon had Adam's shirt—and Adam had no other copy. Now Buff, to give him his due, could have philosophized all day on the destruction of the sugar-houses; but the loss of his shirt went very near to his bosom. Adam lay despairing, when his good genius knocked at the door, then immediately opened it, and walked into the room ; the landlady very civilly tripping down stairs.

" I believe, sir," said the stranger, " you are Mr. Buff ?"

" I am, sir," said Adam, suppressing a shiver.

" I think it very fortunate that I find you as I do"—Adam looked a doubt—" I was fearful that you might be dressed and from home." Adam cleared his throat, and still made a cravat of the blanket. " You perceive, I have used no ceremony; it is n't my manner, sir. To begin: you are quite without incumbrance, Mr. Buff?"

" Quite," answered Adam, with much decision; and was, in his turn, about to question his interrogator on the object of his visit, when he deferred in silence to the prosperous appearance of the stranger, who—though apparently about sixty—was dressed with all the care of a beau. Twice was Adam about to speak, when his eye fell upon the white shirt-frill—ample as our great grandmother's fan—of his visitor, and a sense of inferiority made him hold his peace.

" Mr. Buff, I have heard you are a philosopher?" Adam meekly inclined his eye-lids on the blanket. " Such a man, I have some time sought. It matters not, how I have discovered you—that, in good season, you shall know. It is my wish to place in your hands a most valuable, nay, a most sacred deposit." Adam instinctively opened both his palms. " That is, if I find you really a philosopher." Adam looked a Socrates. " This morning, if you please, we'll enter on the business."

" I will wait upon you, sir, at "—

" No—no—no. I couldn't think of parting with you: when you are dressed, we'll go together," said the visitor, and Adam's face looked suddenly frost-bitten. " But, bless me ! do you rise without a fire, this weather ?"

" Man, sir," said Adam, " never so well asserts his dignity, as when he triumphs over the elements."

" Very true—and pray, don't think me effeminate ; but I always like my shirt aired," said the old gentleman.

" Mine, I hear, was aired last night," said Adam Buff, and the engines rattled through his brain— " though without my consent to the ceremony."

" Ha ! a careful laundress," said the visitor, and Adam smiled a sickly smile. " The very man, I wanted," thought the old gentleman ; then, rising from his chair, to the keen delight of Adam, he walked to the door. " Real philosophy takes little time to dress, Mr. Buff—if you please, I'll wait below," and the speaker left the room, Buff smiling benignantly on his exit.

Adam leapt from his bed, and securing the latch of the door with a friendly wooden peg, proceeded to array himself with the speed of an actor, and the simplicity of a monk, who had never dreamt of flax—the true order of sanctity, as the lives and habits of hooded saints will testify, rising not from fine linen, but rigid horse-hair. However, whilst Adam dresses—alack ! have we no other word to paint the imperfect solemnity?—we have time to explain the purpose of the visitor.

Jonas Butler was a ruddy bachelor of sixty-two—and an ardent admirer of philosophy. We will not roundly assert that he always understood the object of his admiration, but his devotion to it was no whit the less from his ignorance: nay, we question, if it was not heightened by imperfect knowledge. Philosophy was his idol—and so the thing was called philosophy, he paused not to pry into its glass eyes—to question the paint smeared upon its cheeks—the large bead dangling from its nose—and its black and gilded teeth—not he; but down he fell upon his knees, and lifted up his simple hands, and raised his pullet voice, and cried— "Divine philosophy!" Doth not the reader know some Jonas Butler? What a fortunate thing that philosophy is really so musical a word—that it smacks so full-bodied upon the tongue—and that, moreover, it may be so successfully used both in attack and defence—in coming on and in coming off! Never shall we forget its triumphant use by Mr. Butler, on one memorable occasion. A small parcel had been sent him from Yorkshire, and on arriving at the Saracen's Head, was forwarded per porter to the house of the philosopher. "My friend," said Mr. Butler, "you have brought this about two miles?" "About two." "And you wish to charge

me half as much as the carriage for two hundred —
I won't pay it." We feel our utter inability to describe the storm that here ensued—the indignation
of Mr. Butler, the abuse of the porter. At length,
when the tempest was at its height, Jonas laying his
three right fingers on his left hand, exclaimed in a
voice of deep determination — " Very well — very
well; all I say is, this, fellow—all I say is this ; I'll
pay the imposition—pay it with pleasure, if—if you
can show me the philosophy of it." The man stared
as at a magician—growled an oath—took the proffered lesser sum, and left the house. Poor simple
fellow ! he was brow-beaten by an unintelligible
phrase—for though a porter to a coach-office, he
could not describe the philosophy of an imposition !
But to the object of Mr. Butler's call on Adam.

To the old gentleman the world was one large
easy chair, wherein he might eat his venison, drink
his port, take his nap, or, when he pleased, philoso-
phise in grateful equanimity. He had, however,
one tender care—in the newly-breeched person of
his nephew, Jacob Black ; a boy whom he was determined to make a practical philosopher. " Ha !"
he would say, as he looked down upon the nascent
victim, " the statue is there, if we can but cut it
out." And Adam Buff was chosen as the moral
sculptor.

The sound of feet was just audible on the stair-

case, and Mr. Butler turning in the passage, saw
Buff stealing as softly down as though his landlady
was sick, and he feared to disturb her.   Buff was a
heavy man, and yet he trod as upon the points of
nails, and shrugged his shoulders, and vainly tried
to compose his wrinkling features.   So walks a saint
who hath lost his outer cuticle.

Mr. Butler and Adam turned into the street.
" A dreadful fire last night," said Mr. Butler.

Buff clapt his finger to the top button of his coat,
lifted the collar a little about his neck, and answered
—" very destructive, indeed."

Butler and Buff walked on.   One moment,
thoughtful reader.   Behold the pair as they recede :
could you not, even without our preface, divine
from their habits, their separate bearing, the dis-
tinctive character of each?   Look at Jonas Butler ;
a thickish, middle-sized person, in lustrous black—
his hat as smooth and jetty as a raven's wing—a line
of cambric snow above his coat—his foot, taking
the pavement as it were his own freehold—and, in
every limb and gesture of the man, self-comfort,
self-content.   Now, look at Adam ; though a full
head higher than his patron, he does not look so
tall—he does not walk, but touches the earth as if
by sufferance ; and there seems at work in his whole
frame, an accommodating meanness to lessen himself to the dimensions of his companion.   To walk

at his full height seems to him a presumption — he
bends and limps out of pure courtesy; to make
nothing of himself would be little more than to
show a due respect to his associate. Never mind
Buff's coat—that is a vulgar sign and type of
misery—heed not his hat, that hath braved as many
storms as a witch's sieve — shut your eyes to the
half-sole of the left shoe—but look at the man, or
men, and tell us, if ye do not look upon a prosperous
patron who has lured a starveling from his garret
by the savoury steam of a promised dinner. Is it
so? Yes, sir, it is. Fie, reader! fie: it is a philosopher leading a philosopher!

Walk on, Adam Buff! and for the urchin trun-
dling his hoop, now sometimes at thy side, sometimes before, sometimes behind thee; frown not on
him—he is not what he seems. No; he is not a
smutch-faced schoolboy, but fortune in disguise—
the hoop is her dread wheel; and thou, henceforth,
art her chosen leman.

" Sir,—he has not a shirt to his back!" How
often does this avowal convey the dreariest picture
of human destitution. All our sympathies are expected to be up and crying for the victim. A whole
nunnery might have wept for Adam; yet was he in
his dearest want, most rich. It is true, the conflagration of the preceding night had put our hero

to the coldest shift that poverty can lay on human flesh; and yet, like thrice-tried gold, he came forth pure and glittering from the fire !

CHAPTER II.

" Ha ! the fire !" exclaimed Mr. Butler, pausing and directing the attention of Adam to the smoking ruins. " Bless me ! very extensive, indeed," and the two stood, and meditated, though with very different feelings, on the devastation. Mr. Butler eyed the scene with the tranquillity of a philosopher who had lost nothing by the calamity; glancing at the blackened walls and smouldering rafters with admirable self-possession. Adam, however, was made of weaker flesh; for there was visible emotion in his face, as he tried to make out the attic of his laundress from the fifty domestic nooks, now laid open to the profanation of the public eye.

" A fine property but yesterday, and now," said Mr. Butler, taking snuff, " a heap of ruins."

" Gone to tinder," cried Adam, brooding on his own peculiar loss.

" Yes—it is hard, to have our household gods played upon—to see our home, filled with all home's sweets, blazing like the pile that burns the phœnix,"—observed Mr. Butler very profoundly. " To be stripped, perhaps, to the skin in this inclement season," and Butler looked on Buff, who shivered at the touching supposition. " And yet, Mr. Buff, what is nakedness, when we have philosophy ?"

Adam was about to answer in, doubtless, a deeply feeling strain, when an alarm of a falling wall suddenly brought the crowd upon him. Mr. Butler had already taken to his heels, showing that philosophy can sometimes run like an ostrich—but Buff, either not possessing so much philosophy, or having greater bulk, was slower in his motion, and thus unluckily impeded the retreat of a gigantic drayman, who revenged himself of the impediment, by dealing out to Adam an impressive blow on the cheek. Many of the mob who saw the outrage, saw that the blood of Buff was up, for he turned round, looking death and instinctively clenching his fists. " A fight ! A fight !" exclaimed the crowd in a burst of pleasure, and some providently called for " a ring." The drayman stood prepared—Mr. Butler, who had philosophically looked on, approached Adam ; it was an eventful moment for Buff, who stood breathing heavily, and measuring the figure of his assailant. " Better strip, sir," said a disinterested counsellor from the crowd—whilst another, who had stuck his tobacco-pipe in his hat-band to devote himself more entirely to the service, said in the blandest tones, his eyes twinkling up in the face of Buff—" I'll hold your coat, sir." The offer seemed to decide Adam, for he placed his hand to his top button—and when the crowd hoped to see a fine anatomy, Buff pulled still higher the collar of his coat, cast a look of scorn on the grinning drayman, and loudly proclaimed him to be unworthy of his notice. Saying which, he tried to step from the mob, who closed about him, and with derisive yells and hootings hung upon his heels. However, the reward of Buff was near; for Butler made up to him, and squeezing his hand, exclaimed, " I honour you, Mr. Buff—I reverence you ; you have shown a philosophy worthy of old Greece,"— (it was lucky for Adam, he could not show a shirt)— " you have shown yourself superior to the low and ignorant assaults of—ten thousand devils !" shouted Mr. Butler, in a higher key, and leapt like a kangaroo. And with all his philosophy, well he might ; for the individual who had offered to hold Adam's coat, having been repulsed in his kindness, had seized the hose of one of the fire-engines, and with unerring aim had deluged not only Buff, but his patron. A roar of laughter from the crowd, applauded the skill of the marksman. Mr. Butler stood dripping and melancholy as a penguin. Three times he called at the top of his voice " a constable !"

and "constable" was kindly echoed by the mob.
However, no constable appearing, Mr. Butler called
the next best thing—he called a coach. The coachman obeyed, and descending from his box, opened
the door: for a moment, however, he paused at the
reeking freight before him—however, humanity and
his fare prevailed, and he admitted the half-drowned
men, and touching his hat, and striking-to the
door, he asked if he should drive " to the Humane
Society ?"

" To —— Street," said Mr. Butler, being too
wet to understand the attempted joke. Away
rattled the coach, the wags among the crowd shouting—" do you want umbrellas, gentlemen ?" " I
say, coachman—why didn't you wring 'em before
you put 'em in ?" Mr. Butler sat as silent as the
image of a water-god; and Buff uttered no word,
but shook like a poodle new from the tub. The
coach arrived at Mr. Butler's house. " Well, sir,
what is your fare ?" asked Mr. Butler, freezingly.

" Why, sir—let me see—six shillings," said the
coachman very confidently.

" Six shillings !" cried Buff—" why, your fare is—

" I know what my fare is for passengers—but we
charge what we like for luggage."

" Luggage !" exclaimed Buff, and he looked
round for the *impedimenta*.

" Luggage. The fare itself is half-a-crown; very

well—the three-and-sixpence is for two buckets of water." Mr. Butler, not being himself, paid the money, without even alluding to the philosophy of the extortion.

" Walk in—walk in—excuse me—but a minute," said Mr. Butler, in broken syllables, shaking with cold, and preceding Buff into a most comfortable parlour, wherein a fire glowed a grateful welcome :— the host hurriedly stirred up the coals, and instantly quitted the apartment. Buff, being left alone, silently " unpacked his heart" against the ruffian who had drenched him—then eyed the fire—and every man believing that he can poke a fire better than his neighbour, again vehemently stirred it, and expanded his broad back to the benign influence of the caloric. As it crept up his anatomy, his heart dilated with hopes of good fortune ; and his ire against his enemy began to escape with the steam. " It was well for him I had no shirt," thought Adam. (Simple Buff! it was better for thyself. Thou mightest, it is true, have been declared the conqueror of a drayman—when thy very destitution palmed thee off a victor of thine own passion. The juggling of fortune ! when what seems to the unthinking world pure magnanimity, may only be a want of shirt.)

Adam stood, with all the fire at his back, and all his philosophy in his eyes. He surveyed the apartment, furnished with a most religious regard to

comfort, and thought of his own home in Seven
Dials. Struck by the contrast, in the humility of his
soul he felt for a moment a creature of a different
species to that inhabiting the nook he stood in.
" Thus it is," thought Adam, bending his melancholy eyes upon the glowing carpet—" thus it is,
one man walks all his life in a silver slipper upon
flowers, whilst another—yes another better than he,"
Adam could not suppress the comparison, " treads
upon sanded deal from the cradle to the grave.
One man is doomed to feed his eyes with luscious
pictures"—(Mr. Butler had on his walls some charming fruit-pieces)—" whilst another, turns pale at a
milk-score." These truisms were unworthy of a
philosopher—but then, Adam had had no breakfast :
they were certainly beneath a man despising all
creature-comforts, but then Buff was soaked to the
skin. This latter accident was but too evident, for
he stood to the fire, enveloped in steam : Solomon's
genii released from their brazen vessels, never rose
in clouds of denser vapour : an utilitarian would
have wept—that is, had there been any use in
tears—to have witnessed such a waste of motive
power.

" Bless me ! what a smother !" suddenly exclaimed
a feminine voice, and Buff, at the sound, cast his
coat-tails off his arms, and coughing, loomed a little
out of the surrounding fog. The speaker, seeing it

was not the chimney, but a gentleman who smoked, was about to let fall a curtsey, when Mr. Butler, entering in a hurry, prevented the ceremony. "Mrs. Black, my sister," said the host, "Mr. Buff;" and the introduction over, Mr. Butler, with a warm cloth morning-gown upon his arm, made up to his guest.——"Now, my dear sir, you had better put off your coat; you see, I—I have changed," and Mr. Butler complacently glanced at his rich ruby-coloured dressing-gown, lined with fur, to his toes—"Come, or you'll catch your death of cold," and the benignant host pressed the garment upon Adam.

"Cold, sir?" said Buff, with an inexpressible smile of contempt at the suggestion—"I hope, sir, I have learned to subdue any such weakness."

"Nay, now, I insist—you are wet through—you *must* take off your coat," said the hospitable Mr. Butler.

Buff put on a still more serious look, assuring his patron, that even if he felt the wet inconvenient— and which he further begged to assure him, he did not—still he would keep on the reeking garment as a matter of principle. "Consider, sir," said Buff, securing the top button of his coat, and bending his brow—"consider, sir, what a miserable thing is man, if a pint, nay, a quart of water is to distress him. To despise the influence of the elements has ever been my notion of true philosophy. When we think

of the Scythians, sir—of the Parthians—nay, of our
own painted progenitors, the ancient Britons—
when we reflect on their contempt of the seasons—
of the blaze of summer, and the ice of winter—how
inexpressibly little does man, that lord of all created
things, appear, creeping beneath an umbrella."

" As you please, Mr. Buff," said Butler, astonished and delighted at the stoicism of his guest,
" as you please; though I think you practise a little
too severely. For there is no certain proof that
even Diogenes did not turn up his barrel when it
rained."

" What ! won't the gentleman change his coat ?"
asked Mrs. Black with all the kind surprise of a
woman. " Why, he's very wet," and with a passing
shadow on her face, she glanced at the stream that
had meandered from the coat into the polished
steel fender. " Very wet," she repeated.

" Wet !" exclaimed Mr. Butler, unable to repress
his benevolence—" aye, I'm sure, Mr. Buff, you're
wet to the shirt."

Adam spread out his fingers over his heart, and
with a firm voice replied, " Not at all, sir; I assure
you, upon my honour—by no means."

" At all events, Mr. Buff, you'll take a little
brandy," said the philosopher in the furred gown;
and as he spoke, the brandy was brought in. Filling
himself a bumper, Mr. Butler pushed the bottle to

Adam, who, apparently unconscious of the action, filled his glass. " I assure you, Mr. Buff," and the host looked a world of meaning in the face of his ingenuous guest—" I assure you, the real spirit— there's a curious history about that brandy— I could tell you *how* I got it."

Adam was above vulgar prying; therefore, filling his glass a second time, he gravely observed—" It is worthy of remark, Mr. Butler, that there is no nation so savage—no people so ignorant as to be shut out from the light of distillation."

" Very true, Mr. Buff; it is thereby that the philosopher recognises the natural superiority of the human animal."

" From pine-apples to simplest grasses," continued Buff, calmly sipping the brandy, " man ransacks the whole vegetable kingdom for a false and fleeting enjoyment. The reflection is humiliating," and Adam emptied his glass.

Mr. Butler, absorbed by the merits of his brandy, observed—" It comes direct from France."

" It may have been broached before," said Buff, in allusion to his doctrine.

" Oh, dear no ! Don't think it—certainly not," said Mr. Butler, with some vivacity; alive to the virgin character of his liquor.   Adam bowed.

By this time, the coat of Adam, attacked by the fire without and the brandy within, became suf-

ficiently dry to insure him from the pressing in-
vitations of Mr. Butler to change it for another
garment; and although Mrs. Black continued to
look at the habit, it was not its humidity that attracted her attention.   We have before insinuated
that Adam's coat, like the cloak of the famous ale-
wife, Eleanor Rummin, immortalized by the court
poet, was—

" Wither'd like hay, the wool worn away."

Hence, the lady wondered when her brother in-
formed her that " Mr. Buff would stay to dinner."
Indeed, she ventured to cast a look of remon-
strance, instantly smiled down by the complacent
Mr. Butler, rendered more than usually genial by
French brandy and Siberian fur.

" He is a most extraordinary man—a wonderful
man," said Mr. Butler in a low voice to his sister.
" You see—you hear—a perfect philosopher,"—and
the old gentleman pointed triumphantly to Adam,
who, seated in an easy chair, his feet stretched out,
his hands in his breeches' pockets, and his mouth
open, slept and snored profoundly, his senses sweetly
shut up by strong liquor and a blazing fire.—
" See—he stands on no ceremony; though a perfect stranger, he falls asleep."

" I call it excessively rude," said Mrs. Black.

" What women think rudeness," observed Mr.

Butler, " is often the deep composure of a well-poised mind. Had that man lived in Greece—had he only lived two thousand years ago,"—

" I wish he had," said Mrs. Black, and she looked at her steel fender.

" His head would have descended to our mantel-pieces!—My dear Betsy, you have no idea of the self-denial of that man." Mrs. Black cast a feminine glance at the brandy-bottle. " None whatever—had you seen the magnanimity—the utter contempt with which he received a blow—as I live you may observe the mark on the left cheek"—

" Without returning it?" asked Mrs. Black.

" Without condescending to look at the rascal who struck him. And then, when he was wet to the skin—no, I never knew such stoicism—I never"—

At this moment, Adam awoke with a deep-mouthed yawn, and flinging his leg still further out, the heel of his whole shoe came down like an axe upon the tail of a little spaniel, that like a pad of black velvet lay at his foot, and had uncurled its threadpaper queue for the sole purpose of having it trod upon. The blow being given, the dog as in duty bound, yelped and howled like forty dogs, and its mistress instantly taking it in her arms, increased its yelping twenty fold. A common man would have been disconcerted at the mischance, the more especially as the injured party was the property of

a lady. Buff, however, was above such weakness;
for he leisurely raised himself to his full length,
and a distant room yet ringing with the cries of the
spaniel, he tranquilly remarked to Mr. Butler—
" I have often, sir, been struck by the inequality
of fortune suffered by dogs. Here is one, couched
upon a pillow—fed with chicken, sweet biscuit, and
new milk; caressed and combed and decked with
a silver collar, yea, sheltered like a baby from the
wind and rain.—And here is another, harnessed in
a truck, fed with offal or fed not at all—beat with
the stick of a cruel master"——

" Or kicked with his iron heel," said Butler, drily.

" Or kicked with his iron heel,"—repeated the
imperturbable Buff—" sleeping on stones, or"—

" Dinner is ready, sir," said the servant.

Buff immediately left the whole canine race to
their varied fortunes, and straightway followed Mr.
Butler to the dining-room, where he found a new
guest in the person of the family doctor, earnestly
pressed by Mrs. Black to stay and dine. Mr. Butler, philosopher as he was, dined just like a common
man; and though Adam Buff had shown himself
an extraordinary person under other circumstances,
at table he was very little above an average feeder.
There was but little conversation during the repast,
and that taken as a whole not more than ordinarily
interesting.

" Mr. Buff, will you favour me with a potato?
Stay, they don't seem very choice—and in the
article of potatos," said the philosophic Mr. Butler,
" I cannot admit of mediocrity."

" Right, sir; very right, sir," said Adam Buff;
and then with a severe look—" a potato, sir, like
Cæsar's wife, should not be suspected."   Many a
judge with a high character for impressiveness, has
passed sentence of death with less solemnity than
was manifested by Buff in his opinions on potatos.
But, to give Adam his due, he was one of those
rare persons who by their manner elevate and dignify whatever they condescend to touch upon.   Let
Buff talk of shrimps, and he would look so big, and
talk with such magniloquence, that it would be impossible to think *his* shrimps a whit smaller than
other people's lobsters.

The cloth removed, Buff relaxed a little from his
philosophic sternness, and in the playfulness of the
moment, proffered an almond-cake to the spaniel,
seated on the table immediately before its mistress.
The dog—says the naturalist—is a generous animal : there are, however, many exceptions to the
rule ; nor is it to be wondered at, considering the
kind of people amongst whom dogs are sometimes
brought up.   Now, Mrs. Black's spaniel was famous
for its beauty and its ill-temper; never since the
birth of folly—and we are dating before the flood—

did any living thing so presume upon its long ears. Hence, when Buff advanced a cake, the spaniel, resenting the injuries of its tail, barked most vehemently.

Mr. Butler, looking at the dog and then at Buff, said to the latter—" *Timeo Danaos, et dona ferentes.*"

" Pray, Mr. Buff, don't tease her," said Mrs. Black—" I can't answer for her temper."

" We shall be the best of friends," said Adam, who continued to press the sweet bribe upon the spaniel. Now, Adam, though, as appeared in a former page, an observer of dogs, knew not the extent of their vindictiveness. Thus, he continued to press and press the cake, whilst the eyes of the spaniel were lighted up like two topazes, and its bark grew more dissonant with use. It was only the work of an instant, but when Adam thought, in his pleasant way, to force the cake between the long white teeth of the furious little animal, the creature, stung by the new indignity, sprang forward, and bit Buff through the fleshiest part of his arm. Adam jumped up—but he swallowed the unuttered oath: Mr. Butler looked alarmed; and the professional gentleman mildly inquired " Has she bitten you, sir ?"

" I knew she would," said Mrs. Black, passing the ears of her favourite through her fingers.

" You had better take off your coat, sir, and let me look at the arm," said the doctor, and Mrs. Black, still fondling the culprit, rose to retire.

" By no means," said Adam with vivacity, and begged Mrs. Black to remain. " It's nothing— nothing at all," and, with a very pale face, he swallowed a glass of wine.

" Now, really Mr. Buff," said the host, " you push your stoicism too far—upon my word you— why, the little beast has drawn blood—yes, she has bitten through your very shirt."—

" No, no—not at all—oh, dear no," said Adam, pulling up a smile to his face; whilst Mrs. Black ceased to caress the dog, and looked seriously at Buff.

" Should the animal be mad," remarked the professional man, " I need not to a gentleman of your intelligence even hint at the consequences."

" Bless me ! Mad !   Now, really Mr. Buff, your coat must come off," said Butler, with great earnestness.

" I am sure, sir, there is nothing to be alarmed at," said Mrs. Black, having given the dog in charge to her servant to lock up — " nothing at all, yet it would be satisfactory if the doctor were only to look "—

" Don't disturb yourself about it, madam," replied Adam very blandly—" I assure you, I don't feel it."

"There is nothing like providing against the worst," said the doctor. "I can cut out the wound and cauterize the flesh, and you'll be comfortable in your mind in five minutes." Adam turned white, red, and yellow at the words.

"Certainly—certainly," said Mr. Butler—"for, only think, if the dog should be mad—now, take off your coat."—

"I am sure there is no danger, but"—urged Mrs. Black—"if she should be mad,"—

The doctor had taken out his case of instruments, and with Mr. Butler, was pressing upon Adam; who, felt it necessary to make a vigorous demonstration of his will, in order to keep his coat upon his back.

"Gentlemen — Mr. Butler," said Adam with great earnestness—"I—I am no believer"—the voice of Adam faltered——"in—in canine madness. I have no faith in it, and will submit to no operation. And even if my opinions were otherwise, I—I could not pay so ill a compliment to Mrs. Black, as to suppose a dog belonging to that lady, could by any possibility be out of its senses. I trust, sir," said Adam to Mr. Butler, at the same time throwing a side-look at his sister, "I trust, sir, that when a man takes up philosophy, it is not incumbent upon him that he should lay down gallantry." Adam delivered himself of this in a manner that silenced all opposition. Mr. Butler again took his seat at the table, again considering Adam the first of stoics : the doctor said nothing, but thought the wounded Buff the greatest of fools ; whilst Mrs. Black retired from the room, admiring in the generous stranger so wonderful a combination of the nicest delicacy with the strongest fortitude.

CHAPTER III.

" WELL, Betsy, and what is now your opinion of Mr. Buff?" Thus asked Mr. Butler of Mrs. Black the morning following the assault of the spaniel.

" I trust," said Mrs. Black, evading a direct answer, " that nothing serious will come of the bite. I'm sure I wouldn't let Mr. Buff know the dream I had just before I woke"—

" Dreams ! A man like Mr. Buff is no more to be moved by dreams than the Great Pyramid. What was the dream, Betsy?" asked the brother with ill-concealed curiosity.

" I thought that we were all walking down Aldgate, when suddenly Mr. Buff started at the pump, foamed at the mouth, and ran down Fenchurch-street, barking like a dog."

" I never knew such a practical philosopher,"

said Mr. Butler. " I have met with twenty people who could talk Zeno, but here is a man who continually acts him. You should have seen the moral majesty with which he received the blow of the drayman. A common man would have stript and fought."

" Especially of his size," observed Mrs. Black, upon whom the full figure of Adam had had its weight.

" And then to be soaked through his shirt, and think of it no more than if he had been sprinkled with lavender !"——

" He must have excellent health—yes, he must be very strong," said Mrs. Black.

" And when bitten by a filthy beast of a dog"— continued Mr. Butler——

" I have given it away," interrupted Mrs. Black.

" To think of it no more than the prick of a pin. Nineteen men out of twenty would have gone mad with the mere apprehension of madness. Mr. Buff finished his two bottles with the equanimity of a saint."

" And then his politeness," urged Mrs. Black. " To refuse to show his wound out of respect to my feelings !"

" There never was such magnanimity," said Mr. Butler.

" Or such sentiment," added Mrs. Black.

" Well then, Betsy, do you not think Mr. Buff
of all men the very man to direct and ennoble the
disposition of my nephew? Do you not think him
the very man for your son?"

Mrs. Black had a still higher opinion of Adam
Buff; she thought him the very man for herself;
and it was only three months after the introduction
of Buff into the house as philosophic tutor of the
little boy, that he became the lawful guide and instructor of his pupil's mother. About a fortnight
after the ceremony, Mr. Butler died quite unex-
pectedly.

(Does not the fate of Adam Buff prove that he
who is loved by fortune may take no care for a
shirt?)

We regret to add, that the conduct of the prosperous Adam tended to strengthen what we believe
to be the fallacy of ill-nature; namely, that men
often flourish from the very want of those merits,
for which they are accidentally rewarded.

Adam Buff had not been married six weeks, ere
he had been held to bail for beating, with very little
provocation, two watchmen and a coalheaver.—He
had discharged the favourite servant of his wife, for
having accidentally sprinkled him with about a
spoonful of clean water;—and had ordered the
Persian cat to be drowned, for that in pure playfulness, it had struck its talons through his silk

stocking, immediately stript from the leg for the eye of the family doctor. And then what a life did he lead the laundress !——" I have washed for many, many particular people," said the poor woman with tears in her eyes, " but never——never in all my life did I meet with a gentleman so particular in his shirts as Mr. Buff !"

JOB PIPPINS:

THE MAN WHO " COULDN'T HELP IT."

CHAPTER I.

PUT away temptation from the heart, eyes, ears, and fingers of Job Pippins, and behold in him a model of self-government. Born an Esquimaux, we can answer for him, he had never yearned for grape-juice—blind, carnal beauty had never betrayed him—deaf, he had given no ear to bland seductions—rich as a nabob, we are convinced he had never wished to pick a pocket. Superficial thinkers may call this negative goodness. Very well. Will they, at the same time, tell us how much character in this world of contradiction is made up of mere negatives? Consult those everlasting lights, the daily and weekly newspapers. Are not certain bipeds therein immortalized for not going upon all fours? Timbrels sounded before decent ladies and gentlemen, for that they are neither ogresses nor ogres? A duke runs into a farm-house from a pelting shower; warming his toes at the hearth, he—yes—he "talks familiarly" with his rural host! At this the historian flourishes his pen in a convulsion of delight. Was ever such condescension—such startling affability? Of course, it was expected that the distinguished visitor would command the baby at the breast to be carefully washed, and straightway served up to him in cutlets! A gentleman "behaves himself as such," and therefore let us sing to him a carol of thanksgiving. And shall gentlemen only have their negatives gilt with refined gold? Shall the great family of Pippins have no leaf to cover their nakedness? Shall there be no voice to plead for—to extenuate—to——

Here, Jenny, take away this foul black ink, vile compound of gall and acid, and bring us a honeycomb. And, Jenny, dear, relieve us of this last small handiwork of old Mulciber (that he who wrought mail for Achilles should now nib pens for stock-brokers!) and give us a feather, dropt from the wing of your pet ring-dove. So; we are in a charitable mood; our heart opens—our sympathies begin to flow. We will indite the apologetic history of Job Pippins. Yes; it shall be to us a labour of love to turn ebony into ivory.

At one-and-twenty, Job Pippins, being his own master, had little restraint to complain of. In truth, no mortal could be more indulgent to—himself; no man more readily forgive, more speedily forget, the faults and follies of his own flesh. Sorry are we to say, the benevolent example was entirely lost upon the world about him. The first important incident of Job's life will show how, in the very fulness of his hopes, he was driven from his native town—slander, like a mortal snake, hissing at his exiled heels. At once to begin our domestic tragedy.

Sir Scipio Mannikin was the pearl of men. The purity of three maiden aunts was incarnated in a masculine tabernacle. Yes—in Sir Scipio a leash of spinsters lived again. Should sceptics doubt, let them read the printed wisdom of Mannikin at Quarter Sessions, and acknowledge the metempsychosis. Briefly; the only remarkable difference between the knight and any of the three immaculate maidens may be defined in one short word—shaving. Happy had it been for Job had Sir Scipio shared in the same contempt of the operation with his lamented female relations!

Profoundly certain are we of the happiness—the calm, the complete joy—of the young Lady Scipio Mannikin. How could it be otherwise? Thirty years younger than her husband, she could gather, in the spring of life, the golden fruits of autumn. Was she too vivacious?——her wild sallies were checked and guided by the hand of experience; was her heart ever and anon about to run from her mouth?—a look from Sir Scipio would freeze it at her lip. Did she talk idly of the beauties of this world?—her moralizing spouse would convince her that, saving his own estate and his own person, the whole earth was but one large dunghill, and the men and women miserable worms crawling in it. Thus mated, we hear the silver voices of our female readers cry, " Happy, happy Lady Mannikin !"

We are convinced that it was only a combination of the rarest accidents that filled the house of Sir Scipio with the choicest of all things : his very doorposts, if we may use the figure, were greased with the fat of the land. He had the best cook—the rarest wines—the handsomest horses—the most superb wife ! It is a pleasure to know this : it is a consolation to all who, like ourselves, wish to look curiously into the hearts of men, to find the temperate and the unworldly thus appointed—to see them thus providentially rewarded. You will hear a good, lowly creature sing the praises of pure water —call it the wine of Adam when he walked in Paradise—when, somehow, fate has bestowed upon the eulogist the finest Burgundy. He declares himself contented with a crust—although a bene-

ficent fairy has hung a fat haunch or two in his
larder.   And then, for woman, he asks—what is
all beauty but skin-deep?   Behold the lawful bed-
fellow of the querist; why, destiny has tied to him
an angel—a perfect angel, save that, for a time, she
has laid aside her wings.   Our heart thumps, and
our blood glows, when we find the lowly thus recom-
pensed.   Yes; it is delightful to see these humble
folk, who tune their tongues to the honour of dry
bread and water, compelled, by the gentle force of
fortune, to chew venison and swallow claret !

" A steady, respectable young man ?" asked Sir
Scipio of his butler, with a searching look.

" They say, Sir Scipio, the lightest hand in the
county."

" A lad of morality ?"—

" He skims a beard off like froth."

" A dutiful son, and a peaceful neighbour ?"—

" Lady Bag says he dresses hair like any mermaid."

" He may come."

And Job Pippins was straightway summoned to
shave Sir Scipio Mannikin ! Job crossed the
threshold, and the *lares* of Mannikin Hall gave a
feeble wail.   However, weeks passed on, and Job
reaped new laurels with Sir Scipio's beard.   His
hand swept softly as the sweet south along the
stubbled chin, and played like any butterfly about

a peruque. That consummate genius should ever lack self-government !

About this time a domestic accident occurred to Lady Scipio—she suddenly lost her maid. The girl had been found guilty of receiving a valentine, "a filthy thing," in the words of the knight, " with two hearts on one arrow, a couple of disgusting pigeons at the top, and loathsome love-verses at the bottom. A person who could receive such things was not fit to be about Lady Scipio." Kitty White —to the regret of her mistress——was thrust from Mannikin Hall. And what is most extraordinary, the poor girl—albeit her suspicions fell upon two or three—could not, to her dying day, precisely determine who had ruined her.

Indignant virtue is ever heedless of worldly consequences; otherwise Sir Scipio had retained the delinquent for at least another day, for Kitty was wont to raise to herself a crown of glory in the hair of her mistress, which she displayed with a taste only inferior to that of the superb Pippins himself. Now it so happened, that the day following the departure of the wanton maid, was appointed by Sir Scipio for a solemn festival to the stomachs of the heads of the neighbouring clergy : for a week past two turtles, in the kitchen of the knight, had lain upon their backs, resignedly awaiting the destroyer. Out of pure respect to his guests, Sir Scipio wished his

lady to appear in all her brightness.   It was provoking that the guilt of Kitty had not remained
unknown until after the feast !   There was no remedy ; for once, at most, the tresses of Lady Scipio
must fall into a masculine hand.   Yes ; Job Pippins—(again the *lares* squeaked and shuddered)—
must dress the hair of Lady Mannikin !

Now, in those days, ladies wore powder.

CHAPTER II.

WE now approach the fall of Job.   We have deferred as long as possible his ignominy—accident,
we should say—but it is in vain to procrastinate,
and so, we at once produce this Tarquin with a
razor.   Compose yourselves, dear ladies, but—but
enter Job Pippins !

"Upon my faith, a very handsome young man—
a most genteel youth ! There is a delicious wickedness in his face—ha !—the rogue has an eye like
a hawk.   A very proper young fellow !"

But, madam, you forget—we called him a—a—
Tarquin !

"No doubt, sir—no doubt.   A very charming
young man."

(Now we really did think that our maiden aunt

knew at least the heads of Roman history. To be sure, she is at times a little deaf. Thus, when we pronounced—Tarquin, she may have thought we said—Adonis.)

" A perfect figure—neither too tall, nor too short," says the Dowager Lady Maudlincourt, looking at Job with the eye of a drill serjeant; " erect as a staff, and elastic as a cane." And the judgment of the dowager has passed into a proverb : no woman was ever so celebrated for the legs of her footmen.

Behold Job in the library of Sir Scipio, who had somewhat fantastically determined that his lady should receive our hero in that ark of learning, the husband himself sitting leering by. The tresses of Venus were unbound, and—oh, character ! and oh, daily bread ! But let us not anticipate. Job, with steady hand and innocent thoughts, proceeded in his task. He saw that Lady Scipio was awfully beautiful; and a feeling of reverence pervaded his fingers as they moved about her lovely head. He touched her hair as though it had been her heart-strings; and here and there disposed a curl at her neck, as if he laid a jewel worth a million there. Sir Scipio held in his hand Boetius, and in his eye Pippins.

And still Job lingered at his task, and still he felt his terrible trial. He seemed petrified by what the historians of weddings call—the novelty of his situation. To have beheld Lady Scipio and the barber, you would have thought that Diana had at a word called from a block of marble the bloodless image of filthy man, to dress her golden hair—a senseless statue, made and animated for the nonce.

" Mr. Springe," said a servant, half opening the door.

" I'll—yes—I'll come to him," answered Sir Scipio, and he quitted the library. As he left it the sun, which until that moment had thrown a blaze of light upon the Mannikin arms emblazoned in the windows, withdrew its glorious beam.

Already did Job approach the termination of his trials; already was he within a moment of deliverance, when the enemy of man made him his own. The locks of Lady Scipio were duly curled—and bound—and placed;—already was her head a thing for Phidias, when the last ineffable grace was to be showered upon it—when the " new fallen snow" of the powder-puff was to descend, like odours shaken from the wings of a thousand little loves. Lady Scipio held her mask to her face, and Job Pippins took the powder-puff in his hand !

Job walked twice or thrice around her ladyship and trembled. He tried to puff, but his unsteady hand, in fitful gusts, sent forth the powder above, below, about, but not upon the head. Again, Job

addressed himself sternly to his purpose; he gave a
" hem !" calling up resolution to his heart, and
nerves to his fingers. Again, like a lion in a den,
he made a circuit, breathing hard for virtuous self-
possession. Never—never was barber so tempted!
Be the reader judge.

We said Lady Scipio help a mask to her face;
we told not the truth. It is most certain that she
covered her forehead, eyes, and nose, with a little
black vizard, but then—her lips !——her lips were
ripe, red, and naked to the eye as the lips of Eve.
And these, pouting apart, and breathing Araby to
the senses of Job, said, in their delicious rud-
diness, a thousand, thousand things the tongue
could never utter. And then the eyes, the watchers
of the treasure, were closed !——the fruit seemed every
instant to grow towards the hand, and the awful
dragons were asleep! Nevertheless, Job tried to
puff.

Man of flesh can do no more. Ay, well done,
Job; puff, and turn thine eye from the peril. That's
right—look at the bust of Seneca; banish the weakness crying in your heart, by the force of lofty
thoughts. Very good; cast another glance towards
that thin folio in vellum. That, Job, is " Thomas
à Kempis," a capital tome for men in thy condition.
Good again; let thine eyes shun the balmy evil, and
feed upon " the whole Duty of Man." Ha, Job!

now, indeed, hast thou triumphed—now art thou safe from the tempter. Yes, Job; puff—puff—but keep thine eyeballs fixed upon Plato! What a god-like head, eh, Job? What strength—yet what serenity in that magnificent brow! Yes; Plato, Job—Plato is—

" Smack"—" sma-a-ck "—" sma-a-a-a-ck !"

Astounded reader, will it be believed—was ever such effrontery, such hardihood known? We have heard of robbery beneath the gallows—of pockets picked with the fruit of picking pockets swinging in sight of the incorrigible thief—but that a man, with Plato in his eye, should commit a carnal sin with his lip !—

Would we could show how Job Pippins kissed Lady Scipio Mannikin! Does the reader recollect the first four or five quick, sharp, splitting notes of the blackbird, pounced upon a worm—shrieking, whistling, exulting, hysterical? No; they want rapidity, intensity, volume. In our despair, we must even put up with the words of one of the housemaids, who, albeit, she was spared a sight of the operation, vowed that Job " tore up kisses by the very roots !" We fear, too, that the description of the maid may be thought obscure; however, we hope we know when to prefer feminine impressions to our own. And now, gentle reader, it is our most painful duty to call your attention to a family pic-

Vol I. Page 43.

THE FALL OF PIPPINS.

Published by Henry Colburn, Great Marlborough Street 1836.

ture.   The last kiss is doubtless still ringing in your ears, and the roof-tree of Mannikin Hall still vibrating with the claps of kisses.

Imagine, most imaginative reader, a woman, young and lovely, starting at some loathsome thing: say, a boa at once.   Her arms flung up—her lips wide apart—her eyes full of horror—her bosom compressed by a loud, loud shriek—about to come! Such is Lady Scipio.

Next, behold a very comely young man at her feet—his hands clasped and shaking—his jaw dropt —his eyelids down—and his knees grinding the floor, in the desperate hope of falling through! Such is Job Pippins.

Now, attentive reader, look to the right, and you will see at the door a portly gentleman of fifty—his face, generally a lightish purple, is now a favourable black.   Indeed his present colour, supported by a flattened nose and voluminous lips, for a brief moment make Lady Scipio a Desdemona.   Such is the knight—such the outraged spouse!

Glaring over the shoulders of Sir Scipio are two sea-green eyes, the curious property of Samuel Springe, the man of business—a sort of human lurcher—to the lord of the Hall.

One eye, and only a part of the nose of the footman, are visible between the arm of Sir Scipio and the door-post.   Though but fragments, they speak volumes.

Brief was the horrid pause.   Sir Scipio—speechless and champing foam—seized the presented stick of Springe; and, raising it high in air, the skull of Job had been no better than a crushed egg-shell—had not the uplifted weapon happily caught the projecting prongs of an enormous pair of antlers hanging over the door.   Thoughtless of the impediment, Sir Scipio flung his whole weight upon his arm—Springe pressed forward—the footman, " eager for the fray," was no less impetuous, when —with a thunder that seemed to shake the steadfast earth—down came the honours of the chace—down fell the horns; and, assisted by Springe and the footman behind, down fell Sir Scipio upon them !   Then indeed his lady shrieked; and well she might.   Would not any woman scream, seeing her husband all but gored to death by his own antlers ?

Sir Scipio roared and screamed, whilst Springe and the footman, like kind friends, strove to relieve him of the horns; but, somehow, the more they tugged, the more Sir Scipio became entangled. The whole mansion was alarmed—servants of both sexes thronged to the spot—the family at the next house threw up their windows—and still poor Sir

Scipio was as firmly fixed to the antlers, as though they were a part and parcel of his natural person. And then, roaring to be left to himself, when that indulgence was allowed him, he freed his body of the forky incumbrance with incredible dexterity.

(Reflecting reader, if ever the accident of Sir Scipio happen to thee, bawl not—groan not—speak not—lest thy misfortune be published to assisting friends and curious neighbours.)

The knight, with his clothes in very strips, fell into what was called his easy-chair. Pippins—with unheard of stupidity, he had not taken to his heels —dropt upon his knees, and the spectators—their ears opening like hungry oysters — formed in a ring!

Sir Scipio seemed, for a moment, to borrow the orbs of his man of business; and heavily turning his majestic head, as though a weight had newly fallen there, he looked with very green eyes at his crimsoned wife, dyed that hue with fear—with agitation for her spouse. And then the knight, turning to Job Pippins, and lifting up a forefinger——

Had Sir Scipio been the spirit of ague—his forefinger the little wand with which he shook the bones of nations, Job had not trembled more vehemently as he looked upon it. People may judge somewhat of his emotion, when we state that the three shillings and sixpence in his left waistcoat-pocket jingled

very audibly.   The man himself might have acted
the hypocrite, but who shall doubt the feeling declared through gold and silver ?

And Job trembled—and his voice rattled in his
throat—and, at length, shaking with compunction,
yet sharpened to a scream by the intensity of its
purpose, it cried, " I—I—I—couldn't help it !"

And Job Pippins could *not* help it.

CHAPTER III.

WHAT is man, woman, or even child, without
character ? The skeleton in the closet of an anatomist is less loathsome—hath stronger claims on our
consideration—our sympathy.   No matter though
it be the bony outline of a condemned rogue ; the
penalty has been paid, and with commendable
charity we bear no malice towards the departed.
Such was the placability of Sir Scipio.—With a
proper abhorrence of crime, he would hang the
knave who should steal an apple, and then, with a
fine converting morality, utter a religious discourse
on his relics—on mortal weakness, temptation, and
the last account.   Whether Job feared this double
purpose of the knight—or, whether, urged by his
affrighted conscience, he fled the town, we care not

to enquire. This, however, we know; some fortnight after the affair at the Hall——(by some it was
called an assault, by some an intended elopement;
whilst some swore that, but for the kindness of Sir
Scipio, Job had been trussed at the assizes)——the criminal was snugly ensconced in the chimney-corner
of the Hare-and-Hounds, a sufficiently respectable
alehouse some ten miles from Job's native town.
It had been his determination to travel straight to
London; but Sally, the daughter, stood at the door
of the inn, and——how could he help it?——he entered.
Job possessed in no mean degree three things—according to Heloise—most dangerous to the sex; he
wrote well, talked well, and sung well. Hence, his
reputation in divers kitchens; and as he was one
of those wise people——

> " Qui ne trouvent le laurier bon,
> Que pour la sauce et le jambon,"—

or, as we would nervously translate it—

> " Who think the bays not worth a damn,
> If flav'ring not some sauce or ham,"—

Job was content to take his reward from the spit:
and, after all, how much of what is thought by idle
people fame, is merely sought for as the representative of so many legs of mutton! We may
make fame an angelic creature on the tombs of
poets; but really how often do bards invoke her as

a bouncing landlady? Yes, yes—and let the truth be fearlessly whispered at the graves of fifty of the laurelled—the noblest niche is the larder. Let us not forget Job.

A few days after the arrival of our fugitive at the inn, he possessed not a penny; and having, for at least a week, lived on his accomplishments, his landlord began to cast significant looks towards the door. It was three o'clock and Job had not dined. With his nose flattened against the window-pane, Job sat with his eye fixed upon an opposite mile-stone (" 120 miles to London,") when who should amble up to the house but Cuttles, the clerk of Job's parish. Job felt himself dipt in cold water.

" I was mortal certain I should find him here," cried a voice that to Job seemed to saw through the very wainscot. " Service to ye, Miss Sally,— nobody run away with you yet? Well, well—stop till I'm young again, and"—and what was to be the consequence to Sally, Job heard not; but in another second the door opened, and he heard in the sweet twang of his native town—

" So, Mr. Pippins !"

The speaker was a stringy little man of about fifty; with one of those faces which have but two definite expressions, frowning command and sim-pering servility. On the present occasion he wore his hardest look; which, nevertheless, was not so terrible as the fright of Job would indicate. But the fact is, Job saw not Cuttles in his physical truth; no, he heard the greeting of the clerk, and before his eyes appeared the executioner of the county, holding in his ready hand a massive chain of wedding-rings; each syllable uttered by Cuttles was a rattling of the links. Conscience is terribly imaginative. Job, it will be seen, had good cause for his perturbation.

" Well, Job, as what is done can't be undone," (now, whence Cuttles had culled this fragment of philosophy we know not; for in his day, it was not used by all fathers and guardians at the end of all farces), " we must make the best of the matter." Job whistled. " Now, Job, I come to you as a friend; and so, from first to last, tell me how it all happened." The parish-clerk crossed his knees, having edged his chair towards the offender.

" She was always a bold thing," said Job, sullenly.

" Ha !" cried Cuttles, and he gaped as though he was to hear with his mouth. " Well ?"

" And one fine evening last June, as I was leaning looking into the churchyard—I'd been to shave Mrs. Dodds's poodle—I shaved Dodds when he died—I—I—" Job, wheeling round, looked very gravely in the face of Cuttles, and asked, in even a tone of solemnity, " Did you ever taste the ale at this house ?"

Cuttles evidently knew something of the human heart; for, without a reply, he knocked and cried, " Sally, a mug of ale." Pippins meekly added, " the best."

" Yes; you were staring into the churchyard," suggested Cuttles, as Job set down the emptied mug.

" Why, the poodle brought it into my head, and I was looking for Dodds's stone, when she came behind me, and said, ' Job, you merry tinker' "—

Cuttles stared, and pushed his chair away, " She never was so familiar ?"

" Wasn't she ?" cried Job, with something like a groan, and a look of bitterness. " Wasn't she ?"

" But what expressions ! Well, there is no knowing any of 'em," observed the parish-clerk.

" Like bees—you never see their sting till you feel it," cried Pippins. " ' Well, Job,' said she, ' you merry tinker,' "—again the parish-clerk, like a monkey watching for nuts, lifted up his eyebrows, " ' give me a kiss !' And saying no more, she threw her arms about my neck, and gave me such a salute, a team two fields away went gallop off at the noise."

" And so meek—so modest—so delicate !" cried the wondering Cuttles. " Well, Job, if all this be true, you have been hardly used. However, being come upon the business, I must hear all. And after that, Job,"——

" After that, I—you wouldn't think it, Master Cuttles," said Job, with a confidential air—" but, upon my honour, Sally's father not going out, I hav'n't used my teeth since seven this morning."

Cuttles, with mysterious generosity, ordered something to eat, whilst Job timidly pressed the mug on the notice of Sally, who, with incredible speed, produced cold fowl and ham, and a new supply of " the best" ale. Whilst Job employed his teeth, Cuttles filled up the pause with brandy and water. Hunger and thirst somewhat abated, Cuttles returned to the examination. " Well, Job, she kissed you, you say, and after that?"——

" Mr. Cuttles," said Job, and the clerk stared at the altered tone of the speaker, " I don't see why you should be so curious—you may take away, Sally—I know the worst, and there's an end of it."

" The worst!" echoed Cuttles. " I've brought you twenty pounds."

" I tell ye, Cuttles, it's no use. I'll shoulder walnut first."

" Walnut!"

" Ay, go for a soldier. A drum before her tongue. Four words are as good as a thousand— I won't marry her."

" Marry—marry Lady Mannikin !" and the parish-clerk stared, confounded.

" Why, Cuttles, didn't you mean—eh—didn't you come about Susan Biggs?"

" Phoo !—(by the way, we have made Joe, the boy at the White Horse, marry her; yes, he had five pounds and a leg of mutton dinner)—I come about the affair with her ladyship."

" I—I couldn't help it," said Job, evidently relieved by the information of the clerk. " I suppose all the world abuse me?"

" It was very wicked, but you have friends, Job." Pippins looked doubtingly. " It certainly was not right, after the kindness of Sir Scipio, to seek to deprive him of her ladyship,"—Pippins gaped—" to seduce the wife of your patron,"—Pippins stared—" to take advantage of his confidence to fly with her to a foreign land—to—"

" Mr. Cuttles !" roared Job, striking the table, and leaping to his feet.

" However," continued the clerk, unmoved by Job's vehemence—however, there are Christian souls who feel for you. A committee of ladies have taken your case into their consideration ; and though they doubtless think you a most shocking person—indeed, after the hearsay evidence, there can be no doubt of the guilt of both of ye—they send you by me, as a trifling mark of their compassion, twenty pounds."

" Twenty pounds !" echoed the bewildered Pippins.

" And more," continued Cuttles; " Miss Daffodil, the chairwoman of the committee, bade me say, that should Sir Scipio, preparatory to a divorce, take the matter into court, the damages, whatever they might be, should be defrayed; that though you were a dangerous, wicked man, you should be held harmless."

" Twenty pounds—court—damages !" exclaimed Pippins, in a running breath. " What *do* you mean ?"

" Pish !" answered the clerk, with a wink, and emphatically thrusting his fore-finger into the belly of Job; " pish ! Now, hearken, lad; don't think to leave us; come back; take a better shop; and, my word for't, this little matter about her ladyship will bring ye treble custom."

" Do you think so?" asked Pippins, after a pause.

" Certain; and if Sir Scipio should only bring his action for crim. con."——

" Crim. con. !" shrieked Pippins.

——" Your fortune is made." So saying, Cuttles, with a sagacious nod, finished his brandy and water; then, drawing his breath, looked benevolently at Pippins.

Job was puzzled; again he asked, but with deeper seriousness, " Mr. Cuttles, what *do* you mean ?"

" There—there's the twenty pounds; you, of course, will pay the reckoning;" and Cuttles, indifferent to the question, put down the money. " And now, Job, you rogue, do tell me the whole matter;" and the clerk rubbed his hands, with epicurean anticipation. " Tell me—you and your ladyship were going to France? I hear the servants say France; nay, that the postilion—but come, Job"——

" Mr. Cuttles, losing my wits, I do confess I kissed Lady Scipio Mannikin; I—I—couldn't help it; and then"——

" Yes, yes; and then"——

" And then, as though I had done murder, I fell upon my knees; and then, Sir Scipio coming in, had well-nigh ended me; and then, I found myself flung out of the door; and then—and here I am. For her ladyship, they who speak a word against her are cowards and villains."

" Then it isn't all true?" asked the clerk, staggered by the earnestness of Job.

" The Lord forgive all liars !" cried Job, " there's nothing true but what I've said."

" And there was nothing—nothing but a stolen
kiss ?"

" Nothing !" vociferated Job, in so loud a tone
that Sally and her father rushed into the room.
" Nothing !" and Job solemnized his assertion with
an oath.

Immediately, Cuttles snatched the twenty pounds
from the table, and took his hat.   " As such is the
case, Mr. Pippins—as there has been no ingratitude—no violence—no seduction in the affair—I
shall take back the money to the ladies.   As they
have subscribed under misrepresentation, the cash
must certainly be returned to them."   And in three
minutes, the clerk was in the saddle, trotting home-
wards to lay his stewardship before the committee.
We have heard that the discretion of the clerk was
for a long time an applauded theme at the very
best tea-tables.

" What a fool to speak the truth !" said the
landlord, when he had learned the story.   " What
a fool !"

Job coloured to the eyes, and raising himself to
his full height, said, with a certain air of pride—
" Master Nip, I couldn't help it."

CHAPTER IV.

" 109 to London."

Yea, mile-stones to the penniless adventurer are serious things.   To yourself, prosperous reader, now carried post onward, and now comfortably seated on Jessy, your mouse-coloured mare, mile-stones are no more than so many unseemly lumps of granite; but how different to the poor traveller, with his unpatronized face turned, for the first time, towards that land of milk and money—London ! Worked on by his hopes or fears, every stone that leads him nearer to the goal, speaks better or worse tidings; nay, may to his fancy assume the face of kindly greeting or squint-eyed scorn.   Thus, every block may be as of a long line of squab, uncouth guards, such as we see in Arab fairy-land, each growing in hideousness upon its neighbour : and thus, more and more scared by the low brows, hanging lips, and savage eyes of the petrified figures, the foot-sore traveller feels his courage fail and his heart fairly die within him, as he passes the last terrible dwarf, and snuffs the smoke of the mysterious city.   Think of it, ye poets !   If, as the great teacher says, there be sermons in smallest pebbles, what profound thoughts, what glorious images, what ennobling, sweetening sympathies may be struck from out a London mile-stone !

" 109 to London." Job Pippins sat upon the stone, staring at the sinking sun. The sun sank, and Job turning his head, saw the London waggon—like a plethoric elephant—slowly approaching him. In an instant, he was greeted by the waggoner with loud cries for help. He ran to the waggon, and to his astonishment saw the bay cob of Sir Scipio Mannikin tied behind. Ere Job could put a question, the waggoner showed his teeth and scratched his head, with an air of satisfaction; " I say, I ha' got a dead man in waggon."

" A dead man !" cried Job, with more horror than curiosity. " A dead man !"

" Picked un up, in middle of road ; the cob war standin' loike a lamb beside un. I shall tak' un to next house, the Barley Mow."

" For God's sake, stop !" exclaimed Job, and jumped into the waggon. In an instant he recognised the all but departed knight. Struck by apoplexy, he had fallen from his horse. In less than a minute, Job had torn off Sir Scipio's coat, bound his arm, and produced a razor, the waggoner looking silently and serenely on. However, when he beheld the weapon, he asked—" What wilt do, mun ? what wilt do ?"

" Bleed him," replied Job, with exquisite composure. " I fear his heart has stopped."

" Loikely—I do think it be Grinders, the lawyer of ——. Cut un deep;" and the waggoner opened his eyes to watch if the lawyer really had red blood, or japan ink. " Cut un deep," he cried encouragingly, " though if it be Grinders, by what I hear, it be a shame to disturb un."

" Grinders! pshaw, 'tis Sir Scipio Mannikin."

" Wounds!" roared the waggoner, " noa, mun, noa; don't meddle wi' such folks in my waggon." Saying this, he sought to stay the hand of Job, at the moment applying the razor to the arm of the sufferer; but in so attempting, drove the weapon half through the limb. Job turned pale, and the waggoner groaned and trembled. " We shall be hanged, mun, hanged — hanged — hanged!" he shouted forth, and corroborating echo blandly repeated—" hanged—hanged—hanged." The waggoner untied the cob, mounted it, and galloped away like any St. George, leaving Pippins in the twilight with his lacerated patient. The blood flowed, and Job began to count the pulsations of the apoplectic knight, who in about ten minutes came to a kind of consciousness; for beholding Job standing over him with a drawn razor, he started back, and his teeth chattered. At this instant, the gallop of horses was heard, and Job looking out, beheld the waggoner flying along on the knight's cob, followed *sed haud passibus æquis,* by a barb, which, from its height, points, and wooden paces, was doubtless descended from the famous steed of Troy, carrying a short round man, in a broad-brimmed hat, who, at a distance, looked like a black cushion on horseback. Providentially, as the knight afterwards observed, the landlord of the Barley Mow had broken his leg correcting his wife, and had called in Doctor Saffron, who, providentially again, happened to be Sir Scipio's surgeon. Doctor Saffron took up the wounded arm, and looked at Job—" Is this your doing?" Job looked yes, but spoke not. " Miracles do happen in our art, Sir Scipio," said Saffron consolingly, " so perhaps the arm may be saved. Bleeding, fellow !" he cried, turning fiercely upon Job—" I call it capital carving."

" I—couldn't help it," said Pippins, and he wiped his razor.

" Humph ! you found Sir Scipio lying in the road?" said the doctor.

" Rolled up loike a hedge-pig," said the waggoner.

" Ha !" and the doctor caught the eye of the knight—" Ha !" he shook his head three times—" Ha ! turtle—turtle !"

The waggoner stared, for how was he to know that Saffron alluded to a turtle-feast (we have be-no hospitable countenance. Job briefly enumerated his wants. Had he talked to a grim head carved in oak, he had moved it just as soon to sympathy. Its owner drew back, and was about to fling-to the door with emphatic denial, when his eye gleamed, and his mouth widened into a grin, and passing his horny fingers through his grey wiry hair, he cried, " Humph! It's cold, too—well, come in. Moll, the stool." The thing ordered was "quoited" at Job, who sank resignedly upon it, expanding his breast, and spreading out his palms to a roaring coal and wood fire. Job tried to look at the best possible ease; and yet the place in which he found himself, and the group surrounding him, were not calculated to possess him of calm luxurious feelings.

The walls of the hut were formed of wattles, coated with mud; the whole roughly roofed with thatch and furze. It seemed a hovel raised for a season—a place thrown up by stealth; a cabin for a Timon or a coiner. The furniture was of a mixed kind: on a table made of rough deals was an elegant draught-board of ebony and mother-of-pearl; beside it a small Etruscan bronze lamp; the stool, hospitably awarded to Pippins, was the only legitimate seat; the three masters of the dwelling—for each seemed magisterial—supporting themselves on empty casks. In one corner lay various articles of clothing on a heap of straw, dry leaves, and rushes

—cloaks, coats, jackets, some of them evidently made for others than their present possessors. Job looked at the opposite wall, where a large fragment of mirror—Eve had her fountain, Molly her looking-glass—held by nails driven into the baked mud, showed him his company. As he looked—despite his vivacity and constitutional courage—Job somewhat desponded, yea, did once or twice shift himself uneasily, as a fresh-whipped schoolboy, on his form. Truly Job saw no " wreathed smiles" to comfort and assure him. The man, the elder of the three, who let him in, was of middle stature; a fellow with the eyes and beak of an eagle, and the throat of a bull; he sat with his arms squared upon the table, leaning his chin upon his hands; he looked like a wild beast couching ere it springs. He wore a loose white flannel jacket, old leathern breeches, and a striped shirt, which, open at the neck, his broad tanned chest looked like a worn hide. And so sat Phineas and glared at Job.

Bats and Mortlake were much younger than their friend—ay, let us say, friend Phineas. Bats was ugly to a merit. His face was scarlet, as if newly flayed; his eyes small and weak, one of them ever glancing at his nose, that turned a widened nostril up to meet it; his teeth were scattered, and stood like rusty broken nails; his brow he might have covered with his two fingers, and hair of vivid red, in close, lumpy curls, terminated the prospect. This Gorgon, be it noted by the way, had dared to look at Molly; and to him she became as stone. Mortlake, the junior of the three, had a reckless, gipsy look, that might have been called handsome, but for the scowl that too frequently darkened it. The pair sat, now glancing at Job, and now at Phineas, whose sudden hospitality had evidently puzzled them. A pace from these stood Molly, leaning, with folded arms, against the wall. There was something wild, nay, even dangerous in her demeanour, but nothing vulgar. She had the figure of a huntress—tall, round, and finely developed. Her eyes were black as death and swift as light; her dark hair hung in long curls down her cheeks and back, bringing into fine relief the pale, yet perfectly healthy flesh. Her swelling, disdainful lip showed a glimpse of teeth white as whitest curds. Job gasped as he caught her face in the glass; a queen in her coronation robes had not so much awed him; she seemed so strange a mixture of the angel and the devil. Silence having continued to a painful time, Bats, in the depth of his humanity, tried to lead the conversation. " What's o'clock ?" he asked.

At this instant, the silver sound of a repeater was heard in the hut, and at the same moment Job jumped to his feet, and pulled from his waistcoat-pocket a splendid gold watch. He held it in his hand, looking amazement. The eyes of Bats and Mortlake glistened as they leered at the chronometer; Phineas showed no surprise, having marked the splendid chain and seals dangling from Job's pocket ere he entered the hovel. " I say, friend," said Phineas, calmly, " time must be worth something to you, to score it with such a watch as that."

" It isn't mine," cried Job, and the perspiration broke upon his forehead. " It isn't mine."

" Ha! ha! ha!" and the three laughed at the unnecessary information.

" A mistake," cried Pippins. " I got it in the oddest way, but I couldn't help it—I tell you it isn't mine!"

" Ha! ha! ha!" again roared Job's hearers.

" I—oh Lord!—I shall be hanged," said Pippins to himself.

" To be sure," observed Mortlake, comfortingly, " and some day we all shall. Then why the devil should *you* make such a fuss about it."

" These gentlemen," said Molly, with a wicked smile, " are so particular."

" You can't think how I came by it!" exclaimed Job, and again the fellows chuckled in derision. Job hastily felt his pockets, lest he had unwittingly other of his neighbour's goods about him, when he pulled out a handkerchief fairly soaked with Sir Scipio's blood. At sight of this, Phineas rose with a grave look, Mortlake gave an expressive chuck with his tongue, and Bats uttered a low, long, expressive whistle.

"What! he was game, was he? Well, as it's all over now, tell us," said Phineas, "how it happened."

"First tell us," broke in the cautious Bats, "where's the body?"

Vain was it for Job to persist in the truth——vain to dwell minutely on the operation performed on the knight——or the accident which had transferred the watch from the fob of its lawful owner to the waistcoat-pocket of its present possessor;——all he said was only met with increasing peals of laughter. "Well, gentlemen," said Job, half-nettled by their merriment, half-fearing their nods and looks, "dark as it is, and long as the road may be, I shall set out for Mannikin Hall. Sir Scipio at least must believe that I only borrowed his watch to count his pulse." Saying this, Job made for the door; when Phineas, setting his broad back full against it, remarked, with provoking gravity, "Travel to-night? You don't know who you may meet: how do you know you mayn't be robbed?" "Yes," said Bats, "you'd better stay with us, there's a great deal of opposition on this road." And without waiting for

a reply, Phineas made fast the door, crying, whilst engaged in the task, " Molly, the gin !"

In brief time, the unresisting Job found himself again upon his stool, a horn of gin drawn by the hand of Molly between his fingers, Molly herself, with her large lustrous eyes melting on him, on his knee, and his three new friends ranged before him. The wind grew louder without, and the fire ruddier and warmer within—the faces of the three hosts, as the light played upon them, in a short time looked to Job faces of the jolliest, frankest dogs that ever emptied pitcher—the mud walls lost their darkness—Molly lost her scorn—and Job found his voice.

" Another horn—one more," cried the princely Phineas, " and the song will melt in your throat, and run out."

" A little water with it," said Job, with a late temperance, for his eyes stood like doll's eyes in his head ; " a little water," and Job somewhat coyly held forth the vessel.

" Well, if you must ; but I never mix my liquor at home ; the water about here is so bad."   And saying this, Bats filled up the half-emptied horn of Job with pure spirit.   " And now, now the song."

Job, as we have before remarked, was a singer. He had ditties for various complexions ; black, brown, or fair, he could with small preparation adapt himself to the locks and eyes of the presiding divinity. Taking another draught of inspiration — looking a passionate look at Molly—and seizing her wrist, and drawing her hand half through his hand, he held the compressed points of her beating fingers as he sang—

> " Oh ! my Molly's a thief, I must own ;
>   Only look at her eyes,
>   They belong to the skies,
> And her voice for some angel's is known.
>
> " Oh, my Molly's in debt I avow—
>   Yes, she owes for her lip
>   Where the honey-bees sip—
> For her breath to the jessamine bower.
>
> " Oh, my Molly is cruel as fair ;
>   Once a raven was shot,
>   Snowy white without spot—
> She had ta'en all his black for her hair.
>
> " Who my Molly is, hope not to guess—
>   No; she is not the girl,
>   Who talks di'mond and pearl,
> For what gem in the world 's worth her *yes* ?
>
> " Oh, my——"

But at this stage of the slip-shod verse, Job fell from the stool, breaking down in the unfinished song. As he lay insensible upon the earth, Phineas

bent over him, but was startled from his purpose
by a knock at the door.

" Who the devil's that ?" muttered Bats between
his teeth.

CHAPTER V.

BATS cautiously opened the door, and one stride
brought the new visitor close to the prostrate
Pippins.

" What carrion's this ?" asked the new comer,
jerking his toe against the shoulder of the bacchanal, happily insensible of the enquiry.   Bats
was about to explain, when the querist stopped
him by a gesture of impatient command, and by an
evidently educated twitch of the hand, possessed
himself of the repeater, temptingly peeping from
the pocket of Job.   Phineas's face fell into shadow
at the dexterity of the operator.   If there be, as
we devoutly believe, honour among thieves, sure
we are it is alloyed with envy : a man with a hand
like a ham cannot complacently view the snaky
palm of a more perfect brother.   Hence the bile
of Phineas at the adroitness of Skinks, who, indeed,
bore about his person ample *prima facie* evidence
of superior talent; his coat was finer, his———but
we must attempt a sketch of Skinks.

Our new friend was a highway Hercules. Could he have condescended to eat what dull people call honest bread—that is, as Skinks thought, bread without any butter—he might have passed a useful life in a caravan. Many a man, with far less pretensions than Skinks, has lived very respectably as a giant. With no assistance from the shoemaker, Skinks stood six feet three. No man had a more ingenuous face, for he looked the varlet that he really was. His skin was sallow from midnight watching; (his works, we mean pistols, like the Greek's orations, constantly smelt of the oil); his voice had sunk, beneath the night air and brandy, to a raw and rugged bass; and his temper, tried by several juries, had suffered somewhat from the ordeal. His language was generally laconic, but sustaining and sympathetic. Many a trembling, sinking passenger had he, with one word, prevailed upon to stand. His strength was amazing; for often, like Milo, had he stopped a carriage in full career with only his fore-finger—on a trigger. So much for the man of clay. His dress was worthy of its tenant; he wore a claret-coat, "smeared" with lace that passed for gold—black velvet breeches, and boots—certainly from the last of the ogre, who, when we were young, was wont to take three leagues at a step. A three-corner hat, bound and looped with bright metal, half-cocked upon his head, fearfully harmonized with a brace of pistols in his belt. A huge pigtail hung, like a dead snake, down his back. Such was the man who now with folded arms looked contemptuously below on Pippins—asleep and dreaming—we know not what, for verily there are deep things in drunkenness !

And where was Molly? Drawn to her full height, her face flushed, her bosom heaving, and her terribly black eyes fairly eating the Colossus before her—he all the while as insensible of the attention as his prototype of Rhodes. " Lucius, Lucius," cried Molly—and at length Skinks, by a growl, acknowledged the appeal. " Molly !" and he sat down, and Molly sank upon his knee, and wreathed her arms about his neck—Skinks, in deep contemplation, slowly winding up the repeater he had plucked from Job, the heart-strings of Phineas cracking at the sound ; and Bats gasping and glaring with jealousy at the " happy pair," for Skinks had a bear's love for Molly. It might be he was drawn towards her by a sympathy, independent of affection ; her father had been hanged, and only for shooting a gamekeeper.

" What luck ?" Mortlake ventured to enquire of the serious Skinks. " Any thing upon the road ?"

" The road !" echoed Skinks, with the disgust of a man who feels he has mistaken his profession— " That a man of my standing should be brought to

rob on foot ! May the hound that shot my mare—
well, well," and Skinks ground his teeth, strangled
a rising groan, and breaking into a whistle, tapped
with his fingers on the back of Molly—Bats choking in commendable silence. " This is the first
prize I've drawn these ten days," and Skinks somewhat ostentatiously displayed Sir Scipio's repeater.

" 'Tis easy to bag the bird when another has
springed it," said Phineas, and his lip quivered.

" What now !" growled Lucius, " what are ye
but hands and feet—dead flesh, if I had not the
head to move it ? Jack-of-the-Gibbet, though a
scarecrow of ten years' hanging, were as serviceable
a rogue. Springed it ! Well then, we'll take Blen-
heim from Marlborough, and give the victory to
the drummers."

" Why, in such matters," sullenly replied Phineas, " I don't know if there ar'n't sometimes worse
used folks than drummers."

" Hold thy tongue, Phin," counselled Molly—
" thou'lt ruffle Lucius."

" The hangman ruffle him and band him, too !"
muttered Phineas indistinctly.

" Who growled there—thou, Phineas, or the
dog ?" and Skinks determinedly put aside Molly,
and advancing towards the rebel, looked him into
quaking. Skinks stood for an answer.

" A dog," said Phineas, in a tone not unworthy

of the quadruped. Skinks sank tranquilly on his seat, and Molly resumed her throne upon his knee.

"That's the worst of Phin," cried Bats—"he doesn't know common sense. He'd rob a captain of all that makes his commission worth a farthing; the profit and glory of other people's work."

"Be still, Bats—be still," and Molly knitted her brows, and turned towards the offender, who glowed a deeper scarlet at the reproof; his very hair seemed to grow redder as Molly spoke.

"It's meanness of spirit," pursued the quickened Bats, "to quarrel about a trinket like that, Phin. All such knick-knacks are the fair perquisites of the captain for expenses and news upon the road."

"Well said, Bats!" and Molly smiled graciously upon the talking snake about to sting her.

"To be sure; I shouldn't wonder if the captain means to give that watch to the blue-eyed girl at the Plough. She's a kind thing, and the captain loves blue eyes, Phin; he says they're so innocent."

Egypt's asp was not a surer reptile than Bats. Molly, struck to the heart, where an old, old wound was festering, sprang to the earth, quivering, like an arrow newly-fixed, with passion. Her eyes looked molten with rage, her large throat dilated to a pillar; her coal-black tresses were stirred as by the air, and her lips moving with inarticulate sounds, she leapt like a cat on Skinks, and tearing the watch from his pocket, with the swing of an Amazon dashed it to the floor. Skinks jumped to his feet, whilst the wheels of the repeater prettily described circles around him. (It is the privilege of beauty to make us forget time; even Sir Scipio would have been puzzled to identify his own repeater.)

Skinks could ordinarily master his feelings, but not when bound up with a gold watch and chain. He applied a terribly significant monosyllable to Molly, and with his clenched mallet power first, struck—

Wimper not sweet Cupid! Dry thine eyes, and feed thy mother's doves—and thou, fair Venus! shriek not a second shriek—and ye, eternal Graces, huddle not like frighted fowl together. The face of Molly was not profaned; at his last public hour Skinks was spared that tighter pang; for, happily, Bats rushing before the fair, received on his more appropriate nose a blow that fairly pasted it to his cheeks. Down, of course, he fell; but falling, cushioned his *os sacrum* on the belly of Pippins, who, by the profoundest grunt, acknowledged the deposit. But the blood of Bats, as might be seen from his nose, was up, and in a second so was Bats himself. Seizing a bludgeon, nearly as hard as Skinks's fist, he made at his assailant; when Molly—we will not stay to analyze the mixed feelings of gratitude and

love that moved her—clawed up the draught-board,
and striking it with vehement precision on the
skull of her preserver, she split the checkered tablet, holding the astonished Bats in a square collar
of polished wood. Had Skinks been a common
man, he might have struck his powerless foe; but
Skinks had magnanimity, and tickled by the dilemma of his enemy, he roared a laugh; and Mortlake and Phineas, like true courtiers, joined in
chorus. Bats dropt his club, and wiped his nose.
Molly, releasing her prisoner, folded her arms, and
with the look of an injured empress, sank, wordless,
on a tub. Bats still tried coaxingly to raise his
nose, though looking as he would not have objected
to a new one, cut by Taliacotian cunning, from
the heart of Skinks.

The impressive sound uttered by Pippins on the
fall of Bats, awakened the attention of the captain
to the sleeper, " Where did ye pick him up, Bats?"
asked Skinks, in a most honied tone. Bats was
not to be mollified by such peculiar attention, still
his soul rankled with his late injury, still he glared,
and, silent still, he felt his nose. Phineas gave the
necessary information; in few words condensed
the protestation of Job as to the accident which
had possessed him of the watch, and then, with a
speaking wink of the eye, pointed out the bloody
napkin !

E 2

" Got it honestly, eh ?" said Skinks, with a smile
of a Judas. " Ha ! the thief's above his business.
Pick up the pieces, Phin;" and he pointed to two
or three fragments of the watch glittering on the
floor. " Let's look at his honest face," and the obedient Phineas turned Job upon his back, he having
rolled over when relieved of Bats. Skinks took
a burning brand from the logs, and stooping near
Job's feet, stretched it within singeing distance of
his cheek. " Ha ! ha ! ha ! an old bird, my lads.
I know him as I know my nails—a nursery thief—
a bread-and-butter footpad. Why, he was tried
at York for stealing a coral and bells from the
mayoress's baby. I saw him in the dock ; somehow there was a crack in the indictment, and Bill
Ticket—for that's his name—crept safely through."

It is to be feared that when nature made Job
Pippins she did not break the die, but in the same
mould made one William Ticket ; for that the
story of Skinks was cold, malicious slander we cannot believe. No ; in possessing himself of the property of Pippins, he was sustained by the virtuous
conviction that he was punishing a too lucky, a too
dissimulating thief. William Ticket was despoiled,
happily for him, in the person of Job Pippins.

" I'll tell ye what we'll do," said Skinks, oracularly ; " we'll"——

" Ugh !" roared Pippins, flinging up his legs as

though under a galvanic battery, the toes of his
thick-soled shoes striking the under jaw of Skinks
against its brother like a plate of iron. Skinks blasphemed—and Bats, smiling for the first time, took
his fingers from his nose.

Job was not a salamander; a red hot spark from
the blazing wood had inopportunely lighted on his
cheek, as the too near Skinks was about to pass
sentence—a sentence, we fear, in which the jaw of
the judge was made more evident than his justice.

Sentence was passed—immediately carried into
execution, and where, and in what state was the
culprit—where was Job?

CHAPTER VI.

IT was a pleasant morning in the month of fickle
April; the sun was up in his brightness—the fields
steamed with odours—the birds sang and twit-
tered—the limping hare now hopped along the
mead, and now sat and licked her dewy paws—
the rooks cawed their sweet domestic cares—the
hedgehog rejoiced in his new-warmed blood—the
snail, like creeping envy, crawled its slimy way—
the lambkins frisked, and still Job Pippins slept.

Thy hand, reader; step this way. Thou art in

a most delicious meadow, within three yards of the sleeper. See yon dry ditch; there—there lies Pippins!

We paused, and our heart rose within us as we looked upon the dreamer. Touched by the softening influence of the season—for in spring-time our heart turns to a ball of honey—we exclaimed, "Ha! here is penniless worth upon its couch of nettles; thorns at its side, nightshade at its head, and crawling, creeping creatures round about. Poor soul! The toad still squats at thine ear, and the raven is thy constant serenader!" Saying this, and dropping tears beyond the average size, we walked on; for Job began to yawn, and we were fearful he would ask our hospitality. Sentiment we can, and ought to bestow upon the wretched—rolls and and butter cost money.

Job woke, and as he woke his temples were pierced by nails driven to the head by one short stroke, and then some half-dozen lancets were struck into his skull, and his eyes were turned to two lenses, burning hot, and his tongue was an unmanageable bit of hard, dry leather, retaining a high flavour of the tan. In other words, Job felt the last night's gin—such being the compunctuous feelings of those (our authority is a late member of Parliament, an eminent water drinker) who indulge in spirituous liquors.

Job was in his shirt; and, like Hamlet in the same garment, pale. However, casting his eyes on his linen, he more than "rivalled its whiteness," for he turned to a corresponding yellow. The vestment—that "most domestic ornament," his shirt—was stained with unseemly blots of blood. Whether he had merely "assisted" at a tragedy, or had been a principal, was a doubt that, for a second, withered him like lightning. Then it all came upon him—the hut—Molly—the drink—the —the—and then he passed into that confine where darkness swallows all things. An insect ticked its little note. "The watch!" cried Job, and stood upon his feet; the trees, and fields, and herds, whirling round him—and the blood glaring like red fire—and Job, gaspingly applying his hand to his flesh, and feeling that at least he ought to have a very serious wound.

It was, we repeat, a balmy day in April, when Job Pippins, reduced to his last garment, stood in a field with the wide world about him. Hatless, shoeless, hoseless, he stood upon the grass, the bold zephyrs playing with his shirt—his tattered flag of terrible distress. And Job began to feel the sickness of hunger; he looked at the cows, and yearned for his breakfast. Job resolved and re-resolved. Should he try to regain the hut, whence he had been so inhospitably sprited? Then he thought, what availed a naked man against four men and one woman? Should he run to the first house and publish the whole story? Again, who would put faith in a man with so slender a wardrobe? At this moment of indecision, a bull in the next field, annoyed or scandalized at the appearance of Job, leapt the low fence, and unhesitatingly ran at him. Job paused no longer, but made for the next meadow, and scaling a five-barred gate, saved himself in the main road, the bull shaking his horns, and casting a reproachful look at the fugitive. The destitution of Job was perfect, as he thought, without a new affliction; a few seconds before, and he could have dared fate to do its worst, in the firm belief of its inability. Vain, blind man! He was then the sole proprietor of a whole shirt; and now he stood in the London road, with almost all the hinder part of his one garment impaled on the dead brambles surmounting the fatal five-barred gate. The retreat of Job was most ignominious; he had not even saved his colours. (Moral: let no man with one shirt despise the frowns of fate.)

Job stood in the road, his heart sinking deeper and deeper still as he wistfully beheld his tattered property held by the thorns, and still vigilantly guarded by the bull, who to Job looked as though he felt the full importance of the trophy. In the impotence of rage, Job at length with a disdainful action turned his back upon the bull, who took the insult with the most commendable philosophy.

And now, thinks the reader, Job is at the zero of his fortune. He is naked, hungry, penniless, and where shall he find a friend? The river— yonder river, that like a silver thread intersects those emerald fields—that shall be unto him clothes, meat, and lodging. Mercy on us! suicide? No, no; Job had a just value of life: when it was only worth throwing away, his opinion was, that nothing further could hurt it. The river, it will be seen, was Job's Pactolus.

Quitting his foe, Job made for the stream, while his fancy peopled its banks with a hundred racing, leaping, shouting schoolfellows, with whom, des- pising birch—despising the deep moral of the primer tale, in which the impartial pedagogue flogged alike for swimming and for sinking—Job was wont, in boyish days, to dive. Job sighed as he thought of those happy, reckless hours: then what was a shirt to him? His father bought it, and his mother made it !

Job crawled and slinked across the field, and was already among a clump of alders, overhanging the stream. Was the great enemy of man cooling his burning limbs in the bright waters? Or had some pitying angel, softened by the nakedness of Job, lighted among the trees? Was it a temptation

E 3

of the devil, or was it the beneficent gift of a kind spirit? Job was perplexed: well he might be.

Reader, put thyself in the moiety of the shirt worn by Job; think thyself thus naked, weary, hungry, destitute; and then imagine a very handsome suit of clothes—hat—gloves—shoes—walking-cane—all that "makes the happy man," lying, a golden waif, at thy foot,—no visible second person near. What wouldst thou do? No matter; listen what Job did.

Job sat himself upon the grass, changed his equivocal shirt for the ample piece of ruffled "aired snow" before him, tried an experiment with the shoes and stockings, which answered the fondest hopes of the essayist,—girded his loins with the providential pair of breeches—donned the vest and coat,—took his—yes, *his*—hat, gloves, and stick, placing the cravat in his pocket, to be tied in moments of better leisure, and—Job was always a fast walker—in three minutes he was again in the main road. Again he passed the noted gate—there was still the bull, his glaring eye still upon the remnant of the shirt. As Job glanced at the rag, he flourished his cane, and smiled supreme contempt.

Job journeying onward, something weighty struck at his leg. He put his hand in his coat pocket, and pulled out a purse; it contained eight guineas and as many dollars. This was too much;

Job sank against a tree, and overcome, one hand holding the purse, and the other placed upon his heart, thanked Providence !

How long Job might have dwelt in the grateful reverie we know not, had he not been disturbed in his thanksgiving by the noise of an approaching cart rattling along at full speed. Two men were in it, who, as they passed, greeted Job with a wondering whoop; and one of them added to the exclamation the following curious enquiry :—" I say, Bill Ticket, when did you cut your teeth?"

" It's plain," thought Job, "the clothes belong to Ticket." Job paused—he had surely seen the men before; and yet they passed so rapidly, that—but then Job was not aware that, possibly they were going to see a swimming-match—a very private meeting—between a young Oxonian and the Dolphin. We know not that such was really their destination—we can only speak to the match.

As the suit worn by Job had a local reputation, he saw, with unaffected pleasure, a returned post-chaise halt when near him, and heard the postilion ask his honour " if he'd ride?" Job entered the chaise, pulled down the curtains, and went whirling off to the next town, a distance of ten miles. At least twenty times, in the solitude of his carriage, Job pulled out his purse, and counted his money.

The postilion had orders to stop outside the town—Job had business in a neighbouring village. There, he thought, he would calmly pass the day— it was yet early morning—and at nightfall travel towards London. Job had not breakfasted, and, as he crossed a bridge, the inn on the opposite side seemed to open its doors wider to receive him. At this instant he heard a shriek, and looking, saw a girl tearing her hair, and clapping her hands, and pointing to what seemed a mere ball in the water, though, on closer inspection, it appeared to Job a child's head. Job leapt into the stream, and swam in the direction of the child, whose neck was all but in the grasp of his preserver, when, for the last time, it sank. Job—the tailor had made his coat somewhat too tight under the arms —though an expert swimmer, was trammeled in his movements; he dived and he dived, as though in a well he was diving for truth, and still like many divers therein, brought up nothing. Again he went down, and he rose with the body of Augustus Faddle, son and heir of Nicholas Faddle, Esq., proprietor of yonder splendid mansion, Ladybird Lodge, with the lawn sweeping down to the water's edge.

CHAPTER VII.

" A perfect gentleman ! the fineness of his linen declares that," exclaimed the laundress of Ladybird Lodge, talking of Job, at the time a distinguished tenant of the best bed-room of the house. " A perfect gentleman ! you might draw his shirt through a wedding-ring !"

" I wonder if he's married," said an under-maid, looking at the footman.

" Swims like a duck," replied the inconsequential functionary.

" If Master Augustus had been drowned, what a shocking thing ! And to-morrow, too, with such a dinner for his birth-day !"

" Well, I suppose the gentleman will stay to dinner. I'm sure if he could eat gold, it isn't too good for him." (Job had long been of that opinion.)

The above is a brief extract of a conversation, animatedly pursued in the servants' hall, on the philanthropic swimmer put to bed in the Blue Room— Nicholas Faddle, Esq., hovering about the providential visitor, with clasped hands, and all but streaming eyes, and now calling him the guardian angel of his race, and now recommending another half fowl—(Job breakfasted in bed)—and now insisting on a few more layers of hot blankets. It was in vain that Job again and again bulletined his convalescence; the grateful father insisted that, after so generous an action, he must be greatly exhausted. Then he rang for more coffee and toast —then he rushed to the next room to clasp the little Augustus, preserved from a watery grave, and now pickled with hot salt—then he returned to Job, and vehemently declared that the doctor— the family doctor—must see him.

"A clever man—pratice of two thousand a-year —an extraordinary man. Doctor Saffron—you have heard of Doctor Saffron?" Job had heard the name, but, we fear, doubted his skill, for he resolutely declared his determination not to admit him. "If he had done any thing to serve Mr. Faddle he was glad of it—but he had a mortal antipathy to all doctors."

"Well, well! Yet if you'd only let him feel your pulse, and show him your tongue." Job frowned, and bit his lip. "Enough—I won't press it; but if you should catch cold after saving my blessed child—where *are* the hot blankets?" And Faddle snatched at the bell with most benevolent fury; he then ran out, and Job finished his first fowl, and tenth cup of coffee. And still he ate,

luxuriously pressing a bed of down, over-canopied
with richest silk. At length, somewhat appeased,
Job sat up in the bed, and was beginning to rumi-
nate, when the too careful Faddle re-entered the
room, bringing with him the infallible Doctor Saffron. Instantaneously Job dived into the eider, as
though it was another stream, and another child
within it.

" Forgive me, I can't help it, my dear friend,
do speak to the doctor—do "—Job maintained a
dignified silence. " Well, then, only your pulse
and your tongue. You may be ill and not know
it—mayn't he, doctor ?"

" Nothing more likely," said the wise Saffron.

" I ask no more—only your pulse and your
tongue."

Job, finding there was no escape, ventured to
put out his arm—Saffron pressed it, taking out his
watch—Job felt a qualm as he heard the tick-tick
of the repeater. " Humph !" said Saffron, " so"—
releasing the limb—" if you please, sir, your
tongue."

Job now adroitly pulled his night-cap—a gorgeous family affair, with a most exuberant tassel—
down to the tip of his nose ; and drawing close up
to his under lip the snowy sheet, he resignedly
dropt his tongue upon it. With a keen imposing
eye, Saffron pondered on that most musical organ.

" Ha—furred "—he said—" much furred! Yes—
the effect of the water."

Job said nothing; but he thought—" gin-and-
water."

" Well, sir," proceeded Saffron to the all but
invisible Job, " we must have a few ounces of
blood."

Job shook his head and drew his mouth into an
eyelit hole.

" Now, do—pray, do let the doctor bleed you,"
and Faddle rang the bell. " Pray do—lives like
yours, my dear kind sir, are not—bid Nancy bring a
basin—I say, lives like yours are not to be trifled
with. Indeed," and Faddle spake in the most winning modulation, " indeed, the doctor must bleed
you."

Still Job shook his head, but the invincible Saffron stood with his ready weapon. " Some practi-
tioners, sir, would await the slow operation of
aperients, but in cases such as these, I always
attack the bowels with the lancet."

" To be sure," acquiesced Faddle, his own bowels
being no party to the operation.

" This way, Nancy," said Saffron, and a serious-
looking damsel, with a very handsome china bowl,
a piece of Nankin worthy of the blood of Pippins,
approached the bed. " Now, sir, your arm, if you
please—never been bled, perhaps? 'tis nothing—

nothing I assure you—'twill not confine you—no, you may get up to dinner."

" I should hope so," said Faddle ; " and, doctor, you dine with us to-day, of course ?"

It was with some anxiety, that Job awaited the answer of the man of life and death.

" And to-morrow—certainly."

A groan died in Job's throat, and with the resignation of a martyr he extended his arm. So long as the doctor remained in the house—so long Job felt he must be very ill, and keep his bed.

" Beautiful—beautiful," cried the encouraging and self-complacent Saffron, as Job's blood fell like a rivulet into the basin, Nancy becoming whiter with every drop. " Beautiful," and Saffron looked as a miser would look at molten gold. " There is nothing like bleeding, Mr. Faddle—only last night Sir Scipio Mannikin was saved by it—pray keep your arm still, sir—yes, Sir Scipio should raise a tablet to the lancet."

" Razor," thought Job.

" Sir Scipio !" cried Faddle, " he's Augustus's godfather—he dines with me to-morrow."

" No shivers, I hope?" kindly enquired Saffron of the patient, seeing the bed begin to shake under him. " No shivers?" Job pursed his mouth into a negative, and continued to shake.

" It's impossible he should come," said Saffron,

" though he's out of danger, thanks—thanks to a providential accident that threw me near him in the hour of peril. Steady, Nancy. Apoplexy."

" And, of course," asked Faddle, " you bled him ?"

" Of course he was bled," responded Saffron.

" Any more news of *that* affair ?" questioned Faddle in a low significant tone.

" What, the—the barber ?" and Saffron leered and gave a shrug.

" For myself," said the liberal Faddle, " I don't believe the scandalous rumours of wicked people,— I think her ladyship, though merely the daughter of respectable people, and married from a third-rate boarding school, I think her incapable of—by the way, doctor, what sort of fellow is this Pippins ?"

" You never saw him ? Oh,—a—a"—

" Good looking, I hear ?"

" Why, women have odd tastes, Mr. Faddle. I don't see much beauty in a narrow sloping fore-head, high cheek bones, freckled skin, a nose stolen from a pug, and eyes that belong to a fish. How do you feel now, sir ?" asked the doctor of Job.

Job set his teeth, and with some difficulty at self-command, nodded his head.

" I knew you'd be better. As I say, happily for the ugly, women have odd tastes. For my own part, and I trust I am as far above prejudice as any man—for my own part, I should be sorry to be upon a jury, with only the evidence of his looks."

"It's very odd—I hear a subscription has been raised for him?" said Faddle.

"Shouldn't wonder if the women give him a piece of plate—that is, if he be not hanged before 'tis ready. For they're after him."

"Why, nothing new?—nothing?"—

"Oh, I don't know what hasn't been missed since he was last at the Hall—and only last evening—but by-and-by you shall know the whole affair. All I say is this; I devoutly hope the scoundrel will be hanged! How do you feel now, sir?" gently enquired the doctor.

"How do you feel now?" softly sounded Faddle.

"Fainted—fainted!" cried Saffron: "Water, Nancy—water! and that thick cap—away with it," and Saffron's own hand was stretched to grasp the tassel, and in another half second the face of Job would have lain bare before its libeller, had not the patient resolutely griped his head-dress, and shouted, "Better—much better—very well, indeed."

"I told you so," said the satisfied Saffron—"now, you see," he added with the look and tone of a triumphant demonstrator—"now, you see what bleeding is. Take away, Nancy," and Saffron bandaged the arm. Nancy bore away the blood, and was soon beset by the anxious servants. They all gathered around the bowl like spirits evoked by a German wizard. The under-butler, having duly scrutinized the gory contents, half-shut his eyes, nodded thrice, sucked his lips, and said oracularly—" It's very plain—he's a gentleman born." In matters of blood, profoundest heralds have had their blunders—let us not ask too much of an under-butler. Return we to the patient.

" He had better keep his bed to-day ?" asked Faddle benevolently.

" Yes— to-day," sentenced Saffron.

" What may he take ?"

" Let me see. Why, to-day, I should say he may take—a—whatever he likes."

" What! with the beginning of a fever ?"

" My system," said the emphatic Saffron. " If what he eats does him no harm, 'tis plain he's better; if on the other hand, it does him harm, to-morrow the symptoms will be stronger, and we shall have the surer authority to go upon."

So saying, Dr. Saffron took his hat and cane, and returned to the convalescent Augustus.

Faddle crept closer to the patient. " My best friend—the preserver of my child, the saviour of my house—what would you like to take ?"

Job replied, with a tremulous voice, " A glass of rum and water, hot, with sugar."

It was a fanciful wish for a feverish patient; but
it was complied with to the letter—no, not to the
letter. With the guest of Jonathan Bradford at
the Oxford inn,—

> " He said not if a lemon he would like ; "

but the under-butler, like the aforesaid provident
Jonathan, in the simple language of the dramatic
poet,—

> " Brought one."

And now draw the curtains, and tread softly,
for Job is sleeping. At his earnest desire, he had
had a private interview with Jacob Gorse, the man
especially ordained to paddle Augustus in the boat,
but whose wilful negligence had endangered the
child's life, and lost to himself his place at Ladybird Lodge. Job, we say, talked to Jacob ere he
was thrust from the door. What he said to him
here matters not; doubtless he gave him some
golden rule for his future days—some amulet to
wear at his breast—some phylactery to bind around
his brow. Job slept; he slept in down; and he
who but in the morning was shirtless, and "couldn't
help it," was now guarded as the eye and heart of
a princely house—a jewel—a talisman—a wonder-
worker; nor " could he help it."

Had he dived in his half-shirt, perhaps he had
not slept in the Blue Room.

CHAPTER VIII.

THE next morning all was animation in and about Ladybird Lodge. The birth-day of Augustus was to be solemnized with unusual splendour. At an early hour, Faddle, the grateful father, was at the bed-side of Job, who declared himself unable to join the dinner-party, at which, next to the epergne presented to the host for his breed of bulls, Job was expected to be the principal attraction.

" And was ever any thing so unfortunate? Dr. Saffron can't see you; he has been up all night with Lady Gemini, and doesn't, he writes, expect to get away before to-morrow. He can't come."

" Do you know, I think I'll try to join you." Faddle pressed the hands of Job between his own. " Yes, I—I think I shall be well enough; but—but"——

" Very true; your wardrobe"——

" Quite spoilt—impossible that I can wear any thing again."

" Of course, of course. Let me see—will you pardon what I am about to say? I have a suit; I'm sure 'twill fit you—'twas made for me. I never wore it but once—when I was sheriff of the county,

and took an address to court. I may say it—a
handsome thing; a chocolate cut velvet, with flowers down the skirts, and nosegays embroidered at
the pocket-holes;—breeches to match—and white
satin waistcoat, flourished with gold. I'm sure
they'll fit you—ha! I was much thinner then—
sure they'll fit you."

And Faddle, evidently exalted with the project,
ran from the chamber in active pursuit of his plan.

We pass the process of the toilet. Enough for
the reader, if we present to him Job Pippins—we
beg Job's pardon—John Jewel, Esq., arrayed in
the very court suit of the ex-sheriff of the county—
a suit originally purchased in the vain expectation
of knighthood. Whatever may have been the suspicions of the frank and overflowing Faddle, the
portrait drawn of Pippins by the hand of Saffron
made the masquerade perfectly secure; for Job
looked and moved a new-made count. Had not
the dinner-bell summoned him away, Job had
pined, a new Narcissus, at the mirror. But the
truth is, he was a remarkably pretty fellow—a
truth published by the general stir and simper of a
bevy of ladies, gathered to do honour to the natal
day of Augustus, and, incidentally, to reward, with
gentle words and sweetest smiles, his happy life-
preserver. Job wore his arm in a sling—an additional and touching claim to the sensibilities of the

women.   As he entered the room, and cast his
eyes bashfully around him, there was in his face a
look of confusion, which, though it might with
some take from his breeding, with others it added
considerably to his merit.   A cynical male guest
whispered to a companion—" The fellow is looking
round for applause."   Perish all such ill-nature
like a pestilent weed ! When Job looked round, he
looked for—Doctor Saffron.

Job had suffered, as he thought, the whole round
of introduction, when Faddle brought him to a
young fellow, who, for limb and figure, might have
passed for Job's twin-brother.

" My dear Mr. Jewel, I must make my friend
Frank Triton known to you : your tastes, your
accomplishments, must, I am sure, most closely
ally you."

Job and Frank mutually bowed, when Faddle,
in a sort of trumpet-whisper, audible throughout
the room, applied his mouth to Job's ear—

" Splendid fellow ! he's almost beat the dolphin."

Job bowed still lower to the possible conqueror
of such an adversary.

" Beat the dolphin ; but—by-and-by"——And
Faddle significantly lifted up his fore-finger, and
smothered a chuckle, sliding off to an unexpected
guest, introduced by Frank.

" Mr. Jewel, Mr. Wigmore."

Mr. Wigmore raised his broad back a hair's-breadth from the mantle-piece, and having "thrown his head" at Job, returned to his easy position.   He was certainly less polished in his look and manner than any of the company, and yet Job felt less at ease before him.   The women—bless them !—fluttered around Job, and still his bravery was the theme of their silver tongues.   For the ten thousandth time, Mrs. Faddle, "as a mother," thanked him ; and then grandmothers, aunts, cousins, all put in their peculiar claims to thank him in their various capacities.   Then came enquiries touching his health.   How was his head—how was his arm—how was his fever ?   To all such queries, Job, considering the shortness of the notice, replied very gracefully—

" Quite well, I thank you."   At last, by the number of questions confused and bewildered, Job, without knowing when he answered, or to whom he replied, bowed mechanically, and still said—

" Quite well, I thank you."

A dead silence for a second ensued, and Job found himself in front of Mr. Wigmore.

" How's your gums, sir ?"

" Quite well, I thank you."

General attention was drawn upon Mr. Wigmore,

who, insensible as a target, received the eyes of the company. A titter crept through the room, and some of the men laughed outright.

" It was only yesterday a fellow asked about my teeth," thought Job. And he looked timidly in the dead-wall face of Wigmore. It was an anxious moment for Job, when, happily for him, the servant arrived, and Mrs. Faddle was led to her chair by Job Pippins John Jewel, Esq.

The dinner began with more than ordinary gravity. That great event in every twenty-four hours, on the present occasion, received its more than legitimate attention at Ladybird Lodge. Job acquitted himself with praiseworthy elegance and heartiness, and whilst one fair feeder whispered of his grace, Mr. Wigmore loudly complimented him on his appetite. Faddle, and not for the first time, wondered why Frank had brought his friend. But Job, it must be owned, was all watchful politeness; and he had his reward. Dr. Lullaby, an exemplary clergyman of eighteen stone, sat near the turtle. Thrice—in those days of innocence men were not restricted alike to one wife and one soup—thrice the doctor had been helped, and still he sat with one eye slumbering on the last ladlefull. Often he wished to ask, and as often repressed the ignoble weakness. Job saw the internal struggle. Again

the doctor turned to gaze—sighed—and was about
to turn away his head for ever, when Job, with the
dexterous hand of a juggler, seized the ladle, and
ere the doctor could wink, its contents lay melting
in his plate.   The doctor's face was radiant with
pleasure, and thrusting his right hand under the
table, he clawed hold of the hand of Job, and
squeezing it until the knuckles went like cracking
walnuts, he cried in a subdued voice, spasmodic
with delight, shaking on the last word—" *That's—
that's—friendly !*"   Few saw the deed, and none
but Job Pippins heard the thanks.

Nothing of further importance occurred until a
splendid turbot mutely put in its claims for applause.
They were briefly acknowledged by the doctor.—
" This fish, Mr. Faddle, was caught in a silver net."

" I think it is the finest fish that swims," rashly
observed Frank Triton.

" What ! better than the dolphin ?" asked Faddle,
with the thrust of a gladiator.

" Ha ! ha ! ha !" roared Wigmore ; and a timid
lady, only six months a widow, jumped in her chair,
as in a menagerie we have seen a lady jump when
too near the bars.

" What *is* this about the dolphin ?" asked Mrs.
Faddle, with the eyes of wondering innocence.
Faddle gave a sidelong look at Triton, who re-

turned an expostulatory glance, and Mrs. Faddle sat unanswered.

" Do you know, sir,"—and Wigmore, in thorough bass, addressed Pippins—" do you know, sir, how they are going on with the pearl fishery ?"

" Not the slightest notion," said Pippins, with new-born dignity.

" It must be a very hazardous employment for the poor men," remarked the widow.

" Not at all," said Triton—" not at all—for they only employ such as are predestined the other way."

" Is that true, sir ?" said Wigmore to Job, appealing to him as a first authority.

" I should think the fishery doesn't employ all such," said Job, blindly jumping at what he thought might prove a hit.   Faddle rubbed his hands—the doctor hemmed, and Wigmore, for a second, wrinkled his brow.

" For my part," said the widow, with a recollection of youth, " I prefer pearls to diamonds."

" Which would you take, sir ?" said Job, becoming in his turn assailant, to Wigmore.

" Oh, I should certainly take," replied Wigmore, smiling a grim gallantry, " whatever the lady took."

" Then I say, pearls," concluded the widow.

" Pearls," decided Wigmore ; and again he put a smile into his face that would have dissolved Cleo-

patra's union. Then turning round to Pippins, he
bluntly asked—" What do you think of coral, sir ?"

" Really Wigmore," interposed Triton, feeling
tender for his own reputation, " you catechise Mr.
Jewel as though he were a merman."

" Very right—very right, Frank. Pearls and
diamonds !—he has saved the richest pearl for me,
and all I say is,—and what I expect my friends to
say is,—God bless him !"—and something of the
father stole into Faddle's eye, and his wife looked
with all her heart in her face as she turned to Job.

" Ha ! you should have seen Mr. Jewel. I'm
told he dived, and dived like—like"—

" Like a dolphin," said a young fellow, wickedly
supplying the simile. Again the men shouted, and
the women wondered—and Faddle, looking with a
laughing desperation at Triton, cried—

" I'm blest if I don't tell it." Triton after many
unsuccessful appeals, resigned himself into the
hands of Faddle. " You have heard of the man
we call the dolphin—I beg your pardon, Mr. Jewel,
you're a stranger—well, we have a fellow here,
who, I really think, could swim against a whale.
However, my friend Frank thought himself a match
for him, and—ha ! ha !—yesterday morning, it was
agreed that nobody should know it, and with only
one for an umpire, the match was to be decided.
Well, though Frank was only next to the Dolphin

himself, he hadn't a chance; and so he was about
to return to his mother earth, when he found that
the water nymphs—the pretty river-goddesses with
their 'pearled wrists,' as Mr. Milton says, I remember—conspired to 'take him in.' And how
do you think they managed? Why, they had
stolen his clothes." The gentlemen shouted again
at this reduction of Frank to a state of innocence,
but the women, by their staid looks, clearly thought
it no joke. By the way, Pippins indulged in no
unseemly merriment.

"True, Mr. Jewel, true—in other words, some
hang-dog thief had run away with them." Job's
jaw fell like the jaw of a dead man, and he sat as
upon one entire and perfect blister.

"They hadn't left him—ha! ha! ha!—they"—
and here Faddle, with praiseworthy prudence, put
the edge of his hand to one side of his mouth that
the intelligence might reach Job's private ear alone
—"they hadn't left him even a shirt"—Job's teeth
chattered—"no not even half a shirt." Job

" Thought of the murders of a five-barred gate,"

and the table, and the guests spun round, and he
distinguished no face, save the face of Wigmore
looking sternly at him.

"Arn't you well?" cried Mrs. Faddle, and there
was a general move towards Job.

" It's my fault! I would make him come down. Is it your head, Mr. Jewel?" said Faddle.

" Is it your arm?" compasionately asked the widow.

" Is it," asked Wigmore, we mean Captain Skinks —for it was he, indeed—" Is it your teeth?" And as he put the question, his fingers played with the chain of Sir Scipio's repeater.

" Thank goodness!" and Mrs. Faddle pointed to the object without—" Thank goodness! here's Doctor Saffron on his horse!"

" My bed—my bed!" roared Job, and he leapt up, and actually fought his way through the guests —gained his room—and plunged into bed.

Dr. Saffron lost no time, but immediately followed Mr. Jewel. Again the doctor had his finger on Job's pulse—and again Job wore his nightcap down.

" Humph! I think—I"——

CHAPTER IX.

" I think—I think," repeated Doctor Saffron, his fingers still upon Job's pulse,—" I think it was very fortunate I came." Now, whatever Job thought, he said nothing. Saffron rose from his seat, stroked his chin, thrust his hands in his pockets, and pronounced sentence—" A little more blood."

" I thought so," said Faddle, and beneficently smiling, he added—" Nancy, a basin."

" Some sixteen ounces, and a blister on the chest," said Saffron. " Yes, that will do for to-night."

" His dinner couldn't have hurt him; he was only helped three times to haunch," said Faddle, piteously.

" Well, I promise you," protested Saffron with more than professional earnestness, " if he isn't much better to morrow, I'll shave his head." Faddle pressed the doctor's hand in token of thanksgiving. " You have pigeons at hand, I hope?"

" You know we're very fond of 'em, doctor. But you can tell best—would they quite agree with his stomach ?"

" Stomach ! pooh—soles of his feet ! if we don't take great care," and Saffron lowered his voice to a most confidential tone, " if we don't take great care, this may be a case for Doctor Lullaby." Faddle winced—" I tell you, there is no time to be lost." At this moment Nancy made her appearance with a riband and the fatal china bowl. Again Saffron stood ready with his lancet, again he was about to approach the sufferer, when he was chained to the spot by the loud snores of the patient. " Bless me ! he's asleep," cried Faddle, and again

Job snored in corroboration; the very curtain rings vibrated with the sound. " You'll never wake him?" asked Faddle, as Saffron laid his hands upon the bed clothes; " won't sleep do him good, doctor ?"

" Quite cure him," replied Saffron, with a sarcastic smile. " Six hours of such sleep, and he'll want none of my help." And Job snored with greater vehemence. " Don't be deceived by that," said the doctor to the host, " I've heard many a patient do that, and, I give you my honour, with all my care, it has turned into the sleep of death."

" Well, I thought sleep must be a very balm," said the superficial Faddle.

" And so it is," sharply returned the doctor, " but in some cases balm is the deadliest poison: this is one of them. Sir—Sir," and the doctor shouted to Job, when a gentle knock was heard at the door. The footman, with a fine respect for the sick man's chamber, only edged in his cheek, and in the softest voice begged to ask whether the doctor would be able to attend the dinner-table, or whether a cover should be put aside for him ?

Saffron, absorbed by his professional duties, apparently gave no ear to the mission ; but pausing near his patient,—who continued at a short notice to perform wonders, for every snore was an improvement in tone and body on its predecessor,—his face bent into a smile, and he resorted to his snuff-box,

F 3

and having taken a pinch, observed—" Ha ! well —that's better—yes, much better. What did you say?" and he turned to the still lingering footman, who repeated the question.

" I think, friend Faddle, we may venture to leave him for a few minutes;—but, hark ye, Nancy, let me be called, if there's the slightest alteration." Still Job snored, and still the doctor, until beyond ear-shot, applauded every note with—" that's well —better— better—better."

When the doctor appeared in the drawing-room, every voice—save the *ferrea vox* of Skinks, alias Wigmore—cried for news of the patient. Saffron answered in general terms, which, translated into particular replies, assured the enquirers, that if Mr. Jewel recovered, he would no doubt live;—if his disease proved mortal, there was as little doubt he would die: that these were most learned deductions was evident from the fact that everybody seemed perfectly satisfied with them. The dinner was re-commenced with an avidity that promised to more than fill up the previous hiatus. Once—for the turtle lay at his heart—Doctor Lullaby uplifted his voice amid the unfeeling din of knives and forks, and nodding to Saffron, took off a bumper of port with "to your patient, doctor." There was an unostentatious kindness in this—a benevolence very far beyond the wine.

We like not to linger—though in truth, we have
been accused of the low disposition—but we protest,
we like not to dwell upon the darker colourings of our
nature; no, had we our own task to choose, we would
distil the essence of our brains into mottoes for
threadpapers ;—we would prick sweet natal verses
with baby-pins in satin cushions; we would indite
the philosophy of a quadrille ;—and pen the biography of Lady Mary's bullfinch. And oh, ye twelfth
cake images ! how truly—how beautifully would we
paint this much mistaken world ! How would we
prove the very flag-stones to be best white lozenges ;
—December mud, real black-currant jam ;—all
acts of Parliament, sweet apple-fritters ;—Newgate
itself, a mass of barley-sugar ; and Bedlam Hospital,
a piece of mere blancmange. The pillory should
be a tasteful sweetmeat ;—and the very gallows built
of candy ! A professed beggar of twenty years'
duplicity should be a worthy object of the picturesque;—and a man who lives by cutting throats, a
person with an eccentric turn of intellect ;—infanti-
cide should be a provident care of little children ;—
and bigamy, in man or woman, an ennobling spirit
of universality. The world we inhabit is really a
paradise ;—and yet—yet they issue four-penny
pieces !

However, as we are not permitted to be one of
those very choice writers who. like Prometheus,

make their own men, but are compelled to take men
ready made to our hands, we must not disguise the
fact, that in a very, very brief time the patient of
the Blue Room was utterly forgotten by at least nineteen out of twenty of the guests, Doctor Saffron
almost included.   It was very strange, but had it
been a dinner to solemnize the funeral of one of the
family, the feeders could not have eaten more
heartily.   Not a soul left his place, and—as he
ought to have done—went beating his breast upon
the lawn, or watering the gravel walk with his tears.
And yet, there was one—one who thought of Job—
one whose appetite had been struck dead at the tenth
mouthful by what the doctor called his dangerous
relapse.   The fair widow—none of your silly spinsters
with hearts like green oranges—had a heart, soft and
ripe as a medlar.   Whether from having lived with,
and, alas ! buried, a husband twenty years older
than herself, she had become a deeper thinker—
had acquired a keener vision into the soul of
things than many of her evenly-paired acquaintance,
we know not enough of young widows to decide ;
but of this we are certain, she had, from the first,
appreciated the merits of Job at their golden value:
five feet ten inches—a handsome face—apparent
good temper, and, despite the doctor, sound constitution, were not lost upon a woman of her experience.   " She was not a maudlin girl," as her own

maid ingenuously avowed, " to give herself red eyes for a bread-and-butter face and curly hair." With the widow, the whiskers of Mars were of greater worth than the locks of Adonis.

The selfishness of the table proceeded in all its tumult, when the widow, seated next to Doctor Saffron—he had attended her poor husband in his last illness, and she felt a great confidence in him—ventured to put a list of queries touching the sufferer, as she tenderly thought him, up stairs. The doctor was a man of system, and cared not to have his patients laid upon the dinner-table. Moreover, in the present instance, he was ferociously hungry; having been well nigh worn out in his late attendance on Lady Gemini—whose medicine, by the way, at that moment haunted him.

" And, my dear doctor, going on well, you say?"

Turning the drum-stick of a goose in his mouth, he replied—" Well as can be expected;" never taking into account the extraordinary expectations of some people.

" You think there's nothing serious in the case?"

" Serious! no—not at all. I've—with great pleasure"—and Saffron honoured a challenge to wine—" I've sent for a nurse," and again he filled his mouth with goose.

" A nurse!" cried the widow, " so bad as that?"

The doctor, getting a free passage for his voice,

gently declined his head, and in a soft professional tone, breathed into the quickened ear of the widow —" No milk."

" Doctor !" cried the widow, blushing like a peony.

" Still, her ladyship,"——

" Ladyship ! why, my dear doctor—he ! he !— who *are* you talking about ?"   And the widow simpered.

" Your dear friend, Lady Gemini—hasn't Mr. Faddle told you ?   At last, a charming little boy."

" Very true—I never was so delighted to hear any thing.   But the preserver of *our* little boy ?"

" He's—he's in bed ;" and Saffron, becoming restless under the examination, turned from the widow and rolled his eyes up and down the table, seeking what he might devour.   At last he lighted upon a huge turkey in chains ; and with epicurean gusto, insinuated his advice to the carver ; the widow unconsidered, with downcast head, talking at his side.

" And—and dear doctor, what may be his complaint ?"

" The breast," said Saffron to the man with the turkey.

" Love !" thought the widow ; then aloud, " He's a remarkably fine young fellow."

" The leg's a poor thing," said the doctor.

" Well, I'm certainly no judge, but—tell me this, hasn't he a good constitution ?"

" Not a bit of liver left," exclaimed Saffron, with deep regret.

" God bless me ! There's no going by looks," sighed the widow. " Though a little pale, he looked so perfectly handsome."

" No ham," replied the doctor to a gesture of the carver, and then for the first time since his seduction by the bird, was Saffron conscious of the rustling of the widow's black. The lady for some time said nothing, but somewhat bewildered, she fervently hoped that the talk of the doctor had been of turkey.

Disgusted at the selfish manners of Saffron, the widow resolved on continued silence. It was in vain—her philanthropy was neither of the deaf nor dumb. Just as the doctor had changed his plate and prepared himself for a new encounter, the widow began in her silveriest voice—" But my dear doctor, *do* tell me—*do*"——

Saffron laid down his knife and fork (he had returned to the venison), and with a piteous look of remonstrance and a tone almost vibrating with the *pathetic*, appealed to the widow. " For goodness sake, madam ! do not talk to me while I am eating —*do not*—pray do not—here have I swallowed three pieces of fat without tasting them."

A magistrate, who until that moment had never spoken, rolled his eyes in his head, and cried " Shameful."

Hath the reader seen a duck pluming itself in a summer pond? In like manner, stung by the rebuke of Saffron, did the widow work her head and neck. The doctor cared but little for the involutions, and was proceeding gravely with his task, insured, as he presumptuously deemed, from further hinderance. A delicious collop—no less—was on his fork—his fork near his mouth—his mouth gaping, when, with a long-drawn sigh, down fell the head of the widow on the doctor's shoulder. There was a general stir at the table—a general cry of " fainted !" The magistrate chewing his meat, authoritatively pronounced—" decidedy fainted." Wigmore carried the widow from the room, followed by the hostess and another female friend, who relentlessly urged the doctor from his plate. In the moment of desperate disappointment, Saffron could have thrown up his diploma, so that he might have executed his dinner.

" Was ever any thing so unlucky !" said the host. " First that Mr. Jewel should be ill, and then that Mrs. "——

" Sympathy," said Triton, with a wink of wickedness. " Sympathy."

" Don't Frank," cried a dear female friend of the

widow, benevolently strangling a laugh. " Don't."
But we are forgetting what is due to the new
patient.

" We had better get her to bed," said the doctor, with the down look of an injured man.

" The Cane Room," said Mrs. Faddle, and one
of the servants led the way. Wigmore ran up
stairs with his hysterical burden, and Saffron, with
funereal gait and aspect, followed. Wigmore, having surrendered the widow to the doctor and the
women, was proceeding to join the company, when,
about to pass the door of the adjoining chamber,
he recognised the voice of the male patient, at first
he thought loudly laughing, but his head yet rang
with the hysterics of the widow, and his ear was not
sufficiently fine to distinguish the sex of a note.
However, once at the door of the sick man, it
would have been unkind to pass it ; therefore, turning the handle, Wigmore thrust his skull into the
room, and, grinning like a shark, asked " If Mr.
Ticket was any better ?" Nancy was about to
speak. " Say Wigmore—Captain Wigmore—called
to ask ;" and then, with a departing kindness, that
quite puzzled the girl—" take care of his teeth."

" Ticket and teeth ?" said Nancy, " what can he
mean, sir ?"

" What can he mean ?" echoed Job to himself,
and again an ague fit came on. In a few minutes

another knock at the door, and Bodkin, the widow's maid, entered flutteringly, fairly sweeping the ground with curtsies. She begged very many thousand pardons, but would Nancy go to her mistress—the doctor was about to bleed her—and for herself, she loved her so much she could not hold the basin? If the gentleman didn't mind she would stay, in case he might want any thing. Job raised his eye above the counterpane and nodded assent. Exit Nancy.

"And what," asked Job, in a feeble voice, well worthy of cultivation for a representative of the sick, "And what may ail your charming mistress?"

"I can't tell, sir—the doctor says her complaint is just the same as yours."

"And what is that?" said Job to himself in great perplexity.

"And I think he called it sym—sympathy. But whatever it is, he says bleeding is the only cure for it. He has bled you, sir"——

"Damn him!" said Job.

"And he'll bleed my mistress."

Job said nothing.

"Yes, sir—he said you are both to be treated just alike. He has written home for blisters for two. I hope, sir, you won't let him shave your head—pray don't, sir."

"And why not?" asked Job, touched by the interest the woman seemed to take in him. " Why not ?"

" Because my mistress has such beautiful hair, and as you're both to be treated alike—Oh, sir ! you should see it out of that filthy cap; for my part I wouldn't wear a widow's cap to please the best dead man that ever was buried. I"——

Bodkin was arrested in her eloquence by the return of Nancy, who told her she was wanted in the next room. Bodkin with a mysterious glance at Job, heaved a deep sigh, exclaimed, " My poor mistress !" and departed.

" In the next room !" thought Job; and he fell off into a brown study, which held him tongue-tied for many minutes. When next he spoke, he asked, quite unconscious of the syllables, " Nancy, is she rich ?"

" Very comfortable they say, sir."

" In the next room !" again thought Job, " and to be treated both alike !" And the widow's face, despite the dead man's cap, glowed prettily between the curtains.

CHAPTER X.

FOR three whole days—three anxious nights—
were Job and the widow next room neighbours.
Their feelings, toned, as the doctor avowed, and
as they firmly believed, by the same sickness,
sweetly harmonized. They could hear each other
cough, and conscious of such advantage, that usually
unmusical operation, sublimed by the tender passion,
became almost dulcet. Great things have of late
been done upon the Jew's-harp, but they are as
nothing to the cough of our widow. Ere the
second day was closed, so assiduously had she
practised, so frequently had she changed and modulated the note—now coughing *affettuoso*, now
con espressione, now *allegretto*, and now *fortissimo*—
that she was the Philomela of a slight cold, the
very nightingale of a "hem! hem!" Guileless
widow! Little did she know that the woman who
in certain situations coughs—is lost.

The listening heart of truant Whittington, gave
the words it wished to bells. A spirit came through
the dewy air of evening—a spirit speaking golden
promise—a visible advent of the great future—
touched the brain of the little tatterdemalion of
Holloway—clapped his little hand, and made his

truant feet tread the green meads back to fortune
and to London.   " Turn   again,   Whittington !"
Thus   rang   the   bells.——" Write,   Job   Pippins !"
Thus coughed the widow.

Job wrote——

" Blue Room, Ladybird Lodge.
" Mr. Jewel would feel great happiness at knowing how Mrs. Candy passed the night.   Mr. J.
has been *much concerned* at her cough——fears it is
very troublesome to her.   Can nothing be done to
relieve it ?"

————

" Cane Room, Ladybird Lodge.
" Mrs. Candy returns her best compliments to
Mr. Jewel, and earnestly hopes that he has passed
a better night.   Has been much interested in his
cold——fears that the rookery is too near the Blue
Room for a delicate patient.   Begs to assure Mr.
Jewel that there is no danger in her little cough—
she has it every spring.   Hopes it has not disturbed
the rest of Mr. J."

————

" Blue Room, Ladybird Lodge.
" DEAR MADAM——Although I listened all night,
I was agreeably disappointed at not hearing you
above three times——may I therefore hope on your
part for a most refreshing sleep, with a considerable abatement of cough?   I fear that those nasty

sparrows were up too early for you this morning.
I trust, however, that your complaint has not suffered from their noise.

Yours, most truly, dear madam,

JOHN JEWEL.

" P.S.   If you have taken all your medicine,
mine is not quite out.   Need I say it is at your
service ?"

" *Cane Room, Ladybird Lodge.*

" DEAR SIR—Your anxiety flatters and distresses
me.   I would deny the fact—but I have ever been
the worshipper of truth.   Not once did I close my
eyes last night.   In happier days, I slept like the
lady in the fairy tale.   But there are afflictions,
there are losses—and since my late bereavement—
but let me pass the theme ;—I have done.

" I did not sleep—but there were stars in heaven,
sir—and there was the vestal brightness of the soft,
full moon—and the nightingale was singing in the
wood—and the little airs were creeping about my
window-panes—and the leaves were tapping at the
glass—and there are associations of youth—childhood, I would say—and there are feelings—I mean
sentiments—touching emotions, which the boun-
teousness of nature—oh, Mr. Jewel !—what would
this world be without sympathy !

" AGNES CANDY.

" P. S. Could you spare a powder ?"

" *Blue Room, Ladybird Lodge.*

" MY DEAREST MADAM—My heart is torn to inform you that I have no powder left. But I have sent to Mr. Faddle, and horse and man are by this time gone.

" And you were awake all night, and—odd circumstance—so was I ! And I was looking at the stars, and thinking whether love was there ! And I was gazing at the moon, round and bright as a new wedding-ring ! And your name is Agnes ! Oh, madam, did you ever see the *Bleeding Nun?* If you have, then have you seen a wounded heart—but I'll say no more. And yet, what a fool was *Raymond* to run away with a ghost ! Should not *I* —I say, should not *I* have known my own, own Agnes?

Thine ever, my dearest madam,

JOHN JEWEL.

" P. S. I have now nothing left but one little bottle and a poppy-head."

" *Cane Room, Ladybird Lodge.*

" DEAR MR. JEWEL—Your criticism on the drama does honour alike to your judgment and your feelings. The improbability, so lucidly developed by your own instinctive goodness, has, I own, often struck me; but never so fully as now, touched by your diamond of a pen. Oh, sir ! why will you not condescend to write for the stage?　A task so easy—and the reward so great!　For the sake of the expiring drama, *do* forget you are a gentleman, and write a play.

" You spoke of *Raymond* deceived by a shadow. Alas! hath not many an *Agnes* been alike betrayed? How many an elopement—how many a stolen match—but whither am I wandering?

" I hear that you are about to quit your room. I am rejoiced at your convalescence. How delightful—as the old gentleman in *The Stranger* more than insinuates—to feel well after being ill! To breathe the fresh air—to move again among rural objects—to sit in the dusk of evening—such an evening as this day promises—in a jessamine bower—such a bower as that at the end of the second garden to the right of the acacia, as you enter by the little gate through the private arbutus grove —I say, how delightful in such an evening, and in such a place, to inhale the fragrance of the jessamine's creamy blossom—to sit and talk of our hopes in the next world, and our pleasures in this!　Oh, sir!

" Farewell, yours truly,
" AGNES CANDY."

We do not intend to criticise this correspondence; we merely vouch for the letters as true copies.

That the widow should promise jessamine blossom in April, we put down to the unthinking liberality of the generous sex. For is it not in the power of woman to make even the dead twigs of life bud?— and, to give to very stinging-nettles the form and fragrance of delicious hyacinths?

There are to our mind few letters so interesting from their origin, from the place, feelings, and sentiments which begot them, as these missives, written with only a thin partition between the writers. A matter-of-fact lover would have thought of a gimblet. Job, however, in the height of his passion, knew what was due to female timidity and his host's wainscot!

Job lay in a sweet pensiveness in bed, the last letter of the widow between his finger and thumb— when Faddle tapped at the door. " Better?—oh, yes—much better"—cried that soul of hospitality, glowing benevolently at Job, who received the news with a smile of interesting langour. " And the widow—she vows she 'll leave her room to-day !" Job felt the blood in his cheek, and crumpled the letter under the clothes. " He! he ! Saffron's given ye both up !"

Job's lips moved, and we think he said—" Thank God !"

" He swore there was no making ye better or worse. He ! he ! Medicine was thrown away upon

ye.   Oh ! I had almost forgotten—your trunk is
come."

"Trunk !" echoed Job, forgetting in the moment
that he had spoken of a small, but handsome
wardrobe, left at a distant inn, to be forwarded to
him, whenever he should write for it—he pursuing
a rambling tour throughout the country, led onward by its objects of the picturesque.   And yet,
had Faddle certified to Job that his "elephant,
harnassed and mounted, was at the door," Job had
not been more astounded than at the announcement
of his "trunk."   Were the fairies back again ?

"A young man left it.   Nancy, let John bring
it up.   Ha ! ha ! widow," and Faddle tapped play-
fully at the wall, in answer to a light feminine
laugh from the next apartment.   The laugh was
repeated.   "Ha ! ha ! my lady," responded Faddle : and then looking archly at Job, sagaciously
said—"You can't tell me who's in next room ?"

"My trunk !" cried the rapt Job.

"Ha ! ha ! my lady—oh, here is the box ;" and
the servant put down a square wooden repository,
very like one of those precious coffers made for
precious legal wigs.

"Trunk," repeated Job, eyeing the box as if it
contained a lighted bomb-shell.

"Your name, however," said Faddle, reading
in sonorous tones the direction on the lid—"*John*

Jewel, Esq.!—Ha! you are right—very right," commended Faddle, contemplating the limited dimensions of the box—"never take a tour of pleasure with much luggage. A clean shirt, and a change—quite enough. I suppose, now, you have some of your sketches there?"

Job tried to speak, but could only effect a ghastly smile, which Faddle liberally translated into the affirmative.

" I must see them—where's the key?" and, at the same moment, impatiently placing his fingers to the lid, it yielded to the action. " Unlocked !" exclaimed Faddle, and the lid stood up. " Why, Mr. Jewel—humph !—eh—ha, ha !—why, what is this? Sketches? Ha! ha !"

Job dissolved into a cold jelly, and the roots of his hair turned to ice, as Faddle, with a fine homage to art, carefully removed a pen-and-ink drawing from the inside of the lid, and held it in a light most favourable to its beauties. The connoisseur beheld, scratched with bold, though rugged touches on the back of a printed dying speech—(the valedictory oration of a celebrated sheep-stealer)—a gallows; the perpendicular and horizontal beams fancifully constructed of two baby corals, and the figure of a man, with that mortal inclination of the muffled head, depending therefrom.

" An odd subject—a very odd subject," ex-

G 2

claimed Faddle, "and what is this written under-
neath?—oh! I see," and Faddle, his eyes growing
bigger, read with a tone of wonder, " *That's the
Ticket!* Well, Mr. Jewel, I—ha! ha! I can't for
the life of me compliment you on the taste of your
design, but" and Faddle gave a look that heralded
a joke, " but your execution is perfect."

Job grinned from ear to ear with ill-suppressed
horror. He tried to speak, but not a word would
come. He lay in silent agony—fairly nailed by
terror to the bed—watching the looks and hands of
the interested Faddle, who, his curiosity conquering
his good manners, rapidly twitched up the few
articles of dress tumbled into the box. The freedom of Faddle, may, to be sure, admit of this excuse; had the garments been of velvet and brocade,
he had not rudely laid his hand upon them; but
openly displaying their coarse web and plebeian
cut, they were at a thought plucked forth, and
thrown about at pleasure.

" *Your* wardrobe, Mr. Jewel? *yours?*" cried
Faddle, holding a doublet between his fingers, and
his face wrinkling into a thousand lines of fear and
doubt, as though he held a serpent by the tail,—
" *yours?*"

Faddle waited for an answer, but Job was struck
dumb by the mysterious apparition of his own
breeches!

Yes; the box directed to " John Jewel, Esq.," contained the whole of the wardrobe, *minus* the shirt, of Job Pippins. Job raised himself upon his elbow, and with a peculiarly pale cast of thought surveyed the remains—the slough of his baser days. His higher nature (he was in the blue bed in a fine cambric shirt, lace ruffled) looked down upon his sordid first life. In that moment, the purified intelligence contemplated the squalor " shuffled off." No wonder then that Job, looking at his late breeches, after some time doubted his identity.

" This is some shameful trick," cried Faddle; "some infamous hoax." Job smiled in acquiescence. " A stupid piece of would-be wit." Job shrugged up his shoulders in pity of the inventors. " But it shall be seen into." Job shook his head and blandly smiled a—no. " But it shall ! That a guest of mine should—no, Mr. Jewel, no,—it shall"—A sudden thought, with a rush of blood to his face, came upon Faddle; slapping his thigh with great force and precision, he exclaimed, " If now, it should be"——

A slight tap at the door, and enter the hero of the river—Frank Triton. " How-d'ye-do, Jewel, how-d'ye-do ?" asked the visitor, with that graceful freedom which distinguishes the truly well-bred. Job smiled faintly, and immediately there grew at his bed-side a clump of alders, and a bright river

ran through his chamber.   "How-d'ye-do, sir?"
and Frank offered his hand to Faddle, who gathered
himself up, and at a short notice, looked as dignified
as a leaden statue.

"Mr. Triton, as a gentleman,—and a man of
honour,"——

"Hallo!" cried Frank, evidently unused to such
terms of conjuration on the part of the speaker——
"Hallo! what the devil now?"

Faddle remained stern to his purpose, and began
de novo.   "Mr. Triton, as a gentleman, and a man
of honour, do you know any thing about this?"
and inclining his fore-finger towards the box,
Faddle looked and stood the incarnate spirit of
interrogation.

"About what?" cried Triton with a tongue of
brass.

"About this, sir—and this—and this—and this?"
and Faddle pointed to the various articles of dress,
the *exuviæ,* of Pippins scattered on the floor; and
as he compelled the eye of the questioned to jerkin,
vest, and doublet, it was plain from the shifting expression of the beholder, that he was not all guilt-
less.   Frank tried the first resource of detected
crime; he essayed a laugh relentlessly nipped in
the bud by Faddle.   "No, sir, no, this is a serious
matter; I look upon myself as insulted, and again
I ask you if you know any thing of these clothes?"

Triton hung down his head, and subduing a laugh, and then biting his lip,—with a look of confusion, turned over the vestments with his cane.

" Enough, sir—quite enough—I see the joke, and a very poor one it is, belongs to you.   How Mr. Jewel may receive it, I know not.   Nay, sir, no denial.   Now, I recollect—there was nobody but yourself and your new friend Mr. Wigmore present,"—(at the name of Wigmore it was observable that Frank switched his cane)—" when I spoke of Mr. Jewel's wardrobe; and I repeat, how he, as a man of delicate honour, may consider this affront, sir, I "——

Here the attention of the speaker was turned towards the bed where Job lay with a slate-coloured face, and his teeth rattling like dice.   Whether it was fear, or conscience that touched him, we will not enquire; Mr. Faddle liberally translated the emotion into indignant rage.   " Of course, any gentleman so put upon, would be in a fury."   And then the host, his softer nature returning to him, began to play the part of peace-maker.   " It was wrong ; it was very stupid of Frank—but he was a wit, and wits are very foolish people—and Frank, if he would but leave off his wit, would be a very fine fellow, and so Mr. Jewel would pardon the jest, and think no more of the rags sent in the box ?" Job strove to make an answer, but still he lay dumb and bewildered.

" Come, come, forget and forgive. Now promise me, my dear Jewel, you'll think no more of the trumpery, will you, now ?"

" I'll—I'll—try to forget it;" magnanimously answered Job.

" That's right, the brave are always generous; and the man who would jump into a river"——

Job looked piteously at Faddle—" Well, well, I'll say no more of that ; but you'll shake Frank's hand—yes, you'll shake his hand ?" Job had some conscience, and still kept his hand in bed. " Come, I must have your hands upon it—I say I must;" and Faddle with a powerful philanthropy, pulled the hand of Job from beneath the sheets, and fixing it in the hand of Frank, bound the two in his own, and kept shaking them to make their friendship mingle.

" Now, now, I'm happy," and Faddle walked from the room, confident that he had planted the olive ; and pondering on the courage and generosity of Job, who was at once a hero and a sage, and "couldn't help it."

Job, left alone with Frank Triton, was about to lannch into general topics—when Frank put to him the following question—" Pray, sir, can you tell me any thing of Mr. Wigmore ?"

One moment before, Job was for turning upon his side, when the query, significantly put, kept him on his back. No beetle with a corking-pin through its bowels was ever more cruelly fixed. Job groaned.

CHAPTER XI.

"PRAY, sir, can you tell me any thing of Mr. Wigmore?" Frank, with cold ferocity, repeated the question.

Job felt the whites of his eyes turn yellow, as he replied—"No, sir."

"Very odd; humph! I thought he recognised you at your meeting?"

"No, sir," repeated Job, with some improvement of tone.

"Why I thought he alluded to an old complaint of yours. Didn't he speak of a—a toothache?"

"Never saw him in my life till I saw him down stairs," said Job, with growing confidence; and what was more, with truth; for it will be remembered that when the great captain entered the hut, Job was sleeping in the arms of spirituous liquor.

"He has something the air of a—a gentleman;"

G 3

said Triton doubtingly. Job was silent. "And yet, yet," continued Triton, after a pause—"yet, it's very odd."

"I thought he was an old friend," remarked Job; becoming interested by the manner of his visitor, and really anxious on his own account to know something of the mysterious Wigmore. "An old and valued friend?"

"Only an acquaintance of a few hours. I'll tell you, Mr. Jewel, how it was. You have heard of the affair of the swimming match?" Job tremblingly nodded an affirmative. "Returning to dress, I found some scoundrel had stolen my clothes. Without a rag—a stitch—you can easily suppose the perplexing delicacy of my situation." Job could. "At the very moment of my destitution, who should saunter to the bank but Mr. Wigmore. He professed the deepest sympathy for my loss, with the most benevolent zeal, ran to a neighbouring hut, and in a few minutes returned with the very garments you see before you, borrowed from the wife of a cottager."

"Indeed?" said Job, looking at his old familiar dress with the eyes of a stranger. "Indeed?"

"So he said, but the fact is, Jewel, one doesn't like to own one's self tricked; and, in the first place, the hang-dog who stole my coat stole my purse with it.—You are the first to whom I have owned so much, and"—here Frank confidently laid his hand upon the hand of Job—"Pray let it go no further."

"Nobody shall know it from me," stoutly promised Job.

"However, I don't so much care for the fellow who took my purse; he'll meet with his reward—yes, I already see the knot under *his* ear." Job instinctively clapped his hand to his jugular. "What's the matter, Jewel?"

"Weakness—only weakness," said the dizzy Pippins. "And—and—he—Wigmore borrowed those clothes from a cottager?"

"So he said; but, between ourselves, I know not if they didn't come from the bones of Jack-of-the-Gibbet. Look at 'em, Jewel," and the speaker weighed the doublet at the end of his cane—"isn't there a Newgate cut about 'em?"

"Very Newgate," confessed Job. "But," said he, hastening from the subject, "what makes you suspect Mr. Wigmore?"

"I'll tell you. Struck by his friendly offices, and thinking him something of a character, I asked him to the house of a friend I am visiting, and then our talk falling upon"——

"Won't you try to come down?" said Faddle, knocking at the door, and speaking as he opened it. "Won't you come down, Jewel? The widow will be up, and there's somebody below, who—why, what's the matter? You are friends still, I hope?" anxiously asked Faddle, as he marked the look of constraint on the face of Triton, and the perplexed countenance of Job. "Still friends?" he bawlingly repeated.

"To be sure—good bye, Jewel, good bye—mum! —not a word," added Frank in a low tone, but not low enough to escape the pricked ears of Faddle— " not a word; we shall meet, and then"—and then in a louder note, " Good bye—wish you well—good bye."

Faddle inwardly blessed his benignant stars that had brought him up stairs. " A feigned conciliation—a sham truce—'we shall meet'—yes, yes— very good—thank God! there's a magistrate!" All this passed through the beating brain of Faddle with incredible celerity; however, disguising his sagacity, he again addressed himself to Job— " You'll come down—you must come down—here, John, take this rubbish away"—and Job's late habiliments were again boxed, and carried from the presence. " You must come down—I have some friends here whom you must know. Her ladyship was just now in the next room—ha!—I declare—look upon the lawn—her husband is come —there is Sir"——

Job looked from his bed, and though the outdoor object had suddenly moved, Job too clearly recognised through the under branches of a larustinus, the well-known ninepin calves of Sir Scipio Mannikin. Job sunk back upon his pillow, and wished to render up the ghost.

"You *will* come down?" repeated Faddle, his back turned upon the sufferer.

"In the evening—yes, in the evening." The doubting looks of Faddle compelled Job to peculiar emphasis; and the host, affecting satisfaction, left the room. We say affecting, for Faddle was not to be duped.

And again Job was under the same roof with Sir Scipio and Lady Mannikin! with the individual mischief—the sweet perdition of his hopes! What was to be done? As he asked himself for the twentieth time the perplexing question, his eye fell upon the *vera effigies*—in pen and ink—of William Ticket, scratched on the dying speech, fallen like a sybil's leaf upon the bed. As his eyeballs hung upon the black lines, his imaginative fears made them undulate and tremble, and he saw, not William Ticket, but Job Pippins in his mortal throes! Nor were the terrors of Job without the best authority; for at the very time that he lay in the Blue Room steeped in the cold dew of horror, his garments, accidentally waylaid in the hands of John by the inquisitive Sir Scipio, were recognised as the identical covering of the kiss-robbing—artery-cutting—repeater-stealing barber!   Great was the astonishment of Sir Scipio, and many and curious were the looks passed between his stern self and gentle wife (Mercy married to Justice, but with no power over the sword,) as the story was told of the delivery of the box at the Lodge, the theft committed on Frank Triton, and the accident which put him under temporary obligation to Job's vestments.

" There is no doubt that the scoundrel," said Sir Scipio, and no man, from constant practice, gave more sonorous expression to the epithet— " that the scoundrel has joined the gang of ruffians prowling hereabout.   Yes, yes"—and he looked at Lady Scipio as though he were about to promise her a delightful treat—" there'll be a pretty cart-full.   And this, madam—this is the fellow you have pitied!"   Lady Mannikin spoke not; but, assuming the privilege of her sex, she passed her handkerchief across her eyes.   She, indeed, spoke not; but, oh, the eloquence of her cambric!   Yea, there is a tongue in pocket handkerchiefs!

Faustus in his agony shrieked—

" Lentè, lentè, currite noctis equi ! "

Not so, Job; he lay and prayed for night—" thick night."   He had made up his mind—he had determined to escape.   It is true, he thought of the widow with a touch of tenderness that—then again he thought of his neck, and the widow passed away. Marriage was a doubtful good—but hanging was a certain evil. To stay for the widow, was to go to the assizes; Hymen and Jack Ketch were in his case so intimately allied, that he must have them both. The evening came on, the stars appeared, and Job, with a heavy, heavy heart, looked abroad into the grey sky, and asked himself where he should sleep. He rose from his bed—precipitately dressed himself—went to the door—touched the handle— withdrew his fingers—sat down, and again and again ruminated on the policy of his departure. Now, he thought of the good dinners, the soft bed, and the servants in livery. And now, all his hopes would be extinguished by a black cap! No: fly he must; so, resolving to creep down stairs, silently gain the garden, and thence get into the open road, he with a sinking of the heart, and pausing once to listen for the widow—he listened and he heard her not—he placed his hat upon his head, and was about to open the door, when—his arms dropt to his side, and he fell—*come cadde un corpo morto !* —he fell into a chair—the door was double-locked !

At the first burst of perspiration consequent on this discovery, Job could not have parted with less than two pounds of solid flesh. All was known— Sir Scipio had found him out—he was a lamb shut

up for the knife! He listened, and he heard
the clouted shoes of the parish constable ascending
the stairs! No; it was his own heart thumping to
get through his waistcoat. Job wiped his forehead,
and tried to think. He had, with very many people,
great presence of mind—but not in critical situations. He walked to the window; but he gathered
no counsel from the stars. He cautiously opened
the casement, to contemplate the possibility of " a
drop." Bacchus—bountiful Bacchus—prevented
his taking it. Never was the jolly god so beneficent
to wretched man! A vine, of at least some fifty
years growth—a vine, with arms of cable strength,
grew up the wall of the house, offering the firmest
footing to the fugitive. Had the purple toper
visited Ariadne as Romeo visited Juliet, he could
not have set up a better ladder. Job's feet and
hands were in a trice among the fruitful cordage
—and so lightly did he descend, that never a bud
was lost to his helper.

Job stole along the garden, and, silent as a mole,
made in the direction of the high road. Creeping
down one of the green alleys that intersected the
grounds, he was suddenly struck motionless by a
voice that touched his heart-strings. He laid himself flat upon his belly, perspired, and listened; an
umbrageous lilac curtained him around. " Two
husbands before I'm thirty?" exclaimed a female

voice in a note of perfect satisfaction; the speaker
was no other than Bodkin, the widow's maid.
" Two husbands—a lord for a twelvemonth—and
a third marriage at forty," was the reply; and Job
gasped in agony as he recognised the deep, winning,
subtle tone of Molly of the hut, removed to the
precincts of Ladybird Lodge for the ostensible purpose of telling the future destinies of the anxious
household. For the last three days it appeared
Molly had secretly driven her trade; every domestic, from the butler to the scullion, had crossed her
hand and looked on future life. " And now you
must tell me about my mistress." " The widow?"
asked the black-eyed sibyl. " Will she—will she
marry Mr. Jewel?" " If nothing worse befal him,"
was the unsatisfactory reply. " Worse!" cried
Bodkin; " can any mischief threaten so sweet a
gentleman?" Job was generally above vulgar superstition; but in the present case he thought there
might be something in a fortune-teller. " At this
moment," pronounced Molly, her voice deepening
with her subject, " I see a gallows and a church—
a noose and a wedding-ring—a coffin and a bride-
bed. Yes, yes, I smell the flowering hemp and the
marriage roses."—" God bless us," cried Bodkin,
with sudden religion—" hang a gentleman!"—
" And why not?" replied the prophetess, quite unmoved by the probability of such a catastrophe.

" Hang Mr. Jewel !" still exclaimed Bodkin—
" Why, what can he have done?" There was a
sudden rustling of the leaves—a quick footstep—
and then another shrill, feminine, anxious voice,
asked—" What can he have done?" A delicious
tremor went through the bones of Job as he heard
the voice of the widow. It was, indeed, Mrs. Candy;
won to the imprudence by the strong weakness of
love, she had prompted her maid to touch upon the
future fate of her mistress, herself hid the while
among the bushes. Molly answered not; when
the widow, with new fervour, laid a dollar in the
gipsy's palm, and again repeated, with deeper
tenderness, " What can he have done?" Molly
was meditating, if possible, a satisfactory answer,
when—when——

Job, worked upon by a thousand sweet emotions,
and fearing to betray himself, lay and wriggled on
the grass like a wire-snake in a pantomime. " Holding his breath for a time," and digging his face into
the turf, two or three green blades unhappily entered his nostrils; and thus, when Molly was about
to divine, Job published a loud sneeze. There was
a death-like pause !

" A cat !" cried Molly.

" A man !" exclaimed the maid, with deeper
knowledge; and instantaneously the three women,
like a leash of startled hares, ran bounding off.

Molly and Bodkin, not weakened by the weight of
sorrow borne for the past six months by the widow,
secured their retreat—but the widow, running with
a more matron-like step, and accidentally coming
in contact with Job, as he rose upon his knees,
was locked—nay, double-locked in his nervous
arms. Of course she was about to give a scream
that would have split the "unwedgeable and gnarled
oaks," but Job exclaimed, "'Tis I—your Jewel,"
and added to the evidence of voice the testimony of
touch—and the scream of the widow, merely snapping a stay-lace, died mutely in her throat.

"You wicked man!" said Mrs. Candy, "after
such an illness to venture in the night air. Pray—
pray return to the house."

"Impossible," cried Job, deeply impressed with
the imprudence of such a step. "Impossible—my
fate is fixed."

"What *can* you mean?" asked the widow with
most peculiar astonishment.

"I say, my fate is fixed—but wherever I go,
madam, the recollection of your charms, your virtues—the sweet hours of sickness passed in the
Blue Room—Oh, ma'am! I am the unhappiest of
men!"

"Don't say so," urged the widow, though at the
time thinking the unhappiest of men the most pic-

turesque object in creation. " Don't say so. What has happened?"

" Oh, ma'am! I am a wretch hunted by evil fortune—a miserable, ill-starred man—a victim to accidents that—why, why was I born?" exclaimed Job, throwing his head up to the stars for an answer.

" I see it all!" cried the widow—" I see it all— tell me, sir—pray tell me—I have heard the story from Mr. Faddle—but I thought you were secured —and now it all comes upon me—but weren't you locked up?"

" I—I was!"—and Job's teeth chattered at the recollection.

" And yet you have eluded him—and—oh, yes— the fortune-teller spoke too truly—flowering hemp! —yes, your life, your precious life is forfeit to the law! they'll—they'll"—and the widow grew hysterical with the conviction, and she laid her head upon Job's shoulder as she finished the sentence— " they'll hang you."

Now, although Job had withstood the torment of his own fear of the gallows, he could not bear up against this touching corroboration, and the tears started to his eyes, and he stood dissolved, with one arm round the waist of the widow.

" And you have met—and you have shed his blood!"

" I did it for the best," said Job, his thoughts recurring to the apoplectic Sir Scipio in the waggon.

" No doubt—no doubt," replied Mrs. Candy
with feminine charity—" but the world, Mr. Jewel
—the world judges not of best intentions. And
where—where is he now?" she asked with timid
curiosity.

" In the Lodge."

" But are you certain of the worst?"

" Certain—I saw his legs among the branches,
and"—a new gush of sorrow on the part of the
widow awakened Job to new attentions.

" But this"—and Mrs. Candy wiped her eyes
with marked decision—" this is no place for us—
I mean for you. You must fly—you must quit the
country—in a brief time the affair will be forgotten,
and then you may return—and"——

" True, madam, true; 'twould be the safest—
wisest plan—but, since you have shown such kind
concern, I will confess to you that I cannot leave
England without"——

" Nay, Mr. Jewel"—

" I cannot stir from this spot without"—money,
Job was about to say, but the widow was impatient—

" You are a man of honour, Mr. Jewel?"

" I am, ma'am," and Job, anticipating an offered
loan, put his hand upon his heart very boldly.

" Then—then be our two fates one—England, farewell—I'm thine for ever," and she sank upon Job's neck, and his knees knocked together with his new responsibility.

At this moment, shouting voices were heard in the direction of the house. Sir Scipio and Faddle were loudly encouraging searchers and pursuers.

" No time is to be lost !" exclaimed the widow— " this way—this way !" And Mrs. Candy wound through the bushes, Job mutely and wonderingly following her, the shouts growing louder—and a brace of pistol bullets being fired, as Job swore, within a hand of his curls. For a few moments let us leave the fugitives to their fortune.

Faddle, morbidly fearful of the irascibility of Job, had locked his door to prevent what he otherwise looked upon and published as certain, a duel between Messrs. Jewel and Triton. He had unburthened his bosom to Sir Scipio, who, as a magistrate, proposed that the inhabitant of the Blue Room should be bound in heavy articles of the peace. For some time did they wait for the bell of Job— when Faddle, attended by Sir Scipio, proceeded to the Blue Room, where they found the window open and their Jewel gone. The affair was clear as day to Faddle: his guest, incited by his delicate sense of honour, had dropt from the window to keep a mortal assignation. On this, butler, footmen, grooms, lacqueys, all were armed, and all scattered about the grounds to seize the would-be homicides. They found not Frank Triton, for he had that day consented to be chairman at the Walton Club—a knot of brothers of the angle—and at the time of the search, was certainly about to measure his ground under the table; neither did they find John Jewel, for he—however we shall return to him;—but they found, rolled up among the shrubs, armed to the teeth with crow-bar, centre-bit, and all the other implements of their " dreadful trade," three gentlemen with one purpose, Phineas, Mortlake, and Bats, the triumvirate of the wattled hut. Two of them having fired in resistance, and thus satisfied their self-respect, modestly surrendered. Bats fought, but valour was in vain. Let us return to the lovers.

They had crossed the bridge, when they espied a post-chaise rapidly approaching them, sent, as it appeared, for Doctor Lullaby, yet a visitor at the Lodge, for a grand christening next day at Wiggledon Park. The widow possessed sufficient arguments to induce the postilion to take herself and her Jewel in and turn the horses' heads. Away they rattled, Job sitting, in the estimation of his affianced wife, a new-blown hero by her side; she full of tenderness—he full of hope, when—the horses stood fixed. Job let down the glass to call to the

postilion, when a horse's head looked into the
chaise, and he heard in, he thought, well-remem-
bered notes—" Stand—your money !" The widow
screamed—" Wigmore !" and felt for her purse.
The horse withdrew his head, and when Job, trembling on the verge of dissolution, rose to give the
treasure to the highwayman, he saw the animal with
his forelegs stubbornly folded under him, and his
rider tugging at the reins and digging with his
spurs. Nor was the postilion blind to the accident,
but lashing his horses, started on, and the wheel
striking the head of the highwayman, knocked him
senseless into the road. In four-and-twenty hours
the passengers of the post-chaise were wedded man
and wife.

Poor Wigmore—we mean the luckless Skinks—
was found by a compassionate countryman, who
recognised the horse as the property of Frank Triton, esq., it was a fine animal, but with one extraordinary defect, that of going upon his knees. The
captain was delivered into the hands of the law.
His further history is to be seen in that interesting
miscellany which for the past few years has supplied
the playhouses with their most touching dramas.
It also contains brief notices of Phineas, Mortlake,
and Bats. As for Molly, she became an honest woman : she married a sheriff's officer, and wore diamonds from the small and uncertain profits of a

sponging-house. Poor Skinks! in an evil hour did he boast of his knowledge of horse-flesh—of his power to cure any steed of any known or unknown vice, and, in a no less luckless hour did Frank Triton, taking him at his word, lend him his bright bay without naming its particular defect.

And what became of Job Pippins?

He married the widow—made the grand tour—sent, anonymously, fifty pounds to Frank Triton for his purse and clothes—a handsome repeater for Sir Scipio Mannikin (and though he was dead, the present was not lost upon his successor)—returned to England—kept a comfortable house—and having plenty of money, was a decent, respectable, neutral kind of fellow—a frank, jolly dog, whom the luck of accidents had made so, and " couldn't help it." There are more than one Pippins !

JACK RUNNYMEDE:

THE MAN OF MANY "THANKS."

CHAPTER I.

JOHN RUNNYMEDE was descended from a long line of placemen; hence, with him, the love of country was an instinct. He was the last of his race, and though he had not inherited even one slice of the nice white loaf—(the envied *manchet*)— one of the smallest of the gold fishes whereon many of his ancestors had fattened and grown great, his patriotism—strange as it may seem—was in no way weakened by the disadvantage. Fortunately, John had no son: we say, fortunately, for the child of the unrewarded patriot might have lapsed into the rebel: the declension is not impossible; for public virtue, like flowers, may not be propagated beyond a certain point. Happily, there is no such blot upon the escutcheon of the Runnymedes: the death of John was worthy all the lives of all his progenitors.

Whilst we refuse ourselves the pride of exhibiting the genealogical tree of our hero—a tree, determined by the heralds, duly paid for the discovery by a rich cordwainer of the family, to have first struck root in the court of the Conqueror—we will admit of no negative proofs of its antiquity and greatness. That a Runnymede has been known to sit in the stocks, shall be no evidence that a Runnymede has not sat upon the bench; that another has been whipped for picking pockets, shall not annihilate a Runnymede once high in the exchequer; that one of the family has rung the bell of a scavenger, shall not deafen us to the appeal of him who once carried a milk-white wand in the presence. It is with the tree of genealogy as with the oak of the forest; we boast of the timbers it has given to a state vessel, but we rarely talk of the three-legged stools, the broomsticks and tobacco-stoppers made from the ends and chips. Now, that John Runnymede was the son of a prosperous wheelwright, ought not, in the belief of the reader, to affect his descent from even the courtiers of the Norman. Enough of the blood of Runnymede.

" Yes—yes—have my vote? To be sure he shall : Mr. Sidewind is a true patriot—a man who ought to die in Parliament—a man of principles—a practical man." Such was the loud avowal of Jack Runnymede, solicited for his vote by Mr. Sidewind's agent for the borough of ——, but no matter, we will not speak ill of the dead. Jack, be it understood, had inherited the great right of voting with a very small property; and as that right, at the time of our narrative, was exercised by a very few, it was the more precious to the possessor. "Ha!—the purity of election; the proud privilege wrested by the bold barons from a tyrant—yes, yes, thank God! I'm an Englishman." This was the constant thanksgiving of Jack, closing broken sentences on the value of Magna Charta—trial by jury—habeas corpus, and other political treasures enjoyed by Britons: and so strong was his gratitude for these inestimable benefits, that it sometimes escaped him under circumstances not particularly demanding its avowal. Thus, one day walking with his friend Fibb—an oily tradesman and a great patriot—he was stopped short by a crowd, gathered to behold the public whipping of a petty larceny offender. As the culprit came along, yelling under the lash like a wild Indian, Runnymede profoundly observed—" This, politically speaking, is a cheerful sight."

"Cheerful!" exclaimed Fibb, suddenly thrusting his hands into his pockets, and pursing his mouth, like a squirrel cracking nuts—" Cheerful!"

" Politically speaking," answered Jack. " When we consider the cost of this ceremony—the erection of a prison to secure—the salary of a judge to condemn—and of a hangman to whip an offender who, it may be, has only stolen to the value of a groat— I say, it is a sight to make us venerate the laws— yes, to make us bless our stars that we are Englishmen."

" So you said to Sir Peter Polygon, when he stood upon the hustings, covered with mud," said Fibb.

" And I said true," returned Jack. " Nay, suppose he had been killed by the mob—was there not freedom of election, and would he not have died an Englishman? By the way, you voted of course as usual?"

" Humph—why—no, not this time," said Fibb, and he gently rubbed his second chin along his neckcloth.

" How so, been bribed?—to be sure, it's no affair of mine—like myself, you are free—you are an Englishman. And yet I—I thought your principles were fixed?" cried Jack.

" And so they are—immutably," said Fibb, and he played with his watch-chain—" hav'n't I the autographs of King Alfred, and Oliver Cromwell— and Algernon Sidney—and Kosciusko, and Lord Russell? But in this instance, the court candidate is the friend of Mr. ——, the manager."

" What ! of the play-house?" asked Jack quickly.
" What is that to you?"

" A great deal : I think I know something of the
drama; yes—I've taken tea twice with Mrs. Siddons, and once sold her a looking-glass;" and
Fibb nodded his double chin ; " very often go fly-
fishing with John Kemble;—well, I'm on the free-
list, and the manager wrote me a letter—in a word,
if I hadn't voted as I did, I should have been
scratched.—Still, understand, I hav'n't altered my
principles, though I have changed my voice." And
Fibb, with his hands in his pockets, went up and
down upon his toes.

" You astonish me," cried Jack—" I couldn't
have thought it possible."

" Nor could I, until tried," observed Fibb; " and
to say the truth, it cost me a struggle.   Indeed, I
should have flung up my free admission, and voted
according to my conscience, but for Julius Cæsar."

" What has Julius Cæsar to do with an Englishman?" asked Runnymede.

" Understand me—Julius Cæsar in the play-bill.
Did you ever see the Brutus of ———?" Jack shook
his head. " Then I pity you. Ha ! you can't conceive the majesty—the beauty—the dignity—the
power of his Brutus. I have seen it from behind
the scenes. Well, I—I could not resist; so I went
and voted for the manager's friend, and at night

took all my family into the boxes to Julius Cæsar. Wonderful thing ——'s Brutus! So lofty—so noble—so different from anything that's mean," said the unconscious Fibb, and he hurried home, possibly to contemplate his autographs of the patriots of all nations.

The next day Jack was to quit town to exercise, as he justly said, the noblest right of an Englishman—namely, to choose a man to make him new laws, and to mend the old ones if required. This was the third time Jack had been called upon in the capacity of an elector—and never had his attendance been so necessary to the success of his cause—for a spirit of opposition menaced the return of the old member, accustomed to take his seat for the borough of —— as he would take his easy chair. If, before, Jack felt himself to be only one Englishman, his dignity on the approaching event was multiplied by at least three. Nay, had he been about to return the whole Commons, he could not have entertained a stronger sense of his importance. " Happy land—glorious laws—heaven-born liberty —Magna Charta—habeas corpus—trial by jury"— all passed through his brain, and quickened his blood as he stept into the mail that was to convey him to the borough of ——. He was about to seat himself for his journey, when he heard himself, in no bland accents, called by name—" Mr. Runnymede."

" Who calls Mr. Runnymede?" asked Jack, thrusting bimself half out of the vehicle, and dilating his nostrils as if to snuff the enquirer.

" I've a little affair, Mr. Runnymede"—

" Not now," said Jack—" not now, my good man—when I return—little affairs, indeed !"

" Well then, it's a big affair—and you must come out," saying which, the speaker grasped the arm of Jack.

" I tell you, I'm going to the borough of —— to give my vote"—cried Jack.

" *Give* your vote," echoed a porter derisively.

" Yes, sir," and Runnymede was full of the patriot—" give my vote, or do what I like with it. I suppose I may do what I like with it. Thank God ! I'm an Englishman," and as Jack finished the sentence he almost fell in a heap upon the pavement ; hauled out of the mail—for the coachman had taken the reins, and no time was to be lost— by the man who had so anxiously addressed him. " What is this—what is this? Thank heaven ! there's the law—and thank—"

" We must do our duty, Mr. Runnymede," said the fellow, interrupting Jack in his thanks.

" And I must do mine," said Runnymede— " and my first duty is to give my vote—yes, to get"——

" Two thousand pounds," cried the man.

" Not so much as that," said Jack unconsciously

" Every farthing—for that's what the writ against
you says,"—gravely observed what proved to be a
bailiff.

" A writ—and two thousand pounds—from
whom?　I don't owe two thousand pennies," exclaimed Runnymede, white with astonishment.

" All the better if you can prove it," said the
catchpole.　" The writ's at the suit of Henry
Parsons." ·

" Don't know such a man," shouted Jack—" and
two thous——why, what for?"

" That would be very ill manners in me to ask,"
said Mr. Eyes, the bailiff.　" Come, sir," he benevolently added, " don't get a crowd."

" But I tell you, I can't come—I "—at this moment the mail went off—" I shall lose my vote—
I"——

" Shall I call a coach, Mr. Runnymede, or will
you walk?" asked Eyes, without any comment.

" But you shall suffer for this," and Jack buttoned his coat very resolutely—" yes, yes—there
are laws—thank heaven, there are laws !　Parsons—
two thousand pounds !　I see it—you've taken me
for another man"——

Eyes smiled—bent his brows—and meekly observed—" Never did such a thing in all my life, sir."

" But you have—I know you have—never mind

H 3

—it's no matter—I'm in your custody, it's true—I shall lose my vote—my candidate may lose his election—but I don't care—there's satisfaction to be had—yes, thank God! I'm an Englishman!" Nor had John Runnymede ceased his many thanksgivings, ere he arrived at the modest dwelling of Mr. Eyes.

The prisoner was courteously shown into the private room of his gaoler, where company was assembled helping the time with whist. "Is the pig done?" and Eyes spoke in a low voice to his wife.

"Trumps led—not quite," said Rebecca; then bowing a welcome to Runnymede, and attending to the play—"a small club."

"Pig for supper," thought Runnymede—"so, Eyes has really changed his religion with his name," (for the reader must learn that Eyes had long been known in the Hebrew world as Isaacs). It is extraordinary that in his perplexing condition, Jack could have thought of supper; a metaphysician may account for this from some association of ideas: for ourselves, we should as soon imagine Mutius Scævola with his hand over the red coals, asking the Etrurian king what time he went to dinner?

"The pig must be done," said Eyes to his wife, who nodded assent—"A little heart"—then to her husband—"I'm sure, if it isn't done, it won't be for want of brandy and tobacco."

" Brandy and tobacco!" thought Jack, and looked suddenly in the face of Eyes, who mistaking the object of the stare, said—" It's too late to get bail to-night, Mr. Runnymede; but you'll be very comfortable here, I assure you."

" I never knew anybody half so lazy," said Rebecca aside to her mate—" if you don't—(another trump)—if you don't manage something—(another —my trick)—you'll lose the pig; his discharge came to-day—so you must—(trump again)—so you must."—

The attention of Eyes was called to Runnymede, who sat, violently knocking the floor with his toe, and brooding in a savage joy at the prospect of legal satisfaction for the violence committed upon him.   Never had Jack felt so much an Englishman; never had the all-healing law appeared so gracious and so bountiful.   The whole country—yes, the empire would thrill from one end to the other at the knowledge of his wrongs.   He jumped up, animated by the thought.

" You'll stop with us to supper?" said Eyes, with unusual hospitality.

Runnymede was big with the thought of satisfaction; and replied with dignity—" I thank you —I'm not partial to pig."

" Pig," said Eyes; and " pig," said his wife, Rebecca.

Jack, however, had some compassion, and therefore gave the bailiff another chance of saving himself from certain destruction.—" Mr. Eyes, before I retire to my room, I do solemnly assure you as a gentleman and"—

(" The Jack of Spades," said a lady at whist)—

" As a gentleman, and what is more, as an Englishman, that I know no Mr. Parsons—that I owe no two thousand pounds. If this be no mistake, there are some scoundrels in the business; who to blame I know not—but it strikes me that the"—

(" Honours are divided," said Rebecca, and she made the cards.)

" Shall I show you to your room?" asked Eyes, who had heard enough. " If there is anything wrong, it can't be helped to-night; and to-morrow there's no business—but on Monday morning"—

" Monday! The election will be finished on Monday—I—but, no matter—thank heaven! there's the law—yes, thank God! I'm an Englishman," saying which, Runnymede followed Eyes up stairs. Just as the chamberlain had reached the first flight, he heard his name roared out, coupled with no complimentary epithets—

" What, Eyes! thief—catchpole—vermin of the earth—cannibal scoundrel!"—

" Mr. Noland—Mr. Noland," cried Eyes in an

offended tone, and approached the abusive prisoner, who sat in a chair—in a room, the door of which was opened to the passage. Jack stood behind Eyes, and with some difficulty made out a man—who sat rocking in a chair—from clouds of tobacco smoke issuing from a short pipe, buried to the bowl in his mouth. He had hung a night-cap on the side of his head;—and, his eyes filled with a sullen fire—his brow bent—his mealy face stained with red blots—his chin bristled with a fortnight's beard—and his sensual lips moving like worms with suppressed rage, he kept rocking his chair, and growled up into the face of Eyes—" You robber of the gallows! when am I to get out?"

" I hope, Mr. Noland, you have wanted nothing? Didn't Rebecca send you the brandy?" asked the master of the house.

" Brandy! yes—yes," said the prisoner, and taking a bottle from the table, he flung it on the floor, and laughed in his throat, as the empty vessel was shivered into pieces.—" There's the brandy!"—

" Well, you shall have more, Mr. Noland—only, as a keepsake—do me this one little *pictur*"—said Eyes.

" I won't—not a touch—not a touch. I'll work no more for gaol-birds. Damn me! I'm a gentle-man—do you mean to say I'm not a gentleman?"

and Noland rose staggeringly from his chair to assert his gentility. "What! because I don't put dolls upon canvas—and smear petticoats of velvet, I'm not a gentleman," and he fell like clay into his seat: his head rolling from side to side, he growled— "Humph!—velvet—what's velvet? Is any man's straw like mine? Any man's straw, I say? Sir——! oh yes, Sir——! *Sir!* paints lords, and so he's a sir!—can he paint a pig? Can he paint a pig, I say? Makes judges' wigs, too—and fine ladies curls and"—and he laughed with fixed teeth; "ha! ha! I should only like to catch him at bristles." Eyes approached the table, at which Noland sat, and bent his head towards a half-finished picture of a sow and her litter, devouring it with the looks of a connoisseur. As Eyes stooped, rapt by the art, a violent sense of his own merits came anew upon the artist, and staring for a minute to take good aim, he caught the unconscious bailiff by the neck, and grasping it like a Cyclops, beat his head upon the table, roaring above the voice of the injured officer, "I say, put 'em all together—can they paint a pig? Tell me that—can they paint a pig?"

This loud interrogative, with the cries of her husband and the voice of Runnymede, brought Rebecca and her whist-party up stairs—"Goodness me! Eyes! Mr. Noland!—what's the matter?" exclaimed the wife; when the artist let go her husband's neck, rose, and in simpering drunkenness addressed the lady—" What! Mrs. Isaacs!"—

" Isaacs," cried the lady, disdainfully.

" Beg your pardon, but as I had the happiness of knowing you before you were a Christian, Mrs. Eyes—I"—and here, catching the officer by the shoulder, the artist roared a laugh, and again throwing himself in the chair, shouted—" Well, what do you think of the pigs? Was there ever prettier meat?"

" Beautiful—beautiful, Mr. Noland," said Eyes, rubbing his neck, and glancing at the unfinished picture—" like life, I declare—I'm sure you can almost hear 'em grunt."

" Almost? Quite!" cried Noland, and his clenched fist fell like a smith's hammer on the table.

" I never knew anybody work so quick as you," said the officer, with a horrid smile, to the painter—" why, you could finish it to-night?" Noland made no answer, but looked doggedly at the speaker, and pointed his fore-finger towards the pieces of the broken bottle.—" Rebecca, love," said Eyes, " some brandy for Mr. Noland."

" And Mrs. Isaacs—Eyes, I mean—more tobacco," was the amended order of the artist. " Now, I say—you old thief, when am I to get out of your stye?"—and Noland spread himself in the chair, awaiting an answer.

" Your discharge must come on Monday—but you'll dine with us to-morrow, Mr. Noland? Yes—for the last time," said the bailiff;—" but you'll finish the picture?"

" Ha!—that is—I may come to dinner if I provide the pork. It's always been so, eh? Never mind—I'll mend all this—yes, yes—you rascally man-trap—this is the last time you catch me—this is—oh, the brandy!"——

" Good night, Mr. Noland—good night," said Eyes.

" We shall expect you to-morrow at dinner," said Rebecca, first prompted by her husband—and the visitors bade good night to the artist, leaving him silently glaring at the bottle.

" I only hope these painted things may be worth half what they cost us," said the bailiff's wife, before she slept.

" Hav'n't I got twenty out of him, and only for a little liquor and meat—and whenever one discharge has come, hav'n't I got something else put in against him, and all on purpose to keep him here and paint?*   Why, by-and-bye, when he's dead—them pictures will be a fortune to us!   Do you think I'm a fool?" and the bailiff fell into a sweet slumber.

And where, it will be asked, was Jack Runny-

* A true story.

mede? In bed; in a room with bars at the windows, and the door locked, and twice bolted on the outside; a prisoner for the sum of two thousand pounds, he, as he really and truly averred, not owing two thousand pence. " It is no matter," said Jack as he turned restlessly from side to side— " I shall be amply repaid for this—yes, thank heaven! there is the law.—I am deprived of my liberty by the perjury of some scoundrel—I am cheated of the exercise of a dear privilege, and at a moment shut up here in a cage like a wild beast—but what of it?—there's a remedy—a certain, a glorious remedy—for, thank God! I'm an Englishman!"

CHAPTER II.

THE next day passed as pleasantly with Jack as the company of his host and hostess would permit: as for the painter, his dinner with a new supply of brandy and tobacco was carried up stairs, Eyes remarking that it was a pity to disturb him at his work, if his heart was set upon finishing it. The Monday morning came, and ere Jack—active as he ever was, with the feelings of a Briton—could be up, Eyes, his keeper, was at his bed-side; and in the most conciliating tone and with a smiling face,

observed " That there was no occasion to send for
bail—he could, upon consideration, take Mr. Runnymede's single signature to a bond—he was a man
of honour"——

" And, thank heaven ! an Englishman," added
Runnymede ; and no baron witnessed Magna
Charta with greater dignity, than possessed Jack
as he affixed his name to the bail-bond. This ceremony performed, a few minutes saw him in the
office of his attorney.

" Bless me ! Mr. Runnymede—I thought you
were gone to ——, to vote for Sidewind ?" said the
man of law.

" Look at that," said Jack, and he threw down
the copy of the writ politely afforded him by Eyes.

" What ! Eh ?—Parsons—two thousand pounds,"
said Mr. Candidus.

" Don't know the man—don't owe a penny,"
said Runnymede in a voice almost rising to a
shriek—" there —arrested—as I was in the mail—
carried off, I may say by force—locked up, and
couldn't even send a note—but, thank heaven !"——

" Who's the attorney?—Oh ! Ha ! ha ! Allwork,
of Lyon's-Inn ! Phoo—an election trick ! You've
lost your vote," observed Candidus, unnecessarily.

" To be sure I have—but I possess the proud
birthright of a Briton. Yes—thank heaven ! I'm
an Englishman—and satisfaction"——

" My dear Mr. Runnymede, what can we prove?"

" Prove! Hav'n't I been locked up—I—a free-born Briton—hav'n't I been kidnapped—incarcerated for more than six-and-thirty hours?"

" But Allwork isn't worth powder and shot," said Candidus.

" No more are carrion crows," replied Jack, " but they shoot 'em for all that."

" Yes—but in this case, the sport is very expensive. See here, Mr. Runnymede; if Allwork prove true to his employers, we can only go against him. Very well; if we should get a verdict—and it is by ' *ifs* ' that the profession lives—if we should get a verdict"——

" I shall punish the pettifogger," exclaimed Runnymede, swelling with expected triumph.

" And you'll pay your own costs," replied Candidus, very meekly—" and they'll not be a little."

" But I've lost my vote. Can't I prove damages?" asked Runnymede.

" That fact rests in your own bosom," remarked Candidus, and he rubbed one hand with the other, and his eye twinkled.

" It's no matter, Mr. Candidus—I'll not trouble you—good morning—you may be right—I dare say you are—but I can never be convinced—no, never while I breathe the air of Albion, that a man is to be locked up by another man, as you say, not worth powder and shot—and the culprit is only to be punished at the further cost of the injured party. No, sir—I have a respect for your character—for your great legal knowledge—but I can't believe this—no—I can't—for, thank heaven! I'm an Englishman."

Jack Runnymede quitted the office of his friendly adviser, determined to seek another more learned in the law than the simple Mr. Candidus. In an unlucky moment he ran against Earwig, a man of multifarious information; a man who, having no history of his own, made himself proficient in the history of every other person. He knew the boarding-school, its mistress, nay, the names of all its teachers, from which the Countess of ——— eloped with a marching ensign, and the sign of the public-house at which the fugitives were overtaken. He could point out the apple-tree which the Lord Chancellor robbed, and knew the usher employed to flog him for the delinquency. No man was more keenly alive to the frailties of his fellow-creatures; no man had a stronger relish of defect in all things. To have discovered the spots in the sun, was to him greater than the discovery of the laws that govern it.

" Why, Jack?—Where now?—What's the matter? Something wrong? Yes—I'm sure, there's something wrong?" said the acute Earwig.

" Wrong! Do you know a fellow, named All-work, of Lyon's-Inn?" asked Runnymede.

" To be sure I do; but his name's not Allwork," replied Earwig with decision.

" No?"

" No. His name's Chuff—John Chuff. He's Essex—from Prittlewell: came to town—made a little money—I won't say how—but old things came up—so he leaves London; after a time, comes back—in mourning, deep as a raven; crape about his hat enough for a buccaneer's flag; the death's head was in the hat—ha! ha!—his aunt had died—and had left him her property, if he'd take her name. He took both. Hem!"

" But I hear," said Runnymede, " that he's not worth powder and shot."

" Very wrong. He is worth powder—and shot—and rope," said Earwig, with peculiar emphasis on the last word.

" And he changed his name? Why, what was it came up? Tell me," cried Runnymede anxiously.

" Don't you know? Once stole two ducks"——

" Never?" exclaimed the incredulous Jack.

" And a hand-saw"—continued Earwig.

" It's impossible," cried the charitable Runnymede.

" And a chisel," asseverated Earwig, becoming enthusiastic as he repeated the iniquities of Chuff.

" Are you sure of all this?" asked Jack.

" Know the farmer who lost the ducks—have seen the carpenter who owned the tools—once dined with the magistrate who committed the thief to prison—and have read the culprit's name in the gaol books. Depend upon it—'tis all true. Mind— 'twas before he took to the law—and somehow— after a year's hard labour—he got into an office— and so on, and so on—and now, John Chuff is Arthur Allsides! All true—no, no, I'm too sorry for the actual faults of my fellow-men to circulate slander! We have all our failings, Mr. Runnymede—and a little charity costs nothing."

" Now—now I have him," thought Jack, and the whole day and part of the night did Runnymede employ, considering the best means whereby, despite the cold, prudential advice of Candidus, to obtain satisfaction of Allsides. The morning came; and Jack had not determined on his mode of revenge, albeit his purpose was become unalterable. The following paragraph in the paper did not, it may be conceived, tend to soothe his stern resolve:—

" —— Election. On the close of the poll this day, the numbers for both candidates were, curious to relate, equal; on which the returning officer gave the casting vote for the new candidate. Mr. Sidewind is, consequently, no longer member for the borough of ——."

Runnymede cast the journal from him with inexpressible disgust. "And the money that must have been spent!—and that I should have lost the proud prerogative of an Englishman!—but—yes—yes—yes," and he rose to answer the promptings of his soul, for he tugged at the bell of the coffee-room, and exclaimed in a tone that made the waiter bend back—"pens, ink, and paper!" Two or three minutes, and these most fatal implements lay before Jack Runnymede.

Oh, Jack! hadst thou no good genius—no friendly sylph to dry the ink up with its fanning wings—to waft the paper, like thistle-down above the chimney-tops—to seize the pen, and fly with it beyond the moon? Hadst thou no good spirit to serve thee? Wert thou—a second Cato—left to stab thyself with a goose-quill? Meddling, though well-meaning, people pause not to snatch rope, steel, or poison from the wretches who would employ them; and yet, so inconsistent is mankind, a simple Jack Runnymede is every day permitted by half-a-dozen spectators to slay himself with paper, pen, and ink! Alas! is there no kind of death, save that which gives work to the undertaker? Better had it been for Jack to have had plumes above his hearse, than a grey goose feather under his nose!

"There, Mr. Candidus—there, sir; I think you'll call that something. See; no sneaking anonymous

—no, no; I never withhold my name from my sentiments, for, thank heaven! I am"——

" What is all this, Mr. Runnymede?" asked Candidus, as he put on his spectacles, and took up a newspaper, flung by Jack with a rejoicing air upon the office-table.

" Look, sir,—look," and Jack emphatically tapped his fingers on a letter to the editor, Jack's work of yesterday—" there, sir; read—read."

Mr. Candidus cleared his throat and read—

" *TO THE EDITOR OF* ——.

" *Sir,—It is the proud boast of every Briton that for every wrong he may find a remedy. The law, sir, with its ample shield, protects the poor from the tyranny of the rich, and in the scales of English justice a peer in all his robes weighs not the weight of a feather more than a naked ploughman.*"——

" Naked ploughman," repeated Jack to himself, evidently enamoured of the picture. Candidus continued—

" *No, Mr. Editor,—in this our happy, sea-girt isle, the marble palace of the duke,*"——Candidus paused.

" What now?" asked Jack.

" I never saw a ' marble palace' in England," said the unimaginative attorney.

" No matter for that," said Runnymede. " Go on." Candidus obeyed.

" *The marble palace of the duke can no more harbour oppression than can the straw-thatched cottage of the peasant. In Magna Charta, Mr. Editor, the name of every English subject is supposed to be written*"——(Candidus, seized with a cough, blamed " the easterly wind," and then proceeded)——" *is supposed to be written, and liberty his god-like legacy. Yes, Mr. Editor, liberty is the vital blood of an Englishman ; rob him of liberty, and you deprive him of life : it would be more easy for a Briton to exist without a heart than to respire without his liberty.*" (Again, the easterly winds demanded a protracted cough of the attorney.)——" *Liberty, Mr. Editor, rocks the cradle of an Englishman—guides his infant steps—walks with him through life—and bends above his grave. Socrates had his good genius ; an Englishman has his liberty.*"

" Very true—very excellent," said Mr. Candidus, through his cough, and about to take off his spectacles.

" Go on—go on," cried Jack with animation, " for now, we come to it." Candidus adjusted his spectacles, and resumed.

" *If, then, Mr. Editor, liberty be all this—and who is base enough to deny a tittle of it ?—what shall be said of the wretch, who for the basest purpose seeks to rob a Briton of his birth-right—to deprive him of the sacred legacy bequeathed him by his forefathers ?*"

And yet, such a miscreant is found to exist. To be sure, the man who is guilty of one species of theft must be capable of another; and he, whose oblique morality cannot, like Hamlet, distinguish ducks *from* a handsaw, *or in other words"*—

"What *is* all this?" asked Candidus, looking as through a fog at Runnymede.

"Go on," said Jack, rubbing his hands, "go on —'*ducks*' from a '*handsaw*'—that's a slight touch I think."—

"*Or, in other words, he who in his youth has not hesitated to steal poultry from a pond,—he who has not stickled to rob the farmer and the artisan, can in later years hardly be supposed when tempted by lucre, to respect the liberty of his fellow. The matured abettor of perjury is the natural growth of the early thief!*"

"Mr. Runnymede!" cried Candidus.

"I think that's a tolerable period," said Jack in a glow of vanity. "He'll not sleep to-night. But go on."

"*In a word, Mr. Editor, and to prevent the slightest misapprehension as to the person pointed at in these hasty remarks,*"—

"Hasty," repeated Candidus with a sigh, and an unutterable look at the smiling Runnymede.

"*I beg most distinctly to state—for* magna est veritas—*that I allude to Mr. Arthur Allwork, of Lyon's-*

Inn, alias John Chuff, Prittlewell, Essex ; whose in-famy, if heaven spare me life, I trust to hold up to the disgust and execration of every true-born Briton. At present I must beg to be excused from entering into further details"——

"Yes—that's enough for the present," said Run-nymede complacently.

"Quite," answered the attorney, and proceeded to finish the epistle——

"*——into further details,—and beg to subscribe myself your constant reader, and very humble servant,* JOHN RUNNYMEDE."

"That's a letter," said Jack.

"It is," said Mr. Candidus, looking compas-sionately at the writer—"and it is all your own work ?"

"Every word of it," cried Jack, with all the sus-ceptibility of an author — "every syllable, Mr. Candidus."

"And you have, doubtless, made your mind up to the consequences?" asked the lawyer. "You are prepared to stand an action for libel ?"

"Libel! my dear sir, do you think me capable of falsehood ?—why, it's the truth, sir—every word, the truth ; and as an Englishman,"——

"Well, well, Mr. Runnymede, if you will ruin yourself, you must, I suppose, be allowed to select your own means. If you will jump into a well after truth, you mus'n't complain if you are left to drown there a martyr." This said, the attorney addressed himself to some papers before him : Jack, however, could not silently assent to the position of the legalist.

" No, Mr. Candidus; no, sir; even were a man —an Englishman so to perish, the verdict of the world would be "—

" Suicide, under temporary derangement," continued the cool Mr. Candidus, finishing the sentence.

The generous spirit of Runnymede shrunk from further contest with a mind incapable of elevated sentiment; and returning the fatal gazette to his pocket, he bade a frozen " good day" to the lawyer, who, with an eloquent shake of the head acknowledged the civility, and again fell to his papers.

Runnymede walked with the stride of an injured man towards his lodgings. He had expected " loud applause and aves vehement" from his legal friend, who, on the contrary, to the mind of the sufferer, had read a homily on the profitableness of falsehood. Jack had knocked at his own door, and had his foot upon the scraper, when he was addressed by a thin young man, with a yellow face, in very brown black.—" I believe, sir, your name is Runnymede ?"

" It is," and Jack seemed to speak with new pride.

"John Runnymede?" asked the circumstantial stranger.

"John Runnymede," replied Jack very sonorously.

" Then, sir——."

Mr. Candidus was a true prophet——Allwork had not lost an hour in the pursuit of a remedy for his bleeding reputation. The stranger at the lodging door of Jack had, in a manner not to be misunderstood, made known to him that Allwork would appeal to the laws of his country for vengeance on his slanderer.

" The sooner the better," exclaimed Jack with a radiant smile——" for thank heaven ! I can then make known the truth——yes, thank heaven ! I shall then feel what it is to be an Englishman."

CHAPTER III.

JACK RUNNYMEDE sat in the office of Gregory Bricks, Furnival's-Inn, a skilful and, upon his own showing, a pious attorney at law, concerned for Jack in his coming trial with Allwork. The chivalrous defendant had disdained the mean advice of the conscientious Candidus who had counselled, if it were possible, an arrangement with the vilified

party.　Hence, in great disgust, Jack sought another Mentor.

"And when—when, Mr. Bricks, shall we get into
court?"—asked the impatient Runnymede.

Bricks had opened his mouth to reply, when he
was called into the outer office, to meet a client
who, swelling like a frog, awaited the coming of
the summoned attorney.

"Mr. Bricks," said the stout stranger—"this is
shameful, sir; there's that Pierrepoint—just dashed
by me on horseback—on an Arab mare, sir; an
Arab mare.　The saddle—the saddle—for what I
know would pay my bill."

"Well, sir, and—heaven illumine me! what can
I do?" asked Bricks.

"Do, sir? why, serve the writ—do!"

"It's mighty well" replied Bricks with ineffable
composure "to say, serve the writ; but we can't
do impossibilities.　The bailiffs—heaven illumine
them!"—

"Heaven!" echoed the visitor, in a voice sound-
ing of the other place.

"What I mean to say is this, sir; no lawyer can
do more than issue a writ; the rest"—and Bricks
turned up his eyes towards a portrait of Coke—
"the rest is in the hands of the Lord."

The visitor looked an irreligious doubt.　"He
should pay me, if he pays anybody."

"To be sure; but if he doesn't pay anybody— heaven turn his heart!—you can't complain of partiality." Thus spoke Bricks.

"Some debts," said the dogged creditor, "are nothing more than book accompts. Some trades- men if they're never paid can't be wronged: they're safe from loss: now it's very difficult"—and there was a tone of experience in the *dictum*—"it's very difficult to cheat a tailor, or nine times out of ten, a wine-merchant."

"I can't say—I never tried," said Bricks lan- guidly. "But you don't call a wine-merchant safe?"

"Yes I do—that is, very often—if you return the bottles. In fact, bad debts are only bad in any trade but mine. A man can't pay his tailor, his bootmaker, his hatter, and there's an end of it— it's a simple contract, and he can't meet it. But, sir, in an accompt for walking-sticks, there's what I call a moral obligation."

"An article of luxury, to be sure," said the lawyer.

"Especially when a man rides on horseback," added the tradesman.

"Let me see. Heaven direct us!—I am afraid" —and Bricks spoke with a sigh—"I am afraid, we can't make him a bankrupt!"

"He doesn't owe me quite enough," suggested the creditor.

" That's a pity," rejoined the attorney. " And then he's a gentleman—ha ! the Lord have mercy upon us !—those gentlemen give us a great deal of trouble."

" He'd a stick a week for two months," roared the creditor. " I shouldn't have cared for the mounted dragon's-blood—nor the pheasant—nor the partridge-eye—nor the iron—nor the ivory— nor the green-ebony,—but—but," and the poor man seemed softening into tears—" but the uni- corn I can't swallow."

Indeed, it was too much to expect of any man. We know that Vincent de Beauvais assures us that in his time unicorns were commonly to be caught by chaste virgins, devoted to the sport. Now, whether in latter days, there are fewer ladies qualified to take out the needful licence, or whether they prefer to hunt other animals, or whe- ther unicorns themselves are become scarce, we shall not here linger to enquire. Certain it is— and the most superficial observer must have re- marked it—a unicorn is not every day devoted to the bucks of London. And thus, when our trades- man had possessed himself of that, which the tem- porising scepticism of modern times consents to call a unicorn's horn—and thus when exquisitely mounted, it was yearned for by fifty opening purses,—it was unkind, it was unprincipled of Henry Pierrepoint

not to assuage his thirst for walking-sticks with
dragon's-blood—not to soothe himself with partridge-eye;—but, careless of consequences, reckless
of a previous bill—thoughtless of the low profits of
the honest tradesman, struggling with a wife and
five children—(though six is the catholic number)
—we say, it argued in the debtor a foolish brain,
and we fear a perverted heart, under such multiplied circumstances of aggravation, to rob a man
of his unicorn.   We are inclined to think that Mr.
Bricks was of our opinion; for touched by the suf
ferings of his client, he called in the senior clerk.

" Mr. Terms, really, with the blessing of heaven,
this Mr. Pierrepoint must be arrested."

" Yes, sir.   We'll do our best, sir: but there is
no catching him,"—said Terms.

" Pish !" cried the owner of the unicorn; and
the chief clerk looked with sudden dignity from
the goose-quill he was cutting into a pen with the
same coolness that a lazzarone sharpens his knife.—
" I say, pooh !" cried the undaunted dealer in dragon's-blood—" I saw Pierrepoint myself to-day—
he was on an Arabian mare, I don't mind expense
—for my spirit's up—and I will have him."

" Come, Mr. Terms—how—how, under Providence, may he be served with a writ ?" asked Mr.
Bricks.   ·

" You don't mind expense, sir ?" said Terms

speaking as though his mouth were lined with velvet.

" No—I don't !"—and the man of sticks wiped his brow, and struck his fist on the desk.

" Well, the surest way I know to serve him with a writ is this,"—

" Name it, sir—name it."

" You say he rides an Arab mare ? "

" I saw him—this very day, I saw him."—

" Then the likeliest plan to serve the writ is,"—

" Yes ? "

" To mount a bailiff on a Persian horse ;" and Terms nibbed his goose-quill.

We will not detain the reader by any further description of this pending suit of a bundle of sticks : the tradesman fell in with a less expensive mode of service, subsequently suggested by Terms, and quitted the office, additionally comforted by Mr. Bricks, who—under Providence—assured him that Mr. Pierrepoint would soon be in a gaol.

Turn we now to Jack, lapsed into profoundest slumber. We can take it upon ourselves to an-swer, that saving the employer or his clerks, no man since the invention of vellum, ever slept so soundly in the office of a lawyer as, at the hour we speak of, did Jack Runnymede : there was no such snoring in the recollection of the oldest solicitor.

" Mr. Runnymede !" cried Bricks; and at this

moment, the inn clock struck five—" Oh !—Baldwin, where's my watch ?" and the attorney spoke to a boy at the desk.

" Not done yet, sir," and the boy puckered his lips.

" Not done !—and—what are you laughing at ? Not done ?—why, I sent you for it this morning, and what did the fellow say ?"

" He told me to tell you, sir, that you couldn't have it."

" The scoundrel—God forgive me !—who did you see ?"

" I saw his journeyman, sir; and when I said I came for Mr. Bricks's watch, after some talk he said he'd bring"—Baldwin was interrupted in his sentence by a loud knock at the door, which opened, discovered the journeyman true to his word.

" Oh, my watch ?" said Bricks, prophetically, and he again went into the outer office.

" Your watch, sir," replied the man with a slight difficulty of speech, contracted that afternoon at the Blue Posts.

" There wasn't much the matter with it—'tis an excellent watch ?"

" Quite a trifle, sir—and as you say, a capital thing," and the man produced the chronometer.

" I have had it these twenty years, and 'twas always true as the sun—it never stopt before. What could ail it ?"

" Look, sir ; " said the man, exposing the works
of the watch, and putting a glass in the fingers of
Bricks—"look, sir ; somehow or the other, there's a
long, thin hair got in the balance-wheel."

" I see it—I thought some such trifle," said the
lawyer.

" I have but to use these pliars—draw it out—
and your watch goes on as well as ever."

" Heaven be praised !—well, make haste—for I
have an appointment, and shall be past my time,"
urged Bricks.

" Well, I sha'n't do it," cried the man, and grasping the watch in one hand, he leaned his folded
arms upon the table, and his eye flashed, and his
face darkened as, in defiance, he turned it towards
the lawyer.

" You won't pull out the hair?—heaven illumine!
—then, give it me," commanded the attorney.

" What ! you've forgotten me, Mr. Bricks ?"

" Eh ! Joshua Daly?   Bless me !—I made—that
is, you were a bankrupt fourteen years ago."

" I was.   For twenty years I'd never missed a
bill—never let a man ask twice; an accident—a
trifle—a hair in the balance-wheel—stopped me at
a second.   If you recollect, I showed you what it
was—showed how a little time would serve to pluck
out the hair, as I may say, and set me going again.
You wouldn't hear me, Mr. Bricks—you know, you

would'nt;—and now"—and Daly threw up the window.

" What are you going to do, man ?" cried the attorney.

" I'm going to teach you this lesson : in future, not to break a poor fellow to pieces for one little hair in the balance-wheel. In your own words, Mr. Bricks, I'm going to make a bankrupt of your repeater."

And ere the words were clearly uttered, the golden watch of Gregory Bricks was shattered to pieces on the stones beneath. The owner stood speechless and aghast. The spoiler took the door in one hand, and holding up his fore-finger, exclaimed to the dumb-stricken lawyer—" you'll recollect the hair in the balance." So saying, he vanished : next morning the shop was found to be let—nor master nor man was there.

Most men have one absorbing desire. The ruling passion of Mr. Bricks—we cannot deny it—was to make bankrupts : and few there were, however flourishing in appearance, who were proof to his inclination. We are disposed to think he would have found a deficit even in the accompts of Crœsus. And then he laboured with such apparent pleasure in the vocation, that we are convinced he thought he was working for the ultimate good of the gazetted. " Better make him a bankrupt," was his

constant advice to a consulting client.   He seemed
to look upon a tradesman as Columbus looked
upon an egg : to make him stand the firmer, it
was with Bricks indispensable that he should first
be broken.

CHAPTER IV.

MEN, falling asleep in a conservatory, have been
known to die an aromatic death—to sleep sweetly
for ever.   The constitution of some bodies must
puzzle the physicians.   Jack Runnymede, albeit
visited by the nightmare, woke in perfect health in
the office of Gregory Bricks.   The *genius loci* had,
it is true, spell-bound the brain of the sleeper.
He had seen visions of drollery and terror—a
strange, phantasmagoric jumble of the ludicrous
and shocking.   He had in slumber essayed the
facilis descensus Averni — had had its mysteries
arrayed before him; and that so vividly, that
although he was really in the office of a lawyer, he
could have taken his oath, he was in

"A place too caloric to mention."

Jack dreamt that he was in the Arcady of the infernal regions—and there, lying on a brimstone
bank, his tail coiled like a sleeping adder, was

Beelzebub himself, piping as "he should never grow old." The devil puzzled Jack; for looking stedfastly at him, the dreamer saw in the infernal musician, now the likeness of one man and now of another. His face was perpetually changing to a resemblance of fifty people—and some of them most respectable inhabitants of earth—known to Runnymede. And now, would the devil look like Jack's first love, and now would he wrinkle the brown lips of his present landlady. And the music the devil played was, to the ears of Jack, not unlike a great deal of the music of this world. And what think you, was the devil's occupation? That of a shepherd: yea, as he piped, he kept his eye upon a flock of sheep. In five minutes, Jack was as familiar with the devil as though he had known him all his life. But, we have been told, that such is always the case with those determined upon his acquaintance. We give the fol-. lowing conversation from Jack's own lips.

" A good day to you, shepherd."

" A fair, bright day to you, my gentle swain." (When the devil *is* polite, what courtier can beat him ?)

"Lord have mercy upon us ! " —— (the devil frowned)—" what dog is that ? " And Jack stared at the creature for the first time.

" Good Lex—good Lex," said the devil, patting the dog's head with a look of deep affection.

" The devil has a loveable nature to like you," thought Jack, staring at the dog. " Of what breed may he be?" ventured Jack to ask aloud.

" Lex is a bitch," said the devil gravely. " Do you want a little pup?" The appearance of the animal promised fecundity; but Jack paused. After a moment, again he asked—" What breed?"

" None in particular, but sometimes all," replied the enigmatical devil. " Sometimes the pups of Lex begin as lap-dogs, pretty little spaniels—then they turn to mastiffs—then to lurchers—and then, and that's most common, they often end as blood-hounds. Will you have a little pup?" again asked the devil.

" I'll never keep a dog," said Jack, timidly rejecting the favour.

" Lex will eat any thing. Before now, her pups have devoured a whole mansion, and after that picked white the bones of their master. Will you have a little pup?"

Jack shook his head, and resolutely answered, " no." The ingenuous praise of the shepherd was sufficient for Jack; and the bitch herself had a sinister look, quite worthy of her master's eulogium. Her hair was strong and coloured like rusty wire——

her ears hung flapping down like a judge's wig—
and her eye had something in it terribly human.
"No Lex for me," repeated Jack. The devil again
took up his pipe, and played what Jack in his ignorance thought a jig.

"A very fine flock," said Jack casting his eyes
upon the sheep. "How goes mutton, now?"

"Heavy," replied the devil, and again he
piped.

"Pretty creatures! What a fine thing is a sheep
to us!—his meat fills our bellies—his wool clothes
our backs—his guts delight our ears. Every thing
about him is made a blessing to man."

"*Especially the parchment,*" said the devil; and
he cocked his eye, pulled Lex by the ear, and once
more played his pipe.

"They'll make fine meat," observed Jack viewing the broad backs of the flock. "Fine meat!"

"Meat," said the devil, and he laid down his
pipe, and rose to what seemed his full height, and
with a fine satanic frown, reiterated—"Meat! do
you take me, fellow, for a butcher?"

"No," stammered Jack, and he felt as he could
hide himself under a mushroom—"No, you are"—

"Shepherd," and the devil shot up six feet
higher as as he spoke—"shepherd to the honourable society of attornies. We kill for skins

to-morrow.   Graziers breed meat—law parchment is from the devil's own flock."

And so saying, the devil vanished with a rattling sound, and Jack looked about in his dream, and found himself in the office of Mr. Bricks, with all the lids of the japanned deed-cases flung open, and from fifty boxes, at least a hundred figures, puppet size, the incarnation of the goodness, guilt, and folly of the writings therein, arose.   From one marriage-settlement rushed forth a brutal pigmy, haling by her long flaxen locks, his one year wife: from another, gaily tripped a self-contented gentleman, light and airy beneath a hundred weight of antlers.   Now, a grey-coated, white-haired, yellow-faced little hunks, would emerge from a will, followed by a crowd of poor relations; flinging a shilling at them, the old gentleman gives his money-bags to trustees for a chapel.   And now, from title-deeds would rise a stately mansion, and now, it would change into a house-of-cards; and the trunks of forest oaks dwindle into dice-boxes.   From the will of a fond old miser who had left all to his nephew, Jack saw a grey-haired wretchedness, hoarding farthings in a rotten sack,—from the last testament of a doting husband tying up his wife from a second marriage, was seen the disconsolate widow seated on the knee of a fox-hunter.   Talk of churchyards and catacombs and blasted heaths, thought Jack in his sleep, there is no such place for spectres as the office of an attorney.

He had just arrived at this conclusion, when the lid of the private strong-box of Bricks rose up, and out came a thing about a span high, the diminutive likeness of the lawyer himself. In his hand he held a gazette wet from the press : as he looked upon it, some half-dozen bankrupts, with their wives and little children formed in ring about him. The attorney-ghost then laid the paper by, rubbed his hands, placed them behind him, and as he looked at the faces surrounding him, his own face glowed like a Dutchman's above a bed of tulips. Jack watched the attorney with breathless interest ; indeed, the conduct of the spectre commanded deep attention ; for, having carefully surveyed the crowd about him, he grinned like an ogre—turned up his large coat sleeves, and seized a bankrupt, the heaviest of the lot. To the terror of Jack, he shook the man in his teeth as a cat shakes a mouse; he then peeled him like an orange, sucked him dry, and threw the carcase down. And in like manner, he treated every man about him. The heart of Jack quailed with horror, and his tongue turned to ice. But when he saw the blood-thirsty ghost seize one of the children, and begin to suck its bones as a child would suck honey-comb,—Jack could endure it no longer; he jumped from his seat, exclaiming—

"Bricks! you old scoundrel!"

"What!" cried the indignant attorney; and then in a milder tone—"Heaven illumine me! scoundrel! Mr. Runnymede!"

"Eh!" and Jack sank in the chair, and rubbed his thumbs in his eyes, and gaped at the lawyer in the flesh, opportunely arrived to hear the opinion of the dreamer. "Is it you, Mr. Bricks? Well, I declare—I ask pardon—but I was having such a scandalous dream about you."

"You shouldn't even dream scandal—I won't swear that it isn't actionable," remarked the lawyer, glancing seriously at the Abridgment of the Statutes.

"Forgive me, but as true as I am here, I dreamt that I saw you eat six bankrupts, and afterwards begin to crack the bones of their children," said Jack.

"Pooh—*that* isn't likely," tranquilly remarked Mr. Bricks, not descending to specify the particular improbability; "that isn't likely. But Mr. Runnymede—to business"—

"To business," echoed Jack with a look of alacrity.

"This may be a difficult case, Mr. Runnymede, —but you shall have justice—more, sir, you shall have law!" Jack started.   "What's the matter, sir."

"Nothing," replied Jack—but he spoke not ingenuously; something *was* the matter : it was this. The reader cannot already have forgotten the vision of the satanic shepherd : and the truth is, when Bricks with one of his hardest smiles—and there are smiles that make some faces look more stony—said, "you shall have law," the speaker seemed to Jack to wear the very shape and countenance—to speak in the self-same tones of the infernal pastor, when he smiled and asked—"will you have a little pup ?" Jack started at the extraordinary similitude.   "All we want," said Runnymede with an effort "is justice; and with truth on our side,—can we, as Englishmen,—with the blessings of Magna Charta —the invaluable right of trial by jury ?"—

"Very right, indeed, Mr. Runnymede—very right; no, I think we are pretty safe.   You spoke of witnesses"—

"The men, Mr. Bricks—the very men : I have no doubt that with some little cost and trouble— and to keep sacred the rights of a Briton, what is money, what is toil ?—I can produce the very men ; the owner of the duck—the carpenter, the owner of the handsaw," and Jack already looked big with anticipated triumph.

"Ha ! yes—very likely ;" said Mr. Bricks, "but

unfortunately, by the course adopted by the plaintiff, we shall not be allowed to produce witnesses." It was in vain that the solicitor sought to impress this fact on Runnymede; our unsophisticated hero quitted the office of his adviser, strong in the ignorance of his prejudice, and fully determined on the pursuit of truth!

CHAPTER V.

THERE was little in the appearance of either of the two gentlemen who, on the morning following Jack's scene with Gregory Bricks, took their seats in an Essex coach, at the door of the Flower Pot. And yet, if the noblest motives of humanity—if the glowing thoughts of the best benefactors of the world, could be seen as well as felt,—what a halo of light would have shone around the heads of John Runnymede and Thomas Earwig, inside passengers! Yes; they were about to set forward in search of that which scoffers call an *ignis fatuus*, but which wise men know to be a diamond; though perhaps the wisest have sometimes quarrelled for the identity of the jewel. They had avowed themselves the seekers of truth. Shall we—can we— narrate the many trials they endured? The cross-

roads — the bye-lanes — the highways travelled ?
No—we will not—cannot venture on the voluminous theme; but, for the present remaining silent
on the perils they encountered, return with Jack
Runnymede, still hot upon the game, to London.
From hamlet to town—from town to city—from
parish to parish—he had tracked the carpenter, the
owner of the handsaw !

It was nearly noon, when Jack Runnymede
stood before the house of the proprietor of a London
theatre; of the gentleman who had last employed
the carpenter. Jack ascended the steps, and
knocked at the door. Ere the knock was answered,
Jack had time to consider the brief dialogue of two
persons on the pavement, only a few yards from
him.

" Well, Snowden, are you engaged for next season?" was a question put to a rotund person, with
a very satisfied set of features.

" No,—no; nor I don't mean to apply. I—the
fact is—I shall not demean myself by making the
first overtures," said Snowden.

" You won't apply?" said the somewhat astonished querist.

" Certainly not—most assuredly not. At least,
this—this is all I will do,—nothing more—nothing
more. If I go up three steps to Mr. Snob's door"
—Snob, be it understood, was the name of the

proprietor—" Snob himself must, and shall, come down the other three."

Jack counted the steps—whereof he stood upon the topmost—and found there were exactly six. The door being opened, Jack was shown into a room, and his name promised to be taken into Mr. Snob, who had that morning a more than usually crowded levee. Either Jack's ears were extraordinarily sensitive—either the wainscot was of the thinnest—or the speakers more than commonly high and animated in their tones, for Runnymede, at first very unwillingly, overheard the whole of the conversation.

" I assure you, madam, in the time of Mr. Leg— this, you know was originally Mr. Leg's theatre"— a fact, Mr. Snob never failed to insist upon at least once in a sentence—" in his time, no lady ever wore a cross in Mandane."

" That may be, sir,— very likely ; but public taste is much altered,"—said the *prima donna.*

" It has, indeed, ma'am—it has, indeed. In those days, we had royalty itself once a week in the boxes ; and now, where does royalty go ? To the opera, ma'am—to the opera. In the time of Mr. Leg,"—

" I don't care for Mr. Leg, Mr. Snob. Either I am permitted to wear my diamond cross and rosary in Mandane, or I quit the theatre," said the spirited vocalist.

"You may introduce the ballad,—yes, you may sing *Wapping Old Stairs* in ' Artaxerxes,' if you please; but I do assure you, in the time of Mr. Leg,"—

"Very well—very well, the ballad is one point; but you must concede the cross. I should like to know, what is the use of having diamonds, if one isn't to wear them?" asked the lady.

"But don't you perceive, madam, that to wear a rosary in the time of Artaxerxes," the critics had recently questioned the propriety of the act— " don't you perceive?"—

"It's no use talking, Mr. Snob; for the last time I tell you, either I wear my diamond rosary and cross in whatever part I please, or I quit the theatre. Another time, I'll secure the privilege by having it put in my articles." And so determining, the lady left the vanquished proprietor.

"Well, sir," said Snob, in a very altered tone; and Runnymede at first thought the gentleman spoke to some intrusive cur; " well, sir, you must write us another comedy."

"Really, Mr. Snob, with my other duties, it is impossible that I can compose so elaborate a work as a comedy," said the author; for it was a dramatist, and not a dog.

"Impossible, sir!   And why—why not?" asked the proprietor.

"You must concede, sir, that my labours as a manager require that I should be here every morning from ten at noon till twelve at night?"

"Very true, sir—I know it," said the acquiescing Snob.

"And that, sir, every day of the week—you grant that?"

"Certainly—of course;" accorded the proprietor.

"Then, sir, how is it possible," asked the author, "with my time so engaged—I ask you, how is it possible that I can write a comedy?'"

"How is it possible," retorted Snob in a tone of amazement, "why, sir, hav'n't you your Sundays?"

It was evident that the dramatist had not another word to say in defence of his idleness; for without venturing a further reply, he quitted the apartment for the next person in waiting, who proved to be the tailor of the establishment.

"Well, Spangles, and what do you want?" was the question.

"I'm come, sir, if you please, about the new gaberdine," replied the tailor.

"About what?"

"The new dress for Mr. Trout's *Shylock*."

"Oh! well, let me see——ha ! in the time of Mr. Leg, *Shylock* was always played in"—

"Yes, sir, I know—and we have the stock dress in the wardrobe, sir ; but Mr. Trout won't have it on any account. He says, the character of Shylock has been quite misunderstood in consequence of its being played in black : he says that, in fact, Shylock was a very decent sort of person until he grew wicked ; that, indeed, he means well, but people won't let him do what's right ; and all this he intends to convey to the audience by means of the colour of his gaberdine,—and therefore, he says that he won't play Shylock in black, but in a word, he must have a dress of—a—a benevolent colour."

"A benevolent colour," said Snob, musing— "well, I suppose, Spangles, you must get it," and the tailor departed, we presume, on his curious mission.

Mr. Trout in his choice of a benevolent hue, doubtless received his theory of colours from Sir Anthony Sherley, who, in his travels in Persia, in the sixteenth century, says "The king's disposition is noted by his apparel which he wears that day : for that day, which he weareth black, he is commonly melancholy *and civil ;* if he wear white, or green, or yellow, or any other light colour, he is commonly merry ; but when he weareth red, then all the court is afraid of him, for he will be sure to

K 2

kill somebody that day; I have oft-times noted it!" We regret that we cannot make known to the reader the precise hue of benevolence; or whether indeed of one colour, or colours intermingled; as, however, Mr. Trout noted extraordinary contradictions in the character of Shylock, perhaps—though we have searched in vain a file of papers to discover the truth—perhaps, he played Shylock in a harlequin's jacket.

Jack sat with extraordinary patience, expecting every minute to be called in, but every minute disappointed. "Oh, John!" and Mr. Snob spoke to his footman, "has the messenger returned from Mr. Hackney?"

"Yes, sir—half-an-hour ago, sir."

"And has he written the last act of the play, yet?" enquired the manager.

"Not yet, sir—but the messenger said he was hard at work."

"What! he saw him then?" said Snob.

"No, sir, he didn't see Mr. Hackney himself," replied the footman.

"Then how could he tell that he was employed on the play?"

"Why, sir, he said he knew he was, for he saw the scissar-grinder at his door;" and with this proof of Hackney's industry, Snob seemed perfectly satisfied.

"I believe, sir, I have the honour to speak to

Mr. Snob?" asked a feminine voice, which Runnymede concluded to proceed from one of the ladies whom he saw pass into the manager's room, for Jack's door being open, he had a full view of the parties as they crossed from an ante-chamber into " the presence."

" I am desirous, sir, of obtaining a situation for this young lady, for genteel comedy. She has had some little practice in the country, and"—

" Hem! she's"— and Snob spoke almost in a whisper—" she's very pretty; and I think would look well at night. Pray—quite in confidence, now—pray, inform me, whether the young lady is under any protection ?"

" What may you mean, Mr. Snob?" asked the lady, somewhat quickly.

" I mean, is there any gentleman of rank or fortune—any nobleman, for instance—who,—the fact is, these matters, when they *do* exist, bring good private boxes; and if a protection of influence,"—

" Oh! dear, no, sir; I am happy to say, nothing of the kind—nothing."

" Indeed! Well, I am happy too, to hear it. Well, madam," and Snob spoke in a cold, decided tone, measuring syllable by syllable; " I have no vacancy whatever in my establishment." The ladies withdrew; and a gentleman, from his easy

step and confident air, a great man, as Rummy-
mede had wit enough to think, with the manager,
entered the room.

"Well, Mr. Snob, here we are—another poor
season.—You see, if you'd have taken my advice,
how business would have flourished."

"Now, what—what would you have had me
do?" asked Snob.

"Do! why, strengthen the company. Now,
listen; what do you think I'd do, if I had this
theatre? I'd have working people—twelve men,
eight women, all good;" said the speaker, in a
voice like that of a cock with a cold; but, nevertheless, speaking very oracularly. "Now, mind
what I'd do. I'd bind people to me by friendship—yes—I may say by friendship. I'd go to
Bootle, and I'd say to Bootle, 'Bootle, what will
they give you at Drury Lane?' 'So much.' 'Very
well, Bootle, I'll give you more! 'Then I'd go to
Simcox, and I would say, 'Simcox, what will they
give you at Drury Lane?' 'So much.' 'Very
well, Simcox, I'll give you more!' " And thus the
speaker ran through the twelve men and eight
women, "all good," putting to each man and woman the same question of, "What will they give
you?" and replying thereto, "Very well, I'll give
you more." When he had despatched the whole
twenty, for he did not spare poor Snob a single

case, he continued, "Yes, ladies and gentlemen, I'll give you more—more—more than you can get anywhere else, and, therefore, I trust you will come to me quite *con amore!*" Such being the philosophy of the speaker's *con amore.*

Snob was, it would appear, much struck with the position so profoundly put by his adviser: indeed so sensibly struck, that he could say nothing.

"And what is all this you're going to do? Have beasts and birds?"

"Why, the fact is, in the days of Mr. Leg, it certainly was not so; but we must succumb to the spirit of the times. I did think of reviving 'Valentine and Orson,' only an accident took off the bear."

"If you please, sir," said John, entering, "there's a man at the door, and he won't take an answer from me; but he wants to know, as he hears you are going to have beasts—the man's a market-gardener, sir—he wants to know if you're open to a contract for the litter?"

"Tell him to call to-morrow," said Snob; "and, John, as I don't feel very well to-day, tell the prompter to bid the ladies and gentlemen come in here to the reading of the piece."

"What!" said the *con amore* philosopher, "you don't read the farce to-day? You know, I've Shylock upon my head—I can't be hurried."

" No, the farce next week," said Snob.

" I hope it has been altered according to my direction. I must have all the jokes of Prigly; the two bailiffs must be cut out, as they weaken my scene: the old woman must be reduced to lines, saving the best for me; the escape through the practicable fire-screen belongs, in fact, to my part; and all the spice of the jew Aleppo must come from my mouth."

" I have given Hackney the necessary directions, and, of course, he will abide by them," said Snob, to the satisfaction of the great actor; for he took his hat, and much to the relief of Snob's buttons, every one of which was worn with the same thumb and finger, departed.

A sudden rush of ladies and gentlemen, convoked to the " reading " in the parlour of Snob, kept Jack fixed to his seat. At intervals, three or four carriages drove up to the door, conveying the principal artists to assist at the ceremony. The piece about to be read was " The Beggar's Opera."

Let not our readers suppose we are about to introduce the immortal John Gay in flowing peruke —albeit, we are wont to see him in a cap—let them not hope that we are about to take them back to that free, fresh, and truthful age, when men and women were painted as they were; when vice was lashed nakedly at the cart-tail of opinion;

and the fine gentlemen of the day hid not their faces with their hats, and cried, " Fie, shame !" at the castigation. In those happy days of simplicity, a thief was called a thief, and a harlot a harlot. Now—now, with a sweet and "candied tongue," we dulcify iniquity; and whatever be the rogues we treat of, to serve the stomachs of this weaker age, we must be sure and cook our locusts with honey. The books of some modern writers is marvellously like the shop of the modern confectioner; if even a murderer be there, he is sure to be there *in sugar*.

Immortal John Gay ! " Orpheus of highwaymen !" He did not cut out life as young ladies cut their romances and watch-papers, after what pattern they will ; he simpered away nothing of its reality into conventual no-meaning. He did not consider pen, ink, and paper as the means of making lies endurable. He did not make mere filagree of literature ; and choosing a prison-yard for his arena, he never thought to plant thyme there for bees, or pansies " freaked with jet " for the button-holes of the holiday-making felons. Look at *Peachum* and *Lockit;* a brace of social ogres. *Peachum,* with a lacker of good-breeding upon him ; *Lockit,* begrimed with the dirt and damps of a prison. All *Peachum's* views of life have been taken from high ground, and high

K 3

examples.   We could swear he had been, in early
life, valet to a statesman. *Lockit*, on the other
hand, is a fellow risen from under-turnkey. When
Mrs. Peachum, unconsciously "meddling in matters of death," insinuates compassion for the doomed
Bob Booty, her husband, resolved upon a "decent execution," observse, with an elegant sophism
far beyond his sphere—"No gentleman is ever
looked upon the worse for killing a man in his own
defence ; and, if business cannot be carried on
without it, what would you do ?"   Again, his
maxims on play ; " The man that purposes to get
money by play, should have the education of a fine
gentleman, and be trained up to it from his youth."
Next, of what he considers the value and purpose
of his child ; " My daughter to me, should be like
a court-lady to a minister of state, a key to the
whole gang." You hear nothing of this from
Lockit ; he could as soon speak Arabic. He is
cold, venal, brutal, from the vulgar sense of
self-interest ; *Peachum*, on the contrary, from the
taint of high society.   He has been behind the
curtain, and seen the wires.   All that he does, as
keeper of a gaol for felons, as the go-between,
the patron and betrayer of thieves, is but a repetition of what he has seen elsewhere—the translation
of the fine words of high life into the slang of
Newgate. The cold, murderous look with which he

meets *Macheath*, his *son-in-law*, after his betrayal by *Jenny Diver*, is but the " pale reflex" of the light of cabinets. *Peachum* is, morally, to the corrupt statesman, what the statesman's dried preparation is to himself physically; we see all the injected arteries and veins of his past being laid bare before us. The mask of flesh is torn away, and we come at the loathsome truth. *Peachum's* wife is worthy of him; quite " bone of his bone, and flesh of his flesh." It is clear she has, in former days, been the trull of two or three lords, and at length taken for a sum of money by her present protector. Her half-advocacy of *Polly*, pleading for the tyranny of love, with the loose-hung tongue and rolling eyes of a Covent-Garden Venus, and that most candid avowal, " Well, Polly, as far as *one woman can forgive another*, I forgive thee," convince us of her interchange of sentiment with *Peachum;* and that "not being married," they have long lived "comfortably together." And then, *Polly!* what a beautiful vindication is she of the purity of nature—of the simplicity of truth— of its possible triumph over circumstance. *Polly* is a flower blooming in the chinks of Newgate stones. But every character in this beautiful work is stamped with truth and individuality. "The Beggar's Opera" is, what a dainty bibliographer would call, " a young man's book;" a terse, vivid essay on

men and manners.   All its characters are real flesh
and blood, and the sentiments they utter, good or
bad, the coin which passes current in the world.
It is a book for all men of all grades; from the
courtier in his levee-coat, to the felon in his chains.
The opposing saints, St. James and St. Giles, may
read it together.   It is, we hold, a redeeming
point in the character of a dead statesman, that he
was wont, it is said, to recreate himself from the
cares of office, by sitting down to the piano and
playing over and singing all the songs—and what
songs they are!—of the opera; beginning with
Through all the employments of life, and ending
with, *Here I stand, like the Turk, with his doxies
around!*   To the prime minister " The Beggar's
Opera" is a kind of note-book, illuminated with portraits of his best friends.   He may, at a thought,
allot the characters among his particular official
intimates, his panders, his dependents, and his pe-
titioners.   Here he sees a *Lockit* in the governor
of a colony; and here a *Nimming Ned* in a general,
famous for saving goods " out of a fire."   Here a
Mat-of-the-Mint takes the air, not upon " the
heath," but in the " House."   He has *Jenny Divers*
in carriages, and *Molly Brazens* on the " back
stairs."   But to return to the company in the room
of the proprietor.

The ladies and gentlemen had assembled to read

"The Beggar's Opera" for impurities: they were convoked to present to the moral world, a family edition of John Gay! The proprietor, wisely mistrusting his own unassisted powers of mutilation, had called about him the several severe and acute minds to be found in his company; and doubted not that, under the chastening fire of such an assembly, naughty John Gay would come out bright and pure as newly-minted gold. The reading was about to commence, when a lady—she was to represent *Captain Macheath* in a blue frock coat, white trousers, round hat, and straw-coloured kid gloves—requested that the ceremony might be deferred for the arrival of her mamma, who had promised to attend to point out to her the improper passages. Nothing could be more reasonable than such a request; and yet it was most ungracefully acceded to by Mr. Snob, who insinuated that the lady herself was surely a sufficient critic on such a theme. The lady, holding her eyelids rigid, looked in a straight line at the opposite wall, and saying nothing, tapped the floor with her foot. In an instant, carriage wheels were heard—the knocker sounded—there was a rustling of silk in the passage—a sudden smell of musk—and, enter the mother of Captain Macheath! The coachman had been attacked with the cholera, which accident, she begged might be received as an excuse for the delay.

The reading began, and—as the parties read from an already purified text—no objections were made to the author, until *Mrs. Peachum* came to—

" What business hath he to keep company with lords and gentlemen ? he should leave them to prey upon one another."

On this, Mr. Snob, with a knowing elevation of shoulder and earnest screw of the head from right to left, ordered the passage to be expunged ; as he had no doubt it would be offensive to the boxes. " There were not less," said he, " than six lords and an honourable in the house last night," and the prompter drew his quill across the passage.

Next, *Mrs. Peachum*—who had played the singing old women for thirty years, and wore at her neck the portrait of a gentleman, her first deceiving love, in the costume of George the Second—suggested purification.   Could she say such things as these ?—

" She loves to imitate fine ladies, and she may only allow the captain liberties in the view of interest." And again—" All men are thieves in love, and like a woman the better for being another's property."

At this there was a general expression of disgust in the faces of the company. *Captain Macheath* looked at the flies on the ceiling ; *Macheath's* mother suddenly shifted herself with a gesture of unutterable loathing ; *Mrs. Peachum* glanced at the portrait of her first love in the costume of George the Second ; and Snob, again lifting his shoulder

and screwing his head, passed sentence—" Mark
it out."

" Pray, who was it wrote this piece?" asked one
of the company, a tall, thin, pale young man, with
yellow-ochre whiskers, at the same time distending
the fingers of his right hand, and digging them
through his hair, shining with macassar.   He
might have been taken either for a rope-dancer or
a prosperous haberdasher.

Let us, beginning with his leather, describe him.
He wore boots, to which the famous glass-slipper
would be dull and wrinkled : under the boots were
brilliant straps tugging down trousers of eye-pierc-
ing white, the legs whereof were perfectly cylindri-
cal. He had a waistcoat of gorgeous crimson velvet,
worked with gold butterflies : about this ineffable
vest was an interminable tangle of the precious
metal; indeed, he seemed a coxcomb hung in gold
chains.   His shirt was studded with eight diamonds,
secured by golden links, delicate as twisted spider's
web.   Over this he wore a coat of grass-green, and
on one corner of his head—after long and painful
practice no doubt—he had contrived to fix a
small white hat; a thing so light and aerial, that
like the cap of Mercury, it seemed a cap with
wings.   In his hand he held a cane, surmounted
with a brilliant topaz, on which he would now rest
his lips, and now stretching himself backward, would

look up, and seem to whistle. This gentleman
was, in his own opinion especially, first singer.

" Now," and he repeated the question,—" who
wrote this stuff?" There was a pause, and several
of the good people looked at one another. *Captain
Macheath* opened her eyes wonderingly—*Captain
Macheath's* mother shrugged her shoulders, expressing happy ignorance—and *Mrs. Peachum* put her
hand to her head to assist her in remembering the
" fellow's name."

" Gay—John Gay," said the prompter.

" Of course—Gay—John Gay," corroborated
Snob, and again he screwed his head, as he gave in
his testimony.

" No gentleman, whoever he was," said the first
singer.

" Let us go on," said Snob, and the reading
proceeded to the speech of Polly :—

" I know as well as any of the fine ladies how to make the
most of myself, and of my man, too. A woman knows how to
be mercenary, though she hath never been at court or at an
assembly; we have it in our natures, papa: if I allow Captain
Macheath some trifling liberties, I have this watch and other visible marks of his favour to show for it. A girl who cannot grant
some things, and refuse what is most material, will make but a
poor hand of her beauty, and soon be thrown upon the common."

Captain Macheath observed to *Polly*,—" Of
course, you'll never say that ?"

" Certainly not, child ;" said the mother of the captain.

" No, dear; you had better come to the song *Virgins are like the fair flower*, at once," advised *Mrs. Peachum*, and so it was determined. The ceremony went on to the speech of *Mrs. Peachum*:—

" If it had been only an intrigue with the fellow, why the very best families have excused and huddled up a thing of that sort; 'tis marriage, husband, that makes it a blemish."

" Now, sir," said the lady with the portrait of her first lover, " you can never expect me to speak that ?"

" Cut it out," said Snob, with a rose-coloured sense of the improper—" cut it out," and thus they proceeded cutting out Gay to the accompaniment of virtuous sneers and virtuous indignation. We should cast away time and space to particularize every proved enormity, every expression of disgust. Let it suffice, that poor Gay was scrutinized, as poor Quellenec was reviewed by the ladies of the Louvre; a fact, as Bayle says, described in noble latinity, by M. de Thou—(*Oculis curiosis*, &c).

The first singer was among the loudest in his horror at the several abominations, curiously searched for only to be cut out; but when the reading had proceeded as far as the scene, " A tavern near Newgate," the scene in which the beauties of Hockley-in-the-hole and Lewkner's-lane, are assembled

for the recreation of Captain Macheath,—the vocalist foamed over with zealous morality.

"Infamous—shameful—the fellow ought to be
shot—shot!—shooting's to good for him—disgusting—disgrace to a barn,"—and the first singer rose,
and turned upon his heel, and rapped his boots
with his cane, and ran his fingers through his hair;
then hooked his thumbs in the arm-holes of his
waistcoat, and swayed from right to left, and left
to right, his "little state of man" convulsed with
virtuous rage.

At length, the reading was got through; John
Gay was made fit for decent company—the black-
amoor was after great scrubbing, rendered white—
the company rose, and were about to leave,
when Mr. Snob observed to the ladies,—"Oh,
about the dresses for the new piece? Is Mrs. Sleeve
here, John?"

"I've been to the wardrobe, sir, and she's coming
down, directly," and ere the words were well out,
Mrs. Sleeve presented herself.

"Now, Mrs. Sleeve," said Snob, "you will take
the orders of the ladies for their dresses, and mind
and be very particular with the fleshings." Mrs.
Sleeve answered with a curtsey the command, and
Captain Macheath, the *Polly*, and, indeed, all the
ladies who had assisted at the purification of the
author of the Beggar's Opera, went to get themselves

measured for silk flesh-coloured legs and blue satin
slips (not a little above the knee), for a piece of a
mythological character; Snob, as the reader has
heard before, dwelling on the necessity of succumb-
ing to the spirit of the times, and therefore determining to introduce to an enlightened public real
beasts and all but real nakedness—"roaring lions"
and "splendid women!"

"Now, mind, Mrs. Sleeve," said the *Captain
Macheath*, after some conference with the empress
of the wardrobe—"mind; a bright sky-blue satin,
and remember, not too low."

"Where, where," asked Snob, somewhat anxiously, "is Mrs. Centipede? we must arrange about
herself and the Cupids."

"Heaven lies about us in our infancy," saith the
poet; Mrs. Centipede, the dancer, was evidently of
the poet's opinion,—hence she always had, to be
hired at the shortest notice, some threescore children from two to six years old; by virtue of their
years, the tuition of their mistress, white muslin
frocks, and buckram wings with foil-paper spots,
angels of the most agile order. It was a delightful,
a touching sight, to see Mrs. Centipede in the midst
of her whole sixty, twisting, turning; she like a
graceful humming-top, surrounded by little tops
with pegs. Mrs. Centipede was an excellent creature; every Sunday she was to be seen at some

church.   A rival dancer said with a sneer, she attended there to bespeak her pupils as they were
brought to be christened : we do not believe it ;
sure we are, she went, urged by her religious duties,
and not to obtain children ; though, we must own she
had them very young ; and again, they were so
forward.——In many instances her pupils, three
days after they were short-coated, could dance.
Happy ! guileless little creatures ! promoted from
the vulgarity of mortal childhood to spirits of a
heavenly order ! Not banished to bed with the rooks
and the lambs, but kept awake, curled and painted,
to receive at midnight the cheers and loud applause
of an adult, discerning public ! Other children drink
milk-and-water and eat bread-and-butter ; these
happy creatures sip nectar, and munch ambrosia.

"How about my dress for Venus ?" asked Mrs.
Centipede in a low voice of Mrs. Sleeve, as the
dancer slided into the apartment.

"For Venus !" Now, Mrs. Centipede was a
woman of about six-and-thirty ; and we may say,
she danced with her age admirably, inasmuch as
she looked nearly double.   She was thin and
gaunt ; her face had something of the gipsy caste,
rigidly marked : her hair, which she wore in profusion, was coal-black——and her eyes, large and
rolling, were of the same colour.   They had a restless action, as if continually watching the evolutions

of her sixty pupils. In her manner, albeit she was Bermondsey born, there was a kind of French polish; how obtained, we know not; though it was once stated by a lady who kept a rival academy, that Mrs. Centipede's first lover was the French Hercules, and won her virgin heart by pulling successfully against two horses. To be sure, the representative of Venus had, now and then, the advantage of the very best society. Several scions of nobility, besides two or three bankers' sons, would condescend to visit her academy, especially on quadrille nights. It was to such patrons that she owed a presentation to the Blue Coat School for her little " cousin."

" The dress for Venus? " said Mrs. Sleeve, " Oh, Mr. Snob has ordered that to be entirely new."

" Very well," said Mrs. Centipede, with great meekness—"and for the wings for the children, why, I think old gauze will be as good as any;" saying which, she glided like a ghost away.

" Well, Snob, have you thought anything more of that matter ?" asked a young gentleman, having somewhat unceremoniously lounged into the presence of the proprietor.

" What matter ?" interrogated Snob.

" The—the girl ?" answered the young gentleman, with easy self-possession.

" Oh ! very true, my lord ; the young lady has, I have no doubt, considerable talent."

" Upon my life, Mr. Snob," said the young gentleman, " I do think she's equal to anything," and the speaker smoothed down a moustache, like a bit of mole-skin, upon his lip. " I've known the young lady some time, and, though I don't pretend to know much about plays—the fact is, you begin so devilish early—yet she has very fine eyes."

" Very fine eyes, my lord," and Snob twisted his head in admiration.

" And her foot, and ankle—upon my honour, I do think in some of your things, Snob—in what at the club we call leg pieces,"—

" Leg pieces ! ha ! ha ! capital, your lordship— capital."

" I do think, she'd make a good show; I have no interest in the girl, at all—none, I assure you— she's a pet, yes I may say, a pet of my sisters, and so I—I thought I'd drive down to you."

" I'm sure, I'm very obliged to your lordship. Ha! sir, if we had a few more such patrons of the drama !" and Snob sighed.

" You know, Snob, that is, understand—I shall often come to the house, so as I shall want a seat,— why—yes—I may say, whatever you give the girl in salary, I'll pay you again in private boxes."

"Your lordship is very good. The young lady can dance?"

"Like St. Vitus: Mrs. Centipede had her when she was very young. Now, understand, Snob, it's a bargain—the engagement and the private box." Saying this, his lordship walked away, shown out by the proprietor.

And all this time, where was Runnymede? He continued to sit with laudable patience in the back room. For a time, he was an interested listener to the trial of Gay, but his vigilance relaxed, and at length he sank into a deep sleep.

"I'm sure, sir—I'm very sorry—I beg your pardon—but I'd forgot you were here," said John, waking him.

"Well—never mind; now, I hope I can see Mr. Snob."

"Mr. Snob, sir—I'm very sorry—but"——

"But what?" asked Runnymede somewhat soured.

"The truth is, Mr. Snob had ordered the horses —he felt himself a little better—and so, shortly after the reading, Mr. Snob went out."

"Out?" exclaimed Runnymede.

"Out," repeated John.

CHAPTER VI.

" I have found him—I have found him at last !"
exclaimed Jack Runnymede to Earwig, his diligent
companion in the pursuit of truth. It was even
so ; disappointed of an interview with the courteous
Mr. Snob, Jack applied to the porter at the stage-
door, from whom he obtained a clue which, being
diligently followed for many days, led him at length
to the carpenter. " Now, now our evidence is
complete," and Jack's face shone with satisfaction
—" now, what can withstand the justice of our
cause ?" Mr. Bricks looked graver and graver,
assuring the unsophisticated defendant that, however laudable his endeavours, they were made
wholly inapplicable to the case, by the proceeding
of the plaintiff. At this Runnymede would smile
incredulously, and with invincible complacency
observe,—" But I tell you, my dear sir, I have
proof, sir—proof—proof."

" Very true, Mr. Runnymede ; I have no doubt
of it ; and very praiseworthy it is of you to have
gone to so much cost and trouble for the sake of
truth ; but when truth can be of no use,"—

" No use !" exclaimed Runnymede.

"We may," continued the placid Bricks, "pay too dearly for it, only to keep it by us."

"Impossible—quite impossible; truth, sir—truth is"——

"Mr. Runnymede," said Bricks, interrupting Jack in his fervent praise of truth, "I envy your simplicity. You are an excellent man, Mr. Runnymede; but, if I may say it, a little too romantic. This, sir—the Lord help us !—is a wicked world we live in. Perhaps it's right it should be so; but for my part, I think it the duty of a Christian always to take things as they come."

"Especially," observed Earwig—" especially, when the things happen to bring their own recommendation."

"But, Mr. Bricks, I tell you, I have the wit-nesses. I have the man who lost the ducks, the man who was robbed of the handsaw and chisel; the copy of the commitment of John Chuff, alias Arthur Allwork,—and what is more—I have the late turnkey of the county gaol, who—if the plaintiff should endeavour to shelter his iniquity under his 'alias,'—is ready to swear to his identity. And now, Mr. Bricks, I ask you as a lawyer and a Christian, whether any thing can defeat the justice of my case? What, sir,—as an Englishman dignified by Magna Charta I ask it,—what can be stronger than truth ?"

" Process by criminal information," answered Bricks. " But we shall see, Mr. Runnymede—we shall see. Nothing is certain in this world—and more especially in that part of it, known as Westminster Hall."

" Of course, you would like to see the witnesses?" asked Jack, and he rubbed his hands, as if about to invite Bricks to a great treat.

" Just as you please," replied the attorney, with philosophic indifference ; " it can do no harm. Are they in London ?"

" Are they in London !" echoed Runnymede. " Mr. Bricks, this is a cause in which I would spend the last farthing—shed the last drop of my blood."

" The law is much obliged to you," said Mr. Bricks.

" We have had our Hampdens, and our Pyms, and our Eliots, to little purpose, if the birthright of"——

" But you spoke of the witnesses, Mr. Runnymede? You say you can produce them?" interrupted the attorney.

" I can, Mr. Bricks. It has cost me much trouble —much expense—but, sir, I would have walked overland to Crim Tartary in such a cause. I have the witnesses—have them safe, Mr. Bricks, safe," cried Jack, with a triumphant look. " I have taken apartments for them. Nobody save my dear friend Earwig and myself can get at 'em. If they go out, I accompany them——if they stay at home, I lock 'em up. You see, Mr. Bricks, there can be no tampering—no tampering. Ha ! ha !"

" Very vigilant—very circumspect," said Bricks. " You ought to gain the cause, Mr. Runnymede."

" Ought ! Must !" exclaimed Jack, very energetically. " Will you dine with me to-day?"

" Not to-day. The truth is, I——I have promised Mrs. Bricks to accompany her to the consecration of a chapel in our neighbourhood. But I——if you'll promise to keep early hours——I'll sup with you."

" And then," said Runnymede, with a gracious smile, and laying his hand upon the attorney's shoulder, " then you shall see the witnesses."

In the evening, Mr Bricks was punctual at the new lodgings of our hero ; but to the surprise of the attorney, learned that Mr. Runnymede and his friends were not at home. Earwig, however, was deputed by Jack to receive Mr. Bricks, and assure him of the speedy arrival of his client.

" Mr. Runnymede," observed the attorney, as he warmed himself by Jack's fire, " is a very foolish man."

" Very," replied Jack's " dear friend Earwig."

" This affair will cost him some money—will put him to some inconvenience," said the placid lawyer.

L 2

" A fine of five hundred, and I suppose not less than six months' imprisonment," remarked Earwig.

" That's about it," answered Bricks; " and then the expenses will be something."

" The Runnymedes have always been fools," observed Earwig. " Why, there was Jack's father— I could tell you things about him, that "——

Unfortunately for Mr. Earwig's reputation as a story-teller, the sudden noise of a hackney-coach, followed by a knocking at the door, checked him in his theme, for he immediately exclaimed, " Here he is—witnesses and all !"

" Oh ! I suppose he has been for them ?" said Bricks.

" Been for them ? Bless you ! they live here. The fact is, your excellent and stupid client "——

But at this moment the door opened, and the first witness presented himself. He was a tall, burly man, with large unmeaning features. His nose had been cut in two in some Arcadian fray, which injury added nothing to the agreeableness of his visage, or the harmony of his voice. He bobbed his head at Bricks and Earwig, and sat down in silence. The example was followed by an elderly man, with a rustic, care-worn look, who seated himself, smoothing his grey hair with his rough hand. " Servant, gentlemen," said a third witness, ranging himself with the others.

"Hope you hav'n't waited?" cried Runnymede, running in, and taking both hands of Bricks. "But the fact is, the good people here had not been out for two days, and as I wouldn't have them moped, I took them all to see the wild beasts."

"How very kind of you!" exclaimed the benevolent Bricks.

"Never was a kinder gentleman in this world," cried one of the witnesses, made impatient with gratitude.

"Should ha' died but for him, and never know'd what an elephant war like," said another.

"Something like a gentleman," asseverated the man with the injured nose, "took us to Bedlam last Monday."

"Yes, we've wanted for nothin' since we've been here," said a bouncing country wench, in gay gown, cap and ribands, entering with a child in her arms.

"And, pray, Mr. Runnymede," began Bricks "am I to understand that these are?"——

"Very right," cried Jack, "first business, then supper. These good people are my witnesses. This good man's name is"——

"Giles Hurdle," said the old rustic, rising, and still smoothing his hair.

"Giles Hurdle," continued Jack; "this good man was the owner of the two ducks"——

"Duck and a drake," was the correction of Giles.

"They're all the same"—Giles shook his head—"quite the same," insisted Jack. "The ducks stolen by Chuff."

"I could swear it through three bibles," exclaimed old Giles.

"A valuable witness, Mr. Runnymede, if—if—but, however, proceed," said Bricks.

"And this good man is Joseph Squarewise, the carpenter, who lost the handsaw and the chisel," said Jack, and the carpenter bowed a silent affirmation. "And this good person's name,"——

"My name," said the man with the damaged feature, "is Mark Griggers. I was turnkey three years at Chelmsford gaol, and had the custody of John Chuff."

"There—there—there, Mr. Bricks,—can anything be more satisfactory?" inquired Runnymede, with glistening eyes.

"And who," asked Bricks, evading an answer, "who may this lady be?"——

"Mr. Griggers's daughter, sir," said the girl with a curtsey, "and this is my little boy."

"And all witnesses?" inquired the attorney, with a malicious smile.

"No—not the young woman; only the fact is,

Mr. Griggers had promised to give her a trip some day to London, and"———

"And, all things considered," said the late turnkey, "I thought no time could be like the time present."

"I'm only so sorry," cried Mr. Griggers's daughter, "that baby's christened."

"Why, my good woman?—may I ask why?" inquired the attorney.

"Because, I'm the greatest sinner as is alive,"—and the mother looked gratefully towards Runnymede,—"if I wouldn't ha' called it arter that gentleman. He deserves no less, that's what he doesn't. Would you think it, sir, he's bought baby this black hat and feathers? and if he gets the cause—and the Lord send he may! tho' I know nothin' about it—if he gets the cause, I know he'll gi' baby a lace cap."

"And pray, Mr. Giles Hardle, what may you think of London?" asked Bricks, in the way of self-amusement.

"Why, sir, I doan't know," answered Giles; "but I do think all but lawyers be a pack o' rogues."

"Indeed! And for the lawyers, Mr. Giles?"

"Why for them, I be sure they be," said Hardle.

" He'll make a remarkably intelligent witness," said Earwig confidentially to Bricks.

" You were never before in London, I presume, Mr. Griggers? Ha! so it struck me. What do you think of it?" asked the attorney.

" For London," replied the turnkey, " I don't think so much of it."

" Sorry for that," observed Mr. Bricks. " Very sorry."

" And as for Tyburn," continued the turnkey, with a melancholy look—" why it quite disappointed me."

" And Mr. Squarewise, what"———

" The supper's ready, sir," was the sudden announcement of the servant.

" Ha!" exclaimed the turnkey's daughter, " and Dick isn't come back. Kept out by that Jonathan!"

" This way, Mr. Bricks," said Runnymede, shewing him from the room, " we shall find our supper here;" and Jack led the attorney, followed by Earwig into another apartment, the witnesses being left to feast by themselves.

" Here's to our cause!" said Earwig, in due time, filling a bumper.

" With the help of the Lord!" added Bricks, tossing off the wine.

"Nothing can stand against such witnesses," exclaimed Runnymede, flushed with hope. "Nothing."

"What do you think of the girl, Mr. Bricks?" asked Earwig, winking and nodding his head at Runnymede. "Jack can choose a witness."

"Mr. Earwig," replied Bricks with sudden gravity, "Mr. Earwig—I think the—that is, I—I am a married man."

"Upon my life! I insist Earwig, I"—and Jack coloured to the brows at the jocular insinuation of his bosom friend—"I intreat that you give over such levity. The girl is the daughter of the most important witness. Her husband is with her, and"—

"He is? What! is he a witness too?" inquired Bricks.

"Not at all; only as Griggers would have his daughter with him—she of course," said Jack, "couldn't leave her husband, who insisted upon bringing his cousin."

"Well, I meant nothing—'pon my honour, no; but really, Mr. Bricks, as a man who knows something, don't you think Jack has a fine taste in ribands? How well blue becomes the wench, doesn't it?" asked Earwig.

Mr. Bricks almost laid down his knife and fork,

L 3

and with increased solemnity assured Mr. Earwig
that he was a married man.

" What a strange fellow you are !" said the
sensitive Runnymede. " As for those ribands, Mr.
Bricks, the fact is, I—I thought I could do no less
than put the witnesses into decent attire."

" I thought they were very smart for their condition," said Bricks. " Then you have fitted them
out ?"

" It cost me very little," replied Runnymede,
" and as they were to give evidence for me in a
court of justice, why, when I was about it, a gown
and a few yards of riband "——

" And a hat and feathers for baby," added
Earwig, staring at Bricks.

" Didn't make much difference," said Runnymede, not noticing the playful malice of his bosom
friend.

" Well,"——and for the second time Mr. Bricks
made the declaration——" you ought to win the
cause."

" I shall win it," cried Jack. " By the way, I
hav'n't shown you a copy of the commitment of
that rascal Chuff, alias Allwork. Here it is !" and
Jack produced the document, his eyes glistening
like the eyes of a bride at nuptial diamonds, as
he read it. " There—what can stand against that ?"

"I hope it will be received," observed Bricks, "but as an honest man and Christian lawyer, I must express my doubts."

"Aye, you are perhaps right to express yourself cautiously," said Runnymede. "And here—here's his conviction."

"What! for the ducks?" asked the lawyer.

"No. The fact is, the case for the ducks didn't stand; but he stole them for all that. Hurdle's ready to take his oath to it."

"Didn't stand! Why not?" inquired Bricks. "Wasn't it proved?"

"Proved, beyond the slightest doubt; only the prisoner had the advantage of a slight mistake," said Runnymede.

"What was it?" asked the attorney, rubbing his hands, and smiling at the anticipation of a flaw.

"Why, the indictment was for stealing two ducks; but it was proved by the cross-examination for the prisoner, that one of the birds was a drake."

"Then of course they could not convict," exclaimed Bricks.

"No: but he committed the robbery for all that," answered Jack.

"What a lucky escape!" cried the lawyer,

tickled by the good fortune of the prisoner. "What a lucky escape!"*

"But he was a thief for all that," repeated Runnymede, who had no professional taste for chicane to gratify.

"Yes, but if the drake were not admitted against him, my dear Mr. Runnymede—if as I say the drake were not admitted against him,"——

"He stole it," Runnymede spoke for the third time, "he stole it for all that." Bricks shook his head. "But say nothing of the ducks," cried Jack with animation, "I can go upon the saw—I can stand upon the chisel."

"Let us hope the best," said the pious attorney, "let us hope you may stand upon the chisel."

CHAPTER VII.

THE trial—the important trial—was set down to be heard, though, for the sake of Runnymede's witnesses, we are happy to state not before sufficient time had been afforded them to see, under the kind auspices of the defendant, all the sights of the metropolis. As the day approached, Mr. Bricks very prudently attempted to prepare his

* See *Sessions' Reports*, 1836, for a similar case.

client for the worst; still, we regret to say, with
very little success, Jack deeming failure impossible.
It was in vain that the attorney spoke of forms of
court, of the peculiarity of the law of libel—Jack
replied to all these intimations with an unbelieving
laugh. "There might have been cases," Jack
would allow, "which failed from a want of evidence;
but in a case like his, in which truth was as clear
as the light of heaven, to fail was impossible."

The morning came, and Jack Runnymede rose
as to his wedding. As he rode towards Westminster Hall, accompanied by his witnesses, he
felt himself an invulnerable champion in the cause
of truth. Saint George did not ride out to fight
the dragon with greater confidence, with keener
ardour for the fray, than swelled the bosom of
Jack Runnymede on his meditated destruction of
a false attorney.

With the sweetest smile upon his face, and with
the airiest step, our hero entered the court. Many
friends nodded to him; he acknowledged the
greeting with a new smile, and then his eye falling
upon Chuff, alias Allwork, he looked as he would
have withered him in a blaze of indignation. Mr.
Allwork indulged himself with a slight cough—
rubbed his hands—and, judging from his manner,
turned to whisper something droll in the ear of
his counsel.

The judge took his seat—the jury were sworn.
Runnymede had gazed intently at them, feeling assured that he had never beheld gathered together
twelve such honest looking men.   The cause was
begun; for a full account of which we refer the
reader to the law reports.

The libel was proved; and Runnymede's counsel,
not being permitted to justify the statements of
Runnymede by means of witnesses, contented himself with flourishing before the eyes of the libelled
man, the copy of his committal to Chelmsford
gaol; and, at the pressing request of the astonished
Runnymede, pointing out the turnkey in the person of Mark Griggers, waiting in the body of the
court, to be examined.   Allwork threw a look at
his late keeper, but showed no signs of previous
acquaintance.   The counsel next touched upon
the presence of the owner of certain ducks—upon
the ease with which one Joseph Squarewise, a
carpenter, might be produced to speak to a certain
saw and chisel; and ended his address with a most
eloquent appeal to the love of truth on the part of
the jury, who under the direction of the judge,
found John Runnymede guilty of a libel against
Arthur Allsides.   When the foreman delivered
the verdict, a female in the gallery exclaimed,—
" there goes the lace cap of poor baby!"   Jack
looked up, and, whilst the court rang with laughter,

to which, by the way, Mr. Bricks contributed more than his due share—beheld the melancholy face of the turnkey's daughter.

"I told you how it would happen," said Bricks to Runnymede. "You see—we've lost it."

"Lost it! it's impossible that with my witnesses ready—with so strong a case"—

"An excellent case," observed a legal gentleman, "never heard a better case if—if you had been allowed to prove it."

"And pray—what—what remains now?" asked Runnymede, all astonishment.

"Nothing—but"—and Bricks stroked his chin, and stared in Jack's losing countenance.

"But what?—speak out, Mr. Bricks! Let me know what remains to be done," exclaimed Runnymede.

"Nothing more than this: you'll be brought up for judgment."

"It can't be!" cried the unbelieving victim. "Judgment! and what—what follows, then?"

"Why, it's a very flagrant case," said Bricks.

"It is, indeed," said Runnymede.

"To call a man a thief—and a perjurer; it's a serious matter, Mr. Runnymede," observed the attorney.

"But it's the truth, sir—the truth—the truth!" raved our hero.

"That may be—I don't dispute it: but you see, Mr. Runnymede, truth in cases such as this is like green peas in winter, if you will indulge in a luxury, you must pay for it. Now, let me advise you—this is an ugly business—therefore, let me advise you to make the best of it," was the counsel of Mr. Bricks as he walked arm-in-arm with Runnymede from Westminster Hall, the unappropriated witnesses Hurdle, Squarewise, Griggers, with his daughter, her husband and his cousin, slowly following.

"I wish to make the best of it," said Runnymede, "that has been my wish throughout."

"Well said," observed Bricks. "So, authorise me to treat with Mr. Allwork—after all, he's not so unreasonable a gentleman."

"Gentleman! a thief—a perjurer—a—gentleman, indeed!" exclaimed Runnymede in uncontrolled rage.

"You mus'n't say these things; as your lawyer and as a Christian, I say you mus'n't. Now, listen; I'll make an offer to him, and, perhaps, he'll be satisfied with a fair sum of money and an apology."

"An apology! Do you think me a Hottentot, Mr. Bricks?—a barbarian—a beast? An apology —and from a truth-telling Briton? No, sir! I wonder that the departed great, gathered there"— and Runnymede stretched his arm towards the

Abbey—"do not move in their tombs at what is perpetrated there," and Jack violently flung his arm from Westminster Abbey to Westminster Hall.

" If you are brought up for judgment," said Mr. Bricks, unmoved by the energy of his client, " I won't answer for the term of imprisonment."

" Imprison me ! No—impossible. I reverence the laws, and I can't believe it—imprison me ! If such an outrage were committed, do you think I have no remedy ? Yes, sir—yes ; I have a remedy —for, thank God ! I'm an Englishman."

Runnymede, deaf to the voice of his adviser, remained unshaken in his sense of security. " It was enough that Allwork had, by some unaccountable means, obtained a verdict : he would not dare attempt to push his triumph farther. No—scoundrel as he was—he could not be so utterly lost to shame." Such was the conviction of our hero when, after the lapse of some weeks, he was briefly desired by Mr. Bricks to hold himself in readiness to receive judgment.

" It can't be—it's impossible," exclaimed Runnymede. " However, I'll attend the court—of course I'll appear—but he never can be so infamous— the law can't allow it ;" and with this belief John Bunnymede appeared before the judge, who sentenced him to pay a fine of five hundred pounds, with the further punishment of eight months' imprisonment.

"And for writing the truth?" cried Runnymede, quite aghast.

"A very gross case of libel," observed a barrister to half a dozen professional friends.

"Very flagrant—very gross, indeed," replied five of the six.

Jack Runnymede was conducted from the court by the officer whose painful duty it was to see the libeller safely bestowed in one of his majesty's prisons. Jack, having seated himself in the coach, ventured to ask his companion "If he had ever known such an atrocious business?"

"Very common, sir," replied the officer; "but your's is rather strong."

"Strong! I—it's so atrocious I can hardly believe it," said Runnymede.

"Ha! sir, very few words in such a matter cost a good deal of money—fewer words than go to an ounce."

"But it's notorious—the rascal is known to be a thief and a perjurer," cried Jack.

"What! Mr. Allwork? To be sure he is, sir; and that made it so very simple of you to call him so," observed the astute officer.

"But the business sha'n't stop here—no, I'm determined it sha'n't—I—"

" We're very near home, sir," said the officer, endeavouring to soothe his charge.

" I should be a traitor to my country—to myself, if I remained quiet."

" You may be very comfortable where you're going—with money, sir, everything at the best."

" There is the right of petitioning left me," cried Runnymede.

" You can have a room to yourself," said the officer.

" And with good spirits,"—exclaimed Jack.

" Sorry to say, sir, no spirits allowed ; that is, if known : but plenty of wine," was the intelligence of the officer.

" You mistake, my friend. What I meant to say was, that, as a Briton, I had the right of petition."

" To be sure, sir."

" That, therefore, I would address parliament."

" Can't do better, sir—it will help over the time, with rackets."

" Thank heaven ! there's Magna Charta," cried Runnymede.

" And there's the Bench," said the officer, and the coach stopped at the prison gate.

Runnymede entered the lobby and was delivered to the keeper. " Thank God ! I'm an Englishman," cried Jack, as he looked around, and saw himself in the court-yard of the prison.

CHAPTER VIII.

THE fine inflicted upon Runnymede for his
wicked and malicious libel on Arthur Allwork was
the least punishment. There were certain expenses
which, combined with the disorder of his affairs in
consequence of his imprisonment, made it not un-
likely, that Englishman as he was, Jack Runnymede
might grow grey in captivity in an English gaol,
despite the blessings of Magna Charta.

"They can't keep us here—you may take my
word for it, they can't," Runnymede would avow
again and again to his fellow prisoners for debt, the
marshal of the gaol, oddly enough, holding them
all the while. "There's Magna Charta—and, yes,
thank God! we're Englishmen!" And this was,
one day, the proud declaration of Jack to a miserable, ragged wretch, a three years' prisoner for
a debt of five and forty shillings.

"What's Magna Charta?" asked the squalid
debtor.

"The glory of Britons; it gives us our liberty,"
exclaimed Runnymede.

"I wish I could get some of it," said the prisoner.
"Why don't you try it yourself?—How's it to be
had, in bottles?" asked the fellow, with a grin.
"If it is, I suppose that's why it's stopped at the

gate. Magna Charta !" roared the man, with a horrid laugh.

"My friend," said Runnymede, "respect the laws—remember that"—

"Oh, of course—I must respect the laws. Look at my rags !—ha ! ha ! feel my soft hands—hands I wish to make hard with work,—but the laws make me take my leisure here, and lounge like a gentleman."

"Is your debt heavy ?" asked Runnymede.

"Why, blessings on the laws ! yes. It was two pounds and odd, for physic for my dead wife ; but the laws—charming laws !—made it more than ten. You can't think how a poor man, with all the world at his back—and that's load enough, my master— must love the laws, when they strike his working-tools from his hand, and send him to walk here, with his fists in his pockets."

"And your debt was only two pounds ?" asked Runnymede.

"A shilling or two over ; now, it's ten and more : but then the difference is for bits of paper made by the laws, and dealt out by the lawyers."

"And there is one of the craft," cried Runnymede with some disgust, as a yellow-faced, low-browed specimen of the species crawled by.

"Yes that's Blacklamb, the hump-backed lawyer of Clement's-inn. But bless you, sir ! I've no malice against such as he—poor vermin! not I—they can't help it.   I should as soon think of blaming a snake for its rattles."

"Then where does your anger fall, if not upon the snakes?" inquired Jack, interested by the quaint earnestness of the debtor.

"Why, upon them that make it profitable to breed reptiles," answered the prisoner; and tossing his head, he abruptly walked away.

The time of Jack's imprisonment flew by, and in a week, if certain arrangements could be made, he hoped to enjoy his freedom, when—for the darling thought had never left him—he determined to obtain redress, even at the foot of the throne, for the wrongs committed upon him.   His admiring country should feel proud of him as an Englishman.

We have, however, premised that new difficulties beset Runnymede.   His affairs were become desperate, and his liberation was rather to be hoped than expected, even with the sacrifice of every shilling of his property.

"If such things were known to be done by the people in the moon," said Jack bitterly, as he looked over the bill of Bricks, "what asses, what fools, what knaves, what villains, we should call them!" Jack tried to read every item, but he became heart-sick ere he had proceeded three inches down the paper. Sea-sickness is nothing—nausea in its perfection is to be had only from such documents as that perused by Runnymede. However, Mr. Candidus, Jack's real friend, stirred himself in the business, and after a month's delay, the fine and all the expenses were paid, leaving our romantic hero without a farthing.

"I'm going—farewell," said Jack to a fellow-prisoner. "When I get out, thank God! I've the spirit of an Englishman, and can push my fortune : good bye," and Runnymede was about to quit the prison, when he was stopped at the lobby. "It's all right—you have my discharge, you know."

"Yes — but there's gate-fees," observed the functionary in the lobby.

"But the debt's paid—I owe nothing," replied Jack.

"Gate-fees—or you must go back," said the man in authority; and Jack Runnymede, without blessing his stars that he was an Englishman, begged the money of Mr. Candidus, to rescue the champion of truth from the clutches of the turnkeys.

"You never mean to tell me that I have no remedy," said Runnymede to Candidus. "If I am an Englishman, there must be justice for me."

"There is a remedy; but, Mr. Runnymede, by this time you ought to know that nothing in our way is to be done without expense."

" But I am determined to proceed against Allwork; there has been gross perjury; I am determined"——   .

Mr. Candidus checked Jack's ardour, stilled his
roarings for revenge, with these words, accompanied
by a most benignant smile. " Mr. John Runnymede, you must know that law costs money; now,
before you make an unalterable determination, had
you not better put your hands in your pockets ?"

There was something in the words, but there was
more in the manner, of the speaker. Jack Runnymede, despite his yearnings for satisfaction——despite his strong desire to assert his rights as an
Englishman—felt the magic of the appeal. Without another word, he wished Mr. Candidus good
morning, and sallied into the street.

John Runnymede stood in the highway of
sumptuous London, the undone votary of truth.
He turned and turned, and again stood undecided, whither to go. " Why—why was I not
born a baron in the days of John ?" Such was
the vain and fretful question of the dinnerless
Runnymede. " Why was I born in an age when
public virtue is of no account ? But no—it is impossible that my countrymen can be dead to the
voice of my injuries; they must rise, as one man,
to aid me, if I can but make the evil known." And
then Jack thought of calling a meeting of Britons

to obtain redress of his wrongs. Or—the idea particularly pleased him—if he could get up a procession of his countrymen to march, with appropriate flags, to the houses of Parliament! He might call a meeting; yes—thank God! as an Englishman, he had that right.

No sooner had the thought possessed him, than Jack became assured of speedy satisfaction. He should be cheered—quoted by his countrymen as the brave assertor of their rights. His life would be written by a hundred glowing pens—his portrait would be carved and printed on wood—it would adorn newspapers—it would hang, with pictures of the cardinal virtues, on the walls of thousands of cottages. Thank heaven! with all his sufferings, he was still proud of his country—yes, with the right of petition, he felt that he was still an Englishman. The power of money might, for a time, be strong—but there was a moral influence which neither gold, nor rank, nor sophistry, nor tyranny itself could destroy! Jack Runnymede felt his nature sublimated by these ennobling thoughts; and his blood seemed turning to ichor, as he strode, like a giant late for dinner, onward.

Jack had resolved upon the means of action. He would exercise the prerogative of his birthright —he would call a meeting of his countrymen: he would go armed with a petition to the senate—to that august assembly, whose benevolent ears were ever inclined to the complaint of the meanest subject and purified of every selfish, narrow feeling, met and meditated only for the subject's good!

With this determination, the penniless Jack Runnymede sought the house of a printer, known to him in better times. Jack, as he walked, composed the few striking sentences that, printed in enormous type, and exposed to the public eye, would call tens of thousands of Englishmen to the place of rendezvous—where, beneath the canopy of heaven, (for what room, even could he pay for it, would be sufficiently extensive to contain the number of his hearers?) he would detail his wrongs, and move the adoption of certain remedial measures. Yes, Jack had completed the " call " to his countrymen, and was advanced in his address: the rain fell from a November sky, but Jack, in the ardour of his purpose—in the " fine phrenzy " of his soul—felt it not, so completely was he possessed with his address to a visionary multitude of tens of thousands. Thus rapt, Jack Runnymede, to the astonishment and amusement of the passengers, unconsciously committed the strangest antics. Still striking or flinging about his arms and muttering " the sanctity of the person of the subject," he " quoited " a harmless muffin-boy into the middle of the road, — and when he rounded a period with "universal toleration," he gave a flourish with his arm that almost knocked to the earth an inoffensive quaker. Touching upon "the social contract," he covered himself with soot from a sweep; and arriving at the "glorious boon of Magna Charta," he went plash to his knees in a mound of mud. Jack could sooner extricate himself from the mire than from his address; and in a minute, he had joined the thread of his speech, and was again pouring forth a stream of eloquence to the hoped-for multitude. Jack had twenty times dwelt upon "the liberty of the subject."—Again he touched upon the glorious theme—" I say, gentlemen, the liberty of the subject cannot be violated! I say that—thanks to the blessings of Magna Charta!—the liberty of an Englishman is inviolable! Neither King, Lords, nor Commons, can lay a finger upon an Englishman, if"——

Jack had not breath to finish the sentence, for a huge hand grasped him by the collar, and a voice, harsh and deep as if the speaker had availed himself of a trumpet, exclaimed—" Messmate, we want you."

Jack Runnymede, convinced of the inviolability of the person of an Englishman, indignantly screwed himself round, when he beheld a man in a hairy cap and rough coat, not too closely buttoned to hide a cutlass and a pair of pistols.—The man,

M 2

however, was not in a sanguinary mood, as he held
in his right hand nothing more than a short, knotted
cudgel no thicker than his arm.   Besides, he was
evidently a good-tempered person if not too much
put upon : for he met the burning glances of Runnymede with a smile and a nod, and the heartiest
assurance that "he would be nicely provided for."

"My good man," said Runnymede, "you mistake the person—you do, indeed."

"Mistake ! I ax your pardon—we've been arter
you this week," said the leader in the hairy cap.

"Me ! I—I have not the pleasure of knowing
any—any of you," and Jack, aghast, surveyed the
faces of the press-gang surrounding him.

"Mayhap not," said the captain of the gang,
"but we're never above beginning the acquaintance.
You're a lucky griffin, I can tell you."

"Lucky !" exclaimed Runnymede.

"Hav'n't you a twin-brother?" asked the captain, with well-affected interest.

"No—not at all—I assure you," said Jack,
trembling.

"Well, you're as like him as one gull's like
another.   It's only three months ago that we fell
foul on him, just in this water—and, would you
think it?—last Tuesday only—wasn't it Tuesday,
Ben"—and the proprietor of that name wiped his
mouth, winked, and answered "Tuesday,"—"only

last Tuesday he hoisted his flag as port-admiral of
Baffin's Bay. Now, you're so like him—ha! ha!
isn't it his very bowsprit?" and the humourist pointed
his finger to the nose of Runnymede.

"Not quite so much bowsed up," cried the
critical Ben.

"Quite his run. Well, you are so like, that the
Lords of the Admiralty couldn't, if they would,
make you less than post-captain. Come, shake out
your canvas, shipmate," added the speaker in an
authoritative tone, and Runnymede, either through
ignorance of the mandate, or with natural obsti-
nacy, moved no step; when, after a very brief
pause, he felt the knees of two or three of the gang
rudely struck on that part of the anatomy which
honour has selected for its favourite seat. Here—
here was an affront upon the inviolability of the
British biped! Jack Runnymede felt himself almost suffocated with wrath.

"I—I tell you, my good friends"—Jack could
say no more.

"You may call us friends," said Ben, "'specially
when you know what the fat of junk's like: won't
you go to prayers three times in the middle-watch,
for all the good we've done you? Come, heave
ahead!"

"What—what is it you want with me?" cried
poor Runnymede, in despair.

" Want you for a bit of—of curiosity," said the jester in the hairy cap.

" Curiosity ! curiosity !" cried Jack, almost ready to weep.

" Yes;" replied the wag of the gang, " want to see how you'll float, as the devil said when he pulled the marine out of the chains."

" Stay—stay—one minute.   Am I"—Jack was in agony as he put what he felt to be a vital question—" am I to understand, that you wish to press me—that you wish to drag me from my home— my ?"——

" Why, you know your wife's tired of you," cried the hairy cap, " you know she is.   Bring him along, lads."

" All I ask is this—do you intend to use violence —do you intend to press me for the fleet ?" roared Runnymede.

" And nothing less, by ——."   The single oath was lost in the clamorous assent of the whole gang, who, like a pack of hounds, hung about the free-born Briton, yelling, cursing, screaming, fighting.

Jack fought desperately : a hundred times he wished for a sword—a pistol—a poker—any deadly weapon.   " The law—thank God !—the law was on his side, and he might with impunity murder any number of his assailants."

" What a smart hand he'll make in a boarding-

party!"—was the derisive eulogy of one of the *gang*, as Jack, having seized a bludgeon from one of his enemies, cleared a circle about him, and then retreated with his back to a wall. Flourishing his cudgel around him, Jack Runnymede, like a gallant Briton, roared, at the pitch of his voice— " Remember—I warn you—it's illegal—against the law—in violation of—of—dearest rights—Englishmen—fellow-countrymen—succour—it's your cause —your's as well as mine—Britons—your rights!— your".——

Strange as it may appear to the reader, Jack Runnymede calling upon the dearest hopes of his countrymen—appealing to them by their most sacred rights—by their love for their homes, their spouses, and their babes,—was suffered by staring Englishmen to be carried, like a carcase away,— not one British finger moving in his defence. Jack had been seized in the Minories; hence, only a short time elapsed ere he was safely stowed in the Tower Tender. " It's illegal—you can't do it—you have violated the rights of the subject," cried Jack, foaming; and with his clothes torn to tatters in the struggle, he found himself in the floating prison " Sir, you as a gentleman must know that this is contrary to the law," said Jack to an officer.; " you must know that,"——

" They've pressed you, have they?" asked the officer.

" They have grossly violated the liberty of the subject," was the reply of Jack Runnymede.

" I don't admire impressment," observed the officer, drily.

" You can't, sir; as a gentleman and a man of education, you must know that a pressed man is"—

" Not worth half a volunteer; therefore, my man, suppose you take the bounty," suggested the officer.

" Bounty, sir! Although my appearance may not bespeak it, I assure you, I am a gentleman," cried Jack.

" Glad to hear it; gentlemen make capital sailors. Away with him," was the brief order of the officer, and Jack with little ceremony was introduced to nearly a hundred companions, among whom were at least fifty victims to a violation of the law.—Jack Runnymede was received by his new friends with a cheer which, at least, betokened hospitality.

" This is a gentleman," exclaimed one of the ragamuffins, as he caught a glimpse of Jack— " this is a gentleman come here to wear out his old clothes," which pleasantry was received with clamorous applause.

Runnymede was stunned—sick—stupefied by the scene around him. One roared a song in utter desperation—another blasphemed—a third hallooed —and more than one groaned in bitterness, and sobs as from a bursting heart told the deep torture of the sufferer.

Jack, touched by the intense agony of one man, forgot the acuteness of his own suffering. The poor fellow was gathered in a ball in the corner— his trembling hands covered his face ; tears trickled through his fingers ; and his whole body heaved and quivered, as if he struggled with some burning poison. He fought against his grief, and yet, at intervals, he could not master it—it would burst forth in querulous moaning.

" What's the matter ?" asked Jack—" what's the matter ?" Still the man was silent. " What's the matter ?" Jack repeated, laying his hand upon the man's shoulders.

" Keep off—or I'll murder you," roared the man, and Jack started as from a maniac. At length, Runnymede ventured to observe—" I'm—I'm in trouble, friend, as well as you—but why take it so hardly ?" For some time, the man remained silent, and only received the proffered sympathy of Runnymede with bitter scorn. At length, won by the superiority of his manners, and the kind ex-

pressions of our hero, the man briefly told the story
of his present misery.

" I'd been five years at sea. I'd come home—my
wife"—and here the sailor grasped his throat with
his hand and paused—" my wife, with our little
girl,—I hadn't seen the child"—the man writhed
with anguish—" I hadn't seen her since she was a
babe. My wife and child met me—there was her
old father, too—well, they met me at the Docks—
we went on—I was going home—I'd forgot something I'd left aboard—I told 'em to wait at the
Black Dog—I went out, turned the street—the
gang boarded me, and—and"—and the man
dashed his fist against his skull like one frantic.

" And your wife, my friend—your wife?" said
Runnymede.

" 'She's waiting for me—waiting for me—and
I'm in the Tower Tender," on this, the sailor
laughed like a demon. " Waiting for me! ha! ha!"

" But there's a remedy—I tell you, my friend,"
said Runnymede, " there is a remedy."

" What?" asked the sailor, moodily.

" What they've done is against the law; every
man may plead his *habeas corpus*, and"—Jack
Runnymede was proceeding, when the man he was
attempting to comfort turned fiercely round upon
him.

" Why, d—n your heart ! " be cried with intense bitterness—" if you ben't a lawyer."

" Whoop !" roared fifty voices—" whoop! we've got a lawyer."

" No—no—no ! Upon my soul, gentlemen," exclaimed Runnymede, " I am no such thing."

" What are you, then ?" bawled two or three.

" I—I—I'm a pressed man," said Runnymede, in a weeping, puling voice, and the sorrowful tone drew a burst of laughter from many of the hearers.

" Well, but you're something more than that? What line was you in ashore? No gammon among friends. Speak out, like a man ! Warn't you once pumped upon ?" demanded a volunteer, whose confident manner, and flippant speech displayed a person of town accomplishments. " Warn't you never pumped upon ?"

" Never"—answered Jack Runnymede.

" Nor never in the Stone Jug ?" continued the querist.

" I don't know what you mean, my friend," said Jack, very meekly.

" Oh ! d—n pride ! I mean Newgate, and you know it," was the indignant reply.

How strange are the accidents of life ! thought Jack Runnymede; feeling himself become an object of contempt and laughter to the majority of his associates, on the score of his good character and gentility; and with this thought, he briefly stated to his hearers, that he, like most of them, had had his troubles.

"A sneaker, take my word for't," exclaimed Jack's catechist to his particular companions, who unhesitatingly adopted his opinion.

"Don't despair my good fellow,"—said Runnymede in a low voice, and after a long pause, to the disconsolate seaman. "I tell you there's a remedy"—

"Remedy! what remedy? Ar'n't we all here, like stolen niggers?—Hav'n't I lost my wife—my child?—torn from 'em, for what I know, never to see their blessed eyes again?"

"Yes—very true—you are dragged from your home,—as you say, from your wife and child—but still you may thank God"—

"For what?" roared the wretched husband and father.

"Why, that it's against Magna Charta—that it's in violation of the law—and that, in short, though treated like a beast, you are an Englishman."

CHAPTER IX.

NEXT morning, a vessel sailed for the Nore with Jack and his companions, the number being augmented by some half-dozen captives made by the gang in the course of the night. To all, not utterly inconsolable, Runnymede dwelt upon the legal remedy for the abuse under which they suffered. "And how, my good friend—how was it, that you fell into their hands?" asked Jack of a melancholy new-comer.

"I was torn from my bed," answered the man, "the gang had heard that I had been to sea—they got in at the window—and"—

"And didn't you resist?" inquired Runnymede.

"I maimed one of 'em, I think—but 'twas no use;—I was hauled off—my wife screaming—the children in their bed-clothes crying—my old mother kneeling and cursing the gang,—and—there, mate, don't talk of it," and the man trembled from head to foot.

"Got into your house!" exclaimed Runnymede, "took you from your bed? Why, my dear friend, they can't do it."

"What do you mean, by 'they can't do it?'" asked the man, with a scowl.

" Why, it's against the law; in open violation of that great principle which admits the meanest hut of the humblest Englishman to be his castle. I tell you again, my good friend, they can't do it."

" Well, if they can't do it, then I'm not here; so if you can persuade me to that, messmate—if you can make me believe that I'm now at home at breakfast, with my—there, let's have no more of it," cried the poor fellow, choking with emotion.

The vessel arrived at her destination ; Jack and his companions were placed on board the guard-ship at the Great Nore, to be distributed to various ships as hands might be required. " Thank God !" said Jack to himself, as he stept aboard and saw several officers—" thank God ! here are gentle-men :—they must at once admit the flagrancy of the case—yes,—in another hour I shall be ashore." Jack stood eyeing the officers, making to himself an election of one for the depositary of his secret, when he found himself violently pushed, and heard a voice braying in his ears, " Tower Tender-men all aft," and Jack turning with indignant looks to make a lofty speech to the boatswain's mate, was fortunately hurried on among the crowd of his fellow-voyagers. The list was read, John Runny-mede answered to his name, and with his fellows was dismissed. " Why don't you take the bounty ?" asked a sailor, who, from his superior appearance, together with a heavy switch, formed of three pieces of plaited ebony, adorned with a silver top and ferule, under his arm, Jack considered to be a person in authority——the ebony being, no doubt, the insignia of his office. " You may as well have the bounty."

" You are very good, sir, indeed," replied Jack, to the boatswain, for it was that intelligent disciplinarian, opening his eyes at the elaborate politeness of the pressed man, " you are very good, sir ;" said Jack Runnymede, " but——I have other views."

The boatswain was puzzled; he knew not whether to laugh or swear. He scratched his cheek in doubt, and Jack with the greatest civility, again addressed him. " I beg your pardon, sir——but I do assure you, I should accept it as a lasting favour at your hands, if you would have the kindness to inform me, where I can see the captain of this vessel."

There was something in the politeness of Runnymede that quite disarmed the boatswain ; he felt himself quite overlaid by the fine manners of the ragged pressed man. Jack paused and smiled in the boatswain's broad blank face for a reply ; he then repeated " the captain of this vessel ?" (the vessel being a seventy-four.)

" The captain?——why, you see——he's gone to dine with the admiral——I'm sorry, we can't man a boat for you,"——said the satirical boatswain.

"Don't mention it," observed Runnymede, joining his hands and making his lowest bow.

"Perhaps, the first lieutenant will do?" suggested the boatswain, "he's next in command."

"You're very good—very kind, indeed," exclaimed Runnymede, suddenly seizing the hand of the boatswain, who quite unused to such a mode of hanksgiving from such a person, instinctively raised his ebony wand to acknowledge it. He was in a noment disarmed by the vivacity of Runnymede—"the first lieutenant—where can I find him?"

"Just now, he's at school—in the gun-room," answered the boatswain.

"What! have you a school aboard?" asked Runnymede.

"And nine-pins, and cricket, and everything you like—here, Splinters, show this gentleman the way to the gun-room; he wants the first lieutenant." Splinters looking at the boatswain, was perfectly assured from, as Wordsworth says, "the shooting lights of his wild eyes," and from the courteous epithet bestowed upon the pressed man, that there was some game to be played to his disadvantage, and therefore with great alacrity conducted Runnymede to the door of the gun-room. What was his astonishment to hear the "evening bymn" chaunted by boys' voices!—the school closing every night with that solemnity. Runny-

mede edged himself into the school-room, and saw
standing on each side a desk some half-dozen little
midshipmen looking, Mr. Dickson, the first lieutenant being present, very serious; and at another
desk, boys of the second and third class, with the
children of the warrant-officers and sailors attached
to the ship. Mr. Dickson very frequently attended
the performance of the "evening hymn," the
master of the ship, a choleric Prussian, whose berth
was on the starboard side of the gun-room, as frequently mounting to the deck until the hymn was
ended. On the present occasion, however, Mr.
Dickson had another duty to fulfil: for, in addition
to his official labours, he had taken upon himself
the task of watching over the morals, and punishing
the transgressions of all the children in the ship;
who, although no more than seven or eight years
old, were in common with adults submitted to the
visitation of the "cat."

The "evening hymn" concluded, the more serious
punishment was about to commence. The culprit
was led in: he was, in the present instance, a pale,
thin little boy, perhaps seven years old. He
shivered beneath the stony eye of Mr. Dickson,
who stood with his old bare cocked-hat hugged
under his arm——his withered features set with determination——his shoulders slightly bent——the very
personification of stern duty in repose. The child

begged for mercy, but Mr. Dickson nodded to the boatswain's mate. The boy was tied up; and the first lieutenant proceeded to dilate upon the enormity of the culprit's offence: he had dared to spin his peg-top on the after-deck, and had more than once been detected trying experiments on the temper of the he-goat, that animal we presume, for his great services to his Majesty's fleet, being an object of particular interest to Mr. Dickson. " Now, little boy," said the first lieutenant, and he seemed overflowing with kindness towards the offender, " you will be flogged for these offences; you know, little boy, that peg-tops are not allowed in the ship,"—" I didn't—indeed, sir—I didn't," cried the child—" and you know, little boy, that the goat is not kept to have his beard pulled. Hem! hem! Boatswain's mate,"——and Mr. Dickson, eyeing the " cat," spoke quite like a father—" one tail, boatswain's mate;" and with one cord selected from the nine, the child was taught to eschew peg-tops as long as he was afloat, and to have on all occasions a particular respect for all he-goats belonging to his Majesty's fleet.

Jack Runnymede was so confounded by the ceremony—so astonished at the importance which Mr. Dickson threw around the peccadilloes of the boy, and more than all, so disheartened by the appearance of the officer himself—that he did not venture to accost him, but resolved to keep his complaint for the ear of the captain alone. " What —what kind of a gentleman is Mr. Dickson?" Runnymede, purely out of curiosity, ventured to inquire of a sailor who had, as Jack thought, a communicative countenance.

"What sort? Why, he messes by himself, and sells his rum," answered the sailor.

"Has he been long in the service?" asked Runnymede.

"You can see that by his coat, for he never had any other."

"And does he attend the—by-the-bye," and the thought suddenly flashed upon Jack—"if there's a school, I suppose there's a schoolmaster?"

"To be sure; only just now, you see, he's in a bit of trouble."

"On what account?" asked Jack.

"Why, he thought, you see, he was all right, and let his hair grow; but they have docked him again."

"And is it against the rules of the service that a schoolmaster should let his hair grow?" inquired Runnymede wonderingly.

"You see, he wasn't a regular schoolmaster— he was only on trial. He come down here among a batch of marines—a volunteer, as you may be"— said the sailor.

" I'm a pressed man," said Jack, with a sigh.

" It's all the same," said the philosophic tar.
" Well, they drills him and gives him brown bess,
and mounts him on the gangway. One day,
captain coming up the side sees Nankin's hands—
for that's his name—' Dickson,' says the captain,
' that marine's either a scholard or a pickpocket.'
You know, he might ha' been both, but the captain wasn't to know that—' either a scholard or a
pickpocket,' says the captain, ' he's got such smooth
hands.' Well, they wanted somebody to learn the
ship's boys, and they tries Nankin, and finds he
can read, and write, and sum ; so they promotes
him to the gun-room ; and bit by bit, he casts his
red and pipe-clay, and has the d——d impudence
to let his hair grow."

" I see," said Runnymede. " He wished to quit
the marines ?"

" Proud as a mermaid with a new gold frame to
her looking-glass," said the sailor. " Well, he
gets on—and gets on ; and from messing with the
carpenter in the fore cockpit, he gets right aft with
the master's mate—sings songs to the purser's
clerk's wife—wears boots when he goes ashore ;
and more than all, only yesterday—I heard him
myself—ordered the bumboat-woman to bring him
off a tooth-brush."

Jack stared as the sailor, with great seriousness,

touched on the last vanity of Nankin; then asked, " but what—what crime has the schoolmaster committed?"

"Why, he got leave to go to London two months ago. Well, Mr. Highropes—he's the flag-lieutenant—was in London too. Would you think it? the lieutenant going to—I think they call it Fox-Hall—quite a grand place, who should he see there but the pot-hook marine, Nankin, with a long coat, and a squeeze hat under his arm? Well, when the lieutenant takes out a lady—some 'oman of quality no doubt—to dance, Mr. Nankin, with no respect to his officer, has the impudence to think of dancing too!"

"And—and was this the only offence committed by the schoolmaster?" inquired the astonished Runnymede.

"And quite enough, aboard a man-of-war, I can tell you," answered the sailor, with a significant nod.

"Why, they never dared—that is—he was never punished for?"——

"Warn't he? He hasn't got over it yet: directly he comes aboard, captain sends for him; tells him to rig in red again—to mess forward, and to give up his truck, that's his head, to the barber."

this worthy soul. Who'd have thought to have met a
man with the countenance of a hermit in a seventy-
four?" Jack knocked at the door of the old man's
berth.

" Who's there ?" asked the aged tenant, in a
high, shrill voice, with something of a northern
accent. " Who's there ?"

Jack was clearing his throat to answer, when
he heard the tittering of voices, and then a rapid
movement of feet, and he turned his head to detect
the cause. In this position, he received a violent
blow that felled him to the deck, accompanied by a
high-sounding oath, as he almost believed, uttered
by the venerable inhabitant of the cabin.

" D—d dogs !—hope to 'lmighty I've killed some
o' ye !" and then Jack was convinced that it was the
white-haired reader of the bible who had committed
the assault.

" What—what have I done ?" asked Runnymede, gathering himself up, rubbing his neck, and
still upon his knees, staring in the face of the man
of ninety winters.

" Hoot ! who are you ?" asked the cock-pit
Nestor.

" I—I'm a pressed man," said Runnymede—
" but—I"—

" What brings ye to my berth ? I thought ye
were just one of the d—d midshipmen."

At these words there was a shout of laughter from unseen parties, between whom and Mr. Mac Acid, the venerable speaker, there was unremitting warfare. Jack Runnymede, hoping nothing from the enraged aspect of the old man, crawled away.

Young midshipmen, like young dogs, very soon discover the antipathies of those it is their destiny to live with; but unlike the more useful animal, the young midshipman does not avoid the prejudices of the party, but takes every opportunity of revenging himself upon them. Such was the state of things between the juvenile midshipmen of the guard-ship—for, of course, we do not include the midshipmen of forty and fifty—and Mr. Mac Acid, the gunner; for he was not, as Jack had hastily concluded, a divine. Thus, it gave a particular edge to the pleasure of flirting with the carpenter's black-eyed daughter, that the time and place for such relaxation, was "evening, the fore cock-pit," close to Mac Acid's berth. There had been many skirmishes between the gunner and the boys, but the midshipmen generally made a safe retreat, the candle of the gunner being extinguished by the enemy, and sometimes carried off. On the present evening, Mr. Mac Acid, like a thrifty officer, sat conning his volume—for it was not the bible, but his book of stores—with his door ajar, and a heavy cane at his side, prepared at all points for the enemy. When his stick smote the neck of Runnymede, how, for a brief moment did the old man rejoice! To kill a spider, a rat, a pole-cat, a snake, great as may be the satisfaction to those who loathe them, was as nothing to the delight that Mac Acid would have felt at the destruction of a young midshipman: we verily believe that the extacy of the sport would have carried the old man off. "Is there no way, Mr. Mac Acid," asked the good-natured captain of the gunner, "is there no way of reconciling you to the young gentlemen? Can't you by any means be brought to stomach a midshipman?" "I think, sir," replied the venerable Mr. Mac Acid, shaking his white head—"I think I could like one in—a pie."

CHAPTER X.

EARLY next morning, Runnymede was awakened by a voice bawling, "lash and carry—lashand carry;" which command was translated to Jack as an imperative order to the sleepers to pack up their hammocks and bear them upon deck. The order was lost upon Jack, who having no hammock—no bed, no blanket—had lain upon the bare plank. The season was cold November, but, thanks to the

number of sleepers there was no lack of warmth.
Once in the night, Jack went upon deck, resolved—
despite of the season—to walk until morning in the
open air: he was, however, driven down by the sen-
try, lest—for, as a pressed man, he was an object of
peculiar distrust—he should attempt to swim ashore.
It was past three in the morning eré Jack could
fall asleep, and then he was harrassed by dreams,
in which he thought himself, with twenty bold
barons, assembled in a cave at Reigate, concocting
Magna Charta. At length, " up rose the sun," and
up rose the boatswain's mates; and one of these
gentle officers, by the united aid of his voice and
his foot, awoke Jack to real life. Jack, however,
never ate such a breakfast: the savory cocoa gave
comfort to his bowels, and hope to his heart;
hence, when the boatswain's mate piped " Tower
Tender-men all aft," Jack stept along the deck
" like man new made." Fortunately, he was not
aware of the outrage committed upon him during
the night, or the consciousness of his ludicrous appearance might have humbled him. On board ship
there is a great contempt—perhaps a very laudable
one—for long-tailed coats ; hence, Runnymede
had fallen a victim to the prejudice, for whilst
in his slumbers—perhaps at the very moment he
was suggesting the most vital article of Magna

n 2

Charta—his grass-green long-tailed coat was ruth-
lessly abbreviated into a jacket.

Runnymede stood in a line with his companions of
the Tower Tender, whilst a lieutenant-commander,
newly appointed to a gun-brig—to be manned,
rigged, and sent to sea in a week—looked at the
lot to make, by favour, a selection for his ship's
company.   As the officer paused before Runnymede, Jack jumped from the deck, and exclaimed,
" Thieves !"

" Hallo, my man — hallo," said the officer,
" you've lost something ?"

" Look, sir—look !"—and Jack turned his back
to the lieutenant, and with his hand behind him,
exhibited his dishonoured coat.   " There's thieves
aboard—thieves !"

" Shouldn't at all wonder," said an officer, casting
his eye along the line of " Tower Tender-men."

" But, my dear sir," cried Runnymede to the
lieutenant-commander, who smiled at Jack's simplicity—" my dear sir."—

" Anything in the pockets?" asked one of the
ship's officers.

" No, sir—but the—tails "——

" Ha ! never mind them—sailors ar'n't monkies,
they can go better aloft without tails."

Jack was silent ; but he eyed the face of the lieutenant-commander with increasing trepidation, as the officer picked out his men. " If—if," thought Jack, " he should choose me — if — ha !—I say," and Jack beckoned to a short, thick Creole, with his hair cropped close behind, in a blue jacket, and blue worsted pantaloons. Jack judged of the whole by part, and knowing the pantaloons, concluded that it must be the schoolmaster who was in them.

" Do you know that man, Nankin ?" asked Dickson, the first lieutenant, seeing Jack make signs to the pedagogue.

" Oh dear, no, sir !" replied the schoolmaster, with earnest rapidity.

" He seems to know you: perhaps, met you in London ?" said the mild lieutenant, casting one of his feline looks at the swarthy scholar.

" Indeed, sir, no !" said Nankin, the blood rising to his tawny cheek at the word London.

" Silence, my man — silence, you're not ashore now," said the first lieutenant to Runnymede, who, if he talked at all, assuredly only talked with his fore-finger; for he continued, though in vain, to beckon to the schoolmaster, who, in a minute afterwards, vanished from the deck.

The draught of men for the gun-brig was completed, the boatswain's mate piped " Curlew's men, away," and Jack Runnymede, to his exceeding satisfaction, remained aboard the guard-ship one of the unchosen. The gun-brig was destined to a three years' station at the West Indies, and two of Jack's pressed companions, whose stories we have briefly touched upon, were among the number selected for foreign service ; Runnymede continuing to the last to assure them, that no authority *could* press them, and that the humblest Englishman had a castle in his meanest hovel.

It happened unfortunately for Jack Runnymede that, only a few days before his arrival on board the guard-ship, it had been resolved to adorn her hull with a new coat of paint; and though Jack was neither by taste nor education, fitted even for that lowest walk of the art, he was considered by the boatswain's mate to be fully equal to the task of scraping clean the timbers preparatory to the decoration. Being a most servile task, it was allotted to the most ignorant; and the known accomplishments of Runnymede, were not calculated to obtain very considerable respect on board a man-of-war.

" There—lay hold," said a boatswain's mate to Jack, and he held forth an iron implement of about eight inches long, of the shape of a garden hoe.

" What's this?" asked Jack.

" Lay hold—and no palaver." Runnymede obediently took the scraper, still staring at it with vacant ignorance.

"There—go over the larboard quarter gallery," said the mate.

"And what—what is to be done with this?" asked Jack, with a helpless look, now at the scraper, and now at its donor.

"Done with it! here, come with me;" and the mate griped Runnymede's collar.

"Really, my good sir"—said Jack, gently resenting the liberty, "I must beg that—I assure you—I am unused to"——

The boatswain's mate stared at Runnymede, and then, with rare good-temper, croaked a laugh, and kept shaking Jack by the collar; then suddenly letting him go, he pushed him violently onward. Runnymede was again about to remonstrate, when he was confused, cowed by the savage demeanour of his task-master, who drove him towards the quarter gallery, where he saw a single plank slung in ropes over the side.

"There—do as he does," said the boatswain's mate, pointing to one of Jack's Tender companions, who, standing on the plank, resignedly laboured with his scraper.

"I—I couldn't stand there if you'd give me the ship," cried Jack——"and I scrape! Really, my good man, we had better understand one another I—the fact is, I'm a gentleman."

"I know'd that; do you think we'd let anybody

but gentlemen scrape the ship? To be sure you are — there, scrape away now till eight bells, or by ——" and the boatswain's mate nodded at Jack, and winked with terrible meaning. "Over with you!" he roared out, and seizing Runnymede by the collar, the fellow fairly dropped Jack on the plank. "Now—scrape! scrape!"—and poor Jack began to scratch a little harder than a mouse at the rock-like timbers of the guard-ship.

"This is a queer go," said Jack's companion, whose removal to his majesty's navy had, it was more than probable, lightened the labour of some of his majesty's turnkeys. "A very queer go."

"You know," said Jack, continuing to scrape, "you know, they can't do it."

"That's plain," replied Fogleton, for such was the name of Jack's fellow-workman.

"They may think they can do it, but they can't; they have no power to make us do this—take my word for it, they hav'n't," and Jack scraped.

"Else I don't know what liberty's like," said Fogleton.

"Liberty, my friend—liberty is the essence of an Englishman's being—thank God! there's *habeas corpus*," cried Runnymede, scraping.

"That there is," answered Fogleton, looking warily about him for the boatswain's mate, "that there is."

"And trial by jury, eh?" asked Jack.

"I should think so," replied Fogleton; and he spoke as a man perfectly acquainted with the fact.

"And, thank God! we have Magna Charta," exclaimed Runnymede.

"I believe we have, too," said Fogleton.

"Magna Charta, which insures the liberty of the subject," cried Jack, still scraping.

"So I have heard," remarked Fogleton. "But, I say, if we have all these things, how the devil is it that you and me's here?"

"Oh! what they've done, they can't do," answered Runnymede, "there's a remedy. Thank God! we're Englishmen."

"Oh, I'm proud of my country," said Fogleton, "for my part never wished to leave it. As Englishmen, we ought to be proud of—of—of—everything. Phewgh! if the cold don't cut my fingers to the bone."

"It *is* cold; but you are right, my friend; though we have suffered a little inconvenience, we have our remedy. As you say, we ought to be proud of everything: look at our wooden walls —ar'n't they glorious?" asked Runnymede.

"Very fine; very fine, indeed; specially to sing about, but," and Fogleton blew his fingers, "but damned hard to scrape."

N 3

" Never mind ; as I've said, they can't make us do it—there's a remedy—there's "——

" Quarter-gallery, there !" roared the boatswain's mate.

Runnymede, looking up, inquired, very politely—

" Beg your pardon, did you speak to me ?"

" Can you play the fiddle ?" asked the mate, of Runnymede.

" I could once do something on the violincello," answered Jack.

" The—the—why, what's that ?" inquired the puzzled mate.

" What is it ?" cried Fogleton, contemptuously, " why, a wiolinsellar's a fiddle come to its full growth."

" Can you do anything besides ?" questioned the mate.

" I could once play a little on the German flute," replied Runnymede.

" D—d if your fortin isn't made," rejoined the mate, quickly; " here, tumble up !" and Runnymede scrambled from the plank to the deck, and resigned his scraper in favour of, possibly, a more musical instrument.

" Do they have concerts aboard ?" thought Jack, as he followed the boatswain's mate to the waist.

" The fiddler's dead and the fifer's sick," said the mate, " and we want to get the water up."

" And do they raise water by music?" asked Jack.

" There! play away," cried the mate, thrusting a sixpenny cracked fife, carefully bound with tin at either end, into the hands of the musician.

" Really, it's impossible, sir, that I could play on a thing like this.——I do assure you," and Jack raised his shoulders, and flung back his arms, with that deprecating look, which probably the reader may have seen in the face of a singer, very ill indeed with an apocryphal cold.

" Blow—blow away!" roared the mate.

" Well, if you insist upon it—I—but am I to play here?" asked Runnymede.

" Strike up!" growled the boatswain's mate; and Runnymede, to the horror of his own ears, essayed a slow movement.

" That won't do!" cried the mate, " playing the fife like a archbishop—strike up a jig!" Jack obeyed; and as he played a quick tune upon the wretched pipe, about a dozen men hauling a rope, stept to the tune, raising butts of water from the hold. Jack had only once played through the tune, when the boatswain's mate applauded his performance in the most unequivocal way. " Well, Squeak may die now as soon as he likes, for I'm

d—d if you hav'n't more wind than him!" Thus
afloat, as on shore, is the old servant forgotten in
the new comer. " You're all right for life," continued the mate, charmed with Runnymede's art—
" no; we'll never let go of you."

Bad as the fife was, it was not to Jack quite so
bad as the scraper ; and he went on playing several
airs, his reputation increasing with every tune.
The men paused for two or three minutes, and
Jack took breath.   At this juncture, and a little
before the men were about to resume their work,
and the inspiriting influence of music would be
again in demand, the short, thick, Creole schoolmaster appeared upon deck.   Now, Runnymede, despite of all that he had heard of Mr. Nankin, believed him to be a gentleman ; and, possibly, a
scholar; and hence felt confident of obtaining his
sympathy and his assistance.   It was Jack's wish to
dispatch a letter to Mr. Candidus: " He will, I
am sure," thought Jack, "on knowing where I am,
bring me to London on *habeas corpus ;* yes, thank
heaven ! *habeas corpus* is not suspended—and I can
avail myself of its mercies ; for, thank God ! I am
yet an Englishman."

In an evil moment did Mr. Nankin present himself to the eyes of Runnymede ; for, careless of the
wants of the water-drawers, Jack stept away to
address the pedagogue ; and heedless of the cry of

"music," "fifer," "lubber," from the sailors, sought to secure the services of the scholar. "I trust, sir," said Jack, taking off all the hat that was left him, "I trust, sir, that my situation as an unfortunate gentleman will be my apology for addressing you?" Mr. Nankin bent his large black eyes very disdainfully on the miserable figure before him, and, endeavouring to brush up the hair, which by the indulgence of the captain, had been suffered to remain three weeks uncropt, was about to turn away: this action of Nankin brought to Runnymede's recollection the peculiar miseries of the schoolmaster. "Ha! sir," said Jack, staring at Nankin's hair, "they can't do that, sir—they can't, indeed."

"Do what, man?" asked Nankin, "Do what?"

"It's an offence against the person, sir, for a man to cut another's hair against his will. But pardon me, sir—I was about to say—Oh!" shrieked Jack, "Oh! my God!" and with these exclamations Jack sank doubled to the deck; he then rose writhing like a snake, and he ground his teeth, and his face was purple with pain.

The reader may recollect that in a by-gone page we spoke of the boatswain of the guard-ship, and further, of an implement, his constant companion, formed of three ebony twigs twisted, and bound with metal. Unhappily for poor Runnymede, the boatswain, taking his noon-day walk, espied him absorbed in his address to the schoolmaster, the men vainly calling for "the fifer." Without a word—a syllable—the boatswain, with his huge hand, grasped his weapon,—and, as if he would have put the strength of a whole life in one blow, smote Runnymede a little above the hips. The effect of the blow we have endeavoured to describe.

" You want another—do you?" asked the boatswain, shaking the ebony at poor Jack, who was speechless with pain.

At length, Runnymede was capable of stammering —" You—you—can't do it! You know—you—can't do it."

" What! you want another?" and the boatswain was evidently desirous of a repetition of his peculiar enjoyment.

" Oh! you—you shall suffer for this," cried Jack, " see if you don't suffer for this! I'm not to be struck in this way—for, thank God!"—

" What! you *will* have another?" and never before did the boatswain exhibit so much self-denial.

" You know, you can't do it!" repeated John, as we think, very unnecessarily.

" Come; blow away! Come—rig out your fife! blow!" and the boatswain held aloft the plaited ebony.

Oh, life! how terrible are thy changes! Think, gentle reader—think of Jack Runnymede,—nursed in comfort—written down " gentleman"—a man, who had twenty times in his life, shown his acute taste by hissing a false note at the opera,—think of him, a pressed man aboard a guard-ship—his coat lessened to a jacket—the rim rent from his hat—his shirt in tatters,—with a vile, cracked fife in his hand, wherein he is ordered " to blow," for the inspiration of a very mixed company of thieves and vagabonds, and the penalty of his disobedience, a scourging with plaited ebony !

" You won't blow ?" asked the boatswain, with rising wrath.

" I—I"—and poor Runnymede, his blood boiling, and his flesh quivering, endeavoured to form his mouth to the fife, but produced a sound very like that of the wind whistling through a key-hole.

" Well, then, if you won't blow," cried the boatswain, and he brandished his weapon.

" What will—what—what will you have ?" inquired poor Runnymede.

" Give us ' Jack's alive,'" exclaimed the boatswain, with unintentional satire.

Again Runnymede vainly whistled in the fife, and again the boatswain threatened. Jack caught the glowing eye of his executioner, and, after an effort, burst into full strain.

(As this incident is positively true, we humbly conceive that it may be of especial interest to those unfortunate gentlemen charged with the government of singers: we are convinced that in many cases, when the public have been grievously disappointed by the absence of a favourite " from sudden illness," that with the proper administration, or even with the serious threat of ebony, no such annoyance had ever taken place.)

The required quantity of water being drawn from the hold, Jack hoped that he might be allowed to retire below, and——if he could beg or steal a sheet of paper——dispatch a letter to London. Jack, however, was doomed to be disappointed; for in a few minutes a cutter, with a large black bull painted in her mainsail, came alongside. Beef by the half-carcase was to be hoisted aboard, and again the music of Jack was to lighten the labour of his shipmates. "If I'm made to play whilst they hoist water, and get aboard the beef, I suppose they'll want my fife at their dinner," and then Jack cursed the vanity that made him publish his accomplishments.

" What ! you won't blow ?" roared the boatswain, as Jack stood with one hand to his back, the other holding the fife. " You can't eh ?" and again the threatened ebony drew music from the pressed man. " I see, you can play," cried the boatswain, " so, if there's any hitch, I'll give you double allowance the next time."

" It's very well," exclaimed Jack, " but you can't do it: yes, yes—there's *habeas corpus*—you think you have me safe enough, but no —no—thank God ! I'm an Englishman."

About a month had elapsed, and still Jack Runnymede remained the Orpheus of the waist. At length he contrived to get a letter put into the post-office; a letter to Mr. Candidus, who was immediately to obtain the freedom of his client by means of *habeas corpus*. Mr. Candidus, however, acting upon his own discretion, thought, under all circumstances, his client would be more certain of a dinner, if remaining aboard a man of war. Jack had been of great service to Mr. Sidewind, whose party were now in office; nay, Sidewind himself, newly crawled into parliament through not a very open borough, had a small place in the ministry; hence, he was enabled to serve an old constituent; moreover, he did serve him.

A letter " on his majesty's service" was received by the captain of the guard-ship, recommending to his notice " an unfortunate person, a very respectable man — a man of superior breeding— named John Runnymede. He was fully competent to the duties of a captain's clerk."

Jack Runnymede was summoned to the quarter-deck, and informed by the captain of his good fortune. He was immediately given into the care of the master's mate, Mr. Dark, who took him down to his berth in the after cock-pit, where Jack had the additional advantage of messing with Nankin, the tawny schoolmaster; a person, as he himself averred, of the very highest connexions in town.

Candidus had presented ten guineas to poor Runnymede, with which he was enabled to make a very respectable appearance; although, with strange taste, he refused to purchase the blue worsted pantaloons of the schoolmaster at a few shillings, Mr. Nankin himself having a great many pair of them, and therefore capable of parting with one sample to a friend at a moderate price.

"Capital fellow, Mr. Sidewind—yes, it was no matter how he voted, I always supported him," said Runnymede. "See what it is to have a vote, sir!" he would exclaim to Nankin: "in some countries 'twould have been little use; but, thank God! I'm an Englishman."

In a week, Jack Runnymede quitted the guard-ship, being appointed captain's clerk in a frigate.

CHAPTER XI.

"No, sir—no—I shall proceed by criminal information." These were the words of a white-haired gentleman of fifty to a dingy, squab man of the same age. "He has accused me of peculation,"—

" Well, but you know, between ourselves," said
the dark man.

" I know what you're going to say—that he can
prove it—never mind that : I won't let him. I
may do as I please on that point, for thank God !
I'm an Englishman."

The first speaker was a retired purser in his
majesty's navy—and no other than Jack Runnymede. The short black-looking man, Nankin the
schoolmaster ; who, discharged at the peace, had
somehow swollen himself into an attorney of dirty
employments.

Jack Runnymede had, with great industry, made
himself a fortune. He was therefore particularly
sensitive to an attack that had been levelled at his
character as purser. He was resolved to punish
the scandal ; no matter whether the charge were
true or false—he was the best judge of that. The
law gave him protection—for " thank God ! he
was an Englishman."

Shortly after this, Mr. Runnymede was solicited
for his vote. " Pray, sir," he asked the candidate,
" what are your opinions on the law of libel as it
stands—arrest for debt—and impressment ? " and
putting his arms under his coat-tails, Mr. Runnymede awaited an answer.

" In its present operation I am opposed to the
law of libel—certainly, to arrest for debt—and

most assuredly to the infamous and inhuman system of pressing," was the reply of the candidate.

"My service to you, sir," said Jack Runnymede, "you don't have my vote. Your politics may be very well for a garden of Eden, sir, but not for this country. What! change the law of libel? leave open any man of property to the scurrility of shirtless vagabonds—create litigation by abolishing imprisonment for debt—and sweep us from the world as a naval power by doing away with impressment?—No, sir; not while I can lift my voice, will I consent to this.—By losing one or all of these, I should cease to be grateful, as I am, for my country—should no longer bless my stars that I am a Briton—no longer thank God that I am an Englishman!"

CRESO QUATTRINO:

THE MAN WHO "DIED RICH."

It was noon, and the citizens of learned Padua swarmed towards the Palazzo de Ragione. It was plain, there was some show afoot: some quacksalver hot from Venice; or, perhaps, some beatific Filippo Neri, with new-made relics, fresh from Rome. Of a surety, it was something rare and strange that drew hundreds as one man towards the same spot.

"'Tis forty years since such a thing was seen," said an old man who, his shaking hand grasping a staff, and leaning on the shoulder of his grandson, hobbled onwards as though he hastened to a shrine where youth and health might be had for kneeling.

"Ha! ha! that I should live to see this!" crowed a withered beldam, and she clapt her hands and sprang forward like a witch at the Sabbath.

"Could any man have looked for it?" asked a grave tradesman of his neighbour, as they both went with the crowd.

It seemed that all the people of Padua were assembled at the Hall. It was with much labour that the city-guards kept the multitude close-wedged, so vigorously did every one press to behold—what?

A criminal, in shameful nakedness, seated on a low, round stone at the end of the Hall—on the *Stone of Infamy.* The culprit was an old man, with that in his face which makes old age terrible. Years lay heavily upon his back, but a defying scorn had, for a time, flung off the load, and he sat upright as a staff. He sat, and his eyes glowed like burning coals upon the crowd that pressed to stare at him. He looked back the looks of hundreds, who quailed from his eyes as from the eyes of a snake. Many a rejoicing foe who came to chuckle at the sight shrank back, still fearful of his ancient enemy. There was a tumult in the heart of the old man—a fire in his brain—as he caught the eager face of many a fellow-citizen; and he would tighten his arms across his breast as though holding in a passion that swelled to burst it. Old Creso Quattrino sat nakedly upon the stone of infamy—his grave was dug at his foot—and yet no despot from his throne could have looked more fiercely, more contemptuously around him. The crowd heeded not the fate of the victim, but—his grave was dug at his living foot.

Creso Quattrino was the youngest son of a noble, though impoverished house. His elder brothers talked of glory, and cut their daily bread with hired-out swords. One by one, they died in their vocation, and still the eulogy that Creso uttered over each was—" fool." Creso, in early life, became a trader; it was his one hope to " die rich;" it would be his glory to quit life leaving heavy coffers. Fortune smiled upon his desire; and ere the mouth of his first brother was stopped with the bloody mire of fame, Creso could have thrice outweighed the helm, cuirass, and sword of the immortal warrior with merchant's gold. His four brothers, hired by four different states, died in battle. " They have their laurels," Creso would cry, with a sneering humility,—" I have only ducats. They are sleeping on the wide bed of glory, and when the historian shall some day make known that in such a skirmish such a king was repulsed, such a duke was victorious, such a count kept his ground with a trifling loss, he will write in everlasting words the glowing epithets of my happy brothers."

This humour increased with the wealth, with the years of Creso. With him, gold was power—

was reputation : no strength could overcome it—— no shame could tarnish it. He looked upon his ducats as kings look upon their mercenaries—the instruments of his will, the sure doers of his behests, however vile and ruthless. He was that squalid despot—a tyrannous miser. And he would *die* rich !

Creso was past forty, when, with his gold he bought himself a wife — a creature of lustrous beauty—the eldest child of Marco Spori, a poor trader of Padua. Marco was doomed for a petty sum in the books of the man of wealth ; early and late he toiled to pay his creditor, and still some new misfortune made the labour vain. Creso, with a grim smile, would proffer further aid, and then would praise the gentle looks of Marianna.

" No, Messer Quattrino," cried Marco, awakening to the meaning of his patron, " Marianna is wedded."

" Wedded !" exclaimed Quattrino, and his face darkened—" wedded ! "

" In promise," said Marco, " 'tis all as one, Messer Quattrino ; if I understand you rightly."

" Betrothed ? To whom, friend Marco ?" asked Quattrino, with constrained composure ; for love—or call the feeling by a grosser name—before unknown to the miser, had made him like one possessed.

" To Pietro Leti."

" Doubtless, some wealthy merchant ? No ?
Humph ! A scholar, perhaps, with a tongue sil-
very as Satan's ? Is your future son-in-law, good
Marco Spori, of the ' Inflammati,' or ?"—

" He rents a little vineyard," replied Marco,
unmoved by the malignant banter of his creditor.
" His father lived and died upon it—a happy old
man. Why should not Pietro ?"

" And you will give your child—the tender, the
beautiful Marianna, to hopeless poverty ? You will
blast that beauty with early care ? You will fling
her a prey to the tooth of want ?" said Creso.

" She will be poor—granted. Wherefore should
she not be happy ?" asked Marco.

" The poor cannot be happy. Never open your
eyes, man ; I speak a plain truth—a truth the rich
well know, but never preach. No ; it is their trick,
folding their purple round them, to hymn the praise
of low estate—to paint the happy carelessness of
rags—the excellence of appetite begotten by hard
drudgery. Poverty ! Of all the arrows shot at our
miserable nature, is there one that is not made the
keener if whetted on the poor man's hearth ?"

" That is true," said Marco, despondingly—" too
true, Messer Quattrino."

" What is your state now, while I speak, Marco
Spori ? Are you not hunted—even as a wild beast,

hunted?   Have you a tranquil thought?   Is there one fibre of your heart that is not pulled at by a care?   You have children, too—things sent, they say, to bless and crown you.   But, then, good Marco, they sometimes want a supper; and oh! the blessing."

" Do not, Messer Quattrino—for the saints' sake ! do not," exclaimed Marco, lifting his clasped hands entreatingly.

" There is no physician, but gold; trust me, there is not; and when gold fails, believe it, there is no comforter but death."   Such was the creed of Creso Quattrino.

Marco sought his desolate home.   As he lifted the latch, his heart quailed at the laughing voices of his younger children.   Marianna read the thoughts of her father in his eyes.   He sank upon a stool, and for a moment, hid his face in his hands; then, looking vacantly at his daughter, he uttered—" Yes; 'twill be the best—that I should have thought of it !—it will be the best."

" What, father?   Tell me, what?" asked Marianna, winding her arms about his neck.

" To end this,—and there is but one way. Yes, I will make myself a show for the people of Padua —what matters it ?   'Tis but an hour—and shall I not be free ?"

" Father !"——

" Every hope has left me, Marianna; turn where I will, I meet with scornful or with threatening faces. But there is yet a law in Padua, a kind law for the bankrupt," said Marco, shuddering.

" What law? You do not mean ?"——

" The *Stone of Infamy*," cried the father, his flesh quivering as he spoke. " 'Tis but to sit an hour there—to sit and be stared at, and, such is the good law, my creditors are paid."*

" And you will sit upon that stone ?" asked Marianna.

" I must—I will," groaned Marco.

" When, father—when ?" cried the girl.

" To-morrow — if heaven will make me live— to-morrow," said Marco, and his head fell upon his bosom.

Marianna quitted her home, but in less than two hours returned. Her father sprang to his feet, as at the coming of a ghost. " Blessed Mother ! Marianna !" cried Marco, staring at the white face, the cold eyes of his child. " What is this ?" he exclaimed, as she held a purse towards him.

" Gold, father ! gold," said Marianna.

" How got—how come by ?" raved the father, for suddenly the wildest fears possessed him.

" You are saved from shame,"—said the girl— " from worse than death."

* See Moreri.

" How ?   Speak ! Marianna ; how ?" exclaimed
Marco.

" I am the wife of Creso Quattrino," answered
Marianna ; and as she spoke, she fell like a dead
thing to the ground.

From the night Marianna became the wife of
Quattrino, she smiled but once ; it was when she
kissed her new-born girl—a babe that, in one
brief hour, was motherless.   For three years, had
Marianna lived a life of silent anguish.   Her
husband loathed her for the indifference with which
she looked upon his wealth—for the coldness with
which she listened to his golden schemes—his
bargains made from ignorance or want.   He felt—
and the thought haunted him like a demon—that
he had bought a victim, not wedded a partner.
He felt himself, with all his wealth, humbled before the simple nature of Marianna ; her gentleness—her meek endurance—galled, enraged him :
there was one to whom his bags of gold were but as
hoarded ashes.   Reproach at length subsided into
neglect, then turned into disgust ; and, when the
miser looked upon the dead face of his wife, he
smiled in sullen satisfaction.   There was an in-
truding, though a silent, witness taken hence :
even in the chamber of the dead, Quattrino breathe
more freely.   For the child, that should be to him
a blessing—he would mould it to his own heart—

there was no mother, no Marianna, with her
speechless lips, yet cold, accusing eyes, to thwart
the lessons of a thrifty father.   The girl should
wed a prince; yes, he had already gold sufficient,—
and time could not but treble it—to buy a throne.
Auretta was scarcely three days old when, in the
imagination of her parent, vain-glorious, drunk
with wealth, she was a royal bride.

Years passed, and every year, Creso Quattrino
became more hardened with his wealth.   Fortune
seemed his handmaid, so constantly did he prosper.
His dealings were with men of all nations: he
scrupled not to furnish the infidel with arms, heedless of the penalty; for Mother Church denied
the Christian rites of burial to such ingrate traders.
"It matters not," thought Creso, "so that I *die*
rich, I am well content to risk the rest."

"Humph! where shall we meet to talk of this?"
Thus one day spoke Quattrino to Jacob, the
travelled Jew of Padua, with whom our Christian
merchant was wont to have many dealings.

"Why not at your house, good signor?" asked
Jacob.   "Ere this, we have driven a bargain
there."

"It has been noted; therefore, 'tis fit we deal
more privily.   Art thou not a Jew?'"

"I thank Abraham! yes.   I am a branded,
despised Jew: I thank Abraham!"

" And I—I am a Christian; is it not so, Jacob?" asked Quattrino, a withering smile curling his lip.

" I have heard that you were baptised, Signor Quattrino," replied the Jew.

" And our close and frequent communing may damage me in the confessional," said Creso, and still he sneered.

" Thy confessional! where may that place be found?" inquired Jacob.

" Where I lay by my ducats, Jew.   Understand me; our church hath eyes, and ears, and—hands; and long ones."

" All this I know—all this I have felt," replied the Levite.

" This war with the Turk—if 'twere known that thou and I helped the wicked infidel to cut good Christian throats—dost know what might happen, Jew?   Thy bones would crack for it."

" Ugh!" and the Jew shuddered.

" Nay, more and worse; my coin would shrink: the priestly hand—thou knowest how huge its clutch—would be among it.   I thank my good god Plutus! the war flourishes.   'Twas a hot fight the last—there are widows wailing in Venice, Jew."

" I thank my God! the God of Abraham, for it!" cried the Jew with deep devotion; " I have cause to hate thy brethren—God knows it!"

" Saidst thou brethren, Jew?   To me all men

are brethren—'tis the good creed taught me by my gold. Blessed talisman ! Glorious property ! softening the haughty—strengthening the weak; giving to him, who rightly knows its use, a power and mastery beyond all other might. The Turk bids for my aid : I sell him arms, wherewith he cuts a thousand Christian throats, making Christian children fatherless. And why is this ? I will tell you. Why is the Christian slaughtered? The goodly, peaceful creature covets a fair patch of earth —a glittering city—the dominion of a stranger's river. He is an infidel who holds it—it is enough ; the unbeliever's land is soaked with human blood ; the city is besieged—a hell of flames is roaring round its walls—the breach is made ; rapine, murder, and lust whoop through the streets—and the flag of victory flies over blood and ashes. The Christians have conquered ; and with sweet humility, and deep thanksgiving, they make the church roof echo with a loud *Te Deum !* With brazen face and iron heart, they thank their God, that they have prospered in a work, that devils might have blenched at."

" Do I hear Creso Quattrino, the merchant of Padua ?" asked the Jew looking astonishment.

" These hideous mockeries, good Jacob—this wanton tyranny of the strong—have made me look upon the doings of this world as a grim, fantastic, wicked, foolish mask. Virtue, justice, honour! What are they? words—tinkling syllables for sweating slaves, like bells to drudging camels. There is but one thing certain—gold! Grasp that—you grasp power; a power, that though the poor may hate, they must acknowledge. Grasp gold, and you pull the heart-strings of that godlike creature, man, as boys work puppets."

" I love my ducats, good Signor Creso; and yet, amongst my own people, there is, I think, something I love more," said Jacob.

" More—more than thy ducats, Jew?" asked Quattrino.

" Aye; the respect of men—their kindly greetings; need I add, the smiles of my children?" said the Jew, and Creso bit his lip.

" The smiles of children!" and as Creso spoke, a sudden desolation stared from his eyes.

" That is a wealth!" cried the Jew, " that is a wealth!"

" Can it be tested?" exclaimed Creso; " tell me, Jacob—tell me, how?"

" You are yourself a father, Signor Quattrino— the father of a beautiful maiden; a thing of goodness, of gentleness."

" Thou didst know her mother, Jacob?" asked the merchant.

" Auretta is her mother's self—her very self,"

cried the Jew. "'Tis twenty-three years ago—alack ! time slides, time slides ! But I have tarried long. Where shall we meet to-night, since to thy hearth the Jew brings peril ?"

" By the Palazzo de Ragione—by the *Stone*. Humph ! See you not, Jacob, that I preach truly ? The *Stone of Infamy !* Poverty, at the fount of this world, is christened infamy : christened ! branded with a burning brand. The *Stone of Infamy !* Right—very right,—'tis fitly called ; for did a glistening angel sit there, men would loathe it."

" By the *Stone ;* good. The hour ?" and the Jew prepared to depart. " The hour ?"

" Stay : not there. There is thanksgiving at St. Antony's for our victory, for we claim it, over the infidel ; I must be there."

" You, there ?" and the Jew gazed and then smiled grimly. " You at the thanksgiving ?"

" Aye ; being beaten, the infidel hath greater need of arms. You thank at the synagogue—I at the cathedral. Meet me at nine," and Creso Quattrino turned to seek his solitary home—solitary, though a daughter dwelt there. " The mother's self—her very self," he muttered as he took his way—" would she were not so !"

On the marriage of Marianna, Pietro Leti quitted his native Padua for Florence, where he found a wife in the daughter of a thrifty vine-grower, who,

o 3

dying, bequeathed his son-in-law a small estate; and in a few years Pietro became a prosperous man, with wealth enough to send Luigi, his only child, to study at the school of Padua. It was to give a meeting to the young scholar that the Jew had hastened from Quattrino.

"I have waited, Jacob," said Luigi, with an impatient look, as the old man entered his dwelling.

"I crave your pardon, gentle sir—sudden business with the Signor Quattrino, held me."

"Ha! Quattrino. Thou knowest him, then? I had heard so. Thou art friends?" added Luigi, earnestly.

"We sometimes trade together—nothing more : our friendship is bounded by our ducats," said the Jew.

"Dost know his daughter—hast ever seen the beautiful Auretta?" and the youth coloured, and his voice trembled.

"Seen her? Aye, a thousand times. Thou mayest have heard thy father speak of her mother ?" said the Jew, fixing his eyes upon Luigi.

"Auretta's mother? Never. Why should he speak of her ?" inquired Luigi, moved by the scrutinizing glance of the Jew.

"I'll tell you. The story, youth, may haply save thee much misery—may profit the beautiful Auretta."

"Oh, speak! good Jacob—speak!" exclaimed the impatient boy.

"Thy father was to have wedded the mother of Auretta—they were betrothed."

"Betrothed! 'Tis strange I never heard of this. Betrothed!   What barred the match?" asked Luigi.

"Poverty.   To save her father from the direst shame, poor Marianna became the wife of the rich Quattrino.   Her daughter—I have heard the merchant vaunt as much—is destined for a prince."

"A prince!" cried Luigi.

"No less: and be sure of it, young sir, Quattrino's wealth may make even princes stoop to wed Auretta."

"Stoop to wed her—stoop, Jew?"

"But we did not meet to talk of this," said the old Jew, marking the earnestness of Luigi—"we met not for this."

"True.   Well, Jew, shall I have the money?" asked Luigi.

"A thousand ducats—and the security?" and Jacob paused, and stared in the face of the scholar. "The security?"

"Thou knowest I am my father's heir.   Thou knowest, he has no child save me.   Draw what bond thou wilt, I am content to sign it."

"Death is a slow pay-master," said the Jew.

"But the surest, Jacob," replied Luigi.

"A thousand ducats? 'Tis a large sum for a scholar. Truly, what need hast thou, a bookman, of a thousand ducats?"

"Say, to spend in a revel—to buy a gondola—to purchase music—a sparkling stone—nay, to cast into the Adriatic,—what matters it to thee? Shall I have the money, or shall I seek a readier merchant?" asked the youth, and he rose to depart.

"Stay, gentle sir—thou shalt have the money. This night at nine—I'll have the deed prepared."

"Where shall we meet?"

"Here," replied the Jew, and the youth took his way from the house, and, with hurried steps, sought the mansion of Quattrino.

"Blessed St. Mary!" cried Auretta's nurse, as she met Luigi at the door, "my master— know you not, he is at home?—should he see you,"——— .

"Go—say I beg some words with him," said Luigi.

"Are you mad, young master?—Are you mad?"

"Fear not, good nurse—I have conned my lesson; fear nothing. Say, a student craves a meeting with the merchant." The nurse obeyed, and the young scholar stood in the presence of the haughty, purse-proud Quattrino.

"Now, youth," said Creso, "what trade would you drive with me?"

" I would purchase your dearest treasure, Signor Quattrino," replied the simple-hearted youth.

" Aye? thou art young for a merchant. What treasure, child?" asked Creso.

" Thy daughter," answered Luigi; and the old man gasped at the word.

" My daughter? Truly: thou wouldst buy the heiress of Creso Quattrino? Doubtless, thou comest to market with a ducal crown, a countship,—nothing less? Thou wouldst buy my daughter—thou, — a student? but I err—I see, thou art a prince, a noble gentleman, jesting in the bare gown of a poor scholar."

" I am called Luigi Leti," answered the boy.

" Leti!" exclaimed the merchant.

" Son of Pietro Leti, once of Padua, now of Florence. You may have heard of him, Signor Quattrino?"

" And thou dost love my daughter—thou dost love Auretta?" asked Quattrino, waiving an answer.

" And would win her—win her at thy hands," replied Luigi.

" Knows she of this meeting? Doth she sanction thy request—hast thou," asked the merchant, with deep dissimulation, " hast thou her heart? Thou hast? And what — what may Luigi Leti offer a doating father for this priceless gem?"

" The harvest of my sword," answered Luigi.

"Thy sword? A student's sword?"

"Creso Quattrino, my soul abhors deceit: 'tis possible I might have won the jewel of thy house despite thy will."

"Is it so?" cried Quattrino, and his heart laboured with hate—with thoughts of ruthless vengeance. "My daughter would have flown from me—would have wedded with a poor scholar? Thou art a brave, a noble youth, Luigi; thou hast rightly said, thy heart abhors deceit. I read that glad assurance in thine eyes: give me thy hand," and the subtle merchant pressed the palm of Luigi, smiling in his face. "I see thy purpose, youth—thou wouldst not rob an old man of his only joy; thou comest to tell me this?"

"I come to ask a promise," said Luigi.

"Speak; the openness of thy nature hath won me: my heart yearns towards thee, Luigi; trust me, it does. Humph!" and still Creso smiled upon his victim—"thy features make me think of days, that—well, well, they're past. How is the good Pietro? He wedded happily—very happily. I have heard much of the virtues of thy good mother. But thou comest to ask a boon? Name it, good Luigi—name it."

"I have closed my book—have thrown aside my student's gown; and in three days take ship from Venice," said Luigi.

" Take ship—whither ?" asked the gladdened merchant.

" For the war against the Turk," replied the youth.

" A brave lad ! a pious lad ! Ha ! ha ! thoult make rare work among the heathen. 'Tis a pious purpose."

" Wilt thou promise me, Signor Quattrino, if I return to Venice with an honoured name—with glory won upon the infidel—wilt thou promise me Auretta ?"

" Thy laurels 'gainst her ducats ? Thoult prove a lucky champion, if thou dost compass it."

" Shall I have thy word, Signor Quattrino ?" asked Luigi.

" Thou hast her word already—is it not so ?" questioned the smiling merchant. " Nay, I warrant me, 'twas not the timid girl who put such hard conditions ? Doubtless, Auretta would wed thee, though thou shouldst never cleave a turban ?"

" Shall I have thy promise ?" pressed the youth.

" Thou hast made me thy friend for ever, Luigi. Like a thief thou mightest have robbed me of my dearest wealth—nay, more, have laughed at the despoiled old man thy wit had beggared. Not a gallant in all Padua, save thyself, good Luigi, would have dealt thus openly. Well, simplicity

should win simplicity.   When dost thou purpose
to depart ?"

"In three days."

"Thou art equipped then — everything prepared ?"

"I have secured the means.   At nine to-night I
meet Jacob the Jew,"—

"Though an Israelite, an honest man.   And he
advances thee the means? To-night, at his house?—
aye, indeed," said the crafty merchant.   "Well,
thou must sup with me to-night: say, at ten, good
Luigi; then we can talk of Auretta.   Thou wilt
not fail—nay, I must see thee to the door;" and
Quattrino, with well acted courtesy, attended the
duped Luigi to the threshold.   As the merchant
stood at his door, a messenger from Venice arrived,
bearing a letter for Quattrino.

"I pray, signor," said the man, "that it may
bring good news—but there are grievous rumours
in Venice."

A moment, Quattrino glared at the messenger;
then hurriedly broke the seal.   Another moment,
and he staggered like a drunken man.   "Gone !
lost ! sunk !" he screamed, and his face grew
livid.

"Signor—good signor !" cried Luigi, grasping
the arm of Creso.

" 'Tis true, then ?" asked the messenger.

" My argosy,—worth a princedom—and sunk !"
—groaned Quattrino.

" Say not so, good signor; hope the best," said
Luigi.

Quattrino looked as one stunned at Luigi, and
then grasped his hand, and with a forced smile,
said—" No matter : the loss shall not spoil our
supper.   Mind—at ten to-night, Luigi; at ten to-
night," he repeated, the messenger standing by, " I
shall expect you.   The news shook me a little—
but 'tis over.   Remember, Luigi—at ten," and
Quattrino, followed by the messenger, turned into
his house.

As the clock struck nine, Luigi knocked at the
door of the Jew.   The deed was speedily signed,
and Luigi, with the counted ducats bade the Jew
good night.   Ere the Jew could place the deed in
his chest, he heard the cries of Luigi and a noise
of struggling men.   The Jew rushed into the street,
when Luigi, making to the house, fell into the old
man's arms.

" Holy Abraham ! what has happened ?" exclaimed the Jew.

" A villain set upon me—I am slain !" cried the
youth, and he slipped from the feeble hold of the
Jew, and fell dead upon the earth.

The neighbours ran into the street—the watch

came up—the Jew was seized on suspicion of the
murder, no man save himself being found near the
body.   His creed was sufficient evidence of his
wickedness—he was a Jew, and that of itself, was
witness against him.   His house was ransacked by
the officers of justice, and all his papers seized.

"Thou art innocent of the murder?" said the
officer, "well, it matters not; thou wilt have work
enough to answer for thy treasons."

"I will confess all—everything—but spare
my life—let me be saved from torture," cried
the Jew, and he tore his beard, and howled in
agony, when he beheld the discovered papers
proving his correspondence with the agent of the
Turk.   "I—I was not alone in the bargain,"
exclaimed the Jew—" the Christian merchant—
there is proof of it—Creso Quattrino was my
partner."

Ere midnight, Creso Quattrino and the Jew
Jacob were fast in gaol—prisoners to the state.
The assassin, hired by the merchant, had done his
work; but the blow that did a murder, helped to
reveal a treason.

The wretched Jew was doomed to the wheel—
the Christian merchant obtained his freedom, but
only with the loss of all his wealth.   He was fined
for his treasons to an amount that absorbed his
every possession, leaving him a debtor to many,

who, in their time, thwarted and oppressed by
Quattrino, resolved to revenge themselves of his
past tyranny. Quattrino stood in the streets of
Padua without a home, without a meal, save at
the hands of charity.

"And it is come to this? And I shall die poor,
—after all,—a beggar !" he cried, half-resolved to
end his miserable life; and then the hope, vain as
he thought it, the hope of future fortune, made him
bear the load of life—no, he could not die a
pauper.

"And now, signor? The five thousand crowns
between us—I have need of them," said a creditor
to the broken merchant.

" Give me time—a little time, good Battista,"
solicited the humble Creso.

" Aye, and more than thou hast given to any
man: my crowns, to-morrow, or the gaol," answered the creditor.

" The gaol ! What—a felon debtor ! Thou
dog—thou cur, that"—

" Is it so?" said the creditor. " Well, then, to-
morrow look thou to lie in debtor's straw."

All night Quattrino wandered through the
streets. His reason reeled beneath his misery.
He paused before the Palazza di Ragione ; and as
he stood, a monk—who had been to confess a dying
man—approached him.

" Blessed St. Antony ! " cried the friar, " is it the merchant—is it Signor Quattrino ? "

" No.   The merchant is dead—I am his ghost, damned to wander where the rich man lived in glory," answered Creso.

" What was thy wealth ?—perishable dust ! My son, there is better wealth hoarded for thee."

" Where, monk—where ? " asked Quattrino.

" Wealth eternal," replied the friar.

" Humph ! Canst lend me ten thousand present ducats ? " demanded Creso.   " Look there ! Is not that the *Stone of Infamy ?* And now, see,"—and Quattrino griped the arm of the friar,—" see, who stands there and beckons me to it ! Dost not see him ? Look—'tis young Luigi—he, the scholar, who was slain. He beckons me to sit there : me ! Creso Quattrino, the princely merchant of Padua, throned on the *Stone of Infamy !* Ha ! ha ! " And with a yell, the pauper Creso rushed from the shuddering friar.

The next day Quattrino encountered Battista. " Now, merchant ? " said the creditor—" my ducats, my ducats, good Messer Creso—my ducats, or the gaol : there—for who in Padua hath not felt the bitterness of thy oppression ? there thou shalt rot and die my debtor."

" Die thy debtor ! Thy debtor ?—a crawling chapman !—thou, who in my days of wealth didst

cringe before me like a beaten hound?—I defy,
and spit at thee!"—exclaimed old Creso.

"Arrest him at my suit; to the goal with him,"
cried Battista to a ready officer.

"Hold—hold!" shouted Creso—"I—I claim my
privilege—the privilege of a citizen of Padua!"

"What privilege?" asked the officer.

"The—the"—Creso stood convulsed with passion—"I will not die thy debtor—I will sit upon
the *Stone!*"

The crowd that were gathered about Creso
and his creditor, echoed "the *Stone!*" and looked
astonished at each others' faces—and then, as
rejoicing at a promised feast, whooped and shouted
—"Quattrino on the *Stone of Infamy!*" "Creso a
bankrupt!"

The next morning Creso, the golden merchant,
as he was called, became a spectacle of shame and
wretchedness to the men of Padua; for one hour,
he sat upon the *Stone of Infamy!*

"Now, Quattrino, the time is up—thou hast sat
the hour—thy debts are paid," said the judge.

"I am no debtor, by the law of Padua?" asked
Quattrino, and with an effort he rose from his
ignominious seat, and griping the arm of one of the
guards with the gripe of death, he looked as one
risen from his coffin. "I die no debtor!" he gasped,
and fell, huddled, to the earth.

"Santa Maria! he's dead," exclaimed Battista.

"Ha! ha! he's dead!" screamed an old crone.

Ere the beggar Quattrino was borne from the Hall, there was heard a cry of "The argosy—the argosy!"—and a messenger from Venice hurried through the crowd to the self-poisoned criminal. Quattrino's vessel, rumoured as lost, rode in the Adriatic, freighted with unbounded wealth.

"She's safe!—she's here!" exclaimed Quattrino and he writhed with the poison, "in port! safe in port! Ha! ha! I die no pauper—I die"—and with his eyes glazing upon the messenger of fortune the miserable Creso "died rich."

END OF VOL. I.

PRINTED BY WILLIAM WILCOCKSON, ROLLS BUILDINGS.

JOHN APPLEJOHN'S HUMANE INTENTIONS.

Published by Henry Colburn Great Marlborough Street 1835

MEN OF CHARACTER.

BY

DOUGLAS JERROLD.

" We must admonish thee, my worthy friend (for, perhaps, thy heart may
be better than thy head), not to condemn a character as a bad one, because it is
not perfectly a good one. If thou dost delight in these models of perfection,
there are books enow written to gratify thy taste; but as we have not in the
course of our conversation, ever happened to meet with any such person, we
have not chosen to introduce any such here."

FIELDING.

IN THREE VOLUMES.

VOL. II.

LONDON:

HENRY COLBURN, PUBLISHER,
GREAT MARLBOROUGH STREET.

MDCCCXXXVIII.

PRINTED BY W. WILCOCKSON, ROLLS BUILDINGS, FETTER LANE.

CONTENTS

OF

THE SECOND VOLUME.

JOHN APPLEJOHN:

THE MAN WHO "MEANT WELL."

CHAPTER I.

BELOVED reader,—we beg your company up Chancery Lane on a visit of introduction to our well-meaning friend, John Applejohn. Our pén, being fallen from the wing of truth—and that truth has wings, they who have pursued her can best testify—we could not, if we would, be silent on the objects skirting your path. No: the feather in our fingers, like the wand of a magician, sways us to its purpose: we are but the obedient instrument of a compelling power. Otherwise, incited by the waywardness of our temper, we might indulge in fictitious evil; we might delight to build a dungeon, hurrying you from a thyme-covered bank in Arcady; we might, with savage haste, depict a band of cannibals, eating as at an assize dinner,—whereas, we are bound to show a ring of placid Brahmins, taking their bloodless meal beneath the great banyan !

We have entered Chancery Lane. Behold a gentleman in glossy black, with pale and contemplative face; with half-closed lids, and eyes, hare-like, thrown back: he glances at an opposite arch, the entrance to a solemn Hall, where nothing is heard save notes of sweetest sound—justice tinkling her golden scales! The arch to common eyes is built of coarsest stone: it is a piece of purest ivory, worthy to frame the looking-glass of truth; whose silver-voiced sons pass rustling in and out, arrayed in her sable garb—for truth, a milk-white virgin in the sky, became an Ethiop when she touched the earth; albeit that these her children ofttimes deny the change, vowing her blackest black to be the whitest white. And in and out these goodly creatures pass,—wisdom on their brows, hope in their eyes, and peace and love upon their lips. Their awful heads bear curled treasures, snatched from the manes and tails of steeds of Araby, whitened with powdered pearls which Venus' self might weep for. The phœnix might nestle in one of these—by the profane illiterate denominated wigs—deeming it his chosen spicery !

And see that loitering band of middle-aged and venerable men. What a halo of benevolence surrounds each head and glistens on each face ! With a wise contempt of outward show, they are clad in

threadbare raiments ; yes, though able to appear
in purple and fine linen, they meekly choose to
stand in faded black and amber-coloured cotton.
And yet these practical philanthropists will, in the
kindest spirit of intelligence, speak of their abounding wealth: nay, to serve their fellow-creatures,
they have been known to swear to it. They have
made oath to their possessions,—wealth in bonds,
and granaries heaped with yellow corn ; and this,
when the reckless vulgar have called them—men
of straw !

A little onward, and we halt at the simple dwelling of the sober scrivener. Old Egypt, with her
paragraphs of pictures, comes upon us, as we contemplate the labouring scribes. How wise the
craft,—how profound the mystery ! Look at the
ample skin ;—with what occult wisdom is it over-
wrought ! How thickly is the true meaning
shrouded from the common brain, perplexed and
reeling at the cunning of the art ! Grope manfully
through the labyrinth of words, and though you are
but a vulgar man, you will apprehend the sense as
easily as would the eyeless Sampson. Is not the
device most exquisite? Is not this cobweb writing
—("the wise convey it call")—most admirable? But
ere you hope to seize its purport in its pure simplicity, first learn to tell us what language speaks
the painted dog of Cheops?—what his cat?—what

the ibis ?—and what the mystic crocodile ? Even
the stamped lion and unicorn at the margin of the
deed, with their open, ingenuous faces, seem to
wonder at the mystery they are called upon to
make valid and to dignify.

Not so fast : tarry and consider these goodly rows
of tomes, in coats of leather made sacred to the law.
Do you not feel a sudden bowing of the spirit ?—
an awe, as if the sages of long-departed time rose
silently as vapours from their tombs, and stared
upon you ? Ponder on the mighty brains conserved
in the leaves before you. Marvel at the untiring
spirit that hath painted right and wrong, and both
in colours softening delicately down, that where the
separate lines begin or end, it asks some fifty spirits
more to tell. Musing on the books, our fancy
changes them to different things : now, they are
pieces of pure crystal—now, wedges of thrice-as-
sayed gold—now, pots of honey for the hungering
—medicine for the sick. Here, the stricken stranger,
bleeding with his wrongs, may pause and read his
glorious remedy. Here, the wan widow gathers
hope for her just cause—and here, the orphan dries
her sorrow, comforted by strong assertion. And
here, the man, hurt by some neighbour's tongue,
may learn if he be surely hurt or not ! Survey the
shelves : they bend with the weight of grave opinions ;—and learn this further good, that to a single

point there run a hundred opposite lines. Look again : the place is thronged with forms. We are led back to the days of the first Henry—of that foolish bully, John—of pious Edward. And there are the "forest laws :" and with a thought, we have the villain driving his swine to the beech trees, the immortal man but little raised above his grunting charge : we see the sport of nobles, and the pain of serfs, and we sigh for the days of the picturesque when the life of a man was of no more account than the life of a deer. Talk of vendors of romance ! give us the window of a law-bookseller for the bloody tales of iron life. See, there—"State Trials" in a massive row : the books are gone—but there is an array of faces ! Time, the great cleanser, has been there at work. There, the miserable man of lies, his ears clipped to the skull, is a preacher of truth ; and there, the leprous traitor loses his loathsome scales, and smiles on passing generations a bright-faced martyr !

Turn we from the houses, to the passengers and loiterers at doors. Certain provinces are distinguished by the comeliness of their inhabitants. Throughout this vast city, as far as watchful experience has shown us, there is no place in which we meet with so much human beauty, certainly of a peculiar character, as in Chancery-lane; the more especially when the courts are sitting. Look at that slim,

short, young man, at the end of an alley ; his eyes
rolling and twinkling in their sockets, as though he
feared a tiger was at hand, but where he knew not.
He stands but a few paces from his own sweet
home, like a spider advanced upon its web. His
face shows him to be a descendant of the patriarchs ;
it has an anxious though not a melancholy beauty :
he has a mildly drooping lip and the eye of a
moulting hawk. No man has watched some of his
fellow-creatures with greater zeal ; and if the labour
have deepened his spirit, it has also sharpened it.
There, again, is a man of a quite different mark :
his acute study of the law, his intimate knowledge
of its green winding alleys and its mossy nooks, has
repaid him with advantages he cares not to conceal :
witness the sapphire, larger than a beetle, brightening in his breast ; his fingers ringed to the joint
with flashing gems ; his chain of gold swinging in
massive loop at his velvet vest. His face of fine
Mosaic outline, is, with intense legal investigation,
become a face of *terra cotta :* yes, it is a baked
brick cut into a countenance.

And there are two or three of the humbler
priesthood—the working clergy in the cause of
right ; the toiling souls who bear the insignia
and the types of law,—who do " personal service"
to a thousand men, and think but little of the act.
And there is the portly broker—the smooth-faced

sworn functionary; he with universal judgment, who—on the sanctity of his oath—philosophically and arithmetically proves the worth of all things!

Obedient reader, shall we proceed? It is a hot June evening, and the pent air burns and stifles like the heat of an oven.

Stay; who have we seated on this step,—his elbow on his knee, his face in his hand? Who is he, that on a sultry night in June sits on the step of a house——one of the dozen places of ease to the larger gaols? Who is he—who can he be?

Reader,—he is John Applejohn; a simple soul of good dispositions,—a man who "means well."

CHAPTER II.

"I am very sorry, Mr. Applejohn—very sorry, indeed; but you must know I am a father and"—

"To be sure," said John, "or how could I marry Sarah?"—and our hero looked innocently into the face of a tall, big man, rustic in his dress and manner, who now tapped his leather gaiter with an ash stick, and now scrambled his fingers through his thin grey hair, and now coughed, and tried to put a resolute look into his broad, healthy, unthinking countenance, which in its general expression might

have typified the strength and hearty virtues of that
worthiest of knights, good Sir John Barleycorn.

"I am very sorry for you indeed, John—Mr.
Applejohn,"—and the sorrowful speaker passed
the wide cuff of his drab coat round his hat and
fell into deeper melancholy.

"Why,—master Twopenny"—and John stared,
and his mouth widened and grew rigid, and his
blood sank from his face as he spoke—"no, no—
there's no harm come to Sarah? No!—Sarah's
well?"—

"As well as you'll let her be," said Twopenny.

"As well as I'll let her be—I?" cried John in
amazement—"but come in—come in, master Twopenny," and John fluttered into a small room, and
Twopenny, sighing, and slowly rubbing his cheek,
heavily followed.

If we know anything of the brain of the reader,
we think we can divine the cause of his present
discontent. Of course, he is dissatisfied at the apparent irregularity of our plan. We are bold to
ask a little patience at the beginning, though we
may want the effrontery to solicit the favour as we
proceed. Does the reader recollect the time, when
his unformed taste led him to the playhouse? If we
may, without offence, call back his thoughts to those
days of vulgar ignorance, we may demand of him,—
if he have never known the future hero or heroine

of the scene exhibited in a vision by a benignant
fairy? Has he never beheld the sleeping loveliness,
all unconscious of the exhibition, made to dawn upon
the enraptured lover, and then fade away to " slow
music ;"—to be shown, it may be the next minute,
in rags and tatters drudging at the hearth? We have
wished, but with all humility, to imitate the tricks
of Puck ; and though, perhaps, Chancery-lane may
hardly be considered fairy-land, we have with the
gentle waving of our goose-feather, introduced
John Applejohn seated there upon a step ; and, now
with the same mild tyranny, have wafted him to his
own small shop, which he has just quitted for the
back parlour, yeoman Twopenny hanging at his
heels.

" Sarah ?" cried John as he fell into a chair.

" All's well," said old Twopenny, leaning on his
stick, and lowering himself into his seat : but did a
sentinel cry " all's well" in the tones of the farmer,
we have no doubt that the crew would run upon deck
in their shirts, to learn the extent of the calamity.

" But, farmer Twopenny," began John ; when
the old man flung up his broad hand, knitted his
brows, shook his head, and having growled a clear
passage for the coming inquiry, asked deeply, yet
very distinctly—

" Mr. John Applejohn, what do you think of
brandy ?"—

(Now, it is uncharitable to question the extent of
knowledge of any man; the more so of that kind
of knowledge which may be learned in secret, the
unostentatious student shunning the staring eyes of
the Argus world. We will not therefore venture
an opinion on the wisdom of our hero in the
article of brandy: we might underate his acquire-
ments, and we would do injustice to no one.
"What do you think of brandy?" How familiar
—how common–place the query !—yet what a
world of different meaning may be put in it !
How wide the field of speculation opened by the
syllables ! How august the persons to whom they
may be whispered ! Let us imagine a man of
philosophic mind—a magnate of the land—a man,
whose tongue, "like to a summer brook," is running
with continual music.——See him rise to the assembled peers: hear him in the very passion of eloquence arraign some giant wrong—see him paint
some general vice—and listen to the shouts, the
treble cries of admiration that burst and ring about
him. And all he has said—every word he has
uttered—is born of a stern, a sober spirit vowed
eternally to wisdom and to right. He sits down,
the roof above him, the floor beneath, echoing,
shaking with admiring clamour. Bless us ! a wasp
has stung his lordship on the ear ! By no means,
—his lordship it is true jumped, and put his hand

to his wig; but it was when a wicked, satirical
little gnome, inquired of the peer, palpitating with
his new triumph—" My lord, what do you think of
brandy?" We should offer an impertinence to
the imagination of the reader, did we attempt to
follow fully out all the cases in which the question
is inevitably provoked. To a learned professor,
the anchorite of a college,—to him, whose daily
wont it is to speak of temperance as the mother of
many virtues—to the physician writing upon dietetics
—to the fair one, deserted in middle-life, and grown
roseate with weeping—to one and all some vagrant
imp might ask—" Dear professor—excellent doctor
—lovely lady—what do you think of brandy?")

We declare that no time has been lost to the
reader by the above paragraph, for John Applejohn has not yet hit upon what he deems a satisfactory answer; thus, he echoed the question—"think of
brandy? Why, farmer, as for brandy, in its way"—

" Then what do you say to rum?" demanded
Twopenny, and he looked inquisitorially at the
hesitating John.

" I can't say that I much like it," said John
shortly.

" Ho! then,"—and farmer Twopenny, with the
manner of a confessor putting a tremendous question to a shameful sinner, asked—" then what's
your opinion of gin?"

" Poison," and John looked as if he had uncon-sciously swallowed a mortal draught.

" Ho! ho! well, I'm blessed ! Then, Mr. Apple-john," and the old man seemed to become irritable at the capricious taste of our hero—" then, sir, if it be none of the three,—perhaps, you'll be good enough to tell me what you think of wine ?"

" A little wine is a great comfort," said John ; and there was an honesty in his speech and face enough to make a reasonable man of his opinion. The farmer, however, showed himself, as we think, far from reasonable ; for no sooner had John pub-lished his short sentiment on wine, than Twopenny rose to his feet, rapt his leg with his ash-stick, and gave a long whistle.

" Why, what is all this—what is," and then a light fell upon John, " why, now, farmer—I'm sure, I'd quite forgot ; you see, things are all at odds here, and will be till Sarah comes to take 'em in hand—but if you'd wanted anything to drink, you needn't have beat the bush for it. I'm sure I"— and John was about to quit the parlour, when his arm was vigorously grasped by the farmer, who shook his head till his cheeks quivered with the mo-tion, and roared louder and louder—" Not a drop— not a drop—not a drop," accompanying the last three words with an action of the wrist that brought John once more into his chair.

"Why, what is the matter?" cried the bewildered John.

Twopenny drew a long sigh, pulled out his pocket-handkerchief, and returned to a former sentence; again he said—"I'm very sorry, Mr. Applejohn,—very sorry; but you must know that I am a father, and"—

"To be sure you are; well?"—

"And the happiness of Sarah isn't to be thrown away? You'll allow that?"

"Certainly: thrown away!" cried Applejohn shuddering at the very thought.

"And as the chances run that a girl may only get one husband, a father ought—now, you must allow this without any offence, Mr. Applejohn—you must allow this—a father ought to take care that he should be a good one. Now, you will allow this?" said Twopenny, gently touching the knee of the astonished John.

"It isn't to be denied; and I hope, Mr. Two-penny"—

"Gently—gently, if you please; but you after me. I always thought well of you, Mr. Applejohn"—John bowed thankfully—"I thought you a moral young man, and more than that, a good workman; if you did but know your own worth, Mr. Applejohn! No man's name stands higher for buckskins—there doesn't," and the old farmer solemnized

his assertion by savagely slapping his own leg—
" no, there doesn't ! And yet, what are good gifts,
if folks will cast 'em away ? Pearls to pigs, Mr.
Applejohn—pearls to pigs."

John looked at Twopenny, and became assured
of the real state of the case; it was evident to John
that the old man had drunk himself through all
the grades of intoxication, arriving at that dreary
point where something like a sad sobriety ensues.

" No, Mr. Applejohn, I couldn't ha' thought it;
I'd never ha' believed you were born to drink."

"Drink !" cried John emphatically, and then
immediately restraining himself in deference to the
unguarded condition of the farmer. " What shall
I do with him ?" thought John.

" Yes,—drink; it's worse than the black art when
it fastens on a man. Drunkenness ! why it's as bad
to a young man as what they call chemistry," declared the farmer ; though it is our belief that when
he associated drunkenness with chemistry he meant
—alchemy.

" True, master Twopenny—very true," cried
John, humouring the old man whom he thought
fast sinking into tipsy maudlin, though in truth he
was every moment becoming more soberly pathetic.
" True, master Twopenny,—and yet a little—little
drink,"—

" Oh ! that's it, that's it, John Applejohn—a

little !" and the farmer pushed his chair away; then, pausing a moment, looked upon the floor, and repeated "a little !"

" Now, master Twopenny," and John waxed serious, " what have you seen in me ?"—

" Seen ? A little drink ! Seen ? Tell me this, John Applejohn—tell me this," and Twopenny brought his chair back, and with his broad fingers patting John's wrist, looked into the young man's simple face, and asked in a voice of subdued earnestness, " John Applejohn, did you ever see a pumpkin in a bottle ?"

John paused ere he replied: it was a delicate question to answer at a short summons; he taxed his memory—he believed he had seen some such phenomenon.

" And do you know how it got there ?" John shook his head in ignorance of a mystery which, we have no doubt, has paralized wiser heads than his. " You don't know how it got there ?" cried Twopenny—" I'll tell ye ;" and with " bated breath" and serious visage, Twopenny leaned over to the ear of John, and took it upon his own sagacity to say— " they put the pumpkin in when it was little." Saying which, the farmer drew back, anxiously awaiting the effect of the intelligence upon John ; who, we presume, was not altogether astonished by

the published secret, for he stroked his chin, and
calmly remarked——" Indeed." On this, Mr. Twopenny slowly rose to his full height.

" Well, Mr. Applejohn, then I've nothing more
to say—you know my mind ?"

" He is very drunk," thought John.

" Now, we understand one another," said Twopenny.

" Not quite," said John meekly.

" No ! why, this it is then ; a man"——and the
farmer spoke with great solemnity——" a man is a
pumpkin."

" Excessively drunk," thought John.

" He begins to drink little by little—but the
thing grows and grows, until at last, he cannot free
himself—he can't get out,—he can't get out, John,"
cried the farmer in a tone of reproach.

" Very true," said Applejohn, dimly apprehend-
ing the moral application.

" And so I am come to the religious determination that you shall never marry my Sally," said the
stern Twopenny.

John had scarcely breath sufficient to ask, " why
not ?"

" Because," cried the farmer with a searching
glance——" because, you are found out."

" Found out !" gasped Applejohn.

" Found out," repeated Twopenny " you sha'n't have Sally; for I'm determined, when she takes a husband, she sha'n't marry a pumpkin in a bottle." The farmer said no more; three strides took him into the street—John as if stunned by a blow followed to the door, and staring after his visitor, remarked to himself—" How very well he walks—and yet, how very drunk !"   Now, in very truth, farmer Twopenny was sober as a Hindoo.

CHAPTER III.

THREE days had passed, and every morning John Applejohn had leaned, with a beating heart, at his door-post. The fourth morning was come, and John was again watching.   A shepherd, gazing for the folding-star—a sailor looking for the land—a place-hunter at the levee of a minister—feels nothing to the lover waiting for the postman.   Thrice had Giltedge passed the door of John, and with a short shake of the head, had sent him almost exanimate into his parlour: again the postman approached the habitation of the lover.   With what attributes do our hopes and fears invest the meanest objects ! Behold Giltedge, a plain pock-marked man, in a red coat, holding in his right hand a bundle of written papers. To some he comes as the image of death—a walking skeleton: for see, he holds the shilling in his grim mouth, as he calmly feels for twopence change for a tenpenny missive, the black seal of which has made that woman cold and white as stone: the seal is broken—she is a widow—her blue-eyed boy is fatherless. The postman strides onward, his red skirts streaming to the wind: he stops short and gives, what seems a passionate pull at the third-story bell. What a spasm of the heart has that worn man, the three-pair lodger, suffered at the sound! and what a sweet look of love and resignation—of comforting meekness—has his wife cast towards him, ere she leaves the room to struggle with her tears, as she descends the stairs to meet the summons! She returns—the letter in her hand —and still a smile upon her face. The wafer yields its charge; at the first glance the husband sees the walls of a goal—the instruments of lawful rapine. The miscreant owes forty shillings; and the wise and benificent law—as expounding itself in that short letter—tells him that if he cannot pay the forty, the sum shall to-morrow be made nearly eighty; and in a few fleet days, the last sum shall be doubled, calm justice sweetly smiling on the deed. That he cannot pay on the instant forty shillings makes him a criminal; poverty is very properly in the eye of the law, guilt, for never can we consent to believe that the law would punish misery. Besides, there is an importance in high cost; that some five shillings should serve to recover a hundred would greatly diminish the dignity of law.

While we have talked, the postman has proceeded up the street, and to the hopeful imagination of John appears a very different person from Alexander Giltedge. No; to John, the postman looks no other than the boy pictured in the valentine to Sally; the red coat fades into the common light—the stockings vanish—the shoes are gone—the hat is exhaled—and Giltedge with bare legs, a light blue scarf across his naked shoulders, and between his dove-like wings, cometh mincingly up the street, holding between his small finger and thumb—a letter from Sarah. We are right; for John has snatched the offering of love, and with the other hand presented the precise amount of postage. "Paid," says the Cupid in the scarlet coat, and passes on. John rushes with his prize into the back room. His thumb is on the seal, when he pauses a moment, and sighs deeply: another moment, and the seal is broken. John reads, and as he reads, we are sure the fiends rejoice.—

"My dear John,—Did I ever think I should live to see this day! It is better that I should have died—much better that I had never been born! My father makes me write this, and though I mean every word I write, my heart bleeds at every sylla-

ble. It is in vain they tell me that I ought to thank
heaven for my escape; I have tried to do so, but I
can't—and yet I feel it very wicked not to be grateful. Oh, John! could I have thought it of you!
though I tremble to think of your deceit. You,
who always seemed so sober—and now to be found
out! But I won't upbraid you, John, although
my heart is breaking. I have said all I could for
you to my father, but he is harder than any flint
against you. For your own sake, John, leave off
this dreadful habit: think what it must lead to—
and shun liquor more than you would shun a fever;
for that only hurts the body—drink kills a good
name. When I think of you as I first saw you—
and think what this wicked course will make of
you—how it will leave you without friends, without
health—a jeer for the world, and a burthen to
yourself, I could—for all my father says—cry myself blind to save you. Do, John, pray do, step
back from the pit that is open at your foot; and do
not forget that although you and I—my father makes
me write it, has made me promise it—although you
and I, must never meet again, you will never cease
to be remembered by—SARAH."

(A few words added as a postscript had been
carefully marked out.)

John looked up from the letter, with gaping
mouth and an unconscious stare: it *was* paper, real

paper that he held—and, yes, the hand was the hand of Sarah !

" Good morning, Mr. Applejohn." The greeting was repeated, ere John was conscious of the presence of a visitor, who, having thrice knocked without an invitation to enter, had opened the door. " Good morning,—eh ?—not very well,"—observed the considerate stranger.

" A—a sick headache," said John. " I—sit down, Mr. Warp,—I—excuse me—but a minute," and John all but reeled from the apartment.

Mr. Warp threw his eyes up to the ceiling, and ejaculated—" So early in the day, too !" And then, a flood of charity setting in upon him, his benevolence suggested—"perhaps, drunk last night, and not recovered yet." This amiable extenuation was in full force, when John returned : his face was haggard, and his eyes wandering. " Quite plain,'' concluded Warp—" never been in bed. And a young man who might have done so well, too !"

" And now, Mr. Warp—what's the business, sir ? —for the truth is, I—I who was last night one of the happiest fellows," and John sighed deeply, and covered his eyes with his hand.

" Yes, Mr. Applejohn—very true : wě may think ourselves as happy as kings at night,—but the next morning, Mr. Applejohn—the next morning," and Warp tapped his forehead, and then pointed his middle finger to his stomach.

John, who heard the words but saw not the action of Warp, concluded that he had uttered a moral reflection on the uncertainty of human bliss. " Ha ! Mr. Warp, if I could have thought what would have followed, I shouldn't suffer what I now do."

" It's sure to happen, Mr. Applejohn—it's sure to happen, unless we are very lucky, indeed, in what is set before us."

John was so possessed by his grief that the entire ignorance of Warp on the subject never occurred to him. " I didn't think there could be better," said John.

" Perhaps, then," Mr. Warp remarked, very acutely, " perhaps, then, you mixed a good deal ?"

" No—no,"—said John with affecting vehemence —" I know, I have enemies—I'm sure of it; but the bitterest foe I have can't accuse me of that. No man could be more constant. And now, what to do with myself I can't tell," and again he put his hand to his head.

" Have you tried nothing?" asked Warp. John was silent. " Then take my advice.—I was young myself once, Mr. Applejohn, and know what a little attack of the sort is—take my advice; try my remedy—you have nothing to do but to take"—

"What?—take what?" interrupted John with sudden impatience.

"Take a hair of the dog that bit you!" saying which, Warp sat bolt upright, as though suddenly pulled by a string. He sat erect, and nodded smilingly at the sufferer.

"A dog! bit me! why,—what dog?" asked John, staring at his adviser.

"Why,—he! he!—hav'n't you heard the saying?"—(the hypocrite! he must have heard it, judged Warp)—"he! he! a hair of the dog that bit you. That is, if a great deal of brandy did the mischief last night, a little drop of the same may bring about a cure this morning. It threatens to be very sultry—I have a long round to go—and I'll take mine in a glass of cold spring water."

"I should be very glad, Mr. Warp—but I never keep spirits—never taste 'em"—

"An abandoned young man!" thought Warp; and then aloud—"Mr. Applejohn, you will perhaps excuse what I am about to say. I speak for your good, sir; I am older than you, and having been twice in business myself, know what lying is. Let us however hope, that what, in the way of trade, passes in the shop, is not put down to our last account: but, sir, in the confidence of your back parlour, never tell a lie."

"I never do," said John somewhat fiercely, "and

as for the place, Mr. Warp, I can't see how you are to make white in the parlour what is black over the counter."

" You are a young tradesman, and pardon me if I say it, you have much to learn.   A man may in the way of business, be so conceited of truth, that he shall talk himself to utter ruin.   In what I said, respecting the little drop of brandy—'the hair of the dog,' which you didn't understand, hem !—I advised you as I would have advised my own child, if I had one."

" No doubt, Mr. Warp—but—you see, you have mistaken my illness—I never drink, never—and now, in a short word, Mr. Warp what is your business ?"

" My business is from the firm.   I am desired to say that, in consequence of matters to which it would, perhaps, be indelicate in me to more particularly allude, our house cannot suffer you to open an account."   And this Mr. Warp uttered in the tone and with the look of a pedagogue, prefacing the birch with a short speech to the child about to suffer.

" Very well, Mr. Warp; I suppose there are other houses," said John with great resignation.

" True, Mr. Applejohn—very true; but character flies, sir; yes, sir, character has wings; and, of course, the lighter it is, the quicker it goes."

" Character ! why, does anybody dare ?"—asked
John, his eyes flashing—" does anybody dare ?"—

Warp shook his head, and smiled cynically:
"You mus'n't talk in that manner : you're a young
tradesman with no capital, and everybody dares.
It may be all very well for men established, but it
doesn't answer for young beginners : at all events,
if they must do these things, they should have a
proper respect for their own interests, and do them
snugly, and in private."

" What things ?—what do you mean ?" exclaimed
John with rising violence, for the letter had been
sufficient to excite him, without new aggravation.

" I am not one of those men, who have no kindness for my fellow-creatures; no, no, I have seen too
much of life—have known too much of trouble for
that—twice in the gazette, and four compositions
are enough for any man ; all I say is, keep it quiet
—don't let the world be any wiser. Perhaps, it
isn't right to get drunk ; perhaps not ; but it is very
wrong indeed in a young man with his way to
make, to let the world know it."

" Drunk ! you can't mean me, Mr. Warp ? Nobody ever saw"—

" We do such things in that state, we don't
know who sees. Did I see a young tradesman"—
and Warp looked knowingly at John—" generously

inclined to the bottle—a young man, whose credit
depended upon his character,—I should say, give
not more than one day in the seven to the enjoyment. Then invite a friend,—come here into your
back parlour—take especial care that you have no
necessity to leave the room for anything,—then let
your housekeeper lock the door outside, and go to
bed with the key. The next morning, she opens
the door; you have been happy, but you are now
sober; you are in your shop betimes; you have
never been seen in an ale-house; never recognized in the street; never been brought home by
the watchman,—and you are to your customers and
neighbours, and consequently through them to the
whole world, not only a superfine man, but the
very pattern of a tailor."

" And is that all a man requires?" asked Applejohn coldly.

" He may want—yes—he! he!—he may want
the 'hair of the dog,'"—and Warp winked wickedly.

" And what is all this to me?" cried John.

" Don't treat the matter so lightly, Mr. Applejohn : remember, that we live and make money by
character, and therefore it is our bounden duty to
take care of it. Answer me this—I put it as a
friend—answer me this. If a barber were reported
to have fits of madness, would you trust your throat
to his razor?"

" Certainly not," said John; and then he thought
—" though I shouldn't mind just now."

" Very well. If you were a gentleman—for the
case is quite the same—would you trust the cutting
of your cloth,"—

" No real gentleman sends his own cloth," interrupted Applejohn.

" Very true—but hear me out: would you trust
your cloth to the shears of a drunken tailor ? I see
you wouldn't—that is, if he was known; for there
is the mischief—there the shocking evil. For a
young beginner to be known to drink is utter ruin
not only with his clothier but his customer. I
don't blame you for getting drunk, Applejohn—
upon my soul, I don't"—and Warp spoke with
impressive benevolence,—" but I must and do condemn you for sitting down and exposing your
drunkenness in the open street. You don't know
who saw you — indeed, you don't," and Warp
quitted the house. He walked at a quick pace
down the street; and suddenly pausing at a corner,
looked vigilantly about him: he then rapidly passed
a threshold, above which an enormous bunch of
grapes glittering in the sun, typified the *aurum
potabile* to be had within.

" You don't know who saw you !" These words
rang in the ears of Applejohn. It was plain some
mortal enemy had been at work ! John Applejohn
a drunkard ! when the naiad of the stream was no

c 2

more temperate than he ! Oh, it was some foolish trick passed upon him—and yet, Sarah to join in it ! No: it was clear enough ; some wicked, spiteful wretch—perhaps, a rival—had vowed his ruin ; and this was the cruel slander raised to crush him. However, he would not be destroyed without an attempt to clear the matter up ; he would trace the villainy to its spring-head, and punish the cowardly delinquents. He had already grown strong in the resolution, and was about to quit the house on the sacred errand, when he was encountered at the door by his landlord.

"Could I say a few words with you, Mr. Applejohn ?" asked the man.

"Just a few ; for I'm in a great hurry," answered John.

"I won't keep you a minute," said the landlord, and immediately proceeded to open the business. "I've been thinking, Mr. Applejohn," he observed, very considerately, "that, perhaps, as you are only just setting up, you'll find this house too heavy for you."

"I hope not," said John.

"I am sure, I should be very sorry to be in any way the innocent cause of hampering a young man beginning the world,"—

"You are very good, Mr. Pantile—very good," remarked his grateful tenant.

"And though, for the house itself, the rent is

very little; still, as I told you, in this parish the rates are very heavy."

" Light—very light—next to nothing, you said, Mr. Pantile."

" Never could have said that—never could. However, that doesn't signify. What I am come to say is this : if you have any misgivings about your prospects—and as I wouldn't stand in a young man's light—I—yes, I'll tell you what I have made up my mind to do : I'll take the lease off your hands, and all I'll ask of you is the rent for the present quarter." And as Mr. Pantile said this, he looked at John as placidly as a fox looks at a goose. " Don't think, Mr. Applejohn, that I am led away by what folks say of you—no, no; when I was as young as you I had my fling: I led a life of pleasure—I may say, I was quite a rhapsodist" (it was not very clear to Mr. Pantile, what he meant by the word) —"quite a rhapsodist; and therefore, if you think the house too big for you—and though I speak against my own interest, I think it is—I—at a word, I'll take it back again."

" You are very good, Mr. Pantile—very good— but I shall keep the house,—and as for what my enemies say against me—and, if I must say it, a man who can fine-draw as I can, can't expect to be without enemies,"—

" You know best," said the landlord, " but as I

have received a letter from Mr. Twopenny, telling
me that you shall not have his daughter, and
therefore not the three hundred pounds,"—

" And has Mr. Twopenny written as much to
you?" asked John tremblingly.

" And who can blame him? I used to get tipsy
once, for as I said, I was once a rhapsodist—but
you know, Mr. Applejohn, excuse ourselves as we
will, if we will but think as a father, we can't
blame any man for keeping his daughter safe from
a drunkard." Mr. Pantile then unceremoniously
departed.

Here was another blow, and again John sat irresolute and astounded. Like Ugolino, he sat staring
at the wall; when a little boy—an uninspired
Metastasio—from the pastry-cook's, entered with a
parcel. "Shall I put it on the table, sir?" John
started, and stammered " yes;" and the little boy
deposited his burthen close to the arm of the absorbed Applejohn, and went away. John, heaving
his deepest sigh, let fall his hand upon the parcel :
yes, with his hand upon his wedding-cake, he sat
and thought of ruin !

CHAPTER IV.

WE will spare the reader a recital of the many attempts made by John upon the obduracy of the farmer. At the opening of the second chapter of our history, John was within a few fleet days of marriage. His house was in order—his credit good —his name unspotted; and lo! at a breath he had lost his bride—his credit—and his name. It was in vain that John asked to be confronted with his accusers,—the assassins of his reputation. No, no; farmer Twopenny was satisfied, and further ceremony was unnecessary. Nor was John more successful in his appeal to the employers of Mr. Warp; they had nothing to say to Mr. Applejohn; or only this—they begged to decline his orders except for ready money. For three whole nights did John lie wide awake, reviewing every deed of his past life—a fearful employment for some of us in the deep, dark midnight. But John—for any evil he had done—might have whistled with the spirits of the tempest gibbering at the casement. He could only arrive at one conclusion—a dreary one it was,—that some profligate wretch, like to himself as pin is like to pin, was reeling drunkenly about the town, and he, the innocent John Applejohn, was doomed to bear the punishment due to the bacchanal! And with this comfortable thought John would fall asleep. Alas! his waking misery still haunted him. Now, he would be hunted for picking pockets, the real thief—his fatal similitude —safely off with the booty: now, he was to be hung for sheep-stealing, and there in the crowd, was the guilty rascal grinning and making faces at him. At last, all his troubles were over, and he was married to his beloved Sarah: he goes to his happy home at eleven at night, and knocking at his door, is old from the window to call to-morrow, as Mr. John Applejohn has been in bed these two hours! Such were the visions that wore our hero of a night, and gave him the look of a spectre all the day. However, as yet John had only taken the first step in infamy: though almost a confirmed water-drinker, he was nevertheless judged an irreclaimable drunkard. He surrendered his house to Mr. Pantile, who, rhapsodist as he deemed himself, cancelled the lease; the no less willingly that he had previously had a higher bidder for it.

We are convinced that fortune is not always blinded. No; she has at times, a vigilant eye for the luckless Applejohns of the world, or could she always contrive to keep out of their way? Were she really and truly blind-folded, it is impossible

that she should not, at least once in a life, run into
the embraces of the poor souls who, for a whole
existence, stand with open arms to receive her.
Fortune had turned from John, and he stood alone
with nothing but his poverty, and what is the same
thing, a thousand imperfections. And yet John,
though bleeding inwardly with undeserved injuries,
looked upon the men of this world and loved them:
yes, there was no man, woman, or child, to whom
he did not mean well. An anatomist might question the fact, but we are convinced that John had a
heart as big as his whole body.

"The Bottle of Hay" was, at the time of our
story, a noted sanctuary for unemployed tailors.
There, about three months after his rejection by
Sarah, was to be found the pennyless Applejohn.
The nights were growing long and chill, and the
parlour fire of Mrs. Grump, the lone and portly landlady, meekly imitated the beneficence of the impartial sun, for it dispensed its light and warmth
gratis to the destitute tailor. And there the keen-
eyed might behold through clouds of circumambient
smoke, the pensive John fixed in a corner, his blood
now simmering with martial heat, listening to a
martial song, in which the singer with a note of
gratifying confidence, assured the listener that any
numbers of French were considerably less than one
true Briton,—and that to expire, covered over with

c 3

wounds was the only really respectable way of
going out of this sublunar world.   Then would
John think of a distant country, and of that soft
delicious bed, with death the maker—the bed of
glory !   A brief five minutes, and the stern desire
for cutting throats would pass, a second singer,
with a voice like that of a cuckoo, breathing
"Cherry Ripe," and, with the magic sound, carrying back our tailor through the orchards of Kent
to the house of Sarah !

  "Mr. Scarlet; what may be your real opinion
of the present state of the land force?"   Such was
the comprehensive question put by an inquiring
visitor at the "Bottle of Hay," to a some-time tenant
of that respectable hostelry.

  "Shameful," replied Mr. Scarlet, with the manner of a man who had long since made up his mind
on a subject.   "But what are we to expect from
the present ministry?   What do they care for the
honour of the country?   Ha ! if we had real statesmen in office—there'd have been war these six
months.   Yes; by this time we might have lost a
thousand troops.   Shameful," repeated Mr. Scarlet.

  "A shocking loss of blood," remarked a philanthropist.

  "Blood, sir?   What is blood?   Think of glory,
sir," said Mr. Scarlet.   "But we stand disgraced

in the eyes of the world, when a few battles, if we had got nothing by them, would at least have kept up our character. If the British lion doesn't get up and show his teeth, and lash his tail, and roar a little, foreigners will soon think him dead outright. And then for our fine young gentlemen,—why isn't it dreadful for a man as loves his country, to see 'em—poor fellows!—put to the shifts they are, to get rid of time, when the trouble might be taken off their hands in a minute? And yet people talk of the blessings of peace! Pshaw! Why, all things show peace isn't the natural state of man."

" Mr. Scarlet"—it was the waiter, with his head in at the door, who spoke—" Mr. Scarlet, your wife has sent your little girl over to say, that if you don't come home, she'll come and fetch you."

" Peace isn't the natural state of man," repeated Scarlet, who we think had not heard the threat of his wife, pronounced through the waiter.—"No—it isn't," and hastily finishing his liquor, he quitted the parlour.

" He knows the true interests of the country," said a sartorial smoker: "yes, he knows the value of war."

" To be sure he does," remarked another—" he's an army tailor."

And with such sweet discourse, the hours were passed in the parlour of " the Bottle of Hay," until

time and Bill, the boy, called the tailors to bed.
In a long narrow room, at the top of the house,
Mrs. Grump had benevolently caused to be disposed
twenty couches—each couch, if the parties made
themselves small, and were mutually accommodating,—capable of holding, if not containing, two
sleepers. It is a startling truth little known by
the profligate rich, that when trade was very bad,
there might be seen sleeping in the house of Mrs.
Grump, forty passive tailors—yes, in " the Bottle of
Hay" might easily be found full two score unemployed needles !

John had retired to bed ; tailor by tailor came
in, and each and all having less sorrow, or more
liquor than John, soon gave loudest evidence of
perfect rest. Triton with his horn had not been
heard among that sleeping band. The clock of
the neighbouring church struck one: at the very
moment, the door opened, and John saw Mrs.
Grump in a broad-bordered white nightcap, and a
lighted candle in her hand, walk as softly as her
weight would permit her, into the dormitory. She
was followed by a man almost as big as herself.
" Another of the unemployed," thought John, as
he now eyed what he believed to be a journeyman
tailor, pretty far gone in his thread of life. The
man wore a close drab-coat, buttoned to the chin ;
an oil-skin travelling-cap and a red handkerchief

pulled over his head, and tied up to his nose, favoured the curious spectator with a very imperfect view of the face of the stranger. Mrs. Grump and the new-comer moved slowly up the room; the landlady so shadowing the light with her right hand that its rays might come tempered to the countenances of the sleepers, showing them in fine *chiaro scuro* to the inquisitive new-comer; without waking the owners. "A constable, no doubt," thought John—"some robbery,"—and then the causes of his late ill-luck fell forcibly upon him, and in his terrified imagination, he pictured the officers of the peace in search of him, the guilty likeness of the real thief. John closed his eye-lids, and heard the visitors approach his pallet. Suddenly, they stopt; and John, in sudden perspiration, awaited the arousing hand of the stranger. There was a pause, and John lay voiceless with apprehension.

"You'll cut me off dis fellow," growled the man in the oil-skin cap.

John opened his eyes and saw the back of the mysterious speaker, slowly moving towards the door, the landlady with the light preceding. "You'll cut me off this fellow," continued to ring through the brain of John, conjuring up the most grotesque and terrifying forms to fulfil the sanguinary mandate. Twice in his sleep—for sleep came

to him at length—did John suffer decapitation :—
once by the Christian axe, and once by the heathen
scimitar.

CHAPTER V.

"MR. APPLEJOHN, if you'll go to Mr. Zweifler's, there's work for you." Such was the grateful
intelligence conveyed to John while at his frugal
breakfast, by Bill, the boy; and in less than twenty
minutes, our unemployed hero stood in the presence of Carl Zweifler, a German by birth, a
tailor by trade, and a benevolent brute by disposition. Whether the scepticism had been
brought upon him by a succession of bad debts, or
whether Mr. Zweifler was a born doubter, it would
be arrogant in us to attempt to decide; certain it is,
that though by the hard destiny of business he was
compelled to give credit, he had really no faith in
any man. He looked upon all the world as a brotherhood of villains sworn and linked together to
cheat one tailor, and that defenceless animal to be
—Carl Zweifler.

"I am come, sir, hearing that you wanted a
workman," said John, and he had scarcely spoken
ere he felt himself grow cold beneath the light blue

eyes of the old man; the nocturnal visitor of the bed-room——" I am come, sir," John repeated, and then stopt.

" Teeves——teeves——all teeves"——said Zweifler,—— " ha !——well——dere's de oder villains,"——and pointing to a staircase, John followed the direction of the finger, and found himself among a circle of his peers. John was ignorant of the grateful truth, but he really owed his present place to the ingenuousness of his countenance. It was the custom of Mr. Zweifler, when in want of mercenaries, to visit " the Bottle of Hay" in the middle of the night; and at that solemn time to select from the sleepers ——the selection always suggested by the expression on the face of the sleeping——the required member or members. Hence, when Zweifler, pausing at the bed of John Applejohn, said in professional phrase to Mrs. Grump,——" You'll cut me off this fellow," he merely implied, " you'll send this man to me to-morrow morning." We beseech the reader not to dismiss this whim as a puerile invention on our part; by so doing he would commit great injustice towards Carl Zweifler, who always defended what seemed to more superficial tailors an eccentricity, on the ground that " no rogue ever looked so much a rogue as when he was asleep."

John Applejohn continued to sew and reap in the house of the master tailor; and already six

months had elapsed, when John stood in the opinion
of his employer, not altogether so atrocious a
villain as when he first entered his service.　It was
a long time, however, ere Zweifler ceased to attribute the rigid industry of John on Mondays to
some deep-laid scheme of deception ; some unheard-
of plan of infamy.　The attention and sobriety of
his journeyman somewhat irritated the old tradesman, as they seemed to insult his theory of the iniquity of all mankind and of tailors in particular.
" The devil is not so black as he's painted," observed the homely John Applejohn in reply to the
uncharitable creed of Zweifler, one Monday more
than usually satirical on his laborious servant; and
the manner of John more than the matter of the
proverb struck the misanthrope ; for, with new-born
benevolence he rubbed the tips of his fingers under
his black velvet skull-cap, and twinkling his light
blue eyes, he said with a faint smile—" Not so
black?　Well—well—berhaps not : berhaps, after
all, de deyvil is a piebalt."

It was Monday, and John sat alone upon the
board, a study for Hogarth, in his illustrations of
industry.　He was employed on the last button-
hole of a new black coat—the livery of woe for
Benjamin Gruelthorpe, Esq.; son and heir of
Emanuel Gruelthorpe, deceased.　John glanced
from his work, and saw old Zweifler looking

seriously on. The old tailor knit his brows at the garment—shook his head—and groaned through his teeth.

" Nothing the matter with the coat, sir ?" asked John deferentially.

" No, no; goot poy—goot poy: de oder teeves are at nine-pins, but you are goot poy," and never before had Zweifler so unequivocally praised the industry of his now solitary workman.

" Why, sir, the funeral takes place this afternoon," —said John.

" Ha ! ha ! Vhat music it will pe, when de cold clay goes tumblin' on de old man's coffin !" and Zweifler laughed bitterly.

" Mr. Gruelthorpe has died very rich ?" said John inquiringly. " His son,"—

" Son !" cried Zweifler, and he approached still nearer to his journeyman, and with subdued voice, and moistened eyes, said—" John Applejohn, do you know what a son is ?" and then without waiting for a reply, went on—" I will tell you, John Applejohn—I will tell you, what it is to have a son. It is to hear an angel at your ear at his first leetle cry: it is to feel an angel at your breast de first time to put him dere : it is to have your heart every day grow pig and pig, and your eye to have better light to hear his tongue—to see his leetle steps ! It is—it is—but—but you want some silk, John,"—and the

old man, his eyes gushing tears, turned rapidly up
the room, John pausing at his undrawn needle in
silent wonder.   In a few minutes, the old tailor
with a composed face and dry eyes returned, and
threw to John the unnecessary skein of silk.   There
was a pause of some minutes; at length, John
ventured to observe—" I understand, sir, that
Mr. Gruelthorpe's funeral will be very fine ?"

"Very—very fine," said Zweifler, "why not—
why not ?"

"I'm told the grave is to be twelve feet deep,"
remarked John.

"Deeper, deeper," replied the old man earnestly.
"All such graves are."

"Such graves ?" and John looked up.

"Dere is a story in my country about 'em, John.
While you press de coat, I'll tell it you, John—I'll
tell it you."

"Is it true, sir ?" asked Applejohn.

"As heaven," answered old Zweifler ; and John
worked and listened to the tale we are about to
narrate, omitting the peculiarities of the old
German.

"Hans Pfennig," said the old tailor, "lived in
the little town of Cuxhaven.   He had been a
merchant in his younger time, and had returned from
a far land to die in his first home.   He was so old,
no man remembered him a child : he lived, solitary

as a raven—and like the raven, was shunned as a
thing of evil omen. He was known to have the
wealth of a king, and yet he wore the rags and ate
the scraps of a beggar. He was a man to make
men shudder as they looked upon him—mothers
would catch their children up from his path, and
flee away with them as from a fasting wolf: and so
he lived, with the hate of his neighbours breathing
upon him. Days, and weeks, and months passed,
and no man had seen Hans Pfennig. The priest
and some of the townsfolk bent their way to the
lonely hovel of the miser. There they paused, and
looked in the face of one another ; for the door of
the hut was closed, and long grass waved before it.
The door, by the order of the priest, was broken in ;
and Hans Pfennig was found, seated in his chair,
dead and withered. The hut was ransacked, and
oh ! the gold and jewels dug into the light of day.
The shed stood upon a mine of buried wealth.
Well,—a distant heir was found : and the bell was
tolled, and the grave was dug for Hans Pfennig.
The day of burial came; and if the dead might be
made to move, the body of Hans Pfennig had sat
up in its coffin, tortured back to life by the gold
bestowed upon its dust. Never, since man returned
to clay, had simple citizen been so attended ! The
bearers brought the body to the grave : the coffin

was slung within the ropes, and every eye was bent upon the bier descending to the bottom. The ropes were found too short; and staringly, but silently, the diggers tied more rope to either end; they lowered and lowered, and again the rope was out. 'More rope,' cried the grey-haired sexton, and shook his palsied hands; and the people at the grave stood, as if death-struck, and the priest made the holy sign and the cross was raised. 'The belfry —the belfry,' cried the sexton, and two men ran to the church, and brought back a coil of rope, anew provided for the bells. Again they give more rope, and the body of the miser sinks and sinks. 'Pull up the corse,' exclaimed the priest; and twenty men tug at the rope but cannot lift the dead. As they pause, they hear a clawing at the bottom of the coffin, with smothered shrieks of laughter. Aghast, they quit the rope, when the coffin rushes—rushes—down as into the unfathomable abyss! 'Who dug the grave?' 'I—ten feet deep,' cried the sexton. 'Not you, sexton—not you,' said an old monk. 'Last night, I walked here, and I saw things not of this world digging on this spot. There was moonlight, and I saw the glittering of their golden spades!' 'Golden spades!' cried the young heir. 'Aye, son; they made the miser's last bed; for he who hoards the treasures of this

world, and looks unmoved on this world's misery,—
has just this reward; his grave is dug by devils with
a golden spade!'"

"Mr. Gruelthorpe's mourning, sir? a boy has
just come about it—and he desires that one of the
men may take it home, in case"—the servant was
proceeding,—

"Shall I step with it?" asked John, who had
almost breathlessly folded up the coat as Zweifler
finished his legend. Zweifler nodded assent, and
John hurried away with the suit of solemn black to
the disconsolate heir of the muckthrift.

Benjamin Gruelthorpe had been rescued from
the ignominy of earning his own bread by the
lamented death of his venerable parent, who at the
age of three-score and five had dropt like a medlar
from the tree of life. Benjamin was determined to
act justly by the world; yes, the first moment that
he learned his loss, he resolved on speedily rendering
back to men the heap of wealth his sire had slowly
gathered from them. Old Gruelthorpe had a
thousand times crucified his soul for a guinea; his
only child the airy Benjamin, flung away his
inheritance as if his one earthly task was to
arrive as soon as possible at his last shilling. With
kindly impulses, he had never been taught to look
upon his father but as an obstacle to his pleasures;
and, capable of affection, he heard the death of the

old man, with that beating of the heart which tells
the prisoner he is free.   Benjamin lost not an hour
in asserting his new importance; and ere the dead
miser was laid in his grave, his spendthrift son had
quitted the counter of a pawnbroker for lodgings
at a London hotel; where, swathed in a silken
morning gown and stretched on a couch —a bank
of crimson velvet—he awaited with resignation in
his soul and a newspaper in his hand, the coming
of the tailor.

Applejohn arrived at the hotel, was instantly
shown up to the chief mourner; who, turning
his head, and running his fingers through the
thousand flaxen rings with which that head had
been adorned, deliberately opened his mouth, and
hazarded a conjecture.   " I 'spose—the tailor ?"
John bowed, and took the suit of sables from the
bag.

" What's o'clock ?" asked Benjamin languidly
of a tall, grave-looking person, in whose face there
were all the deliberative cares of a landlord.

" I should say, sir," replied Mr. Oldjoe, a man
who evidently never committed himself—" I should
say, sir," and he looked at the chronometer on
the mantel-piece, " seven minutes and a half to
ten."

" And Scutcheon, the undertaker, is punctual ?"

" As death, sir," said Mr. Oldjoe, swallowing a

laugh at his own wit, and then looking more than commonly grave at the great sacrifice.

"How is it, Oldjoe?" and young Gruelthorpe, having donned the black coat, turned his back upon his host—"How is it—a fit?"

"If I had'n't seen you put it on," said the landlord, rolling one eye at the tailor,—"I could have sworn you had been born in it."

"Well, that will do. Oldjoe, let the fellow have something," said young Gruelthorpe, exposing his want of gentility by the order.

"What should you like to take?" asked Oldjoe of our tailor, as both descended the stairs.

"I never drink—never," said John with emphasis: and he spoke truly, at least in a vinous and spirituous sense; for, since his rejection by Sarah, he had confined himself to the drink of simple people —the simple element.

"I'm glad of that," said the landlord, with a happy look—"very glad. No—no man who drinks, could make a coat like that. I'm so glad you won't have my champagne—won't touch my burgundy— can't abide my claret—and would feel poisoned at my straw-coloured brandy. I'm glad of it: but you don't know why? I'll tell you; because it affords me the opportunity of recommending my soda-water."

"Is it so wonderful?" asked Applejohn.

" It's as good as brandy, without any of its bad character for drunkenness," asseverated the imperturbable Oldjoe. "Wonderful! bless you, it's so strong, your goose could swim in it. Here,— Godfrey,—a bottle of soda-water for this gentleman; —the best."

" Have you two sorts of bottles?" questioned John.

" To be sure; five shilling and three-and-six-penny; one for gentlemen, 'tother for the poor." At this moment, Mr. Scutcheon entering the hotel, took the attention of the landlord from our temperate tailor; and Oldjoe quitted John to show the page of death to young master Gruelthorpe.

" Oh! the—the undertaker," said Benjamin, still upon the sofa—his hand still among his curls.

Scutcheon bowed, and his long silk hat-band rustled an avowal of his trade.

" Have you removed the—the,"—the afflicted son with the tip of his third finger tried to displace a possible tear from the corner of his right eye—" the —the body?" and Benjamin, smoothing the collar of his shirt, sighed tolerably deeply.

" To my own house, sir," said Mr. Scutcheon, looking big with the feelings of hospitality. " Last night, sir—in the hearse, sir—from the residence of the deceased." The residence! Emanuel Gruelthorpe had died in an obscure and filthy shed—

a hovel hardly fit to shelter cattle. The residence! The residence of a rat.

" I hope everything has been attended to with regard to my feelings?" said Benjamin.

" Oh, sir! you may rely upon the character of our firm for that," answered the undertaker.

" Oldjoe;"—the landlord crossed to the sofa of young Gruelthorpe, who spoke in a low and confidential voice to his host, Mr. Scutcheon being too much rapt by the character of his firm to overhear their conversation. " Oldjoe," said Benjamin in little above a whisper—" we shall dine at seven, mind; a good show."—

" A spanish mahogany coffin," said Scutcheon, doggedly enumerating the triumphs of the firm on the body of the deceased.—

" Your best plate," whispered Benjamin.—

" Silver plate and silver handles," said Scutcheon.

" There'll be eight of us to feed," continued Benjamin.—

" Fourteen mourners," said the undertaker, " to make 'em spread, in seven coaches."—

" I hope the haunch will stand us all," observed the son.—

" And six to bear," remarked Scutcheon.—

" Oh! and don't forget the singers, for after dinner," warned young Gruelthorpe.—

" I have engaged two," said Oldjoe.—" Wonder-

ful men ! been offered any terms by a Russian duke
who lived here—but patriots, sir; wouldn't leave
their country."—

" After dinner, we must have—humph !—what
d'ye call it?" whispered Benjamin.—

" *Non nobis,*" replied Oldjoe, in an equally
reduced voice.—

" Then we shall be met by the charity children,"
continued the undertaker.—

" I suppose they can sing anything?" asked
Gruelthorpe of the landlord.—

" Sing ! You'll have ' *When Bibo thought fit*' and
' *Pretty painted fly*' to admiration," said Oldjoe.—

" The whole to be wound up with a hymn at
the vault on the virtues of the deceased," said
Scutcheon.—

" I say, Oldjoe; the champagne—the claret, eh ?
prime," said the chief mourner, still whispering.—

" And for the vault," said the undertaker in a
loud voice, arriving at the climax of his good things
—" And for the vault,"—

" Trust my cellar," cried Oldjoe to the heir in
a raised note.—

" It's so dry," exclaimed Scutcheon ; " instead of
putting your father in it, you might keep wine
there."—

" Wine !" cried the roused Benjamin ; " oh !"
and, slightly colouring, he rose from the sofa, put his

hands into mourning, took his hat from his estimable landlord, and tripped solemnly down stairs to the funeral coach.

We should be unjust to Benjamin did we pass in silence the magnificent evidence of his filial love as displayed through the kind cares of the undertaker. The very grave-diggers paused in admiration of the coffin! Never had "food for worms" been more daintily dished up.

" Anything in the papers?" asked young Gruelthorpe the next day of Oldjoe.

" The arrivals at 'the Hotel' in the *Post*," said the landlord.

" I mean, about the—the funeral," said Benjamin, putting his hand to his head all unused to the fumes of burgundy.

" Not a word, sir;"—said Oldjoe.

" No! well, well, it's best—I'm glad of it; such matters should be kept quiet. Some soda." The draught, that at five shillings, we presume, was brought and swallowed; and Benjamin stretched himself upon the couch in deep study.

" It's very odd, sir, that we have heard no news of the balloon," said Oldjoe, with his immovable dead-man face—" though, I suppose we shall, sir, as soon as intelligence arrives."

" And not a word?" said Benjamin in a state of abstraction.

" Not a word, sir. By-the-bye, sir, that's a shocking accident—that ' death by charcoal.' Captain Nitre, sir; house newly painted—dried by charcoal fires—went in too soon—died. Heard there were charcoal fires in the house of the dowager Lady Littlebit—she, who has the next suite of rooms; folded down the paper, as in duty bound, at the very paragraph. An excellent lady—a woman who doesn't fly in the face of Providence. Directly she smells the charcoal, she rings the bell —' Mr. Oldjoe' says her ladyship, ' I shall stay with you another week.' Poor Captain Nitre."—

" D—— that fellow !" cried Gruelthorpe suddenly.

" What ! the captain ?" said Oldjoe calmly.

" No—no—no. Captain ! I mean the fellow who dined with me—that Linepenny—he promised to put a full account of it in all the newspapers !"

Yes; whilst the mercenary Oldjoe discoursed of things pertaining to his proper interest, the young heir was meditating on the funeral of his departed father.

CHAPTER VI.

IT was evening, and John Applejohn sat alone in the house of Mr. Zweifler. The mansion had been left in the care of the maid-servant who, about dusk, addressed herself to the humane feelings of John. She had to step a little way, and would Mr. Applejohn—she would not be out ten minutes —would he be so very good as to take care of the house until she came back? John lived only to grant favours; though possessed of but limited power, he had the widest will to be useful. Hence, he was left in charge of the dwelling, and had remained its sole inhabitant about three quarters of an hour —for women, under some circumstances, have a most incorrect notion of the course of time—when he heard footsteps on the staircase. He thought it was the maid returned, but looking over the banister, saw two men, cautiously bearing a load wrapt in a sheet, enter the front room of the first floor. There was something mysterious in their measured step—their profound silence. John felt his heart suddenly beat, and a sense of fear held him motionless. He knew that one of the men was the accepted tenant of the apartment he had entered——that, contrary to the usual custom of Zweifler, the tailor had intrusted him with a key, by means of which he had now silently entered the house: but who was the other man—and what could it be—for there, indeed, lay the mystery,—that they bore between them? Whilst John stood thus perplexed, he saw the door open and the two men——their burthen being left in the room——reappear. John held his breath, and watched, and listened.

" There, my man," said the lodger in a soft voice, and put something into the hand of his coarse companion.

" What's this?" asked the fellow, affecting admirable ignorance of the coin, as he frowned sulkily upon a piece of silver. " What's this?"

" A shilling," replied the lodger, condescending to become instructor.

" Why, you never mean it?" said the man in a tone of remonstrance, almost subdued to the pathetic. " You never mean it?"

" Indeed, I do," answered the gentleman, firm in his meaning. " Isn't it your fare?"

" Perhaps it is, if you count by distance," said he who proved to be a coachman.

" What by then, if not by distance?" inquired the lodger.

" Come, come," remarked the coachman, and a

gleam of benevolence lighted his broad face—" I won't *split*."

" Split!" exclaimed the lodger in a voice that seemed to leave the operation entirely at the will of the charioteer.

" You know,—I can tell what I've brought— but when a gentleman is a gentleman, why then," but the coachman did not proceed with the consequence.

" Brought! Why, what have you brought?" asked the lodger.

The coachman took his own nose between his finger and thumb, gave a short, quick shake of the head, as if moved by some sudden disgust, and said—" I sha'n't get the coach sweet for a month."

" Ha! ha! I'll give no more," said the lodger, and he turned into his room leaving the coachman at the door. The man stood, eyeing the barrier with a look of doubt. Should he strike his leg through the pannel—or should he quietly turn the handle, and go in and fight? Thus irresolute, he again cast his wandering eye upon the shilling; when, like the duke of Austria, he pocketted his wrongs " because his breeches best might carry them." The fellow lumbered down the staircase, growling, " a murdering set of shabby villains," and closed the door with a violence that admirably conveyed his indignation and contempt of the first-floor lodger.

It was the pure and firm belief of the coachman that he had been hired as a humble labourer in the fields of science; retained to convey a dead body to the lodgings of a surgical student intent on a most laudable and interesting pursuit. If the man had any faith in his own nose, the taint of death still hung,—nay, as he had asserted, would continue to defile the inside of the vehicle, for, possibly, a calendar month: and for this pollution, he had received a—shilling! Only twelve penny-worth of civet to make clean the abomination! No reasonable man will allow that it could be done at the price. Hence, the coachman was justified by the meanness of his employer, to charge him with murder: with the driver shabbiness was synonymous with homicide.

A great poet has said—"We murder to dissect." We know not if on the evening in question, John Applejohn was altogether of the opinion of William Wordsworth, but certainly he had a startling notion that blood had been shed—a belief strengthened by the avowal of the coachman, that if properly remunerated for the secrecy he would disdain to peach. And then, suddenly came upon the affrighted tailor the mysterious visit of old Zweifler to "the Bottle of Hay"—(for, at the time, John

had not discovered the object of his master in such
a practice ;)——the solemn words, " cut me off that
fellow !"——his strange looks——his doubts of all men
——his frequent tales of devilry and witchcraft !——
And then John recollected, that Germans were to
be especially mistrusted——and then he firmly believed in some fearful contract between the lodger
in the first floor and old Zweifler.   John had
never thought anything of the rumour,——but now,
he remembered, that several tailors having been
employed by Zweifler, were shortly after found
missing !   Such was the credulity of John——such
his overflowing benevolence——that he was resolved
to rush into the street, seize on two or three of
the passengers, and bring them to apprehend the
murderer in the first floor.   Already had the simplicity of the tailor painted to him, a victim with two
or three mortal gashes.   Perhaps, a youth, the
hope and stay of a poor widow !   Perhaps, a girl,
some lovely lost one !   Tears were in the eyes of
John, at the spectre of his own imagination : he
was determined, and was about to run down the
staircase, when he heard the lodger open his door
——saw him come out——lock the door, put the key
in his pocket, and descend.   In a minute the street
door was opened and shut, and John Applejohn,
in his own strong conceit, remained alone in a
house with a murdered body.   He turned as cold

as the corse itself—if, indeed, it was yet cold—and
his teeth struck together, and his hair stirred.   At
length, with a vigorous effort he called back his
scattered spirits, and walked down stairs. He panted
with horror as he approached the door—the thin
partition between him and a slaughtered corpse.
Macbeth—even when played by Macready—when
grasped and dragged by the invisible hands of the
witches, and held writhing at the chamber of
Duncan—has not a more awful face, than had
our paralyzed tailor.   He stooped, his whole
body shaking like a deer's tail, and put his eye
to the key-hole.   The room was dark !   He
rose, and with new courage resolved to get a
light.   He departs, and in a few minutes returns
with a lighted candle, and a bundle of keys—
miraculously left by old Zweifler in the tailors'
room.   Yes—John had determined to appease his
own doubts, ere he gave the alarm : the mystery
might be satisfactorily explained, and then what
could he say for himself at having raised a tumult ?
If, on the contrary, an assassination had really
taken place, on discovering the fact, he had only
to throw up the window, and give a loud call of
murder.   With this benevolent intention, John
tried every key in the fond hope that one might be
found to open the Abomeleque's room—the Blue
Chamber of blood and mystery.   Alas ! the good

intentions—the excellent meaning of Applejohn
were not seconded by fortune: no key would
stir the lock. John had tried every key, and cast
his eyes upwards with a look of despair, when, to
our pain we speak it, he saw a nail—a crooked nail
in the wall. John had a vague recollection that
locks had been turned back by so small an implement as that above him. The devil walked
behind the tailor, and grinned in deep satisfaction, as he beheld John Applejohn arm himself
with a hammer to wrench out the nail. Fixed
upon his knees, his face to the door, with one
hand guiding the bent nail, the other grasping
the candle-stick, John laboured hard in the cause
of justice. A stranger beholding him would have
felt tolerably well convinced that John was working
at the lock with a most felonious intention; whereas,
he was a labouring disciple in the sacred cause of
humanity. He appeared to vulgar eyes a house-
breaker, when in truth he was never so much a
philanthropist. Still John laboured; but not effec-
tually. He paused and wiped his brow, and
again addressed himself to his work. At length,
the bolt moves—again—another turn — the bolt
is back! John is rising from his knees, when
he is pinned to the floor by a hand fixed in his
collar,—and four knuckles embedded in his jugular;
—this sudden action is accompanied by the following
words :—

"Teeves—teeves—lights,"—the candle had been knocked down by John's assailant—"murder!"

"Murder — thieves — murder — murder," was taken up by a female voice—for the maid had just let herself into the passage, and was followed by the first-floor lodger, who immediately proceeded up stairs, the girl quickly attending with a lighted candle.   Luckless John Applejohn!

We beg the sympathy of the reader for our unfortunate hero—our man of virtuous intentions. He remained still upon his knees, and the hand of old Zweifler still at his neck; the bunch of keys—fifty dumb, yet speaking witnesses beside him; and—oh! guilt, guilt beyond the cunning of defence—the crooked nail between John Applejohn's thumb and finger!

"Teef—rogue—oh, oh! dis is your work on Mondays!" cried Zweifler, pale with passion.

"Mr. Zweifler, as I live—I—you don't know what I know," said Applejohn.

"I should have been hanged dirty years ago if I had,"—said the tailor.

"Betty," said the tenant of the first floor, "you had better go for an officer."

"No—no—no," said old Zweifler with rapid vehemence—"No—no."

"Yes, Betty—do—go for an officer," cried John—"I wish for an officer. Then it will all come out."

" Come out !" exclaimed Zweifler.

" Come out," repeated John. " There's been murder done. The body is now in that room. I saw it—with my own eyes saw it ! Oh, you needn't stare," cried John to the astonished lodger—" I saw you and the coachman—heard him say he wouldn't turn king's evidence, and all I wanted was first to be sure that"—

" An unblushing, bare-faced thief ! And you think that this fetch will save you ? Caught in the fact, and now have the impudence to trump up this defence," and the lodger opened the door, and entered the room followed by John and the amazed Zweifler. " See, sir ; see," and the speaker uncovered the object, carefully swathed in linen—" see, sir ; a lay figure of the Venus," said the tenant artist.

Zweifler turned a fierce eye upon Applejohn, who, astounded at the discovery, stood for a moment speechless. At length he stammered out—" I—I did it all for the best : may I die this minute, if I didn't mean well." The old tailor shook his head incredulously.

" Run for an officer," again repeated Mr. Dolce, the artist ; and again Zweifler countermanded the order.

" No," said the old man, " no : I trusted him, and he has deceived me."

"Mr. Zweifler, as true as there's a heaven," exclaimed our luckless hero.

"Go, John Applejohn, go; I leave you to your conscience, go; I will not hang you—no: you shall not dis time die with a rope at your neck—but you shall live with a halter round about your heart! Go, John; go," and the old man's eyes filled with tears as he turned from Applejohn, who passionately, yet vainly pleaded against the damning evidence of the keys and nail. In fine, our well-meaning friend was thrust out of doors, Betty vainly begging that he might be detained until she had searched her boxes.

John stood in the street, bewildered, broken-hearted! He tried to walk, and staggered like a tipsy satyr. In the whole world there was not a more sober—a more honest man. He had been cast off by his first love as a drunkard, and was now spurned and branded as a thief. When somewhat recovered from his stupor, his first feelings were those of vengeance on all mankind. If he were treated like a wretch, why not *be* the sot and knave? From that moment, he would drink and rob—he would laugh at sobriety, and think the honest man a masking cheat. For a brief instant was John Applejohn an embryo tippler and cut-purse—an undaunted ragamuffin; and then, his true nature returning upon him, he leaned against the railings

of a house, and cried like a baby. Poor John
Applejohn !

CHAPTER VII.

WHILST in Mr. Zweifler's service, John had
lived with the closest economy; hence, on his
expulsion from the house, he was master of a few
pounds by means of which he hoped to be borne
far away from uncharitable, heartless London; the
scene of all his misery, all his disgrace. Surely
there was some green spot in the world where
good intentions must bring forth good fruits; some
land, where if a man sowed wheat, he would not
gather hemp; a harvest all but got in by the most
unfortunate of tailors. It was about a fortnight
after his last sorrow, when John stood at the window
of a map-seller, " the world before him where to
choose." What a spot was England in the painted
sheet ! He had suffered injuries, but never before
had he thought so meanly of his native country.
France was open to him—so was America—so Van
Dieman's Land. John had in idea thrice circum-
navigated the globe, and yet remained undecided
in his choice of a home; like a dog that turns round,
and round, and round and fain would, yet cannot

curl itself up to rest.   Visions of prosperous felons came upon John as his eye sailed up Sidney Cove !

" What ! you are looking for lodgings to let ?—plenty of 'em there, unfurnished too," and the speaker pointed to a map of Egypt.

Applejohn turned, and looking up, beheld Mr. Oldjoe in his walking-dress.   He wore a sky-blue neckerchief, a pink and yellow striped waistcoat—claret-coloured trowsers, and a green coat, heavily studded with metal buttons, bearing in *alto relievo* the portraits of a fox and goose.—Judging Oldjoe by his dress, he looked a harlequin *incog ;* whilst his face had the rigid solemnity of a tax-gatherer.

" Mr. Oldjoe ! is it you ?" said John timidly.

" It was, yesterday," replied the delicious wag ; and he nodded familiarly to a reverend gentleman, at the moment passing in his carriage.

" Bless me !" cried Applejohn, " isn't that the Archbishop of"—

" To be sure ; didn't you see me nod to him ? I always support the established church," said Oldjoe with more than clerical seriousness.   " No pride about me."

" Good day, sir," and John was sneaking off.

" Wait, my little man, wait ;" and Oldjoe took a card-case from his waistcoat-pocket, and John held out his hand for a card.   Oldjoe stared at him,

as if unconscious of anything ridiculous, and leisurely extracted from the case a handkerchief of
about two inches square. "Always carry your
comforts in a little space," said Oldjoe brushing
the end of his nose, and then returning the lawn to
its small depositary. "Ha! why didn't you bow?"

"Bow, sir?" said John.

"Didn't you see him?—one of the judges: always
be civil to 'em, you don't know what may happen,"
odserved Oldjoe, whilst Applejohn coloured to the
eyes, for he thought, but without truth, that the
admonition was intended to reflect on the occurrence at Zweifler's, of which Oldjoe was entirely
ignorant. "Stop—stop my little man;" for Applejohn was about to slip away—"Mr. Gruelthorpe
wants you."

"I—I am not with Mr. Zweifler at present,"
said John.

"All the better. You are not married?" asked
Oldjoe.

"No," replied John, hesitating for a sigh.

"And have no children? Now, be sure," observed the wit.

"None in the least," answered John.

"Have no objection to travel for all that?" said
Oldjoe—"I know you hav'n't: I watched you at
the maps. What do you think of Sierra Leone?
Take out enough black with you, and you'd make

your fortune in a twelvemonth; yes, although one suit of mourning lasts three in a family, and is then as good as new."

" I shouldn't prefer Sierra Leone," said the tailor.

" No—I see you're not avaricious.   Just like my friend, Lord Ladle—takes out his pension in blankets for the poor, and yet none of 'em know it.   Mr. Gruelthorpe is about to travel, and wants a confidential tailor.   Now, what do you think of it ?" and Oldjoe looked down immoveably on John.

" I have nothing to keep me in London," said the desolate Applejohn.

" Well, when I return from sea, I'll settle the business for you," said Oldjoe.

" Are you going to sea, Mr. Oldjoe ?" asked John in some surprise.

" Yes; let me consider—the wind's north-west: I think, north-west?" ventured Oldjoe with grave deference, and Applejohn with equal gravity, and we believe with equal ignorance, observed—" North-west." " Well, then, I shall be back on Friday—call on me at two on Friday.   As for the wind, I know that will be all right—so say two on Friday," and with never a smile on his blank face, Oldjoe strided off.

" What an extraordinary man ! and how very

humorous," thought Applejohn, whose spirit
was lightened by the communication of the arch
wag, and he looked forward to Friday with
renewed hopes. The day came, and John presented himself at the hotel; the day passed, and
no Oldjoe appeared. Doubtless, thought John, he
is still tossing on the briny wave. Early next
morning, John was at his post; and still no landlord
had been visible. John waited until noon, and it
then struck him that as accidents did sometimes
happen on the main, it would be a waste of time to
wait any longer for an introduction by a man—
who, it was by no means impossible, might at that
moment be drifting out to the North Sea, without
the remotest intention of ever returning. Thus,
after much thinking, John resolved at once to
solicit an interview with Mr. Gruelthorpe, and
induced a humane waiter to carry the humble name
of Applejohn to the superb young heir; who, never
having heard the name, and being at the time sadly
in want of bosom friends of fashion, thought this
might be a stranger of some mark, and immediately
ordered that the gentleman should be shown up.

"Oh!" cried, or rather groaned young Gruelthorpe, in the depth of disappointment as the tailor
showed himself.

"I have been so bold, sir,"—began John with all

humility, when he was interrupted by the sudden appearance of Oldjoe.

"I've caught the duke—said I should—safe!" cried Oldjoe, whose charm of original drollery had made him a familiar favourite with young Gruelthorpe. "Lord Nelson couldn't have done it better."

"What duke?" asked Gruelthorpe, "and where have you been these three days?"

"Been to sea. Look here," and Oldjoe exhibited a telescope two yards long. "My motto like the marines, 'by sea and by land.' Heard he was coming."

"Who was coming?" inquired the astonished guest.

"The Russian duke; got scent of his highness, and would hook him. We got down to the Great Nore; and there we lay to. A whole day and night, and no signs of the duke. I was determined to have him; so I said, 'my boys, put the helm up for St. Petersburgh!' I had hardly said this, when sweeping the horizon, as my friend, Sir Edward Codrington would say, I saw a steamer; I knew by the look of her that there was royalty aboard. 'Lobsters from Heligoland,' said Telamaque my interpreter; for I've left off French myself, it's so common—'Lobsters from Heligoland, said Telamaque—' a duke,' cried I. ' Steer down upon her,' said I—' they're putting on more coals, and I'll board her in the smoke.' I lay in this manner, with my eye at my glass, and with that sagacity which makes me first in the trade, discovered the duke himself eating caviare in the cabin. ' Easy, lads, easy,' said I : ' easy, and I'll board her on the larboard paddle-box'—I hadn't said ' box,' when my foot was on it—and I was actually standing in the state cabin, in front of the duke himself, who was still eating caviare, with my card in my hand, before his highness knew it.—Count de Grasse was never so completely taken," said Oldjoe, with inexpressible gravity.

" And the Russian duke will absolutely be your guest ?" asked Gruelthorpe.

" He couldn't refuse me. He couldn't with any decency. Look here ;" and Oldjoe exhibited the collar and cuffs of his coat trimmed with fur six inches deep. " Do you see this ?"

" What of it ?" questioned the heir.

" Real silver bear,—every bit of it bear. The Russian duke saw the delicate compliment paid to his country, and could refuse me nothing ! Mr. Gruelthorpe," and Oldjoe spoke with new seriousness—" there is nothing like studying national prejudices. As an innkeeper, I've been taught the value of it."

" Indeed, Mr. Oldjoe."

" Bitterly taught it. There were four of us in opposition went out to take the Persian Princes on their passage here.—Well, how do you think I lost 'em? By my ignorance of national prejudices," said the solemn tavern-keeper.

" How?" asked Gruelthorpe.

" Why, the successful landlord—the man who got them to his house—boarded 'em in the channel with a sample of boiled rice:" and had Oldjoe sworn an affidavit to the fact, he had not sworn with a more collected visage.

" Then you tavern-keepers stop these people on the water?"

" There never was such a look out for foreigners on the high seas, as since the peace. If there's a mortality among the pilots," said Oldjoe, "and a war should break out, there isn't an hotel-keeper westward who couldn't take a fleet through the channel."

" And have many crowned heads fallen to your lot?" asked Gruelthorpe.

" Crowned heads, sir!" said Oldjoe, letting the exclamation pass for an answer. " Crowned heads! you've seen me wear a ring on my right little finger?"

" I can't recollect the circumstance," said Gruel-thorpe.

" Yes, yes,—you must recollect it. Hem! Donna Maria's own hair," and Oldjoe stroked his chin and looked away at the opposite wall. " But it's hard work—very hard work. To go out in all weathers; to brave the wind and fog, and—hem! hem! h—m!—yes, I've caught it," and Oldjoe, for he was musical, threw up the lid of a piano, and stooping his long back over the keys, confused them with his fingers, as he tried his singing voice :—

" ' What shall I do, to show how much I love her ?' "

" Do you hear that ?" asked the vocalist—" My falsetto has an edge like a saw. You see, they ar'n't all profit, these dukes."

" And when does his highness come, Mr. Oldjoe ?"

" To-night. He was to land at—oh ! my little man," and for the first time Oldjoe deigned to notice the taciturn tailor.

" I came yesterday, sir," said John, " but as you were not here, and hadn't arrived this morning, I thought I had better speak myself on"——

" Yes, yes; just like the world," replied Oldjoe with an injured look, " you didn't care whether I was shipwrecked or not; you'd have eaten your cold mutton all the same."

" I assure you, sir,"——

"You would;" said Oldjoe sternly—"you know you would; and if you could have got em, pickles with it. However, I am above thinking of these things. Mr. Gruelthorpe, you want a valet—here's your man."

"Why isn't this—yes—isn't he a tailor?" inquired Gruelthorpe, scrutinizing the countenance of John.

"It can't be denied—he is a tailor. But, sir, this is the age of economy—must go with the times, sir; I have reduced my own soda a shilling a bottle,—now, if you can get your body servant and your tailor in one man, eh?"—

"Perhaps, 'twould be convenient," said Gruelthorpe, and a few preliminaries being entered upon and arranged, John Applejohn was duly accepted. He, however, mainly owed his good fortune to the fact, that three previous candidates for the office, had instantly withdrawn their claims on learning the plebeian origin of Benjamin Gruelthorpe.

CHAPTER VII.

JOHN APPLEJOHN had a proper affection for his own country; yet we will not attempt to deny it—certain late events had excited in him an unusual

desire to travel. Perhaps, for such yearnings will
now and then possess us, he felt a sudden wish to
increase his small store of knowledge; and by
contrasting the characters of foreign tailors with
the habits and manners of tailors at home, to
establish some subtle theory on the important subject, but too long neglected. Be this as it may, a
great author in an essay "on tying the cravat,"
assures us that " there is nothing so laudable as the
pursuit of truth." Thus, John having endured
little but falsehood and calumny at home, received
the order of his master to prepare for a journey
abroad, with renewed hopes of enjoying a just interpretation of his good intentions; for, happy are
we to assure the reader, that all the unmerited
injuries inflicted upon John had failed to sour the
sweetness of his temper, to chill the honest blood
that flowed within him. He had lived in what
very virtuous people call this very wicked world
five-and-twenty years, and was almost as simple as
when he first snuffed the air. The consciousness
of his well-meaning was an armour against the
knocks of fortune—balm and spikenard to his hurts.
Strong in his good intentions, he could not consider any evil but as a passing accident—a mistake
to be cleared up by and by. We verily believe that
he would have put his head into a halter, with hardly
a wry face at the injustice of the sentence, strong

in the assurance that in a very little time, a very handsome epitaph would sweeten and make white his memory. Happy John Applejohn !

Benjamin Gruelthorpe had too long delayed, as he conceived, the most important step in his life. He had been his own master nine months,—had delighted the devil, the patron of all misers, by casting away with a free hand the money which his father had sinned for; but was yet only at the alpha of his manly knowledge. Foreign travel was indispensible to even a common education; and though at the time Benjamin quitted London he had not made up his mind to the extent of his peregrinations—though he had not then determined upon going as far as Tadmor in the Desert,—he had firmly resolved to see the Palais Royal. It was in the laudable pursuit of such useful knowledge that Benjamin Gruelthorpe, Esq., attended by his servant, put up at the ——, Canterbury, on his way to Dover. We do not give the name of the inn for various reasons. In the first place, no landlord, licensed to take in travellers, can be answerable for the characters of those whom it is his duty to feed and lodge. And a happy circumstance it is, that at least nine times out of ten the host is left in blissful ignorance of the practices and dispositions of those who give their orders. Were it otherwise, who, save Beelzebub himself, could keep a tavern?

Who could have the head and heart for the ago-
nizing business? What lacerations of spirit, doomed
to obey the commands of the profligate, the selfish,
and the extravagant, knowing them to be so!—to be
compelled to put a two guinea dinner before the
orphan-eating executor—the best claret to the
voluptuary who starves his wife at home! Or if
all orders were to be obeyed with a " conscience
and tender heart," what a capital, solemn farce it
would be to have some moral Quixote, keeper of
the Swan on the London road! Oh! for a Boni-
face of the true La Mancha stamp. True it is,
that the days of chivalry are gone—that, as Mr.
Burke says, they departed the very moment that the
vulgar took to rob upon the highway in common
with barons and knights : then, there ceased to be
a distinction; and chivalry, though still in mail and
with all the trappings of its order, was *in articulo
mortis.* If, however, we were called upon to name
the precise time of its death, the very point at
which the vital spark of chivalry fled for ever, we
would fearlessly give the day on which King
Alfred hung up his golden bracelets by the road-
side, and when, so debased, so sunk was the national
spirit, that throughout the whole degenerate kingdom no hand was found bold enough to pull them
down, and valorously pocket them. Then chivalry
became what we see it now, an armed statue on a

dead man's tomb ; and then, indeed, well might a
highway bard, weeping at the quenched spirit of
his land, and comparing the types of chivalry with
its former living self, exclaim in a pathetic note—

> " Ah ! woe is me ! these high-born sinners,
> Altho' they liv'd so stoutly,
> Seeing they never pray'd themselves,—
> Yet their statues pray devoutly."

Quixote a tapster ! the Knight of the Rueful
Countenance, landlord of the Swan ! We cannot
readily dispossess ourselves of the animating idea.
Nay, we see the madly moral host driving his conscientious trade. A guest with a diamond on his
finger has ordered a platter of hashed venison.
" Are you sure, sir," asks our Quixote landlord
—" are you sure, sir, that a mutton chop wouldn't
harmonize better with your pocket ? Very true, I
see that stone on your finger; but, my dear sir,
is it paid for ?" " Waiter," cries a guest, " bring
me a bottle of your best port." " John," says
Quixote, " take the man a pint of beer; nay, sir,
you must allow me to say beer—you can have no
wine in my house; for you know it was only this
morning that on the score of poverty you refused
your laundress the just claim of two-and-sixpence."
" Another glass of brandy-and-water," cries a red-
faced, prosperous looking man.—" Water, sir, but
no brandy," says Quixote. " No brandy ? Do

you think I can't afford it?" asks the astonished guest. "By no means," says the landlord—"of course you can ; but then, sir, your health ; consider your health ; you have had two glasses, and no man drinks a third in my house." " Bridget," cries the waiter, " take a night-candle to the lady in number nine." " Bridget, I'll take it myself," says Quixote, and away he goes with the burning taper. " The candle," says Quixote. " Very good—we have had a long journey, and want to go to bed." · " An excellent bed," says Quixote—" down, and sheets like snow ; an excellent bed ; but first, madam, permit me to look at your marriage certificate." This is how all landlords ought to act ; and then, how inns would flourish, think the temperate and good—how vice would fall, how virtue raise its head ! Yes, Cervantes was unjust to his genius when he made his hero a knight ; he should have created him a tapster. Never was there such an opportunity for exhibiting the efficacy and the reward of good advice. But to our travellers at Canterbury.

" I don't care, if I see the Cathedral" said young Gruelthorpe with the air of a man about to confer an honor, and that after much deliberation. Knowing no one in the city, he bethought himself of the tombs ; having no letter of introduction to so much

as an alderman, he resolved to call on the Blac
Prince. Nothing, perhaps, could so well illustrai
the inexperience of our traveller as his deplorabl
ignorance of the social state, not of Canterbur
alone, but of every place dignified by a cathedra
How often—tarrying in a cathedral town—hav
we witnessed the benign effect of primitive mar
ners. To what other influence are we to ascrit
the meckness, the loving-kindness, the neigh
bourly charity of all the inhabitants? The sma
distinctions, the delicate shades of place and foi
tune, seem wholly forgotten in the active prir
ciples of brotherly love. The purple raiment
not hastily caught away from the passing touch o
coarser web—the finest lawn makes common caus
with any linen bands—the silken apron shrinks no
from poor prunella. Let pride, and pomp, an
heartburnings for precedence swell, and strut an
smoulder where they may, they never have been—
they never can be—found where man finds a cathe
dral. All who live within the glad sounds of it
chimes, live peaceably as sheep within a greel
enclosure.

"I don't care if I see the cathedral," said Benja
min, and sallied from the inn followed by his trust
Applejohn.

"Would you like to walk inside, sir?" asked al

old woman, as young Gruelthorpe stood gaping at
the exterior of the edifice. " You had better walk
in, sir," said the dame, in a like hospitable tone to
that which may have fallen on the ear of the reader,
tarrying before a caravan, arrested by the outside
portrait of the giant or the dwarf within.

Benjamin entered the cathedral, and the old
woman unceremoniously began her task. " This
cathedral was once the palace of King Ethelbert
the King of Kent who made a present of the same
to St. Augustine,"—

" Very handsome of him," said Benjamin,
" wasn't it John?" asked Gruelthorpe, unbending
to his domestic.

" Very like a gentleman," replied John.

" And went and lived upon the Reculvers here
gentlemen," continued the old woman, " is many
monuments as your eyes may detect. Them in
the wall is called mural monuments the cause unknown. That monument is of Orlando Gibbons
who came to play upon the organ when King
Charles the first was married and died of the small
pox that fatal accident happening in 1625,—under
your feet there was many archbishops and friars;
but in the civil wars the gravestones was dilapidated the ornaments absconded and the bishops
deprived of their brass a shocking thing for any
christian to relate. You will find more of this in

Mr. Weever," said the old woman, and she paused
and looked at Benjamin.

" I—I—I'm aware," said Gruelthorpe, sucking
the head of his cane.

" When the new pavement was put down the
remains very handsomely dressed of archbishop
Tibbald was found in a leaden plate.   That gentleman laying on his side is Sir John Boys in his
doctor's robes."

" Very much injured ;" John observed deferentially, " by time, no doubt ? "

" And the soldiers," continued the guide. " He lost
his nose and other faculties in the great rebellion."

" Lovely thing, that," said Benjamin, gazing at
one of the windows, the sun lighting up the glories
of the stained glass—" a lovely thing."

" It has been much admired," observed the old
woman, slowly rubbing her hands, and then placidly
folding her arms.

" Very beautiful, indeed, sir," said John " I don't
wonder at your liking it."

" Liking it !" exclaimed Gruelthorpe "it's glorious ! I'd give any money to have it."

" No money would buy it, sir," remarked the
woman.

" Besides, sir," said Applejohn, " where could
you place the window—where could you possibly
put it ?"

" Put it! Pooh—fool! I mean, I'd give any money," and Benjamin continued to stare at the radiant glass, " yes, any money to have those very colours in a waistcoat."

" Beautiful by candle-light," said the old woman, rightly falling in with the enthusiasm of Benjamin ; and then instantly proceeding with her duties. " You are requested to bear in mind gentlemen that you are now arrived at the martyrdom where Becket was massacreed and on that very account where Edward the First and his Queen was married. Erasmus a learned Dutchman although according to great authors a love-child came here on his visit to King Henry the Eighth his statue is in the market-place of Rotterdam—he kissed the sword which killed St. Thomas and wrote a book in which he proved that he who could be the greatest fool would in the end be the same as the wisest man. That image in oak is archbishop Peckham in very good repair being five hundred years old."

" A great age," observed Applejohn.

" 'Straordinary, how bishops *do* last !" said Gruelthorpe, and still he sucked his cane.

" Several archbishops and friars lay here so much defaced that if their dearest relations was again alive they wouldn't know 'em. You are now in the chapel of St. Michael : over there," and the

woman pointed upwards, " was once an orga
and is still. Those saints in the panels is S
Augustine and St. Gregory barbarously fire
at by Oliver Cromwell's soldiers the marks of th
bullets still to be seen by the curious and human
observer."

" Another window !" exclaimed Gruelthorp
and possibly he thought of a second waistcoat.

" That window is the eastern window," said th
woman, " there you see is a white stag with a crow
upon its head resting under a tree a greyhoun
doing the same thing. That is a tomb of alablast
the figures upon it the figures of Margaret sist
of the Earl of Kent and the Earl of Somerset an
Duke of Clarence her two lawfully-married hu:
bands; they are all laying together in expectatio
of a happier state."

Applejohn looked at the placid faces, the con
posed forms of the effigies, and then catching th
eye of his master, observed—" Very solemn, thi
sir."

Young Gruelthorpe took his cane from h
mouth, pulled up his shirt-collar, and replied-
" 'Straordinary."

" And was all this done at the request of any
the parties?" asked John Applejohn, pointing
the tomb.

" Under the living eye of the widow herself wh

died sensible to the last the guide thanks you for what you please," and the woman dropping a curtsey, and holding forth her hand, implied by the action that her task was done.

" Is nothing more to be seen ?" asked Gruelthorpe, laying a half-crown in the hand of his instructress. " Nothing more ?"

" There is Becket's shrine," answered the guide, " and the Black Prince, both the property of another woman."

" Property !" exclaimed John.

" She shews 'em," briefly replied the matron, who hobbled hastily away in search of new-comers.

" Wonderful thing ! this, sir," said John, raising his eyes to the roof with a feeling of awe at the enormous fabric above, around him. " I don't know how it is, sir; but whenever I come into a place like this, I feel myself now as small and as mean as a fly, and now as big and as mighty as a giant."

Benjamin Gruelthorpe, with his cane in his mouth, nodded.

" And then, sir, to hear the organ in a church like this ! I declare, sir, it seems to me as if a river of blood flowed from it."

" Blood !" said Gruelthorpe, with a hazy look. " 'Straordinary !"

" I don't mean that, sir ; I mean, that when]

hear the organ peal, every little vein in my bo
seems filling and filling from it, and my hea
grows as great as a drum, and I shoot up fifty fe
high, and I seem as if, big as the church may b
it isn't big enough for me; and I could cry ar
fight, and pray and kneel, and I still seem to g
higher and higher, and bigger and bigger."

" 'Straordinary!" repeated Gruelthorpe.

" It's true, sir; quite true. When the orga
plays in such a place as this, it seems like a—a—
don't know what to call it—a river emptying itse
into me."

" An organ a river? Humph!" and Grue
thorpe sucked his cane.

" There's magic in it, sir—I mean, lawful magi
or something like it. For when it plays, I've see
or I've thought I've seen, the faces upon tl
monuments almost smile."

" 'Straordinary!" cried Benjamin.

" Ha! sir—it is very strange, very strang
indeed; but, I want to ask you one question.
hope it's not an improper one?"

" I hope not," said Mr. Gruelthorpe, with a
air of dignity. " I hope not."

" I want to ask you, sir, if—now, I hope I'
not asking anything that anybody would thir
wrong?" and John hesitated.

" I trust not," said Benjamin; " only, dor

presume on my good-nature, John; in what you may be about to ask, you will, I trust, be pleased to recollect that you are my servant, I am your master."

" Oh ! sir, never fear : I only want to ask you something about a church organ," said Applejohn.

" Very well—go on," observed Gruelthorpe, somewhat relieved ; for he feared some delicate family question on the part of his domestic. " Well —what about the organ ?"

" Why, sir, hav'n't you thought, when you've heard it in full play, that the organ was really and truly"—and John paused.

" Really and truly, what ?"

" Really and truly—a—a bit of the next world ?" and John looked anxiously in the face of his master.

Benjamin Gruelthorpe took his cane from his mouth, ran his fingers through his hair, and making answer, said—" I—I can't say."

" Depend upon it, sir, it is ; and nothing else," said Applejohn. " Ha ! sir—this is a terrible place," and John raised his arms in wonder and veneration. " A terrible place !"

" I see nothing terrible in it—very fine," said Gruelthorpe.

" Why, it is fine, sir—but to me, it's more terrible than fine. And yet I think better of my-self, when I think that men, perhaps, as weak and as mean as I am, helped to make it," said John.

" Very possible," observed John's master.

" And doesn't it make you prouder, sir, that you're a man?" asked Applejohn.

" I hope, I have something better to be proud of," replied Benjamin Gruelthorpe.

" You see, sir, though I'm a poor, ignorant fellow myself, it does my heart good, puts hope into me, when I think of the wonderful things done by creatures, who with all their wisdom, were only men. The very thought of it gives me a lift with myself, sir."

" 'Straordinary !" remarked Gruelthorpe, gazing about him. " To be sure," said Benjamin, scarcely knowing what he said, " a solemn place like this—that's a sweet pretty figure, in the pink gown—a solemn place like this is likely to make us think of to-morrow."

" Oh ! yes, sir, and of yesterday," replied John. " I'm sure I could stay among some of these figures until I should feel that I quite knew 'em; it makes us older to think of 'em ; hundreds of years older, sir. I wonder, where you and I were, sir, five hundred years ago."

" Very 'straordinary," observed Gruelthorpe, somewhat tickled by the solemn speculations of his servant.

" You know, we must have been somewhere, sir," said Applejohn.

" Why—I—-I should say, John, it's a—that is—
it's a long time back, John."

" And only to think that—that—I don't know
what I was going to say, sir," was the candid
avowal of our hero, who felt himself getting fast out
of his depth. " I know no more what I was going
to say, sir, than, saving the presence of the tombs
about me, than a jackass."

" 'Straordinary !" exclaimed John's master at
the coarse comparison of his servant. The truth
is, in any other place John would have compared
himself to a ninny, a blockhead, a goose; but a deep
sense of his forlorn ignorance took the strongest
image, and he could abide with nothing less than
a jackass.

" As you have said, sir," remarked John, after a
pause, and desirous of renewing the theme—" that's
a beautiful window."

" Splendid colours," said Benjamin.

" I suppose there's some meaning in all those
figures, and in that white stag, sir, and the dog?
They ar'n't there for nothing ?"

" By no means," answered Gruelthorpe. " No
doubt, they're portraits. Some of 'em beautiful
faces ; never saw any more beautiful, never. 'Straordinary !"

" Ha ! sir," exclaimed John with a groan, and

still gazing at the heads in the painted window.
" Ha! sir."

" What the—I mean, what's the matter?" asked
Benjamin.

" You talked of beautiful faces, sir? I'm afraid
it's sinful: but there's a face in that window that's
as like as"—and then John turned to his master,
and with pathetic earnestness observed,—" but you
never saw Sarah Twopenny?"

" Perhaps, you would like to see the cathedral?"
asked a prim old woman, coming up to Gruelthorpe, and without waiting for a reply, added—
" this way, sir, to the shrine." Benjamin obediently
followed the woman, and John, tearing himself from
the painted window, walked after his master.

" This, ladies and gentlemen," said the female,
addressing a party already awaiting her lecture,
" this is the monument of the famous Edward,
known as the Black Prince, in consequence of his
wearing armour of that colour. He died at Canterbury, at the palace of the archbishop, a prelate
celebrated for his hospitality. You will observe that
the monument is in excellent preservation, being
as good as new. That is the figure of his Royal
Highness, double gilt. There you see, hanging
above the monument, is his Royal Highness's
gauntlet or glove worn in those days. You also

see his scabbard, being a remarkably small one for so great a hero."

" Pray, pardonnez moy, but—my good woman —if that ere is the scabbard, what is, scusez moi, become of the sword ?"

This question was put in a remarkably small voice, by a little, dapper person, who, at every word patted his head, as if to assist him in the delivery of English. He wore a moustache not unlike a very old tooth-brush.

" An illustrious foreigner, no doubt," thought young Gruelthorpe.

" The sword," replied the woman, " was feloniously stolen by Oliver Cromwell, and never returned. That is his Royal Highness's surcoat, which he wore against the Frenchmen, beautifully quilted."

"'Straordinary !" said Gruelthorpe.

" It is not so sure that he licked the Francois," said the man with the moustache, patting his head.

" People are left to their own opinion," said the severely precise guide, looking sourly at the doubter —"'specially foreigners."

" And pray, what tomb is that ?" asked a pretty country girl, whose figure in a pink gown had received the praises of the critical Gruelthorpe.

" That, my young lady, is the tomb of Arch-

bishop Courtney, who died in 1396. The ce
rious have called it a cenotaph," said the guide.

" 'Straordinary," cried Gruelthorpe.

" Shameful !" exclaimed the foreigner.

" My good woman, what do you call a—a—w
you called just now—what is it?" was the inqu
of a visitor, and Gruelthorpe and his man J
listened attentively for the interpretation.

" A cenotaph," replied the woman with c
siderable dignity, " a cenotaph has nobody in

" A tomb to let," concluded John.

" The idle and malicious assert that the ai
bishop is buried at Maidstone; but it is no s
thing. We warrant all his mortal remains to be h
That is the monument of Dean Wootton, the
protestant dean : you perceive that he is in the a
tude of kneeling. The sculpture is much admired:
head particularly, which the dean himself had
upon his travels, expressly for the present occasic

" Ha ! a dean should always be prepare
thought John, with much simplicity.

" And now, ladies and gentlemen, you see
very spot where you might once have seen the v
shrine of St. Thomas à Becket. He was buriec
a coffin of gold, mounted with precious stones,
smallest of which was larger than the largest kno
egg of the largest known goose."

" And what became of 'em ?" asked the suspected foreigner. " Disez moy."

" They were stolen by the authority of his blessed Majesty, Henry the Eighth," answered the guide. " The face of the martyr was shewn in"——

" Granny," cried a little boy, who had run to the woman, and kept pulling at her skirts,—— " granny, dumplings is done."

" The face of the martyr," repeated the woman, putting aside the boy, " was set in gold, and adorned with jewels, and whatever you please, ladies and gentlemen, to bestow upon the guide will be received as a token of your liberality."

" Those fellows played pretty tricks, then, sir," said Gruelthorpe, making up to the man with the moustache.

" Ye—yes," said the foreigner. " Dat is,—wee."

" Capital jugglers, sir," said Benjamin, and to his astonishment, the foreigner silently acquiesced in his opinion by slightly raising his shoulders, and then abruptly turned away. " Humph ! I see—shocked his religious prejudices," said Gruelthorpe ; and with his eyes bent upon the pretty figure in the pink gown, Benjamin quitted the cathedral.

CHAPTER IX.

"This is very dull work, John," said Gruel
thorpe, who, having dined and drunk his bottle an
a half, sat with stretched legs before the tavern fir
"What's to be done, John?"

"Shall I try and borrow you a book, sir
Bless me! there's one upon that table," and Joh
gave the volume to his master.

"Humph! What's this? 'The London D
rectory,'" and with not another word, Gruelthor
flung the book upon the floor.

There are men, who left to themselves in an ir
at Canterbury, might have found matter for curio
thoughts even in "The London Directory." F
is it not a register of the social triumphs of man-
the *libro d'oro* of civilization? Pleasant, with t
rain pattering at the window, the coals burni
briskly, with ease and snugness for our fire-si
gods, to glance down the page of "The Lond
Directory." After all, are the leaves so barre
Now, we read the names of living pin-makers, a
now, we think of the mitred abbots of the olden d;
Now, look we down a long line of traders, wor
men, all ministrant to a kingdom's comfort,—a

now, look we to the olden time, when the comforts
of a nation's hearth were the luxuries only of the rich.
A few worked tapestry for barons and knights—
our " Directory" gives us hundreds of paper-
hangers for the walls of shop-keepers. An earl's
floor was strewed with rushes ; now, have we carpet-
makers for artisans. The light of heaven struggled
through holes in cabin walls; now—see our " Directory"—it comes flooding through unwrinkled
glass ! Even the substantial man must have adjusted his beard at some clear brook ; now, may
the cobler shave in a mirror. The riches of India
—the spices of the Moluccas—blaze and are fra-
grant in the pages of the " Directory." When
Ethelbert talked with good Augustine, where did
the Kentish ladies get their ivory fans—where did
housewives buy their cloves and ginger—where,
where did the little boys of Canterbury get their
pennyworths of figs ? The " Directory" awakens in
us recollections of bold discoverers—hardy enterprize
—cunning invention—patient toil ; and all for the
wide family of England, not for the tyrannous and
haughty few, made tyrannous by the sense of ex-
clusive enjoyment. The " forked animal" man, cons
the page of the " Directory," and sees a thousand
merchants offering ten thousand triumphs won by
the ingenuity, the skill, the labour, and daring of
his kind. He reads the name and abode of a dealer

in oil, and he thinks of the bold mariner harpooning
the leviathan amidst " regions of thick-ribbed ice."
A "grocer" in the next line sends his thoughts
far, far away among the mandarins. A " tallow-
chandler,"—and he is riding in the Baltic, that the
good folks at home may not go to bed without a
candle. Canterbury had its pilgrims—its picturesque processions of shirtless monks, bully knights,
and beardless squires ; but they are gone,—and
seated in the parlour of our host, for the bridle of
the churchman,

> " Gingeling in a whistling wind as clere
> And eke, as loud as doth a chapel bell,"—

we hearken to the horn of the London mail—and
for "The Golden Legend," we have " The London
Directory." However, let us leave the volume on
the floor, flung there by the impatient and drowsy
Gruelthorpe, who saw in the book only so many
names printed upon paper, bound in calf-skin.

"What will you do, sir ?" asked Applejohn,
anxious for the amusement of his master.

" I 'spose there's no company to be had, John ?"
inquired Gruelthorpe despairingly. " I should like
to cut the throat of an hour or two with cards. I
'spose there's no gentlemen in the house ?"

" Shall I go, sir, and"—

" Go to the devil," replied Gruelthorpe, yawning
and flinging himself upon the sofa.

John quitted the apartment; yet, pausing on the outside, he stood considering the means of catering for the pleasures of his master. Never—never did servant cogitate with better intentions. It was in vain; John could decide upon nothing; he therefore descended the stairs, determining to sally forth into the city, to give loose to his fancy, already filled with abbots and abbesses, noble ladies and mailed knights.

On his way to the street-door John unhappily passed a room, wherein he beheld the foreigner he had that morning met in the cathedral, seated with two persons of a somewhat mean appearance, though apparently in familiar intercourse with the great man himself. There was, however, this marked distinction—the meaner men smoked pipes, the illustrious foreigner whiffed a cigar.

" I—I wisits one of the canons to-morrow; so, Gobye, mind you keep sober," said the foreigner.

" Sober as the town-pump," said Gobye.

" And be wery particklar, Tipit, with that ere wine. You know, when we was last at the duke's"—

At this moment, the door closed, and John Applejohn did not hear what occurred at the duke's. He had, however, heard sufficient, and ran back to his master.

" What does the savage want?" cried Gruelthorpe, as his servant broke upon him.

" If you please, sir, there are some gentlemen down stairs, who I have no doubt will be very happy to join you."

" Are you sure they're gentlemen?" asked the cautious Gruelthorpe.

" Sure of one of 'em; for he wears moustachios, a gold chain, and six rings. But you've seen him, sir; he was at the Black Prince."

" What! the foreigner?" and the eyes of Benjamin glistened.

" The very person, sir; and I'm sure he's a gentleman, sir—for I heard him just now speak of visiting a duke."

" Good heavens!" exclaimed Benjamin, and he rose, and approaching the glass, adjusted his scattered curls.

" Shall I say, you'd like his company, sir?" inquired John.

" Stay. I'm afraid you can't speak French enough to be understood by him,—for he's evidently from Paris; I'm sure of the accent," said the acute Gruelthorpe.

" I think I can make myself understood, sir, in English; for he talks a good deal better than when we heard him," and John, interpreting a nod from his master as consent, ran down stairs, and made his way into the presence of the illustrious foreigner, who, with his friends, John invited in the name of

Mr. Benjamin Gruelthorpe, to help over a dull hour with the vivacity and intelligence of their society.

" Shall be too much proud," said the foreigner, tapping his forehead with his fingers.

" Werry 'appy, indeed, to drink a glass o' vine with any gem'man," declared Gobye.

" Is he at de top of de stairs ?" inquired the exotic visitor.

" The first floor, sir; I'll conduct you to him," and John quickly advancing, heard not the friendly warning bestowed by the foreigner upon his two companions.

" Now, lads," said the Frenchman, with a pure Parisian accent, " be wide awake, and no gammon."

" I hope, gentlemen, that—'straordinary !"— exclaimed Gruelthorpe, and he stared at the scurvy companions of the foreigner as they swaggered into the apartment.

" My good friends—my varee good friends—my bones amies," said the foreigner, introducing Gobye and Tipit.

Gruelthorpe bowed, and proceeded. " I hope, sir, that you will excuse the liberty of a stranger, who finding himself alone in a dull town"—

" 'Tis varee dull—varee dull, indeed, to stranger;

but to me who know avery bodie upward and downward,"—said the foreigner—

" 'Straordinary!" exclaimed Benjamin, and showed his teeth. " You possibly visit the heads of the clergy here?"

" Oh! all of de heads of de church—from de dromedaries"—

" Dromedaries!" cried Gruelthorpe—" 'straordinary!"

" Ha! ha! I mean de—de—humph!—de"—and the illustrious foreigner with a desolate look at Gobye and Tipit, continued to tap his forehead.

" Dromedaries," said Mr. Gobye, " you mean prebendairys."

" Ha! ha! 'tis all as one—prebendayries; but you see, I am foreigner."

" A Frenchman, I presume?" asked Benjamin.

"Do you parley French?" inquired the foreigner, staring at Gruelthorpe.

" Not—I—that is—not in the slightest," said Benjamin.

" 'Tis great pity, for I am French," said the foreigner.

" May I inquire your name?" asked Benjamin.

" My name, sare, is Signor Smugcard, at your service *à jammy*."

" You may go, John; I shall not want you this

hour or two—pray, be seated, gentlemen. Oh !
John, send the waiter to me," such were the words
of Gruelthorpe; and his trusty and well-meaning
domestic, rejoicing that he had found society for
his master, despatched the waiter for orders, and
then strolled down the streets of the ancient city
of Canterbury.

CHAPTER X.

JOHN wandered he knew not, cared not, whither.
Thinking of Sarah Twopenny, of the roaring sea
that might for ever divide him from her—for Mr.
Gruelthorpe had resolved to take ship from Dover
the next day—of the malicious tongues that had
killed his innocent fame, John, unconscious of the
distance, strolled far from the inn ; and had made
nearly a circuit of the city, when he paused at a
monastic ruin. All about him was dark, silent,
and desolate. Now John, albeit he had never
owned the failing —nay, was determined to keep the
weakness a secret even from himself—was somewhat superstitious. He did not think it impossible
that ghosts might walk ; and, granting the possibility, he thought Canterbury a very likely place
to meet with them. For all he knew, the Black
Prince might wander restlessly abroad in search of

his stolen blade ; Margaret, the Earl of Kent's sister, might take a walk arm-in-arm with her noble husbands, Somerset and Clarence; nay, the shadow of Thomas à Becket himself might roam about the city, gibbering for his golden coffin. As these thoughts fell upon John, the soles of his feet seemed to grow into the earth—the crown of his head became ice—and scarcely breathing through his nostrils, he slowly turned his head from side to side.   At this instant, a light blazed through a casement of an isolated part of the ruin—John started at the light, and almost fell to the earth. He then crept close to the window, hearing voices within.

" I tell 'ee, he's the devil himsel—or his sarvin' man, surelye.   I seed un do things, that I thought the floor would ha' opened, and swallowed un clean," said one.

" What did he do ?" asked another.

" Do ! The Lord ha' mercy on us ! I seed un make a half-crown dance like mad in a sugar-basin, and nobody by.   More than that, he made port wine run under the ground fro' one pot to 'nother, and not a drop wasted.   Then he borrowed a real gold weddin' ring and fired it off with gunpowder; then he biled a egg in a sarcepan, and broke the egg, and took out of it a bird"—

" What ! biled ?" exclaimed a shrill, female voice.

"No! as raw and as live as any chicken; and who'd think it?—there was the ring 'bout bird's neck! Well, he gives the ring to the lady, and she looks at it, and puts it on her finger, and smiles at her husband sittin beside her, as much as to say, it's as right and as tight as ever."

" And did he do nothin' else?" asked one of the company.

" Nothin' else! If I was to tell 'ee what he did, ye'd all say I was the greatest liar on two legs," cried the narrator.

"No—no—no! Tell us," exclaimed half-a-dozen voices.

" Well, then,—but mind 'tis all true. A good while arter this — and you should ha' seen un make any card o' the pack come to him."

" Come to him," cried one of the listeners. " What! without touching it?"

" Without touching it? why, he laid the pack down—and walked away, and then whistled— phewgh!—just so; and may I die this minute, nay worse than that, may I never taste another drop o' ale, if the Jack of Clubs didn't jump out o' the pack, and follow un about the place for all the world like any dog."

" The Lord ha' mercy on his poor soul!" said a pitying female voice.

" Soul!" exclaimed one of the party—" he

ha'n't as much soul as ye could lay on a sixpence. Such folks never have. But go on—arter that?"

" Arter that, he brings out a—a bladder full of magic ; and, just as if he was askin' a neighbour to take a sup o' malt, he puts his hand on his breast, and begs to know if any lady or gen'lman would ha' a little ? He stood and stared at me ; but I gi' un sich a look, I could see it went right through his back-bone. Well, only to think o' the fools o' this world ! There was Shankton, the button-maker, near Northgate ; he goes up to un, and takes one bladder, and Bill Mousebite, the cheese-monger, that married his daughter, goes and takes t'other. Shankton sucks at the bladder, and then stands still and stares, and then he bursts out into a laugh, quite scandalous. There he stood, laughin' away, some folks cryin' shame on un, for he ha'n't buried his wife a month, and it warn't decent. Still he stands, laughin' like a cat. Well, Mousebite his son had sucked another bladder, and looked quite fierce to see his own father-in-law grinnin' there like any cow-boy through a collar; then Mousebite says nothin', but runs straight up to un, and gi's Shankton, wi' his double fist, sich a smash upon the nose, the blood spirted from it like water from a flower-pot ! Down falls Shankton like a bull,—but, would you believe it, wi' the blood pourin' into his open mouth, he kept grinnin' and rollin' with pleasure, whilst Mousebite, lookin' fiercer and fiercer, slid about, and worked his arms like a windmill, and knocked down six men that tried to hold un?"

"All the black art," said one of the hearers.

"Black enough for Mousebite; for no sooner does Shankton come to his senses, than he rubs his nose and looks quite penitent, and wants to gi' his son-in-law to a constable for the 'sault. Then the chap that conjured wanted to persuade un 'twas all the magic,—but Shankton buttons his coat in a passion, runs home, takes out his will—he had left every thing to Mousebite and his wife—flings it in fire, smokes sixteen pipes in his rage, and afore he goes to bed, orders his maid to dress and clean hersel' the first thing, for he'll marry her the next mornin'."

"But he didn't marry her?" cried a woman.

"No; 'cause why? he was ashamed when he woke to shew his nose to the parson. While it was gettin' well, he'd time to listen to sense; but for Mousebite — he's cut un off with a halfpenny."

"But warn't the blow all through the conjuror?" inquired a hearer.

"That's what they say to Shankton, but he won't believe it; he swears his son must ha' had his wits about un, or he wouldn't ha' hit so hard."

" Now, isn't it a shame, that the mayor lets men
like the conjuror ?"—observed one of the party, who
was abruptly stopt by the historian of the magician.

" Men !   He's not a man.   He's the devil himsel'—I'm sure o' it.   I could swear it : there's somethin' about un not like a common conjuror.   I
ha' seen 'em chew fire, and take pison at fairs—but
none like this chap : no, no,—there's a somethin'
about un, that—oh, yes ! its plain he's the devil
himsel', he's so much o' the gen'lman."

" Here, Deborah—another mug of ale," cried
one of the company, and the words of the speaker
went to the heart of John Applejohn, and warmed it.

John, though at first considerably alarmed, had
at length listened with more curiosity than fear,
becoming assured that the narrator of the works of
the wizard, dwelt upon the tricks of some wandering
mountebank endowed with greater cunning than his
brethren.   The words " a mug of ale" still trembled at John's heart-strings : he felt satisfied that for
money there was liquor to be had within ; and, as
rain began to fall, John Applejohn entered the
only habitable portion left by time and fate of the
Abbey of St. Augustine, and now made sacred by
the destinies to the sale of malt and hops !

John immediately found himself among the
company assembled in the ruin ; and, ere his ale
could be brought him, was tempted to conversation

by an elderly man, who, from his voice, John immediately recognized as the person who had so long and so eloquently descanted on the exploits of the conjuror. " 'Twill be a wet night, sir," said the man; and John replied that the rain had driven him into the house.

" Ha! that's the stuff against cold and wet, and wind," observed a lean, thin old man, with a sharp face and a bright eye; and he bustled about the fire, and rubbed his hands, as though, like John, he had just sought shelter from the night. " Deborah, girl," he cried, " a mug of ale; and mind, the abbot. I hope, sir," and the man approached John, and looked inquisitively at his liquor, " I hope, sir, as you're a stranger,"——

" I am a stranger," said John.

" I hope, sir, that you have the abbot there?" and the man pointed his fore-finger to John's mug. " Nothing less, as a stranger?"

" It's very good, sir," and John tasted the ale, and smacked his lips. " Very good."

" But not the abbot, I can see," said the old man, and to the surprise of John, he took away the mug, and calling Deborah, began with serious looks and in angry tones to take her to task for the slight put upon a stranger.

" The ale will do very well—very well, indeed, sir;" said John, putting out his hand for the mug.

" Excuse me, sir, as a citizen of Canterbury, I
have its reputation at heart, sir ; I cannot permit a
stranger to be deceived in his ale. Perhaps, you
will allow me, sir ? " and the man inclined the edge
of the mug to his mouth, as if awaiting the consent
of John to taste the liquor. Then instantly taking
a draught, and making a wry face, he seemed to
shudder, and gave the half-empty vessel to the
girl, telling her in an authoritative tone to take
it away, and not in future to impose upon a
stranger. The rest of the company remained silent,
eyeing Applejohn and his new and disinterested
friend.

" Ha ! this will do—ha ! ha ! this is the abbot,
sir," said the man, as he poured from the replenished mug of Applejohn. " Look, sir—look,"
—and the man held up the glass to the light—
" don't you see him, sir ?"

" The ale looks very bright," said Applejohn.

" But don't you see the abbot, sir ?—look ! There,
sir—look at his broad, bright, fat face ! I can see
every feature of him—his cheeks, nose, chin ; his
winking eyes, look !" and the man held the glass,
and gazed upon it, as though really rapt by the
vision of a fat monk. " Can't you see him in the
ale, sir ? What dimples the jolly old fellow has !
Ha ! ha ! look, how he shuts one eye and chuckles
at us."

Applejohn stared suspiciously at the man—was he a lunatic? "I—I can see nothing," said John, having stared at the ale, whilst unseen by him the visitors winked and nodded at each other. "Upon my life, sir, I can see nothing," and John put down his glass.

"Ha! sir, that's because you're a stranger to Canterbury. Notwithstanding, my service to you," and the man pledged him. "Perhaps, you never heard the story."

"Never. It must be something odd?" surmised Applejohn.

"Not so odd, as true, sir. Deborah, another mug of ale, for this gentleman. Sir, I have five minutes to spare, and I'll tell you the story."

"Has it a name, sir?" asked John. "What story?"

"It has a name, sir;" and the speaker, having softened his throat with another draught of ale, began the legend of—

"The Abbot of the Ale-cask.

"Many hundred years ago, the good king Ethelbert, moved by the pious prayers of the saintly Augustine, built him this monastery for the black monks. And in this very place they lived and revelled, prayed and drank, confessed and carved, until the stormy times of Henry the Eighth, who sent hither his commissioners to take an honest account of the revenue of the abbey, and then to turn the monks out of house and home. In Anno Domini 1539, their revenues were found to be one thousand, four hundred and thirteen pounds, four shillings—tell me, if I'm wrong, neighbour Stot," said the speaker to the man who had discoursed of the conjuror, and who nodded his willingness to assist the narrator should he stumble—"four shillings and eleven pence halfpenny."

"'Twas a close reckoning," said Applejohn.

"Sir, they were men of conscience, and didn't miss a farthing; men of conscience, sir—Deborah, fill again. They sent the monks packing, as in duty bound. Now, the abbot of that day was called Hilary, the Maltster; an excellent churchman, and a pious lover of good ale. It was a sight to behold his resignation when the officers came to drive him and his brethren hence. 'At least, my lord'—it was a lord, wasn't it, Stot, though I forget his name?"—Stot took his pipe from his mouth, and nodded—"'at least, my lord,' said the abbot, 'you will suffer us, if we must leave our darling abbey behind, at least you will permit us to carry away our ale?' And big tears ran down the abbot's cheeks as he looked in the unrelenting face of the commissioner; who not at all moved by the sorrows of the churchman, said, 'the devil a drop,' and the abbot and all the monks shuddered when his lordship swore.—' The devil a drop,' cried his lordship, and the wicked soldiery with their halberds drove the abbot and the brotherhood from the gates; and the good Hilary went beyond the seas, and died of a broken heart, brought on by small wine."

" Is it true, think ye?" asked Applejohn.

" There's more to come, sir. Deborah, another jug—more to come, sir; isn't there, Stot?" Stot nodded. " The body of the good Hilary—of Hilary the Maltster, lies at Cologne; they show you his tomb, sir, shaped like a hooped tankard, and curiously wreathed with hops cut in white marble. The tomb is shown in the church of—of—but that is no matter; the body of the abbot was buried at Cologne, but his unlaid ghost haunted the abbey of St. Augustine. Don't be alarmed, sir, but drink;" said the narrator, as Applejohn shifted on his seat, " drink, sir; for the abbot is the jolliest of spectres."

" And does the abbot still walk?" inquired John.

" Not if the ale be of the true quality—but, you shall hear, sir. I said, his spirit haunted the abbey: it is true. When Queen Elizabeth, on a progress, in the fifteenth year of her reign, slept up stairs"—

" Up stairs!" exclaimed Applejohn.

" That virgin sovereign did not close her eyes

for two nights: and what, sir—what think ye kept her gracious majesty wide awake?"

John considered a moment, and then answered —" Perhaps, the fleas."

" Sir, you're a wag," cried the story-teller, and hid his face in the mug, whilst the rest of the company laughed outright.   " No, sir; the affair was hushed up by the privy council, but the ghost of Hilary, the abbot, danced a saraband in the queen's chamber, with a hooped flaggon in his hand and a cask upon his head, crying aloud the while, ' hops !—your highness,—hops !' "

" Is it true, d'ye think?" again asked John.

" A maid of honour confessed the story on her death-bed.   Nay, more; when Charles the First and his bride Henrietta lay in the same chamber, the abbot wouldn't let 'em have a bit of quiet, but flourished his flaggon, and danced, and still shouted —' hops ! your blessed majesties,—hops !' "

" And did they ever get rid of the abbot, or does he still dance?" questioned the credulous Applejohn.

" At length, a brewer took the monastery—an honest man," answered the story-teller.   " 'Tis said, the first night his mash-tubs and his boilers were brought in, there was heard solemn chaunting at midnight in the vaults."

" But did the abbot never appear again—did he never more cry ' hops?' " asked John.

" He did — and would this very night, if the brewer gave him cause," said he of the legend.

" God bless me!" exclaimed Applejohn, " what cause?"

" Once, 'tis now ten years ago, there had been a great brewing, and either 'twas the dishonesty or the carelessness of the men, but the liquor was marvellously bad. Well, the poor brewer suffered for it; for, at midnight, in came the abbot, and this time with all his monks; and they dragged the poor brewer from his wife clean out of bed, beat him mercilessly with their flaggons, and screamed, and shouted, and hallooed 'hops! you rogue—hops! —hops!—hops!'"

" And—and what—what—when the abbot is pleased, does he appear then?" asked John.

" Then," answered the man, " then is he to be seen at midnight sitting astride a barrel of the best ale, with a full flaggon in his hand. Should the brewer appear, then does the abbot smile with benignant drunkenness upon him."

" And all this is true?" again inquired Applejohn.

" True as death; and, my friend," added the man very solemnly, " it teaches us this valuable moral."

" I don't see," said John—" what moral?"

" The moral is plain as your nose; and tells you,

if you would sleep soundly of nights,—never—never to stint your hops."

" What! is the gentleman gone?" said Applejohn, surprised at the sudden disappearance of the narrator.

" Yes; he always goes, when he's told that tale; and he always does tell it to a stranger," said Stot, grinning.

" A very entertaining man," said Applejohn.

" Aye," answered Stot, " very; and was once the most thrivin' cooper in Kent—a scholard, too; only, you see, he thought anything o' the barrel, but makin' it."

" Does he often come here?" inquired John.

" Yes; he commonly drops in, to look out for a visitor; but he do'n't always score so much for 'em as to-night."

" What's to pay?" asked Applejohn resignedly of Deborah, who on giving in the reckoning did not forget the accompt of the communicative cooper. " A very entertaining man," repeated John, as he discharged the joint bills. " Pray, gentlemen, as I'm quite a stranger here, which is the direct way to ——?" and John named the inn where his master sojourned.

" I'm going by the house; will be proud to show you," said a middle-aged man, who from his sleek, plain appearance, John took for a small trader. "Good night, gentlemen," said the man, immediately laying down his pipe, and taking his hat.

"Good night," said John, and he followed the civil stranger from the house. As he crossed the threshold, a volley of laughter burst from the company, whilst more than one of the party cried, "hops! you rogue—hops!—hops!"

"Very agreeable company frequent that house, sir," said our simple hero.

"The only really honest folks in Canterbury," replied his companion, and with the familiarity of an old friend, he took the arm of Applejohn, and walked with him to the door of his inn.

"Your master has been asking for you," said the waiter as Applejohn entered the house; and, without a moment's delay, John hurried to young Gruelthorpe.

"So! Mr. Applejohn," said Benjamin, "I find you have friends in Canterbury."

"Friends! sir—not that I know of," answered John. "Bless me!" and he looked round the apartment—"is the company gone, sir?"

"Oh! you'll see them again—no doubt. So, sir, I find you know this conjuror?"

"I—I have heard a good deal of his tricks, tonight. An extraordinary man, sir! I don't much believe in bargains of the sort—but—I hope there's

no understanding between him and Beelzebub,"
observed John, conceiving that his master alluded
to the magician of whose necromancy John himself had that night heard so much. " I hope not,"
repeated John.

" Perhaps, you've reason—no doubt, you have;
because the bargain may include some of his friends,
eh? You have doubtless good reason for your
wish."

" None in particular, sir; I only speak as a
Christian," said Applejohn.

" There, fellow," and Gruelthorpe flung five
sovereigns on the floor—" pick 'em up."

" Certainly, sir," replied the obedient domestic,
and immediately gathered the coin from the carpet,
and held the money towards his master.

" Take it for your wages, and"——

" I thank ye, sir," interrupted John, " they're
not due yet, and with your leave, I wouldn't draw
any beforehand."

" You're no longer my servant, fellow," said
Gruelthorpe.

" God bless me !" said Applejohn.

" I thought you an honest man, but——but now
I know your character—I've found you out."

As Gruelthorpe uttered these words, Applejohn
saw himself upon his knees, with the crooked nail
in his hand, and old Zweifler gnashing his teeth

above him. Yes—it was plain to John that some
enemy had recognized him, and informed Mr.
Gruelthorpe of the accident in the house of the
tailor, whence, a victim to his good intentions,
John had been thrust forth, a detected house-
breaker.

" Upon my soul, sir !" said John, almost bursting into tears, " what I did, sir, I did for the best;
don't, don't cast me off, sir, because of appearances,
sir; for, upon my soul and body, sir, I—I meant
well."

" Meant well !   Never tell me—'twas a regular
scheme of robbery," said Gruelthorpe.

" It wasn't, indeed — I know the crooked nail
was against me, but for all that"—

" Crooked nail ! I"—and as Gruelthorpe spoke,
new lights seemed to break upon him—" I shouldn't
wonder if in your time you've been tried for
burglary."

" No—never—never tried !   As I'm a living
sinner, and an honest man,—never tried !" exclaimed John.

" Well, well, you might have cost me more
money—the first loss is the best," said Gruelthorpe, with resignation.

" And have you, indeed, lost anything?" inquired Applejohn with real interest.

" Have I lost anything?   I think you took care

of that by the company you brought me. You say, sir, you know the conjuror who is here?"

" I heard of him to-night," said Applejohn, ingenuously.

" No doubt—no doubt," answered the sarcastic Gruelthorpe—" and do you recollect a few of his tricks ?"

" One, especially. I hear he can make the Jack of Clubs walk out of the pack, and follow him about the room like a dog," said John.

" Why, you impudent scoundrel !" shouted Gruelthorpe, " it isn't enough that you bring a mountebank here to rob me, but you must laugh at me afterwards. Begone, fellow."

" I bring a mountebank—I rob !" cried Applejohn, and he stared vacantly at his master. " A mountebank ! "

" I suppose you can read ?" asked the satirical Gruelthorpe.

" Write and cypher," answered the innocent Applejohn.

" Then read that—left by your friend ; the friend you brought me, that I mightn't feel lonely. Well, if ever I believe in a foolish face again !" and young Gruelthorpe flung himself upon the sofa. " Read, scoundrel ! if your blushes will let you ;" and John's master pointed to a piece of paper lying, with the cards, upon the table.

John took up the paper, and read as follows:—

"' SIGNOR SMUGGARD, ILLUSIONIST,
("' *From all the cities of Europe, and from London in
"' particular,*)
"' *Presents his profound and heartfelt respects to the nobility,
"' gentry, and public of*
"' THE ANCIENT CITY OF CANTERBURY,
"' *And begs to state that he will have the honour of exhibiting,
"' for three nights only, his hitherto*
"' UNRIVALLED TRICKS !'"

"D—n him!" exclaimed Gruelthorpe; "read on! I—I wonder at your audacity;" and the master stared at the self-possession of his innocent servant.

"'Unrivalled tricks,'" repeated Applejohn.

"Go on, sir!" roared Gruelthorpe—and John obeyed.

"' *He will pick the pocket of any gentleman of the company,
"' and he shall never know it.'*"

Gruelthorpe groaned, and rolled upon the sofa.

"Bless me! Ar'n't you well, sir?" asked John, approaching his master.

"Read on, sir!" bellowed Gruelthorpe.

"' *He will blow any lady's wedding ring into a million count-
"' less pieces, and afterwards*
"' TRIUMPHANTLY RESTORE THE FRAGMENTS!
"' *He will put the current half-crown of the realm into a
"' Glass Vase, and make it*
"' DANCE ITSELF INTO LITTLE SIXPENCES !

"' *He will tell any lady's thoughts!*
"' BUT,—
"' *Upon the honour of a gentleman,*
"' *Pledges himself that they shall be eternally buried with him,*
"' IF AT ALL IMPROPER!'

" No man could do less," said Applejohn.

" I wonder at your assurance," cried Gruelthorpe, " but go on."

"' *The Signor will call any card from the pack into his hand,*
"' *at any distance, and from anybody!'*"

" Oh! you scoundrel," exclaimed Gruelthorpe;
" but finish it."

"' SIGNOR SMUGCARD *might set forth a thousand illusions*
"' *performed by him; but it is trusted that it will be an*
"' *overwhelming testimony of his extraordinary*
"' *powers, when he states that his*
"' *Sleight of Hand and Tricks of Legerdemain*
"' *Have obtained for him the approbation of the best judges;*
"' *among whom he is proud to number*
"' ALL THE CROWNED HEADS OF EUROPE!
"' SIGNOR SMUGCARD *will administer the Laughing Gas to*
"' *the curious in risibility.*
"' *Lessons in Sleight of Hand and Tricks in general,*
"' *given by the Signor.*
"' *Gentlemen of the Church attended in private.*
"' N. B. No Dissenter need apply.'"

John, having finished a perusal of the bill, looked
wonderingly in the face of his master, " Has the
conjuror been here, sir?"

" Ere John had put the whole question, his master leapt from the couch——" Why," he exclaimed, " you——you brazen rascal !"

" What's the matter ? What have I done ?" asked John.

" Done ! didn't you bring that scoundrel and his accomplices here ?"

" You were alone and dull, sir, and wanted company, and I thought the foreign gentleman,"——

" Foreign gentleman ! a conjuror from Shoreditch !——Look there !" and Gruelthorpe pointed to a pack of cards scattered about the floor.

" What ! did he get you to play at cards, sir ?" inquired John.

" A little loo—only a little loo," muttered Gruelthorpe, biting his fingers.

" Loo ! What ! loo with a conjuror, if he is the conjuror ? but I took him for a count at least. Loo with him ? Why, sir, you see he can bring any card from the pack. Play at loo with a man who can make the Jack of Clubs follow him like a dog ? Play at"——

How far John might have proceeded in his oblique censure of his master we cannot say, but at this moment he was stopped in the current of his speech by Gruelthorpe, who suddenly caught him by the shoulders, swung him round, and thrust him out at the door.

" There must be something wrong," thought
John, " perhaps, he has lost a large sum of money`;
still, when his passion is over, he can't blame me——
no, that's impossible : because, whatever has happened, I did all for the best. However badly
things may have fallen out, I meant well," and
with this barren consolation John crept to his
room, resolving not again to appear before his
master until summoned. " He'll forget it in the
morning," was the belief of John, who, having
waited up until midnight went, tranquil in his sense
of innocence to bed.

Long ere John was wrapt in sleep, his unforgiving
master was travelling post to Dover.

We, however, should do injustice to the generous
spirit of Signor Smugcard, if we concluded this
chapter without registering his act of courtesy towards Gruelthorpe. That gentleman had in the
best possible temper lost a hundred and fifty pounds
to the signor and his friends, and was still in ignorance of the professional abilities of his antagonists.

" There, I think that will do, gentlemen," said
Gruelthorpe, flinging down the cards.

" You vill play not no more at all ?" asked the
Signor, with truly a winning smile.

" No——not to-night; I don't care much for cards,
but they help over a dull hour," remarked Benjamin.

" You are tout certain, varie quite sure you will play not no more?" inquired the signor for the second time.

" No—no—another time, should we meet, I may be very happy."

" Ha! sare," and the signor heaved a sigh, and looked with melting eyes upon Benjamin Gruelthorpe—" dis vorld is so fool, so entire fool of tings dat are no sure, maybe we sall nayvere meet agane."

" May be," said Benjamin, with proper resignation.

" In dat case, are you tout certain, varie quite sure you will play not no more?" asked the signor for the third time.

" Not to-night," said Gruelthorpe firmly, " not to-night."

" Den, sare, I vish you much good-night; I have been much delight vid your company; and I should tink varie littel of meself, if I did not offer you a place for my illusi-ons."

" Illusions!" exclaimed Gruelthorpe. " What illusions?"

" Gobye," said the signor, " give an annonce—a bill"—and Mr. Gobye took a roll of at least two hundred of those documents from his coat-pocket, and carefully blowing the edges to separate them, put into the hand of Gruelthorpe a bill of entertain-

ment, of which we have already given a copy.   At
the same moment, Signor Smugcard approached
Gruelthorpe, and bowing low, presented him with
two free tickets for the exhibition, saying—"One
for yourself—and one for ladie."   The tickets delivered into the paralyzed hand of Gruelthorpe,
the Signor Smugcard walked across the carpet to
the door as if he trod upon the thinnest sheet of
ice, and then, making his lowest bow, disappeared,
followed by his companions—for he disavowed all
accessaries—Gobye and Tipit.

Benjamin Gruelthorpe glanced at the bill, and
then at the tickets—he had played at loo with a
conjuror !   He rang the bell with his best violence,
and inquired for his servant.   At that moment
John Applejohn entered the house, and in a few
seconds stood in the presence of his enraged master,
when the scene we have already described, was
acted between them.

CHAPTER XI.

" DEPEND upon it, there must be some mistake,"
said Applejohn in the morning, when informed of
the departure of his master by the waiter.   " He
can't have left me behind."

" That's for you to settle with yourself—here, it
seems, you are," said the waiter.

" I did all for the best," said John, " I meant well—time will show, I meant well;" and thus, satisfied with his good intentions, John sat down to breakfast. " If I starve for it, I can't help it," talked John to himself, cutting at a large flank of beef; " I meant well—and good intentions"—here John buttered his roll inch-thick,—" good intentions will sweeten dry bread."

" I suppose, my man, your master will give you a character?" asked the waiter of John, whilst yet at his breakfast.

" He couldn't do less," said our hero, " I've done nothing wrong—I wasn't to tell a conjuror from another man—I meant well."

" There's a gentleman put up here last night from Dover; he's been speaking to master; he wants a servant."

" Tell him I'll be with him in a minute," said the simple John, swallowing his tea. " And now," and John rose from the table, " where is he?"

After some words with the landlord, upon whom the simplicity of our hero had a very favourable effect, John was ordered to hold himself in readiness for an audience of the gentleman in need of a lackey. Two hours elapsed and then John was summoned to the presence.

" The gentleman was a thin, tall, sallow young man, with a sharp face buried in a profusion of

black hair, whilst his cheeks and throat were f
bandaged with whiskers. He was in a morn
gown of bright blue damask, tied about the g
with gold cords, enriched with heavy tassels of
same material. His shirt collar was thrown b
and in his whole air and manner there was to
something inexpressibly impressive and elegan

" Oh ! ha !" said the gentleman, and he pi
his teeth and looked at our hero.

" I—I've understood, sir, that you—you w,
servant," ventured John.

" Well? what then ?" drawled the man in
damask gown.

" I—I want a master," said Applejohn.

" Humph ! ha ! How long have you been
the crows ?" asked the young gentleman.

" I never lived in a family of that name,
swered the ingenuous John.

" Ha ! ha !" and the young gentleman lau
small as through a quill. " I meant, have you
long from the clods—from the fields ?"

" I'm not London born," said John. " I
last with Mr. Benjamin Gruelthorpe."

" The Gruelthorpes of Cornwall — the
copper-men ? — No ? Then I don't know
What can you do ?"

" Whatever you please, sir," replied the
Applejohn.

" Well—ha !—yes—you may follow me to London. I hav'n't time just now to look into your character—and by the way, I think character altogether a d—d imposition. I suppose any rascal can get one for half-a-crown? Eh ?"

" I don't know the price, sir—I never went to market," said John.

" Oh, yes—yes; as for character, any scoundrel can give a brother scoundrel a lift. I had a fellow, a groom, Mr. Rummer," and the young gentleman addressed the landlord, who had introduced John, " yes, a groom; well, he had a character signed I do believe by half the bench of bishops: would you believe it,—the fellow broke open my dressing-case, stole five hundred pounds in banknotes, besides a miniature set with the superbest diamonds ?"

" Dear me ! sir," said Mr. Rummer, " a very heavy loss."

" Oh ! d—n the money; 'twas the miniature that —by the way, Mr. Rummer, you remember that separation in high life ?"

" I—I think I "—stammered Rummer.

" Oh yes! you must recollect it; all brought on by that confounded miniature; the thief was taken, the portrait was recognised, the exposure was inevitable; there was a meeting of the families, and —ah ! poor thing, she's now in Wales."

" And didn't you punish the thief, sir ?" inqu
the landlord—" didn't you make an example ?

" D—n examples ! There again 's the gre
mistake—as if any body was ever the better fo
ample ! Though certainly, I think I should
had the fellow hanged, only as the affair happ
just before I started for the county,"—

" Started for the county !   I hope you
ceeded ?" said the landlord.

" No, Mr. Rummer, no ; bribery and thr
sir ; bribery and threats. I lost the election,
so you see I might as well have hanged
scoundrel after all."

" It was very liberal of you."

" D—n liberality !" said the fine young ma
" in fact, Mr. Rummer, d—n every thing."

" To be sure, sir," assented Mr. Rummer.

" Servants," exclaimed the young gentle
fixing his eyes upon Applejohn, " are the gre
villains that ever chewed. I've been ruine
'em, Mr. Rummer ; that is, if I could have i
ruined. You recollect that I was about t
married to Lady Barbara ?"

" I—I—oh, yes ! I heard something of it,"
the obliging landlord.

" Something of it ! Settlement and every t
signed. Well, I had written a little poem ;
afraid it has somehow or the other got into p

—it's a trifle. I flung it off at the opera, standing
one night in Fop's Alley, looking at Lady Barbara
opposite; we'd had a little tiff that morning. I
dare say, you never met with the poem? it begins—
tut! I never—no I never can remember my own
lines. Yes, I have it—it begins—

> ' Fare thee well, and if for ever,
> Still for ever fare thee well.'

"I think, sir, I can show you where those lines
are in print," said the well-meaning Applejohn.

"When I need you for my librarian, I'll inform
you," said the young gentleman, darting a withering look at John.

"But about Lady Barbara, sir?" said Mr.
Rummer, who appeared to pay the greatest deference to his guest.

"Well, lovers' quarrels, you know, Mr. Rummer,
—there's a proverb, I forget it, about 'em. Lady
Barbara insisted upon my writing the lines in her
album—d—n writing! and oh!"—and here the
young gentleman raised his voice, and spoke with
considerable fervour—"and oh! particularly d—n
all albums!"

"My daughter has one," said Mr. Rummer.

"So had Betty, our housemaid," observed
Applejohn; who, but for his modesty, might have
stated that he had himself, ere his expulsion from
the house of Mr. Zweifler, contributed to it.

The young gentleman vented another look uṕ
John, and then proceeded—"Lady Barbara
sisted ; I gave the album to my other scoundreḷ
a servant to take to my hotel. The ruffian w
to some low pot-house ; was, for the basest p
poses, made infamously drunk, and the album
Lady Barbara—a volume which the greatest naṛ
of Europe adorned, a book in which the greaṭ
authors had writ, in which the finest painters, ṇ
in which my dear friend, Mr. Dolce "—

"Does he know Mr. Dolce ? " asked John
himself, and again he thought of the crooked ṇ

"You have heard of Mr. Dolce, the artist,
Rummer ?" asked the young gentleman.

"His name hasn't yet travelled into these parṭ
said the innkeeper.

"Wonderful artist ! has the best cut coat
London ; " said the young gentleman, "extraoṛ
nary genius—paints ' beauties ' by the score, and
to the life—more than that, wears diamond stụ
Well, even my friend Dolce—but you surprị
me ! not heard of Dolce—not seen his grẹ
work—' Portraits of the Lap-dogs of Spinsters
Quality ?'—no matter, even my friend Dolce ḥ
painted a ' beauty ' in Lady Barbara's album,—wọ
my ruffian of a servant—d—n all servants !—ḷ
the book at the pot-house, while he himself v
brought to my hotel in a beastly state of inebrietỵ

" The fault of his stomach, perhaps ? " suggested the charitable Applejohn.

Again the young gentleman frowned. " But what became of the book ? " asked the landlord.

" Unfortunately," said the man in damask, " Lady Barbara's name was in it—well, the next day 'twas sent to her mansion, contributed to by all the atrocious miscreants, the hackney-coachmen and link-boys, the previous night assembled at the Bag o' Nails. To be brief, Mr. Rummer ; her lady mother, the Duchess—and by the way, that excellent woman had the strangest questions put to her by the new contributors to the album—forbade me the house, and—and it's a long story, but—oh! d—n all servants ! and certainly d—n all albums ! "

" I hope, sir," said Applejohn, " if you think well enough of me to give me a trial, I shall be found honest and diligent ? One thing, I will answer for, sir ; you may be always sure that I shall mean well."

" I think you may venture upon him, sir," said the landlord, resolved to assist John.

" Well, you may come with me to London—d—n London !—must go back to it, though—ha ! Paris is the only place for a gentleman. Well," and the hero in damask stared at John, " as Mr. Rummer seems your friend, you may consider yourself my animal."

G 3

" Thank you, sir. You shall find me everyth
you wish — thank you, sir," and the deligh
Applejohn bowed himself from the apartment,
lowed by the landlord. " Pray, what's my masl
name?" asked John.

" Cramlington," answered Mr. Rummer, "
an excellent customer of mine, and so I keep frie
with him—that is, I listen to him.   I believe
sees the first company in town.   You're in h
I can tell you."

To say the truth, John was in no way displea
at the turn of accidents which had prevented
expatriation.   In quitting England, he felt tha
should have left Sarah Twopenny for ever—retu
ing to London. hope whispered him that the r
take under which he had suffered might be clea
up—that he who was the most temperate of
sons of men would not continue to carry about v
him the punishment of a drunkard, that—tha
and then the incident of the crooked nail m
him despair anew.

The next day, John attended his master to to
Mr. Cramlington rented chambers in, it is eno
to say, the most fashionable part of the metrope
The duties of John were particularly easy, i
much as he was left to himself the greater par
the day, his master generally quitting home ea
in the morning, and not returning until the ev

ing, when he usually dressed for a dinner-party or the opera. Mr. Cramlington was really an eccentric person. In the morning he quitted his chambers attired in the sober suit of a merchant; gold chains, rings, brooches, all set aside; nay, his superb head of black hair, together with his voluminous jetty whiskers, reposed upon his dressing-table until night, their owner sallying forth in a light, natural crop, with his cheeks as bare as his palm. No two persons could be more dissimilar than Henry Cramlington in the morning, and Henry Cramlington at night.

" The fact is, you see, John," said Cramlington, " I wore this wig and these whiskers for a frolic at a masquerade ; and, as there I happened to fascinate a certain lady, who may one day be your mistress, John, I am fearful that a change to a state of nature on my part, might injure me in her good opinion."

John felt particularly flattered by this proof of his master's confidence ; and therefore ventured to observe that he thought Mr. Cramlington's fears entirely groundless.

" No—no—John ; I know more of these things than you can possibly do : I shall keep the secret until I'm married."

" Why, sir," said the conscientious Applejohn, " you'd never enter into the holy state of matrimony under false appearances ? Lead a woman with sham hair and whiskers to the altar, and she not know it ! Pardon me, sir, but I don't like deceit in wedlock."

" Pooh ! pooh ! it's done every day, John. I wouldn't divulge before marriage for the world," said Cramlington, with emphasis.

" I think, sir—I must say it—providing that the lady really and truly loves you, I think you wrong your other good gifts, sir, to rely too much upon the wig and whiskers."

" Not at all : you know nothing about it, John ; d—n me ! you have no notion of the women who have fallen victims to the curling-irons."

" Well, sir, to be sure," and John scarcely suppressed a sigh as he thought of Sarah Twopenny, " to be sure, they are strange animals. One doesn't know what will please 'em. And yet, sir, I must say it—it's too bad to use deceit, when nature's made us the strongest."

" Strongest ! Why, we're fools to 'em—babies— nincompoops—d—n me !" said Cramlington.

" You don't say it, sir ?" cried Applejohn. " What ! all women ?—All ?"

" All. They all love—d—n me !—to cheat, trick, and perplex us. Ha ! that sentiment brings to my recollection a poem I once wrote upon the sex. There were two rather good lines in it—let

me see—d—n it ! never can recollect my own
poetry. Now, I have it :—

> ' Some men to bus'ness—some to pleasure take,
> But ev'ry woman is at heart a rake.' "

" That's hitting 'em hard, sir," said Cramlington's compassionate valet.

" Hang 'em !" cried the merciless poet, " we
can't hit 'em too hard."

" And yet, sir, abuse 'em as we may," said
Applejohn, " for all their tricks, sir, there's a time
when there's nothing like 'em. When sickness
comes, sir, or trouble, or"——

" Very true, John ; I hope I'm not insensible to
the good they have. No ! though I have, in my
time, told the baggages some hard truths, I trust,
as I've shown in another poem——I wrote it after a
fever brought on by pine-apples——I trust, as I've
said in that little poem, I"——

" What did you say, sir——if I may be so bold,
sir—what ?" asked John impatiently.

" No matter——I've quite forgot it : I never can
remember my own lines ; other men's verse sticks
to my brains like birdlime, but I never—d—n
me !—can remember my own. Yes—now I apprehend ; my poem begins somehow as follows—

> ' Oh ! woman, in our hours of ease,
> Uncertain, coy, and hard to please ;

> But when pale sickness wrings the brow,
> A ministering angel thou !' "

" Beautiful !" cried John—" beautiful !"

" There's a good deal more of it," observed Cramlington, " but I've told you, I never—d—n me !—can remember my own lines."

From the foregoing dialogue the reader must be aware of the courteous familiarity extended by the master to the man.   Indeed, there was scarcely a day, that Cramlington would not, for the especial delight and improvement of his servant, illustrate the most common topic by short quotations from long poems, written by the speaker, as he would sigh and say, " in happier hours."   Nay, such an opinion had Cramlington of the natural taste of Applejohn, that he would condescend to sing to him *Vivi tu*, and then gather the judgment of his valet on the performance.

" That's precisely," Cramlington would say, when he had howled the melody, " that's precisely as my friend Ivanoff does it."

" And does he get money by it ?" asked Applejohn wonderingly.

" Money ! thousands," said Cramlington. " Money ! D—n me !"

" God bless me !" said Applejohn ; " well, lottery luck is nothing to the luck of some people."

" All men have luck, John, if they have but sense

enough to make use of it. Egad! that reminds me of a sentiment, tolerably expressed I think in a little sketchy drama I once wrote."

" What! a play, sir?" asked John.

" Yes—but I never would consent to have it acted. The lines are, I think—yes, they run thus:—

> ' There is a tide in the affairs of men,
>   Which taken at the flood leads on to fortune.'

I forget the rest—but 'twas all in the same strain, only a good deal better."

One morning, Mr. Cramlington was more than usually familiar with his domestic. As he sat late at breakfast—he had been at four different parties the previous evening, and had not returned home until daylight—he astonished and gratified John by narrating the many conquests he had made within the last eighteen hours: never did master paint himself so great a hero to his valet.

" But, hang it! it's no use, John—I feel my time is come," said the victorious Cramlington. " Quite sure—d—n me!"

" La! sir," said the simple Applejohn, " I never saw you look better."

" He! he! I mean—plague on't! why wasn't I born a Turk?—I can only marry one, and—but what I was about to say, John, is this; as I may leave town at five minutes' notice, have every thing in readiness for my journey."

"Certainly, sir. Shall you go far?" asked John.

"To Scotland, of course," said Cramlington. "Scotland,—d—n me!"

"May I be so bold as to ask, sir—is it pressing business, sir?" inquired John very respectfully.

"Business and pleasure combined," replied the master, "I—I run off with an heiress, John,—d—n me!"

"Run off? What! relations won't consent, sir?"

"Sha'n't ask 'em—sha'n't ask 'em, John; there's always some difficulty—d—n me!—with relations; as I said in one of my early poems,—

> 'The course of true love never did run smooth.'"

"You never said a truer thing, sir," remarked Applejohn, heaving a deep sigh. "I don't know how it is, sir, but we no sooner love anything, or get anything to love us, than something always happens."

"Hallo! John,—d—n me!—you've been reading my new manuscript poem—I didn't know I had left it about."

"Not I, indeed, sir," asseverated John, "I wouldn't be guilty of such a thing, sir."

"Oh! I'm not angry; but you must have read it—for I have the very same thought, rather prettily turned too. As I only put it to paper last week, I recollect it very well. It begins—

    ' I never reared a young gazelle,' "

" What's a gazelle, sir ?" asked John.

" A *specious* of goat, John," answered Cramlington, and proceeded—

    " ' I never reared a young gazelle,
      To glad me 'with its soft black eye,
      But when it knew and loved me well,
        Was sure to die.' "

" It always happened to my father with his bulfinches, sir," said Applejohn, " the best piper was always the shortest liver."

" Too often the fate of us young poets, d—n me !" cried Cramlington. " However, help me to dress, John—for I've much to do abroad ; and mind, in case I may want them, have my trunks ready at a minute's notice."

Mr. Cramlington was assisted by his valet into his sober suit, and in his own light hair and with his natural, naked cheeks, sallied from his chambers, secure in his present appearance from recognition by any of the five hundred individuals among whom he the last night lounged and tittered. " I shall be home at seven to dress, John," were the departing words of the master.

" He's a very agreeable man, and then, so very

clever," thought John, "who'd have thought he could do such pretty verses?" And Applejohn, musing on the many virtues and talents of his master, set himself to arrange the sumptuous decorations for the night. In this important pursuit, the raven wig and whiskers of the beau Cramlington fell into the hands of Applejohn, who thereupon began to reflect on the uncertain and curious dispositions of the sex, thinking many deep things, too deep we presume, for expression; for with the wig and whiskers in his hand, he looked as gravely as Hamlet gazing on the skull, yet said nothing. John turned his head, and saw his features in a glass: we know not what process of thought tempted him to the trial, or whether indeed he thought at all of the matter, but in a second he had placed the wig upon his head, the whiskers at his cheeks, and stood and gazed in the mirror an altered man. He was so changed, his dearest creditor, had he had one, would not have known him.

John sat in his master's easy chair, and with his head in his hand, first fell into profound meditation, and then sank into deep sleep. He had for three nights sat up late for Mr. Cramlington, and was worn with the service. John had sweetly snored away an hour, when he was awakened by a loud knocking at the chamber door. Forgetful of the borrowed wig and whiskers, John yawned, stretched himself, and slowly rose to attend the summons. He opened the door, and almost fell prostrate when he beheld the terrible countenance of his late master, Karl Zweifler, the tailor.   The old man, without the slightest ceremony, walked into the centre of the apartment, and turning himself round, surveyed at his leisure the appointments about him.   John, tongue-tied with fear and shame, spoke not a syllable.

"Vere is your master, eh?" asked old Zweifler.

"Out," answered John, "quite out, sir."

The tailor turned fiercely round upon John, and exclaiming "teef," "liar," stalked into the bed-chamber of Mr. Cramlington; having opened the bed-curtains, and looked in every corner of the apartment, Zweifler grinned in the face of John, and said—"You vill please to tell me de name of de pig villain."

"The name of my master, sir?" inquired John; and the old man grunted an affirmative.   "Cramlington, sir."

"Oh! mein Gott!" groaned old Zweifler, "Gramlindon!"

"No, sir; Cramlington," was the correction of John; "Cramlington."

"Damn villain!" shouted old Zweifler, "I said Gramlindon. Now, you will blease to write me dat ubon a pit of baper—write me down de name of dat teef your master—write Gramlindon."

"I write it, sir!—I—the truth is, sir," and John was about to excuse himself, when old Zweifler seized him by the collar; again did the knuckles of the tailor, fixed in John's jugular, send an indescribable coldness to his heart. John resigned himself to the old man, who led him to a table, whereon lay pen, ink, and paper. "If you blease," said Zweifler, presenting the pen to John, and addressing him with the most ferocious politeness, "if you blease, you damn villain, to write de name of dat pig teef, your master. Gramlindon! Mein Gott!—Gramlindon," the old man ejaculated in astonishment and horror. "Write," he bellowed, and in his best round hand, considering the circumstances of intimidation, John penned "Cramlington."

The old man took up the paper, and gnashing his teeth, shouted—"Mein Gott! it is Gramlindon."

At this moment, a smart, quick knock was heard at the door, and the old man threw his hands above his head, and roared "Ha! ha! berhaps dis is Gramlindon. Open—you teef, open," he exclaimed to John, who mutely obeyed the order, when a man in a rough coat and low glazed hat, walked in.

"All right, isn't it," asked the man, "Mister Cramlington's?"

" Yes," answered John, and " quite right," said old Zweifler, making a great effort to maintain his composure.

" Have you any business with my master ?" asked John.

" I believe you—I've brought him a reg'lar jewel," said the man, and he seated himself with an air of conscious importance.

" He puys jewels !" exclaimed Zweifler, with a groan. " Berhaps, diamonds. Is it baid for ?" he inquired of the new-comer.

" That's not my affair," said the man, " but I should think my master knows his customer or he wouldn't trust him with such an article. Old fellow," and the stranger addressed himself to John, " have you anything to drink ?"

" Nothing," said John.

" Worse than an uninhabited island, for all it's so fine then," observed the man, looking round the room.

" But what have you brought my master ?" asked John, old Zweifler staring silently at the new-comer.

" 'Tisn't to be matched in all the town, I can tell ye, old chap," replied the man, " if it is, my name's not Bub. I say, your master's going to be married, isn't he ?"—Zweifler groaned—" what's the matter, old un ?"

" But is that your business ?" inquired John,

" what can you have to do with my master's marriage ?"

" You wouldn't ask that, if you know'd what was in my pocket," replied Mr. Bub, with a nod and a wink.

" Berhaps," said Zweifler, trying hard to be polite, " berhaps, sir, it's the marriage zettlement?"

" I should think so ; 'nough to bind any woman to a man for life; I tell 'ee, there isn't the fellow to't in the wide world; and I ought to know something, for I've been in the trade since I could stand upon one leg," asserted Mr. Bub. " Yes, I'm sure when gen'lmen does as Mr. Cramlington does, they means marriage downright, and no inweigling. She's such a beautiful creature ! "

" Is she ?" asked Zweifler, " you're sure, eh ?— beautiful ? "

" Beautiful ! your whiskers black as they are," said Bub, slapping John on the shoulder, " your whiskers"—

" My whiskers !" exclaimed John, and catching his features in the glass, he saw his master's property upon his own face, and felt deep gratitude for the accident that had disguised him from the eyes of old Zweifler.

" Black as they are, your whiskers are white to her," said Bub.

" Black !" exclaimed Zweifler.

" And ears," said Mr. Bub, measuring about eight inches from his fingers, " ears that long."

" Mein Gott !" said Zweifler. " Where does she come from ? "

" Purest breed in the world; takes the water like a duck," avowed Bub, " they say, came first from Spain."

" Mein friend," exclaimed Zweifler, " you are a teef—a damn teef."

" Did a little once in that way when young, and not ashamed to own it," said the ingenuous Bub, " but we don't call it stealing, we don't : to pick a pocket's a robbery if you like ; but to steal a dog is only too much humanity for animals."

" A dog ! what—what do you mean ? " exclaimed Applejohn.

" Mean ! why, look there ; that's what I mean," and Mr. Bub, with a triumphant countenance, drew from his coat-pocket a very diminutive and very beautiful jet-black spaniel bitch. " There— look at 'em," he cried, and displayed the peculiar attractions of the animal, that like certain other animals owed much of its good fortune to the length of its ears. " Worth fifty pounds apiece, the ears alone," said Mr. Bub.

" You seem to make very much of the beast." remarked Applejohn.

" Make much ? Why, there's repitation, for all

trades," answered Mr. Bub, " I tell 'ee I'm almost as fond of that little spannel bitch, as if she was my own flesh and blood."

" Gott forgive ye," cried old Zweifler, "you damn teef !"

" La ! bless your heart, if you was to see what I see with these little things and them as owns 'em, you'd think something better of your fellow creatures for their kindness. Why, there's many an old lady as I know, as treats her dogs and her birds as if they was the best of her."

" Oh lord !" groaned Zweifler.

" Bless you ! I can feel all their pulses through their animals," said Mr. Bub. " You see, they comes to the gardens," by this, it was evident that the speaker was attached to some great menagerie, " they comes to the gardens, and sometimes they just gives me a nod and nothing more, and then I know all's well at home. But when a dowager comes smiling up to me, and says ' Good day, Mr. Bub,' why then ' Oh, oh !' I cries to myself, for I know right well her spannel's caught the 'stemper, or parrot's got the pip. Bless your hearts ! people in our line o' life see a good deal o' human nature," said Mr. Bub.

" And very odd parts of it, too," said Applejohn, interested by the manner and matter of the speaker.

"I believe ye," said Bub, "animals, the lower animals, as we people of science call 'em, does away with all distinctions. For instance, when a duke takes to stuffing,"——

"What do you mean by stuffing?" asked Applejohn.

"Stuffing skins of birds and beasts," said Bub, "to make 'em look like life; why then, in that case, he's no more than a common man. There's two or three dukes of my acquaintance think they knows a good deal of stuffing—that's what I call the practical science of the matter,—they knows nothing about it, though sometimes I humour 'em."

"You find it to your advantage, no doubt," observed John.

"Yes; it tells in for a man better than always speaking the dry truth: but sometimes I can't help having a fling. Why, there's the duke of ——, but I won't mention his name, 'cause I promised him I wouldn't; well, I went on an invite to his place to see a sick ostrich of his; a carpenter had left his basket of tools in the way, and there was a hammer and six chisels missing, and the bird getting melancholy, suspicions fell upon him. Well, to make short, we recovered the tools and the ostrich too. But I was going to say, that his grace takes me all round his museum—*his* museum, after our's!——and, proud as a peacock with two tails, he would show me all the birds stuffed and set up with his own hands. In a man's own house, you know, its only polite to humour him a bit; so whenever he asked, ' What do you think o' that flamingo, Mr. Bub ?' I says ' Very well stuffed, your grace ;' and ' What do you think of that Solon goose, Mr. Bub ?' I answers, ' You stuff a goose better than any man in the kingdom, my lord duke ;' and so on, he being as I could see, mightily tickled with my good word. Well, we went round fifty specimens, and as he was only a duke, and not a bird-stuffer by birth, I did all I could to encourage him——why should we feel envy of any body ? However, one can't always go against one's conscience ; so when we had been nearly all round the museum, his grace stops suddenly before a bird——did you ever see a cockatoo ?"

" Yes," answered Applejohn. " Well, his grace stops ? "

" His grace stops, and looking hard at me, he says, ' There, Mr. Bub——I think that's nature itself. It looks alive——hopping on the twig, eh, Mr. Bub ?' Now, I'd do anything for his grace, but I saw he was getting too conceited. It was no more like the shape or action of a cockatoo, than——however, I looks at the bird, and I shakes my head. ' What !' says his grace, ' what's the matter ?' Then I looks very steadily at him, and I says, 'My lord duke, you'll pardon what I'm going to say?' and he says 'Certainly.' 'Well then, my lord duke,' says I, 'don't you in the house of lords—you'll forgive me what I'm going to say—don't you in the house of lords sometimes vote by proxy?' 'I do,' says the duke. 'Then, your grace,' says I, 'for the time to come, I'd advise you to stuff cockatoos in the same manner."

" That was bold of you," observed Applejohn.

" I know it; but in the cause of science we must risk a little. However, the duke took my advice seriously to heart, for I'm told that his grace has never touched a bird of that sort since. Geese and so on may be stuffed by bunglers, that is ammatours, but parrots and cockatoos is very different things. I assure you, it's enough to do to protect the interests of science. Isn't it a horrid thing that people as ought to know better won't let a lion go for a lion, and a bear for a bear, but they want to mix 'em up with things that don't belong to em?" asked Mr. Bub.

" What do you mean?" inquired Applejohn. " Mix 'em up?"

" Yes; with music. Some of the 'fellows' of our society want to have a military band, like Mr. Polito, in Smithfield. Do you call that science? When science has a real lion, what does it want with cymbals? Isn't it enough to make an

H 2

elephant blush to the tusks to be puffed off with pandæans ?"

"It must hurt its consequence," said John.

"Consequence! hurt it!" exclaimed Bub, "I should only just like to see 'em try to do it if I was an elephant."

"But, mein freind," said Zweifler, who had for some minutes employed himself in the minute inspection of the costly articles to be found in the chamber, "mein freind—how much vill dat damn buppy cost?"

"Cheap at eighty guineas, sir; cheap at"—Mr. Bub was suddenly interrupted by the violence of the old man; for he gave utterance to a yell—raised his arms—clenched his fists at the unconscious spaniel, and, incapable of words, rushed from the place. Mr. Bub, after a moment's pause, indulged himself with a long whistle.

"He doesn't know what he's about," cried Applejohn, considerably relieved by Zweifler's disappearance; "the fact is, I—I think he's my master's tailor."

"That's enough," observed the sagacious Bub; "no wonder, poor gentleman, that it makes him mad to see so much money wasted upon puppies, when he, perhaps, gets so little, eh?"

"But do you really think the dog will cost eighty guineas?" inquired John.

"I know that Lady Lucina—ah! she's dead now, she was the woman for science—although her ladyship was one of the oldest fellows,"——

"Her ladyship, a fellow!" exclaimed Applejohn.

"A fellow of our society—she paid eighty-five for a spannel with a tail that had nothing of the promise of a tail about it that this has. Ha! she was the woman for science. She took as much interest in the monkies as if they was her own family. I may say, she quite lived in the Gardens. There wasn't a Muscovy duck hatched that she didn't book it; kept the young emews' birth-days; and when the first kangaroo was born, why, in honour of science, she give a grand dinner-party to all the fellows. She *was* a woman."

"And dead, eh?" said John."

"Caught her death, watching the sick lion without clogs last hard winter: I give her a hint what would happen, but there was no getting her from the den; she insisted, as she said, upon seeing the last of what she called 'the lordly brute.' Terrible thing, to think how our lions do die: you'd not think it," said Mr. Bub, "but he's a wonderful lion that lasts above a season."

"What is it that takes them off?" asked Applejohn.

"Why, some of our fellows will have it, it's the clay—some, the water; Muzzle, one of the keepers, has an opinion of his own—he swears it's because among the fellows there's such a mob of attornies."

" I can't see how attornies should destroy lions," observed the enlightened Applejohn.

" Why, nor I neither," said Bub, " only you see, some people have great faith in what's called animal magnetism. After all, her ladyship was the woman for science. Do you know," continued Mr. Bub, with increasing melancholy, " of all the folks that come to the Gardens,—and I forget the millions of shillings that we took last summer—of all of 'em, there isn't one in a thousand that comes out of the real love of the thing?"

" Isn't there, indeed?" said the astonished John, " what do they come for, then?"

" I could make your head look like a porkipine to tell you," answered Bub. " Science! bless your soul, they leaves all thoughts of it behind 'em—that is providing they bring out any—with their walking-sticks and parasols at the gate. Science! Bless your heart, sometimes it's matrimony!" exclaimed Bub; " and I've marked, that thèy that come to talk over love and marrying, commonly buy a catalogue to hide what they call their motives."

" Is it possible?" asked Applejohn, with all his simplicity, " Can it really be possible?"

" It's a melancholy fact," answered Bub. " Only yesterday I saw a couple, and I thought by their looks, there really was a love of science in 'em. They was standing just by the Brahmin bull with the catalogue open. I had to walk by 'em, and what do you think I heard? No doubt, you'd suppose they were reading all the particulars about that noble animal?"

" Why, what else?" inquired John.

" The old story; not a bit of science, but all matrimony. I heard the words ' po-shay' and ' consider my pa,' and I was quite savage."

" Why should you be——not an enemy to matrimony, I hope?" said Applejohn.

" By no means," replied Bub, " specially to the matrimony of other people—but marrying is one thing and pure science is another; I wouldn't have the one made the cover to the other; I wouldn't have 'em mixed. You'd think now, I suppose, that when the giraffes first come, it was they that filled the Gardens, and nothing else. You'd think it, wouldn't you?"

" I should," said Applejohn.

" To be sure," continued Bub, " and yet I should like to know what it was that very year that trebled the number of weddings at Marrowbone. Bless you, they get one another's consent in the face of the rhinoceros, and settle the christening before the monkies. I tell you, these things are done every day; and what's worse, there isn't a bit of

science in the whole matter.   But I say, isn't this
dry work?" asked Mr. Bub, very significantly.

"I'm not thirsty, myself," said Applejohn, "but
I should like to have some more talk with you;
you seem to know something, Mr. Bub."

"So every body says," replied Bub modestly.
"I've a good deal to do to persuade people I don't
come from King's College, but I don't."

"I should very much like us to meet again,"
observed Applejohn, anxious to extend an enlightened connexion.

"First business, then pleasure," said Mr. Bub;
"come, give me your fist to this," and Bub wrote
the following receipt for the signature of John :——
"*Resraved of mr. Bub A Spannel Bittch*," to which
John subjoined "JOHN APPLEJOHN."

"John Applejohn," and Bub paused when he
had read the signature.   "If I was you, I should
never think of changing that name—you'll never
get such a droll one again."

"It is a little particular," remarked John, "has
been a very good one.   I'm the last of the family :
the Applejohns go out with me."

"But I shouldn't let 'em, you know—I should
graft," said Bub.

"What do you mean?" asked our simple hero;
and then the metaphor of Bub revealed itself to
John, who sighed as he thought of Sarah Two-

penny. "No; that's impossible," he said; "but I really should like us to meet again."

"Then come to the Gardens to-night at eight; and, as you seem a decent fellow, I'll take you to my society," said Bub.

Applejohn seized the speaker by the hand, and most cordially promised punctuality.

"Clever fellows, there,—men who know life and science; all of 'em first-rate chaps. I'm the chairman. Mind, eight, and no mistake," and Mr. Bub, carefully depositing the receipt for the spaniel in his waistcoat pocket, took his leave.

"A valuable man to know"—thought John—"a man of science—of the purest science;" and admitted to the society of which Mr. Bub was the distinguished chairman, Applejohn reasonably expected to obtain the most useful intelligence conveyed by the most pleasing means. Heavily hung the hours until eight o'clock.

CHAPTER XII.

EARLY in the evening, Mr. Cramlington came home to dress. He was absorbed in admiration of the spaniel, destined that night to become the property of a lady who will in due time appear upon our page, when he was disturbed by a hurried knocking at the door. "John, my wig!" exclaimed Cramlington, and rushed into the inner room to sieze that elegant disguise, John, after a necessary delay, attending the clamorous summons. "Master's at home," cried a gentleman very confidently, and dashed into the room; almost at the same instant, Cramlington issued from the inner chamber, in his satin morning-gown, and with hair and whiskers black as death.

"Ha! ha! my dear lord Slap, how are you? Eh! what's the matter?" asked Cramlington, seeing his lordship's arm in a sling.

"Nothing—smashed my arm last night, but had capital fun. Ha! ha!" and his lordship flung himself down in the easy chair of his host. He was, however, no sooner down than up again—the spaniel with swollen eye-balls and angry teeth snapping at the offending part of his lordship, which falling heavily upon the fragile creature lying in the chair, had almost rendered it a fit subject for the museum of the nameless duke, distinguished by the praise of Mr. Bub.

"Gracious heavens! Slap," exclaimed Cramlington, rushing with open arms to the flattened spaniel.

"D—n the dog! Why, the devil do you litter in your chairs?" cried his lordship, and catching

the dog by its tail of great promise, the born senator, for his lordship was a peer, flung the animal
to the other end of the room, Applejohn providentially catching the beast as it was in full speed
towards a superb mirror.

" My dear lord," cried Cramlington, and then
added, but very deferentially—" d—n me !"

" Suppose I'm bit, eh ? good joke for the damned
newspapers, eh ?"—cried his lordship.

" I hope, my dear Slap, you're not hurt; it is
but a pup, Slap," said Cramlington.

" Nothing hurts me," exclaimed his lordship,
" blood—true blood will stand anything."

" But what's the matter with your arm ?" inquired Cramlington, with great concern.

" Such rare fun last night—never had such glorious fun ! Why, wasn't you with us ? Ha ! ha !
such fun !" and his lordship flung himself back in
the chair, and shouted with laughter at the recollection of the revel.

Cramlington, staring with astonishment at the
opened and injured jaws of nobility, exclaimed—
" Good God ! Slap—what's the matter with your
teeth ?"

" Had three knocked out last night—here they
are though," and his lordship produced three teeth,
two single and one double, from his waistcoat-

pocket, "brought 'em off safe out of the gutter, and more than that, left the field with the pump-handle —such fun !"

" Pump-handle !" exclaimed Cramlington — " what ! another ?"

" Yes—swore I'd have it; carried off St. George's last night—that makes ten pump-handles at my chambers. Glorious fun ! must have a dozen though," said the peer. " However, you must come with us to-night."

" You know, my dear lord Slap, that I'm yours entirely, but to-night," and Cramlington sought to excuse himself.

" Must come; such sport in hand—the crowning joke, d—n me !—the crowning joke, ha ! ha ! I've hired a stable ready to receive him," said his lordship.

" Him ! who ?" asked Cramlington.

" Billy Pitt. Carry him off to-night ! Ha ! ha ! how I shall make those damned editors cackle ! Talking of editors, have you seen what that scoundrel, the editor of—what's the paper—said of me ? I'll give his ears to my terrier, by—but, however, I've condescended to answer him. Read that, Cram—read that," and his lordship flung a letter on the table, which Cramlington opened and read. The contents were as follow.

" *TO THE EDITOR OF* ———.

" *Sir,—In your paper of Thursday, the following base and contemptible paragraph has been kindly pointed out to me :—*

' LORD SLAP AGAIN.—On Tuesday morning, the shopman of Mr. Dobree, pawnbroker, of Charlotte Street, was considerably astonished and alarmed on discovering that the three balls suspended over the shop-door had been violently carried off during the night : information of the robbery was immediately given at the police-office. The most curious, and we must add, the most flagitious part of the mischief remains to be told : for on that very morning, what was the surprise of the footman of the Bishop of L———, to find the Lombardy arms, the property of Mr. Dobree, pawnbroker, fastened immediately over the door of the right reverend prelate ! His lordship, with that kindliness of disposition which has endeared him to his reverend brethren, immediately gave orders for the return of the property to Mr. Dobree : the balls have been restored to their pristine station. It is almost needless to add, that Lord Slap and his friends have been implicated in the transaction. When will this eccentric nobleman have sown his wild oats ?'

" *Now, sir, permit me very briefly to remark on this paragraph, in which it is very difficult to separate the falsehood from the malice. Your readers will henceforth know what amount of belief to award to your fanciful lucubrations, when I distinctly and solemnly state, that the three balls—the ' Lombardy arms' as you are pleased learnedly to designate them—belonging to Mr. Dobree, never were removed to the house of the Bishop of L———. No, sir ; it is a duty I owe to the*

*public and myself to state, that it was the mansion of
the Bishop of E——— that on Tuesday morning last
was found decorated with the insignia of the pawnbroker. You will, I trust, in future abstain from
coupling my name with circumstances, of the truth of
which you appear alike ignorant and unmindful.*

                " *I remain, yours,*

                        " *SLAP.*

    " *P. S. You are pleased to ask, when will my wild
oats be sown? To this I make answer,—about the time
that your hemp will be up.*"

    " That *is* splendid!" exclaimed Cramlington,
" he'll not forget that, I think."

    " The scoundrel!" cried Slap, " I'll have his
ears off—I'll have his ears in spirits of wine to
show my friends—I *will!*"

    " Serve him right—serve him right, d—n me!"
added Cramlington with some hesitation; for it
almost seemed that he considered the oath as the ex-
clusive property of his lordship, and therefore rarely
indulged himself with it in the peer's presence.

    " But you must be with us to-night, Cram; such
fun! Must carry off Billy Pitt," cried Slap.

    " What Billy Pitt? Any rascally editor of that
name, eh?" inquired Cramlington.

    " Editor! D—n all editors! I mean, Billy Pitt,
the minister, out of Hanover-square," answered his
lordship.

" What ! the statue—carry off the statue?" and Cramlington stared at the boldness of the idea.

" To be sure; tired of street-door knockers and pump-handles; they're small game, d—n me ! and make no noise now. But to carry off Billy Pitt— that will make something of a stir, I think," exclaimed Slap, big with the enterprize.

" But it can't be done, my dear Slap," said Cramlington timidly.

" Can't it ! I've engaged fifty fine fellows—such splendid rascals—and, ha ! ha ! I say, Cram, how the tabbies will stare when they get up in the morning and find Pitt walked away—discover the ' heaven-born minister ' removed—oh ! what glorious fun," and the senator was in ecstacies at his anticipated triumph. " Well, Cram, you must be one of us."

" My dear Slap, I should have no objection, but the fact is, the freak involves politics; you know, I swear by Pitt, and "—

" Oh, d—n it ! there's no politics in the business, none at all; I intend to prove that there's no politics in the matter," said Slap.

" How, my dear Slap, can you disabuse the public mind of the prejudice? They'll set down what you mean to be a pure joke, as a conspiracy of the disaffected," observed Cramlington with more than his usual acuteness.

" I've provided against that ; and I tell you how. To-night we shall carry off Pitt from Hanover-square ; well, to-morrow, we shall remove Canning from Palace Yard, and the night after, we intend to steal old Cartwright from Burton Crescent. Eh? Ha! ha !" and his lordship roared with delight.

" Why, you're not serious, my dear Slap ?" asked Cramlington.

" Don't you perceive," said the peer, " as we favour no party, we shall triumphantly assert our independence ?"

" Carry off three statues ! All London will be in an uproar. Three statues—and where will you put 'em ?"

" All settled, I tell you : I've hired two stables and a cow-house to receive 'em. What fun, eh ? Never was such fun !"

" But I'm very much afraid, my dear Slap, that —hang it ! the authorities as they call themselves know nothing of real humour—that you may get yourself into an ugly scrape. It's one thing to run away with a cobbler's knocker, and another to make off with two prime ministers," said the cautious Cramlington.

" That's it," exclaimed Slap—" there's the fun. The thing has never yet been attempted ; 'twill be the greatest thing of the day—Tom Rumpus will be of the party, and Blow, he's only gone to

Bath to bury his aunt, he'll be back in time for the sport. You know my friendship for you, Cram, I wouldn't let you out of the party, no—d—n me! for any money."

Cramlington shook lord Slap's hand with the most cordial spirit of gratitude, swearing that he should never, to his dying day, forget the senator's kindness. " Really, my dear Slap, your condescension overpowers me! That I, a mere commoner, should be thus admitted to your most private recreations,"—

" Don't mention it," cried his liberal lordship, " true genius levels all distinctions; and never, never can I forget the cool courage with which, while I tossed with the mutton-pie man, you laid the train of gunpowder under his very nose, and blew him "—

" Oh, a trifle—not worth naming, my dear lord —quite a trifle," cried the modest Cramlington.

" Trifles show the man, Cram," said the peer; " from that very night, I was convinced you were destined for great things, d—n me. Therefore, you must join us with the statues; look at the glory—look at the fun! There'll be a proclamation out—hundred pounds reward—oh, what real wit!"

" A thought has struck me," exclaimed Cramlington, " a brilliant thought, my lord. The thing

will make just as much noise, and isn't attended
with half the danger; listen, my lord."

"Humph! d—n me! 'fraid there's no fun in
what you're going to say; however, go on," said
the peer.

"You know the statue of the venerable George
the Third—the statue on horseback?" asked Cramlington.

"Cockspur-street—the gentleman with his hat
off?" said lord Slap carelessly.

"The same, my lord.   In meditating upon the
statue of that good and great man"—

"That's right," said Slap, interrupting his friend,
"I like a spirit of loyalty—too little of it in this
d—d levelling age."

"In contemplating the statue," repeated Cramlington, pleased with the eulogy of the peer, "of
that good, great, and temperate man—of that enlightened legislator, and staunch supporter of the
established church, has your lordship never been
struck with his pig-tail?"

"Infant poker?—Yes."

"Well, then, my lord, I propose—at all events
to begin with—that instead of carrying away William Pitt, we saw off the pig-tail of George the
Third."

"No, no," cried Lord Slap, "it's disrespectful;
don't mind removing a minister or two into a cow-

house, but d—n it! won't touch a copper hair of the pig-tail of sacred majesty. Like wit—but d—n disaffection!"

" I applaud your principles, my lord—they do honour to your heart and head," exclaimed Cramlington.

" Have sworn to defend the prerogative of the crown," cried lord Slap, kindling with generous ardour, " and look upon that pig-tail as one of the sacred institutions of my country. Like a harmless frolic, but d—n treason!" and lord Slap, to the astonishment of the commoner Cramlington, assumed all the severe dignity of an hereditary senator. " Cramlington," said lord Slap, with touching gravity, " if we are to remain friends, not a word, not a syllable on the removal of that queue. I would shed the last drop of my best heart's blood in defence of that pig-tail."

" No man can suspect my principles, my lord," said Cramlington, affected by the earnestness of the peer; " when I proposed to saw off the pig-tail of his majesty, I hope that you will do me the justice to believe that to the statue itself I intended nothing personal."

" I know that—never doubted your principles, Cram, but your wit, your capital keen wit,"—

" My dear lord," simpered Cramlington.

" So apt to run away with you. However,

come with me to my rooms—now, I'll not be denied—all the lads are there."

" I'll follow you—upon my honour," said Cramlington.

" Won't leave you—won't, d—n me!" cried the peer; and Cramlington, finding the nobleman determined, hurriedly dressed himself, and having given Applejohn the strictest orders to attend to the comforts of the spaniel, was about to depart with his lordship. "Oh!" cried Cramlington, "has any one been here, John?"

" Your tailor, sir," said the domestic.

" My tailor! My tailor — impossible!" cried Cramlington, and he rolled his eyes.

" I beg your pardon then, sir," said John, " he mayn't be your tradesman, but as I heard he is a tailor, I thought that perhaps, Mr. Zweifler,"—

" Who?" shouted Cramlington, turning pale as paper.

" Mr. Zweifler, sir, he has been here, and "—

" What! do you employ that old German rascal?" asked lord Slap of his astonished friend.

" I—I have known him for—for," and Cramlington turned to his servant—"who—who did he ask for?"

" He asked for—for my master," replied John.

" Aye, for Mr. Cramlington?"

" Yes, sir, I think he asked for you by name;

but he seemed very odd and passionate, sir," said Applejohn.

" Upon my soul, d—n me! I do wonder, Cramlington, that you employ such an old scoundrel; but if the miscreant's pressing, we must give him a hint to mend his behaviour—yes, we must set his house on fire, or play him some such practical joke," said lord Slap, and placing his sound arm in the arm of the confused Cramlington, the nobleman led the commoner away to meet a few of the midnight spirits of the age, to which it is our wish with little ceremony to introduce the reader.

CHAPTER XIII.

Lord Slap and his friend were received with a shout by four gentlemen assembled at the lodgings of the peer, whose arrival was the signal to serve dinner, provided from a neighbouring tavern. " Slap," cried one of the party, whose bold, handsome countenance was not entirely disfigured by a severe bruise, and several cuts, " Slap, my dear fellow, permit me to introduce my young friend Plucky, one of the oldest families in Devonshire,—a gentleman who will be an honour to our society."

" The introduction of my dear friend Rumpus,"

said lord Slap, bowing to the new-comer, a sickly-looking boy of eighteen, " is a guarantee of all the amiable and excellent qualities of a gentleman."

" I trust, my lord," cried young Plucky, in a chirping voice, " that is, I hope to deserve the eulogies of my valuable friend, the Hon. Tom Rumpus."

" No doubt, sir—no doubt, d—n me !" said Slap. —" Come, lads ; let us feed, and then to business."

" Ha ! ha ! my dear Slap—you are the most exquisite fellow—it is the best joke I ever heard," exclaimed Rumpus at the latter end of the meal.

" What, Rowdow ? you've let the cat out of the bag, eh ? d—n it ! couldn't keep the secret, eh ?" and lord Slap shook his head reproachfully at lord Rowdow, who, seeming to taste every word ere he uttered it, slowly excused himself on the score that " he knew Slap wouldn't mind the affair being whispered to Tom Rumpus."

" Yes—yes—that's how a man's brightest ideas sometimes miss fire. We should look very small now, if we were to find Billy Pitt put under the protection of five hundred of the police," said Slap.

" 'Twould be devilish annoying," said Rumpus, " but there's no fear of that. It is the best idea since the carrying off the three balls from the pawnbroker, and hanging them at"—

" Bye-the-by, gentlemen, have you seen what

that scoundrel editor says of the transaction? have you seen how the miscreant garbles the business?" asked lord Slap. " I've written to the ragamuffin."

" Upon my life, you're wrong—you are, indeed, Slap," said the Hon. Tom Rumpus; " I'd treat such vagabonds with silent contempt—or, if they came in my way, with a horsewhip."

" I shall be very happy," cried young Plucky, "very happy, indeed, my dear lord Slap, if you contemplate horsewhipping any body, to go and hold the door, while you lay into the ruffian."

" Sir—d—n me !—eternally obliged to you, Mr. Plucky. A little wine, sir?" and lord Slap pledged his new friend.

" But, seriously, Slap," said Rowdow, " I would not write to the papers."

" No, after all," observed Cramlington, "perhaps it's low."

" It's not only low," said Mr. Smasherton, the last of the four, " but it's impolitic; it makes the scoundrels so devilish conceited; it makes them crow about—what do they call it?—— yes, public opinion,—I think that's the slang phrase. Public opinion !—ha ! ha !"

" What is it made of?" asked young Plucky, "public opinion ! how is it manufactured ?"

" That's a devilish droll question, Plucky. Yes, I should like to have it analyzed; it wouldn't be bad sport to separate the component parts of public opinion," observed lord Slap, and all the party roared with laughter at the suggestion.

"Let's indulge in a little chemistry," said the Hon. Tom Rumpus, "let's analyze it; let us suppose this champaigne so much public opinion, and all of us, chemists as we are, declare what we find in it."

"Bravo !" cried the party, and every man filled his glass. "Do you begin, professor Rumpus," said lord Slap.

"Aye, do," exclaimed Cramlington ; "do, Tom, and as I have said, that is, as Mr. Pope has said——

'Catch the living sparkles as they rise.'

Now, Tom, what do you see ?"

The Hon. Tom Rumpus, held a glass of champaigne to his observing eye, and thus gravely characterized

"The beaded bubbles winking at the brim."

"Now, gentlemen, this fluid is called public opinion—it has been denominated the wine of life, the thing by which we move, and breathe, and all that ; there," and Tom looked closely at the air bubbles,—"there go a crew of shirtless editors— ha !—they're up and out, before you can count 'em."

"I see a mob of 'unwashed artificers,'" said Rowdow, looking steadily in his glass, "and now, where the devil are they?"

"There go my tailors!" exclaimed young Plucky, as the bubbles rose and burst.

"Yes, I should think your tailors break sooner than any other," said Smasherton, and the intended joke was loudly applauded.

"I think—I think," cried Cramlington, staring curiously at the glass, "yes, I'm almost sure I've caught hold of my washerwoman."

"And there's my bootmaker," exclaimed lord Slap—"and there's—eh?—how d—d muddy this wine is!"

"All public opinion, my dear fellow," cried Tom Rumpus; "the greatest part of it to be got only from the dregs: so, gentlemen, let us have done with our practical chemistry. We've analyzed opinion, and find it composed of scoundrel editors—a man's own tradesmen—and muck in general. Talk about ghosts and spectres, the bugbear of all bugbears is public opinion: thank heaven! I'm not superstitious, or I should never have gone to bed without a candle for fear of the hobgoblin."

"Public opinion! Every ruffian pretends to make up a bit of it," cried Rowdow.

"The greatest scoundrel—the filthiest beggar

believes he contributes to the general fund," said Rumpus, "and in these times gives himself airs accordingly."

"Very true," observed Smasherton; "a fellow with a hole in his breeches, with no hat, naked legs, and a broom in his hand, is still to be respected; because, you perceive, my dear friends, there is in the bundle of dirt and rags, that particle of divine gold—a scintillation of public opinion."

"Well, lads, d—n it! ha! ha! let's be proud that we can live without it," exclaimed lord Slap. "Now, to business. Listen; I've hired the men—all the tackle's in order—and you are all determined upon the removal of the minister?"

"I'm told he can't keep his ground," said the innocent young Plucky, who had not been informed of the conspiracy against Pitt, and therefore conceived that his friends talked of politics and not of a high misdemeanour.

"Have you secured him a retreat?" asked Rumpus, "where is he to be put by?"

"Never fear me, lads; I've hired a splendid shed for the prime minister. What glorious fun, eh? what sport 'twill make! I say, boys, if there's a public meeting on the matter, we must all go and speak; we must all express our indignation at the miscreants, eh? ha! ha! what fun!" again cried lord Slap.

"Great pity you hav'n't room for the bronze in your museum, Slap," said Rumpus.

"Has lord Slap a museum?" inquired young Plucky.

"Have I a museum!" exclaimed lord Slap, "look about you, Plucky—not such another collection in the kingdom. But I'll show you a few of the specimens."

"Why the devil, Slap," observed Smasherton, "why don't you have a catalogue for visitors?"

"D—n it! I would,—but the fact is, I hate the trouble of literary composition."

"But what, my dear lord Slap," and young Plucky looked wonderingly about him, "what are the articles in your museum?"

"Look there; lot the first," and lord Slap pointed to a corner.

"Lot!" exclaimed Plucky, "why, my dear lord, they're pump-handles."

"Ten of 'em; brought away the tenth—St. George's—last night. Everything in my collection, my dear Plucky, is the fruit of hard conquest; no d—d presentations. I only want two more handles to make the set complete. However, I have a weightier business in hand just now; I have first to secure two of the principal ministers, and the pump-handles will follow.   Ha! Rumpus, do you see that one?" and lord Slap pointed to one of the ten hydraulic instruments.   "That's St. Giles. Don't you recollect,—the scoundrel policeman had his bludgeon raised at my temple, when you bent that bit of iron over his skull, and we got off? Should have been killed but for that—never, never, my dear Rumpus, do I look at that pump-handle without thinking of you.   Ten of 'em, Plucky; isn't it fun?"

"I had no idea," said Plucky—"capital."

"Look here—number two," said lord Slap, exhibiting a huge bronze knocker.

"Is that an interesting relic?" asked Plucky.

"Very; wouldn't take any money for it.   This knocker was the property of the late William Wilberforce—had a great respect for the man; —watched three nights to wrench off his knocker."

"What is this?" inquired Plucky, reading a label attached to number three, "what is this— '*A trifle from Fulham?*'"

"That is," said lord Slap, "the bell-pull from the gate of the Bishop of London: and there you see number four—for I'm above bigotry of all kind—is the scraper of Doctor Chalmers.   But there's nothing here; come into this room"—and lord Slap conducted Plucky into an inner chamber, filled with the richest and most curious midnight spoils. Rumpus, Cramlington, and others followed.

"What is this—a Highlander?" asked Plucky, staring at a painted image, the size of life.

"Yes; carried him off from the door of a snuffshop. I say, Smasherton, you recollect that night—you'd two ribs snapped—capital fun, wasn't it?" cried lord Slap.

"A stout, stalwart fellow," exclaimed Plucky, admiring the kilted effigy.

"Said to be like Sir Peter Noodle, before he was breeched—that's why I keep it. Great respect for Sir Peter—talks more and says less than any man on the bench," observed Slap.

"And what are these, my dear Slap,—doorplates?" asked Plucky.

"Eight-and-thirty of 'em, — only two more, you know, Rumpus, and I win my wager," said Slap.

"What wager is that, my dear lord?" inquired Cramlington.

"Why, I've laid Slap a fifty that he doesn't carry off forty door-plates with the name of 'Smith' upon 'em, in three months; and I'm very much inclined to fear that I have made an ass of myself; to be sure, there's only a fortnight left of the time," said Rumpus.

" Don't flatter yourself, Tom," cried lord Slap,
" I've already marked out six—but at present all
my thoughts are absorbed by the prime minister.
I say," and Slap pointed to half-a-dozen police
lanthorns, " do you recollect the night we fought
for these—what fun ?"

" Wasn't that the night we sent seventy accou-
cheurs to the lord Chancellor ?" asked Rowdow.

" Yes," answered Smasherton, " and the monthly
nurses to the attorney-general.   Glorious wit !"

" Good heavens !" exclaimed Plucky, " what—
what have we here ?"

" Ha ! that *was* fun.   Tom Rumpus was terribly
drunk, when luckily we met some fellows carrying
home this new coffin—we thrashed 'em soundly—
such wit !—took away the commodity, brought Tom
home in it, and here it is.   The undertakers had
to go back and manufacture another article.   Great
fun," cried Slap.

" By-the-bye," said Smasherton, " this reminds
me of bad news.   I forgot to tell you."

" What's the matter ?" exclaimed two or three
of the party.

" Blow can't be with us in our attack on the
minister.   He's at Bath, you know, and they won't
bury his aunt until Wednesday."

" Shameful," cried Slap, " never mind—must do
without him."

"What, my dear lord Slap, what is that collection of curious caps and ?"——

"Ha! Plucky—there isn't such another collection as that in the possession of any other nobleman in the world. What do you think they are? They are the hats, caps, bonnets, or call them what you will, of all the watchmen of Europe," answered his lordship.

"You don't mean it, Slap?" cried Plucky.

"Taken with my own hands, my dear Plucky—taken in hard fight. I intend to make another tour for the coats,—such fun !—I'll have the whole costume before I've done, from the common dress of an English policeman to the holiday suit of a janissary. That's what I call real fun—true humour—glorious wit."

"You *have* travelled then, my dear lord ?" asked Plucky, deferentially.

"Have travelled ! I'll show you that I have in a minute—here, never mind the rest of the museum now," and lord Slap quitted the room wherein were five hundred articles, among which might be found knockers, scrapers, barber's poles, black dolls, dairy-signs of cows, golden boots, and other domestic instruments, and familiar types of commerce. "You ask me if I have travelled, eh? Here, Mameluke," and Slap called to his servant, "hand me my nose-bag."

" Your nose-bag, my dear lord!" exclaimed the astonished Plucky.   " A peer's nose-bag!"

" Here it is," cried the noble lord, as his servant handed to him a tolerably large velvet bag, crammed with apparently some weighty substance.   " Now, Plucky, lad, you ask me if I have travelled?   I'll just trouble you to cast your eyes over these," and with a word the peer emptied the bag of its contents, which fell in a rattling shower upon the table.

" Stones!" shouted Plucky, jumping at the sound.

" Look at 'em; they are stones—but look at 'em," cried the nobleman and born senator with a triumphant air.

Young Plucky picked up the stones, one by one, and having minutely examined a dozen of them, exclaimed—" Good God! my lord—why, they're noses."

" Every one of 'em—warrant 'em all noses," cried lord Slap; " noses of both genders and of all shapes, from the nose of Diana to the snout of Pan. That's fun, if you like.   A hundred noses!   And now, I think, Plucky, you'll not ask me again if I have travelled."

" Really, my lord, I'm very dull—I don't apprehend; I don't see the connexion of your travels with these noses," said Plucky.

" Don't you? well then, permit me to illumine you, Mr. Plucky; and to assure you upon the honour of a nobleman, whose whole life he is proud to say has been spent in pursuit of the humorous, that these noses are from the most eminent galleries and gardens of the most superb cities of Europe."

" Copies?" asked Plucky.

" Copies be d—d! I chipped them all off the original statues, with my own fingers, my own hammer, and my own chisel," said the peer.

" You did, my lord?" exclaimed the astonished Plucky.

" I did; took me some time to do it, too; for I had to watch my opportunity. However, I flatter myself that I succeeded wonderfully—indeed, I may say that I scarcely visited a city throughout the Continent that I didn't quit it with a broken nose. That is fun, if you like," exclaimed the mutilating nobleman.

" Ha! ha!" roared Rumpus, " don't you call that wit, Plucky? Isn't that life?"

" Capital! I hadn't an idea," replied Plucky, evidently dazzled by the brilliant prospect of distinguishing himself, so suddenly opened upon him.

" However, enough of this, my boys, it's d—d egotism in me to boast of these things," and his lordship gathered the broken noses in a heap, and was about to return them to the bag: seeing the eye of Plucky resting as his lordship thought wistfully upon the fragments, the liberal nobleman asked—" Will you have one, Plucky—one as a *gage d'amitié ?*"

" No—no ; not for the world," answered the modest Plucky, " 'twould be a million pities to spoil the set."

" Take them away, Mameluke—and mind, you scoundrel, that you don't lose one.   Ha ! this is all very well ; still in the matter of noses, I am not yet quite satisfied," said lord Slap.

" What more could mortal man desire ?" asked the Hon. Tom. Rumpus. " You're quite an Alexander, and sigh for new noses to chip."

" No, I shall never rest—you know, those scoundrels the editors of—but no matter ; I never —no, I never shall rest until I have three editorial noses cut from the living animal, and put in excellent spirits, in my museum,—I never shall," exclaimed lord Slap with touching earnestness. " I never shall."

" Well, — well, let us hope the best," said Rumpus.

" Yes—I tell his lordship," observed Cramlington, " to have patience ; all we wish can't be done in a day."

" That's very true," remarked the philosophic Slap, " so, now to business. I'm resolved to-night to pull down the minister."

" What's the question? Must you go to the
' House' to-night?" inquired the unsophisticated
Plucky.

" The house! Pooh—I mean Billy Pitt," answered Slap.

" Now, I hope, my dear lord, you'll be advised,"
said Cramlington. " What think ye, gentlemen,"
and he addressed the general company. " Isn't
the business dangerous?"

" But think of the fun," answered Rowdow,
" besides we've hunted small game more than
enough: we must now do something to take the
town by storm; knockers and pump-handles are
now become a drug."

" I must say," remarked Smasherton, " that I'm
taken with the idea of running off with Pitt; still I
see obstacles."

" D—n it! gentlemen, you don't mean to cry
off?" exclaimed lord Slap with some emotion.

" No, certainly not," said the Hon. Tom
Rumpus, " but don't let us be too hasty."

" Too hasty!" retorted lord Slap rather contemptuously, " why, except the little affair last
night, and the matter with the pawnbroker and
bishop, we've done nothing this fortnight."

" That's true enough; still, I think we had better wait for Blow," was the counsel of Smasherton,
" you know Blow's a host."

By this time young Plucky had been informed by his dear friend Rumpus of the real object of the meeting, and therefore no longer confounded the removal of ministerial bronze with the out-voting of ministerial real life. Assured that the immediate purpose of the society was fun—glorious fun—he ventured to ask permission of lord Slap to be heard. " Hear! hear!" from lord Slap, and " Bravo! Plucky," from Rumpus.

Mr. Plucky rose: and never did young and bashful member of either House propose or second an address in answer to a royal speech with more modesty, with more grace, with a finer sense of what was due to himself and to his subject. There was, for a moment, a slight confusion in the manner of the speaker—his cheek was flushed, and his voice trembled,—but he almost immediately regained his self-possession, and—we give his entire speech—spoke as follows:—

" My lords and gentlemen—When I look around me and observe not only my seniors in age, but noblemen and gentlemen illustrious by achievements, accomplished under difficulties which would have paralyzed not only meaner men, but individuals enjoying equal rank and birth—(' Hear!' from Mr. Cramlington) I cannot,—I say I cannot attribute my present position in this society to any merit of mine save to that—for I consider it a

merit—of being known to my friend, and I am
proud to call him my friend, the Hon. Tom
Rumpus ('Hear!' from Rumpus.) I, my lords
and gentlemen, am an unknown man. (Cries of
'No!') Permit me to say, I am an unknown
man. I bring to this chivalrous society nothing but
good intentions. It would be folly—it would be
base ignorance in me—to think otherwise. As yet,
gentlemen, I feel—all too acutely feel—that I have
done nothing.

"When I look around me and consider the
trophies of my noble friend—I trust he will henceforth permit me to call him my friend ('Hear!'
from lord Slap)—I feel humiliated by the sense
of my own insignificance. I, my lords and gentlemen, can show no pump-handle—I can exhibit no
knocker—I never chipped the nose from an Apollo
—I never plucked a bishop's bell-pull—never bore
away a presbyterian scraper. I have yet my spurs
to win; for it ill becomes me in such a society to
boast of a broken lamp or two—a linch-pin, pulled
in early life from a quaker's gig—cats shoed with
walnut-shells—rats smeared and burned with tur-
pentine—or any other puerile exploit. My lords
and gentlemen, I feel that I am now only about to
start in a course that you have all so gloriously run.
I shall gird up my loins for the race ('Hear!
hear!') Succeed as I may, I yet feel that I can

never approach the inventive genius and invincible courage of a Slap—the buoyant humour and ennobling fortitude of a Smasherton—the airy wit of a Rumpus—the practical satire of a Cramlington—or the playful mirth of a Rowdow (Cheers from all parties.)

"My lords and gentlemen,—I was about to propose a subject for your consideration; yet when I think of my own inexperience—when I remember my own ignorance of public life—I—I—(Cries of 'Hear!' and 'go on.')—My lord, then it does appear to me—I entreat your kindest construction of my motives—but it does appear to me that the removal of the statue, although involving great public confusion, and thereby considerably enhancing the reputation of this society, is a matter requiring the most mature reflection. For my own part, I would say, let the minister remain for another session."

"I beg your pardon, Mr. Plucky, but have you any specific motion to make?" asked lord Slap. "Otherwise, this address is—d—n me!—a little irregular, the statue having been determined upon."

"I have a motion, my lord," ("Hear!") said young Plucky. "Still, my lord, permit me to deprecate"—(Cries of "Motion!") Mr. Plucky coughed, and bowed obedience. "My lord, I observe in the public prints of this morning, that there are three remarkably fine tigers for sale, newly arrived in the East India Docks. Now, my lord, as fun—glorious fun—is as I understand the object of this society, I humbly propose that these tigers be purchased, and on any evening that shall hereafter be determined upon, conveyed in a coach or caravan to the doors of the Opera-House, and there be suffered to escape among the people as they are about quietly to depart for their homes and their beds."

A burst of applause honoured the motion of young Mr. Plucky; and the epithets "glorious fellow"—"splendid wit"—"first-rate humourist" were liberally bestowed upon him.

" D—n me!" exclaimed lord Slap, " there's something in it. How many tigers—three?"

" Just the number," said Rowdow; "one for boxes—one for pit—and one for gallery. I shall vote for the tigers—decidedly."

" Still, I—I would suggest, as an amendment, that the experiment should not be made at the Opera-House—no—some of us may have friends and relations there, and—no ; it might not be considered gentlemanly. I would suggest that the tigers should be taken on a holyday-night to some low play-house, and at a lucky minute let loose among the mob." Thus spoke lord Slap.

" That's better, very considerably better," cried Smasherton.

" I am quite in your lordship's hands," said young Plucky, with great modesty. " If, however, a suburban play-house be decided upon, it would possibly meet the views of all the gentlemen present, should that particular house be selected, (for I am told there is such a place,) which is the especial temple of recreation for sheriff's officers, their wives and families."

" Not the slightest objection," said lord Slap, and it must be owned with great disinterestedness, he being a privileged person.

" Will your lordship, then, be good enough to put the tigers?" asked the Hon. Tom Rumpus.

" A show of hands, gentlemen, for the tigers," was the order of lord Slap, and every hand was uplifted in favour of the animals. " I congratulate you, d—n me! Plucky," exclaimed lord Slap, shaking the young member by the hand—" I congratulate you, alike on the felicity as on the success of your first motion."

" He'll be an honour to the society," cried Smasherton. " He's full of wit—the drollest dog alive—splendid humour," and the diffident Plucky blushed at the many praises showered upon him.

" Mameluke," called out Slap, and the domestic took a whispered order from his master, quitted the room, and in a minute returned, bearing what a casual observer might have mistaken for a large telescope.

" Mr. Plucky," said lord Slap, and from his look and voice, it was evident that his lordship was about to enter upon a very serious business. " Mr. Plucky, you have—d—n me !—this evening proved yourself a speaker of the highest genius ; and it would be to me a matter of everlasting regret, d—n me ! if you quitted the present meeting without some trifling mark of its esteem and admiration. In enrolling yourself a member of our society, Mr. Plucky, a man of your acute intellect cannot have been insensible of the fact, that many dangers await you.——Popularity, or what is much better, notoriety, in these days of competition, is not to be obtained by reading all day in an arm-chair, or retiring to eider-down with gruel at eleven. No, sir ; men who in this age would distinguish themselves, must be up and doing. Midnight brings rest to the mob of men, but not to us. It is very probable that you may, in your pursuit of fame, have an arm or a leg broken—be made to swallow ten of your teeth—or be carried to your lodgings with a compound fracture of your shoulder. These things are to be expected ; happy is he who escapes them. It is my wish, sir, as a token of my regard—d—n me !—and as a testimony of my admiration, to provide you with a solace in sickness, should any calamity in the pursuit of fun—of glorious fun—befall you.   Look here, sir," and to the astonishment of Plucky, lord Slap produced a tin instrument of about three inches in diameter, and as many feet in length.   " I present you with this antidote to melancholy—with this never-failing source of wit and amusement."   Plucky bowed.

" Mr. Plucky, in presenting you with this instrument, I ought to tell you its peculiar use.   I had been knocked down, and my ankle dislocated,—you recollect the night, or rather the morning, Rowdow ?"

" To be sure ; infamous case.   Only for pitching a chimney-sweeper into a pail of milk—brutal affair," said Rowdow.

" I was confined to my chamber, Mr. Plucky, for two months—and this," and his lordship looked gratefully at the engine, " this was my only solace."

" A solace ! How, my dear lord Slap ?" asked Plucky.

" You will perceive, Mr. Plucky, that this instrument is made on the true hydraulic principle, —Mameluke, you scoundrel—empty that bottle of port into the cooler."   Mameluke instantly obeyed the order, and presented the vessel to his lordship, who applying the instrument formed " on the true hydraulic principle," to the wine, drew the whole of it into the tube.   " It is in fact, you see, Mr. Plucky, nothing more than a gigantic squirt; I had it made to hold a bottle. Mameluke, you miscreant, stand further off; back, sir! and keep your d——d hands from your face," cried lord Slap, as his servant, with possibly a fear of the coming event, covered his face and swayed restlessly from side to side. "You will perceive, Mr. Plucky," said his lordship, "you will perceive that—there! bet fifty pounds he had every drop of it!" exclaimed the eccentric nobleman, having adroitly discharged from the instrument, "on the true hydraulic principle," the whole bottle of port into the menial countenance of Mameluke.

"Capital shot!" cried Rowdow.

"That, Mr. Plucky, during my two months' severe illness, was my only solace.——I sat at a third-floor window," said his lordship, "and on an average I hit every night from eighteen to twenty coachmen. 'Twas capital fun to hear 'em swear."

"With port wine?" inquired Plucky.

"No, d——n 'em!——water, or——or anything. By-the-bye, they make a capital kind of thin ink now, which would do splendidly," was the recommendation of his lordship. "I should have died with melancholy but for this instrument, d——n me! However, sir, it is your's; and on presenting it to you, I can only imitate the parting address of

Louis the Fourteenth, d—n me! to James the Second. It is yours, sir, but I cannot wish you better than by wishing you may never have cause to use it," saying this, the peer, amidst the cheers of the company, placed the hydraulic instrument in the hands of Mr. Plucky.

Mr. Plucky attempted to return thanks; he found it impossible, and then briefly apologised for his confusion on the score of his feelings.

" Now, when are the tigers to be tried?" inquired Rowdow, anxious for the sport.

" Why not to-morrow?" asked Rumpus.

" Certainly not," said lord Slap, " how do we know what condition they're in?"

" Oh! they're in capital health—at least so said the paper," remarked Plucky.

" Health! D—n health! don't you perceive," said Slap, " if the tigers have been over-fed, they'll afford no sport? They'll be no more than Newfoundland pups let loose in the mob. The only way to insure glorious fun is to get the tigers into our own possession, and keep them without an inch of meat for ten days or a week at least."

" That's well thought of," said Smasherton; " if they're not sharp-set, we shall throw away our money and our time."

" But, it has just struck me," remarked the

milky-hearted Cramlington, " that, possibly, the tigers may do some serious mischief; that they may wound, or perhaps kill somebody."

" Nothing of the sort; they'll not go beyond a scratch or so," said Slap. " Perhaps, take away a mouthful or two from some fat tailor, who can afford it; or, if he can't, he can advertise to have his pound of flesh back again, it being of no use to any but the owner." This sally was loudly laughed at by all the party, except Cramlington, who returned to the subject.

" But if anybody should be killed? To say the least of it, my dear lord Slap, there'd be an inquest, and all that nonsense; and I do think—it's only the opinion of an individual, certainly,—but I do think that we might have just as much fun with the tigers, without any fear of bloodshed. You see, bloodshed, my dear lord Slap,"——

" What the devil would you have, Cramlington? Perhaps," said Rumpus, " you'd prefer rabbits to tigers?"

" I reject the insinuation of my honourable friend," retorted Cramlington, turning to Slap.

" Then what would you have?" asked lord Slap.

" I would have the tigers, certainly; I would assuredly send them among the mob—one at the pit, one at the box, and one at the gallery—

it will be glorious fun, and I stand to the tigers. Still"——

"Still what?" roared several voices.

"Still, with regard to the animals, I must confess it would materially ease my mind if—if," and Cramlington was almost fearful of giving birth to the tenderness that laboured at his heart—" if they were muzzled." Cramlington sank in his seat, fairly knocked down by the shout of laughter that followed his humane suggestion. "I have finished," said Cramlington with dignity—"I say no more."

A pause ensued, which was broken by Rumpus, who asked lord Slap what was to be done. "You see, we have thought it prudent to defer the removal of the statues, and as we must wait for some time until the tigers are properly starved, there's no fun."

"Has any gentleman anything to suggest?" asked lord Slap. Every man seemed plunged in thought—but no one made answer. There was another pause, and Cramlington shifted himself uneasily towards Slap, and whispered to him, and gesticulated with great vehemence. Lord Slap shook his head,—cried "pooh!" "pish!"—still Cramlington continued to whisper. At length Slap drew himself up, and said—"Well, Cramlington, if you like to put your pig-tail into a motion,"——

" I will," exclaimed the energetic Cramlington, and rose.

" Pig-tail in a motion !" cried Rumpus.

" My lords and gentlemen," said Cramlington, " as there is apparently a great dearth of fun, and as the tigers cannot come off for some time, I have to make a motion." Whereupon, Mr. Cramlington moved that the pig-tail of the statue of George the Third—all for the sake of glorious fun—should be cut off that night, and, neatly enveloped in silver-paper, be sent to the court barber.

" Does anybody second the motion ?— d — n me !" asked lord Slap, looking at the serious faces of the party.

We are proud and delighted to say, that wits as they were, there was no man of the knot found so reckless in his principles as to second the motion.

The motion was consequently lost.

CHAPTER XIV.

LEAVING lord Slap and his companions still sitting, debating the means of fun, " glorious fun," we return to John Applejohn, that we may accompany him in search of his new acquaintance, Mr. Buffon Bub. That profound naturalist had finished his labours of the day; the leopard had gorged his belly full, the tiger had supped, the bear was satisfied, the hyena was appeased; and Bub, "their guide, philosopher and friend," quitted his carnivorous cares to seek the high society of man. Our hero met the naturalist at the garden gate, and lost no time in assuring him that he felt particularly happy at the event. Mr. Buffon Bub received John Applejohn with an unaffected stare of ignorance.

"You surely don't forget me, Mr. Bub? Why, how many hours is it since we met?" asked John.

"Sorry to say, I never could count beyond a thousand," answered Bub, "so perhaps you'll tell me."

"My name is Applejohn. I am Mr. Cramlington's man—I"—John was proceeding, when he found his hat suddenly removed by Mr. Bub.

"If that's the case," asked Bub, staring at the fair locks of John, "who the devil has bleached you?"

"Ha!—my hair," answered John. "You see, that was quite an accident. When we met, I had —ha! ha!—black hair and whiskers."

"And since then, you've taken a fancy to another colour? When do you change again?" asked Bub, with a suspicious look at John.

"The truth is, Mr. Bub, it's quite a secret, but that wasn't my own hair."

" I should think not," observed the naturalist.

" I don't know how it happened—in a moment of forgetfulness I had put on the black wig and whiskers, and the old German coming to the door, I couldn't take 'em off."

" Why not ? " asked Bub.

" Why, between ourselves, Mr. Bub, that man— I believe, however, I said as much—was a tailor, and we had met before, and"—

" Is that all ? I see—he made for you once, and you didn't want to claim his acquaintance?" observed the acute Bub.

" I regret to say," answered Applejohn with a sigh, " I did not. However, I earnestly hope that a day will come, when the affair between us will be fully cleared up."

" Why," remarked Mr. Bub, " in the matter of tailors' bills, whatever comes of 'em, it's as well to hope the best."

" Ha ! Mr. Bub, I could tell you a sad business I had with that old tailor. It's an affair that weighs very heavily upon my heart; however, I assure you, I meant well."

" Every gentleman as deals with a tailor, commonly says he does; for my part, I think good intentions ought to go farther than ready money; but they don't, Mr. Applejohn; the world, you see, hasn't got to that state of perfection to take a man's good meaning instead o' half-crowns."

" More's the pity, Mr. Bub," observed John.

" That's what I say; if it was otherwise, what a banker's account I would have!" declared the naturalist.

" But the worst is, Mr. Bub, the ill-luck that follows a man who means well. I do believe, if I was to make a present of a guinea to anybody, 'twould turn to a farthing."

" Did you ever try?" asked Bub. " If you never did, now's your time," and the naturalist turned up the cuff of his coat, opened his palm, and winked at Applejohn.

" Just now, Mr. Bub, however I might wish it, I can't afford the experiment. Ha! Mr. Bub," proceeded John, possibly desirous of turning the conversation, " has it never struck you that this is a very strange world? I ought to have been a happy man, Mr. Bub, but on this earth there's nothing certain."

" Don't talk in that way, Mr. Applejohn, don't; I can't bear it," exclaimed Bub, abruptly.

" Bless me! what's the matter—anything happened?" asked John.

" He was the pride of my heart! No father could love his child better than I loved him. You may well say nothing's certain. When I come to you with the spannel, he was in the best health and spirits, and now—but I'd promised myself not to think of it, it won't bear thinking of. Only this morning!" and Bub sighed.

"I wouldn't hurt your feelings for the world," said the tender Applejohn, "but—I fear, Mr. Bub, you have had what is called a domestic loss?"

"You may say, domestic; he'd take his meat out of my mouth—bounce right through a hoop when I cried 'jump'—stand upon his two legs, and lash his precious tail like any whip. Don't talk of it."

"Tail! I was afraid you had lost a favourite child," said Applejohn, somewhat relieved.

"I tell you, he was the pride of my heart; and to-morrow they'll skin him. Such a noble creature! It's only on Monday that he set for his likeness for the king's arms—it was painted for one of our fellows as was 'pointed thimble-maker to the crown,—and now, he's gone."

"I see—you've lost one of the beasts?" said John.

Mr. Buffon Bub turned suddenly round upon Applejohn—stared in his face for a second, and then, with a burst of feeling, exclaimed—"The lion's dead!"

"Dear me!" said John. "Did you have him a long time?"

" I had him in a basket from the ship as brought him from his native place; his mother— poor thing ! she'd eaten up a rajah and a company's captain—was killed afore he was weaned; he was caught, you may say with the milk in his mouth; and now he's dead."

" I don't wonder at your grief, Mr. Bub; no doubt the animal was attached to you," remarked John.

" Attached ! I believe he was : he'd roar when I came within a mile of him ; my own wife didn't know my foot better than he did; and now he's gone.   Poor dear Nero's dead !"

" What—what was his complaint ?" asked John.

" I can't say for certain—but I think his death lays at the door of a d—d stockbroker," exclaimed Bub.

" What could a lion have to do with such a person ?" inquired Applejohn.

" You see, the old stockbroker, after he'd had his bellyfull watching the bears get up the pole, wanted what you call excitement, and would teaze Nero—would poke him about to get up a roar. Well, one day the old fellow somehow or another steals in a big blue cotton umbrella; and there he stood, as I heard, laughing away as if he was winning upon 'Change, and poking the royal animal under the right shoulder.   For a time, the lion treated the old fool with proper contempt; but at last, Nero pounced upon the umbrella, dragged it through the bars, and afore you could say 'stop,' swallowed it complete."

" What! the umbrella?" cried Applejohn.

" I come just in time to see the handle disappear down his throat; I could swear to it—round wooden handle, with five bits of mother-o'-pearl, like shirt-buttons."

" And did the umbrella kill the lion?" asked John.

" Why, some of our people said he'd digest it—but all I know is this; after that, whether the disease were what is called sympathy, or whether it were something in the nerves, I can't rightly say; but this I know, from the time that Nero swallowed the umbrella, it never came on to rain that the poor animal didn't swell three times his proper size." And Mr. Buffon Bub narrated this extraordinary event with a gravity which left nothing for Applejohn to hazard even as a doubt.

" And was he the last of the lions?" inquired John.

" The last and the best," answered Bub. " Poor dear fellow! how he used to love me! Ha! Mr. Applejohn, it would have done your heart good to see him and me play together with a shin of beef: how I'd just grease his whiskers with it, and then

take it away to tease him; and then how he'd jam
his nose between the bars, and loop up his lip o'
each side, and drop his under jaw, and push his
paw sideways out, fishing after my jacket; how he'd
keep up a rattling growl, and I talking and chatting
to him all the while—and the ladies and gen'lmen,
countesses and dukes and lords among 'em, perhaps, looking on, and all more delighted than if
they was at a rational play.   And then, when I
throwd him the bone, to see him drop down upon
it like a thunderbolt, and pull it with his two paws
like any Christian under his breast, with his eyes
looking murder at anybody as should touch it!
Ha! that was a brute—and he's dead."

"But another lion may be had," said Applejohn.

"Another lion!   Perhaps it's my fancy, but for
my part, I think that the breed gets poorer and
poorer every day: lions ar'n't what they used to
be when I was a boy; except Nero, there's hardly
a lion that oughtn't to be ashamed to show his face.
Poor Nero!   Well, I'm afraid I've a good deal to
answer for—I didn't always use him well," said
Bub.

"I don't know for certain, but I think I may
venture to say, you did," observed John.

"No, I didn't; sometimes the fine old fellow
would be dead asleep as a stone—dreaming, perhaps, of lounging about in his own native land, for

he used to pine for it, I know he did, sometimes—
and then I'd rouse him up, to make him walk and
show his paces to a holiday party of little school-
boys; and then, poor thing! he'd sometimes sit
down, and pushing his nose through the bars, give
me such a melancholy look, as much as to say,
' Mr. Buffon Bub, if you'd have stumbled upon
me, fast asleep in Afriky, I'm d—d if you'd have
waked me.'"

" Perhaps, there is a cruelty in chaining up the
brutes,—still I don't know"—and John could not
give a decided opinion on the matter.

" Cruelty ! why, though I'm in the business, I
do sometimes feel for 'em.   Poor things ! isn't it
shocking now, for the hawks to be caged up with
the sparrows flying about 'em, and yet can't get at
'em ?   However, it doesn't answer to think of these
things—we must have science, and—poor Nero !"

" I'm sure you must have a tender heart, Mr.
Bub," said John, " I'm sure you must."

" Why, it's a cowardly thing to hurt wild beasts
once in your power; and do you know, I've an old
thought or so on that matter—it's my belief that
folks who ill use poor beasts in this world, may,
perhaps, be hunted for a while in their turn.   I
say, Mr. Applejohn, how should you like to be
clapped in a cage, with the ghost of a lion for your
keeper ?"

"I never heard of such a thing," said Applejohn.

"No more did I," rejoined Mr. Bub, "but it would be droll if it could happen, wouldn't it? and in after matters, Mr. Applejohn, who can say what won't happen? Here's the house," and the speaker suddenly stopt at the hospitable door of an inn much frequented by the humbler lovers of natural history on their way to and from the Gardens. Mr. Bub led his companion into a small room, where some half-dozen persons were already assembled. We pass the compliments of meeting, circulated among all parties, and hasten to place Applejohn quite at his ease, in the midst of his new associates. It was, however, but too evident that the loss of the day had cast a cloud over the society: or it might be that in deference to the feelings of Mr. Bub, the members restrained their usual flow of mirth, for there was a sad propriety in the looks and words of everybody. Mr. Bub, having lighted his pipe, watched the smoke with a moralizing eye, and thinking of Nero, meditated upon the uncertainty of leonine life. At length he observed, "Ha! gen'lmen, that lion was the flower of the flock."

"Are you sure, Bub?" asked Mr. Rough, an eminent farrier of the neighbourhood, "are you sure that Nero had fair play? My opinion is

pison. There's a many malicious people go to
your Gardens. I wouldn't suspect nobody outright; but this I must say, I saw Doctor Hygian
pelting the poor beast with what seemed biscuit—
I only hope, it warn't pills."

" The loss of Nero," said Bub, not condescending to entertain the suspicion of the farrier, " the
loss of Nero will be a great blow to science."

" And the shillings," added the farrier. " But
you must try and get something else. What are
the fellows about ?"

" It's easy enough, to say get something else,
Mr. Rough, but where are we to get it ? I 'spose
though, the fellows will try at something—and that's
what makes me miserable; 'cause, just now, I don't
want to quit England," said Bub.

" And can nothing be had, unless you go to
catch it, Mr. Bub?" asked Applejohn.

" They pays me the compliment to think so.
I contracted a liver complaint going after the
rhinoceros, and they never give me even a
meddle for it," said Bub.

" All your own fault, Bub," exclaimed Mr.
Paunchly, a thriving butcher, whose good fortune
it was to supply dinners to the *carnivora* of the
gardens; " I must say, all your own fault. You
might have writ a book on that animal, and had it
finely bound in scarlet morocco and gilt edges, and

K 3

made your fortune by it. Yes, anybody but you might have gone to court on that rhinoceros."

"In that matter," confessed Mr. Bub, "perhaps, I was a little back'ard."

"A little!" cried the butcher—"a good way back'ard. What's the use of a man having the brains you have, if he will hide 'em in a bushel? You know every thing—you know, you do; and yet you let the 'fellows' run away with all your credit."

"Poor things!" said the benevolent Bub, "it pleases 'em to think they know a little, and why should I take the conceit out of 'em? Because I know every thing about a beast—where he comes from, what he can eat, what family he belongs to, what's his habits, and in fact, all his private and public history—is that any reason, why I should crow over people, who are perhaps nothing more than lords and members of parliament? Isn't the world big enough for us all? as I said to lady Mildmug, when she would tickle the bear with a stick."

"Ha! you shouldn't have let that rhinoceros slip through your fingers as he did," said Rough, "when you had that chance, you should have thought of your family."

"And pray, Mr. Bub," inquired Applejohn, desirous of withdrawing the naturalist from the friendly censures of his acquaintance, "pray, have the fellows done a great deal for science?"

"For my part," said the farrier, "I don't think we get poultry a bit bigger for all they've done."

"We have not, perhaps, been very lucky," said Bub, with a look of mild reproach at the farrier, "but, you know, what I said about good intentions, Mr. Applejohn—science can't always succeed. To be sure, one of our fellows, Mr. Crawthump, coming to me this very day when he heard of the death of Nero, says to me, 'Ha! Mr. Bub, I've told you so; you'll never prosper while you let in the fellows and their wives and families on the Sabbath. While such wickedness goes on, how can you ever expect to keep a lion?'"

"Humph! He's a nice fellow, he is;" said the butcher; "for my part, the only thing I see to complain of is, keeping the poor beasts without any meat on Sundays."

"It does 'em good, Mr. Paunchly," said the meek Bub, "it does 'em good; in a wild state they lives irregilarly. Sometimes a lion eats a whole buffalo, and then, poor thing! goes without for a week; and then they're ragged and bony, and not in the condition that lions are in a state of civil life. Look at Nero; his skin was as sleek as a bishop's apron."

" And Mr. Crawthump would have you shut out visitors on a Sunday?" asked Applejohn.

" He goes further than that; and, as he said, for the better observance of the Sabbath, he proposed on that day to put all the monkies into strait-waistcoats. More than that, I heard that that was to be part of a bill brought into parliament. Just to satisfy myself, I went down to the House of Commons to look out for that clause. Somehow or the other, I 'spose they found out that I was there, and didn't go on with the matter."

" But what I complain of is, the fellows," said Rough, " have done not a bit of good for science. Poultry is just as dear."

" Mr Rough," said Bub, with impressive placidity, " we should be careful how we blame whole bodies of folks for the blunders of some."

" Very right," exclaimed the butcher.

" Excellently said," remarked Applejohn.

Mr. Bub, unconscious of the praise, proceeded —" Many things have been tried, Mr. Rough, but few have turned up trumps. There's Alderman Whitecross, he was one of the cleverest of the fellows, and had a capital plan for what he called the enlargement of ducks."

" Pray," asked Applejohn, " what plan was that?"

" Why he proposed to make the ducks hatch

nothing else but goose eggs : the alderman was not supported in his plan, and flung his fellowship up as he said in very marked disgust. Don't say we hav'n't tried nothing," said Bub. " Then there was another plan for the improvement of asses."

" Whose plan was that ?" inquired the butcher.

" Why, there was no one name mentioned, but there was a great many fellows in that job," answered Bub. " It was a plan to turn all the asses into zebras ; but the fellows, after many months' debate, found there was just as many asses as before."

" But why—why don't they stick to poultry ? When I first heard of the society, I did promise myself a turkey for ten-pence," said Rough.

" Some people, Mr. Rough, are never to be pleased. Poultry ! What do you say to the plan for taming wild-ducks ? Not spent above a thousand pounds, and we've at least seventy ducks as tame as any of your most familiar acquaintance."

" Ha ! something more might be done for poultry," was still the assertion of the farrier.

" We've tried our best in that matter, I must say ? Why, did you never hear of the plan of Mr. Barleymeal, the great Scotch 'conomy member ? Well, he was one of our fellows ; and had a capital plan to lower fowls to just one half the price."

" What plan was that ? 'Twould be a capital

thing for the poor.   What plan, Mr. Bub?" asked Applejohn.

" Why, Mr. Barleymeal's plan was simply this : he showed what a deal would be saved, and what a deal would be got in the way of chickens, if it could be contrived to make every single egg hatch not less than two."

" Two !" exclaimed the butcher.

" Twins from every egg," said Bub, gravely; " and more than that, he put down upon paper rows and rows of figures, showing how many more chickens would be brought to market—how they would lower butcher's meat,"—

" What a fool !" exclaimed Paunchly.

" And many other profits beside. Well, he counted up I don't know how many hundred chicks, allowing only two for each egg, when how it happened it isn't for me to say —but there wasn't above a third of the chickens ever come to light. Still, you can't say, Mr. Rough, that the fellows was to blame. It's plain, to be sure, that the blame lay somewhere ; but for my part I believe the fault was originally laid with the eggs."

" Ha ! all I know is, there's very little what they call science in the matter. The fellows hav'n't made nothing cheaper," said Rough.

" Did you ever see the beavers we've got in a pond, eh?" asked Bub.

" I have—pretty creatures !" exclaimed Paunchly.

" Well, I should like to know what's made hats so cheap as they are, if it wasn't for our breed of beavers," said Mr. Bub—" but science may work itself blind for some people, and get no thanks."

" Why, you don't kill your beavers for the trade, do you ?" asked the farrier.

" Do you think," said Bub, endeavouring to parry the home-thrust, " do you think the poor things is skinned alive ? Then see how cheap all sorts of furs is got since the fellows dealt in bears. Rabbit-skin's gone down to nothing."

" I hope, Bub—I really do hope," said the disinterested purveyor of shins of beef, " that you'll get a few lions : if not, you may as well let all the fellows discharge themselves, and shut up the Gardens."

" Why, I don't know, if we get a good band next summer—though it goes against the grain of a man as loves science to think of it—still, if we get a good band, a loudish organ or so, a juggler to fling about some knives and balls, and two or three pretty little girls in white muslin frocks and red shoes, to dance upon stilts; why, perhaps, poor Nero mayn't be so very much missed. People, you see, call science by itself dry stuff; so they like science with tumblers."

At this moment the door was opened, and a tall, thin, pale-faced man glided into the room, and catching the eye of Bub, nodded to him, and then with a triumphant look, said in a voice little louder than a whisper, " It's over."

Mr. Bub looked at his tall, fragile friend, and scarcely suppressing a chuckle, asked—" How did they do it?"

" Done it safe enough," answered the stranger, " the thing will never be heard of again."

" You don't say so?" cried Mr. Bub, and he shook with inward laughter.

" In the whole course of my professional exist- ence—and I have, you will concede, Mr. Bub, seen something—I never did see such an exhibi- tion," said the tall man, raising his eyes and hands, and tossing his head, " never."

" You don't say so?" repeated Bub, and again he laughed, " Gone to the devil, eh? Call for what you like, Mr. Shadowly."

" What's the matter, Bub? Not a secret, eh?" asked Paunchly.

" Not at all—it's known pretty well, now. He! he!" gasped Shadowly, " he! he! it's a great triumph. Gone to the devil! A great triumph!"

" All comes of people, as without knowing anything of the matter, meddles with science," said Bub.

" And lower a profession," gasped Shadowly, " However, it's a glorious triumph."

" But what's it all about?" inquired Mr. Rough; "do you call going to the devil a glorious triumph?"

" For me," answered Mr. Shadowly quickly, "it couldn't be more glorious for me."

" To be sure, some people know what's best for 'em," remarked the butcher, staring at Mr. Shadowly.

"You see, gen'lmen, this is the whole affair," and Mr Bub addressed the party. " Mr. Allgag, —you've heard of Mr. Allgag?"

" Of the playhouse, to be sure," said the farrier, " didn't I dock his horses for the last tragedy—and didn't he give me a silver horse-shoe, with his eternal gratitude 'graved upon it?"

" I dare say, sir—I dare say," said Shadowly, with a sneer, " Mr. Allgag is exactly capable of such discrimination."

" Well, Mr. Allgag," resumed Bub, "come to us, and wanted to borrow our polar bear."

" And when I had offered to play Hamlet, too!" said Shadowly, and again he threw up his eyes and arms.

" Not only the bear," said Bub, " but the elephant to boot."

" When I offered my Hamlet ! Well," cried
Shadowly, " it's a great triumph !"

" And I must say the gen'lman,"—

" You don't call him a gentleman ? Good
God ! sir," exclaimed Shadowly, " did you ever
hear what he said of my Hamlet ?"

" I only know," replied Bub, " what he said of
the elephant and bear, and that was very much
like a gen'lman. He said, as for all expense,
that might be d—d ; and my opinion is, that no
gen'lman can say more."

" What ! he wanted to hire your beasts ?" asked
Applejohn, who had kept a long silence.

" That was it, sir," said Shadowly, fixing upon
our hero as a stranger—" when there was my—but
go on, Mr. Bub."

" I was asked about the matter, in course ; but
as I have been all my life for pure science," said
Bub, " I spoke up for the animals."

" Very right—very right, Mr. Bub : had the
manager," said Shadowly, " been without resources, 'twould have been a different matter ; but
when there was a Hamlet—the only Hamlet in the
world, to let—but—he ! he ! almost killed one of
the fiddlers,—great triumph !"

" I said," continued Bub " that to take the animals to a play-house was to remove 'em quite out o' their spear ; and though Mr. Allgag thought all I said was said in the way of a private pike against him, it warn't—it was all for pure science; more than that, I said the bear and the elephant warn't used to applause ; and if they got a good deal of it, I wouldn't answer for the tricks they'd play."

" Very right, Mr. Bub"—said Shadowly, the actor—" there is no answering for anybody under such trying circumstances. I recollect when I acted Hamlet,"—

" So you see," interrupted Bub, " very much to the anger of some o' the fellows, who'd have liked to turn a penny, Mr. Allgag went to another place, hired some beasts, and to-night they comes out. This gen'lman—I sold him a tiger skin"—

" For Othello," said Shadowly, " I dress him that way."

" This gen'lman's been to see 'em," said the naturalist.

" And I take it very unkind of you, Mr. Bub, not to let me know of this," said the butcher, " Bears must be fed ; and though I look at what is called the destruction of the theatre, with as much pain and grief as anybody, still, as bears must be fed, I might as well have had the job as another person."

" Not at all, Mr. Paunchly ; 'cause the bear's on
board wages—that is, his master finds him.   What
I did I did upon principle.   I said to Mr. Allgag when he comes about the beasts,—I said, no,
sir ; do you keep your people to themselves—and
let us keep ours.   If they're mixed so much up
one with the other, folks won't soon care about
any of 'em."

" A remarkably true view of the case," said
Shadowly, " but after to-night, I don't think the
manager will trouble you.   He's had a lesson to-
night I think."

" What did they do, eh ? What did they do ?"
and Bub laughed in the expectation of mischief.

" I'll tell you.   In the first place, the play was
so heavy in itself," said Shadowly, " that not even
an elephant could drag it easily to the third act.
The audience began to hiss and whistle, when—
oh ! a great triumph—the elephant, as if indignant
at the treatment,"——

" He's a noble animal, and if he knows it," said
Bub, " won't take impudence from nobody."

" The elephant turned out of the procession,
and walked to the front of the stage.   There was
a dead pause, when the beast raised its trunk,
lifted up its ears, and screamed.   On this, another
shout was set up, when the bear broke from the
man who held it, jumped into the orchestra, and

catching the respected leader in its paws, hugged him within an inch of his life, many of the musicians, in the agitation of the moment, vainly breaking their fiddle-sticks upon the head of the infuriated animal."

" Ha ! ha ! Well, what will science come to ?" said Bub.

" At length, the bear was beaten from the leader, and dragged away ; but with the elephant stoutly refused to appear again, and the curtain fell, amidst the most delicious clamour. Several distinguished critics who saw me in the house—I was somewhat gratified by the circumstance—exclaimed, ' No bear !' ' Shadowly !' ' No bear !' ' Hamlet !' Well, my friends, at such a time it did not become me as a Christian or a gentleman to bear ill-blood to the manager. I forgot every insult I had endured from the man—I saw that he was on the edge of a precipice, and I resolved to save him."

" Very handsome of you, indeed, sir," said Applejohn.

" What do you think I did, sir ?" asked Shadowly, addressing himself to John.

" Perhaps, offered to take the beasts in your own charge," answered John, " perhaps, offered to lead 'em on again."

" Sir !" and Mr. Shadowly drew himself up, and frowned terribly : then, relaxing from his severity, he observed, "but I see, sir, you don't know me. What do you think I did, gentlemen? I immediately quitted the front of the theatre, and went round to the stage-door. 'Can I see Mr. Allgag?' said I. 'Impossible, sir,' said the man at the door, 'he's coaxing the elephant with toast and ale, and won't be seen by nobody.' 'Take my name instantly to him; say that Mr. Shadowly —he knows the name—will, at the unanimous call of the audience, bury every thing in oblivion, and in the present dreadful crisis, serve the theatre by performing Hamlet. Tell him that. I shall retire to yonder opposite tavern, and await his answer.'"

"Very like a gentleman," said Paunchly.

"When the bear had failed, for you to come for'ard in that manner showed you had no malice, and was very noble," said Mr. Bub.

"I went to the tavern, gentlemen; ordered a Welch rabbit—for I always play Hamlet upon toasted cheese; I find it gives a quality, a certain tone to my voice, and in seven minutes was ready to dress for the part. Three more minutes did I wait—no messenger came, and I again went to the stage-door."

"You couldn't do less," said Applejohn.

"Hear me out, sir; and when I have told my tale, think what you please of human nature. I immediately accosted the man,—you shall hear, gentlemen, every word that passed between us. ' Did you take my name to Mr. Allgag?' 'I did, sir.' ' Did you deliver my message to him—my exact message? Did you tell him every word?' ' I did, sir.' ' And what did he say, when you told him that I would bury every thing in oblivion?' ' Why, he said, sir, as you was about to bury every thing, he hoped you'd bury yourself quite at the bottom of the lot.' "

" Ha! ha! that wasn't bad," roared the farrier.

" I've heard worse than that," said the butcher.

" Yes, he's not bad at a joke, that Allgag," observed Mr. Bub.

" He must, indeed, be a very droll person," remarked Applejohn.

Mr. Shadowly had expected many expressions of sympathy; he therefore with inexpressible disgust listened to the praises of the manager's wit, when the brutality—the shocking brutality of the man—ought to have called down execration. Mr. Shadowly rose, slowly put on his hat, and treating every gentleman present to a smile of ineffable contempt, quitted the room.

In half an hour the company broke up, Mr. Bub requesting Applejohn not to estimate the general wit of the society by what he had heard that night, as he himself—it will sometimes happen in the brightest circles—had never known his friends so very dull.

CHAPTER XV.

JOHN returned to his master's chambers where, in the meekest spirit of resignation, he waited the uncertain coming of the libertine Cramlington. " I shall be very glad when he marries," thought John, as at about three in the morning he was roused from slumber by a clamour in the street. " When he marries, of course he'll keep better hours," concluded John; and as he soothed himself with this comforting thought, he heard a tumult without—a loud knocking at the door, with the voice of Mr. Cramlington and others " high in oath." Applejohn opened the door, and in rushed his master, followed by lord Slap, Plucky, and the Hon. Tom Rumpus.

" Glorious fun ! " cried his lordship, " think I've smashed that fellow's jaw," and the peer, sinking in a chair, took a lady's bonnet from his senatorial head, and laughed immoderately.

" Did you hear the scoundrel inquire of me," asked young Plucky, " what right I had to kiss his wife ?"

" D—d insolent ruffian ! " said the Hon. Tom Rumpus, " if I'd been you, I'd have set him on the spikes of the railings, and then have turned him round."

" It would have served him quite right—but if I hav'n't caught the animal, I've carried off the skin," and young Mr. Plucky produced a fur tippet from his coat pocket.

" Gentlemen,—I—upon my word—you know, these people have no idea of real fun,—if they were to proceed against us for a robbery," suggested Cramlington.

" There'd be fun!" cried lord Slap. " I say, Cram, should like to see you in the prisoner's dock —with your nose snuffing the southernwood and rue. But I say, Mr. Cramlington," and his lordship took a severe tone, " you've shown yourself rather nice to-night; in our attack upon that old scoundrel, Zweifler—devilish lucky I thought of him as we passed the door—you hung back like a cur."

" A what, my lord,—was cur the word?" asked Cramlington with considerable passion, for he felt that all the eyes of Rumpus and Plucky were upon him—" a cur, my lord!"

" I—I withdraw the cur,—but you must confess you hung fire," said the peer.

" I—the truth is, my lord, I believe that at the bottom, old Zweifler is a tolerable person, and"—

" It's no matter; as you were so diffident in

making a personal call, you couldn't do less than send your card."

" My card ! my lord, what may I ask ?"—

But the inquiry of Mr. Cramlington was broken short by a knocking at the door, and the shouting of Rowdow and Smasherton. The door was opened, when the two useful and illustrious members entered, dragging between them a remarkably diminutive and youthful-looking person, who in vain endeavoured to escape; they lifted him, despite his struggling, upon the table.

" Caught the vagabond, as he was running by the door," said Smasherton, " sure he's a thief."

" Upon my word, gentlemen, I'm not—I'm "—exclaimed the prisoner.

" Search him," cried Slap, " shouldn't wonder if he hasn't got the crown jewels in his pocket. What's your name ?"

" Tape, sir," said the trembling little fellow, " Maximilian Tape."

" Great historical likeness to Colonel Blood," said Slap; " where's the jewels, you villain ?"

" I—I'm not a thief, gentlemen; I'm a—a—tailor—I'm,"—and the man recognized John—" Oh, Mr. Applejohn ! is it you, sir ?—you can answer that I'm a tailor; you know we've worked together in "—

" What ! " exclaimed Cramlington, turning

MAXIMILIAN TAPE BEFORE THE "LORDS."

very wrathfully round upon John, " are you a tailor ? "

" I—I was bred to the business, sir," said Applejohn, " but I—I"—

"Yes, yes—there's more to be got by a crooked nail than with an honest needle," said Tape, and Applejohn's teeth began to chatter at the insinuation of the captive. Luckily however for John, the gentlemen were too intent upon their immediate sport with the prisoner, to give attention to his sneers at his fellow-workman.

" Silence !" cried lord Slap, " if you're a tailor, prove your words ; come, if you're really a knight of the needle," and lord Slap broke a plate upon the head of the unfortunate little man, " sew the pieces up again."

" Gentlemen—pray, gentlemen, let me go, for my wife's sake," cried Tape.

" Your wife ! Why, you miscreant," said Rowdow, " how long have you been breeched ?"

" I told you I had a wife and family," cried Tape.

" Family !" said lord Slap, " well—d—n it ! you a family ! I shall think less of children after this. How many, you illicit ruffian ?" roared lord Slap.

Maximilian Tape shrank within himself, and gasped in his fear as he confessed—" Five."

" Five !" cried Plucky.

" Five," replied the father, " and I was running for the doctor for my wife, when these gentlemen"——

" The doctor !   Oh ! no wonder, d——n me !" said Slap, " that gentlemen like us are ground to the dust by taxes, when idle ragamuffins like you bring such large families about us."

" But for such villains, I could keep my foxhounds," said Rowdow. " And you're a tailor, eh ? Who's your master ?"

" Mr. Zweifler," said the man ; " if you'll only go to him,"——

" Better let the fellow go," was the advice of Cramlington ; " he's going for the doctor ; consider his poor wife."

" Why, you atrocious wretch, that will make six children. Horrible !" cried young Plucky. " Don't let him go before he gives us pledges."

" I'll give you anything, gentlemen ; but do consider my wife," said Tape.

" Well, then, if we let you go this time," questioned lord Slap, " will you promise this honourable company never to do so any more ?"

" I'll promise anything, sir, that a man should promise," cried the tailor.

" Man !   You a man—if you dare to entertain such an opinion,"—and lord Slap shook Tape by the collar, who promised for the future to eschew

such conceit, if the honourable company would but
suffer him to depart.

" Stop, Slap; don't let him go yet," cried
Rumpus, "as all of us are in the Education Commission," and Tom winked at his friends, " it is
our duty to get pledges for the new baby. Now, Mr.
Tape; if you should be blessed with a son, will you
give us your solemn word not to make the child a
member of parliament?"

" La! gentlemen," answered the simple Tape,
" I hope to bring the child up to some honest
trade, I shouldn't think of any thing else."

" Will you promise not to compel the boy to be
a general officer?" asked Rowdow.

" Or a lord chancellor?" said Plucky.

" Or an archbishop?" required Slap.

" He shall be nothing, if you'll let me go, gentlemen," said Tape.

" No tailor can promise more;" said Smasherton,
" let him go."

" Stop," cried Rumpus, " if you're a true tailor,
you have a needle about you; so, without another
word, write us the promise in your blood."

" I—I can't write, gentlemen. Oh! my poor
wife," and the wretched little man lifted up his
hands entreatingly.

" Vanish, then!" cried Slap, " but mind, you
outlawed rascal, mind, you never do so again." A

way was made for the tailor to the door, and with the agility of a grasshopper the little man skipped from his tormentors, all of whom save Cramlington laughed immoderately at the adventure. "There, now," exclamed Slap, "if that isn't wit, I don't know what wit is."

"Well, what's to be done now?" asked Rumpus. "Why, Cram, you look as lively as old Laocoon."

"Do you know," said Plucky, "I'm afraid that we have unconsciously given pain to one of Mr. Cramlington's relations."

"My relation, sir?" asked Cramlington, stammering and blushing.

"Yes; to Mr. Maximilian Tape: I'm sure he must have been a younger brother at least, you seem so devilishly affected."

"Mr. Plucky," cried Cramlington, his eyes flashing fire, "we are comparatively strangers,—still, sir, permit me to hope that you do not wish to insult me. You do not really mean to insinuate that I'm any relation to that"—

"Ha! ha! Why, really, Mr. Cramlington," said Plucky, "I did but joke—I—of course, I should as soon think you the son and heir of a darning needle." Mr. Cramlington instantly seized Mr. Plucky's hand, pressing it with great warmth of feeling. "But what makes you, Cram, so very bilious in your mirth?"

" Why, the truth is," said Slap, " poor Cram's in love."

" Now, my lord—my dear lord," cried Cramlington, " I—there are sacred subjects, my lord."

" To be sure ; talking of sacred subjects," said his lordship, " I have that old rascal's door-plate in my pocket—there, Cram, it's at your service," and lord Slap flung a brass-plate, with " Zweifler" on it, upon the table. " Bet a hundred I wrench off door-plate or knocker with any born gentleman in the kingdom."

" Really, my lord," said Cramlington, " I hope we're not going too far : I trust that in these attacks on private property,"—

" Private property ! D—n it ! if you're getting sentimental," cried his lordship, " I've done with you. Come, gentlemen—another turn, and then soberly to bed at four. Farewell, Cram,—I suppose you'll stop at home and take gruel to-night ?"

" I am not very well, my lord—if you could do without me," and Cramlington looked imploringly.

" We'll try—come, gentlemen ;" and Slap having donned a hat, the property of Cramlington, quitted the chamber, followed by his sprightly companions, who, we regret to state, did not couple the name of their domestic friend with the most respectful epithets.

" Not thorough-bred, I should say," observed

young Plucky, " no, under-bred, depend upon it—
as I'm a gentleman, under-bred."   In quitting the
party to return to Cramlington, it may be an
equal matter of surprise and gratification to the
reader to learn that the distinguished individuals,
after a fruitless search for humour, retired at an
unusually early hour, soberly to bed.

Mr. Cramlington sat in a pensive mood, with
his eye upon Zweifler's violated door-plate.   At
length, he condescended to address his servant.
" I—I don't think this proceeding quite right.
What do you think, John ? "

" Why, sir, in a poor man I should call it high-
way-robbery ; as it is, sir, I can't give an opinion.
Only this, sir, I would advise you not to let the
property be found on the premises.   Pray, sir,
will you allow me to ask you a question ? " Cramlington bowed assent.   " How long may it be
before you think of getting married ?   I wouldn't
leave you for the world, sir ; but, really, lord
Slap puts a poor man's character quite at stake."

" You are right, John ; I ought to marry : I
have seen enough of society—had enough to do
with titled men.   After all, what is there in a title ?
For as I said, in a song I wrote when quite a
boy—

> ' The rank is but the guinea's stamp,
> The man's the gold for all that.' "

" Oh ! that's capital, sir—that's really capital !
I do think, sir, if you would but talk a little of
your poetry to lord Slap and his friends 'twould do
'em some good."

Cramlington shook his head, and with a languid
smile, said, " I fear not, John—I fear not." This
was no doubt a fixed opinion of Mr. Cramlington,
inasmuch as he never did condescend to bestow a
line of those numerous effusions upon his high
companions, which he so liberally imparted to his
valet. " Yes, John—I certainly will marry : I feel
that without the object of one's heart—what are
those lines of mine ? hang it ! I wrote them so
long ago—ha !—I remember :—

> ' Without the smile from partial beauty won,
> Oh ! what is man ?—a world without a sun. '

I never wrote a truer couplet—I feel it, never,"
said the poet.

" As I'm alive, I could stay here till this time
to-morrow, listening to all your beautiful things,
sir," said Applejohn, " I could, indeed."

" But it's getting late, John ; good night," and
Cramlington rose to retire to his bed ; he paused, and
putting his hand to his forehead, said—" Tut ! the
lines have escaped me ; they were in a tragedy I
once wrote, but I left the manuscript in a hackney-
coach."

" Bless my heart ! sir," cried John, shocked at the loss, " and did you offer no reward for it ?"

" 'Twasn't worth the trouble. Now, I have it—but I do believe they're the only lines I can remember out of the whole play ; but they do strike me as being rather strong. Let me see," and Cramlington, extending his right arm, and grasping his black artificial locks with his left hand, to the passing fear of Applejohn, bellowed the following lines—

> " ''Tis now the very witching time of night ;
> When churchyards yawn, and hell itself breathes out
> Contagion to this world : now could I drink hot blood,
> And do such business as the bitter day
> Would quake to' "—

" For goodness sake ! sir," exclaimed John, frightened by the terrible purpose of the poet.

" Don't be alarmed, John ; I forget the rest—but they're strong ar'n't they ?" asked the bard.

" Shockingly strong, sir," said Applejohn, " and you left the written book in a hackney-coach, sir, —had you no copy, sir ?"

" Hang it ! no—it's gone, and it's no use grieving about it : still I do think, if I had had that tragedy acted, it might have done something ; to be sure, we are never proper judges of our own works, yet I do think that little play one of the neatest things I ever wrote."

" What was it called, sir ?" asked John.

" I never gave it a title," answered the unfortunate poet.

" How unlucky ! That made it more difficult to come at—how very unlucky," repeated John.

" Good night, John—good—ha !—a couplet has just hopped into my head—an original couplet—it isn't bad for a sudden thought—

> ' To both of us a fair good night,
> And rosy dreams, and slumbers light.'"—

" Beautiful !" exclaimed John.

" Tolerable, for a sudden thought," said John's retiring master.

CHAPTER XVI.

EARLY next morning, as Mr. Cramlington sat at breakfast, he was alarmed by a knock at the door. " If it should be Mr. Zweifler for his door-plate," cried John.

" Booby," said his master, dropping an egg-cup at the words, and turning very pale, " booby—how should he know it was here ? "

" That's true, sir;" replied John, " see what a thing is conscience." Another knock. " Still, sir, if it should be Mr. Zweifler for *you*."

" I'm not at home, John," and young Cramlington ran like a startled hare into his bed-room, and closed the door, which he was heard to bolt and lock. Again the knocker sounded, and John's heart sank at the summons. How could he think of confronting the terrible looks of the old tailor! John stared in vain around him for the friendly wig, there was no help for it; he must, in · his natural hair, appear before the man who had caught him with the crooked nail 'twixt thumb and finger. Another knock—and John, in desperation, opened the door. He trembled, and slowly raised his eyes to meet, as he feared, the burning glances of a furious old tailor, when he beheld the smiling, shining face of a damsel of about two-and-twenty; who, simpering at the confusion of John, held towards him a curiously folded piece of paper, and saying, "For Mr. Cramlington," dropt the note at John's feet, and ran away. John stared awhile about him—thought of Sarah Twopenny, sighed, picked up the note, and, walking to the bed-room door, rapped with his knuckles, and, to the great relief of the prisoner within, said—"You may come out, sir."

"Who was it?" asked Cramlington, rejoiced at his liberty.

"A letter, sir; a young woman brought it—she flung it down, and ran away," answered John.

"Why the devil didn't you stop her? Why did

you let her run ?—Now, what a deal of misery or joy, John," said Cramlington, sighing and looking interesting, and turning the note in his fingers, " may be contained in a little piece of paper ! As I have said in an epistle of mine—humph ! I forget, but 'twas a translation from the Latin of a nun, Heloisa—it was something about letters, but no matter." Mr. Cramlington opened the note, and his face beamed with sudden happiness. He sat down, and smiling placidly at Appiejohn, said— " John, my time is come."

" Dear me, sir ! what do you mean ?" asked the anxious domestic.

" Get my trunks in order—my time is come. I shall carry of my lovely Caroline to-night, this note —this precious note—is't not," and Cramlington again folded the note, and flourished it to and fro— " is't not like the wing of Cupid ?"

" Why, sir, if I must say, I think it's more like a cocked hat," said John.

" John, you want imagination ; you want a part of that extraordinary faculty of which I possess so much—which makes every thing out of nothing ; which finds "—

" Talking of finding, sir," said John interrupting his master, " I only wish you could find that tragedy you left in the hackney-coach."

" Pooh ! 'tisn't worth thinking of," said Cramlington.

" I know, sir, I've done nothing but dream about
it all night. That bit, sir, where you make the
' churchyard yawn,' and the ' hot blood,'—that's
terribly fine."

" Nothing to what I have done; however, let
my trunk be in readiness—my coat, cloak, and
everything for a journey for two. I shall be back
at six, and then you must be prepared to attend
me. First I must in person—give me my wig,
John—fly to my darling Caroline. My wig, John."

John with reluctant step retired for the raven
wig and whiskers, and returned with them, stood
looking pensively at his master.

" What's the fellow staring at ?" said Cramlington,
" give me the wig."

" I wouldn't do it, sir, if I was you," said John,
still holding back the jetty decoration.

" Wouldn't do what ?"

" Why, sir, as it comes so near, I'd throw off
disguise, and go to the lady in my true colours.
For instance, sir, if the lady don't like a fair man,
see what a wretched house you'll have after you
marry. I'd give up the black, sir," said Applejohn,
" I would indeed."

" John, you're a fool, and know nothing of the

sex: they love us the better for cheating 'em—they
do, indeed. Though—hang 'em!—we are no match
for 'em; no, they beat us hollow. As I have said
in a little song of mine, in an opera that may come
out some day, for I've been so busy of late, I've
not had time to do the music—in that little song,
I remember, I—the air is rather pretty and all my
own, it goes much in this way;" whereupon, Mr.
Cramlington chirped the following lines to what
John considered a very original air:—

> " 'Tis woman that seduces all mankind,
>   By her we first are taught th' inveigling arts,
> Her very eyes can cheat when most she's kind,
>   She tricks us of our money with our hearts."

" It's too true, sir," said Applejohn sighing.
Cramlington proceeded in a louder voice—

> " For her like wolves by night we prowl for prey,
>   And practise ev'ry fraud to bribe her charms,
> For suits of love like law, are earn'd by pay,
>   And beauty must be feed into our arms."

" I'm afraid it's too true," said Applejohn.—

> " ' And beauty must be feed into our arms.' "

sang Cramlington, and catching his face in the
glass, he stuck his hat upon his head, flung up his
arm, and again repeating the shameful libel on the
disinterestedness of the adorable sex, the singer
quitted his chamber for the street.

" I've thought too well of 'em, all my life," mused
Applejohn left to himself, " if I'd been a rascal,

what a happy fellow I might have been !"   John,
however, made all possible haste to fulfil the orders
of his master : every thing was speedily prepared,
and John waited anxiously for the arrival of the
poet and musician, though not without trembling
at every sound, lest old Zweifler should again appear.   Six o'clock came, and brought back Cramlington ; he was in a very flutter of delight.   Entering the room, he exclaimed—

> "' Blest as the immortal Gods is he—
> The youth who fondly sits by thee !'

In three hours more—a short three hours, and we
shall be galloping to the altar—I shall call her
mine—is my trunk ready ? all her charms—my
great coat ? her warm, devoted heart—mind, my
comforter.   Her blushing face—her—her—if, now,
I could subdue myself for five minutes, I feel that
I could write the most beautiful bit of verse—I"—

" Here's pen, ink, and paper, sir," said Applejohn.

Mr. Cramlington sat down, and taking the goose-
quill between his thumb and finger, brushed his
black locks back, and looked either very much in-
spired, or very hungry.   He then applied three
fingers of his left hand just over the top of his nose—
frowned—looked at the carpet—again stared at the
paper—and rising, put down the pen, with these
remarkable words—" It's no matter."

" Won't you write anything, sir?" asked the disappointed Applejohn.

" I'll throw off an ode in the carriage; there isn't time, now," said the poet.　" I must dress for the theatre—we must be there at seven."

" What! sir—do you go to the playhouse first?" inquired John.

" That's part of the plot, John; part of the plot. The post-chaise will be waiting for us at the end of the street; Caroline will be taken with a sudden faintness at the conclusion of the first act; indeed, she'll be so very ill, that she'll be obliged to go home immediately."

" Dear me! sir—I hope not," cried John, "for in that case "—

" Simpleton! In that case, I shall insist upon seeing her home, leaving her respected uncle and aunt in the boxes—her sister Maria is in the plot— then we jump into the coach, and"—

" I see it now," observed John with extraordinary sagacity.　" Then you'll carry her off and marry her."

" Nothing less, as I'm a gentleman: there'll be a pretty stir, i' faith—a very pretty stir; shouldn't wonder if some of the cousins want to shoot me; but no matter, as I've said in one of my unprinted works—

　　' Come what will, I have been bless'd ! ' "

" Why, yes, sir; and once done, they can't un-
marry you," said John, "that *is* a comfort."

" Sometimes," observed Cramlington; " but,
quick, John—we have no time to lose. Call a
coach, put everything in it,"—

" Do I travel with you ?" asked John.

" Certainly not," was the reply of his master, who
straightway gave his servant the fullest directions for
the business of the night. The luggage was to be
taken to a certain inn, where the post-chaise had
been ordered—the trunk of Caroline had already
been secretly despatched there—the post-boy knew
where to wait, and John was to be at the door of
the theatre, to attend the coming of the happy
couple, and take further orders. We are happy to
inform the reader that all these preliminaries were
effected in the happiest manner. Seven o'clock
was come—was past; Mr. and Mrs. Monteagle,
and their lovely nieces, Caroline and Maria Monteagle, with an interesting cousin, named Frederick
Ponto, new from Bombay, and the happy, exulting
Henry Cramlington had passed the threshold of
that Temple of the Muses—too often made the
Mews for the horses—and were seated in the box—
the post-boy sauntered by his ready vehicle at the
end of the street, and John Applejohn kept watch
beneath a portico, massive if not very picturesque.
The evening grew chilly, and John in his ex-

ceeding tenderness for the health of his master, bethought him of a thick great coat, deposited with the luggage in the chaise: he immediately walked to the end of the street, and was accosted by the post-boy.

" Coming?" was the brief question.

" Every minute," answered Applejohn, taking the coat from the chaise, and returning to his place of watch. He had not remained there many minutes, when he was familiarly accosted by a tall thin man.

" Why, you've never come to see the elephant? Try him again to-night—ha! ha!—be damned again; glorious triumph!" On this John immediately recognized Shadowly, the disappointed Hamlet of the previous evening. " You never came to see this trash?" asked the tall man— " Let me hope, my dear sir, that you make no party to uphold the bear to the destruction of the true drama?"

" Certainly not, sir," answered Applejohn, " I was waiting here for—for"—

" I thought so; I was sure from a certain intelligence of manner that"—and here the speaker grasped John's hand—" did you ever see my Hamlet?"

" Never had that pleasure," said John.

" Only wait a little—they'll be sure to send for

me—I know they will; the elephant can't go through
it; they may try to thrust him down, but they must
fall back upon my Hamlet. You say, you never saw
it? Very well; it's all right. I am not a malicious
man—thank heaven! I'm not a malicious man, or
after the insults I have received from the manager,
I might refuse to come forward.   However, I trust
that my devotion to the true interests of the stage
will render me forgetful of petty annoyances.—I—
I have been three times round to the stage-door,
offering my services—I have my Hamlet's dress all
ready; cloak, star, sword, everything—I am now
about to go for the fourth time; yes, for the fourth
and last time, knowing that the elephant must fail,
I'll step forward to save the house from inevitable
destruction. The manager shall not say, that I
suffered personal feeling to destroy the real drama
at the last moment. Come with me, I'll take you
behind the scenes."

"I'm very much obliged to you—another time
—but I have business, and can't at present stir from
this spot," said Applejohn.

"Stay here, then; I'll send a man round for
you—for I shall be dressing for the part in five
minutes,—I'll send a man, who shall take you into
the theatre. I will—upon the honour of a gentleman," was the assurance of the sanguine Mr. Shadowly, who turned from John, to offer for the fourth

and last time the entire use of his Hamlet to a sinking manager. The reader, however, may judge of
the spirit with which the kind, the benevolent offer
was received, from the fact, that in less than ten
minutes Mr. Shadowly returned with huge strides
to the portico, where John with the coat on his
arm was still waiting. Great was the indignation
in the looks of the actor ! He seized Applejohn
by the arm, and in a loud, whistling voice, exclaimed—

" '———— Now could I drink hot blood;
  And do such business as the bitter day
  Would quake to look upon !'

" I could," exclaimed Shadowly, glaring at the
astonished Applejohn—" I could."

" I say," said John, taking breath, " did you
ever find anything in a hackney-coach ? "

" Talk not to me of hackney-coaches, man,"
cried Shadowly, " what think you of that villain
Allgag—that thief—that ? "—

" Why, as for thief, Mr.—I believe your name's
Shadowly?" and John began to put a very serious
face upon the matter.

" It is, sir; Jaffier Shadowly : but that is not now
the business, it "—

" Oh ! I don't know that : things come out very
curiously; would you be good enough to repeat
those words—those about ' hot blood ? ' "

" What ! you like my way of speaking them ?

There never was man, woman, or child who did not like my way; and yet that villain Allgag! I have this moment made to him my fourth offer, and would you believe it?"—

" Yes; but the ' hot blood?'" said Applejohn.

" Ha! you're a man of taste—I can perceive that you have the right feeling of the art," said Shadowly.

" The—the ' hot blood'—if you please," urged Applejohn.

" But, never mind; you shall see me play the whole part—you shall; and when that elephant and that wretched bear are dug up centuries hence in a fossil state,—why then, yes, even then, my Hamlet,"—

" I beg your pardon, but I insist upon hearing those words again," pressed John, " I must hear them."

" I admire your enthusiasm, young man: it is complimentary—I feel it to be so. Yet, don't be impatient; the words are,"—John appeared to listen with the deepest attention—" the words are—

'——— Now could I drink hot blood;
And do such business as the bitter day
Would quake to look upon!'"

" And you'll mean to tell me, Mr. Shadowly," said John, becoming excited, " you'll mean to tell me, you've never been in a hackney-coach?"

" Often—what has that to do with Hamlet?" asked Shadowly.

" I mean—you know very well what I mean—that you never found anything in a hackney-coach? Now, consider; and confess the truth."

" Found anything in a hackney-coach !" exclaimed Shadowly.

" If you'll give up the property at once, I'll"—John was interrupted in his intended proposition by his master, who called him from the lobby; John ran in great haste to Gruelthorpe, whom he found with a lady trembling on his arm. " Oh, sir ! you don't know what I have to tell you !" exclaimed John.

" Silence, blockhead—run and prepare the coach—silence, I say. What have you there?" said Cramlington.

" Your coat, sir,—only your coat, sir; but I was going to say,"—

" Fool ! give it me—and away," exclaimed Cramlington, snatching the coat from his servant; when the pocket-book—carelessly left in the coat of Mr. Henry Cramlington—fell from the pocket, and was instantly picked up by a lurking thief, who immediately made from the lobby with his prize.

" Sir—sir—stop thief !—sir, you've lost your pocket-book," exclaimed a stranger.

" My pocket-book ! " cried Cramlington.

" Yes, sir—I saw him—I saw it fall—I'll catch him—stop thief ! " roared Applejohn, and was running in pursuit of the offender, when Mr. Cramlington seized John by the collar.

" Let him be—stay where you are—poor wretch ! —I wouldn't prosecute—I "—exclaimed Cramlington in sudden agitation.

" Oh, sir ! you're too kind, sir—stop thief !—you must, sir,—stop thief ! " roared Applejohn, and with a sudden and violent effort he disengaged himself from his compassionate master, and ran, crying " stop thief ! " after the delinquent.

" I—I—I wouldn't prosecute—it's no matter— come, Caroline," said Cramlington, endeavouring to make his way through the crowd too quickly gathered about him.

" But, sir—'tis a duty, sir, you owe to society, sir," said the stranger; " I hope the scoundrel will be caught."

" What's this, Mr. Cramlington,—robbed ?"— asked Mr. Frederick Ponto, that gentleman having followed the fair Caroline from the box, resolving, despite the assurance of Maria that her sister would soon be better, to attend the sufferer to her carriage. " Eh; Caroline—why you seem, very much better ? "

" Very much—very much better," said Cram-

lington, " this way—this way ;" and the lover
endeavoured to hurry his trembling charge through
a crowd of people, all considerably interested in the
loss of the gentleman, and the probable capture of
the thief.

" Hurra ! we've caught him—here he is !—bring
him along !" cried twenty voices, as the robber
was dragged forward.

" I caught him, sir—nearly slipped through my
fingers though !" exclaimed the almost breathless
Applejohn,—" but I fixed my hand in his collar,
sir—and here—here—here's your pocket-book,
sir ! "

" Pocket-book ? Ha ! ha ! Pocket-book ! Hurra
for a pocket-book !" and a roar of laughter from
the mob greeted the display of the recovered property. The reader will, possibly, cease to wonder
at this vulgar merriment, when we inform him that
the pocket-book—an article apparently stuffed with
bank-paper,—the valuable pocket-book of Henry
Cramlington, Esq., suddenly exhibited by the
trusty Applejohn, appeared no other than—a
tailor's book of patterns !

Mr. Cramlington turned pale, and almost fainted,
as he stared at the damning witnesses in blue, black,
grey, green, brown !

" Caroline !" said Frederick Ponto to his cousin,
and offered his arm.

"Frederick!" cried the young lady, and—evidently not knowing what she did—accepted it.

"Positively, a tailor!" exclaimed Frederick—"well, I thought there was a mystery about"—

"Spare my feelings, Frederick—spare my feelings," was the entreaty of Caroline, as bewildered with shame and disappointment, she was assisted into the carriage by her cousin. (We may here as well dispose of the lady, by stating that in six weeks after the above melancholy catastrophe, she became Mrs. Ponto.)

"Oh! you infernal scoundrel!" exclaimed Cramlington, gnashing his teeth, and clenching his fist.

"A wicked thief," said Applejohn, believing that his master addressed the robber.

"But I'll trounce you, I will—yes, I'll—I'll"—Cramlington was speechless with passion.

"You must prosecute him, sir," said a police constable; "this way, sir—this way—the office is open."

"No—no—I don't mean to prosecute—I don't" —and Cramlington sought to escape, but the constables crowding about him, declared with several respectable lookers-on, that it was a duty the gentleman owed to society to transport the thief; and thus, despite of himself, Cramlington was hurried before the magistrate, many vulgar persons among

the crowd addressing himself and the robber on
the way.

" What a shame to rob a tailor !" cried one
benevolent person——" I say, when will my coat be
done ?" inquired a second——" Button, not so short
in the skirts as the last, if you please."——" Jack,
what colour will you have ?—'cause, make your
choice, and he'll measure you." Such were the
sundry calls, gladdening the ears of the astonished
Cramlington, as he was hurried to the office.

" Now, what's all this ?" asked the magistrate as
the constables brought in the robber, the robbed,
and the witnesses. " What is this ?"

" Pickpocket, your worship," answered the constable, and the features of the accused were collateral evidence against him.

" Who has he robbed ?" inquired the magistrate
—" Is this the gentleman ?"

" He's no gentleman," said the prisoner, who
then added with the most profoud contempt—" he's
only a tailor."

" State your case," said the magistrate to Cramlington ; who trembling and stammering, deposed
that his pocket had been picked by the prisoner at
the bar. " Is that your property ?" inquired his
worship, pointing to the pattern-book.

" It—it is," answered Cramlington, blushing to
the ears.

M 2

" You are a tailor, then ?" said his worship.

" I—I was a tailor; but I—I do not practise at present—I am retired—I—I assure you, my lord, this is to me a most distressing situation ; and as I understand that the prisoner at the bar"—how Mr. Cramlington became aware of the domestic fact, we know not—" is married, and has a very —very large family"—

" Gammon," said the hardened culprit, with the most offensive leer at his unwilling prosecutor.

" My good man, don't injure your cause," said the compasionate Cramlington.

" That will do, sir—that will do ; the prisoner is committed for trial," and to the horror of the complainant he was bound over to prosecute the offender.   Mr. Cramlington was about to quit the office, when Applejohn called to him—

" Sir —sir—don't go—there's another thief," for though John was much astonished at finding in his magnificent master only a retired tailor, he was nevertheless determined that his employer should have justice upon all his evil-doers.   " Mr. Cramlington—don't go, sir"—

" Another thief!" exclaimed the magistrate; and then in an authoritative voice to Cramlington —" come back, sir."   That gentleman turned back, and looking at John as though he could have eaten him, *cum grano salis,* anxiously awaited the event.

"Now, what is this?" asked his worship, "what's your charge?"

"If you please, your worship, there's something very mysterious in the conduct of that gentleman there," said Applejohn.

"Mysterious! don't talk in that manner here, sir, have you any charge to make?" asked his worship.

"If my master will let me, please your worship, I think I can get out something that may lead to the discovery of a dishonest transaction that"—

"Come, come; you beat too much about the bush for an honest man. Have you any charge to make?"

"I think I shall have, your worship. If you'll first allow me to ask of that gentleman—it's you, I mean, sir,"—and John addressed himself to the tall, pale Shadowly who had come among the crowd to witness the proceedings against the pickpocket.

"And what are you, sir?" asked the magistrate of Shadowly.

"My name, sir, is Jaffier Shadowly; I believe, pretty well known—despite the baseness of some parties—pretty well known, indeed, sir."

"Have you any charge against this man?" inquired his worship of Applejohn.

" I can take my oath, sir, to a certain fact; there may be some mistake in the matter—on the other hand, there may be robbery.   Mr. Shadowly, will you just speak over those lines, you spoke to me— Mr. Cramlington, pray, sir, attend; you'll be astonished, when you hear 'em—those lines you spoke to-night?"

" Your worship," asked Mr. Shadowly, with a smile and a graceful bending of the body, " have I your permission?"

" Strange case, this," said the magistrate, somewhat amused—" go on, sir; but don't be long."

" Your worship," said Mr. Shadowly, " I am proud of the opportunity so strangely afforded me, of showing you how infamously I have been treated by the champion of that system, which has crushed the native drama of the English stage, which has"—

" Go on with your business, sir; I have the cases of two or three pickpockets to listen to; I can't have my time wasted with the native drama. Go on."

" I obey, sir;" said Mr. Shadowly, preparing himself.

" Mind—the very lines," cried Applejohn.

" I know my cue without a prompter," replied Shadowly with a sneer; and then, fixed in his favorite attitude began :—

" ' 'Tis now the very witching time of night ;
When churchyards yawn, and hell itself breathes out
Contagion to this world.   Now could I drink hot blood' "—

" There—there ! " exclaimed Applejohn, incapable of longer silence.   Mr. Shadowly threw
at him an annihilating look, and repeated the
words—

" '——————— Now could I drink hot blood ;
And do such business as the bitter day
Would quake to look on.' "

" There, sir—there," cried Applejohn to his
master—" isn't that enough ?   Won't you make a
charge ? "

Mr. Cramlington bit his lip, and shook his head
with looks of great confusion at his well-meaning,
but too officious servant.

" What is all this ? " inquired the magistrate.

" Why, your worship, I should like to ask Mr.
Shadowly if he didn't get that speech out of a
play ? " asked Applejohn.

" Out of a play ! " echoed Shadowly—" why,
did you never hear of the sweet Swan of Avon ? "

" Never mind swans or geese neither, that's
nothing to do with the present charge,"—said
Applejohn.   " Let me ask you one thing—it's no
use, sir, I will speak," said John to his agonised
master, " you'd let people take the eyes out of your

head, and say nothing—I only want to ask you, if you know any more of that play?"

"Your worship," said Mr. Jaffier Shadowly, with a deeper smile, a lower bow than before, "it will give me infinite pleasure to go through the whole of the part, before you—and if any gentlemen of the press are present, I hope for their liberal treatment under the circumstances.—The whole of the part, your worship, beginning with the line—

'A little more than kin, and less than kind,'

and ending with, for I play it from the original edition—

"Why does the drum come hither?'"

"What is this jargon about?" asked the magistrate; and then to Applejohn—"Have you any charge to make?"

"In a minute, your worship," said John. "You confess, Mr. Shadowly, that you got all that from a play?"

"Why," replied Shadowly, with a pitying smile, "why, of course."

"Then, your worship," exclaimed John with energy, "I'm prepared to swear that what he's got he hasn't got honestly: I am prepared to swear upon the information of Mr. Cramlington, that that play is my master's property!"

" Your master's property!" cried all except Cramlington.

" My master's property," asseverated John; " he wrote it—it was never printed—and moreover he told me that he lost the written book—left it in a hackney-coach!" A shout of laughter followed this declaration.

" Pray, sir," and the magistrate with very creditable gravity, turned to the retired tailor, Cramlington—" pray, sir, am I to understand that I sit before the author of Hamlet?"

" Really, sir," replied Cramlington, quite confounded by the disasters of the night, " I trust that I am not called upon to bear the blunders of my servant. I did certainly speak of a book, a manuscript copy, left by me in a hackney-coach, and my domestic—a simple person, as you perceive, sir— he has confused the—the—your worship must perceive the"—poor Cramlington tried to smile, and rushing from the office, stammered—" the very ludicrous mistake!"

" There never was so easy a man as my master," said John to Shadowly; " you've had a lucky escape, I can tell you; if it had been some men"—

At this moment there was a sudden noise in the passage, and immediately John, to his consternation, saw Mr. Cramlington, his respected master, dragged back to the office by the rude hand of Carl

Zweifler, followed by his diminutive journeyman, Maximilian Tape.

"I have got de teef—I have got de teef—my vindow—my door-blate!" exclaimed the old tailor.

"Silence—silence! What is this?" cried the magistrate.

"I vill hang him—I never did tink to hang a man—but mein Gott!—I vill hang dis teef," and Zweifler stood with his clenched hands, and his eyes glaring like a hungry cannibal upon the unfortunate culprit, involved in the fun, the glorious fun, of his noble friends—Slap, Rowdow, and party.

"What is the charge?" said the magistrate. "Take off your hat, fellow—take off his hat, officer."

The officer with more zeal than civility struck at the hat of Cramlington, and knocking it from his head, knocked with it his superb black wig, and the bushy whiskers thereto appended. Henry Cramlington stood confessed at the bar, with bare face and flaxen locks! Old Zweifler had proceeded with the greatest vehemence—"Dis teef—dis tamn teef," when the old man turned round and staggered back—"mein Gott! de teef is mein son!"

"Your son, my good man? He seems a very tricksy, disreputable person. Well, he has robbed you, it appears? What"—added the magistrate—"what have you to say against him?"

" He is mein son !" cried the old man, and he wrung his hands—" mein own son !"

" Do you proceed against him ? State the charge : we can't sit here to be trifled with. Do you proceed against him ?"

Old Zweifler drew himself up, buttoned his coat, and turning from the prisoner, said with great energy—" My heart is ion—I *do* broceed."

" What is your charge ?" asked the magistrate, taking up his pen.

" I go to ped last night—I but my head ubon my billow—dat billow vich he, de brisoner—Gott help me ! mein own son—has stuffed with dorns.—I cannot sleeb—I—ven he was porn, he made my heart twice as pig—and now he is proken it."

" Proceed," said his worship. " Come to the charge, my good man."

" Last night—my vindows is proke—'tis not enough to preak my heart, but he preaks my vindows—my vindows is proke—and my door-blate stolen away."

" And you believe the prisoner, your son there, to be the thief? You charge him with stealing your door-plate?" Old Zweifler made no answer ; and again the magistrate addressed him. " Attend to me, my good man. You charge the prisoner with stealing your door-plate ?"

" Mein Gott !" exclaimed the old German,

trembling with emotion, " mein Gott ! de brisoner is mein own son—and de brisoner cannot pe a teef !" and with these words old Zweifler threw himself round, and fell upon the neck of the accused —" Oh, Ludwig ! Ludwig ! vy have you proke my heart ?" and the old man wept bitterly.

" Let us go home, father," said young Zweifler.

" You say home—to my own home—mit me? To stay mit me ?" cried the father.

" To stay with you—to—I'm ashamed of myself, father—I"—

" I dank Gott ! mein son is ashamed of himself ! Oh, I dank Gott for dat !   You hear—he is ashamed ?"

" Have you no charge, my good man ?" asked the magistrate, very drily.

" Charge !   You hear—he is ashamed !   What charge—ven he is ashamed ?" cried old Zweifler.

" Clear the bar," said the magistrate, who added in a low voice, " foolish old man."

Old Zweifler and his son were about to quit the office, when they were met by two or three officers bringing in for judgment the chivalric Plucky, and his spirited friend, Tom Rumpus.   The prisoners paused at young Zweifler.

" He's got another head certainly ; but I'm ——," said Rumpus, " if it isn't his coat and waistcoat."

" He makes his own," cried a voice in the crowd.

" Mein son, mein own son, Ludwig Zweifler," exclaimed the old tailor, clapping his blushing offspring on the shoulder, and to his confusion, making him confront the contemptuous glances of his late high companions.

" A tailor! I told you, Rumpus—ha! ha!—I told you," said Plucky, " that the fellow was hatched under a goose; he showed so many white feathers."

The Hon. Tom Rumpus and Plucky were then conducted before his worship. We have not space for a detail of the proceedings: it may be sufficient to state that an old woman, on her way to the bar to appear against the prisoners, called them " a couple of murdering villains who wouldn't let a poor soul roast her apples in peace and quietness."

We have now to account for the appearance of old Zweifler at the office. He had only that evening discovered a card-case flung through his dining-room window on the previous night by the humourous lord Slap, who had with great skill extracted the missile from the pocket of young Cramlington; against whom the tailor had come for a warrant, when he found in the libertine of high life his own graceless flesh and blood. By means of false name, false wig, and false whiskers, the young tailor had disguised his real self; and assisted by large sums of money, which he had found very little difficulty to raise on post-obits at anything per cent., he had by degrees wriggled himself into what he believed to be the very best society; lords Slap and Rowdow, Rumpus, Smash-erton and Plucky, being the choicest samples of that elevated and enlightened sphere. Thus, he had stumbled upon an introduction to the Mount-eagles, and had every prospect of improving his acquaintance with Caroline into a secret marriage, when the stolen pattern-book revealed his plebeian self, and the half-kindled torch of Hymen was extinguished by a thimble! The book—the accursed book—by some horrible accident had been left in a coat which the unfortunate hero had worn in the pursuit of his business, and added to the travelling wardrobe by the too zealous Applejohn. Old Zweifler had learned that his son had been very often seen to enter the lodgings of Mr. Cramlington; and hence the appearance of the old tailor at the chambers in search of his scapegrace offspring; who, at length humbled and ashamed, returned to the shop-board, became a tailor to the very nails, and at this moment keeps his country-house and carriage upon broad-cloth.

Ludwig Zweifler, otherwise Henry Cramlington, sleeps under the paternal roof: but where—where is John Applejohn? What was the reward of all his noble intentions? Listen: he approached his late master, who caught him by the collar, twirled him round, and—but that John was quick of motion, he had received the most ignominious rebuke that one gentleman can inflict upon another. John escaped the graver injury—but his ears were offended by the epithets—" scoundrel—vagabond —thief!" and a very unequivocal recommendation never to trust himself in the presence of the speaker again. John had ruined his master—as his master then believed; yet, who is bold enough to say that John did not mean well?

CHAPTER XVII.

AGAIN was John Applejohn upon the world; again was he in the terrible position of a man who, with the best of appetites, has not the best of characters; the evil being in his case considerably aggravated by the fact, that the satisfaction of his stomach depended upon the purity of his name. It is true, he was a tailor—but his reputation was stark and dead, hanging from a crooked nail! John was well nigh reduced to his last pound, when loitering in the Park, gazing at the ducks, fed by happy little boys and girls, he in the melancholy idleness of his spirit wished himself one of the web-footed, well-fed animals; and stood, "chewing the cud" of the silly fancy, when a well-known voice roused him from meditation to look upon the pale, sharp face of Jaffier Shadowly; grown paler, sharper, since last John saw him.

"How are you,—do you see that bird? I think that's—yes that *is* the hernshaw.   Some Hamlets always say 'hand-saw'—I always keep to hernshaw. By-the-way, speaking of Hamlets, you wouldn't think it, I hav'n't come out yet.   No: I hav'n't, indeed."

"I fear, Mr. Shadowly, I behaved very ill to you about that play and the story of the hackney-coach: the truth is, I'm very much afraid my master, as he then was, didn't always speak what"—

"Never mind it—don't say a word about it. What are you doing now?" asked Shadowly.

"I want a place: I went to Mr. Bub, to get something to do with the beasts; but he said even the places of the men who carried the intestines to the bears wer'n't to be had without great interest with some of the fellows."

"And would you—I believe your name is Applejohn, — would you condescend to administer nourishment to a bear?"

"Not by choice," answered John, "only when a man wants nourishment for himself—I"—

Shadowly put his hand upon John's shoulder, and looked steadily at him. "You have voice—figure—face?"

"All three," answered Applejohn.

"Then, you sha'n't starve; no—I—I have long wanted to bring up an Horatio according to my own style; just now, I have I think an offer for Hamlet—come with me." John obediently followed his friend, and after some minutes' walk eastward, Mr. Shadowly entered an alley, where cast-off clothes wooed the pockets of the poor and economical: Shadowly paused at a door, and said with some solemnity—"Here the agent lives."

"Agent! what for?" asked John Applejohn.

"For the true interests of the drama," answered Shadowly: "follow me."

"Stop—stop," cried John; "what is all this—agent for the drama? Does he get places for people out of work?"

"Your question, Mr. Applejohn," said Shadowly, "is put in homely phrase, but I believe it contains the true character of Mr. Goodfellow's occupation. Follow me, and fear not."

John followed his patron, who conducted him along a dark passage, and up a very winding and very narrow staircase. Halting at the second floor, Mr Shadowly knocked.

"Open locks—whoever knocks!"

was exclaimed in loud sonorous tones from within, and Mr. Shadowly turning the handle of the door, entered the dim apartment, followed by John.

"Mr. Shadowly! The very man who"—

But ere we proceed, let us endeavour to describe the person of Mr. Goodfellow. In his youth he had been called a handsome man, and his face at five-and-forty put in strong claims to the compliment. His black hair was flecked with grey, but his eye was full of vivacity, and his mouth expressive of kindliness and good humour. His shirt collar was flung back over what had been in former times a white linen jacket, edged with blue riband; he wore grey trowsers, made for him as it appeared in his more dapper days; and a pair of russet shoes, with rosettes of faded scarlet worsted, were lowered to his slippers. Mr. Goodfellow sat in an arm-chair, upon which were the remains of white-wash and Dutch metal, and with a huge book opened before him, was evidently employed on the future fortunes of the good people who composed his levee. The agent rose to greet Mr. Shadowly, and "proud to be introduced to any friend of his," welcomed Mr. Applejohn.

"The very man I was thinking of, Mr. Shadowly; sit down, sir—there, sir; upon that throne," and Goodfellow pointed to a rush-bottomed chair, with very many of the rushes wanting. "On that throne, sir." And this, Mr. Goodfellow delivered in a loud ringing voice, and with a manner that would have exalted even a three-legged stool into the dignity of an arm-chair. Indeed, nothing mean and petty seemed to enter into the enlarged and magnificent mind of Mr. Goodfellow; every thing with him was upon a grand scale; his alchemic tongue would turn pewter pots to gold by the very tone in which he would speak of pewter pots. Thus, when he said to the representative of Hamlet—" On that throne, sir," it was impossible from the loud musical voice and the heroic look of the speaker, to consider it merely a rush-bottomed chair in a very advanced state of dilapidation.

" Mr. Goodfellow," began Shadowly, "I want to"—

" I beg your pardon," said the agent, with mingled sweetness and dignity—" I beg your pardon, Mr. Shadowly, but when you entered the mansion, I was engaged with Mr. Strongbow, an illustrious musician, sir, who will by and by when he is somewhat more matured,"—here, Mr. Strongbow, a little withered man of at least sixty-five, in a thread-bare brown coat, with tarnished buttons, drab breeches, and leather gaiters, rose and bowed to the tragic actor.

It is said that babies feeding at the breast, catch the expression of their mothers. Mr. Viotti Strongbow had lived so long upon his fiddle, had for so many years hugged it to him, that his head and the head of that which fed him were alike as twins. Every particle of his visage was a piece of fiddle—and his voice was the voice of cat-gut. He rose, we say, bowed and sat.

"Mr. Strongbow first," said Goodfellow, "you know, Mr. Shadowly, order is heav'n's first law." Mr. Shadowly bowed an acquiescence to the truth, and the agent turned his smiling face to the musician.

"'Twouldn't buy me rosin," said Strongbow.

"The salary, I must say it—is moderate; yes, the remuneration is inadequate. I own it—I blush and own it," said Goodfellow.

"What could the manager mean by offering a musician such a salary?" asked Strongbow.

"The manager," replied Goodfellow, "is a great reader of Roman history,"—

"What of that?" inquired Strongbow.

"And therefore knows that Nero fiddled under great difficulties."

"It's no matter to me," said Strongbow, "what another musician has done. I have had my difficulties too."

"All of us, sir—all of us," said the agent, casting up his eyes, "within this vale of tears."

"And I say, seven shillings a week, and to travel

a journey of a hundred and fifty miles is—oh! it can't be done," said Strongbow. "I had rather wear a green shade—put a dog in a string, and go into the street at once."

"No, you would not, Mr. Strongbow—I know too well your love of the art—of its dignity, sir. Seven shillings, I own it, is low: still, you must bear in mind this important fact. In the large and populous district in which the theatre lies,"—

"It isn't a regular built theatre of course?" said Strongbow.

"Why," replied Goodfellow, with one of his sweetest smiles, "why, I believe the manager is bound in his lease to allow a farmer to thrash corn in it."

"Ha! I understand—oh lord!" and the musician groaned, and if possible looked more than ever like his fiddle.

"Still, sir, don't despond—one of the qualities of true genius is hope, sir, hope. I was about to say that in the populous district—populous though scattered,—there is not, I am credibly informed, although the people have an embryo passion for music, there is not a single fiddle. Hence, Mr. Strongbow, the advantage of the engagement must press itself upon you: for combining in yourself the whole of the orchestra, when private parties are afoot, you will not be injured by unprincipled competition."

" There's something in that—still," cried Strongbow, " seven shillings."

" In the cause of music, sir—in adoration of that immortal maid," said the agent, " I will upon my own responsibility advance a shilling, trusting to my persuasive powers—feeble though they be—to reconcile the manager to the unlooked-for augmentation."

" Eight shillings—well ? But you say, it's a village. Humph ! I don't know," said the musician, " I had rather it had been a market-town."

" There you are wrong," replied the agent, " permit me to say, very wrong, indeed. Market-towns, Mr. Strongbow, are busy only on market-days ; calves or corn once a week ; but in villages, sir —in villages, there is an equanimity of disposition among the inhabitants—a serenity of mind I may say, disposing them as much at one time as at another to the patronage of our art."

" I suppose, the manager wouldn't advance a fortnight's salary ?" said Strongbow, gloomily.

" Really, Mr. Strongbow," answered Goodfellow, " I think I may venture upon my knowledge of that gentleman's finances to assure you, that such an event comes not within the range of human probability."

" I thought not," said the fiddler.

" Sir, I'll not pay the ill-compliment to your instinct to suppose you could have thought otherwise," rejoined the agent.

" I don't know,—eight shillings," and the musician hesitated—" it may do in summer, but when winter comes,"—

" Ha ! " exclaimed the agent, " then—then will come your harvest : for in that primitive village, Christmas, sir—Christmas is kept in all its ancient splendour. See—see what you'll make by the waits —they have not heard the waits there these twenty years : there is in that otherwise happy district, an adult generation who have never heard the waits ! Mr. Strongbow, in that district, I perceive it—you are destined to be the envied man who shall bring back the simple music of our forefathers."

" Well, I—I think I must close, but I'll let you know," and the fiddler walked to the door.

" Mr. Strongbow," exclaimed Goodfellow in his loudest voice, and putting on his most important look—" Mr. Strongbow, I have a duty, sir, to fulfil ; I must have nothing left to surmise ; I send my despatches by the post to-night—I must have a definitive categoric answer."

" I'll let you know in time," said the musician.

" Ere the postman shall strike upon the bell, if you please," said Goodfellow, and the fiddler being gone, the agent turned him to a slim youth who appeared at the ripe age of seventeen to have grown beyond his strength.   His lip was graced with a moustache made apparently from the nap of a dirty white hat ;   his dress was remarkably shabby, but there was an exulting, hopeful spirit in his eye, as he approached the table of the agent. " Now, young gentleman, if you are determined to leave your shop, and turn actor, I—I think I can send you to grass somewhere in Essex."

" Pray, sir," asked the young gentleman, with a very thick lisp, " pray, sir, what is the ighest salary ? "

" Why, Mr. Butter, adventurous managers, mark me—adventurous managers, I say—offer for first tragedy fifteen shillings a week : but, sir, I should be wanting in duty to you, myself, and to those gentlemen the managers, did I not without equivocation or mental reservation, assure you that such a sum is perfectly illusory—mark me, sir, perfectly illusory.   However, as you are determined to regale your nostrils with the lamps, I can put you in a company where you will have great practice."

" That, Mr. Goodfellow," said the tyro, " is in course my great hobject."

" Great practice, sir; you may do every thing, from Richard the Third to carrying on a table."

" I'm hup in Richard," said Butter.

" And the other," observed the agent, " may be compassed with a very little study."

" I should like the young tragedy and the eroes," said Mr. Butter.

" A most profitable line, sir: by the way, you wear pantaloons—of course ?"

" Sich a pair !" exclaimed Mr. Butter.

" The patronage of boarding-schools follows as a matter of certainty," said Goodfellow. " Your benefits, sir, may be enormous, but—I deceive no man—they may be most contemptible."

" I'm not a bit afeard," said Butter; " the thing isn't hall together new to me. I've took lessons from Mr. Vimper; and give him seven shillings for a book of Amlet."

" Gracious heavens !" exclaimed Shadowly, "you play Hamlet?"

" Mr. Shadowly, permit me," observed Goodfellow, " to request a taciturnity—a courteous taciturnity." Mr. Shadowly gracefully acknowledged the reproof. " Seven shillings, Mr. Butter, for Hamlet ! When that divine emanation of our glorious and transcendant bard,—of that great creature, is given forth to the world, price sixpence?"

"Yes, I know hall that," replied Butter; "but Mr. Vimper marked vhere I vas to throw hup my hies, and lift my harms. He said throwing hup the hies and harms in the proper places was the greatest part of helocution."

"Eyes and arms are useful in our art, I don't deny it. Well, Mr. Butter, as for salary,"—

"Ha! that's hit," said Butter.

"As a young man you can only expect to enter a commonwealth; that is, a company established on the justest principles, where every person shares according to his merits."

"I can't have no hobjection to that," cried Mr. Butter.

"Then, sir, Essex—Essex is your destination. Do you know the county? It offers peculiar advantages to the young aspirant. There are marshes—very many marshes—much water in Essex. Answer me, sir; are you fond of eels?"

Mr. Butter with great emphasis replied "Wery."

"Sir, you're a happily constituted man: whilst in Essex, you may snap your fingers at fortune—for there, sir, eels abound. You have nothing to do but to pull off your shoes and stockings, if after

a moderate term you persist in wearing them,—
and wade for your dinner."

" Vade, Mr. Goodfellow—vade, sir ?"

" Catch eels, sir; catch eels. There requires, I
own, an art—a certain dexterity of hand, and
tenacity of finger to catch an eel with the naked
palm; for eels, sir—I deceive no man—eels"—and
Goodfellow gave the sagacious look of a discoverer,
—"eels *are* slippery."

" I can old anything," said Mr. Butter, looking
at what he considered a very sinewy hand.

" Then, sir," observed the agent, " hold yourself
in readiness to walk, or if you are luxuriously inclined, and have the money, to ride to Essex on
Thursday. Enough, sir; a letter shall be sent to
you to-morrow. Stay, sir; you are about to enter
upon a thorny, but a most glorious profession."

" I ham," replied Mr. Butter with great fortitude.

" There are prizes in it, sir—great prizes; somebody must have them. There are blanks, also—a
very considerable number of blanks; somebody
must have them too."

" We all ope for the best," observed Mr.
Butter.

" Nobly said, sir; nobly said. But, sir, I was
about to give you a little wholesome advice against

the guile, the cupidity of rustic landlords.   Mr.
Butter, you must sometimes have a bed—hay isn't
in the fields all the year round, or salaries would
be much reduced.   Well, sir, it is possible amidst
the multitude of human affairs, that if you take a
lodging, you may not always have the money to
pay for it.   Such a calamity has occurred to the
very lights of the profession.   Now, sir, mark me :
under such heart-rending circumstances, you owe
a solemn duty to your manager never to go home
in your dress,—if that dress be the property of the
stock.   For strange, incredible as it may appear to
you, an unsophisticated creature, blushing on the
threshold of active life,—monstrous as the fact may
present itself to you, I have positively known a
landlord so lost to the feelings of humanity, so
callous to every touch of common tenderness, as to
detain the costly property thus thoughtlessly placed
in his possession, until every shilling of his avaricious demand upon his unsuspecting victim was
paid down upon the nail; aye, sir,—upon the
nail !"

"You don't say so ?" exclaimed Butter.

"I wonder not, sir, at your simplicity—'tis the
concomitant of youth ; but, sir, be advised by a
man who has had landlords.   Pay while you can,
sir ; but when you can no longer pay, exhibit the

purity of your principle—the excellence of your good intentions, and your love of tranquillity—by quietly removing yourself from a roof under which you can no longer rest in peace. Farewell, sir; farewell, and prosper.—Remember, sir; the sandals of John Kemble are not yet occupied."

"You'll *see*," replied Mr. Butter, and he quitted the room, in his own conceit, with the sandals already at his soles.

"And that fellow is to be an actor!" said Mr. Shadowly. "Well, Mr. Goodfellow, if ever he should come to London, he'll never set the Thames on fire."

"Very likely not, sir," replied the agent; "still, the New River may be in considerable danger."

"And has the blockhead ever played?" asked Shadowly.

"I have seen him expose his anatomy as Richard in private," said Goodfellow. "A very thin slice of Gloster indeed, sir."

"But doesn't he in the most atrocious way misplace the *h*—the *w*—the *v*—and"—

"He does; it can't be denied, sir, he does;" said the agent, "and yet, sir, he is an honest lad, a very honest lad—he gives you in the course of the night the full number of letters; nay, I know not, if you wait patiently, whether you hav'n't more than the number by way of interest, for the delay."

" Mr. Goodfellow, as we are now alone, shall we not imbibe?" and Mr. Shadowly took from his pocket a bright half-crown, and held it forth to the agent.

" Sir !" exclaimed Goodfellow, with an expression of arch-wonder in his face, " that is a half-crown ! You are out of an engagement, sir—return it to your pocket; put the money in your purse, I say."

" Nay, but Mr. Goodfellow, I insist"—

" A half-crown, sir ! I give you my honour, sir, and I speak it not to your disparagement, nor to the disparagement of your friend whom I have not the felicity of knowing,—but, sir, I pledge you my honour as a gentleman, that I have had six eminent men, most eminent men in the profession with me this morning,—and yet, sir, I would have defied the united muscular exertion of ten Israelites, exercised upon any one of those men, to have shaken from him half of half-a-crown ! Put the money in your pocket, Mr. Shadowly—half-a-crown is not often beheld by the conscious walls of this cabinet. When you are in pay, sir,—when you're in an engagement,"—

" Allgag must come to me—nothing but my Hamlet will save him," said Shadowly.

" Then, sir, come hither, and show me silver or gold, and I will imbibe with you. But now, sir—

now, Tom Goodfellow himself will play the host. What does your friend take ?" asked the agent.

" Anything, sir," said Applejohn, who marvelled greatly at the dignity of Goodfellow, " anything, sir; though I want nothing."

" The usual thing, I suppose—we can't do better ; " observed Goodfellow to Shadowly, who nodded acquiescence. " What, ho! within there !" exclaimed Goodfellow—" What, ho! I say—Fabuletto !"

In answer to this call, a little boy of some ten years old, one of the twelve children of Goodfellow, ran from the next room. " Yes, father ?"

" Fabuletto," said the sire, placing sixpence in the hand of his offspring, " Fabuletto, child—a pot of metropolitan ponderous fluid : and haste thee, good Fabuletto ; " and had Ariel been discharged upon the errand, he could not have " done his spiriting" more quickly ; for ere Applejohn had ceased to speculate upon the mystic command of the agent, Fabuletto returned with a pot of foaming London porter.

" Doubtless, sir, you drink from the metal ?" and Goodfellow pressed the beverage upon Applejohn, who drank.

" I will give you, gentlemen," said Shadowly, taking the pewter-pot, " I will give you the revival of taste—the regeneration of the drama."

"I would drink that toast, sir," said Good-fellow, seizing the pot, "I would drink it, lacking other liquor, in

> 'The ruddy drops that visit this sad heart;'"

and the agent emptied the vessel, and reversing it, whilst about three drops trickled to the floor, exclaimed—"Peace! the charm's wound up." He then flung the pot into a corner of the room, and resumed his official chair. "Now, Mr. Shadowly, to business. I have an offer for you, sir; you have staid too long in London, sir; you would be very wrong to play anything but first business."

"Especially to the persons who are now in possession of it. No, sir; I have made up my mind to do nothing second: in a word, not to grind colours for artists who can't paint."

"Very right, sir—very right. Of course, Mr. Shadowly, you can play every leading part?"

"I can play Hamlet," said Shadowly.

"Certainly: but I mean you can play all the first tragedy?"

"I—I flatter myself I can play Hamlet."

"He, sir, is a heathen—a beast—a wretch devoid of sense, who doubts it!" said the agent. "But if another tragedy were put up?"—

"I think no tragedy so good as Hamlet."

"My opinion, Mr. Shadowly—my opinion; 'tis

the prime work of the immortal bard. Still, you know other parts—other"—

" I should always prefer playing Hamlet," said the actor.

" As I said, sir, I have an offer for you—an offer not far from the metropolis. You could take all your friends down in stage-coaches, or, perhaps, the whole of your connexion in a gig."

" I must open in Hamlet—nobody near town has seen it."

" Open in what you please : the town is Greenwich," said the agent.

" Small theatre," observed Shadowly, with sudden melancholy ; " very small."

" By no means, Mr. Shadowly—'tis a new theatre—a theatre erected under extraordinary patronage, and for three days only—a most extensive building."

" I must open in Hamlet," said the actor.

" You will find the proprietor of the theatre a most obliging person, and if you can persuade him," said Goodfellow with his usual gravity, " that Hamlet will suit his purpose as well, or perhaps better than anything else, I have no doubt that he'll oblige you."

" Well, that's settled," and already Shadowly saw himself in the inky suit of the Dane. " Now, how much am I to have ?"

N 3

Mr. Goodfellow raised his eyes to the face of the actor, smiled and said—" Sir, you've been too long in London."

" I feel I have—I have wasted my time in solicitation, when, had I gone into the country, I might have brought managers crawling to my feet. But to return to the salary—what am I to have?"

" I am glad, sir, for your own sake—for the cause of the drama, that you are at length awakened to your just value. You have been much wanted in the country, sir; trust the word of Tom Goodfellow—a word never yet nailed to the counter of public opinion, as a bad one. You have been much wanted, sir."

" I think so—I'm sure so," said Shadowly: " but how much am I to have?"

" In the country, you would have been followed —sought for—asked to the mayor's balls—the churchwardens' wives' tea-parties—the—I am glad, Mr. Shadowly, profoundly glad that you have at length determined to migrate into the rural provinces of merry England."

" All my friends have long advised me. But the question is, how much am I to have?"

" In Greenwich, sir, you will find a"—

" But, my dear Goodfellow," and Shadowly laid his hand upon the agent's shoulder, and stared in his face,—" how much am I to have?"

" Oh ! I understand you; I perceive—the *pecunia*—the 'last infirmity of noble minds,'—the salary?" said Goodfellow, suddenly enlightened.

" Exactly it: how much am I to have?" asked the actor, for the sixth time.

Mr. Goodfellow threw himself back in his chair, folded his arms, and looking sorrowfully at the actor, said—" Mr. Shadowly, estimating, as believe me on the faith of man, I do estimate your extraordinary powers, I should feel myself a beast, if I could tell you."

" You can't tell me what I'm to have?"

" I can't sir—my tongue would cleave to my mouth, did I attempt to wound your high-minded ears by giving utterance to the sum proposed."

" What! very low, eh?" asked the actor.

Mr. Goodfellow spoke no word, but drew up his features at the question, as if suddenly suffering excruciating tooth-ache.

" Still, I have I hope fortitude—let me know the amount—come, speak out," said Shadowly.

" No, sir; not for the worth of this sublunar world would I speak it—but—but, Mr. Shadowly, I will constrain my hand to write down the sum— I will put down the salary in round numbers." On this, the agent wrote on a scrap of paper, and burying his averted face in one hand, with the other, which he made to tremble exceedingly, gave the document to the tragic actor.

Mr. Shadowly took the paper, glanced at it, threw it upon the table, and said—" D—nation !"

" I expected no less from your greatness," said Goodfellow, venturing to look up, " but let not your just displeasure fall on me."

" To offer me such terms—me !" cried Shadowly.

" They are low, sir ; degradingly low ; and yet, sir," said the agent, " it should not be forgotten that provisions are very cheap at Greenwich. The terms are very low, even for Greenwich ; and yet that picturesque borough to the student of human nature presents peculiar recommendations."

" What are they ?—I don't know 'em," said Shadowly.

" The pensioners, Mr. Shadowly ! If, in the extraordinary changes that I forsee—and from my position I may without vanity say, that I am enabled to forsee much—if, from the changes that the drama must yet undergo, from the vicissitudes that its professors, its highest professors—among whom I of course include Mr. Shadowly—must suffer ; if you should be compelled in the ' sere, the yellow leaf' of your days to take to the old men,—mark you not, sir, the advantage you would have over all competitors, from a previous study of the habits, the manners, the bye-play, so to speak, of those picturesque antiques, the pensioners of Greenwich College?"

" Pooh! I—I learn anything from such persons!" exclaimed Shadowly, with an amazed look.

" Despise not such instruments, sir; believe me, that in the pursuit of that high calling to which destiny has exalted you—for it is a high calling, sir, the display of human passion,—you may learn a touch of nature, aye, sir, a miraculous touch from the vilest beggar in your path. I will give you, sir, a practical instance of what may be done even at Greenwich. Are you aware, sir, that a gentleman—who shall be nameless—was instructed in every step of his celebrated nautical hornpipe by a pensioner now living in the Hospital? That hornpipe alone, sir, is worth a thousand a year! The actor has marked his sense of its value, by giving to a splendid pile of buildings at Hastings, of which he is the happy proprietor, the significant name of Hornpipe Crescent! Despise not Greenwich, Mr. Shadowly."

" But the salary—the salary"—

" It is low; still, let me hope you have not forgotten the collateral advantages?"

" I don't know—I—after all," said Shadowly, " it would be worth something to show that rascal Allgag that I *can* get a situation."

" That feeling of triumph," exclaimed the agent with great animation, " would alone be worth twenty pounds per week. When—when he has lost you, Mr. Shadowly, then—then will come his sense of your value—then will begin his everlasting remorse. Shall I say you accept the offer?"

" Hang it !" cried the tragedian, " the salary is an insult."

" Disabuse thy mind of that, I pray thee, gentle coz,—think not so hardly of the manager. I know the man—the meekest, best of creatures. 'Tis not his estimation of your genius that offers the salary : 'tis not his mind that speaks, but—alas !—his pocket. I can perceive, Mr. Shadowly, by the varied expression of your countenance, that you will take the man's offer."

" Be it as you will," said Shadowly.

" Your hand, sir," exclaimed the agent, rising to grasp it. " 'Tis done. You will have a multitudinous audience. By-the-way, I had forgotten to state, that the salary is only for three days—it is not to be considered for the week."

" That materially alters the sum," said Shadowly, " that doubles it. Ha ! a very different thing : I play only three times for"—

" More than three times," replied the agent.

" More than three in three nights ?" asked the actor ; " how is it possible?"

" Why, you will be convinced of the popularity of the drama in Greenwich, when I inform you that at this season of the year—you will open on Whit Monday—the manager has played, and every time to overflowing audiences, not less than twenty times a day. Call you not that encouragement of the drama?" asked the agent.

" Twenty times ! Why, what theatre is it? What's it called?"

" It might be called, from its proximity to that lovely place, it might be called the Park Theatre. Think of Greenwich Park," said Goodfellow— " fine historical associations about it; Queen Elizabeth used to walk there."

" Is it a regularly constructed theatre—regularly built?" inquired the tragedian.

" Built with the greatest care; it is put up and taken down again like clock-work."

" What ! is it moveable ?"

The agent smiled, and said—" Thespis began in a cart, Mr. Shadowly; and I should be guilty of an affectation, I trust foreign to my character, were I to attempt to deny that the theatre of which I speak is carried away from place to place in sundry waggons."

" You surely do not mean, Mr. Goodfellow, to insinuate that the theatre is—a—a booth at a fair ?"

" At this festive season of the year," answered

the agent, " the nymphs and swains make holyday.
The drama is not merely a harmless, it is an
instructive recreation : you will have the proud
satisfaction of blending tuition with amusement, for
the benefit of thousands of your common species."

" But in a booth—in a common booth—with walls
of canvas !" exclaimed Shadowly.

" I am told, sir," observed the agent, " that the
great Greek tragedians—I do not read Greek myself—always acted in the open air."

" What might suit the Greeks," observed the
English actor, " would be extremely disreputable
in a British artist.   Act in a booth !   As I have
said, to canvas walls !"

" At first, when I was solicited to become agent
for the manager, let me confess it, Mr. Shadowly, I
thought as you do.   What ! said I to myself, I !
Tom Goodfellow—I who have expended my best
energies in support of the true drama—I, who
every week, send youths—young, callow mission-
aries of considerable promise—into the most remote
corners of this extensive empire, to disseminate a
taste for the true theatre—I have a letter here, sir,
from a haberdasher's apprentice, a youth sent by
me to the Isle of Skye ; he has played Richard
there"—

" Has he ever played Hamlet ?" asked Shadowly.

" Not yet ; but he has played Richard and

Coriolanus three times, and speaks in the highest terms of the docility of the natives.   Nay, he is so much pleased with the people, that having left his trunk behind, he has conformed to the insular prejudice, and wears a kilt.   But, sir, I am wandering from my theme.—As I said, I felt as you feel with respect to the Greenwich Theatre.   In the vanity, the ignorance of my heart, I thought the agency beneath me : but, sir, a little cool philosophy set all right.   I thought with you of the canvas walls—of a theatre built without the aid of a single brick.   And what, said I, my better mind coming to me,—does the artist, does the true actor, the genius, the mighty mover of the passions depend upon the materials, the insensible materials that form the building ?   Am I an agent for bricks and mortar—or for the throbbing sons of genius ?   Am I to estimate an actor by trowel-work ?   Are the wondrous depths of tragedy to be measured with a carpenter's chalk-line ?   Perish the folly ! I exclaimed—it is the man and not the building.   If the actor ride in his carriage, does his carriage elevate the art ?—no : it is the art that has given him the vehicle.   As genius is an endowment which no money can purchase, it is therefore above all the extraneous advantages obtainable by lucre.   A diamond is a diamond, though you shall put it on the finger of a beggar."

" That's very true—very true, indeed," said Applejohn, venturing to speak.

" It is true, sir," observed Mr. Shadowly, "only permit me to say, that on the finger of a beggar, nobody would believe it to be a diamond. Why, sir, does not mendicant genius every day offer the ' precious jewel in its head' for sale—and yet, because the holder is mendicant, does not the world believe the jewel to be of no value? Men, sir, have died with jewels in their brains; and not until the men were dead, were the gems owned to be of the true water.—Now, when I am dead, why then my Hamlet will be confessed the"—

" It is already confessed, sir, by men who know what Hamlet is, to be prodigious: but then, sir, the judgment of the few is but a razor against that block of stupidity called public taste: time, sir— time is wanted to cut through the stone. But, sir, the time will come when your Hamlet will be a household thing," said Goodfellow.

" Do you think so?" asked Shadowly, touched by the energy of the agent.

" Think so! We shall have your image, sir, in pottery—we shall see your Hamlet upon twelfth-cakes with a sugar-plum skull in his hand. But, sir, you must be seen to be appreciated. Now, sir, the Greenwich Whitsuntide Theatre will hold a thousand people: you will play Hamlet—that is all the marrow of him—fifteen times a day for three days. I will not pay you so ill a compliment as to conceive that the house will not be crammed. Now, sir, see what you have done! You have played Hamlet to five-and-forty thousand people"—

" So many?" asked Shadowly, moved by the flattering prospect.

" No—I am wrong: of course, many will see you repeat the part seven or eight times; it will not always be entirely a new audience: I will deduct five thousand for enthusiasts. Well, sir, with that deduction, see what you have done! You have inoculated forty thousand people with the divine *virus* of your Hamlet, and sent them loose upon society to spread your complaint against London managers. Ha! what say you now, Mr. Shadowly?" and Goodfellow looked upon the tragedian as all his own.

" It would be a great triumph to be carried on the very back of the public to the London house," said Shadowly.

" John Bull, sir, is slow to rouse, but when he is roused," observed the agent, " there is no knowing where his tricks will stop. It would not at all surprise me, if you were drawn by the populace to the stage-door, and Mr. Allgag was compelled by the overwhelming influence of public opinion, not only to take you in, but to give you the very highest salary in the theatre."

"I can hardly hope that; still, people can't know what my Hamlet is, unless they see it. And yet, do adequate judges attend the"—

"The Greenwich Whitsuntide Theatre? The best, sir; for there is a very—very limited free-list, and that on the days and nights of your performance will of course be suspended. Besides, it is a well-known fact, that several managers make it a point of their professional religion to attend the theatre to look out for rising talent. Mr. Flyblow—you know him—great man for the Newgate Calendar, always goes to Greenwich; but in disguise, that he mayn't look too much like a gentleman. Well, Mr. Shadowly, what shall we say?"

"Why, egad! I—I have a great mind—the salary is sure, of course—I have a great mind, if only for the freak"—

"Henry the Fifth, sir, played his youthful pranks, why should not you? I shall write to Mr. Phœnix directly, informing him of his good fortune. You are lucky, sir—lucky in one another. And now, sir," and the agent turned to Applejohn, "what may I have the paramount felicity of doing for you?"

"Oh! I was about to say," observed Shadowly,

" don't you think he would do for something? At present, he is very nearly starving."

" All in his favour," answered Goodfellow, " if he would adopt the stage; for he has nothing to lose, except his hunger, which to be sure, may be somewhat difficult to get rid of."

" What should you like to act, Applejohn?" asked Shadowly.

" I ! lord bless you ! Nothing," cried John. " I should die to think of it."

" Don't think of it, sir," said the agent, " but die first. If you have an honest calling, sir, stick to it—if,—what have you there, Spalatro?" and Goodfellow addressed himself to a little boy, another son, who entered, carrying in his hand a neck of mutton. " What is that, Spalatro?"

" Mutton, papa—mother bought it," answered Spalatro.

" Put it in the buttery," said Goodfellow—" what, ho ! come hither, sirrah? What meanest thou by this?" and the agent pointed to a play-bill which half enveloped the joint. " What is this, sirrah?"

" A play-bill, papa," said Spalatro.

" And is it thus, sir, that you desecrate the archives of our art? Speak, sirrah ! is it thus?"—

" The butcher wrapt it up," answered the boy.

" Enough ! his soul is untouched by the softer influences of the profession; but had I a thousand

sons, I would disinherit them all did I apprehend
them in so barbarous an act.   In the buttery," and
Goodfellow waved the boy hence.   " The fair—I
mean the Greenwich Whitsun Theatre opens on
Monday; you will be punctual?"

" Depend upon me, sir; and on the receipt of
the salary, I"—

" Speak not of it, sir: we are gentlemen both;
what I expect, you will confer.   No more words,
sir.   Farewell, and may the gods of Rome watch
over and protect you !"

Applejohn and   the   tragedian   quitted   Mr.
Goodfellow, and in due time the agent sits down to
his neck of mutton.   And let the reader be assured
of this ;—should some destitute, way-faring actor
make a call whilst a morsel of mutton shall lie upon
the dish, somewhat of that morsel will be set before him, sweetened and recommended by a hearty
welcome.

Were not fortune incurably blind, surely to those
frank souls who do noble things with meagre necks
of mutton, she would now and then send with her
especial compliments, a savoury haunch.   One
man shall be at best a splendid wretch with a hundred covers; whilst a Tom Goodfellow shall play
Lucullus with a neck of mutton.—Yea, on a plate
of sprats shall sup his friends " in the Apollo."

Droll, honest, hospitable Goodfellow,—for every

year of thy whimsical life, may the blessing of three hundred and sixty five dinners fall upon thee !

CHAPTER XVIII.

"Beware, sir, beware of modesty," was the counsel of Shadowly to Applejohn, as side-by-side they walked down the Kent-road. "Beware of the rock modesty; I have almost wrecked my fortunes on it."—John to the pressing solicitations of Shadowly to turn actor, urged his utter ignorance of the art, his want of taste for it, with many other disqualifications too numerous to mention; still, the tragedian would not so be answered: he insisted upon the infallibility of his own judgment, which assured him that John Applejohn was destined to make a very showy figure in the future history of the English stage.

"Bless your heart !" cried the simple John, "in such matters, you can't think what a fool I am; I'm worth nothing."

"Never say that—never own it, though it should be the truth. When a man tells the world he's worth nothing,—'tis no matter whether he is or not, the world always takes him at his own valuation. Now, there can't be a greater folly; because, the same man has only to go into highways and marketplaces, and blow the key-bugle of his own praise to have all caps go off to him."

"Then, with submission, Mr. Shadowly, how is it that you, knowing the use of this, have never done it?" asked the acute Applejohn.

"There it is—there it is! I hadn't courage to follow my own precept out. It doesn't serve, for a man to sound two or three notes, and then blush and take to his heels, astonished at his own impudence; no—he must stand and blow away against all comers; and though his trumpet may be in itself but a poor cracked thing, still in time people's ears become accustomed to it, and then they begin to say a good word for it, then to vehemently praise it, and at last to own that there never was, and never will be, such another trumpet."

"But surely all people can't be so deceived?" said Applejohn.

"Perhaps, not all—but out of the mob, there's always a sufficient number to swear by any tin trumpet be it never so bad.—The only care is, that it be continually blown to them."

"What a pity! that you who know all this, should never,"—

"I know what you would say, John; but it's a defect I have in my face: there is, I own it, there is brass in it, but not enough: now, 'tis of little use to a man to have one cheek metal, if the blushes will come through the other; no, sir; to go through with success, he must be hardcased all over."

Such was part and parcel of the very instructive lecture on worldly wisdom read by Shadowly on his way to Greenwich to present himself to Mr. Phœnix, proprietor of the Whitsuntide Theatre. The reader may, probably, wonder at the sudden intimacy between the tragedian and our hero: the mystery may be explained by one word,—vanity; Mr. Shadowly found in John Applejohn a most deferential admirer, and patronised him accordingly. The praise of John—rapt, astonished by the passionate speeches of the actor—was delicious incense to the nostrils of Shadowly, starving for admiration. The actor declaimed, and John vowed that never in his whole life had his nature been so moved, elevated—never had he caught such glimpses of poetic light!

"I'm sure, Mr. Shadowly," said John, the actor having finished one of Hamlet's soliloquies—"I'm sure, sir, you make me feel proud of myself, that you think me fit for your companion—me, who am a poor ignorant fellow, knowing nothing."

"I'll make a man of you, John: yes, you shall be the first Horatio of the day."

"I can't hope it, sir," and John shook his head.

"The first Horatio, as I am the first Hamlet: we'll storm the town and take it together. I'll read

all Hamlet to you—the whole of the tragedy left
in the hackney-coach," said Shadowly, with a
significant laugh.

"Now, what could have made that man deal in
such wicked lies?" observed John, reminded of
the poetic vapourings of the young tailor.

"What? Why, a strange and ravenous desire
for praise," said the actor. "Of all weaknesses,
perhaps, the most absurd and ridiculous; a folly
that makes a man a laughing-stock to all the world.
But, step out, John; we have little time to lose: I
have a thousand things to settle with Phœnix, for
it isn't often that he has an artist like myself, eh,
John?"

"No, indeed, sir; I don't know much about it,
but"—

"That's why I value your applause, John: you
are not hackneyed in the ways of criticism; no,
no; when I move you, I feel that I have struck
upon the natural note of passion—I feel that I
have done what only real genius can do, eh,
John?"

"You may say that, sir."

"It's easy enough to play conventional tricks—
to have a set grin—to gargle your throat with syllables—to shake your head—to stand and roll your
eyes, and then to tap your forehead, as if there
was something there too great to come out,—all

such pranks are easily played, and catch the ad-
mirers of a certain school.—But I hope I know
how to despise all such antics. I hope that, taking
the divine goddess nature for my guide, I arrive
at the sources of feeling by simple, dignified, unerring means—eh, John?"

"You do, indeed, sir. I never heard anything
like it; never."

"I believe not: yet, I must say, John, if there
was more unsophisticated nature among audiences,
more of that pure, natural intelligence, of which
you possess so much"—

"Not I, sir—I'm sure, sir, I know nothing."

"Know nothing, John! What would I give to
play before a pit full of such ignorance! Then
my Hamlet might hope for fair dealing, then it's
peculiar originality might gain due reward."

"And it must, sir; depend upon it, Mr. Shadowly, it must. If it's all as good as the bits you've
said to me,"—

"Much better, John; very much better."

"Then it must be the noblest thing that human
creature ever listened to."

"That's not the point, John: I was merely about to
say, that I would back your opinion on acting—your
simple, uneducated opinion in all its natural fresh-
ness,—against the voices of ten thousand. Believe
me, John," and Mr. Shadowly took his compa-

o 2

nion's hand, " believe me, I think you the finest
judge of natural acting,—I say, natural acting,
that I ever met with.   I say this ; and I flatter no
man."

Pursuing this pleasant discourse, the two friends
arrived at that point of Greenwich allotted by
authority to the sports of Whitsun merry-makers.
The theatre—the principal dramatic establishment
in the fair—presented itself to the lofty looks of
the tragedian. He paused, and had inward wrest-
lings with his dignity—the struggle lasted but a
few seconds, for putting his hands in his pockets,
he there found conquering odds.   He approached
the unfinished building—he *would* not think it a
booth—and mounting the steps, saw the proprietor
Phœnix superintending " the clink of hammers."

" My name, sir, is Shadowly," said the actor,
with a dignity that inferred he had said all that
could be said.   He repeated to the unmoved
Phœnix—" Shadowly."

Mr. Phœnix was a big, burly man ; with a round
yellow face, small eyes winking in pits of flesh, the
nose of a bull-dog, and the mouth of a fish.   He
wore a loose white coat, red waistcoat, corded
breeches, and top-boots. A gold chain, large as
the chain of a smoke-jack, dangling from his fob
gave token of the man of wealth. He also displayed
a large brooch of hair—the relic of a first love, a

slack-wire dancer, twenty years deceased,—surrounded with superb brilliants. Mr. Phœnix looked at the tragedian with the same intelligence that the reader, passing through a meadow, may have seen suddenly lighted up in the face of an ox.

"Shadowly, sir;" repeated the actor.

"Is it," observed the proprietor—"and what of that?"

"The name is of course, known to you?" and Mr. Shadowly bent himself back.

"Oh! ha! well, how d'ye do? to be sure," and Phœnix nodded a familiar welcome.

"I believe, Mr. Phœnix, I may without vanity say I have made some noise in the world," said the actor.

"By what I've heard, pretty well. I was sorry to hear of your misfortune in London," observed Phœnix.

"'Tis no matter, sir," replied Shadowly, believing of course that the proprietor alluded to the brutality of the manager. "It's no matter, sir. I appeal from Allgag to Phœnix; and have no fear of the result. When can we rehearse?"

"Whenever you like—you've brought all your traps with you?" asked Phœnix.

"They will be here per coach. The young lady who will play with me, I"—

" By-the-bye,—how is she? She was only a baby when I first come into the profession. Times is changed with some of us. Ha! I'm not too proud to own it—but I started in life with nothing to my back but a learned pig."

" Doubtless," said Shadowly, recurring to his immediate interests, " doubtless, the young lady has played Ophelia?"

" Ha! eight-and-twenty years ago—how the time does pass!—she was showed in a caravan: I recollect, she was the very first Spotted Girl as come out."

" Is it possible!" exclaimed Shadowly—" a Spotted Girl?"

" Yes, and when that went off—for the public is so very variable,—she was a wild Zealander—and then a mermaid—and then she took to the rope, and warn't it a little after that, when you married her?"

" I—I marry a—a Spotted Girl!" exclaimed Hamlet.

" My friend's a bachelor, sir," said Applejohn.

" Pray, Mr. Phœnix, do you know who I am—I ask you, sir,—who I am?"

" Why, Jack Shakerly, isn't it"—

" Shakerly!"

" Ha! Shakerly, as married little Nancy Tumtum

the Spotted Girl?—I heard she'd run away from
you in London with the Wild Man from Mada-
gascar—but I 'spose you've took her back?"

"And pray, sir," it was with heroic strength of
mind that Shadowly subdued his mounting rage,—
"pray, sir, am I to understand that you expect a
Mr. John Shakerly and his wife, late Nancy
Tumtum, the original Spotted Girl? Do such
persons make part of your company?"

"Well! I thought," said Phœnix, shading his
eyes with his hand, and staring at the tragic actor,
"I thought if you was Jack Shakerly, you wasn't
half the fine fellow you used to be, when you was
the Indy Conjuror. I thought so," and Mr.
Phœnix made no other reply.

"I come, sir," said Shadowly, and he frowned,
"armed with the introduction of Mr. Goodfellow,
agent."

"Oh! I see—you're the tip-top chap he wrote
about?" said Phœnix, and Shadowly with a sickly
smile acknowledged the homely compliment. "Well,
I'm glad to see you: but, it's only fair in me to
tell you that you'll have your work to do."

"I am aware, Mr. Phœnix, of the arduous task
imposed upon me."

"You come after a great favourite, I can tell
you: never was no one liked more than Bill Gale:
something like an actor—took a pride and pleasure

in his business, as you may judge when I tell you he broke three blood-vessels in as many months."

" I trust, Mr. Phœnix, to achieve equal triumphs by wholly different means. Pray, how much do you act of Hamlet?"

" Why, as for Hamlet, you see we've taken the ghost out of it, and put him in a better piece of our own, and that's all we do of it."

" Not play Hamlet!" exclaimed Shadowly.

Mr. Phœnix thrust his hands in his pockets, and sucking his teeth, tranquilly asked—" Do you want to ruin me?"

It would, we fear, enlarge our story considerably beyond readable dimensions, did we attempt to give a faithful report of the very animated conversation that hereupon ensued between the actor and the manager: the tragedian taking Melpomene to witness, that no power in this sublunar world, no reward to be enjoyed in this transitory existence, should induce him to play anything less than Hamlet; whilst on the other hand, the manager spoke in terms of very equivocal respect of Shakspeare and all his works, and more especially of the bantling prince of Denmark. Shadowly spoke on the side of genius, taste, elevated passion, discoursing largely and learnedly thereon; Mr. Phœnix confined himself to profit and loss: the tragedian soared into the boundless ether of imagination—the master-

showman ensconced himself in his breeches-pocket.
A compromise was at length effected; the negotiation being greatly assisted by the state of Shadowly's finances. It was finally agreed, that the actor
should play the part in the drama written expressly by the author for the Greenwich Whitsuntide Theatre, the tragedian securing to himself the full privilege of introducing as much of
the language of Hamlet as would harmonize with
the mind and feelings of a Barbary corsair, such
being the original character in the forthcoming
dramatic poem. This treaty was no sooner concluded than the dramatist of the booth—he was,
rare union! dramatist and money-taker too,—ventured to appeal against the measure.

" I tell you what, sir," said the dramatist, approaching the stolid Phœnix—" I tell you what,
sir ; I have my bread to get as well as Shakspeare
—choose between us, if you please; all Shakspeare
or all me, but I stand no partnerships."

Mr. Phœnix was a very powerful man ; and his
decision was equal to his strength. Therefore, the
dramatist had no sooner delivered himself of his
" unalterable determination," than Mr. Phœnix
laid his hand upon the bard's collar, with startling
dexterity turned him round, and applying his foot
to that region where, when Minerva kept a sixpenny
day-school in Olympus she applied the birch, he sent

the poet down a flight of steps, calling him a son of not
the muses ; and telling him to go to that place which
we all earnestly hope to avoid, as soon as he could
conveniently reconcile himself to the journey. The
dramatist, fortunately for him, alighted on the head
of the great drum. " Not the first time you've
been saved by my music," cried the satirical
drummer, at the time assisting in the erection of
the orchestra.

" I trust, sir, that some of the soliloquies which
I shall feel it my duty to introduce," said Shadowly,
" will not be found too long ?"

" Don't trouble yourself at all about that," said
Phœnix ; " 'cause if they are, depend upon it,
there'll be somebody polite enough in front to tell
you to cut 'em short. And pray, what line are you
in ?" and the proprietor addressed himself to John.
" What are you ?"

" I'm nothing," said John, modestly.

" I beg your pardon,—he is a young man of very
great promise," said Shadowly, " and if you would
only give him an appearance,"—

" Quite full," replied Phœnix, to the great relief
of Applejohn ; " but I tell you what, could you eat
raw beef ?"

" I prefer it cooked," answered John.

" But I mean in the way of business—because
Solomon's cannibal has struck for wages, and you

may have an opening in his caravan. I think,
young man, you'd do very well for a cannibal—
Solomon gives seven shillings a day besides the raw
meat. That's his van over there," and Mr. Phœnix
pointed to a huge green vehicle.

"Thank you, Mr. Phœnix—thank you, sir,"
said Shadowly, and taking Applejohn by the arm,
the actor prepared to drag his passive friend down
the steps.

"Stop, sir—stop; we begin at five, and you
hav'n't got your part," said the showman to
Shadowly.

"Depend on me, sir; an extraordinary study—
get every line of it while I'm pulling off my boots,"
said Shadowly, and he hurried away, carrying
Applejohn with him. When fairly out of the
hearing of Phœnix, the actor said very confidentially to John—" Now, mark me; not one line do
you hear from me that isn't in Hamlet: a Barbary
corsair! yes, you'll see how I'll civilize him.—But
John," and Shadowly pausing before Solomon's
van, contemplated the human and inhuman wonders
painted thrice the size of life, and exhibited as the
exterior sign of the rarities to be seen for one
penny within,—" John, this really promises something."

"Don't be deceived! bless you, there's nothing

like that when you get inside," said John, " I've been cheated too often."

" Pooh ! Pooh ! I mean, John, that with tolerable dressing—and if you'll pledge yourself to keep the service a secret from all mankind, I'll mark your face for you—with very little pains, you'd make a much better cannibal than that," and Shadowly pointed to the portrait of a wild man with pink flesh, and hair descending to the toes, holding a live rabbit to his ravenous jaws.

" What *do* you mean, Mr. Shadowly ?" asked John.

" I mean, without flattery to assert, that if you'll give your natural qualifications proper play, there's not a cannibal in the fair that can stand against you. John, you're a lucky fellow—here's an opening that mayn't occur to a man in your situation once in his life."

" You really never mean, Mr. Shadowly, to advise me to show myself as a wild man, and eat raw meat ?"

" And why not ? Doesn't the philosophy of life tell you that raw meat is infinitely better than no meat at all—cookery, when all is said, is nothing more than a prejudice ; one of the effeminate inventions of extreme civilization."

" I—I can't answer all you say," replied John,

modestly, " but I'd rather starve, Mr. Shadowly, as a decent Christian, than get my bread by turning half-naked cannibal."

" Starve!" echoed Shadowly, and looking with melancholy eyes on John, the actor asked—" do you know what starvation is? Don't talk of it.—but follow me this instant. I insist that"—

" Ha! What — Hamlet! all full—not an engagement to be had—just hired a wild man—great pity—very man!"

" Mr. Oldjoe!" exclaimed Applejohn, as that eccentric vintner descended the steps of the caravan, followed by a well-dressed boy of about ten years old,—" I hope, Mr. Oldjoe that,"—

" Quite well; never better—for a plain young man, and you know Mr. Shadowly, I never boasted of my beauty,—never could look better. Don't go in—don't think of going in," said Oldjoe, laying his hand on Shadowly's shoulder, " now I and my little boy have come out, there's nothing worth seeing."

" Your little boy, Mr. Oldjoe?" asked Shadowly.

" Child of my mind—offspring of my immortal part—you don't know it; but this little boy's a great man," said Oldjoe.

" Not an English child, eh?" asked Shadowly.

" Look at his open face,—tallow, hemp, and hides, eh? Hush! he's a Russian prince," said

Oldjoe, confidentially, "I'm his tutor; hence, as I say, he's offspring of my mind."

"A Russian prince!" cried Applejohn, "is it possible, sir?"

"His father's now at my house; the celebrated Prince Kickhisownwhiskeroff; with his wife, the Princess Kickherownwhiskeroff, and their daughters, Catharine and Elizabeth Kicktheirownwhiskersoff—sweet girls; one of 'em—but it isn't for me to betray the tenderness of a lady."

"And you are the young gentleman's tutor?" asked Shadowly.

"I have taken upon myself to teach him the beauties of the English Constitution; and so, with the consent of the prince, his papa, I've brought him down to Greenwich Fair. Nice, docile little fellow! Such affection—such sweetness of temper! Do you know why we went into that caravan? You'd hardly believe it in a child: when he looked upon the pictures outside, he burst into tears at the Swiss giantess, and would have it she was his own wet-nurse that he'd left at St. Petersburgh: took the dear baby in to pacify him; whilst there—he didn't think I heard him—I listened to the proprietor making an engagement with a Spitalfields weaver for a new cannibal."

"What a pity!" exclaimed Shadowly, turning to Applejohn—"we're too late."

" Why, you never wanted the engagement ?" asked Oldjoe—" Hamlet come to raw beef?"

" I, sir !" shouted Shadowly, " No ! sir—I trust, Mr. Oldjoe, when fortune comes to the worst, that I have sufficient magnanimity to starve."

" Always thought you a spirited fellow," said Oldjoe; "always said too that Allgag didn't use you well—but you shouldn't mind that, and for this reason—he uses nobody well. Come, Paul, my dear ; you must go in the round-about," and Oldjoe was moving on.

" Prince Paul Kickhisownwhiskeroff in a round-about !" cried the astonished Shadowly.

" To be sure ; you mayn't know it—but little Paul may some day be prime-minister in his own country : can't begin the round-about too early. Besides, as I said to his papa this morning—' Kick-yourownwhiskeroff,' said I, ' of course, you'd wish his highness to know all the ramifications'—that's not a bad word, is it ?—' all the ramifications of English politics ?' On which, Kick. lifted up his shoulders, and made a sound with his mouth as if he was blowing his soup—' I thought you would,' said I ; and therefore, Mr. Hamlet, in the round-about Prince Paul goes."

" But, Mr. Oldjoe," cried Shadowly, " I pre-sume the young prince has never seen me act ? Allow me to state that in compliance with the wishes, frequently expressed, of the nobility, gentry, and public of Greenwich, I have consented to appear for a limited number of days at a"——

" Booth?" observed Oldjoe.

" Theatre!" exclaimed Shadowly, " under the most respectable and liberal patronage that"——

" I tell you what,—Mr. Shadowly! I have a respect for your talents, and as you are one of the sights of the fair, I shall feel that I have not fulfilled my duty to Prince Paul Kickhisownwhiskeroff if he quits Greenwich without seeing you."

" Mr. Oldjoe, though we have met but once before, I then considered your judgement to be"——

" Exactly," said Oldjoe, interrupting the actor —" exactly. And now can you inform me—but were you ever at Bartlemy Fair?"

" Allow me to say," replied Shadowly, with dignified emphasis—" never. This is my first appearance at"——

" I didn't mean that," said Oldjoe.

" I thought you wished to ask about my Hamlet," observed Shadowly.

" Not I, indeed," said Oldjoe; " I wanted to ask you a question concerning sausages."

" Sir!" cried the actor; but Oldjoe was not a man to be startled from his purpose.

" Concerning sausages," he repeated. " By the way, you were never at Strasburg? Ha! Ca—

pital sausages there—once went a pilgrimage of the
Rhine upon a single sausage. Capital tour! Cheap,
savoury, and romantic. But I was about to say,
Mr. Shadowly, if you've been at Smithfield, you
may remember that at the festive season they make
remarkably small yet toothsome sausages, that hiss
away—you know what hissing is, eh?"

" Not as Hamlet, sir," replied Shadowly, stiffly.

" That's extraordinary," continued Oldjoe.—
" Now, I wished particularly to know if sausages
of precisely the same character—cooked by elderly
ladies—and partaken of under the open sky by the
lower orders, were to be had at Greenwich?"

" I think not—I've seen none, sir," said Applejohn.

" That's a pity—or otherwise I should certainly
have treated the little Prince Paul to a sample of real
old English hospitality. However, Mr. Shadowly,
to return to your Hamlet. We have now various
engagements; the first is for his highness to try his
fortune in the lucky-bag; as an infant politician,
who knows what's in store for him? Stop—the
round-about first,—no, not so; the round-about as a
politician he may take according to circumstances.
Next, he must have at least a pennyworth of sticks:
he may knock down a tobacco-box, and save it
until his years of discretion—after that, he must
visit the gypsies; then he must ring-the-bull; then

take a lesson in the curious and interesting game of
pea-and-thimble, the whole to conclude with the
learned pig, and"—

"I don't think there is a learned pig," said
Applejohn.

"All the better for you, Mr. Shadowly," said
Oldjoe; "for I can tell you, we shall then have a
better chance of seeing your Hamlet."

"Sir," observed the actor, "as he is to come
after the pig, the Prince of Denmark is much
obliged to you."

"Egad! Prince of Denmark—so he is! I'd
forgotten—I'm afraid we can't come: the fact is,
the Kicktheirownwhiskersoff family and the Crown
of Denmark have an old grudge between them: I'm
not much of a politician—but I think, yes I think
it's about an old right of catching mermaids in the
Baltic, and pickling them for the London market."

"You are pleasant, Mr. Oldjoe," observed Shadowly with a contemptuous look.

"Always was from a child," answered Oldjoe.
"I'm sorry for the mermaids—very sorry; but so it
is, you see—I can't go against family prejudices.
If, now, you could play and dress Hamlet as the
Emperor of Austria, the prince might take it a
compliment, and"—Mr. Shadowly turned away—
"you won't? Very well—always the case with
geniuses—will do things their own way. I turned

off a waiter yesterday who was a genius—would knock off the necks of his bottles, because he said 'twas beneath a genius to draw corks."

" I—I beg your pardon," said Applejohn, hanging at the skirts of Oldjoe, " but have you heard anything of my old master, Mr. Gruelthorpe?"

" Ha! there, sir—there," said Oldjoe, stopping short, and addressing himself to Shadowly, " there's a fatal instance of prejudice; beware of it, Mr. Shadowly. I've scarcely time to—Paul, my dear," and Oldjoe stopped and spoke affectionately to little Kickhisownwhiskeroff—" Paul, my dear, if you must eat that chanticleer-in-trowsers,"—

" What do you call it?" asked Shadowly, staring at the gallinaceous gilt gingerbread in the hands of the Russian Prince. " Chanticleer-in-trowsers!"

" I assure you," said the solemn Oldjoe, " the name in polite circles.—Didn't you hear of that dreadful case of suicide? A lovely girl of eighteen, a nursery-maid in a noble family flung herself into the Thames."

" When! what for?" asked the tender-hearted Applejohn.

" Last Easter," replied Oldjoe very seriously. " She had been with the children to the fair, and bestowing upon them gingerbread like that in the hands of his Highness—wipe it off, and don't suck the gold, love, if you must eat the bird,—yes, giving each of them just such a cake, she unfortunately gave with it the vulgar name. There was a talk of taking her before a magistrate for corrupting youth—the tutor of the family said that one Socrates had been made to drink bitters for no greater an offence; however, she was only turned away; when, she was so haunted by her conscience, that she drowned herself in the Thames. There was of course an inquest on the body."

" Is it really true ? " inquired John.

" True !" cried Oldjoe with a stern look,—" I was foreman of the jury."

" But, Mr. Oldjoe, you spoke something of the danger of prejudice ?" said Shadowly.

" I did, sir—listen to a tale of blighted love. Mr. Benjamin Gruelthorpe—I'm sorry, John, to have heard what I did of you. I thought you an honest man but it's clear, faces are made differently now—don't speak—I hav'n't time to hear you. Well, sir, Mr. Gruelthorpe—lay this story to your heart,—was in youthful life a pawnbroker; perhaps, you have met him? Never mind; his father died, and left him a heap of money—'tis but a few months since,— a heap of money. He went to Paris, fell in love with an English lady of rank and title, and everything was settled. He had as I say a heap of money, and there were no questions asked. Being one day with the lady of his love, her mamma requested him to put a shawl upon Emily: in a moment of abstraction, he took the shawl, but instead of laying it on the alabaster shoulders of his mistress, he, no doubt thinking of bygone times, held up the article to the light, and stood looking at the shawl, as looks a pawnbroker. Nothing was said at the time," continued Oldjoe in a solemn voice, "but inquiries were set afoot, when the pawnbroker was discovered in Benjamin Gruelthorpe, Esq., and by means of a letter, written in a crowquill hand on pink paper, politely requested to forget the number of Emily's house. Now, sir, there's the effect of early prejudice."

"And what became of my young master?" inquired Applejohn very anxiously.

"When I was last in Paris, John, I endeavoured to discover. Walking towards Notre Dame with my friend Victor Hugo—'Vic.' said I, 'either my dear departed French tutor Têtedeveau, he was an emigrant duke—I've known two or three Dukes Têtedeveaus—who lived at Turnham Green when I went to school, either he misinformed my youthful mind, or not far distant from the towers of Notre Dame stands the Morgue. It was remarkable, but Hugo with little hesitation said—'C'est vrai;' and what was most strange, he at the same moment pointed to the edifice.   I entered the Morgue"—

" Isn't that the place,"—began Shadowly.

" It is," interrupted Oldjoe, " the place for the waifs and strays of death.   I made every inquiry there for Benjamin,—and discovered to my considerable grief that an English gentleman with the recent marks of a pawnbroker had been buried from that benevolent establishment only three weeks before."

" Did you hear nothing more of Mr. Gruelthorpe,—nothing more certain?" asked Applejohn.

" Nothing at that time; but I received a letter yesterday from Dusseldorf informing me that Mr. Benjamin Gruelthorpe was at that moment residing there in the best of health, and in much better spirits."

" Why, then, all you've been telling us about his probable death"—

" I know what you were going to say, Mr. Shadowly, but permit me to remark as a gentleman—how fond these foreigners are of our gold!— look at the little prince, if he hasn't licked the gingerbread bare—how they do swallow our gold to be sure!—but I was about to remark, that we are now come to that very minute when it will give me inexpressible satisfaction to wish you a very good day."

Mr. Shadowly instantly stopt, and with a lofty air was about to make doubtless a very dignified speech, when Oldjoe patted him upon the shoulder, and observed—" Sorry—very sorry that the pickled mermaids won't let me hear your Hamlet ; but if, as I said, you could only make it the Emperor of Austria, I should be too happy. Now, Paul, my dear," and Oldjoe without deigning another word to the actor, addressed himself to the little Russian —"now, Paul, there is first the lucky-bag—then the sticks—then the ringing-the-bull—then the round-a-bout—ha ! won't you think of me when you're prime minister?—and last of all, if you're a very good prince, and keep your hands clean, you shall be rewarded with a swing."

At this moment the prince pointing to a circle of men, exclaimed—" Oh ! oh ! oh !"

" Paul, I see it," was the prediction of Oldjoe. " I see it—you'll be a great man and a greater minister. My little love, that is one of our venerable institutions—that is a game originally invented by the first rulers of the world, and used very much among the Druids—that institution is no other than the thimble-rig !" The boy looked up at Oldjoe, who composing his features, said—" May it please your highness, pronounce thimble-rig."

The juvenile Prince Kickhisownwhiskeroff stared in the face of Oldjoe, and, for a first experiment, pronounced the words with a very creditable accent. "Say it again," said Oldjoe, when the Prince repeated the words. "Ha!" exclaimed Oldjoe, patting the cheek of the Prince, "oughtn't your country to give me a pension? Well, well, I suppose I must be content with an order or two: if, my dear, your father should ask you what you think I'd prefer, you may say the black eagle. And now—hush!—here is the table—here the professors!—You now behold the boast of Britons—the real thimble-rig!"

Shadowly and Applejohn were about to join the lookers-on at the table, when they were accosted by an almost breathless messenger despatched in search of them by Mr. Phœnix.

"He can't want me," said Applejohn.

"He does, though," said the messenger. "I can tell you, we're ruined without you."

"There must be some mistake," said John to the actor.

"None at all," replied Shadowly, and grasping the arm of Applejohn, he led him back to the booth.

CHAPTER XIX.

APPLEJOHN had no sooner mounted the platform, than Mr. Phœnix ran forward to greet him. " You hav'n't settled for the wild man ?"

" Certainly not," said John. " I tell you, I'd starve first. I'm not without a shilling yet, and"— at this moment John placed his hand in his pocket, but immediately started and turned as pale as if a reptile there had stung him.

" What's the matter—are you ill ?" asked Shadowly.

" Not a penny—as I'm a Christian, not a penny !" said Applejohn. " The lord forgive him, whoever he is !—but whilst we stood gaping before the van, some thief has picked my pocket—seven and sixpence, as I hope to be saved."

" Never mind—I'll fill your pocket for you ; " said Mr. Phœnix ; who then taking a studied view of John's anatomy, exclaimed in a burst of admiration—"why, you are the very thing, and not a shade of mistake !"

" I can't do anything," cried the modest John, " upon my word, I can't."

" Ten shillings a day," said Phœnix aside to Shadowly, "and he must do it."

" Let the skin be brought after us," said the actor in a low voice to Phœnix; and then to Applejohn—" John, follow me." Our hero, humbled by his recent loss, desponding at his present state of destitution, obeyed without a word the mandate of the actor; and speedily found himself behind the scenes, among a crowd of artists preparing for the business of the time.

" Gentlemen," said the actor, " my name is Shadowly; the name is, I trust, a sufficient introduction—I greet ye as brethren—men devoted like myself to an elevated art: enough for myself. I have now, gentlemen, in obedience to the wishes of Mr. Phœnix, to introduce to your fraternal indulgence Mr. John Applejohn, who is engaged to represent at a very short notice all the statues hitherto made attractive by the grace and strength of Mr. Jawbone, who, for reasons undiscovered, has absented himself at this critical moment from the theatre."

It is only due to the liberal feelings of the artists assembled, to state that they bestowed the heartiest welcome upon John; who was so astonished at the introduction, so overwhelmed by the cordiality of his companions, that for some moments he stood staring about him, bereft of speech. At length he was able to exclaim—" I play statues—I never did such a thing in my life ! Not for the world ! Mr. Shadowly,—there must be a mistake !"

" Mr. Applejohn," said Shadowly, " I have ventured to answer for your consent in this very tri-fling matter. I well knew the benevolence of your disposition—your readiness to oblige your fellow-creatures—your goodness of heart—in short, all those virtues which I will spare myself the trouble and you the confusion of remembering—and I there-fore on my private knowledge of your admirable character, pledged myself for your acquiescence."

" I wish I could be of any use, but I—I"—and again John stammered and stared.

" Unless you comply," said Shadowly, " Mr. Phœnix must forego the advantages of the present very limited season, and close the theatre. I appeal to your humanity, Mr. Applejohn.—Here are ten gentlemen before you, each with a wife and some with two families—their beds, their dinners for the next month are in your hands."

" But, I don't see how," cried the amazed Applejohn.

" Rival booths, I mean"—and Shadowly hastily corrected himself—" I mean theatres, have a stone Hercules walking outside; such a person has hitherto been the great attraction of this establishment:

Mr. Jawbone, you hear is not to be found—you are the only man with a figure for Hercules—the only man,"—

" But I can't play," said Applejohn.

" We don't require it : all we desire to save the theatre from destruction is,—that you should dress yourself and promenade outside."

" But if I'm known," cried John, " I'm ruined for life."

" Wherefore ruined, sir ?" asked Shadowly.

" What do you mean by ruin ? " exclaimed half-a-dozen voices.

" Are any of these gentlemen ruined ?" inquired Shadowly ; " stand they not as well with the world as they have ever done ? "

" I didn't mean," said Applejohn, and he vainly attempted to apologise—" I assure you, I only meant to say that"—

" That you would prepare yourself this minute; —here is the dress," and Shadowly presented John with an elastic web made to fit the naked figure, muscular developments being assisted by proper padding.

" Anything but that—I couldn't Mr. Shadowly —I"—and John endeavoured to make good his retreat, when Shadowly seized, and then addressed him.

" Mr. Applejohn, I again appeal to your humanity

—still, when you have put on the dress, if you shall continue to feel a diffidence in your natural powers—and you'll have nothing to do but to walk about, as the mob are not to know that you are not Jawbone himself—if, however, you remain doubtful of your abilities, you may doff the dress and"—

"Well, I'm sure I sha'n't like it, but to show you that I," and John took off his coat.

"I expected no less, Mr. Applejohn, from your philanthropy," said Shadowly; who with others assisted John to dress, and in a few minutes our hero to his own consternation found himself clothed, wigged, and whitened for a stone Hercules.

"I can't do it—I should die if anybody was to see me—I—where's my clothes?" and Applejohn looked for his every-day garments. "I should be very happy to oblige you, gentlemen, but I feel that this is—hallo!—what are you about? Gentlemen! I insist! Murder!"—

"Hold your tongue, you fool!" said an actor, one of the four who had suddenly lifted John Applejohn, the new Hercules off his legs, and were now running to deposit him on the platform without.

"If you say a word, we'll pitch you into the mob," said a second of the bearers, and in a trice John found himself set down among the mummers

without.   A loud cheer from the surrounding
crowd welcomed the wretched Applejohn; who, so
much was he alarmed, appalled by his situation,
could see nothing distinctly.   His sight grew dim—
his throat became suddenly dry—the blood sang
in his ears—his tongue was glued to his mouth—
his knees knocked together, and he would certainly
have fallen on the boards, had not a young lady in
a Highlander's costume—one of the gentle actresses,
—caught him by the arm, and to rally him into
self-possession, insisted on his immediately making
one in a three-handed reel, with herself and a grand
Turk.

The fair had now begun.   Showman strove to
out-bellow showman, cymbals clashed, drums beat
—and all was holyday uproar.   As the evening
advanced, the crowd became more dense and more
vociferous, now taunting John with his awkardness
—now, with his idleness, as like a strayed goose he
wandered to and fro, devoutly praying for midnight.   He had in vain begged for his clothes to be
restored to him, that he might cease to be a statue,
and run away.   To all these entreaties Mr. Phœnix
deigned nothing more consolatory than a very
coarse command for John to attend to his business,
with subsequent permission when the fair was over
to go to the same place, whither in the morning
the proprietor had despatched the dramatist.   John

wandered inconsolably backwards and forwards,
when he was rudely accosted by a tall, robust,
clownish, drunken fellow, who had forced his way
through the crowd, and had mounted the platform.
" Perhaps, you don't know me ?" said the stranger,
glaring at Applejohn.

" I—I have not that pleasure," said John.

" Well, then, it's time you did : my name is
Jawbone—I've been in this troop since I played
the fairies"—

" What ! my dear fellow," and John's heart leapt
at the prospect of deliverance—" the Jawbone so
celebrated as the statues ?"

" Exactly : and now, I'll let you know—because
an artist of my standing gets drunk a little—I'll let
you know what it is for sneaking rascals like you
to come and try to take the bread out of his
mouth !"

" I take your bread ? if you'll believe me, Mr.
Jawbone,"—but John was not allowed to conclude
his sentence ; for the tipsy Hercules with a power
worthy of the arm of his namesake, threw our hapless hero from the platform into the midst of the
mob.   Fortunately for John, his weight was very
equally divided upon the heads of half-a-dozen of
his former spectators, who, however, proceeded to
resent the freedom by falling upon the innocent
offender.   A yell from the mob—a rejoicing shout

—attended the descent of John from the platform, and a hundred fellows in the crowd rushed to the spot where Hercules had alighted.   In the midst of this uproar, several sparkish holyday makers broke through the press, and seized upon the astounded Applejohn.—" Here's fun !— glorious fun ! lend me a knife—must have his nose —give a hundred for the nose of a living statue— hurrah !—glorious fun !"   Such were the cries of five individuals who, it may be sufficient to say, are not to be considered strangers by the reader, and who were bearing away with triumphant cries the helpless Applejohn, who roared, but as it appeared roared in vain for rescue, when a sailor broke through the mob, laid right and left about him, and seizing the captive Hercules, swore he would murder any number of rascals who should dare to lay a finger on him.

" Well, I'm glad you sung out !—I knew your voice—but lord ! that I should find you in such a pickle !" said the sailor.

" Why — it isn't Seabright !— Ned Seabright ?" exclaimed Applejohn, and with no further words, he flung his arms about his deliverer, covering him with classic chalk.

" Jack, Jack—how could you so disgrace yourself?—how could—but here they come !—here comes Sarah and her father !"

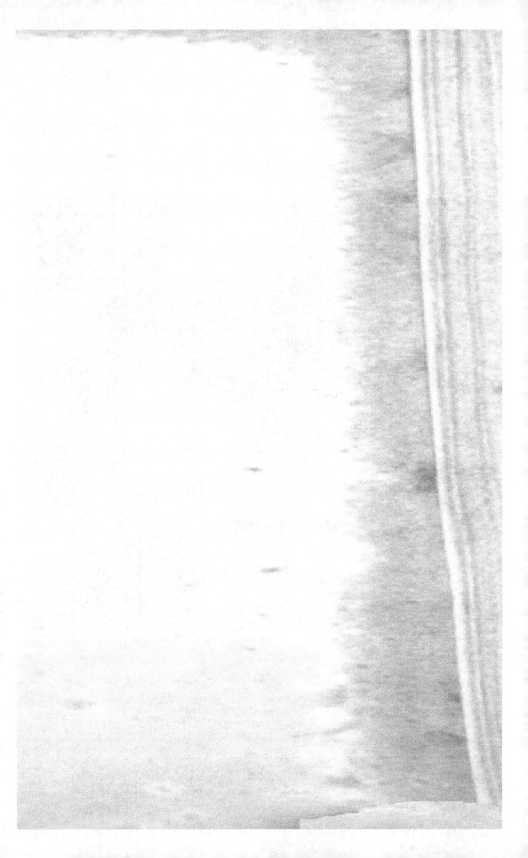

At these words, Applejohn breaking from his friend, endeavoured to escape. " No, Jack; we've had a pretty dance to find you, and now you don't slip your cable, I can tell you. Farmer, give us your coat—here's a hat—and now, come along to the Compasses."

John in silence, the blushes burning through his whitened face, suffered himself to be wrapt in the farmer's great coat, to have his stone-coloured wig replaced by his friend's hat, and trembling with surprize and shame, to be hurried through the crowd to a neighbouring ale-house.

" I ha' done thee wrong," said Farmer Twopenny, holding forth his hand to the confounded Applejohn, who was never so much a statue—" Ned Seabright ha' cleared it all up—and when you're in Christian shape again, if you like to ha' Sarah, why"—

The next instant Sarah Twopenny was in the arms of her bewildered Hercules.

CHAPTER XX.

WE trust that a short chapter will be sufficient to clear up the plot to the satisfaction of the reader, who, we hope, has not forgotten our introduction

of Applejohn, seated on a door-step in Chancery-
lane. " Aye, he was seen there, drunk," says the
reader.

By no means : hear the story. John Applejohn
on the twentieth of June, a burning evening, had
been summoned to a certain hospitable roof in
Chancery-Lane to bail Edward Seabright, master-
mariner, and John's schoolfellow, maliciously arrested for an exorbitant debt. The room of the
prison was stifling hot, and John, awaiting certain
preliminaries walked to the door, and seated himself upon the step. With his head in his hand
he awaited the coming of a humble functionary
despatched upon some cautionary duty. In this
attitude he was seen by an uncharitable acquaintance, and duly reported drunk—for, it was reasonably asked, would any respectable man be found
in such a situation if he were sober ? John meant
well—no man better ; but the story of his drunkenness flew from mouth to mouth ; his clothier refused
him credit—Farmer Twopenny denied him a promised wife—misfortune followed misfortune—and
John, still meaning well, at length found himself
upon the stage of a mountebank, to be flung thence
as a sneaking interloper, an underhand varlet with
a mean design upon another's bread !

Captain Seabright returned to London, having
made a prosperous voyage. He sought for John,

and learned the story of his vice from the Farmer, who dwelt with great emphasis on the drunkenness of Applejohn on a particular night when he was seen sitting intoxicated on a step in Chancery-lane. The sailor immediately explained away the calumny; showed how much poor Applejohn had been abused—tracked him from place to place—and at length, with the Farmer and Sarah came to Greenwich Fair, at the very minute Hercules Applejohn, like a mangy cur, was flung among the bellowing crowd.

If the reader admire simple, honest meaning, cheerfully pursued—despite all calumny, despite all suffering,—for its simple, honest sake, we think he will rejoice that John Applejohn obtained Sarah Twopenny for wife, and that fortune, tired of persecuting him, rewarded him for troubles past with the three great blessings of this mortal stage—health, competence, and the respect of men.

END OF VOL. II.

PRINTED BY W. WILCOCKSON, ROLLS BUILDINGS, FETTER LANE.

MEN OF CHARACTER.

BY

DOUGLAS JERROLD.

"We must admonish thee, my worthy friend (for, perhaps, thy heart may
be better than thy head), not to condemn a character as a bad one, because it is
not perfectly a good one. If thou dost delight in these models of perfection,
there are books enow written to gratify thy taste; but as we have not in the
course of our conversation, ever happened to meet with any such person, we
have not chosen to introduce any such here."

FIELDING.

IN THREE VOLUMES.

VOL. III.

LONDON:

HENRY COLBURN, PUBLISHER,
GREAT MARLBOROUGH STREET.

MDCCCXXXVIII.

PRINTED BY W. WILCOCKSON, ROLLS BUILDINGS, FETTER LANE.

CONTENTS

OF

THE THIRD VOLUME.

———

ISAAC CHEEK:

THE "MAN OF WAX."

CHAPTER I.

" Bright was the sun, and clear that morrow-ing," when Isaac Cheek for the first time stood in the parlour of Mr. Cox. In one hand he held a letter of introduction—in the other, a white hat; or, as we incline to believe, originally a black one, become white with reverend old age. Isaac stood in a most advantageous posture, his legs being adroitly disposed to hide an ignominious patch in trowsers evidently made for the wearer ere he had attained his full growth. His coat was not so much buttoned, as hauled, up to the chin ; with no relief of linen, no manipulated flax, to turn forth " its silver lining" on the beholder.

" Mr. Cox will be with you directly," said Sarah. " Sir" was at the tip of her tongue, but a sudden glance at the visitor from head to heel made her withhold the superfluity.

Mr. Cox entered the room, and seeing a b
standing reverently on the carpet, benevol
coughed to give the poor man courage, and
held forth his hand to receive the missive. I
.... a smile, trod as though he walked
......'s wool, and then timidly placed the lett
th. hand of Cox, who, as he took it, twitche
face as if he had received a stinging-nettle.
opened the paper with the tips of his finge
and, his nose slightly curled as if he feare
plague from the contents, declined his right
upon the writing. He read aloud :—

" My dear Cox,—The bearer of this is re
very clever fellow. Don't judge him by his
which you will at once perceive to be not
promising. If you can employ him in any way
for I can assure you, though outwardly a sl
dog, he is, take him altogether, a thorough-
chap—in truth, a man of wax. Yours truly.
            " JOHN ROBINSO

As Cox delivered these contents—and he (
them over the tongue very sonorously—Isaac (
with an air of conscious worth, passed his
around his hat, in an ostentatious but vain at
to smooth the beaver—and when Cox repea
which with fine sensibility he thrice did—" a s
dog." Isaac pulled up the collar of his coat to
the insinuation.

" And pray, sir, what can you do?"

Isaac had not dined for the last three days; he was therefore fully justified in saying—" Any thing, sir."—No—never since the invention of speech, did man put more bowels into an answer.

" Umph!—ha!—well—just now, I happen to want a—a secretary," observed Cox, dropping himself into an easy chair.

Isaac smiled from ear to ear; and, forgetting the patch, drew himself erect, and placed his hand upon his breast.

" Were you ever in Persia?" asked Cox.

Isaac paused to recollect whether he ever had been at Ispahan. " Not yet," he at length modestly replied.

" Do you know any thing of chemistry?"

Again Isaac smiled a terrible gash in his face; and hoping that the gesture might be translated to his advantage, was silent.

" Very well: and, of course, you keep accounts?" Isaac smiled for the third time. " And you can transact foreign correspondence?" Isaac smiled, but very weakly. " German, French, Italian, a trifle of Dutch, and if you have a seasoning of Russian, why—why, all the better?" Isaac bowed in acquiescence to that opinion. " For the truth is," said Cox, negligently, " I have a great deal to do with many crowned heads. Indeed, pretty nearly all of them have, in their time, passed through my hands."

Isaac felt himself dilate, sublimed with respect.

" As for salary Mr.——, by the way, what is your name ?"

" Cheek, sir—Cheek," and Isaac again coaxed his coat closer to his chin.

" A very odd name. Well, Mr. Cheek, as I have said, we perfectly understand the matter of salary and—as the office is a place of highest trust, —if you can produce any vouchers for your moral conduct—do you know any clergymen ?—I think I may say the secretaryship is yours."

Cheek this time bowed so suddenly and so pro- foundly, that the door—to which he had gradually receded—open at his back, struck by the act of homage, closed with a loud report. " For my moral character, I flatter myself that—yes, sir. I think I can promise"—and here Cheek nodded his head on one side, widened his nostrils, and struck one heel against the other, with an air of the most perfect satisfaction.

" No doubt—no doubt," said the liberal Cox, apparently fully convinced by the self-assurance of Isaac. What you have said is quite sufficient— consider yourself in office. Bless me ! what a head is mine !—I had almost forgotten—would you run with this ?—I'll direct it—'tis for Miss Buckleby and

it is most particular that she should immediately
have it, for in her own words, 'life and death depend
on it.' Ha! Mr. Cheek," continued Cox, "you
cannot well comprehend the value in this little
bottle. Half the wisdom of the east is concentrated
within it. Talk of the elixir!"

A knock at the door prevented the probability of
any such discourse; and the appearance of a grave
young man in Oriental costume, called Cox up
from his seat. The stranger rolled his black eye at
Cheek, and seemed to summon to himself new dignity. Approaching Cox, he saluted him, *more
Persicorum*, and then slowly turning up the room,
squatted cross-legged upon the hearth-rug.

"You don't speak the Persian?" asked Cox
doubtingly of Cheek, who, though not quite assured
of his ignorance, faulteringly answered—"No."

"That's a pity. A most interesting person, and
one of my patients." Cox winked one eye, pointed
his thumb over his left shoulder at the sitter, and
added, in a tone of confidence—"The sixty-ninth
son of the Shah Abbas."

"And all with beards like that?" asked Cheek,
admiringly.

"Ha! there's a long history attached to that
beard: I assure you, it wasn't always what you now
see it. His original want of beard was his misfortune. All his brothers beat him by two spans and

a half; and the Shah, acutely affected by the circumstance, ordered him to be bow-strung. He was
brought from Shiraz under the guns of three English frigates. When I return him to the Shah, I
can't say what his gratitude may send me."

" Why, it's like a muff," said Isaac, his eye im-
movably fixed on the chin of the Persian; who at
that moment smiled, doubtless at some sweet poetic
fancy of the divine Saadi passing through his brain.
" Very like a muff," iterated Isaac, confirming
himself in the simile; and again the Persian
smiled.

" Now, if you will run, Mr. Cheek,—for, as I told
you, this is on life and death—if you will immediately run."

Isaac bowed, took the parcel, and quitted the
room—but Isaac did not run. We doubt not nature had some dignity in her eye for Cheek, when
she sent him earthwards. He was none of your
lank strips of humanity, made merely to measure
ground—things, whose " nerves, and arteries, and
veins" are compressed in their bodies like a skein
of thread in paper. No—Isaac was certainly ordained for a mace or a corkscrew; a mayor or a
butler. His belly was caski-form, his arms and
legs round as bottles, and by the care with which
he used them, apparently as fragile. One foot ever
seemed to wait a concerted signal from the other

ere it followed it. He walked as though he was of the opinion of the heathen philosopher, that the whole world was like unto an egg. And this majesty of movement Isaac had indirectly cultivated at the table, in the few green seasons of his life when the luxury was open to him. Truth to say, he had been a devourer from the bib: there ran a legend that in his babyhood he had killed three wet-nurses. His face more than hinted the weakness. It was not a face of flesh, but a face of jam. And yet Isaac was recommended as "a man of wax!"

Isaac, impressed with the warning of Cox, that life and death were in the errand, pursued his way in the most philosophical spirit, showing by his features that life and death were equally indifferent to him. At length, however, he arrived at—— square; and having solaced himself for ten minutes at one of the corners with the syren air of a ballad singer, whistled her strain and proceeded onward to seek the wished-for name or number. The door was opened, and a woman eagerly exclaimed— " Thank the Lord! I knew your knock."

" I bring a mixture for"——

" Heaven be praised,—yes!—come along, sir— you must give it to the dear creature yourself!" And Isaac was seized by the wrist, fairly lifted up two pair of stairs, and drawn into a bed-room, by

the woman, who shouted in all but hysterical triumph, " Here—here he is !"

Cheek was bewildered by the scene before him.
In the lap of Miss Buckleby, the governess, lay a
little girl of about six years old, clothed in holiday
white and red shoes, screaming like a cat, and
writhing like an eel; whilst an old woman, looking
in its blue face, exclaimed with touching hypocrisy,
" bless its pretty eyes," and another earnestly solicited the honour of " holding it."

" Ha !" cried an old gentleman with powdered
hair, and face as smooth and shining as though made
of Dresden china—" Ha ! Miss Buckleby, I told
you it would be so—those filthy custards"——

" My dear, dear sir," exclaimed Miss Buckleby,
in an affecting tone of remonstrance and a look
enough to melt any heart not harder than sealing-
wax—" My dear, dear sir"——

" Well— I—what I mean to say is, 'tis easy enough
to get another wife, but another child"——and here
the speaker paused, as if struck by some well-
remembered difficulty.

" A slight attack of indigestion, sir," said Miss
Buckleby, looking seraphically at Cheek, and pursing her mouth as though she were playing the
flageolet—" but as the doctor has not come himself,
if you will administer,"——

" Do, sir—pray, lose no time," urged the elderly
but unwrinkled gentleman.

Cheek turned his hand into his coat-pocket calmly
as any automaton, drew forth the more than "elixir"
delivered to him by Mr. Cox, robbed it of its en-
velope, and a cup being presented to him, filled it
from the bottle; and, taking a professional, but
unmanly advantage of the sufferer, poured the
sovereign anodyne down its little throat. The
effect of the medicine may be readily guessed from
the women, a second after, crying with one loud
voice—" pretty creature !"

The whole group—if we except the great operator, Cheek himself, who stood serene in power—
were in a high state of grateful animation. Miss
Buckleby smiled, and looked at the elderly gentleman, who gently pressed his hands together, and
smiled at Miss Buckleby. At this moment of thanksgiving, a genteel young man was shown into the
apartment, and apologizing for the inevitable absence of his principal, produced a phial, uncorked
it, and blandly asked for " a spoon." At the words,
the mouth of every body present—save the mouth
of the little girl—opened as though at the summons
of a magician.

" A spoon—what !—another draught—the child
hasn't strength to bear it," exclaimed the father.

" Another draught !" echoed the young gentleman, knitting his brows, compressing his lips, and swinging round as upon a pivot in front of Cheek, no more affected by the mute challenge than the goat of Esculapius—" Another draught! I beg your pardon, sir—I was not aware that another practitioner—I'm sure, I"—and the speaker, with excited finger and thumb, endeavoured to re-cork the supplanted phial.

" What!" cried the father—" is not this gentleman an assistant of"—he could say no more, so decided was the negative look and gesture of the new visitor. " Then, sir, who are you?" and he spoke to Isaac.

" My name is Cheek," cried Isaac; and had it been Coriolanus he could not have named his name with greater dignity.

" Cheek! and who do you come from?"

" From Mr. Cox."

" Cox!" shrieked Miss Buckleby, and down she fell,

> —" As though that name,
> Shot from the deadly level of a gun,
> Did murder her!"

" And who sent for you?"

" I suppose, Miss Buckleby—for I was told that 'life and death' were on the errand."

" Kind creature!" exclaimed the father "all her anxiety for my dear child—nay, Miss Buckleby," and he pressed her hand, and looked in the reviving face of the maiden—"but why send for another doctor—was not Mr. Franklin enough—why should the child take?"——

"Ben-Hily, Ben-Holy, Ben-Haly, Ben-Hallat's Persian Dye?" asked the young practitioner.

"Dye!" screamed the parent; "Dye!" and the doctor pointed out the Orientalism raised in the bottle.

"I perceive—a little mistake," said Check, with the nerve of a rhinoceros. "I am the new secretary to Mr. Cox—and all our three footmen being employed, and the butler laid up with the gout, and hearing that Miss Buckleby had sent a life and death command, I volunteered to bring the—the elixir."

"Elixir! and do you know its qualities, sir?"

"No, sir," replied Check, evidently proud of his ignorance.

"Do you know the effect of such poison on the human stomach?"

"Poison!" groaned the father—"Poison," shrieked Miss Buckleby; "Poison," sobbed the female servants; "Poison," snorted Check, beginning to be moved.

"Oh, sir!" and Miss Buckleby fell at the feet of the old gentleman—"'tis I who am the wretch—'tis I who should suffer—mine, mine, is the crime."

"What crime?" and seeing Miss Buckleby on her knees, the old man was softened, and repeated in gentler tones, "what crime, Louisa?"

"Red hair, sir—red hair!" and she wrung her hands with a thrilling sense of her ignominy.

"Wretch!" he could speak no more, but recoiled horror-struck from the delinquent. Struggling for expression, he at length, in the laconism of extreme woe, appealed to the doctor—"An emetic, sir?"

"A constable," was the reply, and the speaker pointed out Cheek as the proper subject for a police operation.

"But my child—my child—poison—poison!" exclaimed the parent.

"Don't be alarmed, sir," said the doctor, "the dye is perfectly innocuous. See, sir," and the gentleman applied the Persian dye to his lips.

"Are there no deadly compounds?" asked the gentleman; "no mortal drugs—no mischievous ingredients?"

"Innocent as milk," was the answer. "So, Mr. Cheek, this time you have escaped a jury. Oh, I assure you," and the speaker again sought to calm the paternal fears—"harmless as water. It is composed of—of—yes," and again and again applying it to his tongue, he enumerated the compounds of the incomparable Persian dye.

Cheek was suffered to depart; and though he

had been the unknowing physician—the unconscious cause of cure, for the dye had proved efficient as antimonian wine—still, as he had not healed on the strength of a diploma, he quitted the house, not only unthanked, but threatened and reviled. Such is the gratitude of man! Nor was he for many a day forgotten in the visions of Miss Buckleby, whose all but successful attack on the widower was foiled by the untoward publication of her red hair. And then the mischance of things! That Cheek should have arrived with the dye at the very moment Mr. Franklin was expected to the little girl!

But Isaac was not all desolate; he had caught some words of consolation; and thus, with steady hand, and a serene face, he again knocked at the door of Mr. Cox. The door was opened.

CHAPTER II.

" ARE you any judge of the fine arts?" asked Cox of Cheek, as the secretary with an improved air of self-confidence, seated himself before his master. In truth, so leisurely had he sunk upon the cushion —so little had he respected the presence of his employer, that Cox felt it necessary to repeat the question. " Mr. Cheek, are you any judge of the fine arts ?"

" Which of 'em ?" asked Cheek, and this time never smiled.

" A most exquisite collection,"—proceeded Cox —" every statesman and celebrated pickpocket of more than a century ; and then the set of murderers is, I am assured, unrivalled. You have no friends with money, Isaac ?" asked Cox, familiarly.

" Why ?" said Cheek, in a tone implying a probability of so excellent an advantage. " Why ?"

" My dear fellow," and Cox smiled benignantly, " there is now a fortune to be made. You have only to stoop for gold, and pick it up."

" I don't mind stooping," said Isaac, with proper worldly philosophy. " I don't mind stooping," he repeated more determinedly.

" With your talents and your address—your perfect knowledge of mankind—your fine animal spirits"—Cheek swelled like a pouter pigeon— " your invincible energy of character—you—you want but a hundred pounds." (Alas ! that such merits should want so little to be perfect !)

" Only a hundred pounds !" said Cheek, as if he spoke of as many grains of sand—" only a hundred pounds !"

" And then you might join me in the venture. I have only heard of it since you quitted me. Yes,"

—and Cox spoke as though he communed with himself—"yes it is wonderfully cheap." At length Cox descended from the clouds, and deigned to enter into particulars. An admirable collection of wax-work had been seized for rent—a kind and active friend had given him notice of the fortunate chance—the whole lot was to be had for something approaching nothing—and if some acute, enterprising person like Cheek would but join him——

" And have they got all the murderers?" asked Isaac.

" All of any reputation," was the answer ; " and of course," added Cox, with a fine provident wisdom, " as others come up, we can add them to the stock."

" Well then, Mr. Cox, I think the sooner you and I are added to them the better."

" Mr. Cheek !" and Cox pushed his chair back, as though it went on a railway. " Mr. Cheek !"

In few words Isaac related the accident which had applied the dye, not to the fiery tresses of Miss Buckleby, but to the interesting intestines of her infant charge ; maliciously adding, that the child was not expected to last out the night.

" Why, Mr. Cheek, can such stupidity?—give hair dye to a child?—the Persian dye to"——

" How did I know what it was? You talked of your patients—said the mixture was on ' life and death'—I was dragged into the room—the child lay screaming—what *could* I do?"

" But did it swallow a tun, it couldn't kill it," vociferated Cox.

" That's what I said," cried Cheek. " But if the child goes off, who is to satisfy a coroner's jury? To be sure, I could in my defence publish the recipe."

" You never would be such a scoundrel?"

" Life is sweet, Mr. Cox," said Isaac, and he smacked his lips, and his eyes twinkled mischief.

" The recipe ! publish the recipe—make known the compounds of the inimitable dye !" and Cox spoke and looked as though he touched upon a crime not registered in the calendar of mortal guilt. —" But"—and the features of Cox were scarlet with satisfaction as he triumphantly crowed forth— " before you publish the recipe, you must know it."

Isaac spoke not, but set at Cox like a pointer; the jaw of the proprietor of the Persian dye fell as he gazed on the terribly eloquent eye of Cheek, who, with no more passion in his voice than is struck out by marrow bone and cleaver, dissonantly enumerated all the compounds uttered by the doctor. The face of Cox changed to all colours like the face of a mandril—and his hair rose upon his head like the hair of a spitting cat.

Imagine the sweating drudge of half a century,

the living mummy of a laboratory, at length glorified by the long-sought secret; see him towering among his crucibles, and his retorts, challenging a place with the gods, to whom his "so potent art" has raised him; mark him swelling with the consciousness of immortal strength, the sole repository of superhuman wisdom—and then imagine a subtle spy creeping from a corner, a curious dwarf who watched the last process, hath plucked out the heart of the mystery, and lying *perdu* at the golden moment, hath, at a single point of time, possessed himself of the slow-coming glory of an age: so looked the alchymist Cox—so looked the prying Cheek!

"And is—is the child so very bad?" at length asked Cox, trying to compose his face into a corpse-like serenity.

"I should think anybody would give a hundred pounds for my discovery," said Cheek.

"While there's life there's hope," cried the self-comforting Cox.

"Let the worst come, by selling the recipe I shall be able to fee counsel," observed Cheek.

"'Twould be a stain for ever on the Persian dye," groaned Cox. "Don't you think, Mr. Cheek, that—if it would not be very inconvenient—a little journey out of town—say to Liverpool—packets start every week to America—and in case of the worst"——

"What! quit my country? Leave England?" and all the patriot rushed into the countenance of Cheek. "How could I live, sir? No; I'll wait and face a jury, even if I should be hanged."

Cox looked up, and sudden hope seemed lighted in his features. The current of his thoughts appeared in an instant changed, and clasping his right knee with his hands, and gazing with a look of patronage on Cheek, he observed, "Well, after all, perhaps it would be best."

"That I should be hanged?"

"Now I think again, 'twould be the making of the dye. Consider the advertisement."

"Even transportation might give it a lift," urged Cheek, satirically.

"A trifle like a public whipping could do it no harm," said Cox; and Cheek moved uneasily in his chair. "But, really, Mr. Cheek, if you think the child cannot recover, I must immediately prepare for the increasing demand."

"You may save yourself that trouble," replied Cheek, sullenly, "the child is well as I am; but for the recipe"——

"I see it, Cheek, you are the very man I need; Robinson anticipated all my wants when he sent you. Let us understand each other. As I asked before, have you any taste for the fine arts?"

"I like four meals a day," replied Cheek, "and have a taste for anything that will get 'em."

"Solomon's wisdom goes to nothing better," said the sensual Cox. "Well, about this collection that accident makes a bargain." Cox was not so tedious as to state that he was the landlord of the shed where the collection was *not* exhibited. "You shall be nominally the sole proprietor."

"Nominally?" grunted Cheek.

"You have some conscience, I hope, Mr. Cheek?" asked Cox, but Isaac replied not. "What I mean is, that the exhibition shall be under your name, and that the profits be equally divided between us, the half of the purchase-money being first deducted from your share." Cheek sat pondering silently; and his face became purple with thought. "Consider the advantage of the offer; and again, think of the standing it will give you in society. The sole proprietor of the original wax-work! You shall have possession of all the figures, with, as they say in Parliamentary Committees, 'power to add to their number.' Well, Mr. Cheek?" and Cox waited for the *ultimatum.*

"There's my hand," said Cheek, presenting that piece of anatomy as though it were costly as the palm of Midas. "There's my hand."

" And between men of honour quite enough,"
cried Cox.

" I don't care much for parchment," observed
Cheek ; " and yet it's a necessary evil."

" True, but I can see we want no deed—we shall
agree like brothers."

" And with brothers, says the Italian," and Cheek
spoke with the air of a schoolmaster—" two witnesses and a notary."

" Proverbs, Mr. Cheek, proverbs are the second-
hand wisdom of fools and knaves."

" Mr. Cox !" and Cheek rose like a bear on its
hind legs, to enquire the particular class to which
he might belong.

Fortunately for their infant contract, a knock at
the door called off the attention of the parties. The
Persian gentleman with the beard, not perceiving
the whereabout of Cheek, said in good Petticoat-
lane English.

" Mister Cox, here's Michael Hangelo in the
passage."

" Show him in," said Cox. But it is only due
to Michael Angelo that he should enter with a new
chapter.

CHAPTER III.

CHEEK, who had somewhere heard the name, but knew not the precise species of creature to which it was attached, cast his eyes curiously towards the door for Michael Angelo. He saw nobody, but was startled by a sound proceeding, as at first he thought, from under the carpet. He looked down, and saw upon the floor something nearly three feet high; a figure that seemed as if originally formed of full dimensions, but crushed within a mould to its present dwarf deformity. There was that flesh and bone about him, that if "long drawn out," would have lengthened into a symmetrical life-guardsman. In a word, he was a man shut in like an opera-glass. He was habited in a faded grass-green coat, with buttons up to the shoulders—buttons robbed of their gold in the struggle through life ; a blue velvet waistcoat, its glory somewhat obscured; drab breeches, and speckled worsted stockings; in one hand he held a copper-mounted cane—with the other, he waved a hat, not unlike a decapitated sugar-loaf, bowing as though he bent before the assembled human race.

" Well, sir, I hope we have arranged this

matter, so as to spare your professional feelings."
Thus spoke Cox; and Michael Angelo, with the
intense gratitude of a man of genius, pressed his
hat to his bosom, slid his legs backwards and forwards, and bowed.   "I should have been sorry to
see the figures put up to public auction."

"Sir!" exclaimed Michael Angelo, and his
small voice rang as though it came through a glass
tube—" 'twould have been an everlasting blot upon
the age.   What!   Newton going by the hammer!
Ravaillac knocked down! Jack Shepherd bid for!
To have had that glorious constellation of art scattered to the four winds of heaven! Napoleon, perhaps, bought by the Court of Petersburgh—Vol-
taire gone to the Pope—Joan of Arc possessed by
the grand Turk, and, though I say it, all my beautiful murderers purchased by the managers of Drury
Lane and Covent Garden!"   The tears came into
the eyes of the speaker at the bare thought of such
desecration.

"This gentleman," and Cox introduced Cheek,
who, standing up, and placing his hat before the
patch, received the homage of Michael—" this
gentleman, with a rare feeling towards the arts,
has consented to purchase the whole collection."

"In the name of every artist in Europe—in the
name of the mighty dead, sir, permit me, a humble
labourer in the immortal fields of grace and beauty,

to thank you for a devotion of which, I am sorry
to say, the present time affords so few examples.
No, sir ; we are a money-scraping generation, and,
as I often say to Josephine, my wife, sir, are deaf
and blind to the emanations of the soft and lovely.
Mr. Cheek, what now, flattery apart," and Michael took out a horn snuff-box, and tapping the
lid, continued his question——" what now do you
really think of my twins ? "

" I have not the pleasure, sir, of knowing any of
your family," replied Cheek.

" Ha ! ha ! I should have told you," said Cox,
" that this gentleman, Mr. Michael Angelo Pops,
is the artist to the collection."

Cheek bowed, and Pops, full of himself, continued——" I am not vain, Mr. Cheek ; no, I trust I
am as free from that vice as any R. A. of the lot ;
by the way, sir, it's sometimes lucky to be a stone-
mason, isn't it ?——but can the whole Academy
match my twins ? And yet they rob me——rob me,
every year."

" Rob you !" cried Cheek, " and have you no
redress ? "

" No, sir, no ; they change the material ; I work
in wax——and they commit the felony in stone. Did
you ever see *my* Pitt ? Well, sir, I don't like to
mention names ; but if I hav'n't been shamefully
copied ! however, I am used to these things.——That

makes the third prime minister stolen from me.
Well, it can't be helped ; but if I'd stuck to bronze,
and never fallen upon wax,"—and Pops took half
a handful of rappee to drive away reflection.—Still
he returned to his injuries, exclaiming, with the
look of a Diogenes—" Ha, sir ! genius is nothing
—wisdom is nothing—worth is nothing in this
world, it's the material makes the man ! A Phidias in wax isn't worth a—but, no, I won't mention names—in free-stone. Ha ! it's a great curse,
Mr. Cheek, to be born with a sense of the beautiful ; I, who might have made a fortune as a tallow-
chandler, may starve upon wax."

" Well, Mr. Pops, let us hope for better justice,
as the world grows wiser under the direction of Mr.
Cheek," said the comforting Cox.

" I can see, sir, a man who knows life. Now, the
late proprietor, a very worthy person, was too
much for abstract principles to give fair play to the
show."

" What do you mean by abstract principles?"
asked Cheek, with the humility of a pupil.

" Why, sir, he was for giving a crowd of folks
out of Greek history, and didn't pay sufficient attention to our Newgate Calendar. He'd spare no
money to get up a Cæsar, toga and all, and yet
grudge the expense of a journey to Kingston to
get the face of the first house-breaker of his day—

that's what I call abstract principles, sir. The present wax-seeing people, sir, require excitement; their bowels are only to be come at through blood. Bless your heart, sir, my figure of Mrs. Brownrigg brings showers of shillings (to be sure she wears her original nightcap), while the Venus de Medicis takes never a farthing. No, sir, no; no man who shows wax-work should indulge in abstract principles."

"There's nothing stirring of late, is there, Mr. Pops? No new child with two heads—no piebald girl?" asked Cox.

"No, sir, no; nature has been plaguy dull and monotonous of late; there was a talk of a birth in high life of a little boy with horns like an elk; but I'm afraid, sir, 'tisn't true. When will Mr. Cheek take possession?"

"Immediately," replied Cox.—"Immediately," responded Cheek.

"I need not say, Mr. Pops, that we shall—I mean, that Mr. Cheek will be—most happy to retain your eminent services as artist to the exhibition," observed Cox; and Michael Angelo made a bow, which reduced his height to something above that of a buttock of beef.

"Shall I have the honour of accompanying Mr. Cheek? I have only to call in Parker's Lane to order supper of Josephine—poor thing, she's not

very well—by the way, Aaron," and the artist
turned round upon the Persian with the beard—
on the sixty-ninth son of the Shah Abbas, who
happened to unceremoniously open the door;—"by
the way, Aaron, that bit of rhubarb I bought of
you on Thursday in Shoreditch, turned out none
of the best."

"Rhubarb!" said Cheek, looking knowingly at
Cox, who raised his shoulders, sighed, smiled, and
said, "Ha! Mr. Cheek, the exile is sometimes reduced to melancholy shifts."   Leaving Cheek to
ponder on this sorrowful truth, Cox turned up the
room, and Michael Angelo proceeded to escort the
new proprietor to Parker's Lane.

"You'll not take a coach?" asked Pops, promising
himself that luxury.   Cheek thrusting his two hands
into his pockets, replied with peculiar decision,
"No!"

It was about five o'clock on a sultry afternoon in
July, when Cheek arrived at the mansion of Pops,
in Parker's Lane.   There were outward signs of
the epicurean habits of the dwellers within.   The
door-way, strewn with pea-shells, tempted a frail
sow from her proper path, the road, to dispute possession of the prize with about twenty children,
who swarmed about the step, thick as bees at the
mouth of a hive.   Pops, who fairly disappeared
among the crowd of bantlings, led the way, direct-

ing Cheek by his voice. " Never mind Betsy—
she's gentle as a rabbit," said Pops, as Cheek deferentially drew back from the mountain of living
pork stopping the door. Arrived in the passage,
he was about to mount the stairs, when a brindled
bull-bitch, whose appearance gave the naturalist a
hope that the breed was not likely to be extinct,
lying at the bottom, raised her head as Cheek raised
his foot, rattled a growl, exhibited two rows of
teeth in splendid preservation, and her eye, kindling
like a live coal, threatened sudden mischief. " Never
mind her," said Pops, " she won't bite,"—but
Cheek, with a lack of faith in feminine forbearance,
refused to advance. Pops leapt from the stair, and
valiantly holding the animal by her two ears, enabled the pusillanimous Cheek to ascend. The
weather was extremely hot, and as Cheek mounted
from story to story, the staircase provokingly reminded him of a corkscrew, and that, by an association of ideas, suggested ale. " Another, if you
please," said Pops bashfully, as Cheek paused at
the fourth floor: "only another," cried Pops, in a
tone of encouragement. Cheek turned to renew
the labour, when he was fixed upon the first stair
by the voice, as he considered, of a man with a
confirmed cold, exclaiming—

" Go, my best love ; unbend you at the banquet ;
Indulge in joy and laugh your cares away ;

c 2

> While in the bowers of great Seminoïe
> I dress your bed with all the sweets of nature,
> And cover it as the altar of our loves ;
> Where I will lay me down and softly mourn,
> But never close my eyes till you return."

Cheek cast an enquiring look upon Pops, and was about to speak, when another voice, with a new emphasis, but with a trifling impediment in its delivery, repeated—

> " Wh-e-re I w-will l-l-ay m-e down and so-oftly mo-ourn,
> B-b-ut ne-ver clo-o-se my e-eyes ti-ill you re-turn."

Again Cheek looked, when Pops observed with a smile—" One of Josephine's pupils—Miss Boss—a charming girl,"—and jumping at the latch of the door, made into the room, followed by Cheek, who, unseen, was fortunate enough to hear a repetition of the two lines, under the correcting auspices of Mrs. Pops. Both ladies, their backs turned to him, and the pupil following the action of the preceptress, who, with the edge of her right hand, continued to cut a perpendicular line, and faithfully in the same place, exclaimed syllable for syllable—

MRS. POPS.

" Wh-e-re I w-will l-l-ay m-e down, and so-oftly mo-ourn."

MISS BOSS.

" Where I will lay me down, and softly mourn."

MRS. POPS.

" B-b-ut ne-ver clo-o-se my e-eyes ti-ill you re-turn."

MISS BOSS.

" But never close my eyes till you return! "

At the word "return," Mrs. Pops, with
kerchief in right hand, made the "cut six," and
with the vigour of a dragoon, at the same instant
swinging round to "exit" with a dignity that caused
three teacups on the mantle piece to tremble, and
brought down sundry bits of broken ceiling.   In
this peculiar action—and it was the distinguishing
grace of all the pupils of Mrs. Pops—she was
rigidly followed by Miss Boss, who, unhappily too
near Mr. Cheek, raised her hand, grasping her
kerchief on the word "return," and twisting to the
door, brought her fist with fine energy upon the
nose of the unseen guest.   Had Cribb played tragedy, the hit could not have been more effectual!
Cheek fell against the door, with the weight of a
stunned bull—Miss Boss clasped her hands, and
made so low a curtsy, that she nearly sat upon the
floor—Mrs. Pops shrieked, and woke a child in the
cradle, who answered the maternal note, and two
boys, who at first shouted a laugh, added to the
cry of pain and terror, their ears having been boxed
by the mother for their unseemly merriment!
To vary the tumult, a bantam hen, sitting in a tri-
angular deal spittoon in the corner, quitted her
eggs, and flying on the back of a chair, essayed her
voice ; the cry was taken up by her late companions
in the street, and Parker's Lane rang like the
poultry yard of the Ark.

" My S-tars, P-pops !" were the first words, and
they were spoken by Josephine.   Miss Boss, the
delinquent, said nothing ; but still stood with clasped
hands surveying the blood-dropping nose of Cheek.
She had not even sufficient presence of mind to
offer him her handkerchief, but suffered it to be
twitched from her by her preceptress, who liberally
presented it for the use of the sufferer.   Cheek
took it in silence, and removed from the door: Miss
Boss immediately spied her opportunity, and slip-
ping behind her victim, lifted the latch, and having
flourished her hands about in mute horror to Mrs.
Pops, ran down the stairs like any sylph, but was
immediately followed by one of the boys, despatched
by the instructress.

" I am so sorry," said the host, as he looked up
to Cheek swollen like a bladder.

" It won't be very black," said Josephine, as she
descried the colour gathering about Cheek's right
eye.

" The best remedy in the world," exclaimed
Pops, and jumping on a chair he withdrew a piece
of raw beef from the cage of a jay suspended from
a nail ; and insisted upon its immediate application
to the bruise.

" I hope you're better, sir ?" said Mrs. Pops, her
stutter becoming aggravated with her sympathy.

" What ! is she gone ?" cried Pops, looking

wrathfully round like a balked despot for Miss
Boss.

"She had an appointment, my dear—she had to
meet"—and Josephine bowed and whispered—"she
had to meet *them* in the Park, at the Theological
Gardens."

"She will be so sorry," said Pops, comfortingly
to Isaac.

"A charming girl," cried Josephine—"she is
about to appear in *Statira*, I was giving her the
last lesson. I'm sure she'll be happy to present the
gentleman with a ticket. Do you know, Pops, the
people at the 'Garden' won't let her play unless she
takes three pounds worth of tickets, and, poor thing !
she has no connexion for pit or boxes. But as I
said, I'm sure, if this gentleman will accept,"——

"Josephine, my love," cried Pops, with the air
of a man who has too long deferred a sacred duty,
"Josephine, my love, Mr. Cheek,—the gentleman
who has purchased 'the property.'"

Mrs. Pops made a low curtsy to the new proprietor, and still nursing her infant—for, like *Lady
Macbeth*, Mrs. Pops at the time knew what it was
"to give suck,"—she proceeded to congratulate,
amidst the cries of her baby, played upon like a
bagpipe by the right arm of the pacifying mother.

"I shall be home at nine to supper," said Pops,
"let it be whatever you please." Josephine gave

an anxious look, and timidly asked—" Lamb chops
and *grass*, Michael ?"

" Whatever you please," was the liberal answer ;
and Pops was making for the door, when his wife
called him back with sudden energy.   He returned
to his helpmate, who commenced an admirable
piece of pantomime, unfortunately lost upon the
dull perceptions of Cheek.   Had he been open to
passionately eloquent appeals of action, he would
have understood Mrs. Pops to say—" Pops, have
you no money ?—you perceive that Miss Boss is
gone off ; and although this is the third lesson she
owes us, although this is the third time I have gone
through *Statira* with her, she has not"——

In the midst of the motions, the little boy despatched after Miss Boss returned ; sidling close to
his mother, he gave her eighteen pence, and whispered, in a tone audible to Cheek,—" Now she
says she only owes you for two."   Mrs. Pops took
the money with the dignity of a queen ; and, looking graciously down upon Pops, said— " Very
well, love—at nine."

" A treasure of a woman that, sir," said Pops as
he descended the staircase—" ha ! sir, such a brain ;
a great creature, sir—a great creature."

Cheek who was as literal as a note-of-hand,
merely replied, " Very stout, indeed."

" True, sir—true ;" and Michael heaved a sigh.

" Ha ! sir—but for her figure she'd bring me forty pounds a-week."

" That's a pity," said Cheek.   " How so ?"

" It can't be disguised, sir ; for present taste Mrs. Pops"—(if their be faith in weights and balance she was fifteen stone)—" Mrs. Pops is a *little* too heavy for her line."

" The tight rope or slack-wire ?" asked the dull and innocent Cheek.

" Mr. Cheek, I perceive, sir, that you are not theatrical ?" said Pops, sullenly.

" No, sir, I am not," replied Cheek, as though defending himself from an infamous insinuation.

" Is Mrs. Pops ?"

" Some day, sir," said Pops with an encouraging manner, " some day, sir, I'll show you the spice-box and lemon-squeezers presented to her by the turners of Tunbridge Wells.   Ha ! sir, her *Juliet* was a thing to keep a man awake of nights.   They talk of the *Juliets* and the *Belvideras* of the present time ! put 'em altogether they wouldn't make half of Josephine."   Cheek, at this, looked like a prose-lyte.   " No, sir, there is so much nature about her !"   Cheek looked more and more convinced. " And then, sir, she is so devoted to her art.   She has such an intense love for the profession, that though banished from the stage herself—and, by-

c 3

the-by, I have seen women of as grand a scale, but without her soul, sir——she has won me to consent to her giving lessons."

" To furnish ready-made actresses ?" observed Cheek, with rare acuteness.

" To bring 'em out, sir,——to teach them nature —to show them the established way of developing the passions : in fact, to put young ladies up to all sorts of stage business. You should hear her give a lesson in elocution,—in"——(for Cheek looked puzzled)—" in the proper mode of delivering prose and verse."

" But," said Cheek, her stutter still beating in his ears, " but hasn't she an impediment that"——

" None, sir—that has ever been observed. Her pupils have all done wonders. Some Sunday, Mr. Cheek, I'll walk with you in the Park and point out their carriages to you."

" Bless me ! she must find it very profitable," remarked Cheek, with an eye to business.

" She might, sir, if she was not so particular; but the fact is, if Josephine has any fault, it is that of excessive nicety. 'Talent, my love,' she always says to her young ladies, 'talent, my love, may do a great deal upon the stage,——but, with London managers, there is nothing—nothing like private character.' Now, sir, you saw Miss Boss ?"

Cheek's lips became rigid as a horse-shoe at the question, and passing his knuckles tenderly across his nose, he replied—" Saw her, and felt her."

Pops, magnanimously waiving the injuries of his neighbour, continued, with no allusion to Isaac's nose—" An excellent person, sir ; a good, virtuous, discreet girl ; and, as my wife informs me, an admirable breeches figure."

" Breeches ?" exclaimed Cheek ; but further enquiry on his part was prevented by Michael Angelo, who suddenly stopt in front of a house, saying— " This is the place, sir."

CHAPTER IV.

THE artist, with a dignified waving of the hand, laconically but proudly observed—" Here we are, sir !"

A great moral lesson is taught by wax-work. Pops evidently spoke as if assured of such influence. Certain we are, there is no show so worthy the twelve-pence of a philosopher. Orators and pick-pockets—philanthropists and cut-throats—swindlers and state arithmeticians here shoulder one another, and almost seem to plead a common right to their respective callings. Here is a king eternally opening Parliament—there a minister looking perpetually wise—there a celebrated orator, always about to rival Demosthenes, but never doing so—there a council of potentates and warriors, met to discuss peace, with no likelihood of concluding the deliberation—and patriots always about to sacrifice themselves for the good of their country, and not moving a finger for that purpose. A show of waxwork is a fine exhibition of human *intentions.* And yet, however cunningly fashioned, the figures appear to be the handiwork of death, anticipating or commemorating the image set up.

" And what figure is that? Bless me it's alive!" asked and exclaimed Cheek, as a young creature of about sixteen turned full upon him.

" Eleanor, my dear, you may go home; there'll be nothing more to-night," said Pops to the girl, taking no note of the words of Isaac. The girl—a meek, intelligent, young thing—smiled sweetly upon the dwarf, bent to Cheek, tied her bonnet-strings, and glided silently as a shadow away.

" Your daughter?" asked Cheek.

" Dear, no! Poor thing—poor thing! You saw where she was standing? She knows nothing of the matter, and never shall !"

" What matter ?"

" Why, sir, it's a long story; and it isn't as pleasing as a fairy tale. Well, sir, you see that figure?"

" That in the frieze jacket and leather-cap?" said Cheek.

" The same. Well, sir, you must know that poor Eleanor—she's been, I may say, as good as my own child these eleven years"——

" What, does she live with your family?"

" She's quiet and contented, and wants little—gives no trouble—takes up no room;—and then so trustworthy—she takes the money here, sir, and is true, sir—true as arithmetic. Josephine and she quarrel a little sometimes—that is, Josephine quarrels, for Eleanor says nothing."

" But who is she—where did she come from?" asked Cheek, with, for him, extraordinary interest.

" Why, sir, if you'll promise to be secret, I'll tell you. Eleanor is"——

" Good evening, Mr. Pops," said a languid voice, issuing from a dark pale gentleman, until the previous moment absorbed in the contemplation of one of the figures. " Good evening, Mr. Pops," and the speaker relapsed into profound meditation.

" Do you know who that is?" asked Pops of Isaac in a whisper, standing upon his toes to waft the query softly upwards. Cheek looked towards the visitor, then down upon Pops, and shook his head. " A great man—comes here very often—indeed, he's on our free-list."

" An editor, perhaps?" guessed Cheek.

" Not in the least," replied Pops. " I'll introduce you to him—I will, upon my life," asseverated the artist, big with the honour he was about to bestow. Michael softly approached the great man, followed by Cheek. " Hem !—Hem ! an extraordinary person, that ?" said Pops, diffidently opening the conversation, and pointing to the figure of Mrs. Brownrigg (in her original nightcap), the figure that had stolen the heart, and eyes, and thoughts of the gentleman on the free-list; who made no reply. Pops ventured to speculate that it was impossible to make anything of her.

" A most difficult subject to handle. But yet, I think, with proper treatment," said the visitor, " I think"——

" Well, for my part, I should think such a person past doing any thing for," said Cheek, with virtuous disgust of the coal-hole murderess.

" There would be a difficulty,—but, yes, she might be managed."

" Impossible !" exclaimed Cheek, with energetic horror.

" Perhaps, sir, you are not aware of my treatment of such characters ?" asked the gentleman with ill-disguised pride. " Perhaps—I say perhaps—you have not heard how I managed with"——and here the speaker ran over a list of the most celebrated highwaymen, sheep-stealers, and house-breakers—

" you are not aware, perhaps, what I have made of them?" and the gentleman again cast his eyes upon Mrs. Brownrigg, and again was silent.

" Now do you know who he is?" asked Pops in a half-breath, his eyes all in a glitter.

" I perceive," replied the sagacious Cheek.   " I perceive—keeper of the Penitentiary."

" Lord love you, no ! Why, it's the great author —the great writer of plays, Mr. Victor Nogo !" exclaimed Michael Angelo, with kindred admiration of a brother artist.

" Humph !"—and Mr. Nogo, rapt by the subject, communed with his spirit, almost wholly unconscious of the presence of his hearers—" Yes, it may—it shall be done ! I see the capability of great effects. Ha ! *an illuminated view of the Coal-hole, with the moon rising on the bodies of the victims !* And then —ha !—yes—*An awful storm—the coals suddenly ignited by a flash of lightning—the Coal-hole entered by firemen, and providential discovery of the bodies !* There's three electrical effects ; let me see—*Miraculous recovery of one of the apprentices, who, at the critical moment, produces the whip in court, and thus supplies the only required link of evidence !* Capital ! and then—I have it—*Procession to Tyburn, with the real Jack Ketch, engaged, at a great expense, for the run of the drama ; and the last dying* speech of Mrs. Brownrigg, to orchestral accompaniments ; the cart to be drawn from under her feet amidst a—A BRILLIANT DISPLAY OF FIREWORKS !" Why, I see it—the thing is done ;" and the poet made in his note-book hasty memoranda of the aspirations of his muse. " And now for the title"— and Nogo vigorously scratched his head, still no title came ; he scratched again—again—and then he plucked the brilliant thought away. " I have it !"—and he wrote it down, and the letters beamed to the fancy of the domestic bard like a row of diamonds—" I have it—' THE BLOOD STAINED COAL-SACK ! OR, FORTY MURDERS IN FIVE MI-NUTES !'"—And Mr. Nogo clasped the book, and thrust it into his pocket, with the triumphant air of a magician who had caught and bound to his service some under-working sprite. In very truth, the mysterious note-book was hardly of less power than the potent tome of the Italian necromancer—

" Trassene un libro, e mostro *grande effetto ;*
Che legger non finì la prima faccia,
Che uscir fa un spirto in forma di valletto
E gli comanda quante vuol che faccia !"

Yea, Nogo's common-place book was a book of " great effects." Genii of the mountain, the flood, and the mine—devils with tails and horns of various lengths—dwarfs, giants, griffins, hippopotami—

variegated vultures and huge sky-blue spiders—all were in its leaves, ready at the motion of the master to produce "a great effect!"

"What, sir?—I see you have it!" said Pops, having watched the divine impulse of the poet, the return of the book to his pocket, and the gleam of satisfaction that irradiated his countenance—"Yes, I'm sure you have it; we may shortly expect something—eh, sir?" and Michael Angelo smiled, anticipating the glory.

"Why, yes; I may say it's done. Though, in this piece, I shall not sacrifice myself to language: I shall keep my eye upon effect. Yes, I flatter myself, I know what the public likes. There are dramatists, to be sure"—and Nogo turned to Cheek—"who do prettily enough with words; but then none of them have any effects."

"I have always heard it was a poor business," said Cheek, understanding effects in the spirit of a broker.

"Now, I am not vain; but I do think I know what an audience is made of—yes, I may say, I can successfully reduce a drama to the meanest understanding. By the way, Mr. Pops, you never saw the gilt inkstand gratefully presented to me by Mr. Blaze, of the New Cut, the celebrated maker of blue lights and red fire. Now, if such things arn't triumphs of the drama, I should like to know what are?"

"There's no mistake in silver-gilt," said the tangible Cheek.

"If that isn't genius, I know nothing about it," magisterially concluded Pops. "Speaking of genius, Mr. Nogo, I am afraid you never saw any of Josephine's pupils. Ha! you should hear some of them read."

"I didn't know she keept a school," said the author.

"Not exactly a school; though many of the nobility have pressed her to open an academy for the art, and teach comedy and tragedy, at so much by the quarter—opera, pantomime, and dancing to be paid for as extras. And she ought to do it—she ought; but the truth is—and I am sorry to be compelled to own it—the truth is, Josephine is too modest. Ha! sir, diffident worth may live on dead flies in a garret; whilst confident pretence—but I say nothing. By the way, have you heard that Miss Sappho, since she has retired from the stage, teaches elocution and passion in all their branches? Absolutely has half-a-guinea a lesson for teaching young ladies how to repeat their part of the marriage service with the proper hysterics. Half-a-guinea a-lesson! Ha, sir! you should have heard Mrs. Pops repeat the marriage service."

"Pray, did you ever hear her?" asked Cheek of Pops; who stared, fluttered, and, after some difficulty, laughed at the strange blunder of the querist.

"But, as I said, sir—diffident worth"—Pops, however, spoke to the dreaming; for Mr. Nogo stood in a trance. Pops repeated the words—"But, as I said, sir—diffident worth"——

"I beg your pardon"—and Nogo started into speech—"I beg your pardon; but it will make the bill stronger, and will add materially to the interest of the piece—could you lend us the authentic night-cap?"

"I have no doubt, sir, that—that"——

"Thank you," quickly replied the author, taking the benefit of Michael's doubt, and hastily quitting the premises.

"A great man, sir—a very great man—knows the public taste, sir—and helps to make what he knows," said the eulogistic Pops to Cheek, who had turned round, and with fixed eyes stared on the figure in the frieze jacket and leather cap.

"And now, about that girl?" said Cheek——

"Well, sir; you see, Eleanor—bless me! why, what's the matter?"—and Pops, again interrupted in his projected narrative, turned to the son of the Shah-Abbas—to the Persian rhubarb-dealer — who hastily entered the place; and, in few words, informed the new proprietor and artist that Mr. Cox required their instant attendance at his house on business.

" What can it be ?" asked Pops.

" I thinks—I thinks"—and Aaron rubbed his hands with the glee of an ogre—" I thinks it's a new murder."

" A new murder !" ejaculated Cheek, with a look of timidity.

" And there's pork chops for supper," added the Persian.

" Let us go directly," said Cheek, " it may be very important."

" I shouldn't wonder if he wants us to travel for a new subject," said Pops.

" You've hit it," said the foreigner, with a good knowledge of our idiom.

" Another murder !" exclaimed Pops.

" And pork chops for supper !" added Cheek ; and with these words they quitted the show-room, and betook themselves to the house of Mr. Cox, who, in truth, had projected a provincial pilgrimage of business for the artist and the proprietor.

But a new chapter must be allotted to the commencement of the eventful wanderings of the man —or rather of the men of wax.

CHAPTER V.

THE journey of Cheek and Pops from London to —— was, we are distressed to say, unrelieved by any accident. Not a single highwayman, not even a broken axletree mitigated the monotony of the way; and thus, two and twenty hours after their departure from the metropolis, they were seated in the little parlour of the Silver Stag, eating their breakfast like common people. Cheek was not a professed wit; but now and then he threw a pleasantry away, "like dewdrops from a lion's mane." In the present instance Isaac, jocund of heart, and heavy of abdomen, turned up a face of light, and exclaimed, from the very bottom of his belly, " Why, Pops, this is the land of milk and butter !" The reader of severe taste may see but little in the sentence; we can nevertheless assure him, that for Cheek there was a great deal in it. Pops grunted an affirmative through a mouthful, and again addressed himself to a ham, which he seemed rather to perch upon—so diminutive did he look—than sit to.

It is one of the fatal evidences of the infirmity of our nature that appetite decreases with eating. However, let us not linger on the fallacy of all human hopes—be it sufficient to us to say that Cheek, finishing his breakfast, felt a saddening truth endured by highest genius—he felt how far execution lagged behind conception. The untouched twelfth egg—the last slice of twenty strata of bread and butter—proved to him that he was mortal !

" And now, now to business," cried the artist, wiping his mouth, and pulling down his cuffs. " Our first care must be to get into the gaol. Why, what's the matter?" proceeded Pops, seeing Isaac suddenly wince, as though, like Puck, he was seated on a thistle. " For my part, I've been I may say"—and Michael spoke with a new air of superiority—" Yes, I may say I have done business in almost every gaol in the country."

" They are ugly places," replied Cheek gloomily.

" I have passed many pleasant days in 'em," averred Pops. " The world, Mr. Cheek, the world has no idea of life in a condemned cell. I've met with civilities there that would make—ay, noblemen blush. And then for morals—and for what one may call the decencies of society—oh ! you have no idea how sentence of death brings out the real politeness of a man. There was Jack Fobem—as great a bully as ever blustered—well, two days before he was hanged, you might have taken him for a lord."

" Shall you be long over the present job ?" asked Isaac.

" No—no—trust to me; when I once get into the prison, I have all my tools with me, and I'll bring my man away at a single sitting."

At this moment, the landlady of the Silver Stag made her appearance. Casting a rapid glance now on Isaac, and now on Pops, she proceeded to clear the table. In the middle of her task, she paused—and observed, in the cold, accusing tone of a Siddons—" Where's the other spoon ?" at the same time displaying three in her hand. " I say— where's the other spoon ?"

" My good woman,"—cried Pops, the landlady colouring to the eyes at the epithet—" My good woman"—

" Oh !" exclaimed the landlady, discovering the lost property under the turned edge of the tea-board. " I'll bring your bill directly," she added, anticipating the order for that certain evil.

" What do they take us for ?" asked Pops in amaze, vainly awaiting an interpretation on the part of Cheek. " What can they take us for?" And still Isaac, in his modesty, could not determine. The landlady, with almost incredible speed, returned with the bill. Pops twitched it from between her fingers, and laid the document upon the table, as though it was to be considered that day three months; and then putting his forefinger to his brow, and his thumb to his cheek-bone, asked— his honour sweating blood at every pore—" Pray, madam, do you lose many spoons in this house?"

" No, sir, never; for before some people leave the room, I always take care to count 'em."

Pops trembled from head to heel, and was fairly stricken dumb by the new insult. But for Cheek— true philosopher as he was—he was as proof to such attacks as an armadillo. Whilst Pops was convulsed, strangled for a reply, Cheek maintained magnanimous silence; and whilst the artist could have transfixed the landlady with his just indignation, Isaac, with his forefinger on the table, traced a circle of water round a perplexed gray-coated gnat. *Aquila non captat muscas*, saith the motto—but the motto was not made for Cheek.

" I say, madam—I say, do you know who we are?" roared Pops, whilst Cheek raised a meek look of remonstrance towards the querist. " Perhaps, you are not aware that I am an artist of"—

" I thought so," exclaimed the woman, as though her worst doubts were realized; and she spun herself out of the room.

" They know nothing of us here," observed Cheek, with the indifference of a stoic. " Consider, we are more than a hundred miles from London."

" But fame—fame travels, Mr. Cheek," returned Pops.

" Not always by the stage," answered Isaac, careless of the truth he uttered ; for Isaac was often as unconscious of the pearl he let fall, as the oyster that breeds one. " Not by the stage !" Alas, how many a genius—how many an eighth wise man, having booked his place, finds even at the end o twenty leagues that his fame hath not come passenger ! How many a great mind hath been levelled by mile-stones ! How many a prophet in his own town, removed to the next, looseth his mantle !

" Not to be known here ! Why, my name is on my box !" cried Michael Angelo.

" Perhaps the people can't read," replied Cheek, and Pops seemed somewhat comforted by the probable ignorance. " True, true," he assented, with the small voice of peace ; and then he suddenly knocked his clenched fist on the table, and knitting his brows, and his face turning to an imperial purple, Michael shrieked—" But the spoon, Isaac ! the spoon !"

" That was odd," said Cheek, beginning to whistle.

" Odd ! I call it infamous," vociferated Pops.

" But you must own the ham was capital," observed Isaac, benevolently wishing to give praise where praise was due.

" To be suspected of a robbery ! *Me !*" and Michael cast his eyes towards the sky, as though he expected to see it open.

" And the bread-and-butter delicious," continued the eulogistic Cheek.   Pops said nothing, but his face suddenly became wrinkled like a brook ; he gasped with indignation.

Foolish, foolish Michael Angelo Pops !   How often do we see a little man with a great soul fuming, pelting, wearing out his littleness with his greatness—teasing himself and his neighbours about his reputation ; when a wise, quiet, happy fellow, fattens in tranquillity, thinking only of his " bread-and-butter !"

" If, indeed," and Pops felt strong in what boxers call new wind—" If, indeed, the spoon had been found upon me,"——

At this moment, the door opening, Pops paused in the middle of his sentence, and fixed his eye upon a new visitor, who with enviable self-composure advanced towards the table, and drawing a chair under him, sat down.   As he deposited himself, he winked a brassy eye at Pops, distended his mouth, evidently with an intention to smile, and nodded his head.   We are happily old enough to remember

the late Mr. Pope's *Banquo*; and we have little
doubt that the new-comer had shared in our good
fortune; for his action was a servile imitation of
that great and gentle actor, in his "blood-bolter'd"
capacity. The visitor certainly had not his throat
cut, but his smile more than equalled that advantage
for the expression of the picturesque and terrible.
Pops spoke not—Cheek was silent. Again the
visitor winked—again he smiled—again he twitched
his head.

" Then it wasn't found upon you, eh?" said the
stranger, condescending to speak with a rugged
familiarity.

It is a terrible dilemma for a little man, when circumstances occur which insist that he should appear
very big. To say that Pops rose from his seat is
to impart no idea of the truth; we should rather
say, he shot up from it. Standing upon his two
great toes, and his neck stretched almost to hanging
point, Pops, with a constrained civility—very difficult for a new beginner—asked, if the party addressing him " knew *who* he was?" Were a
giraffe gifted with speech, and placed in the predi-
cament of Pops, its gestures could not be more
dignified.

" To be sure I do, Mr. Pops," was the answer;
and the speaker rubbed his hands upon his breeches'
knees, and laughed a hearty laugh. " Know you!"

D 2

" Then, sir,"—and Pops abated something of the ferocity of his dignity—" then, sir, you are probably aware that I am an artist of"——

" In course I am : why it's all over the town."

" Ha, ha !" and Pops chirped in his throat, and, looking at Cheek, cried, in a side speech not lost on the long-eared visitor, " Isaac—ha, ha !—you see she *may* travel by the stage?" But Cheek was not a man to appreciate a delicate touch ; the surest way to make him sensible of a hit was to knock him down.

" By the stage, eh ? what ! along with you ?" asked the stranger, and again he smiled.

" Yes, yes ; with me," answered Pops, rubbing his hands, winking at Cheek, and feeling even through his bones a glow of satisfaction. " Well, it seems then, sir—I beg your pardon, sir, what may be your name ?"

" Gullet," replied the stranger with apparent " measureless content" at the appellation.

" Well, then, Mr. Gullet, it seems that I—that is, that we—were expected ?"

" We thought we should have you, though not quite so soon," cried Gullet. " Howsomever, I'm very glad that it's fallen to *my* chance to light upon you,—a capital bit of luck."

Pops made a very profound bow ; and even the phlegmatic Cheek declined his head in token of the compliment. Indeed, there was a heartiness, a sincerity in the manner of the speaker, that demanded an elaborate acknowledgment. Cheek began to feel the dignity of his new calling, assured of his importance by the attention of Gullet, whom he addressed with the blandest condescension.

"A pretty neighbourhood hereabouts—eh, Mr. Gullet?" said the nominal proprietor of wax.

"Yes, very pretty; and you'll—ha! ha! I beg your pardon"—and Gullet passed the sleeve of his coat across his mouth, as if to wipe away even the remains of an unseemly laugh—"you'll have a capital view from the castle."

"So I've heard—so I've heard," said Pops. "A very old and beautiful edifice: there are about it a —a great many historical associations?"

"Ever since assizes were held at——" replied Gullet; who, placing his arm on his thigh, bent his head forwards, and looking keenly in the face of Pops, asked with sudden seriousness—"I suppose you've made your mind up to this business,—you know exactly what's to be done?"

"To be sure—to be sure. By the way, how did you happen to expect us here?"

"Why, the mayor received a letter that"—

"That's like Cox," said Michael aside to Isaac —"just like him; cautious, calculating man—he's told our business, and bespoken every civility for us, no doubt.   What ! the mayor received a"——

" Yes ; but I had further intelligence from—— however, no matter for that ; here you are."

" I see how it is," exclaimed Pops, expanding with pleasure—" I have no doubt that you are somehow in the service of the mayor himself?"

" In course I am," said Gullet, staring at the vivacity of the artist.

" And that his worship has sent you to"——

" Why, he knows that you are here by this time."

" And when will he be ready to receive us?" asked Michael, nodding towards Cheek, busily employed pulling forth a shirt frill, large as our grandmother's fan, from a shirt, late the property of Mr. Cox.   " When will he be able to receive us?" repeated the artist to Gullet, who looked earnestly through the lattice.

" He's ready now," was the answer.

" I'll only change my neckcloth and wait upon his worship."

" Nonsense !" cried Gullet, his lip curling and his eye twinkling—" Nonsense ! a man like you would be just as welcome in a coal-sack as in cambric."

" See what it is," said Pops, aside to Cheek— " see what it is to have a mayor who knows what art is."   Cheek smiled.   " Yes, yes ; as my schoolmaster used to say—'*emollit mores, nec sinit esse feros.*'" Cheek opened his eyes; but, after a moment's hesitation, bowed to the latinity.

"His worship," observed Gullet, "never stands upon ceremony. He settles—eh?—but here it comes;"—and as Gullet spoke, the rattling of wheels was heard; and, in a few seconds, a vehicle, something like a taxed cart, rapidly approached the door of the Silver Stag, followed by a crowd of men, women and children, huzzaing—whooping —screaming.

"Now my dear Mr. Cheek," observed Pops confidentially to him, "you see the influence of art. Had there been an ass—a hog in the mayoralty, no carriage had been sent for us—no huzzaing crowd would have gathered about our chariot. No; we might have come, have performed our task, and gone away again like a pair of nobodies. But you perceive there is a taste in the mayor; and, as a natural consequence, taste pervades the mass." It is a hard matter to deny a speculation when backed by servants, carriage, and horses; therefore, Cheek said nothing. Had the mayor not sent a vehicle, Cheek might have spoken.

"Are we to go in that?" asked Pops, his voice scarcely heard for the shouting outside.

"Yes, so let us lose no time." Gullet opened the door—paused—looked round—scratched his

head, and muttered to himself, " D——d fool !
forgot the *cuffs*."

The visitors were met by three other men—as
Pops observed, with a twitch of the elbow to Cheek,
servants to the mayor—on leaving the apartment,
and escorted to the vehicle at the door-step ; where
they had no sooner presented themselves, than they
were met with a shout, which Michael acknowledged
with a bow that would have done honour to a con-
gress ; Cheek humbly followed his example.   This
gesture on the part of the visitors was met with a
new shout from the gathering multitude, as faithfully
and as elegantly acknowledged as the first.   Indeed,
both Pops and Cheek were so employed in paying
their respects to the acclamations of the populace,
that sundry sneers uttered by the malignant were
wholly unnoticed.   Indeed, what man, when he
can bow to a shout, would give himself the
trouble to prick up his ears to a hiss ?   Thus
Pops and Cheek were driven off amidst hurrahs,
and heard no syllable of "d——d villains," "murderous thieves," and such other discords to the
triumphant strain.

" Well, then, Becky, I suppose it be all right for
thee, since Gullet ha't aken 'em ?" said an old beldam,
with yellow face and blue lips, to a big red-cheeked
girl, gaping from the door of the Silver Stag in a
fluster of delight.

" Yes, to be sure it be; now, we shall see if Gullet can't keep his word."

" The reward for the murderers—it be a matter of fifty pounds?" asked the old crone.

" Given by the town, the Lord be thanked!—and Mrs. Mayor, like a good soul, makes it guineas out of her own pocket," answered Becky.

" Well, he's a very little fellow to commit such a horrible murder," said a lank, middle-aged man, with a skein of thread about his neck, and a pair of horn spectacles on his nose.

" Little !" exclaimed a woman, with the voice of a whistle—" little ! ye lazy loitering varmint; you know it's spirit, and be cursed to you—spirit !" and her husband—for the man with the thread was her mate in serious matrimony—cast a wary glance at the direction of her fingers, endeavoured to laugh assent to a verity she had so often proved upon him, and, like a magpie, hopped across the way, and reseated himself upon his bench.

" Then I suppose the big one is the burglar ?" asked a loiterer.

" They've been the terror of the county," remarked another, leaving the question unanswered.

" Becky !" cried a voice from the Silver Stag, " ye idle toad ! come and skin eels."

" Let 'em skin themselves, and be ——," muttered Becky, reluctantly retiring into the house;

and adding something about being "her own mistress in a month."

In the mean time, Cheek and Pops proceeded to their conference with Mr. Mayor.

CHAPTER VI.

Mr. Lionel Mace, the Mayor of——, was, as Pops more than ventured to predict, a patron of the arts. At the very moment he was informed of the apprehension of the two accomplices of the Bridle-road murder, he was giving audience to an actor of considerable provincial celebrity; a man who had refused forty shillings per week for second tragedy at Covent-Garden! As in these days professional self-denial is of rare occurrence, we feel ourselves bound to state the fact, when called upon to name the name of Mr. Flat. The mayor, sacrificing his elegant tastes to public duty, abruptly dismissed the actor on the announcement of the approach of the rival murderers. "But mind, Mr. Flat,—mind sir, if I give you leave to act here, we must have the reglar drama—no nonsense—the real thing—five acts, and no mistake." The manager —for he was no less a dignitary—holding his hat under his arms, rubbed his hands, bowed, and said

—"*Sir !*" No man had a greater command of that simple monosyllable ; by means of it Flat carried on his government. To complaint—congratulation —sympathy—abuse—Mr. Wentworth Flat rubbed his hands one over the other, and said, "*Sir !*" His utmost variety was that of gender : now and then he certainly indulged himself with a—"*Madam.*"

" Are these the wretched men ?" asked Mr. Mayor, as Pops and Cheek were led into the room. " For God's sake, my good man—I beg your pardon !—you infamous villain—don't laugh," cried Mace, as Pops smiled and smirked like a boy newly breeched. Pops looked up at Cheek for the meaning of Mr. Mayor—and Cheek turned to that officer for the like favour.

" He's very small ;" said the town-clerk in a half whisper to the mayor—" very short, indeed ; why, if he committed the crime, he must have jumped to stab him."

" My opinion exactly," said Mace, with, con-sidering his office, more than average sagacity. For the first moment Pops seemed to feel there was some mistake ; whilst Cheek, who had not the dangerous enthusiasm of his companion, was quite convinced of an existing error. Pops coughed, clenched his right hand, raised himself as he was wont upon his toes, and was about to speak. The mayor, however, noted the imprudence.

" Silence! my dear sir,—I mean, you cold-blooded ruffian—say nothing. Have the kindness —I mean, attend to me. You must know, that by the indulgence of the law of England—why, Gullet —how is this? why ar'n't they handcuffed?"

" Handcuffed!" shrieked Pops, his eyes suddenly lighted like the tails of glow-worms.

" Handcuffed!" uttered Cheek spasmodically, blowing out his face like a foot-ball.

" Handcuffed!" repeated Mace, very sonorously. Indeed, the tones in which the word was spoken by the three persons, imparted to a contemplative ear the exact separate feeling and interest of the speaker. Pops was treble indignation—Cheek philosophical sullenness—whilst Mace spoke as an epicure de-prived of a customary luxury.

Gullet, the tipstaff, essayed an excuse. " Don't talk to me, sir—don't talk to me," proceeded Mace, more intent upon venerable custom than upon syn-tax—" don't talk to me ; I take it as a piece of personal disrespect, that I should sit here in pre-sence of the prisoners, without being handcuffed. It's what I've not been used to, sir."

" Prisoners!" cried Pops, and his eyebrows bent more than ever did Cupid's bow bend at the bull's-eye of a maiden's heart—" Prisoners!" and he looked at Cheek, and found some comfort in the plural case. " Prisoners!"

" Oblige me, gentlemen—that is, you wretched men, be attentive. Silence !" and Pops for the third time shut his mouth. " Silence—by-and-by you will be heard. By the laws of England—oh ! yes, it's all very well now, but now it's no matter," said the mayor to Gullet, interrupted by the clinking of two pair of handcuffs, the brightness of which lucidly illustrated the morality of the county : in fact, they were a sort of hand-mirrors, " to show *virtue* her own feature."

" But, Mr. Mayor—upon my honour—I"—

" Silence, sir ; silence, fellow ; don't I tell you that the laws of England allow every man to be heard ? Silence, I say ; and therefore, hear me. In the happy country to which you belong, it is the proud prerogative of every man to refuse to criminate himself. Justice has cotton in her ears, and won't listen to self-accusation. No, gentlemen— that is, no—it is a part and parcel of our sublime policy that justice should give herself as much trouble as possible, in weighing well the evidence, not allowing the prisoner to have any weight in his own case ; he being liberally supposed to know nothing of the matter, and therefore, if hanged, to go out of the world laying his hand upon his heart with the consciousness that he has had no hand in the business. You are quite safe in the testimony of the witnesses ; and, therefore, it is my duty as a

magistrate, to request that you will give yourselves
no trouble, but leave your case to the prosecution.
Now, where is the evidence ?"

" If you please, your worship," and Gullet advanced, and stroked his hair down his forehead,
with as brilliant success as if his hand had been a
blacking-brush—" If you please, your worship, you
must take the prisoners' word for once, because they
confessed to Mrs. Go, the landlady of the Silver
Stag, who sent for me, who"——

" Is Mrs. Go ready for examination ?" asked Mr.
Mayor.

Mrs. Go, playing with the sinister corner of her
shawl, advanced, and said she was quite ready.

" Well, Mrs. Go ?" and each eye of the mayor
looked an interrogative.　" Well, these men confessed to you the murder ?"

" Murder !" cried Pops, and he flung his arms
about, as if in a pulpit or in a fit.

" Murder !" echoed Cheek, in as lively a tone as
though he said—" Marbles."

" I overheard them," said Mrs. Go, mincingly—
" for I scorn to have paper in any of my key-holes
—I overheard them talking of breaking into prison
and taking off the murderer ; and after that they—
I mean the little man there—confessed outright that
he was an artist at such things."

" That is true," said Pops ; and as he spoke, he

felt that he was no longer a little man. "That is true," and he bent his head, as though oppressed with the weight of imaginary laurel. If the schoolmaster of Pops had learned Italian, Pops, at that moment, would have exclaimed—"*Ed io anche son pittore !*"

"Mind, understand me—I don't want you to criminate yourselves—but tell me," said the mayor with a frown—"how do you get your bread?"

"Bread!" exclaimed Pops, as though the question ought to have run—"Pray, sir, how do you obtain your daily claret?"

"Yes—bread?" replied the mayor—"I suppose you eat—eh, sir?"

"That they do," cried Mrs. Go, the landlady, remembering the breakfast. The mayor repeated the question.

"Sir—Mr. Mayor—I perceive some extraordinary mistake—in finding myself before you. I perceive that some error"——

"Your worship," said Gullet, interrupting Pops —"no mistake at all. He seemed quite at ease, when I said you wanted him."

"Very true, Mr. Mayor—very true. I did receive your mandate as a compliment to my profession—and"——

"Profession! why, what are you?" asked Mace. "Profession!"

" I have the honour to be an artist of"——

" You don't mean a painter—a sculptor—a—a something of that sort ?" asked the town-clerk.

" Exactly," replied Pops, with the coldest dignity. " And my visit to this town being an express commission to"——

" Dear me ! dear me ! I see it all, Mr. Mayor," —and the town-clerk whispered to Mace, whose countenance became suffused with the brightest colour, and he laid his hand upon his waistcoat, and bowed his head, and his lips were puckered into a smile, and he seemed to acknowledge some sudden and unexpected honour with the most interesting air of embarrassment.   In a brief time, however, he returned to a sense of his duty.

" Gullet, you have acted with great discretion; but, unfortunately, these gentlemen are not the murderers ; they are persons of quite a different stamp.   Gentlemen, you are discharged ; and permit me to say, that you quit this court without a single stain upon your characters.   Indeed, I don't know if you ar'n't all the better for the accusation; you are discharged, and"——

" But, Mr. Mayor," called Gullet in a state of anguish, the promised reward fading from his eyes —" remand 'em—pray, remand 'em—there's more evidence—there be, indeed ; they confessed that the woman came down with 'em."

" Woman !" said Cheek—" Woman !"

" Yes, Nancy Dawson, that we're after," roared Gullet.

" I protest, Mr. Mayor," said Pops in a solemn voice—" I protest, that I know no woman of that name ; and moreover, that I am a married man, and therefore never travel with a woman."

" What ! you mean to say that you didn't wink and poke your elbow at that chap, and say—'she *did* travel by the stage?' Will you deny that?"

" Mr. Mayor, I recollect—my friend here will recollect—the purport of my allusion. Finding that my humble reputation was known here, I did remark to Mr. Cheek, that fame—fame, Mr. Mayor, travelled by the stage. I spoke of fame."

" Of Nancy Dawson !" insisted the tipstaff.

" Fame ! that bright and glorious maid," exclaimed Pops.

" As great a jade as ever walked," shouted Gullet.

" Order in the court," cried the mayor. " Gullet, you are a good and vigilant officer, and I am sorry for your disappointment. With the blessing of Providence, however, you may yet succeed. These gentlemen are discharged." The accused stepped towards the smiling Mayor ; and Gullet, doggedly fumbling the rim of his hat, departed with the unappropriated handcuffs. Mrs. Go, retiring at the same time, endeavoured, but in vain to console him. " Well, to be sure—it is hard," remarked that excellent woman; "it is hard—and 'twill be a dreadful shock to Becky !"

" I regret, Mr. Pops, the inconvenience you have suffered. Of course you know Mr. Fangleby?" asked the town-clerk.

" Certainly," replied Pops, thinking it prudent to know him at even the shortest notice. " Certainly."

" I—at least on the part of the committee—I requested him to despatch to us an artist of the very highest merit, and I have no doubt that my friend has been happy in his choice."

Pops bowed all over to the compliment. " Will the sessions be heavy ?" he asked, modestly turning the conversation from his own merits.

" So-so," replied the clerk. " There is this case which has made such a stir. For my own part, I don't believe that the wretch had any accomplices : I think it all his trick to traverse. By the way, what do you think of your subject ?"

" The—the subject I am come to take? Why, I—to say the truth—I am rather pleased with it."

" You see, there is plenty of him. There is a fine, marked, characteristic,"—

" I expected no less from all I had heard," replied the artist. " When do you think I shall be able to begin ?"

" Why, we'll settle that over our wine. Of course,
you will dine with Mr. Mayor to-day? Ha, sir !
he has been a great benefactor to the town."

" He looks like it," observed Pops, acutely ap-
prehending a local patron.

" The mark of respect we are about to pay to
him, however admirably executed—and I doubt not
its excellence—will be but small compared to the
benefits he has bestowed upon the happy town of
——. There, sir, I call that an admirable light,"
and the town-clerk pointed to Mr. Mayor in earnest talk with Cheek, near the window. The light
falling through a blue curtain upon the face of the
mayor, softened its general redness with a cerulean
tinge. " You dine at three to-day, Mr. Mayor, of
course?" said the town-clerk, relieving Mace of
Cheek.

" At four—it must be four to-day; for I have to
meet Pig, the iron-master, about a contract—business, you know, Mr. Clerk, business ;" and Mace
thrust his hands into that " ocean to the river of
his thoughts," his breeches'-pockets.

" Well, then, Mr. Mayor, as to-day is to me a
dies non, I will walk with these gentlemen about
the town, and return at four. In our stroll I can
point out to our friends the many records we have
of the munificence of our present mayor."

" Now, don't—don't"—and Mr. Mayor looked

entreatingly at Mr. Town-Clerk: then, recovering himself, he cried, gaily waving his hand, "at four, then, gentlemen,"—and retired through a private door.   Mr. Town-Clerk and his visitors left the hall by the principal entrance; not, however, before one of the servants had pointed out Pops to his fellow as the man who was come from London "to take Mr. Mayor's pictur."

The town of—— is one of the five hundred neat, comely, *too* clean towns in which England rejoiceth. We have walked in its streets until the cleanliness has been oppressive.   We have absolutely yearned for a bit of mud; yea, our heart hath panted for a gutter.   A dead dog in the road would have been accepted by us with thankfulness.   But there was no such fillip to be given to the imagination.   There is a legend of a half-devoured rat being found before the door of a new-comer, but it wants authenticity.   Walking the streets of——, the mind has nothing to repose upon—nothing whereon to expatiate—not a single green cabbage leaf—not even a potato paring.   No; our immortal part shrinks back from the cold touch of surrounding primness. There is, so to speak, a varnish of cleanliness upon all things.   A woman's nightcap looks like that of our grandmother "cut in alabaster ;" and the very boys and girls seemed mangled in their pinafores.

Mr. Town-Clerk led his distinguished visitors from the hall with the air of a man embarked in a most pleasing duty. "Our church, gentlemen," said he, pointing with the finger of triumph to a brick edifice. "They do say, as old as the conquest. I can't exactly say after what order it is built."

"The order of the parish, no doubt," gravely suggested Cheek, looking hard at the structure, and putting both arms under his coat-tails.

"Very good, indeed; very good," said Mr. Town-Clerk, showing a set of very strong teeth. Pops, throwing a look up at Cheek, bit his lip, and whispered "Hold your tongue."

"And there, Mr. Pops—what think you of that monument?" And Mr. Town-Clerk pointed to a black marble tomb with an epitaph in brass letters, and two cherubim heads with palm leaves and trumpets floridly worked in the same durable material. "Mr. Mayor's first wife—a fine woman —best brass—made an excellent mother—capital workmanship—had a tongue to be sure—admirable trumpets—brightened with brick dust every Saturday. The town owes this to Mr. Mayor; but I am sure that he set it up with the greatest pleasure." Then, proceeding up the church—for the party were inside the edifice of questionable order—Mr. Town-Clerk pointed out various tombs, with the oak effigies of the inmates carefully painted. " Pray, sir, keep your fingers off—the paint is quite wet," a truth which the curious Cheek himself discovered, having wiped the scarlet from the lips of an unknown baroness with his thumb. " All these painted by Mr. Mayor," added Mr. Town-Clerk.

" Very handsome, indeed," said Cheek, "quite like life ; it's a pity they haven't glass eyes."

" Ha ! that never struck me ; it might add to the expression. But if Drawly was here, I could show you the candlesticks—all given by Mr. Mayor. Four immense candlesticks."

" Silver !" exclaimed Cheek, opening his eyes at the supposed munificence.

" Silver· plated," said the clerk, dropping his voice on the last word ; and, leaving the church, the party found themselves in another part of the churchyard. " So ! Grim's gone at last. You're making his bed, eh, Roger?" said the town-clerk to the grave-digger, hard at his vocation.

" At last, sir"—said the man—" but he almost put us out of patience. Howsomever, when I seed Doctor Cork's grey pony at Grim's door, I knew as how it was all right. Some said because he was a lawyer he'd never die."

" They mostly hang a long while," said the meditative Cheek. " But, bless me ! isn't it very deep ?"

"His widow ordered it ten feet," said the grave-digger. "All the better for us, you know; it's with us, you know, as with the lawyers themselves; the deeper we go to work the more money we get."

"But why should Mrs. Grim wish her husband buried so deep?" asked Pops, who, influenced by the solemnity of the place, had been some time silent. "Why so very deep?"

"All spite and malice," said the grave-digger with a grin—"it's only to give the devil more trouble."

"You see that shovel and pickaxe," said Mr. Town-Clerk—"both presented to the church by Mr. Mayor."

"I never heard of such benevolence!" cried Cheek, overcome by such frequent manifestations of liberality.

Quitting the churchyard, the party proceeded onward for some minutes, when Mr. Town-Clerk suddenly halted opposite a pair of occupied stocks; constructed with fine providence for the benefit of future generations. The engine was made of stoutest oak, strengthened and guarded with wrought iron. "Look here, gentlemen, said the clerk—"another instance of the kindness of Mr. Mayor. The town owes its very stocks to him; he has not only given us the luxuries of life as are shown in the tomb of the first Mrs. Mace—but, as you here perceive, he supplies us with its very necessaries."

"He'll meet with his reward, assuredly," said Cheek.

"Only let him wait till I get out," said the drunken tenant of the stocks, until that moment considered sleeping.

The party quitted the delinquent in contemptuous silence. However, they had not proceeded far, when Cheek observed—we know not what led him into the train of thought—"No doubt, Mr. Clerk, the ale about here is very good?"

"Why, sir, we support our historical character." Cheek slightly bowed and smacked his lips. "And now, gentlemen, what do you behold?" asked the Town-Clerk.

"Eight ducks in a pond," replied the exact Cheek.

"Very true; but do you mark the beautifully wrought iron railing, securing from a watery grave the peaceful passengers of this happy town? Three adults and a child were, for ten winters, the average number of deaths. The railing and the posts that support it, were, last November, the gift of our excellent Mayor."

"Beneficent man!" ejaculated Pops.

"Very true, sir—and yet the ingratitude of some

folks ! Mr. Mace had been tricked in a contract by Chalybs the ironmonger in the market-place. Well, Chalybs' wife does take a drop; and one dark night, how it happened was never known, Mrs. Chalybs was taken all but dead out of this pond. The very next morning, Mace set his men to work, and in less than a fortnight, the railing you behold was constructed. Now, anybody would have expected the warmest thanks on the part of Mr. Chalybs to our excellent Mayor,"—

" Pray, sir," interrupted Pops, " are you a married man ?"

" No," said Mr. Town-Clerk.

" Oh !" said Pops.

" Instead of which, sir," continued Mr. Town-Clerk, " the rancour of Chalybs has been more violent than ever. On every occasion he"——— here the chimes were heard from the church—" but we shall hardly be back in time for dinner."

CHAPTER VII.

Cheek, in cases of personal emergency—and he held dinner to be one—could be a fast walker. Putting all his soul into his heels, he stept forth, and the town-clerk in his turn becoming follower, Cheek was pursued by that functionary and the trotting Pops. The clock struck four ; the Mayor was a punctual man—the dinner was served—the guests were seated. Mr. Pig the iron-master had been prevailed upon by the mayor to meet "the artist," and Mrs. Mace, and her daughter Angelica, bestowed upon him the like honour. For at least half-an-hour a religious abstinence of speech was observed. The party even took wine—and the mayor had pulled out his best—as fishes take water, in perfect silence; whilst Cheek ate, as the camel drinks, for at least half-a-dozen days ; beads stood upon his brow, and gravies hung about his mouth.

"Mr. Cheek, may I help you to a little plum-pudding?" asked Mrs. Mayor.

"Plum pudding," said Cheek, "is my weakness;" but Mrs. Mayor helped him as if in plum-pudding she wished to try his strength. "I have often been very sorry, Mrs. Mayoress, to observe so excellent a dish so generally neglected. With a strange superstition—for I can call it nothing more —many, even well-disposed people, make plum-pudding only at Christmas ; for my part, with a little beef, a bit of turkey, and a flavour of ham, I do think I could dine on plum-pudding every day in the year."

"This is Angelica's making," observed the mother.

" Is it, indeed?" exclaimed Cheek, "why then, I must"——and he held forth his plate, purely out of compliment to the maker, for a new supply.

And was this all that was said at dinner? asks the reader. We answer, all; assuring the querist that what was said may equal in utility and wit the conversation of even some "cabinet" parties. And in truth we do think, if a legal enactment compelled certain diners to discourse only of plum-pudding, the world would lose but little by the restriction. Plum-pudding may often be more wisely discussed than politics, even by those who eat the one, yet set themselves up to make the other. When men are fully awakened to their true interests, and to the proper use of that golden gift, time, sure we are that they will quit their vain wranglings on what our friend Pops has called "abstract principles," and fix themselves on the solidity of pudding.

" I believe, Mr. Pig," said Mr. Town-Clerk, the cloth being removed, and the wine, cakes, and fruit produced, " I believe, Mr. Pig, you do a little in the arts yourself."

" I should think I did, sir; I should like to know who supplied the iron for the suspension bridge at——."

" Talking of the arts," said Mrs. Mayoress, " how does your book come on?"

"Does Mr. Pig write?" enquired Pops, with an innate veneration for the literary character.

"He hasn't yet appeared in print; but I suppose, Pig," and Mr. Mayor turned to the iron-master, "I suppose, we may expect the history soon?"

"History?" said Pops.

"Yes, sir; *The History of the Origin and Progress of Cribbage*," said Pig, condescendingly.

"It will be vastly interesting," said Miss Angelica.

"Illustrated with the portraits of the most celebrated players. The likenesses"——

"Talking of likenesses," interrupted the Mayoress, "when does the gentleman begin his task?"— and Mrs. Mace looked benignantly at Pops.

"To-morrow, if permitted," replied Michael Angelo with the decision of his great namesake.

"Well, my love," and the Mayoress turned to the Mayor, "What say you?"

"Why, if it must be—it must be," answered Mace in the true spirit of philosophy; and then he added—simpering somewhat—"and yet I could wish Mr. Pops had a better subject, I"——

Here the speaker was interrupted by his shopman, arrived to inform him that Mr. Flat the manager, attended with a list of plays for the inspection of the Mayor, who in his official capacity, had "bespoken" a night.

"Shall we have the fellow up?" said Mace, considerately attending to the feelings of his guests.

"Is he the gentleman who played *Hamlet?*" asked Angelica.

"I don't know—but as he's the manager, I suppose he is; for I've always remarked that these fellows give themselves the best of it," said the Mayor.

"Very true, indeed, Mr. Mayor, and it's terrible for other ladies, where they happen to have a wife—why, there was my wife—I mean"——

Cheek, who sat next to Pops, gave him a vigourous dig with his elbow, and whispered—"Don't, you fool—don't expose us."

The mayor, who had been gathering the voices of the ladies and Pig, heard not the friendly counsel of Cheek; but turned to the man, saying—"You may let him come up; and, stay—poor devil—yes, tell Sarah to bring another glass."

"Now, Mr. Mayor, mind—we must have a tragedy," said Mrs. Mace.

"A tragedy, and a pantomime," suggested Angelica.

"And if I'm to see it, we must have—Oh!—here's the man," and as Pig spoke, Mr. Flat appeared, rubbed his hands, and made a bow.

"Mr. Flat, sit down," said the hospitable mayor.

"*Sir!*" said Mr. Flat, and obediently sat down.

"Mr. Flat, take a glass of wine," and the host pushed the bottle towards him.

"*Sir!*" said the manager, and he filled his glass.

"Well, now," said the mayor, "about this 'bespeak' as you call it; of course I must do as other mayors do?"

"*Sir!*" and Flat was about to relapse into silence, when he opened his mouth, adding—"The world expects no less from your mayoralty."

"I suppose you can give us anything from—from—yes—Shakspeare, upwards?" asked the mayor.

"Or downwards," replied the manager.

"Well, then, ladies—come, choose the tragedy" —said the gallant husband and father; and the manager produced his list.

"I should like *Macbeth*," said the mayoress, "only I have seen Mr. Flat once in it."

"MADAM!" said Mr. Flat, with more than common emphasis.

"Suppose we had *Richard the Third*,—who, now, would play *Richard?*" asked Mrs. Mace.

"*I*, madam," replied the manager.

"And who among you sings the funny songs?" enquired the mayor.

"*Sir! I!*" returned Flat.

" And if we have a pantomime, who will be the Harlequin?" was the question of Miss Mace.

" *Miss! I!*" was the answer of the versatile *impresario*.

" Well, then, we'll say *Richard the Third*, a pantomime, and—eh?"—and the mayor conned the list; " ha! this seems to be a new thing—let us have this."

" *Sir!*" And Mr. Flat received the list. " *Sir!* I beg your pardon—but—the piece you have last selected is chargeable—in fact, sir"—and Flat rolled one hand over the other with considerable animation—" in fact, sir, it is a taxed piece."

" Taxed! A tax upon plays! I never heard of such a thing," exclaimed Pig, " it can't *be*."

" Explain, Mr. Flat," cried the mayor hastily, suspecting an imposition. " Taxed—what!—like soap and tea?"

" Exactly, sir," replied the manager, pathetically. " We must now pay for new plays, as we have all along paid for candles. The government —not that I ever venture upon politics—but the government has given the death blow to the drama."

" Indeed—drink your wine, Mr. Flat—I have never heard of the matter : pray, how long has this abuse existed?" asked Mr. Mayor.

" A little better than three years, sir; since wher I need not tell you how the drama has sunk in the estimation of every rational man. Many causes are ignorantly given for this decline ; but the true one, Mr. Mayor, is this—the tax upon new plays. When dramatists are to be paid the same as tallow-chand-lers, there's an end of the legitimate stage ;" saying which, Flat took off his wine.

" You never mean to say, if you play this new piece," a.... ¹ Pig, with an incredible face, " that you'll have to give the fellow anything as writ it ?"

" *Sir !*" cried the manager, " the matter of three shillings."

" Shameful !" exclaimed Pig.

" Infamous !" said Mr. Mayor.

" Who ever heard the like?" asked the mayoress, looking towards the ceiling.

" I'm blessed !" ejaculated Cheek.

" And to say the truth, Mr. Mayor, the drama you have selected is not fit for the stage—at least, I may say, the stage at present is not fit for it."

" What ! a dull poor thing ?" said Pig.

" A very beautiful thing for the—closet," saying which, Flat imagined that he had passed the bitter-est sentence upon the work of the dramatist. " Now, Mr. Mayor, if I might suggest a light, agreeable, elegant little piece—a most delicious and effective little drama—we have had no such capital bits since the new tax—I should say," and the manager placed his finger on the list—" that this would admirably harmonize with the other entertainments."

" Ha ! What !"—and the mayor read the title—
" Humph ! *The Little Jockey?* What's it about?"

" Is it very genteel?" asked Angelica.

" *Miss !* Remarkably. A young lady, to secure
her lover, forms the heroic resolution of going into
buckskin breeches and top-boots"——

" Ha !" whispered Pops, unable to controul his
feelings—" ha ! Mr. Cheek, you should have seen
Josephine as *The Little Jockey.*"

"Was she weighed before starting?" asked Cheek.
recollecting that " great creature," the preceptress
of Parker's-lane.

" And most fortunately we have a new actress
coming from the metropolis—a young lady, as the
agent assures me, of the most exquisite promise—
and the agent is a man of too high honour to be
swayed by the paltry fee of seven shillings—a young
lady who is dying to have a breeches' part."

" Mr. Flat !" said the mayoress.

" Madam," said the manager, and proceeded—
" If, Mr. Mayor, you will permit me to say *The
Little Jockey?*"

" Well, as I have other business to attend to just
now—*The Little Jockey*—it isn't taxed?" the manager smiled a satisfactory negative. " Well, *The*

E 3

Little Jockey be it then.　You hear?" said the mayor.

"*Sir*," exclaimed Mr. Flat, finished his wine, rolled up his list, and departed.

" And now, my dear." said Mrs. Mace, "about what we were talking of when the man came?"

" Yes, the object of Mr. Pops's visit," observed the town-clerk, who had silently consumed at least a pound of cherries.

"You say you can begin to morrow, Mr. Pops?" asked the mayor.

Pops bowed.

" Well, how shall you treat your subject?"

" I have not yet determined, Mr. Mayor; but I have a presentiment, that it will be one of the greatest hits of my life."

Mr. Mayor chuckled, and filled his glass.

" But, perhaps, Mr. Mayor, yourself might suggest something."

" To be sure, my dear," said the Mayoress. " What do you think of this dress, Mr. Pops? An apple green coat, a sky-blue velvet waistcoat, and black satin *remainders?*"

" Why, madam," said Pops, deferentially, " we like to be as faithful as possible ; and don't you think that dress may be a little beyond the rank of"——

"Beyond, sir?" exclaimed the mayoress, "I can tell you that he wore it the very first day"—

"I beg your pardon—I—I was not aware of that fact—I thought"——stammered Pops.

"I recollect, my dear," said the Mayor, "and every body owned it was very becoming. I think with you that that dress will be the best."

"By the way," said the town-clerk, "I hav'n't shown you where we intend to hang the"——

"No, sir—but in good time—I shall certainly see it," said Pops.

"An admirable place, where every body may have a look—and I doubt not that the execution will afford the most general satisfaction."

"Except to the party himself," remarked the artist.

"Oh! depend upon it," said Mr. Mayor, "you'll not find him difficult. And now, what attitude will you have? Shouldn't there be something in the hand, or"——

"As I said before, we like to be very faithful. Whether I put any thing in the hand or not depends upon the original himself."

"An orange, now, or"—— and Mr. Mayor took one from the table.

"An orange, sir, would be admirable—excellent —if the circumstance were strongly dwelt upon in the newspapers."

" Our own county paper is sure to notice it," said the town-clerk.

" But there's another difficulty," said Pops to the clerk, " people in his situation are apt to be self-willed—and unless we can get the parson to per-suade him, he may in his last moments refuse to suck an orange."

" Last moments ! why, you would not make a death-piece of it ?" exclaimed the quick-eared mayor.

" I should like to give my man to the public just before he was turned off," said Pops, with *gusto*.

" Turned off !" roared the mayor, and " turned off !" shouted the ladies, Pig, and the town-clerk.

" Though perhaps, after all," sighed Pops, " he mayn't be hanged."

Mr. Mayor jumped from the table with a vigour that nearly overturned it, his wife and daughter uttered a shriek, Pig burst into an oath, and the town-clerk exclaimed, " Hanged ! Mr. Mayor hanged !"

" Mr. Mayor ! I didn't mean Mr. Mayor !" cried Pops.

" By no means—not in the least," asseverated Cheek, looking for the door.

" Then what brought you here ?" asked the town-clerk; " were you not sent by my friend Fangleby to paint Mr. Mayor for the Hall ?"

" Quite the contrary," said Pops, meekly.

" What do you mean by quite the contrary, fellow?" said Mr. Mayor, suddenly arming himself with the terrors of office.

" I came to model Kemp the murderer for our set."

" Model a murderer !—*your* set ?" exclaimed the bewildered functionary; when Pops handed to him a catalogue of the wax-work, at the same time introducing the unwilling Cheek as the " spirited proprietor." Mr. Mayor blew like a porpoise; and sat himself down, rolling his eyes from side to side, perplexed for words sufficiently large to mitigate his indignation. At length, in broken sentences escaped—" A couple of scoundrel showmen—dealers in wax dolls—to dare to come and embezzle a dinner with the mayor of——," and Mace was proceeding with invectives, when Pops—the incarnate spirit of the dignity of art—rose to reply.

" Mr. Mayor, we are neither scoundrels, fools, nor mayors—we neither deal in wax dolls nor in hob-nails—and, for your dinner, there is my half-crown !"

" Half-a-crown !" cried Mr. Mace, startled at the spirit of the artist.

" One plate of veal, sixpence—a plate of fowl, eightpence—plum-pudding, fourpence—potatoes, a penny—two bread, twopence—wine, and dear at

the money, eightpence——and a penny for the
waiter !" So saying, Pops stalked with the majesty
of "buried Denmark" to the door.   Here he
paused, crying, " Mr. Cheek——remember——in your
reckoning, there are *two* puddings."

CHAPTER VII.

" Well, Mr. Pops, you have made a pretty business of it," said Cheek ; the couple having housed
themselves at a new inn.

" I have vindicated the dignity of my art," said
Pops, depositing his elbow on the table and his
brow in his palm.

" If Mr. Cox should discharge you ?"

" My honour is without a wound," hastily interrupted Michael Angelo.

" What's the use of one's honour being sound,
with no money in one's pocket, and a hole in one's
shoe?" asked the practical Isaac.   " That people
will be so extravagant——I may say so unprincipled,
as to indulge themselves in honour when they can't
afford the commonest necessaries ! It's a conceit I
hate."

" To be called a scoundrel——a dealer in wax
dolls——a"——

" But—for all you said to the contrary—the wine was unobjectionable," urged Cheek.

" I felt it," said Pops, brooding over the injury, " in my heart's blood."

" And so did I," sighed Cheek; " I'm sure I could have taken a good skinful of it."

" Mr. Cheek, there are insults of which a man of genius is particularly susceptible. It isn't your fault if you can't understand them."

" I thank heaven, I've more sense!" said Cheek with dignity. " To be sure, it's no matter for the genius itself, but it's devilish hard upon the reasonable people who may travel with it."

" Hard!" exclaimed Pops, with the corners of his mouth lowered to his chin. " Mr. Cheek, associated as you and I are, do you know what we resemble?" Cheek shook his head. " I'll tell you, Mr. Cheek—a bat, sir—a bat. You are the mouse lifted by my wings."

" All the worse for the mouse," said Cheek, with more than usual sensibility—" the mouse is much better left alone in his cheese than when flying about upon leather. One eats and gets fat all the year round—the other flits here and there for a few weeks, then goes to sleep for the rest of the twelve-month to save himself from starving. Oh! I'd rather be a four-legged fat cupboard mouse, with bacon and fine old Cheshire, than a mouse, of what you call genius, upon wings, flying at gnats and spiders." Pops replied not, but threw up a heavy sigh. "And now, will your genius tell how we are to get the murderer? After your behaviour, Mr. Mayor will never let you into gaol."

"No matter," said Pops, mysteriously.

"No matter! we can't show ourselves to Cox without him : and how will you get his figure?"

"If the worst comes to the worst," replied Pops, —"by inspiration." Cheek stared, for a moment doubting the sanity of the artist. "Did you never hear of portraits painted, statues made, nay, even books written about, when neither the people nor the books were ever seen or read? And what do you call the faculty that effects this?" said Pops.

"Swindling," said Cheek.

"Inspiration," declared Pops.

"Humph!" observed the sluggish Cheek : "no doubt a good deal of money is made by it, call it what you will. For my part"——

Here the speaker was broken in upon by a message from Mr. Mayor, who, guided by the shrewd advice of Mr. Town-Clerk, brought to the artist a permission to visit the gaol. There was a wisdom in this, worthy of imitation by even higher authorities than the mayor of —— : the privilege so gracefully granted, stopped the mouth of gossip that otherwise might have blabbed the equivoque.

which had made Pops and Cheek visitors at the board of Mr. Mace.

The features of Pops brightened, and he bent himself backwards as he received the grateful intelligence. "You see," he said to Cheek—" you see that on some minds professional spirit is not thrown away."

"No—no," said Cheek—"I must say it," and he stooped to pat the artist on the shoulder,—"I must say it, you behaved like a prince—a lad of proper mettle."

"No time is to be lost," cried Pops, airily; and, accompanied by his admiring companion, he took his way to the gaol. The permission of Mr. Mayor had forerun their appearance at the gate, which, turning on its harmonious hinge, admitted them to the prison. They were shown the way into the court-yard by one of the turnkeys—a fellow who looked a part of the stone building, gifted with motion.

"There you'll find your man," said he, pointing to the area, which they had scarcely entered ere they heard a loud yell, and looking round, saw a man beating a boy, who published in sharp treble the castigation.

"You cruel little scoundrel—how would you like it? Suppose I pulled off *your* legs, eh?" and the speaker, a tall, rather good-looking man, raised his hand over the boy, who shouted for mercy, and promised better behaviour. "A little savage!" said the man, letting the urchin escape, who bounded into the prison, nodding maliciously at his assailant, fixing his thumb at his jugular, and accompanying the gesture with a quick "cluck" of the tongue.

"An impudent rascal!" said Cheek.——"Pray, what has he done?" meaning what had brought him there.

"Look," said the man, showing a crushed butterfly, "this is the third I've taken from him to-day."

"But what is he in here for?"

"He was found getting over an orchard with some apples on him—a young gallows-bird."

"Can you tell me," said Pops, having vainly endeavoured to discover the blood-shedder, "can you tell me where is Kemp the murderer?"

"My name is Kemp," said the champion of butterflies.

"I beg your pardon," cried Pops, flutteringly— "I didn't mean"—

"Don't mention it," said Kemp with the most civil composure, "you only speak according to the indictment."

"I am,"—proceeded Pops, assured by the ease of the culprit—"I am an artist of, I may say, some reputation. You are possibly aware, Mr. Kemp, that some ignorant people have a prejudice against their likeness being taken."

" Yes—they think they shan't live long afterwards," observed the prisoner, crossing his legs and arms, and leaning against the wall. " Well, sir, I hope I am above any thing of that sort."

" I could perceive that, Mr. Kemp, at the first glance. Here, a man of superior habits is soon distinguished. It is the wish, sir, of many patrons of art—and I assure you, we number many of the nobility, gentry, and clergy—to perpetuate your portrait. And as life, Mr. Kemp," said Pops with admirable delicacy—"as with the best, I should say with the healthiest of us, life is uncertain, perhaps you would have no objection to favour me with a sitting as—as soon as your present engagements permit ?"

" And what am I to get for it ?" said Kemp.

" To certain minds, posthumous fame, Mr. Kemp, cannot be a slight reward for a little condescension on this side the grave. Your refusal will, I am convinced, cause the liveliest disappointment to the public at large, whilst your acquiesence will add a gem to our collection that"—

" Collection ! Oh ! then there's to be more beside myself ?"

" The most admirable collection that—but I beg your pardon, Mr. Kemp—this gentleman is the proprietor," and Pops introduced Cheek. Kemp held forth his hand, whilst Cheek—in compliance with the nods and signs of the artist—advanced his fingers as though he was about to put them into a rat-trap. His blood turned to cold water, and he gasped again, as Kemp, not insensible of the disgust, kept squeezing the hand of the proprietor.

Pops observed the malicious enjoyment of the culprit, and the terror of Cheek. To create a diversion he therefore adroitly offered to Mr. Kemp the catalogue of figures already in course of exhibition.

" W ll," said the prisoner, putting aside the proffered pamphlet with his hand—" let me hear if there are any of my friends among them—that is, if I have ever heard of any of 'em. Because company's every thing."

Pops commenced reading with the most confident air; trolling over the tongue the names of statesmen and heroes, poets and members of parliament. Closing the golden list he cast a triumphant look at the murderer. "And now, Mr. Kemp, what say you—what say you to such names?"

" Upon my soul," said Kemp, " before this moment, I never heard of one of 'em."

" And did you never hear of"—and Pops ran through the catalogue of celebrated assassins.

" That's quite another thing," said Kemp, " where do you think I've lived not to have heard of them?"

" Well, Mr. Kemp, if you will but oblige us, I

GREEN INTRODUCED TO A NEW SUBJECT.

can promise you a capital niche between—let me see—oh! between Mr. Wesley, the famous dissenting minister, and—and"—

"That can't be, sir—no, that can't be; any where else—for I trust to die a member of the established church."

"Any such scruples, Mr. Kemp," said Pops, "shall be most delicately considered. By the way, do you smoke?"

"And chew," said the prisoner.

"A little tobacco, then, might not be offensive?" and Pops graciously presented a packet of the odorous weed to the captive, who, deigning no word, accepted the gift and turned away. "A very civil fellow," said Pops.

"But to shake me by the hand!" cried Cheek. "As I'm alive, I feel quite sick."

"It's nothing—nothing; all in the way of art," said the philosophic Pops.

"Don't talk to me—I—feel as if my hand was covered with blood—and"—

"He'll make an admirable subject," exclaimed the rapt professor.

"It seems to me a stain upon my hand that I can never wipe away," cried Cheek, loathingly.

"He'll bring a great deal of money," said Pops.

"Do you think so?" said Cheek.

"An immense deal of money—my reputation on the fact," asseverated Pops.

"For a murderer—he is—after all—a—a decent sort of fellow," cried Cheek; "and you really think he'll attract ? '

"As sure as fate !"

"Well, well—we mus'n't be too hard upon people in his situation—I dare say he meant it as a compliment, and"—and, without finishing his sentence, Cheek became closely reconciled to the tainted hand, for he put it in his pocket.

"Art, Mr. Cheek, is above the prejudices of society. A man who loves his art, will go any where for an expression. I know, sir, I know very well, that this is called low by fine gentlemen, who describe life from drawing-room windows. That's not my way, sir—if you'd give the real thing, sir, you must see it—put your hand upon it—breathe the air of it—live in it. As for any thing else, you might as soon hope to learn Chinese by drinking tea. But here is the murd——I beg his pardon— here is Mr. Kemp."

We are convinced that it was nothing but the high and deep devotion of Pops to his art that compromised his natural horror of the murderer into the exactest civility towards Mr. Kemp. A fashionable portrait painter could not be more complimentary, more considerate towards the little

whims of his sitter, than was Pops towards the
ruffian of ——— gaol. Thus, when the assassin re-
appeared in the court-yard, with a lighted pipe,
blowing clouds of the eleemosynary tobacco, Pops
approached him with all the grace of which he was
capable, asking—" Well, Mr. Kemp—and how is
it?—to your liking, I hope?"

" A little too mild—but quantity will make up
for quality," said the smoker.

" It shall—it shall," replied Pops, quickly ap-
prehending the hint conveyed.—" And—as delays
are dangerous—could you spare half an hour?"—
And Pops appealed most dulcetly to Kemp's consideration.

" With all the pleasure in life," replied Mr.
Kemp, and led the way to his cell. One of the
keepers cast a look of ferocity at Pops, who, alive
to the appeal, placed a dollar in his hand, and
walked on.

" You wouldn't wish to be taken smoking?" said
the artist, about to commence his labours.

" Why, I don't think a pipe improves the
face," said Kemp, being unconsciously of the
same opinion as Minerva. " But, after all, Mr.
Pops, what does it matter, when Tom Kemp is
come to this?" and knocking the bowl of the pipe
against his thumb-nail, the ashes fell upon the
stones.

" We should have some regard to posterity, Mr. Kemp.   The decencies of life are not to be forgotten even at our last moments."

" There—will that do?" asked Kemp, placing himself in an attitude, having first laid down the pipe.

" That would do admirably," replied the artist, " only I have a Henry the Eighth in exactly the same position.   If, now, Mr. Kemp, you could throw yourself into the attitude in which you committed the"—Kemp glared at him—" the most interesting act of your life—I should take it as a most lasting favour.   It might, perhaps, bring out the muscles in a way that should prove an agreeable novelty.   You must not think me pressing—but the truth is, in the exhibition of such subjects we are compelled to be very careful— the theatres run us so confoundedly hard ; there's no keeping a—a —piece of strong nature to one's self for 'em. Thank you," said Pops, bowing profoundly, as Kemp placed himself.   " Flattery apart, I do think, Mr. Kemp, you'll make a great sensation."

" Upon my life, I think so—and I never compliment," said Cheek, with the air of a patron.

" It's unfortunate that we shall miss the Midsummer holydays—otherwise, the young ladies would have abounded."

" You think so?   Well, to be sure," and the

speaker grew an inch, " Tom Kemp has had his
bits of luck in his day."

" Why there's ——, and ——, and ——," said
Pops, naming a few of the illustrious infamous—
" they're especial favourites with the boarding-
schools. Though we've got Lord Byron in his
Greek cap, and Mr. Hume with the " Ready Reck-
oner" from his own library, they stand no chance—a
little more to the left—thank you, Mr. Kemp; no,
they stand no chance with them."

" I suppose we are all in one room?" asked
Kemp, anxious for the future whereabout of his
image.

" We scorn to make any difference. You'll be
in admirable company. No—there's just the same
fame for you as for the best of 'em : if you'd found
out a new world, you'd have had no bit the better
place."

For three days Pops continued at his task, and
succeeded in obtaining a living likeness of one who
was about to become the late Thomas Kemp.
Every day Pops narrated to Cheek—who refused
to pay a second visit to the prison—his professional
success : the head was finished the very day before
the trial of the prisoner came on. As, however,
the whole facts of the case, from the death-blow to
the execution and hanging in chains (the fetters
being the gift of Mace the mayor), are to be em-

bodied in a play for one of the national theatres, we will not wipe the bloom from what is expected to be the greatest dramatic novelty of the season, by any detail of the matter.   Enough for us to say, that Kemp was convicted on the clearest evidence.

On the evening of his conviction, Pops—who had won the heart of the head turnkey by a promise to model his wife's child—gained access to the prisoner.   We are not ourselves in all hours, says the adage ; and Kemp had evidently been put out of his temper by the address of the judge.   To shorten our tale, Pops returned to his inn like a man possessed.

" What's the matter ?" cried Cheek—" my dear Michael, what ails you ?"

" Ails me ?—a ruffian !—that I—an artist—I—who have modelled kings—made a dozen princes —that I"——

" What *is* the matter ?"

" That villain Kemp !" exclaimed Pops, choking with indignation.

" Good God ! he's not acquitted ?" cried Cheek, presaging a lost attraction.

" Not so bad as that—but my head !—would you believe that he has insulted my head?"

" Struck you ?" asked Cheek, very calmly.

" I mean—my head of his head.   Would you think it—you saw the man—now, would you believe that human vanity could be so base—you saw the fleshy pimple on the left side of his nose?"

" I remember—almost as big as a pea," said Cheek.

" Bigger, much bigger, Mr. Cheek; and so I modelled it; when the villain swore that I was a bungler—an ass—a fool that wanted to disgrace him in the eyes of the world, to scandalize him in the grave; and so saying he seized his head and dashed it down upon the stones. Never mind, Mr. Cheek, it's all here; in two days you shall see the head again. Yes, he swore that I had enlarged the pimple out of pure malice."

" Then he objected?"—

" He objected to nothing but the pimple. He didn't mind standing with the knife in his hand with which he had done the murder—nay, before the trial he had sold me the very clothes he wore when he killed the man—every thing from hat to shoes; and with the very weapon, in his identical clothes, he consented to go down to posterity, but he swore that his ghost should haunt me if I dared to put upon his nose a pimple."

" It was hardly as big as a pea," said the aggravating Cheek.

" I say, Mr. Cheek, much bigger—but whether bigger or less, is not now the point; he has insulted me—the artist—and curse me if now I don't give him a pimple as big as a marble!"

We regret this expression on the part of Pops;
but we must beg of the reader his most liberal
extenuation for the many coarse and vulgar subjects
which had, doubtless, narrowed the mind of the
artist. If he had been capable of rising to the
dignity of historian or biographer of great men,
elevated by the task, it is impossible that, out of
personal spite, he could have magnified a little pea
into a large marble. Historians and biographers
are incapable of such meanness.

CHAPTER IX.

" Can nothing be done to bring in these turnips?"
asked Manager Flat of his property-man on the
morning preceding the night of the mayor's state
visit. " Surely, they might be made a feature.
Can nothing be done with them?"

" I have told you no, sir, twenty times," was the
unsatisfactory reply.

" Sir !" was the monosyllabic reprimand of the
manager, and the property-man departed. " Madam !"—and this time the manager addressed a lady
in a faded pink silk, with a reticule as big as a barrister's-bag.

" Good morning, Mr. Flat. Bless me! I hope

the orchestra will be here—I must go through
' *The Boy in Yellow.*' "

" *Madam !*" which implied that every necessary
attention would be paid to the new actress. " By
the way, madam, I believe you dance ?" The lady
curtsied an affirmative. " Did you ever dance the
egg hornpipe ?"

" Never, sir," said the lady with commendable
humility.

" *Madam !* Three seasons ago I got up a pantomime at an immense expense. To effect a proper
illusion, it was necessary that twelve turnip lanthorns
should be constructed—well, madam, the pantomime did not realize, and for three years the turnips
have lain dormant. Yet, for three years have I
considered how to employ them. It now strikes
me that you might dance the hornpipe, substituting
turnips for eggs ; the hornpipe will consequently be
on a much grander scale."

" But, really, sir—as I never saw the egg hornpipe"—

" A very charming thing : the eggs are placed
in a circular direction, and the lady, being blind-
folded, dances in and out of them, breaking one egg
with her foot before she goes off to show a generous
public that there is no deception."

" Yes, sir ; but it's impossible that I could break
a turnip by stepping on it."

"*Madam!*" and the manager looked downwards
—"*Madam!* have a better opinion of your foot."

"Now came still evening on," and several pairs
might be seen straggling towards the theatre, distant
about half a mile from the town, and judiciously
placed at the end of two fields; we say judiciously,
inasmuch as the walk tended to win people from
" the fever and the fret of life," and to purify and
elevate their souls for the true enjoyment of the
drama.   Here and there a little boy, with gravity
in his face, and a bundle under his arm, plodded
towards the temple, to deposit at the stage-door the
meretricious ornaments of the lady or gentleman
who lodged with his mother.   At an early hour, at
least ten persons were descried from the theatre
crossing the fields, and all things promised an enthusiastic and overflowing audience.   Caught by
the general intoxication, Pops and Cheek had resolved to patronise the drama in a way in which
much patronage is awarded, namely, to obtain, if
possible, a free admission.   "Are we not professional men?" asked Pops, as Cheek ventured to
doubt the success of the experiment.

At a few minutes to seven Cheek was to be seen
standing in the middle of the first field looking
loftily around.   A lady passed him with a hurried
step, bending her eyes to the earth to escape his
glance.   With the calmness of Socrates, he looked

on her receding form, when he felt a hand upon his shoulder, and the interrogative " Do you know that lady?" accompanied the action. " I have not that pleasure," replied Cheek. " Humph! well, she looked as if she knew *you*, and started like"— and the speaker, leaving the sentence unfinished, stalked towards the theatre. " Surely I have seen that man before," thought Cheek—" to be sure— yes—Pig, the iron-master. But, where the devil is Pops?"—so saying, he turned to seek, when he espied the artist running from an adjoining field towards him, waving something in his hand, and followed by a boy screaming at the pitch of his voice.

" Would you believe it, Isaac? Who do you think is the *Little Jockey?*" and before Isaac had time to speculate, Pops exclaimed—" Josephine! my wife!"

" Impossible! what! have you seen her?" asked Cheek.

" No! but look here—here she is," and Pops displayed to the proprietor an ample pair of doe-skins.

" She! why, they are"—

" Josephine's—my dear Josephine's."— Cheek looked incredulity—" What!" and Pops energetically grasped the article in his hand—" do you think that I don't know the leather—I'd swear to it from a thousand skins!"

"Oh, goodness me!" cried the boy—"pray give 'em to me—I've got to take 'em to play-house—and I was only showing 'em under that hedge to Billy Rogers, when you"—

"Little boy—you say the lady lodges at your house?"—said Pops.

"Yes, sir; and my mother will kill me."

"Go to the lady, and when she asks you for the doe-skins—tell her that the gentleman who has the dearest right to them—mind, who has the dearest right to them—now holds them, and must be personally applied to."

"Oh, sir—pray, sir!" and the child jumped as if upon hot iron.

"Little boy, don't make a noise. I shall be at that tavern," and Pops pointed to a near pot-house. "That tavern. What is it called, boy?"

"The Horns, sir."

"She will find me there," and Pops strided towards the house, carrying the bundle, and followed by the passive Cheek, whilst the boy, blubbering anew, ran to the stage-door to inform the representative of the *Little Jockey* of her unforeseen destitution. The boy was suffered to pass behind the scenes, and trembling, made his way to the dressing-room in which was the lady, unconscious of her loss, practising her song.

"The boy in yellow wins the day,"

rang through the vaulted roof, when the child knocked at the door.

" Who's there—and what do you want?" asked the fair vocalist.

" If you please, ma'am,—it's—it's—the yellow I've come about. The breeches are gone, ma'am!"

" Gone!" shrieked the despoiled, hysterically. " Gone!" But let us quit the scene of misery that ensued, and return to its unrelenting cause.

Pops and Cheek were seated in the room of " The Horns." Cheek, finishing his glass of gin-and-water cried—

" Ha! there's some sense in this," for, as we have before adumbrated, Cheek was not theatrical.

" I am delighted, Mr. Cheek, that in the acting of Mrs. Pops you will this evening have an opportunity of seeing many quiet touches of nature. Don't be carried away by a want of applause : Josephine's style is a little too true to life to touch the vulgar."

" Isn't it odd," asked Cheek, " that she should leave town without your knowledge ?"

" My dear Isaac, it was indiscreet—very indiscreet ; for which reason I have impounded this," and Pops laid his hand upon the bundle. " But, poor thing! though she loves me with a devotion that is sometimes troublesome—yet her affection for the art is so intense she cannot struggle against it."

F 3

"But I heard it was a young, unmarried lady who was about to appear; I forget who told me, but I"—

"That's all the policy of the manager." Cheek stared. "You see, Mr. Cheek, the marriage state, though a very respectable invention, is not—as present taste runs—is not so attractive for a play-bill. Maids—though supposititious—draw more than real wives. I know a manager, a most respectable man, who won't have a wedding-ring in his whole company."

"She seems to take her loss very coolly," said Cheek at the end of an hour, and at the conclusion of four glasses of gin-and-water; in which number he was faithfully accompanied by Pops, who gradually became all the better for liquor, for he did nothing but eulogize the sweetness, the gentleness, the commanding intellect of his adorable Josephine.

"A woman of a million, Cheek—another glass of gin-and-water—a woman with the mind of a giant, but with the delicacy of a sylph—a creature entirely made of brain and heart—a child of nature, with"——

The tribute of connubial praise was interrupted by the appearance of Mr. Pig, who swelled into the room, and with his sternest looks, and his largest voice, abruptly addressed himself to Pops.

"I believe, sir—indeed, sir, I am well informed,"

—the face of the little boy despoiled of the bundle was here visible at the skirt of Pig—"that you have possessed yourself of the valuable property of a lady engaged at the theatre?"

"I have, sir; and what then?" replied Pops, with all the dignity to be obtained from gin-and-water. "And what then?"

"Then, sir, in the name of that lady, I order you to give it up!"

"You order—you!" and Pops gasped for breath. "Do you know who that lady is, sir?"

"No one better, sir."

"That lady, sir—is—is"—and Pops turned blue with wrath, and Cheek finished the sentence—"his wife!"

"Pooh—pooh!" said Pig.

"Pooh—pooh!" cried Pops in amazement at the iron-master.

"She has made me her confidant in the matter —she has told me that you have some claims upon her—but those claims I am here to satisfy. And let me tell you, Mr. Pops, that you have taken a very unmanly, and—but it's no matter—in one word, will you give up the breeches, and?"——

"But with my life," shouted Pops, flinging up his right arm to its full extent, and hugging the bundle to his heart with the left.

"There's thirty shillings," and the iron-master

put down the sum in silver on the table—"which
will cover your claims upon the lady—thirty shillings, and now"—

Pops, gnashing his teeth, deigned no answer, but
with the edge of his hand scattered the half-crowns,
shillings, and sixpences upon the floor; and then,
stood pale and aghast, still hugging the bundle.

" Very well : you are witnesses,"—of course the
landlady and maid could not be absent—"you are
witnesses that I have tendered the money. And
now, my fine fellow," and Pig buttoned his coat
very vigorously—"we shall see what law can do
for you."   Delivered of this, Pig vanished from
the room.

" My good man," said the landlady to Pops—
"now is the woman really your wife ?"

" Ha ! can you be sure of it ?" asked the maid.

" Cheek—Isaac"—cried Pops, waking as from
a stupor—"you will be my friend ?—my honour,
Isaac—my honour !"

" There's another sixpence somewhere," said
Cheek, despondingly, he having picked up twenty
nine shillings and a tester during the address of
the iron master.

" My heart is broken, Isaac—a glass of brandy,"
sobbed Pops.

" Two," exclaimed Cheek, and moved by sympathy, squeezed the hand of the artist.

"That Josephine—that she—I—but you'll stand by me, my friend—you'll?"—the brandy being brought, Cheek and Pops swallowed it with admirable precision. " And now, Isaac—now we'll see the stuff that a British audience is made of"— and the wronged husband, still hugging the bundle, slapped his thigh, and rushed into the air. Touched by his injuries, Cheek was about to follow his example, when he was stopped for the bill. This he paid, minus sixpence, which he assured the landlady was " on the floor."

The two friends paced with giant strides, towards the theatre. Arrived at the pay-place, Pops—it was, happily, half-price—laid down a shilling, and with Cheek, entered the pit in time to hear *Richard* assure *Richmond* that " the chance was *his.*" The house was filled with the beauty and respectability of the town of———. The mayor, mayoress, Angelica, and Mr. Town-Clerk, with a few private friends, occupied the principal box. Under ordinary circumstances, Pops would have found it difficult to obtain a centre place in the pit, but what could withstand the feelings of a husband, panting for revenge? He sat in the middle of the arena, the bundle upon his knee, vainly beckoning Cheek to advance from the side, to which his deference to the company already seated, attached him. The curtain being down, let us, from our sheer incapability to describe it, draw a veil over the misery of Pops. He sat, the bundle on his knees—his elbows on the bundle—his chin in his hands—his teeth set, and his eyes fixed, sweating with revenge and liquor. The curtain remained down; and—in the brain of Pops—the green-eyed monster continued to rise up! The audience showed symptoms of impatience; and it was with a grin of fierce delight that Pops heard voices from the gallery exclaim—" Little Jockey—Little Jockey !" He wriggled himself on the bench, and plunged his elbows deeper into the bundle, and shifted his chin in his hands. " Little Jockey—Little Jockey !" cried the Arcadians in the gallery, and a deep groan burst from the throat of Pops.

" Why, they *are* a long time," said an elderly matron seated by Pops, and interpreting his groan as a mark of censure at the delay—" They are a long time, sir; but I think it's always best to leave groans to the gallery." The tumult swelled—a cry for " Little Jockey" was mingled with the call for " manager"—shouting, hissing, stamping, whistling, with other sounds at the command of a civilized audience. Apples were thrown upon the stage—two or three candles at the back of the gallery were extinguished—and many of the younger women showed signs of alarm—whilst elder ones, with a fine moral courage, assured them there was nothing to fear. It was very disrespectful to the

mayor, who conveyed his displeasure by sundry
big looks to the rioters—still the storm raged
higher, and it was not until a fine heroic fellow in
the gallery, exclaimed—"let's pull up the benches?"
that the cry for "Manager"—"Flat"—"Manager,"
was met by the appearance of Mr. Wentworth
Flat himself. Strange to say! in an instant, the
roar subsided; not a sound was to be heard, save
the hard breathing of Pops, his elbows still glued
to the bundle.

"Ladies and gentlemen," said Mr. Flat—with
exquisite unconsciousness—"may I ask, what it is
you desire?"

"Little Jockey—Little Jockey!" was roared
from gallery and pit, and Pops laughed hysterically
at the response.

Mr. Flat paused to reply, when a voice addressed
him from the gallery—"Mr. Flat!"

"Sir!" said the manager, putting his hand to
his heart.

"I suppose thee call'st thyself master of these
folk?"

"Sir!" answered Flat, wishing to imply that
he did.

"Well, then, if thee be'st master, why dost not
see that they *does* their work? Where be *Little
Jockey?*"

"Sir!" and then addressing himself to the

audience : " Ladies and gentlemen, is it your wish
that the performance should go on ?"

" Yes—yes—yes," cried the whole audience,
when Flat bowed and retired from the stage amidst
a general burst of applause ; affording another
proof that in this world there is nothing so unaccountable as applause.   There was a further delay
of five minutes, during which Pops continued to
wipe his brow with his hand, keeping one elbow
rigidly on the bundle.   Five minutes more elapsed,
and then a murmur ran through the house, deepened into a groan, and burst into a loud shout for
" Little Jockey."   The call was so imperative that
the manager rushed on, whilst sparks of flame
darted from the eyes of Pops, and he sat with
gasping ears.

" Ladies and gentlemen," cried the manager with
a look of prostrate misery.

" It won't do, Flat," exclaimed the orator from
the gallery.

" *Sir !* Ladies and gentlemen, this is, perhaps,
the most painful moment of my life.   That on an
event like the present—patronized as I am by the
highest authority of the town of ———" applause
from Mr. Town-Clerk and friends in mayor's box,
— " I say, that such an accident should have occurred on such a night, is to me—a—but, ladies
and gentlemen, I remember the proverbial genero-

sity of an English public"—great applause—
" and I feel bold enough to hope"—Mr. Flat
paused.

"Little Jockey," screamed a child's sharp voice
from the gallery, and Pops recognised in its owner
the carrier of the bundle. "Little Jockey!"—
" Little Jockey!" it repeated, growing higher—
" Little Jockey!"

"Give that child the breast," said a cynic from
the pit; and then to Mr. Flat—"Go on, sir."

" *Sir !* The young lady who was to have had the
honour of appearing before you in the part of *The
Little Jockey* has met with a most unlooked for
disappointment. Her dress was to have come down
by the mail—by some afflicting accident it has not
yet arrived"—Loud cries of "shame, shame." Mr.
Flat continued : " As, however, the drama of *The
Little Jockey* is not one of those ephemeral modern
productions produced within the meaning of the
act—one of those tailor dramas depending upon
wardrobe—as its attraction lies in the minute development of the character—the display of passion
—the brilliancy of dialogue—and the exquisite
conduct of the plot—it will, I am sure, be no draw-
back to the enjoyment of an enlightened audience,
if, for this night only, the young lady appears in
the part of *Arietta*, without her usual clothes?" A
tremendous burst of applause; upon which the

manager thinking, with the orator of antiquity, that from the cordiality of the shout, he must have unwittingly said something very foolish, subjoined —"I mean, ladies and gentlemen, without the dress of the Jockey, substituting for it a pair of white trowsers, kerseymere waistcoat, and brown frock, most handsomely lent to her on the shortest notice by Mr. Valentine, the walking gentleman."

"No—no—no—no !"   "Jockey dress"—"cap" —"breeches"—"no, no"—"Jockey dress"—was shouted from various parts of the house, together with "shame"—"robbery"—"give us back our money"—"Jockey dress"—"breeches !"

"Upon my honour, ladies and gentlemen, they have not come by the mail, and"——

"'Tis a lie—a lie—a lie," shouted Pops, springing upon the bench with a bundle under his arm.

The whole audience rose, and there was a general cry of "hear him—hear him ! Where is he?" for the pit having risen to a man, Pops was not visible. Still, though unseen, he continued to cry "a lie—a lie !" and numerous inquirers shouted "Where is he?"—"Give him a lift !" said some; "Hoist him up !" said others ; and, in obedience to what became a general wish, a broad-backed six feet yeoman lifted Pops upon his shoulders, the artist still clinging to the bundle. A general burst of applause greeted the elevation of the gentleman who had given "the lie" to the manager. "Hear him!" rang through the house.

"Ladies and gentlemen," said Pops, "many causes are stated as the ruin of the legitimate drama"—A loud "Oh!" was uttered by the audience, followed, however, by a charitable "hear him!" Pops continued. "The principal cause is in the people that have become managers: they keep no faith with an enlightened public—they"——

"Breeches!" cried an impatient hearer.

"I am coming to them, ladies and gentlemen," said Pops, vehemently. "I say, that managers lend themselves to the grossest frauds—by every kind of trick they endeavour to obtain"——

"Breeches!" exclaimed another voice, upon which Mr. Wentworth Flat advanced a step, and said—

"Sir! may I ask what your oration has to do with the dress of the *Little Jockey*—the dress detained in London?"

"Bravo, Flat!" was shouted, followed by a round of applause.

"Left in London?" crowed Pops, with a malignant laugh. "Ladies and gentlemen, I hold in my arms the complete dress of the *Little Jockey*—and that young gentleman in the gallery can testify how I became possessed of it—and moreover, I can, at two days' notice, produce Mr. Nathan's receipt for the articles, purchased by me for my lawful wife."

" "Your wife !" exclaimed fifty voices, and the interest increasing, a dead silence ensued.

"Yes, ladies and gentlemen ; and I put it to you, whether as wives, mothers, husbands and fathers, you will patronise a manager, who, to strengthen his bill, encourages wives to elope from their husbands and families, and to appear on these boards —boards which a Siddons has trod, and a Grimaldi has tumbled upon—under the protection of a man, who—who"——Pops could say no more, but wept copious tears of gin-and-water.

"Shame"—"shame"—"infamous"—was levelled at the head of Flat, the mayor very significantly shaking his hand in horror of the manager.

"Sir !" said Flat, in answer to the gesture—and then turning to the audience—" Ladies and gentlemen, upon my character as a husband and a father, this is all a foul, a wicked calumny."

"Look, ladies and gentlemen !"—and Pops untied the bundle with his fingers and teeth—" look ! here is the yellow cap—the yellow waistcoat and sleeves—and here the breeches—and—and"——

Pig at this moment appeared at the back of the mayor's box, and Pops, entwining his feet about the neck of his supporter, flung himself forward like a flying Cupid, and the breeches in one hand, and the sleeves and cap in the other, shook them towards the iron-master, exclaiming, "And there— there is the man who has destroyed my peace— there is the man who has ensnared my Josephine —there is the vile seducer!"

Pig turned like blue and white marble at the accusation—the ladies in the box with a short shriek, instinctively clutched their clothes, and started from him, whilst considerably more than one voice cried out to "throw him over."

Even the presence of the mayor failed to allay the virtuous indignation of the house. There never was such a tumult, as the reporter of the county paper subsequently assured his readers, "in the memory of the oldest play-goer." In the midst of the storm, Mr. Flat vainly endeavoured to be heard himself or to obtain a hearing for Mr. Pig, who had advanced to the front of the box, which he kept striking with his clenched fist, in a way to do credit to the best ironworker. At length, the manager rushed from the stage; and in a short time returned leading on a lady—the lady engaged to make her first appearance in the *Little Jockey.* The lady, with swimming eyes, curtsied to the audience, but—and it is an everlasting blot upon the men of the town of ——, that she was assailed with "off"—"off"—"no"—"no"—"horrible"—and other epithets of opprobrium and disgust. "A wretch!"—"Poor dear man!" exclaimed some of the ladies, seeing Pops start, and let fall the Jockey dress, and clasp his hands when the lady appeared. And well he might; for he beheld not a faithless and truant wife, Josephine Pops—but his wife's most promising pupil, Miss Margaretta Boss. "The creature!" cried the ladies, and prepared to depart; the men still shouting and hallooing. However, this much may be said for many of them; many declared that they should have supported the supposed runaway wife, if their own wives had not been present; and that they were indignant for the time, merely to keep peace at home.

We must do Pops the justice to state, that when he became conscious of the injury he had inflicted upon Miss Boss, he tried all in his power to explain away the mistake. He roared, shouted, gesticulated, foamed at the mouth, and continued to point to Miss Boss, who with her clasped hands held to her throat, and her head turning from side to side like a toy mandarin, stood the image of entreaty and despair. It was of no use; the audience took his action for emotion at his wrongs, and his pointing to Miss Boss, as a defiance to her to prove the falsehood of his assertion. And more than all, the mayor's box was cleared of its inmates, save

Pig, who stood manfully forward. All the ladies in the boxes took the hint set by the mayoress —the females in the pit and gallery indignantly tied on their bonnets, and, followed by their reluctant husbands and sweethearts, quitted the house —nearly all the lights were extinguished, and Miss Bass loud in hysterics. Fortunately, the iron-master occupied the box nearest the stage, and vaulting from it at the critical moment, caught the falling young lady in his arms. His action was met by the few bachelors lingering in the pit and gallery, with loud applause, and cries of " bravo," above which might be heard the shrill voice of the bundle-carrier calling " Little Jockey !"—" Little Jockey !"

" This is a pretty business," said Cheek to Pops as they returned over the fields ; " you've ruined the woman."

" I went by the doe-skins," said Pops. " How was I to know that Josephine had sold her the dress? And why—why didn't she explain how she had forgot to pay her for it, when she sent me the thirty shillings' balance by her friend the iron-master ?"

CHAPTER X.

A herald, with a silver trumpet, shouting in the streets of ———, would have failed to convince the denizens of that virtuous town, of the entire innocence of Miss Boss. Not only, as she pathetically lamented, was her character ruined, but her benefit was blasted. Mr. Pig, the iron-master, was injured only in reputation; his pocket was invulnerable. Even the most charitably disposed, canvassing the circumstance, declared "there must be something in it." Mr. Flat had vainly called upon Pops to induce him to give a true history of the affair in the county paper; but Pops declared it to be a fixed principle of his life to have nothing to do with editors. "No, no," said he, magnanimously, "people who can't live down such mistakes, ought to die as soon as possible." Pops being inexorable to the entreaty of the manager, Miss Boss sought to assail him through his friend.

"I believe, sir," said the young lady, whose name had been announced to the astonished Isaac by the waiter—"I believe, sir, I have had the pleasure of meeting you before?"

Cheek instinctively placed the back of his hand

to his nose; and then, recovering his self-possession,
replied, " In Parker's Lane, madam." Miss Boss
bowed.

" Oh, heavens ! sir," exclaimed the lady, plunging at once *in medias res*—" what is to be done ?
Save me, sir—save me !"

" Madam !" cried Cheek, falling back from the
affecting passion of the petitioner.

" It isn't here, sir, as in some towns, where such
a circumstance might be the making of an actress
—but here, a benefit depends upon private character," and Miss Boss sobbed.

" It's a great pity," said the sympathizing
Cheek.

" It's dreadful, sir. But since Mr. Pops is so
cruelly obstinate—since he seems so bent upon my
destruction—you, who know my innocence"——

" I, madam !" exclaimed Cheek, as if accused of
some enormity.

" You, who know my innocence, will, perhaps,
undertake my defence ! You will write a letter—
you will appeal to a generous but abused public—
you will champion the cause of an afflicted, heart-
broken woman—you will be to me a friend, when
all—all—all—all"—and Miss Boss became inarticulate with emotion, and to make her cause
stronger, began to faint. Cheek retreated from
her approaching weakness; but, following close,

and wringing his hand in hers, she fell upon his arm, as the door opened, and discovered Mrs. Josephine Pops and Mr. Pig, the iron-master.

" Very well, ma'am—very well, I am satisfied— quite satisfied—I wish you joy of your friend, ma'am," exclaimed Pig, trembling with passion.

" Joseph !" cried Miss Boss, running at the iron-master, who gathered himself up, and smiled a ghastly smile of scorn, " I assure you, I came here to seek Mr. Pops, I"——

" I know you did ma'am," said the wife of Pops, clapping her hands to her hips. " I know you did ! Yes—I have discovered it all. He must come here to model, forsooth ; and you must come here to meet him ; you—whose fortune I have made —you, to whom I have taught my own by-play of *Lady Teazle*—the pantomime of *Fenella*—the songs of *Polly*—the dance of *Letitia Hardy*—you, to destroy the peace of a happy, faithful, gentle wife, the mother of four children, and who is now"— Mrs. Pops could say no more, but leapt at the bonnet of her pupil, and, clawing it off, she then caught Miss Boss by the hair, who turning round, fixed her hands in the tresses of her assailant. On this, Pig threw his arms around the waist of Miss Boss, and Cheek, paying the like attention to Mrs. Pops, the women scratched, and the men pulled. Cheek and Mrs. Pops had this advantage over their opponents; they weighed more than double. Hence, after much unequal tugging, Cheek and Mrs. Pops conquered by their own gravity; for Miss Boss, letting go her hold, Cheek fell, and still embracing Mrs. Pops, brought her down with him. Nor was this all; for the proprietor, falling against a highly-polished mahogany buffet, split the pannel like glass—and a large china punchbowl on the top, moved by the concussion, descended, breaking into pieces on his head. At this moment, Pops, the landlady, landlord, and all the inmates of the house, crowded into the room. What was the horror of the artist to see his wife lying in the arms of Cheek, screaming, and triumphantly waving in her hand the wig of Miss Margaretta Boss! What the perplexity of the landlord to see his shivered pannel—what the horror of his wife to behold her broken china! Nor must we omit to cast a pitying glance at the fair pupil, despoiled of her wig—blushing, sinking, swooning under the fiery glances of the enlightened iron-master! We think the landlord did not express himself too strongly, when he positively declared that "he would have no such doings in his house."

Mrs. Pops threw one look at her husband, exclaimed—"Oh, Pops!" and adding some words about "further proof," words almost unintelligible from the infirmity of the speaker, rushed up stairs into the bedroom of her helpmate. " Where— where can I get a constable ?" cried Miss Boss, re-solving to throw herself on the laws of her country. " Hallo !" exclaimed one of the servants, tapping the window, and beckoning to a man at that mo-ment on the other side of the way—" Hallo," and in a minute the summons was answered by the ap-pearance of Gullet. " This young woman," said the landlord, " has been shamefully used by these people, and"—and here the speaker pointed to Pops and Cheek.

" My name, sir, is Boss," said Margaretta to Gullet—" My name is Boss, and I charge"——

Gullet looked knowingly at Pops and Cheek, and then turning to Miss Boss, a little familiarly took up her elbow between his finger and thumb, and said, " Upon your soul and body now, isn't your name Nancy Dawson ?"

" Boss—Margaretta Boss—and I want to swear my life against an infamous woman—oh, sir !" and she turned to Pig, who was slinking off, " and after all—all—will you—can you leave me now ?" Pig could, for he did.

" Yes, yes, you'd better come to Mr. Mayor," said Gullet, and he proceeded to hand the injured woman from the room, and she quitted the house, followed by Cheek and Pops, given into custody by the landlord, for the broken china and damaged mahogany.

The inn last patronized by Pops and the " proprietor" was superior to the Silver Stag; indeed, it was the principal hotel, and as Mr. Cox, when he travelled, with a wisdom we cannot condemn, always selected such an asylum, he was—about half-an-hour after the departure of his artist and party for the hall—seated in the best room of the Blue Lion. He had ordered dinner for two; for the sixty-ninth son of the Shah Abbas, alias Aaron Leir, travelled with him. Whilst their repast was in preparation, their discourse fell upon the town, the surrounding country, and its many natural and architectural beauties. A pause ensued, and Cox looked at his watch. " They are very long with the salmon," said Cox.

" How long vill it last," said Aaron, stirring as from a deep study.

" Long! that's as it may be, Aaron," said Cox; " I only hope that it will be able to accommodate two."

" Vot! is dere another?" asked the man with the beard.

" Why, what do you call yourself? I suppose you'll be quite ready for it?" observed the proprietor of the elixir.

"I! my Got!" said Aaron, and for a Jew turned very pale indeed.

"Why, what's the matter—don't you like salmon?"

"Salm—oh—ha!"—and Aaron seemed suddenly illuminated. "Yes—Got help me!—I was thinkin' of de gibbet."

"What! Kemp? Yes; they've soon had him up. An admirable set of irons; and we had a capital view of him. I only hope that Pops—oh!—the dinner." The dinner was served, and silently consumed. "Not an ill-looking fellow," said Cox, returning to the gibbet with his wine.

"Suppose they'd buried him?" asked the superficial Aaron, "vouldn't it be as good as hangin' him in chains?"

"Certainly not," said Cox with his characteristic acuteness. "You see, Aaron, it is a very old custom to hang men in chains, which is one reason of its excellence; the next is, the example it holds out to crime; the next is, the influence it has upon society at large. When a man is buried he's done with; but when he's to be seen at all hours, it makes us familiar with robbery and murder. The boys who by-and-bye will play at pitch and hustle under Kemp, will, I have no doubt, display the great utility of a gibbet."

" It's an ugly sight," said Aaron.

" Very true—very true; but people will get used to it, and by-and-bye think nothing ugly in it;" and by such close, consistent reasoning did Cox speak on the side of the gibbet. " They say Kemp began by robbery—by-the-bye, I had almost forgotten that wicked slut Eleanor. Who'd have thought it? However, as business has called me through the town I can see how Pops is going on, and"—at this moment the landlord entered with the newspaper, and Cox questioning him about the visitors to the town, discovered that Pops and Cheek had but a short time since quitted the Blue Lion for the Mayor. Cox was a man of decision, and rising from the table, he desired Aaron to follow him. They were about to quit the inn when they met, at the very door-step, the poor orphan protected by Pops. She had followed him from London, having been harshly treated by Josephine, to whom she had had cause to complain. When the poor girl saw Aaron, she uttered a cry, and covering her face with her hands, turned from the door.

" Eleanor !" said Cox, " girl—what brought you here ?"—He added sternly, " I wish we hadn't met."

" I—I couldn't stay in London, sir—I—I came to find my father," for so she was wont to call honest little Michael.

" You'll find him if you come with me," said Cox; " I am going to him." The girl, avoiding the glance of the Jew, followed Cox in silence.   They soon reached the hall, and were ushered before Mr. Mace, at the moment listening to a pathetic address by Pops, who was counsel for his wife against Miss Boss.

" Father—father," cried the girl, unable to contain herself, and running and embracing him.

" What ! Nelly—dear little Nelly," cried Pops, kissing her again and again with a loud smack, in defiance of the mayor, who continued to cry " silence in the court."

"Yes—any body before his own flesh and blood;" said Mrs. Pops, looking down disdainfully on the caresses of Pops, who, however, returned to the defence of his wife, pleading with such pathos, that Mr. Mace called the whole party a pack of fools, and desired them to behave better for the future. The damaged mahogany and broken china were to be settled for in private with the landlord. The party were about to retire, when Mr. Cox—whose sudden appearance had sufficiently surprised his servants present—stood forth and begged that the girl might be detained.

" Eleanor ?" asked Pops, with wondering eyes. " What for ?"

" For robbery," answered Cox.

" Robbery !" shrieked the girl, and fell as motionless upon the floor, as though a bullet had entered her heart.

" Ellen—Nell—if this be true—no it isn't—and yet—oh, Lord ! oh, Lord ! if it should"—exclaimed Michael, and he turned a ghastly white, and his teeth chattered.

" She has robbed that gentleman," pointing to Cheek, " in whose service she was employed, of twenty pounds."

" She !" cried the astounded Cheek; " not of a single penny."

" Mr. Cheek, you are not aware that the strong chest has been opened—the money taken out—and, as you here perceive—the thief decamped from London."

" Nelly—Nelly—speak—say it's a lie—tell me— one word—say, a lie—or my heart will break," and tears rolled down the cheeks of Michael. " You hear what they say, Nell ?—they call you thief !— Is it true ? is it true ?"

" No, father—as God looks down upon me, no !" and the poor girl put her hair from her eyes, wiped her tears, and turning her head to meet the glance of Cox, stood silent and erect to hear him.

Cox, though evidently affected by the situation of the girl, and somewhat staggered by the dignity with which she met the charge, stated that, as the

G 3

friend of Mr. Cheek, he had some interest in the property—that Aaron, his servant, had given the alarm of the theft, the box being found on the premises cleared of its contents—that Eleanor alone had access to it—and that before the robbery was discovered, she had secretly quitted London, and had been apprehended as a fugitive only a few minutes since. Mrs. Pops, when called upon for her evidence, stated that Eleanor had returned home one evening apparently in great agitation—that the same evening she had left the house, and that she had heard no more of her until the present meeting ; she herself being induced to quit London in consequence of the "scandalous business" between her husband and her ungrateful pupil. Poor Eleanor heard all this with the face of death ; but when Aaron was required to give his testimony, sobbing violently, she fell upon the neck of Michael. The Jew gave his evidence, never halting for a word ; swore to his finding open the empty chest, and to his immediate communication of the fact to Mr. Cox.

"And now, my little girl," said Mace, softened by her piteous wailing—" Now, my little girl, what have you to say ?"

"Oh, Lord ! oh, Lord !" ejaculated Michael. "Now, Nelly—dear Nelly !"

"I am innocent, sir," said Eleanor; "if I do

not speak the truth, may I fall dead before you."

"But why—why," asked the mayor, "did you quit London?"

Eleanor turned to answer. She was about to speak, when her eye met the eye of Aaron; her throat and face were dyed scarlet, and she exclaimed convulsively, her clenched hands directed towards the Jew, "*He* knows—*he* knows!"

Aaron meekly answered that he knew nothing—he had told all, upon his conscience; and sorry he was to be obliged to do it, but he had told all.

"Then you positively charge this young creature with theft; you would have me send her to gaol?"

Eleanor clung to Michael, stifling her sobs; the tears poured down Michael's face; Mrs. Pops became softened—Miss Boss wept—the iron-master's eyes twinkled—and Cheek tried to cough down his rising emotion.

"What am I to do?" exclaimed the tearful mayor, in great perplexity, his sympathies fighting hard for the accused.

"There's some mistake—there must be some mistake," cried Pops. "Only let me get to London—give me time, your worship, for the sake of my poor Neliy: an orphan, sir,—a poor orphan—a thing without a friend in the world except myself—a creature full of goodness—a helpless lamb, left in this hard world to—to——time, sir for the love of God, sir, time !" and Michael hugged the girl in his arms; and Josephine embraced her too, and cried outright.

" If the charge is persisted in," said Mace, " I have but one course; however, we will have another examination to-morrow."

" And Nelly—you wouldn't put her in a gaol till ——I tell you, sir, you'd kill the dear child," cried Michael.

" What security can I have that she"——

" I'll be bound in all my farm for her," said a fine young yeoman present—" I will, indeed, Mr. Mayor; for I'm sure she's as innocent as any nestling."

" Well—I—Gullet, let your sister take care of her for to-night. Mind, I hold you answerable for her appearance to-morrow. I am afraid I'm straining a little—but really she is so young; and if looks be any thing—I——well, mind you're answerable," said Mace to the constable.

" I tell you, I'll be answerable, Mr. Mayor, to the last penny I have. Poor thing ! there's black work somewhere," said the young farmer.

" There is—there is," cried Michael; " God bless you, sir, for your good thoughts of my poor Nelly. There now, Joe"—and Pops addressed his wife—"go with her—comfort her—talk to her, and I'll see you by-and-bye." Eleanor was accompanied to the constable's house by Mrs. Pops; Cox retired with Aaron to his inn, informing Cheek and Michael that he wished to give them audience there ; and the iron-master offered Miss Boss his arm to the street.

CHAPTER XI.

"Mr. Pops, pray, stay a minute—and, Sandford," and the mayor addressed himself to the young farmer, "don't you go. The girl, it seems, is not your daughter?" said Mace, earnestly addressing Michael.

"Poor heart! no," said Pops; "but I don't know if she isn't sometimes dearer to me. Well, well ; some of us are sent roughly enough into this world, and roughly enough some of us are handled."

"You knew the parents of the girl?" said the farmer.

"I knew her father, poor fellow! You see, it was all on a matter of business, and I—but it is rather a secret. Poor heart! she couldn't help it, and I've never let her know who was her father."

"And why not?" asked Mace.

"Because, sir, I think it would kill her. I'm sure she's such a gentle, high-minded thing, that she'd pine and waste away with the knowledge—

she'd feel the shame in her blood, though not a heart in the world beats with better."

" Pray tell us, sir," said Sandford, " from whence she comes? I pledge my secresy; and my friend, Mr. Mayor, can be as close as the grave. Who is she?"

" About thirteen years ago," answered Pops " I was sent to a man condemned to die. He had done that which perhaps deserves death; though, for my part, I think death for him who dies, hardly a punishment at all. What is it to be snugly put to bed out of all the trouble about us? No, sir; the punishment is upon the poor souls who stand broken-hearted at the grave, not upon him sleeping soundly at the bottom."

" But the girl—Eleanor?" asked the farmer.

" I tell you, I went to her father on business. He had been a thriving, they said, an honest man. Well, troubles fell like rain upon him: he was cheated, robbed where he had placed most confidence—he was turned out of house and home—lost his wife—took to loose company—fell from step to step—and, at last, in a night fray, a man was killed. Eleanor's father was"———

" A murderer!" exclaimed Sandford, with irrepressible horror—" the father of that girl a"———

" Even so, sir—I shall never forget the first time I saw him. It was a beautiful summer's night, and

he was seated on a bench in the court yard. There
were still the remains of better days in his face.
He sat in his frieze jacket and leather cap, with his
arms crossed, looking down upon a child—it was
Eleanor—seated at his feet. She was about three
years old, no more ; and so beautiful, so innocent—
she looked, I may say, a piece of holiness, ay, a bit
of religion new from God. It was an awful thing
to see that child in a place for felons. A little angel
playing in the furnace ! There sat the baby at the
feet of its dying father ; and there, turning up its
blessed little face to the face of the murderer, it
struck its toy—a doll given to it by the keeper's
wife—against the fetters of its father, and smiled
and laughed, and crowed at the ringing music.
The sound went into my heart like a sword—I was
sick, and reeled again."

" And the wretched man ?" said the young
farmer, his lips trembling at the picture of the
artist.

" He looked down upon the child, and the colour
of his face turned with the agony of his soul. For
some time his lips moved, but I could hear no voice.
At last I heard him say—' Yes, Nelly, yes—they'll
hang your father, and you will go to the workhouse—
and you will be flung like a weed into the world—
and you will grow beautiful as your own blessed
mother—and you will be wronged, betrayed—made

a thing of shame—and life will be to you a misery—
and you will curse the hour of your birth—and you
will curse the father that begot you—and you will
lie down in wretchedness and pray for death, and
death will not find you. Oh, God! Oh, God!
who will protect you?'"

"Poor wretch!" cried Sandford, weeping.

"Well, sir, to shorten the story; that night little
Nelly slept with my child. We have had three
since then, and if sometimes their share of bread
and butter has been less because divided among
five, I think the little has done them as much good
as if it had been more. And Nelly—a thief! oh,
Mr. Mayor!"

Mace sat, his eyes swimming in tears. "Well—
well," he contrived to speak—"we must see to-
morrow," and Pops, broken-hearted, quitted the
hall, Sandford walking home with the mayor, resolved to delay his departure from the town until,
as he said, "right was done to that poor girl."

Michael bent his way towards the Blue Lion, in
obedience to the commands of Cox, to whom, after
some talk, he privately showed the result of his
mission in the portrait of Kemp, which he had
restored from the injury committed upon it by the
vanity of the original. It was of little avail, however, that Cox flattered the cunning of the artist:
his professional pride was, for the time, dead;

killed by the sorrow he felt for his dear little Nell.
It was remarkable that Leir did not show himself,
but retired early to bed, assuring the waiter that
the fatigues of the journey, with the anxiety he
suffered on account of the girl—" and who could
think that such an innocent looking thing could
be a thief !"—disposed him for nothing but his bed.
Cox, softened by the concern of Michael, bitterly
regretted the part he had taken in the business.
" However, let the worst come to the worst,
Michael," said' the man of the elixir, " we can
quash the evidence, and so 'she's sure to be
acquitted."

" Acquitted ? and in that way ! no, sir—no ; as
you have gone so far, as you have charged her
before the whole world—before the world you
shall try to prove it—and then, if you fail—the
Lord forgive you, Mr. Cox, for your persecution
of my poor orphan !" Michael was deaf to the
remonstrances of his employer, and quitted the
room supperless for his bed.

" You can't sleep in your old apartment to-night,
sir," said the chambermaid ; and she proceeded to
inform Pops, that after the tumult of the morning,
new company had arrived, and his room was occupied. " But there was a double-bedded room,
where, for one night, he might be accommodated."

Pops was in no humour to contest a point which at ordinary times would have roused his soul of fire; therefore saying nothing, but drawing a heavy sigh, he followed the chambermaid to the double-bedded room.   With a dumpish heart, Pops went to bed, where he lay tossing to and fro, worn and sleepless. In this state Cheek visited him, opening the door with extreme caution.   He came with words of comfort on his tongue, and a glass of brandy and water in his hand.   " Are you awake, Michael?" said Isaac.

" How do you think I could sleep ?" said Pops.

" I thought you couldn't, and so I thought I'd bring you something to cheat you into a slumber," and Isaac sat beside the bed, offering the brandy and water.

" This is no time for drinking," said Michael, and he took the glass.

" Right, Michael—it isn't," and Isaac received the empty glass, which he replenished from a bottle providently brought with him.   " However, it's no use weeping—I suppose I shall find water in the room ?"

" A jug full in the corner," replied Pops, despondingly.

" No, Michael"—and Isaac possessed himself of the water, and " craftily qualified" the alcohol—

" this is no time for drinking. It's a hard thing to suspect a man, but I'm quite certain that that Jew is a monstrous thief."

" As you say, Isaac, it's hard—very hard to have an uncharitable opinion, but as sure as I lie in this bed he's a villain."

" They can't prove any thing against the girl— that's one comfort," said Isaac, and he drank with an air of satisfaction.

" No matter for that—it's a blot upon her," said Michael, and he sighed and drank again.

" As the world goes," cried Isaac, with the bearing of a philosopher, " a blot or two doesn't make us all black. And if—who the devil's that?" asked Cheek, hearing snores proceeding from the other bed.

" Hush!" and Pops raised himself up—" the candle—look!"

Cheek took the candle, and softly crossed the room; looked through the curtains—started back —set the candle down again—took the extinguisher dropt it on the light—sank in the chair by Pops —griped his arm—and whispered, " Aaron, the Jew!"

" Aaron! the girl never told me that."

" Hush! Oh, Michael! now he's asleep, you can't think what a thief he looks."

" Are you sure he's asleep?" asked Pops. " Are

you sure"—again the Jew snored, and began to mutter. " I'd give a penny," said Michael, " for a peep into his brain."

" No doubt it's a show that would be worth the money—though, when all's said, I dare say there's few of us would like to let our neighbour have such a peep."

" It's no use—fight as you vill—I vill have you," —muttered Aaron.

" Silence, Isaac—the devil's talking in him."

" Damn the key—it von't fit," cried the dreamer.

" Do you hear that?" cried Pops, nearly breathless with anxiety. " Oh, good Beelzebub! a little more—only a little !"

" Only twenty pounds—only twenty," and Aaron groaned in his sleep. " Ha! ha! you may cry—who'll believe you?"

" Isaac, do you hear that? Do you hear?" Michael looked about the room—for the moon shone gloriously through the window—and perceived that Isaac was gone. Michael immediately got out of bed, and approached the bed of the Jew, " I'll make him confess, or I'll dig it out of his throat with my nails," mumbled Pops, as he walked on tiptoe towards the sleeper. He flung the curtains apart, and shrunk back at sight of the Jew; his features were so convulsed, and his hands were fixed, like the hands of a drowning man, in the clothes. His face was bathed in sweat—his tongue worked in his mouth—and his whole body heaved and writhed, as if burning poison were in his veins. The spectacle fixed Michael powerless to the spot: for a moment a touch of compassion visited his heart, and he moved to wake the dreamer from the bed of hell on which he suffered,—and then Michael thought of the poor orphan, and paused.

" Only twenty—vell—she did it—I'll swear she did it"—cried the Jew; and Michael, like a roused tiger, was about to leap upon his breast, when he heard the door open behind him, and looking, saw Isaac and Cox appear. " I'll swear she did it," repeated Aaron, as they entered the room, and Michael and Cox exchanged looks; after a pause, Michael quitted the bed, and joined the listeners. " Have you heard enough ?" said he exultingly to Cox.

" And they hanged him for it ! And he began with thieving—look—how he swings round to me —no, no—I can't stand it—hark, hark how the irons creak ! Hark ! hark !"—and the dreamer fought in the bed as if possessed ; and then, by degrees, became less violent, and at length, with a long-drawn sigh, awoke. The next instant he uttered a piercing shriek, and leapt up in his bed, and roared like a maniac. " See—he's there—he follows me—his whole face laughs at me ! mercy ! mercy ! I'm de thief ! my Got ! my Got ! mercy !"

The hearers ran to the bed, and found the Jew insensible. He lay like a stone upon the pillow —his teeth set, and his hands clenched. The landlord, for he had been brought to the door by Cheek, turned from the bed in the direction of an opposite table, when he gave a loud scream, and crying, " Kemp ! Kemp !" fell upon the floor. The horror of the landlord accounted for the last ravings of the Jew, who, waking, beheld on the table the wax head of Kemp, finished to the life, placed there by the artist before he went to bed, and coming out in terrible reality in the moonlight. The handkerchief which Michael had thrown over it, had been accidentally removed by Isaac in his search for the water-jug. The landlord was taken down stairs ; and by the advice of Cox, the door was locked upon the Jew.

Pops would, at that instant, have run to the mayor, but was overruled by the authority of Cox, who insisted that the business should be deferred until the morning. The morning came, and Pops ran to Gullet, the constable, to come and take into custody Aaron the Jew.

" Why, you see," said Gullet, " he's got a little the start of us—for he was seen two hours ago on the top of the —— coach."

The information of Gullet was perfectly true. On coming to himself, Aaron, either smitten by

THE GHOST OF KEMP.

compunction, or half conscious of the revealings of
the past night, lowered himself from the window,
and made his escape. His destined victim—she
had repelled his offered villany in a way that left
him nothing but the savage hope of destroying her
good name—was restored to the arms of Michael,
well nigh mad with joy at her deliverance, and
wholly wild at the escape of the Jew.

CHAPTER XII.

This shall be a short chapter; but we trust a
satisfactory one. "What became of poor Eleanor?"
We care not to describe the whole process of the
courtship, but certain it is, that in time she became
the wife of Richard Sandford, a flourishing farmer.
And what, it may be asked, befell Miss Margaretta
Boss? (We would fain speak of the ladies first).
Did she marry Pig, the iron-master? No; but he
died, leaving her a very pretty annuity: nay, more,
he dedicated to her his second edition of the *History
of the Origin and Progress of Cribbage,* superseding
his dedication to the first issue to an officer's widow,
and supplanting the widow's portrait as an " illustrious player," with a highly finished engraving of
Margaretta. And did the gentle Boss live and die

ungathered? No: she married Isaac Cheek. It will
be remembered that on his first interview he was
seriously struck by her: he had the bruise for a
·week. The marriage was a most happy one;
because as Michael would say, the courtship began at the proper end. As for Michael, assisted
by Sandford, he became the whole and sole possessor
of the " property ;" and, to the great grief of many
historical painters, is now making a rapid fortune
as a " man of wax."

MATTHEW CLEAR:

THE MAN WHO " SAW HIS WAY."

CHAPTER I.

" With such an excellent property, too! Ah, sir!"—

And, as the speaker touched upon property, his voice trembled, and into either eye there stole one large tear, we think quite as large as the Narcot diamond.

" Ah, sir! if Mr. Clear had only seen into himself! for with such a property!"—

The truth is, Matthew, though the dimmest owl, had, in his own conceit, the vision of an eagle. The snail that carries its eyes at the end of its horns —Matthew, by the way, died a widower—had not a more projective look. Seeing nothing, he could to his own satisfaction peer into the very essences of things. But presuming with the reflective gentleman above—we shall duly return to him—that Matthew never did descend into himself, shall we not pause ere we wonder at or blame him? Did you, sir—you who have the good fortune to read us—ever descend into a coal-mine, a tin-mine, or, for you have the look of a traveller, into a salt-mine at Cracow? Surely there must be a sudden suspension of the breath—a rigidity of the fingers clinging to the thing which hurries us from the light of heaven—a dizzying fear of what we go to meet! Yet what is all this—what this sinking below some hundred feet of earth (dear old mother of an ungrateful brood!) to the solemn descent of a man within himself? What is this going through antediluvian strata—layers with the bones of the mammoth and the griffin embedded in them—for, seeing what the earth still produces, we are strong in our belief of a pre-adamite griffin—what is all this in the darkest and most dangerous hour, to the awful sinking into our own soul? There may be green grass flourishing at the very mouth of the mine— flowers blossoming about it—but what, what is below? As we sink are we not astonished at the gloom? See we not incrustations of the meanest things where we thought we hoarded gems? and, arrived at the bottom, where we hoped for a stream of living water, sounds of happy greeting, and a ray of comfortable light, we find no drop to wet our withered lips—we hear the croaking frog or shrieking bat, and—our heart palsied with dread—we grope in darkness, in substantial night?

We care not to pursue the theme, but we simply put it to the reader to consider what would be the revolution of society should it become fashionable for people to sink into themselves? What, should some questionable genius produce a kind of moral diving-bell for the use of families? Fortunately, such an invention is, we believe, impossible; though should it be found otherwise, we have this consolation, that the inventor, sharing the fate of great projectors, would inevitably starve in his triumph; and to support this our belief, we here offer to give any odds against the first seven years' profits of the inventor, compared with the septennial gains of any worker of punch—dancer of French dolls—or exhibiter of the gallantie-show.

Matthew Clear was the sole son of a wise stockbroker. But though he inherited his father's money, he did not come into the paternal sagacity whereof the cash was the golden fruit. It is true, Matthew possessed from nature an inexhaustible fund of conceit, which only wanted good luck to be received and registered as penetration. Falling, as our story will show, upon evil days, men scrupled not to call him a fool, when—had only another card turned up—he had, with the self-same faculties, been dubbed a sage. Such, however, is the fate of mortal man—such the opposite rewards that wait on chance! If your bossom friend beggar himself by haunting lotteries, chide, moralize, be very in-dignant—if he draw ten thousand pounds, con-gratulate, eulogize, embrace him, failing not to hint at the loan of a few hundreds.   Luck, mere luck, makes even madness wisdom.   Our Matthew was not lucky.

At eight-and-twenty, Matthew having paid the undertaker—that two-faced varlet to the blind goddess—had not, if we except the possession of ten thousand pounds—by the way, a great exception—a single care in the world.   Rich, and without relatives, he stood aloof, bright and lonely as a gilt weathercock.   For business—direct business, he had no genius.   Indeed, such deficiency was in his case proper and to be expected.   His father—good, buried man ! though let us observe, not only good because buried—had toiled through fifty years of life—had been especially ordained and appointed to make money for an only son, the said only son being on his part expressly begotten for the single purpose of spending it.   Surely the naughty fiend laughs when he sees paternal misers hoarding their monies in bags with fifty " mortal gasbes" in them.

We know not a more interesting object than an unsuspecting young man, left alone in this world of temptations, with ten thousand pounds.   Who would not rather hug secure mendicity ?   The beggar lies by the road-side, and, like a lizard on a bank, basks in the sun, a careless vagabond; but where the refuge, where the tranquility for the hapless animal born to civet? To the simple inheritor of thousands, there is open to him only one dreadful way to seeming peace. Soon—very soon, Matthew became certain of this truth, for he was speedily hunted, and at the same time, by two mature spinsters and three experienced widows. Five women! and Matthew, be it remembered, was only eight-and-twenty.

"Most beautiful diamonds!" cried Matthew, as he received a necklace from a thin, long, rather yellowish feminine hand—"most beautiful diamonds!" and he looked at the effulgent bait with his one peculiar look, ever called up when he wished to see his way. Matthew lolled on a couch in the handsome room of a most handsome and particularly respectable boarding-house: near him, at his very fingers'-ends, sat a timid, sallow daughter of Eve. Though the lady looked emphatically thirty-four, sure we are she was but thirty-three. She had not a face to "enchant the world" (indeed, who that valued his night-cap would marry such perdition?) but then she had *such* a mind! In a word, she was a most plain woman, most elaborately accomplished. Yes; Miss Julia Lac possessed the surest, the most lasting beauty:—lips wax pale—skin turns—eyes grow dim, but the mathematics

endure till death.   Only boys are taken by pretty
simpletons; for our mature part—and Matthew
subscribed to our opinion—if ever again we fall in
love, give us no angelic semblance—no fragile loveliness looking as though it lived on lilies; but,
Cupid ! for once be grave, and give to our arms a
fine matronly specimen, breathing the camphor of
a museum—in fact, a living learned mummy.   All
the species have *such* minds !   Now Julia Lac was
one of these—a virgin roll of human papyrus.

Still Matthew sat, and—the necklace hanging
across his sinister palm—he still continued to see his
way.   Would we might paint the thousand objects
that floated before him ! we must content ourselves
with a few women, all of whom, curtseying and
bridling, looked wedding-rings at Matthew.   Now,
one with most significant finger would point to a
very respectable freehold, duly parcelled into wood-
land, stream, and meadow; she and the scene would
pass, and enter a second candidate, carrying as a
scroll a bank security.   A third—a fourth appeared;
and Matthew sat intently seeing his way.   Rapt,
he lightly passed his thumb along the necklace;
and, as at the touch of an enchanter, there rose
before him a most ravishing prospect.   All that
India boasts of rich and beautiful beamed upon him.
He saw fairy-land, with all the countless wealth of
Solomon, and his legendary genii.   And there, by

a spell, was transported the lady from his side.
There, the queen of that radiant, teeming spot,
stood Julia Lac; who, with one hand upon her
maiden heart, and the other pointing to her property, said very audibly, at least to Matthew—for
love has sometimes long ears—" This and these are
thine!" Matthew winked, and when he looked
again—miraculous vision!—he saw himself en-
throned in highest state upon a white elephant.

We as surethe reader that Matthew saw all, and
more, much more than this: yet, in his own niggard,
constant phrase, he had only seen his way. Of this
truth we could print the strongest certificate,
namely, the certificate of Matthew's marriage with
Miss Lac,—an event to be dated only three weeks
and some days from the time of his day-dream.
All his acquaintance called Matthew a happy man;
he denied not the imputation, but would droop one
eyelid, duck his chin, and would briefly sum up the
attractions of Mrs. Clear by more than insinuating
that before he committed matrimony he had—seen
his way.

Given up to their mounting affections, the intoxicated couple quitted London, winging their
way, "linked by a silver hook and eye," to a rustic,
myrtle shade, for the honey month. Mrs. Clear,
even at the end of the four weeks, with the most
flattering susceptibility, assured her husband that

she could dwell there for ever. How loathsome was the town become to her ! how poor—how frivolous—how hollow ! Why, at least, for another month, should they quit the dear retreat ? Matthew's blood glowed—nay, simmered with happiness at such appeals; he was suffused to the very nails with hymeneal satisfaction ; but Julia must not forget—there were matters to be settled—she had received no letters about the property—and, for the sake, not only of themselves—and Matthew looked with a gay wickedness into his wife's eyes—for the sake, not only of themselves,—this he repeated, expanding with the tautology—they could not continue to go on there in the dark. Matthew meant they must see their way.

CHAPTER II.

With a thousand silent adieus to Ringdove Nest, did Mrs. Clear resign herself to the chaise ; for, as she beautifully said—and we regret that so sweet a sentiment was wholly lost on the post-boy—her heart was held by the very honeysuckles. Arrived in London, the married pair found fervent congratulations subsided into tepid compliments, and were soon abandoned to their own resources. In seven weeks, the happy couple were become reasonable man and wife, as the following breakfast colloquy will certify :—

" My love" (Matthew *loquitur*), " I thought you had given that filthy bird away ?"

Thus spake the husband, as a loud laugh and a nervous exclamation from a great grey parrot split upon the ear of—shall we say—the complaining helpmate ?

" My dear," returned the wife, with truly conjugal indifference, " is it my fault if I find Nabob so essential to my happiness ?"

Another shrieking laugh from the great grey parrot.

" Happiness !" cried Matthew, as though the wife of his soul had spoken something treasonous to the marriage state. " Happiness !" and Matthew jerked his chair, looking wonder at the audacity of woman.

" Ha ! ha ! ha !" chuckled the parrot ; ha ! ha ! ha ! Hooked him, by —— !"

Perhaps this is the place to give a brief history of Nabob. The bird, when very young, had been presented to Mrs. Clear by a handsome Company's officer, who survived the gift barely a month, being carried off by one of the thousand fevers to be obtained only in perfection in India—all others being spurious. On the lady's passage to England, the bird attracted the attentions of a boatswain's mate, and Julia being an invalid, Nabob was surrendered to the care of his admirer. John Rogers had a tender heart, and, being a boatswain's mate, a sure hand. Like all sailors, he was born the natural enemy of a shark. Every idle moment would he lay in wait for his foe ; and, on such occasions, Nabob was never absent. We have said John Rogers was expert ; he was also somewhat vainglorious ; for, never did he strike a shark, but he roared and shouted—" Ha ! ha ! ha ! Hooked him, by ———— !" What was to be expected of a parrot of any capacity perched on the cathead, continually listening to these notes of conquest ? The bird was no dull scholar, and in less than three weeks, to the admiration of the crew, and we must admit, to the passing disquietude of his mistress, the parrot laughed and shouted in the very key of the triumphant angler. It is true, that, in the brief day of courtship, Mrs. Clear resolved to part with Nabob ; indeed, twice or thrice, when Matthew pressed his suit, the chuckle and the exclamation of the creature broke somewhat dissonantly on the conference, making Matthew pause, and reddening the cheeks of the fluttering spinster. But in the final interview, when Matthew boldly made the offer, and, breathless, stood waiting life or death—to be anticipated in her reply by the ever-laughing, ever-shouting bird, passed the temper of the kindest mistress. As an earnest of her future obedience to Matthew, she declared herself content to sacrifice Nabob. Then, the lady was Miss Julia Lac— now, was she Mrs. Matthew Clear.

" Madam, how is it possible? I say, how is it possible—"

A great statesman, in his advice to young ambassadors, counsels them to take snuff : when sticking for a word, or wanting a moment to baffle a query, the box, as he insinuates, gracefully assists the hesitating. Matthew, failing in syllables, and not being a taker of snuff, threw himself upon a muffin. Mrs. Clear could not speak, but, turning her head with extreme dignity from Nabob to her husband, she looked a very thick volume. We say she could not speak; for at the moment she held between her lips a lump of sugar—the sixth—for the epicurean beak of the parrot ! Sympathetic reader, imagine a seven weeks' wife staring at you with withering reproof in her eyes, and a lump of sugar held mockingly between her teeth ! For Matthew, the vision of a death's-head mumbling a cross bone had not so confounded him.

The breakfast was nearly finished, when the servant appeared with two letters. Being directed to his master, they were handed to his mistress. Mrs. Clear broke a seal. Had she at the same time broken her heart, she could not have published the damage by a louder shriek.　Matthew jumped upright, and ran, or rather slid, to his suffering wife : the poor soul was blue-white with anguish. He was about to fold her in his arms, when, with a subtle power borrowed from grief, she repelled his attention, at the same time depositing him on a distant sofa.　Matthew drew his breath, and, though he stared, for once, could not see his way. Mrs. Clear, recovering her self-possession, cried—" wretch !"

The tale must be told.　The fatal letter was from a lawyer intrusted with the repair of the wounded affections of one of the ladies to whom Matthew, as a gentleman, was contracted.　The lady, being deserted by one man, had no other remedy than an appeal to twelve.　Plainly, the action was commenced ; and the damages due to the heart of the forsaken were moderately estimated at three thousand pounds.　We ask any woman what was left to Mrs. Clear but to exclaim " wretch ?"　Had Matthew from the first impressed upon his future wife the sacrifices he was ready to venture—had he only hinted to her the possibility of other claimants —she would, we are convinced, have exhibited her magnanimity, and, spite of all, have wedded him. But to be tricked into marrying a man with six or seven hearts bleeding at every pore about him, what woman of delicacy could placidly endure it? It is our hope that Matthew lived and died a Christian; yet will we not suppress his heterodox aspirations.   In the present instance, remembering that—counting his wife as nothing—he was pledged to four women, he was criminal enough to wish himself a Turk.   Yes, Constantinople—at least for some seconds—seemed to him a most delightful city.

Left alone, for Mrs. Clear had retired for another handkerchief, Matthew began to calculate all the chances.   Damages might be flatteringly heavy; there might, possibly, be more than one action—women were so vindictive!   Still, had he not, with every deduction made, married the richest of the five?   Were not the Indian possessions of his wife—were not her jewels more than trebly worth the best of any other offer?   Matthew smiled in self-affirmation; bobbed his head; rubbed his hands. All things considered, he was fully convinced that he had—seen his way!

" In this sweet mood," as the poet sings, Matthew cast a glance at the second letter, yet unopened. With a slight tremor, he broke the seal; and as he broke it, Mrs. Clear, with vermillion eyes, re-entered.   Matthew, unconscious of the presence of his injured, yet attentive wife, read on.   In a second, Matthew, his cheeks like lead, exclaimed—

no ! we will not sully our paper with so prodigious
an oath.   The reader, however, must not think it
was lost upon Mrs. Clear, for, had the demon of
mischief suddenly clawed her husband through the
floor, we doubt whether she would have screamed
so loudly—whether, clasping her hands and sinking
upon the chair, she would have portrayed such
eloquent dismay !   He who is not melted when a
woman screams, is a brute.   This is a point of our
religion, though, we sigh to say, it made no part of
the faith of Matthew ; for, as though chiselled out
of knotted oak, he approached his astonished wife,
and, striking the letter with what old Fuller calls a
" dead hand," he puts this unadorned, this naked
query, to the partner of his fortune and his bed :
" In the name of the devil, ma'am, what is this?"

" Mr. Clear !" said the lady, all her spirits conjured to her eyes by the Satanic exhortation.   The
tones of man and wife were admirably illustrative
of their individual manner.   Matthew was loud,
vulgar, confident ; with a mouth opening like a
toll-keeper's pocket.   Julia, soft, hesitating, retiring, used her lips as though she wanted full
confidence in their conduct, and therefore spoke
in guarded fragments.   On the present occasion,
she ventured to repeat—" Mr. Clear !"

" Look here, ma'am ; I am written to for five
hundred pounds for a diamond necklace."

" Well, Mr. Clear ?"

" Well ? Why, I know you showed me a necklace, but—eh ?—it can't be ?"

" You said the diamonds were very beautiful, and —and I took your judgment."

" Judgment ! D—— it, ma'am !" (Mrs. Clear shuddered)—" Weren't they your own ?"

Mrs. Clear, curving her neck gracefully as any swan, said " No."

" No ! What ! not some of your extraordinary diamonds—not some of the family jewels ?" roared Matthew, and he looked aghast. Not getting a reply, again he shouted—"Not your own ?"

" No."

" Ha ! ha ! ha ! Hooked him, by —— !" was the unpremeditated, and untimely proclamation of the artless parrot.

Matthew, seizing a knife, glared with the eyes of a butcher at the bird, which, as conscious of the murderous intent, flew to the extended arms of its mistress. Matthew stood a moment, then fell, as though stabbed to the heart, into a chair. He waxed white and red—cold and hot—played with his fingers upon the table—vehemently rubbed his calf—twitched his neck-cloth—and then, with an air of settled desperation, ventured to look for further particulars into the face of his wife, at the time assiduously pressing the seventh lump on the self-denying parrot. Matthew groaned.

Now, Matthew was not a man to groan without good and sufficient reason; for though few moments had elapsed since the eloquent burst of Nabob, yet had Matthew, struck by the omen, reviewed a thousand circumstances, solved a dozen riddles, tallied fact with fact, questioned, answered, compared, deduced.——What he had lost, with what he had not won, came in terrible contrast upon him; and, assured that he had not——seen his way, he groaned! But, it may be urged against him——to grudge a necklace to a wealthy bride, to a woman dowered with almost an Indian province, was the imbecility of a miser. Very true; yet, by some subtle association, the necklace was to Matthew a connecting link with all the Oriental possessions of his spouse; that gone, he was superstitious enough to give up every thing for lost. In such despair—and though man and wife are but one flesh—he viewed his unoffending partner with the eye of a cannibal; and really, no woman less deserved such a look.

"Five hundred pounds for diamonds for *that* neck!" and Matthew ground every syllable with his teeth—"Ugh! I'd sooner lay out the money in blisters."

Mrs. Clear started up. For an instant the china seemed in peril; but there are insults that "do lie too deep" for porcelain. Mrs. Clear merely did what all women of sensibility always should, inasmuch as they always can, do—she burst into tears.

Matthew was left alone with the parrot. Nabob evidently felt the delicacy of his situation; for cocking his head, leering his eye, and working his black tongue, he edged himself sidelong from the extended fingers of Matthew, like a vulture, seeking to truss him. Securing the door, that he might the more surely effect his sinister design, Matthew stealthily pursued Nabob, who hopped from chair to sofa—from sofa to table—from table to firescreen, evading his follower, until, enveloped in a shawl of his mistress, flung over him with gladiatorial precision by his master, he was soon panting in the hands of the destroyer. Certain we are, that Nabob had resigned himself to sudden death; at his neck he already felt the merciless thumb and finger. "Not body's death but body's banishment," determined the clement Matthew; and, lifting up the window, he delivered himself of a most pestilent remembrancer. Ere Matthew was well ensconced in his dressing-room, Nabob, from the summit of a neighbour's chimney, was contemplating a trial flight to the Surrey hills.

CHAPTER III.

When a man is not to be convinced by an earthquake, what argument can successfully be applied to him? Vain was it that Mrs. Clear assured her enquiring mate that the late terrible convulsion (it was very minutely described in all the journals) had swallowed up every rupee of her Indian property, leaving her nothing in the world save a lively trust in the affections of a husband. Matthew remained a sceptic; for, though his wife discovered the greatest anxiety on every new arrival, expressing a hope that "something might be saved," Matthew would grin incredulously, asking her if her memory would serve to make an inventory of her losses? As the earthquake had proved such a timely friend, it had doubtless not taken all? These sneers he would urge with unrelenting assiduity; but Mrs. Clear—high-minded woman!—disdained to reply to the insinuations. Calmly, and with touching resignation, she would, on such occasions, raise her eyes to heaven, and ask, " What sins she had committed to be married to an atheist?"

All this time Miss Camilla Brown—such was the name of the injured plaintiff—slept not on her wrongs. It is true that, mollified by Mr. Downy, the pacific solicitor of Matthew, the lady entertained certain hints at a compromise. Downy had a heart of honey, and a tongue of silver; a gentle, persuasive, excellent little man, with a real friendship for his client, whom he had known from a boy.

"Ha!" Matthew was wont to soliloquize, "had I not kept my marriage secret from Downy, he had enquired for deeds, and then—and then"—and then, we can take it upon ourselves to affirm, Miss Lac had still remained an unplucked bud.

"Well, Mat," said Downy, at his last conference, "Iv'e made the best of bad. I——where's your wife?"

"Gone to Dorking," replied Matthew, impatient of the superfluous query.

"Dorking again! But I come on business. I've offered the plaintiff five hundred pounds, and I think she'll listen to reason."

"No doubt," said Matthew, drily, "'tis a good round sum for the trouble."

"I tell you, Mat," urged Downy, in a soft yet impressive tone, "if she goes into court with those letters, you're not safe for a thousand."

"If I had but seen my way, I had never written," said Clear with unnecessary emphasis. "That a man should lift a pen against himself! 'Tis a sort of suicide," moralized the defendant. " Five hundred pounds ! Well, if I must, I must."—Downy nodded satisfaction.—" But if ever I have a son !"—

Downy turned his grey eye on Matthew; then, looking upwards, stared at the portrait of Mrs. Clear. Matthew felt the look to be cruelly murderous; for it slew the unborn. From that hour, Matthew never had the hardihood to enjoy even a probable son.

" I suppose," said Downy, " you have heard that Mrs. Melon, and"—

" Another action ?" asked the conscience-stricken Matthew.

" No, she's married—so you're safe from her. But your young widow, Mrs. Undercrust"—(Matthew gasped)—" Ha ! that was a miss, indeed !"

" Phew ! She hadn't a penny certain."

" No; but now her uncle's dead,"

" Dead ! D—— it," said Matthew, and he looked ready to weep, " now she must be very comfortable."

" They say, fifteen thousand," remarked Downy, who unconsciously again glanced at the portrait of Mrs. Clear ; then recollected himself—took up his hat—gave a silent squeeze to her husband, and left him to the sharp reproach of broken protestations.

One morning, some weeks after the visit of Downy, Matthew sat in his easy chair, exhibiting a most perturbed and anxious countenance. Mrs.

Clear was from home; by the way, she was gone to Dorking. From his looks, it was certain that Matthew could not see his way. He took up a book—he threw it down—he paced the room—he stared into the street. At length, he went out. Having wandered in St. James's Park a couple of hours, he returned home. After the lapse of two more hours, the servant announced—

"Mr. Felix!"

Matthew jumped up to meet the visitor, but immediately sank again into his chair. Truth to say, ill luck never had a more significant retainer than Mr. Felix. He looked with a dead black eye on Matthew—shook a sharp, white face—elevated his shoulders, and said, or rather croaked, "Mr. Clear, I am very, very sorry"—

"Lost? lost?" asked Matthew, suffocated with anxiety.

We may here inform the reader that Mr. Felix was formerly head-clerk to Mr. Downy; and that his present object was to inform Matthew of the verdict—not ten minutes returned by a conscientious jury, in the case of Brown *versus* Clear. The reader will remember that we spoke of a compromise. Certain it is, that the plaintiff, won by Downy, had consented to take five hundred pounds with costs: the money was to be paid the next day, when Mr. Felix, who had recently set up for himself, assured Matthew that if brought into court, the plaintiff, left to *his* adroitness, would not get a sixpence. To this he pledged even his reputation. Matthew—seeing his way—broke with his old friend Downy, and gave the case to Mr. Felix, who again and again, in his own graphic and anatomical phrase declared that "Miss Brown had not a leg to stand upon!"

"These things *will* happen," said the comforting Mr. Felix; "the damages"—

Matthew, in a state of strangulation, gasped— "How much?"

"One thousand five hundred pounds!"

The features of Matthew changed like a dying dolphin—"One thousand, five—why—you told me, —yes, you swore, she hadn't a leg to stand upon."

"As a lawyer, sir, I was justified in the assumption; but after what had passed between you and Miss Brown, you, sir, must have known better."

"Passed—between—us?"

"Oh, Mr. Clear! a case of rock couldn't stand against *them* letters. Not a dry eye in court; even his lordship moved; and three times the counsel stopt to recover himself! Seven ladies fainting, and three in strong hysterics, taken from the gallery. How could you write *them* letters?"

With this interrogative, and a passing complaint of great exhaustion, Mr. Felix departed to dine.

Though we anticipate the event a few weeks, we will here state, as an evidence of the mighty power of love,—making the lion to lie down with the lamb, —that such was its influence over Mr. Felix, that though opposed to Miss Brown, he subsequently married the lady, wisely adding his own bill of costs to her private damages.

To return to Matthew, who sat staring and stunned. The unequivocal triumph of his epistolary talents, weighed with him not a feather against fifteen hundred pounds. At length, Matthew began to vociferate. "Fool! fool! And when I thought I saw my way! Fifteen hundred! fifteen! and then the costs! Oh Lord! In all, two thousand pounds! Two thousand! How Downy will triumph! how he'll chuckle! how he'll exclaim"——

"Ha! ha! ha! Hooked him, by ——!"

Matthew stood transfixed. Was it "but a wandering voice," or was it, indeed, Nabob in the flesh? Another laugh dispelled all doubt; Matthew, opening the door of an inner room, beheld the bird of evil omen—beheld—

"Tippoo, my dear, where's your bow?"

Thus spake Mrs. Clear to a fat little boy of about eight years old, with glittering dark eyes, coal coloured hair, and a primrose complexion. The docile infant drew up to Matthew, greeting him with a truly oriental salutation. Matthew, without the slightest return of the elaborate civility, glared at his wife. Mrs. Clear, with an amiable attempt at conversation, taking off her bonnet, observed, " she had been to Dorking." This she said in a tone of explanation to the bewildered look of her husband, who, however, was far from satisfied with the intelligence. " He knew—she was always going to Dorking—but—who—who the devil was Tippoo ?" His wife, with a confidence peculiar to herself, explained.

" A burden had long weighed upon her heart; she could no longer live beneath the pressure. Tippoo was a helpless orphan. She had long known his unhappy parents; she might almost say his mother and herself, bred together, were one. In his last moments, she had promised the father to nourish and protect the little Tippoo. She had brought the dear infant to England—had placed him with a nurse at Dorking. But for the visitation of Providence, which had swept away her property (true, as a Christian, she ought not to murmur), out of her own means, she would have reared and educated the little love; but since the earthquake"—Here, a torrent of tears rendered the speaker inaudible.

Though the presence of Tippoo was thus satisfactorily explained, the sudden advent of Nabob still remained a mystery. There never was so lucky an accident! Tippoo during his residence at Dorking, much frequented the society of certain mercenary naturalists abounding in that neighbourhood; we speak of bird-catchers. On the morning of the day of Mrs. Clear's last visit, Nabob, keeping company with rustic linnets and plebeian sparrows, was caught in a net with a dozen of his low friends, and immediately recognised and claimed by the delighted Tippoo. A guinea rewarded the bird-catcher: and thus, Mrs. Clear in one day repossessed herself of all (except her husband) she held dear in the world,—Tippoo the orphan, and Nabob the parrot.

Mrs. Clear had heard of the verdict; and though considerably shocked at the sum, besides being much hurt at the warm, libertine tone of the letters, her conduct on the occasion was all but angelic. Matthew expected bitter reproof—scorching glances. Alas! he knew not woman. He knew not her deep tides of feeling—the secret sources of her sympathy; Mrs. Clear breathed nought but comfort and content: perhaps, the genial season had its influence: it was a lovely July night, and Matthew was melted.

" Indeed, it was a heavy sum; but a cheerful economy would soon replace it. And, after all, what an escape! For what," exclaimed Mrs.

Clear, with ill-suppressed horror, "what, my dear Matthew, if you had married such a person?" Mrs. Clear evidently waited for a reply; but Mr. Clear said nothing.

At this moment, the domestic group might have kindled a Wilkie. Matthew was seated on a sofa, one hand beside him, the other thrust beneath his waistcoat. On his immediate right sat his wife in a novel position. She had both arms about her husband's neck, with her eyes following his eyes. On Matthew's left knee, after much unseen assistance on the part of Julia, sat little Tippoo, all his faculties absorbed by a large scarlet apple. At an end of the sofa was perched Nabob, silently devouring buttered toast, a vegetable he had much missed in the fields of Surrey. Now, confess, reader—have you not here a picture?

" Is he not a sweet fellow ?" asked Mrs. Clear, turning her husband's head to Tippoo. " And then so mild—so tractable ! Yes, Matthew, he will —he must win upon you ; you will find in the dear child a son,—(some association made Matthew cast up his glassy eyes to the portrait)—" an affectionate son ; and, yes, you will be to him as a loving father?" Matthew sat with his tongue like a stone in his mouth. " Eh, Matthew?" and Mrs. Clear continued with every query to tighten her arms about her husband's neck. " Eh, Matthew?" At length,

Vol. III. Page 170.

MATHEW CLEAR NOT "SEEING HIS WAY."

Published by Henry Colburn, Great Marlborough Street, 1838.

in self-defence, for a blue tinge stole upon the good man's cheek, Matthew uttered a sound which with Julia passed for "yes."

"I knew you would; and you will foster him, and educate him as a gentleman, and provide for his future wants in this stormy, wicked life—eh, Matthew?"—and Julia's arms were still at Matthew's neck. "Eh, Matthew? I say, eh, Matthew?" and Mrs. Clear raised her voice with every question, squeezing, too, with growing force.—"Eh, Matthew?"

This time, Matthew becoming decidedly purple, cried loudly—"Yes, yes!"

"Ha! ha! ha! hooked him, by —— !"—and the parrot finished his buttered toast.

CHAPTER IV.

The expenses of the law-suit, various debts contracted by Mrs. Clear, when she walked "in maiden meditation, fancy free," together with the professional education of Tippoo, in a few years reduced Matthew's ten thousand pounds to little less than four. Unhappily, Mrs. Clear, for all her solitary hint at cheerful saving, had not learned "to sink with dignity." Until awakened by the ring of the

last guinea, she lived in the delusion of the unbroken
ten thousand. It is true, her imagination was
tinged with oriental extravagance; much was to be
allowed for her breeding; though Matthew, we
grieve to say, was quite devoid of the necessary
charity. Nay, sorry are we to add, that as he lost his
money, he lost his temper; as he became poor, he
became less endurable. Indeed, so surely did his
manners fall with his purse, that when suddenly
deprived of every shilling, he appeared—aye, even
to many of his protesting friends—an incorrigible
monster. Poor fellow! he was hardly used; for
he was one of those rigid people who, with ten
thousand pounds, pay their way, praise honesty as
the best policy, and look on the gazette as part and
parcel of the Newgate Calendar. Pity, that such
folks should feel adversity,—that such excellent
principles should be weakened, broken, by evil
fortune! However, so it chanced with Matthew:
he, who with a plum would have been a miracle of
stoical probity, lightened of the best part of his
wealth, began to look with gentler eyes on human
indiscretion. Matthew, rich and prosperous, would
have called that gross iniquity, which the same
losing Matthew practised as wise self-preservation.

"Very well, Mr. Clear, very well; you know
best; but sure am I that Simpson's a villain."
Thus, with feminine foresight, one day prophesied

Mrs. Clear. Matthew, seeing his way, smiled contemptuously; and though he spoke not, he felt, to his own satisfaction, more than a match for Simpson. Had he condescended to reply, he might, we think, have ventured a like ingenuous vaunt to that really proclaimed by a modern master of the revels.——" Beware, sir, beware of that Mr. Bradford," whispered the friendly warning. " Sir," replied the mirror of managers, with an air and look of questioned genius,—" Sir, Mr. Bradford may think himself a b——d rogue; but, sir," and the speaker towered and dilated with a consciousness of power, as he coined the expressive comparative,—" but, sir, he shall find that *I* can be a b——d-*er !*"

" Ha ! what? Simpson—why, the very man in my thoughts," said Matthew; " well—humph ! sit down." But Matthew, despite his hospitable address, looked ill at ease. His eye fell from the face of Simpson, and now, wandered, quite unconsciously, to Mrs. Clear's portrait; and now, dwelt sleepily upon the carpet. Julia rose from her seat; and, uttering half a dozen eloquent footsteps, quitted the room ; we say eloquent, for even the dull, the guileless Simpson, understood the disdain conveyed in them.

Matthew sat, as though his chair became every moment hotter and hotter; and his face, glowing from a dirty yellow into a dingy red, betrayed the increasing heat. On the other hand, Simpson showed a countenance of stone. Observing the confusion of his friend, he, with exemplary politeness, silently awaited his convenience. Preluding the act by a short cough, Matthew jerked his chair, took the hand of Simpson, and squeezing it with the fervour of a Pythias, said or sighed——" My dear Simpson, I am so sorry,"——

" Not a word—not a syllable, my dear friend. Since you can't oblige me with the thousand"—

" Between ourselves, my dear boy, the extravagance of Mrs. Clear is—but no, not even to you should I—can I—expose my own wife. I thought I had the money—I"—

" I wish you had, with all my soul ! But, at once to put you out of agony, I am come to tell you, that I don't want it."

If, before, Matthew warmly pressed the hand of his friend, he could at this moment have embraced him. Yes, no sooner had Simpson declared his independence, than Matthew became perfectly tranquil.

" Indeed," added Simpson, after a brief pause, " 'twas very lucky that we didn't purchase"—

" Lucky !" cried Matthew, and his jaw worked like the jaw of a corpse galvanized ;—" lucky !"

" Very lucky; for, you must know,"— and here

Simpson lowered his voice, took out his box, and impartially showering the snuff up either nostril, continued with syllabic distinctness,——" you must know, that the bonds we were to buy together, have to-day gone down to nothing." So saying, Simpson vanished from the room, leaving Matthew fixed in a chair, an exanimate pauper.

A few words will tell the rise and progress of this domestic tragedy. Simpson and Matthew were bosom—nay, as Simpson thought, pocket-friends. Thus, when Simpson, speaking on the best secret information, assured Matthew that a timely purchase of certain bonds must inevitably " lead to fortune," and consequently to fame,——at the same time, asking for the golden intelligence, the temporary loan of a thousand to participate in the venture ——Matthew, in a rapture of gratitude, and with a religious exclamation, promised the cash. However, Matthew was no sooner left alone, than he began to see his way. Why should he pay so dearly for mere advice? Why should not he himself reap the harvest of his own thousand? The tempter of man triumphed over friendship; for, incited by the devil, Matthew invested every shilling of his fortune in the aforesaid securities, wholly unmindful of the thousand pounds sacredly pledged to the believing Simpson! Thus, seeing his way, Matthew looked upon stark beggary. We think Simpson had an inkling of the sudden destitution of his friend: we believe it, from the calm, cold manner with which he touched upon the fall of the bonds, —from the spark of malice that lighted his dull eye as he glided from the apartment. We may wrong him,—but we have our suspicions.

What was left to Matthew? In no man was the love of country more deeply rooted; and yet, on the shortest notice was he prepared to wean himself from England—to cross the sea—to become an alien and a wanderer. Yes; without breathing a word about the vision, he clearly saw his way to New York. It may prove the worth of Matthew, when we assure our readers that many, many in London inquired most earnestly of his prospects. Matthew employed, as he conceived, the surest means to baffle such amiable curiosity. Indeed, believing himself unequal to the pang, he even took no formal leave of his wife; but promised himself, when he should have seen his way across the Atlan-lantic, to—to send for her. Fortunately, the day he withdrew himself from his home, Mrs. Clear was gone with a party to the London Docks. He had merely told her, that for a few days he should be absent in the country.

It was about a fortnight after this separation, that the fast-sailing ship, " The Good Intent," lay off Spithead: all was prepared; in a few minutes she would put out to sea. A boat approached the ship, containing a passenger, a Mr. Bustard, whose berth had been duly selected and paid for by a friend in the London Docks. The voyager mounted the side; but, no sooner was he upon deck, than a shriek—a piercing female screech went through the very timbers of the " The Good Intent." The men paused motionless at the ropes; the passengers stared, transfixed; but what was the surprise of the males—what the indignation of the ladies,—when a woman rushed to the new-comer, fell " like a guilty thing" at his feet, and with clasped hands, running eyes, and cracking voice, exclaimed—

" Forgive me, Matthew !—pray, forgive me ! I don't deserve that you should have followed me ! Indeed, I don't ! But, forgive me, my only Clear —and I will—I will go back with you !"

Reader, it was even so. Peter Bustard, cabin passenger, was no other than the defaulter, Matthew Clear. And most unluckily, two individuals—their boat lay astern—expressly commissioned to search " The Good Intent" or any other vessel, for the fugitive,—convinced by the words of Julia that they had caught their prey, instantly pounced upon it, and having satisfied Captain Rogers of the legality of the act, proceeded to carry Matthew and his luggage into their private bark. Indeed, Captain Rogers, though evidently interested in the fate of

I 3

Matthew, was too wise an officer—too good a sea-man—to question lawful authority. Otherwise, he had never risen from the rank of a boatswain's mate to the command of his present ship: for, by the strangest accident in life, Mrs. Clear, when a spinster, had sailed to England with the very Rogers, in whose "Good Intent" she was now a favoured passenger.

Matthew was hurried into the boat; his wife, breathless with anxiety, watched him safely seated between the officers. Of course, she expected an invitation to join the party; but Matthew deigned no look, no word to the forsaken. Her magnanimity at the spousal neglect was truly beautiful. She descended to the cabin with the dignity of an injured empress; and from the stern window, with a bottle of hartshorn at her nose, contemplated the "lessening boat;" and though, at least with Matthew, it "unwilling rowed to land,"—Julia, above the weakness of silly Susan, neither "cried adieu," nor "waved her lily hand."

For two or three minutes a deep silence reigned throughout the ship; and the very sea, the breeze, seemed hushed in sympathy with the silent sorrow, the wrongs of Matthew. All, save the oars, was profoundly at rest, when a high, shrill note came over the waters from "The Good Intent,"—a sound driven "like a sword of fire" into the ears of Mat-

thew—a voice that cried through the serene air—
across the glassy wave—

"Ha! ha! ha! Hooked him, by ——!"

It was not to be supposed that Mrs. Clear could
cross the Atlantic without Nabob. Like the sweet
little cherub, the parrot was aloft, perched on a rope
of "The Good Intent."

CHAPTER V.

Law and private malice did their worst; and
Matthew grew old, and lived a beggar. It is true,
in the fondness of his heart he would continue to
see his way; but then he looked through rags, and
the world had lost its glory. He was open to any
offer; but fortune only sneered at his readiness.
In the humility of his soul he thought nothing on
this dirty earth too foul to touch; and yet he walked
with empty hands. Alone in the world—for he
possessed certain evidence of the demise of Mrs.
Clear at Philadelphia—he had little to live for, but
found it difficult to live. Often, seeing his way, he
looked directly at the poor-house. And what added
scorpions to his daily wants, was the prosperity of
early acquaintances—of men with no more eyes
than moles; men, who in truth had never seen

their way, and who, notwithstanding, had jogged dully and prosperously on. Harassed, disgusted, weary of breath, Matthew paused in a desolate hour at a book-stall; and, thumbing over a volume of Plutarch, nerved by heroic examples, he resolved on "self-slaughter."

Reader, pause ere you execrate. Behold Matthew, with but one sixpence—and that begged from an old acquaintance—in his pocket; houseless—hopeless; his coat in tatters; a ventilating rent in his breeches; melancholy eating his heart; a November sky—a November rain; and a hole in either shoe! Is not this an hour in which a man could lie down in a coffin as in a bed? In which he could gather himself to sleep—wrap even a parish shroud about him as he would wrap a warm great-coat—compose his arms upon his breast, and then fall smiling off into death—smiling, at the running, scraping, stamping, shuffling, still to continue over his head, by the lackeys, the flatterers, the debaters, the jugglers of the world above? Yes! Matthew saw his way into a grave, and looking back at what he should leave, the wormy pit seemed to him a warm, comfortable couch; eiderdown at the bottom, and silken curtains at the sides!

Matthew, pondering on the means, decided in favour of arsenic. Composing himself to a look of indifference, he entered the splendid shop of a "surgeon and apothecary." Having, like Romeo, to call about him, he had some seconds to observe the gorgeous show made by the man of drugs.—At length, the apothecary appeared behind the counter. "What may you want?"—

Matthew paused, and a tremor thrilled him from crown to sole. "What may you want?"—

"A—a—a dose of salts," answered Matthew. The salts were delivered, the money paid, and Matthew was again in the street. The reader may marvel at the vacillation of the self-doomed, who, seeking deadly poison, asks for a salutary aperient. We know not whether we can satisfactorily solve the riddle; but this we know, that Matthew, casting up his eyes, beheld in the prosperous surgeon and apothecary, the helpless, and, as he afterwards turned out, the ungrateful, arrogant Tippoo; the boy, whom—held to his pledge by Mrs. Clear—Matthew had "fostered, and educated as a gentleman, and provided for in this stormy, wicked life." Meeting his looks, Matthew thought he was recognised; and whether—for pride is a mysterious agent—he would not suffer Tippoo to suspect that his foster-father was so abased that nought was left him but to die, or whether Matthew had really repented of his wickedness, we cannot decide. We can only assure the reader that, eschewing poison,

he asked for salts; and, the medicine in his possession, he was too good an economist to fling it away.
No, he took it; and, strange to relate, in four-and-
twenty hours, he saw his way with very different
eyes.   From this accident, we venture to suggest
to every morbid genius, to every despairing lover,
who determines to purchase arsenic, first to try a
dose of salts.   Aperients are fatal to romance.

Matthew drudged and drudged, and sank and
sank.   He, who, on the outset of life, saw his way
over its proudest heights, its richest plains, now,
with contracted vision, hung over the books of a
sordid master, a withered usurer.   However, as
the man of money-bags was much older than Matthew, as he had no kindred, and was bountiful in
his professions towards his sole, his confidential, and
his half-starved clerk, Matthew, in bright moments,
would see his way to the miser's fortune.   Hence,
was he all devotion and ductility.   Thus, when his
master testified to an event, it was enough for Matthew: though he himself should have forgotten the
circumstance, yet was his confidence so great in the
veracity of his employer, that he had but little
hesitation in swearing to it.   A law-suit most triumphantly illustrated the fidelity of Matthew.

A certain spendthrift deeply indebted to the advances of the money-merchant, had the dishonour-
able audacity to contest the claims of the lender.

The suit was involved in many niceties ; and what was worse, it fell at a time when Matthew's master was in the hands of the physician, who, to the anxious inquiries of the clerk, shook a death's-head ! The pain of the sick man's disease only aggravated his desire of vengeance. To Matthew he left the evidence of the case, narrating various incidents which, described on what Matthew believed to be a bed of death, had to him all the force and solemnity of an oath. Matthew swore in open court in the spirit of his master ; but vain was the testimony ; the spendthrift gained the cause ; and the sudden shock finished the usurer. He died, leaving every thing he had to build a chapel, bequeathing not even a blessing to his clerk. Hapless Matthew ! It was not enough for the defendant to gain a victory, but he must persecute the conquered. An indictment was filed against the clerk for perjury. He was tried, found guilty, and sentenced ; and for only swearing in the spirit of his master, Matthew was condemned to pass two years in Newgate, and to stand one hour by St. Sepulchre's clock in the pillory !

Poor Matthew ! we saw him fixed and turning ; and we must say to his credit, that he went round and round with the calmness and equanimity of the most practised statesman. We have long yearned to hold a philosophical discourse on the pillory : is not the present a golden time? We pledge ourselves that our essay shall employ one hour, and no more? Well, we do a violence to our feelings, and defer our task.

All was breathless, hushed, in the Old Bailey, as Matthew was presented to the mob. The executioner acquitted himself with praiseworthy adroitness. In an instant Matthew was ready for the sport; and still the silence reigned, as he stood, prepared for the first turn.

" Ha! ha! ha! Hooked him, by —— !" rang from a window of the Governor's mansion. Yes, there was the ubiquitous Nabob! He had been brought to Newgate by a sailor, subsequently doomed to the hulks; had been trafficked with a turnkey's wife for tobacco, and, after various prison vicissitudes, was promoted to the drawing-room of the Governor.

Nothing could exceed the humanity of the crowd. Two or three—at our commencement we particularized one speaker—moralized on the condition of the culprit; but, with a single exception, no spectator offered an affront. Having turned his hour,* Matthew was about to be released.

---

* Ere this passes from the press, the pillory may be abolished —gone for ever with many other " venerable and excellent institutions."

"How are you now?" soothingly inquired the executioner.

"Pretty well—pretty well—if"—

"At this moment, a dastard in the human form flung a handful of mire in the eyes of the sufferer; who, trying to shake it off, merely added:—

"If—if—I—could—see—my—way!"

A kind Samaritan attended Matthew in the prison. He sought to clear the eyes of the sufferer of certain particles. "Look straight forward," said the operator.

"Ha!" groaned Matthew, and he thought—"*If* I had always looked straight forward, how differently should I have seen my way!"

BARNABY PALMS:

THE MAN WHO "FELT HIS WAY."

CHAPTER I.

That philosopher was an ass, who, trembling at the peril inherited with his eyes, resolved to avoid all mischief by putting them out. We know, that in this narrow, gloomy passage, called the world, eyes are, so to speak, edged tools, hurting the wearer. We know that, deceived by them, we often shake and wonder at a stalking giant, when, in truth, the Polyphemus is only a swaggering mountebank on wooden stilts,——and doff our caps to a glistering glory, which stripped of its outside, is more loathsome than an ape. On the other hand, how many with a wise tyranny, use their eyes as the meanest vassals, never suffering them to play truant in the summer clouds——to hang on summer flowers——to loose their time with unprofitable exhalations, or to try to spell the mystery of the stars ! No ; prudently disciplined, the ocular servants help their masters to dress and to undress

——to save them from posts and pillars when abroad ——to eat their meat at home——and to take especial care that no shilling be a counterfeit. Now, Barnaby never thought of trusting his eyes but with the lowest duties, instinctively keeping them from all delicate embarrasments. In the petty, menial wants of life, Barnaby might employ his eyes; in the momentous concerns of this world, he winked, and securely——felt his way.

At the green age of eighteen, Barnaby possessed the ripe fruit of two score. But the truth is, Barnaby had never been a child. In the nurse's arms he was a very mannikin, showing an extraordinary precocity in his choice of the ripest apple and the biggest cake. Left as a legacy to an only uncle, the boy flourished after his " own sweet will," unchecked and unassisted save by the scantily-paid attentions of a well-meaning pedagogue, vegetating in a hamlet some six miles from the Kentish coast. Poor Joshua! he might have learned of his scholar——might have sucked worldly wisdom even from the suckling. We repeat it: at eighteen Barnaby was a match for grey hairs.

Barnaby had a deep respect for his uncle; in fact, so deep, it all but sank to fear. Thus, our hero spared no pains to feel his way to the heart of his relation, who, be it understood, enjoyed the reputation of a wealthy man, albeit, old inhabitants of the town would sometimes marvel how his wealth had been acquired. Palms, senior, dwelt in a huge dilapidated mansion within gunshot of the sea ; his household consisting of an old man and his daughter, a pretty, gay-hearted lass of eighteen.

Old Palms was seated in his oak parlour, steadily employed upon a breakfast, of which beef and Kentish ale, with an incidental drop of white brandy, formed the principal part. Before him sat Barnaby in trim travelling attire. He looked and spoke the creature of humility. Could he have made the transfer, he would have given his soul to his uncle as readily as he advanced the mustard. The truth is, Barnaby was about to enter the world : he had drawn on his boots for the great pilgrimage of life. In a few hours, and he must feel his way through the crowd of London, being destined to the warehouse of Messrs. Noakes and Styles, mercers, City. Hence, the reader may imagine that Barnaby was subdued by the approaching event—that he felt some odd twitchings at the heart, as he stared at the old wainscot, with its every worm-hole familiar to him —that a something rose to his throat, as he looked out upon the sea, tumbling and roaring in concert with a January gale—at that sea which had sung his early lullabies, —that his heart, like the ocean-shell, still responded to the sound. It is reasonable to believe—though we cannot substantiate the fact—that some such emotions rose in the bosom of the pilgrim. Of this, however, we are certain: Barnaby looked with the eyes of a devotee towards a small leathern bag, lying on the table at the right hand of his uncle and Barnaby continued to gaze at the string securing the neck, until, distracted by the appearance of Patience Mills, who—the more serious portion of the breakfast consumed—entered with a dozen eggs.

. Now, Patience had a face as round, and cheeks as red, as any pippin, eyes blue as heaven, and a mouth, as a certain young man on the coast avowed, sweet as a honey-comb. Nevertheless, had Patience been some smoke-dried hag, Barnaby had not visited her with grimmer look. Patience replied to the glance by a giggle, solacing herself, when out of hearing, by muttering "glad he's going." Barnaby looked at his uncle's fingers, and then at the bag. Heedless of the hint, old Palms took an egg.

"Come, eat, Barney; eat. Ye'll have a cold ride to London: the north wind's edged like a scythe. What! not take eggs?"

"Doat on 'em, uncle," cried Barnaby, aroused, like Shylock, from "a dream of money-bags." The fact is, Barnaby had that day determined to like every thing: on that occasion he wished to leave a vivid impression of his meekness and humi-

lity.   " Quite a weazel at eggs, uncle," continued
Barnaby, and he began to chip the shell.   Now, it
so happened that Barnaby had fallen upon an egg
which, on being opened, emitted conclusive evidence
of its antiquity.   Old Palms, instantly perceiving
the work of time, roared to Barnaby to cast the
abomination out of the window.   Barnaby, however, determined to give an example of his economy
—of his indifference to petty annoyance—sat like
a statue, still holding the egg between his thumb
and finger—his uncle applying the same instruments
to his own nose.

" Out with it, Barney !"   Barney smiled a remonstrance, and handled his spoon.   " Zounds !"
cried old Palms, almost grinning through his disgust at what he deemed the ignorance or simplicity
of his nephew—" Zounds ! nephew—why—ha !
ha !—you'll never eat it ?"

Barnaby, mistaking the humour of bis uncle,
nodded knowingly.

" You will ?   I tell you 'tis a musty egg—a bad
egg—pah ! the egg stinks !"

Barney looked as though he believed he had won
his uncle's heart for ever, and then complacently
made answer, " I don't care for eggs *over fresh.*"

Now, we boldly declare the egg of Barnaby to
be a grander subject for the moralist and the ro-
mance-writer than either the egg of Columbus, the

famous roc's egg of the Eastern Princess, the golden egg of Æsop, or the egg of Mother Goose. Reader, pause a moment, and reflect on the prosperity of whole hordes of people, whose success in life is solely attributable to their participating in the taste of Barnaby.

Look at his lordship, sparkling with honours, padded with bank paper! and know ye to what he owes all this? Oh, doubtless to his high statesmanlike qualities—his profound knowledge—his indefatigable industry. Not so, not so; the simple story is, he was wont to confidentally breakfast with the minister, and on such occasions showed that he "cared not for his eggs over fresh." But shall we stay at courts and courtiers? No; from a palace to a workshop there is ever some ductile eater—some omnivorous, obsequious Barney at breakfast—who has made, or looks to make, a figure in the world by not caring for his eggs "over fresh." Many are the ways in which the tale may be told. There is Tom Spangle, a handsome, healthy, six-foot animal of two-and-thirty. He had not a shilling; now, he rides blood, and writes cheques. Do you know the secret of the change? Very well; he married the ancient, yellow widow of an army-contractor. Ay, even so; he cared not for his egg "over fresh."

The avowed taste of Barnaby was not lost upon

his uncle.   The old man looked through the youth with a thinking eye—an eye that seemed to read his moral anatomy—and then uttered a long "hem!" at the same time stretching his hand to the money-bag.   Invisible fingers were playing on the heart-strings of Barnaby, whilst, from the corner of his eye, he saw his uncle slowly undo the strip of knotted leather which " compressed the god with-in."   The bag was opened ; its glorious contents blazed on the table; and as they rang upon the oak, Barnaby instinctively rose to his feet, standing respectfully uncovered in " the presence."

" Barney," said old Palms, and reverently laid his hand upon the gold, " Barney, my child, you see the little board I've set apart for you?"   The life-blood of Barnaby tingled in his very eyes, and his ears rang with music.   " You see the few savings and scrapings I have made for the child of my bro-ther?   For I feared that you, an innocent, unpro-tected, unassisted lad, would need the aid which money can alone afford.   Barney, I trembled for the softness of your heart—the simplicity of your nature."   Here Barney felt almost in peril of tears. " Yes, Barney, these were my weak anxieties, my foolish fears."   Saying which, the old man began to return the guineas to the bag.   During the ope-ration, not a word was spoken.   Barney, scarcely venturing to breathe, stood with his head bent on

his breast, and one eye on the table, silent and subdued.   The tinkling of the gold—the voice of
Barney's fortune, was alone audible; and, as note
followed note, the young expectant became possessed as though he listened to angelic trumpets.
The bag being filled, Palms proceeded to tie its
mouth, talking as he leisurely tied.   "Barney, I
find my fears were the fears of ignorance.   You
need not such a sum as this; you are already rich
in strength—in wisdom."

"I, uncle?" cried Barnaby, sensitively shrinking
from the compliment, and at the same time—struck
by the manner of Palms—breaking into a profuse
sweat.   "*I* strong? *I* wise? Oh, uncle!"

"Come, Barney, why so modest? I say, strength
and wisdom, as the world goes, are yours.   Here
we've a hundred guineas in this little bag; what
then? to a lad of your wit they're of little worth.
You'll never miss 'em.   Now, here," and Palms
slid the coin along the table, "here are five
guineas."

"Five! uncle!"

"Five.   The reward of your skill—of the skill
you have shown this morning."

"Five guineas? skill? uncle!"

"Never doubt it, Barney; take up the money,
and never mistrust that head of thine; for well I
know, that the fellow who, in this working world,

cares not for his eggs '*over fresh*,' will, in the end,
flourish as well though he begin with five guineas,
as with five thousand."

The tone and manner of old Palms forbade any
reply on the part of his nephew, who, nevertheless,
received the eulogy with a sulkiness worthy of the
great cynic. Indeed, had Barnaby pocketed five
snow-balls, he could not have looked more blank
and frozen; could not have mounted the borrowed
horse, ready saddled to convey him to London,
with more reluctant leg, with grimmer counntenance.
No wonder; Barnaby thought he had securely felt
his way: now Barnaby had lost ninety-five guineas.

CHAPTER II.

THERE is a golden volume yet to be written on
the first struggles of forlorn genius in London
—magnificent, miserable, ennobling, degrading
London. If all who have suffered would confess
their sufferings—would show themselves in the
stark, shivering squalor in which they first walked
her streets—would paint the wounds which first
bled in her garrets—what a book might be placed
in the hands of pride!—what stern, wholesome
rebukes for the selfish sons of fortune!—what sustaining sweetness for the faint of spirit! It is true,

the letters might be of blood—the tales of agony
and horror—of noble natures looking serenely, with
the hungry fox gnawing their bowels—of disappointment sinking to despair—of misery, dreaming
of, and wooing death ! And then, how many petty
shifts to mask a haggard face with smiles—how
many self-denials—how many artifices to hide a
nakedness from laughing scorn ! Nor would the
tone be all of wretchedness.   No : beautiful emanations of the human heart—the kindest minister-
ings of human affections would sweeten and exalt
many a sad history.   How often should we find the
lowly comforting the high—the ignorant giving
lessons to the accomplished—the poor of earth
aiding and sustaining the richly-dowered !

Barnaby was in London ; but not—our heart
bounds as we declare it—not to add to the
number of splendid vagabonds, now thrust from
her thresholds to sleep in the market-place, and
now, dining off plate cheek by jowl with my lord.
Barney was speedily warm, as in wool, in the house
of Messrs. Nokes and Styles ; and with the combined wisdom and delicacy of a spider, began to
feel his way to the foibles of his employers.   Nokes
was a man of brass—Styles a thing of willow.
Assured of this, Barnaby immediately felt the propriety of bowing to the one, and bending the
other.

" Look at that lazy brute,—he doesn't draw a single pound," remarked the observing Nokes, as one evening, standing at his warehouse door, he contemplated the progress of a passing waggon.

" Not half-a-pound, sir," chimed in Barnaby; " and yet, I doubt not, he eats his share of corn and hay.   But this it is to be, as one may say, in partnership with those who *will* pull."

" Right, Barnaby;" and the countenance of Nokes darkened, as he watched the easy-going quadruped.

" They who *will* work, *may* work.   Was Mr. Styles here to-day ?"

It is our hope that the query of Barnaby was unconsciously coupled with his profound views of the distribution of labour—that he had innocently let fall a spark on the train of Nokes's smothered feelings.   If, on the contrary, the conflagration were premeditated, the moral incendiary must have glowed at the flattering proof of his success ; for Nokes was all but suffocated.   The blood rushed to his face — retreated — rushed — went back — presenting unto Barney as fine an exhibition of " humours and spirits" as that recorded by the learned Peireskius, who at the cost of some words, sets forth the useful lesson he acquired through " an augmenting-glass or microscope,"—showing how a certain plebeian animal " setting himself to wrestle

with a flea, was so incensed that his blood ran down
from head to foot, and from foot to head again !"
Wise Peireskius ! true philosopher ! who from the
bickerings of small despised animals extracteth
better wisdom, learneth surer self-government, than
the unthinking million carry from a dog-fight, yea,
from a bull-bait ! (Reader, when thou shalt behold
a Nokes bursting with envy, hatred, and unchari-
tableness, think of the learned lord of Peiriesk and
his little monitor—ponder, and let thy soul be
instructed.)

" Lack-a-day ! I'd quite forgot ; 'tis Epsom
races," cried Barney, in self-reproval of his unnecessary question, the face of Nokes again suddenly
resembling a chemist's bottle by candlelight. " Epsom races !" repeated the speaker, in a tone that
left nothing further to be advanced upon the subject.
And Nokes evidently judged the words to be conclusive ; for feeling—like a patriot at a public
dinner—more than he could express, with a wisdom
rarely exhibited on such occasions, he spoke not at
all. He merely jerked out his watch ; and, at a
glance, calculated that in two hours at most he
should be looked for to join his friends at whist.

Mr. Styles, in addition to his love of horse-flesh,
had a passion for the rural and picturesque. He
kept a country-house, under whose hospitable roof
Barney was wont at times to eat a Sabbath meal,

having previously attended his inviter to the parish church. It was a sight to melt the thoughtless youth of Bridewell to behold Barney during service. There he was, pinned to the side of his employer; now seeking out the lessons of the day—now, with open mouth and staring eyeballs (an expression of features not disgraceful to any tombstone), out-singing a numerous Sunday-school, shrilly piping in the gallery. It is true, the clerk would cast a look of bitterness; but then, it was avowed that Barnaby never opened his mouth, that the poor man did not feel shaken on his throne.

" A most comfortable sermon, Barney?" remarked Styles, with a certain air of interrogation. " Most comfortable?"

" I'm a wicked creature, if I wouldn't have given a guinea for Mr. Nokes to hear it. Did you observe, sir, how that gentleman with the scarlet face and powdered head was moved? Pray, sir, who is he?"

" Humph! He's newly retired among us, Barney; I—I forget his name; but they tell me he has in his time been a great player."

" No doubt, sir; no doubt. Every word of the preacher seemed to enter him like a bodkin! A great player! poor wretch! Surely, sir, he can't have made all his money by playing?"

" Every penny, Barney."

" He keeps a coach !" cried Barney, in a modulated tone of polite amazement.

" A house," added Styles, " that did belong to the member of the county—a town mansion—and a shooting-box."

" All won by playing ? Mercy upon us ! The devil offers great temptations !" moralized Barney.

" Say what we will of him, Barney," responded Styles, with exemplary liberality towards a fallen foe; " say what we will of him, I am afraid the devil is no fool."

" And—and"—asked Barney, with a face somewhat uncorded from its first rigidity—" what may the gentleman have most played ?"

" I can't exactly tell, but I believe principally low parts; such as footmen, clowns, and country boys !"

" Parts ! I mean games ! Chicken-hazard—short-whist—roulette — rouge-et-noir — or"—and Barney for some seconds continued the inventory, with a knowledge of the subject, wholly unexpected.

" Games ! Understand me, Barney ; I tell you the man was an actor, a stage-player."

Barney could not subdue a look of disappointment: in a moment, however, he returned to the subject. " Actor or not, I am sure he must have played. La, sir, did you see him when the doctor thundered at gaming ?" Truth to say, Styles was one of those profound sleepers who can sometimes snore at Jove's best bolts——" Ha ! as I said, I'd sell a guinea cheap, so that Mr. Nokes had heard it."

Styles looked meaningly at Barney——drank off a glass of port——clasped his fingers——glanced a moment at his left shoe——and then, as a magpie turns his head, lifted his cheek inquiringly towards Nokes's well-wisher. " Gaming, sir, isn't it a sort of murder ?" Styles nodded : " Wives and babes are killed by it. Isn't it a kind of arson——such capital houses are destroyed by it ?" Styles nodded twice. " Isn't it the worst of robberies,——for the most innocent, most painstaking, most upright of partners may be made beggars by it ?" Styles responded to the last query by a long succession of nods. " Then, sir, and saving your presence, I must say again,——I must say"——and here Barney emptied his glass, as seeking courage for the avowal ——" I would have given five guineas had Mr. Nokes been with us at church this day."

" What do you mean, Barney ?" asked Styles, with the look and tone with which folks usually address a ghost. " What do you mean ?"

" Why, sir, this I mean"——and Barney drew his chair in confidential proximity to his master——"this I mean ; I must say it——I can't help it——but, sir, I don't like whist clubs." And an emphatic blow upon the table made the glasses leap at the aversion of the speaker.

"No more do I," replied Styles; and in the reply proved himself the master of a most difficult science—the art of saying very much in very little. Now, whether the wine was more than usually subtle, or whether the devotion of Barney had suddenly softened his employer,—certain it is, that Styles rapidly became an altered man. He who was usually silent and timid, became loud and self-asserting; inveighing, in good round terms, against the arrogance and imprudence of Nokes, and upbraiding himself for his pusillanimous deference to his dissipated partner.

"I have been a fool long enough Barney," insinuated the modest Styles; an assertion which his no less diffident hearer ventured not to deny. "Yes, yes; I have too long given the reins out of my own hands; have been a nobody in the firm." Barney shrugged his shoulders, and leered acquiescence. "A nobody!—worse than nobody!—a blockhead—a nincompoop—an ass!" Barney, with great moral courage, bowed to the justice of every epithet. "But," exclaimed Styles for the twentieth time, rising at the accomplished number, "I'll be so no longer—I'll"—

We have not the slightest doubt that a most beautiful peroration was, at this moment, destroyed

K 3

—barked down, by a yelping little spaniel, unhappily for oratory, lying with extended fore-paws beneath the chair of Styles; the whole weight of the speaker coming suddenly upon the left leg of Kitty, she howled and barked with a persevering vigour truly feminine; her agony and helplessness were not lost upon a sister; for Madge, a terrier bitch, sprang from an opposite corner, and, in an instant, almost joined her teeth in the neck of the wounded. Kitty howled in a more intense treble; Madge growled vengeance in deep bass; whilst Styles and Barney, having vainly tried to separate the disputants, for a moment stood and looked in each other's face,—the concert of female voices still continuing. " Did you ever see such a tyrannical fury ?" asked Styles, with a hopeless look, pointing at the ravenous Madge.—The appeal was too much for the sensibility of Barney, who—the exclamation struck from him by a yet higher shriek on the part of Kitty—roared out,—" D—— that Nokes !" at the same time aiming an ineffectual kick at the newly-christened. Styles smiled benevolently at the oath. Barney, moved by the sufferings of Kitty, and a blow upon his own shin against the chair, dragged forth the combatants ; Styles tugged at the spaniel, whilst Barney, with the wisdom of the cock-pit, placed the tail of the terrier between his teeth. At this picturesque moment, and most unluckily for Madge, the servant bawled in at the door—

"Mr. Nokes!"

Down, with terrible force, came the grinders of Barney, the terrier quitted its hold, and, tearing out of the room, ran yelling close by Nokes, sometime her unsuspecting namesake.

"There—there—Barney!" cried Styles, and confusedly opened the door of a closet, within which, silently as a spectre, Barney felt his way. Styles, with the suffering spaniel under his arm, seated himself in his chair; the bitch, with female delicacy, squeaking little, but shaking her crushed fore-paw reproachfully in the face of the destroyer. Nokes entered; his countenance was lined and mysterious as lawyer-written parchment; there was mischief in it, though obscured by certain confusion; much malice and no little cowardice. He coughed, but, strange enough, no subject seemed to present itself. Luckily, he glanced at the streaming eyes and quivering paw of Kitty. "So— humph!—a dog-fight?"

"It's very odd," replied Styles, with the learned air of an F.R.S., "it's very odd—but though Kitty and Madge have been together these five years, they can't agree. It's very odd."

"When people can't agree," returned Nokes,

and he looked a Columbus as he propounded the moral discovery, "they had better part. Mr. Styles, for these three months I have been confirmed in this opinion."

" Longer—surely, longer. 'Tis two years since Mrs. Nokes had a separate maintainance."

Nokes, touched by the indelicate allusion to his domestic infelicity, in silence passed his five fingers across his brow, and said, with very cold dignity, " Mr. Styles, fortunately there are partnerships which may be dissolved."

" Fortunately," acquiesced Styles, stroking the head of Kitty.

" You wonder, Mr. Styles, why your dogs can't agree. Perhaps I can explain ; it may be, that one is sporting out of doors all day, whilst the other is left at home to bark and keep house."

" What do you mean, Mr. Nokes ?" asked Styles ; and with forced tranquillity, he placed the bitch upon the hearth-rug. Had an oracle put an interrogative, it could not have been more searching —more impressive.

" I mean, sir, that I have a partner in view, whose habits of business, Mr. Styles"—

" Glad to hear it," interrupted Styles, "for as I have some time contemplated a dissolution, we can the sooner get rid of one another."

" No house can stand against the chance of such bets," cried Nokes. " Hundreds vanishing after hundreds."

" Bets ! hundreds ! No, Mr. Nokes, let us keep to the serious truth ; guinea points, sir,—guinea points don't become a tradesman."

" Guinea points !—guinea—but, as we are happily of the same mind to separate, we won't talk nonsense."

" 'Tisn't necessary," accorded Styles; "therefore, as we understand each other, may I not ask the name of your new partner ?"

" Oh, certainly ; a most industrious, pains-taking young man."

" Glad to hear it," said Styles again. " I think —indeed, I am sure, I have for myself just such a partner in my eye."

" I wish you all success," cried Nokes; "may I know who he is ?"

" To be sure ; a most business-like, prudent person. But, first, the name of your partner ?"

" He doesn't yet know his good luck. But"— and Nokes looked with the eye of a fox over a farm-paling—" Can't you guess?"

" Hav'n't a notion. Yes—I think—I—"

" To be sure," cried Nokes,—" Barnaby; though I hav'n't told him,—Barnaby."

Styles hardly repressed a smile at the credulity

of Nokes; then, with a serious air, observed, " My
good friend, don't count upon him. Allowing that
I myself—though he is quite ignorant of the fact—
were not determined upon offering him a partner's
share, I am sure he would not—and, forgive me,
my friend—he could not, join with you."

" Not!" exclaimed Nokes, and his eyes glittered
like brass buttons—" And why not?"

" The lad is scrupulous; he can't abide cards,"
said Styles.

" You mean bets squandered upon fillies," replied Nokes, sarcastically.

" Pshaw ! between ourselves, the young man
has talked to me with tears in his eyes about
your nightly whist; guinea points, Nokes—guinea
points !"

Nokes leapt to his feet—and extending his arms
—projecting his breast—and throwing back his
head, cried aloud to the vacant ceiling, " Twopenny! As I have a soul to be saved—twopenny !"

Styles, subdued by the fervour of his partner, in
a modulated tone proceeded, " I do assure you,
Barnaby has always sworn to a guinea."

" A household crocodile !" cried Nokes. " Ah,
friend Styles, had you lost as little by the last
favourite,"—

" As little? How much, now—how much?"
asked Styles, with a bridling air.

" Wasn't it five hundred ?"

" A hat—a single hat to Jerry White—he wore it this very day at church—five hundred ! Upon my conscience, and may I die a sinner, but 'twas a hat."

" Barnaby protested 'twas five hundred pounds."

" The hypocrite ! he shall this moment speak to our faces."

" I wish he could ; but though he told me you had asked him here to-day, he vowed he couldn't spend the Sabbath with a blackleg and a horse-racer."

" A blackleg !" screamed Styles, and the exclamation was answered by a shriek in a yet higher note from the cupboard. Nokes at once recognised the voice of Barney, and ran to open the door, when Styles, preventing him, turned the key, put it in his pocket, and hurried his partner into an adjoining room, Barney still raving—as his masters conceived—to be heard in explanation. After a lapse of some ten minutes, employed by Nokes and Styles, in mutual assurances of renewed faith and friendship, the key of the cupboard, with a check for ten pounds, was placed in the hands of Betty, armed with final orders touching the prisoner. The door was speedily unlocked ; and Barney, his hands crimsoned as the Thane of Cawdor's, —blood on his face, and horror in his voice,

rushed out, sank in a chair, and in a tone of
mingled fear and veneration, exclaimed—" The
devil !"   A common household occurrence will explain away the seeming mystery.   The blessing of
increase was upon all things owned by Styles ; even
his cats escaped not the general good.   It so happened that seven kittens, scarce one day old, with
their satisfied mother, were the unknown tenants
of the cupboard, previous to the occupancy of Barney,—who, agitated by the colloquy of the partners, and having no thought, taking no pity, of the
blind, had walked upon the embryo hopes of future
Whittingtons. Two of the kittens being killed, the
maternal instincts of the parent were aroused,—
and when Nokes and Styles left their assistant, as
they believed, yelling with compunction, he was
suffering in various parts of his naked body, from
the teeth and claws of a revengeful cat.   It was
with some difficulty that Betty explained to the
confused young gentleman, the final decree of his
late employers.   They had sent him his salary for
the current quarter, and Betty would lose no time
in opening the door ; a hope was expressed, that he
would not show himself at the warehouse.   Barney
took his hat, and crawled from the house.   The
night was pitch black, and the rain beginning to fall,
—he was soaked to the skin ere he had felt his way
to his comfortless bed in London.

CHAPTER III.

" SIR, you talk of coincidences,"—thus one day
spake to us a valiant captain of the local militia—
" I will tell you, sir, a most remarkable coincidence : it is this, sir :—the very day on which
Napoleon escaped from Elba, I marched with my
regiment to Wormwood Scrubs !"   We are about
to match the coincidence of the gallant warrior for
Middlesex.—Thus, be it known, that the very night
on which Barnaby Palms was turned from the firm
of Nokes and Styles, the soul of Peter Blond,
mercer and hosier, Bishopgate-Without, was summoned to what is popularly called, a last account.
From a subsequent calculation made by the widow,
it was evident that Peter had vacated his house of
clay the very instant Barnaby left the roof of Styles :
yes, as Betty turned the key, Peter expired. Who,
when they have heard our tale, shall say that
Fortune doth not sometimes look above her bandage, to take a peep at vagrant merit ?   Who shall
call her a mere romping hoyden, playing at blind-
man's buff, catching the ill-favoured and the worth-
less, and hugging them in her arms, whilst the fair
and virtuous stand untouched in obscure corners ?

Or, granted, that the goddess doth sometimes approach them, shall it be said, that it is only to show them her beautiful hands, and then to pass on? The truth is, we slander Fortune: because the wise and bountiful creature will not let us at all times and in all places have our wicked will of her, —like unprincipled rakes, we take a poor revenge by calling her naughty names. We are rejoiced to say it, Barnaby was not of these evil speakers. However, to proceed with his obligations to what the unthinking vulgar would call good luck.

The second day after his dismissal, Barnaby, his clear spirit obscured by thoughts of future dinners, walked—we should rather say, was led by his good genius—up Bishopgate-Without. Melancholy grew upon him as he went: balked in his best intentions by the ignorance and hasty prejudice of his employers—disappointed in his hopes of partnership—it might be, misrepresented to his fellow-creatures—the whole earth grew dim and blank. At that moment, so great was his disgust of the worldly wealth which he could not obtain, that in all his previous life, he never felt so serious—so religious. Whilst in this dark, solemn mood, an undertaker's porter walked with the elastic step of death before him, and presented to Barney's meditating eyes, a coffin of satisfactory respectability. Here was an accident—or, as our friend the captain

would have said, a coincidence! Were we not
writing a veritable biography—were we hammering
out a romance (hammering is a wrong term ; considering the facility and the material with which
such things are made, we should rather say glass-
blowing), we would assure the reader, that Barney,
struck by the omen, instantly forswore the world,
lived his future life in an empty vault, and worked
as sexton : but we write a stern, true thing, as the
coming sequel will certify. Thus, as the eye of
Barney fell upon the coffin-plate, his face brightened,—nay, became radiant as the visage of a saint
in a cathedral window. Doubtless, urges the reader,
Barney felt a spiritual ecstasy—a " rapt," as the
mother Maria Teresa calls it ? We do not
speculate—we speak to facts. Barney, having
devoured the inscription, brightened up, smote his
right leg with much vehemence, and with huge
strides walked onwards. The brief notice—that
last short history of the noisiest of us—" Peter
Blond, aged 64," told Barney that Mrs. Blond was
left a solitary widow, without a child, but with a
capital connexion. Shame upon ye, Barney !
And out upon the vile and sordid matters blighting
this beautiful, this liberal world,—that we should so
often look for self-promotion to the coffin-plates of
our neighbours ! In few words—the deceased

interred—Barney became the widow Blond's first man of business.

For three years did Barney, with exemplary skill direct the affairs of the late Peter Blond. For three years did he proceed, cautiously feeling his way, as he believed, to the respect of the trade, and, as he hoped, to the affections of his mistress; who, be it known, had some five-and-twenty years the advantage of her deceased lord, being all that time his junior. The house flourished—the widow had long since cast away an unbecoming mourning— Barney grew sleek as a beaver—and all things promised——no, there was one doubt, one fear would haunt our hero. With a curious superstition, Barney felt all about him insecure, until the church had laid its hands upon it. Besides—and why are we thus tardy in our justice?—Barney had his prin- ciples. As he became prosperous, he felt a growing respect for character; nor was it altogether self that rendered him thus sensitive; he had the feelings of a man, and saw the situation of the widow. Let the following dialogue be his testimony.

" As for the world, Mrs. Blond, depend upon it, the world grows wickeder and wickeder." So saying, Barney moved closer to the widow, whose good- natured face seemed little shadowed by the misan- thropy of her managing-man. The place was the

back-parlour—the time the hour of supper.   The
meal despatched, moral reflections—of which the
above is not an unfavourable sample—flowed like
a stream from the lips of Barney, evidently deeply
impressed with the worthlessness of all living flesh.
" It's enough, ma'am, to make a young man go into
a wood, and turn hermit."

" What's the matter, Mr. Palms?" asked the
still unanswered widow, for the sixth time.

" 'Tis a hard thing to say ; but I really do believe
that all mankind are villains."   (Whenever a gentleman says thus much, be assured, considerate
reader, that he contemplates an instant offer of
himself as a choice exception).

" What—all ! Mr. Palms ?"

" Nearly all, ma'am," responded Barney, showing
his teeth.   " Human creatures ! snakes upon two
legs, Mrs. Blond."

" Why—what—what has happened ?" asked the
widow, her face looking all the prettier for the
earnestness of its expression.

" I am sure, ma'am, if this house had been
roofed with silver, and floored with gold, I could
not have been more contented with it.   Since the
death of your husband, no one has been so happy
as I."

" Mr. Palms !"

" I—I won't say no one, ma'am ; but it's hard

to leave when one might be so very, very comfortable."

"Oh! I perceive, Mr. Palms," tranquilly remarked the widow—"you have in view a better
situation?"

"Better!" echoed Barney, in a hopeless tone,
at the same time venturing a leer of soft reproach
—"better!"

"Then what compels you to leave me?"

"You do," and Barney was almost strangled with
tenderness.

"I! Mr. Palms?"

"For myself, ma'am, I care little what the world
says. I—I hope I am an old file that defies the
tooth of slanderous serpents. But, ma'am, I can't
feel myself a man, and stand by to hear you
wronged. What is gold to a good name!"

"Pray explain, Mr. Palms. In a word, sir,
what"——

"The neighbours, ma'am—the neighbours,"
replied Barney, in deep expressive notes.

"And what of the neighbours?" briskly interrogated Mrs. Blond.

Barney, with exquisite delicacy evading a reply,
proceeded—"I have made up all the books; the
accounts are balanced to a farthing. Since your
affairs have been in my hands, Mrs. Blond, I hope
I may say they have not suffered."

" There never was a better book-keeper, Mr.
Palms. But, sir, you spoke of the neighbours—
what do they say—what dare they say ?"

" Well, ma'am," and Barney did a violence to
his feelings as he spoke, " the woman to the right
tells every body—the Lord forgive her !—that we—
that is, you and I, ma'am, are truly and lawfully
married !"

" Married !" cried Mrs. Blond, in a voice that
spoke a full knowledge of the awful responsibility.
—" Married !"

" That's not the worst."—Mrs. Blond looked
doubtingly.—" That's not the worst : for the woman
to the left, with all her teeth and nails, denies it.
She says,"——

Little Mrs. Blond breathed hard with suppressed
disgust at the malevolence of the world. " And
what does she say ?"

" She swears we certainly are not married ; but
swears as strongly, that—that—we—ought—to—
be." Mrs. Blond sat silent and flushing. Barney,
with profitable insensibility, mistaking the blushes
of offended beauty for the tumultuous confusion of
a surprised heart, dropped upon his knees, and
seized the hand of the widow. At that instant—and
as though by conspiracy—out went the candle !—
at the same point of time, to complete the confusion of the widow, Bobby, the boy, coming to the

door, bawled through the darkness—"Is Mr.
Palms gone home, ma'am ?—may I lock up ?" Barney scrambled to his feet—and the widow unconsciously called for a light.   A light was instantly
supplied by the staring boy, who was directed by
his mistress to attend Barney to the door.   Palms
followed Bobby a few paces, then stopping short,
returned to the widow.   "As I said, dear Mrs.
Blond—as I said, ma'am, what is gold to a good
name ?"   Mrs. Blond said nothing.   Barney, taking silence for his best friend, in plain direct terms
urged his suit.   It was apparent that late incidents
had had their due effect on the prudence of the
widow.   For at his vigorous solicitation, she promised to meet Barney at the church.   That the
ceremony might attract no attention on the part of
gossiping neighbours, Mrs. Blond stipulated that
it should take place at a certain little village on the
Sussex coast.   All this negotiation was the fruit of
scarcely five minutes, Bobby standing with his
finger on the street-door latch. Barney walked "like
man new made" to the spot where the boy, with a
candle twixt his fingers, in fine *chiar'oscuro* awaited
him. Now Barney, looking down upon the urchin,
saw his eyes twinkling with meaning, and his mouth
drawn up like a rabbit's into a smothered titter.
On this, anticipating somewhat his dominorial rights,
Barney boxed the boy's ears, calling him "a

————sneering little scoundrel." He then strided into the street, and like a lover gazed on the moon-light. The clear beam fell upon the house, and as Barney gazed at the golden letters " Blond," he might be dreaming, but he saw them fade and disappear, and in their place beam forth, in lambent brightness—" Palms."

But a few days and Barney was wandering— musing on wedding-rings—on the Sussex shore. It had been arranged by the widow and himself, that they should separately leave town, and meet at the church door on the appointed morning. Barney had engaged the best apartments at the best inn, and in eight-and-forty hours he might call the widow, with all her funded wealth, her stock, and outstanding debts, his own. His feelings seriously directed by the coming event, he attended the parish church with the best intentions. But where shall weak man hide, where temptation is not? Placed immediately opposite to the destroy- eyes of woman, do not our resolutions, though ranite, melt like wax? Thus it was with was stared into weakness, falsehood— theme: a syren voice —at eleven—the ming tempter

l" in the time

of man, it is the four-and-twenty hours preceding
marriage, or, though culprits may differ—hanging.
Now Barney, though brimful of love, was in a
strange town, with nothing to do but to count the
minutes.   Thus, if at eleven o'clock he walked to
the churchyard, it was not to lose his constancy,
but his time.   As for bed, could he sleep on the
eve of the glad to-morrow?   To the churchyard
then he sauntered. The night was dark—the wind
cold—he listened for the " voice of the charmer,"
and heard the owl hoot from the belfry. Thinking
he was tricked, he felt a touch of compunction for
the widow : blushing for his weakness, he turned to
seek his inn, when he felt his hand grasped, and a
low, soft " hush" fell upon his ear.   Ere he could
reply to the admonition, his legs were off the
ground—a bandage over his eyes and mouth—and
his arms pinioned.   Could Barney have been an
impartial judge, he himself would have eulogized
the celerity of the operation.   In a thought, he felt
himself rocking in a cradle : the plashing of oars
convinced him of his error : he was on " the wide
and open sea."

To be sold for a slave was the least Barney
looked for; perhaps to become the property of the
Grand Turk—to be promoted—(promoted !)—to
a keeper of the seraglio ! Barney thought of the
widow, and grew cold from head to sole.   Barney

was blindfolded; yet did he plainly see a gang of buccaniers with moustaches long as ordinary pig-tails. The boat was speedily alongside a very sus-picious looking craft. Barney was happily spared the sight of her.——The captive was lifted aboard, and unceremoniously, as a bale of coarse merchant dise, flung into a corner called a berth. This ac-seemed to be a preconcerted signal with wind and wave; for almost on the instant, a stiff gale sprang from the north-west—the sea rose in mountains, and the vessel, light as a cork, danced upon their tops. In this uproar, what was to be expected of the stomach of Barney, anything but amphibious? It was evident that his keepers had formed a right opinion of its weakness, for with a latent feeling of humanity—let us praise where praise is due—they had taken the bandage from Barney's mouth.

The storm roared itself, like a wilful child, to rest, and the morning dawned upon the wave, bright and gorgeous. It was the wedding morning of Barnaby Palms—and, lying coiled like a dis-tempered dog in his nook, he told the hours struck from the church, where, in brief time, a disap-pointed bride would weep for him. Barnaby sighed; the time wore on—he groaned: another hour, he called aloud; another and another, and he raved and stormed and begged to be put ashore. Coarse and violent as his persecutors had shown

themselves, they still were men ; and knowing that
the situation of Barney was—as the newspapers,
when the fact was known, would propound—more
easily felt than described,—they opened the door
of his prison, and suffered him to feel his way upon
deck. Barney saw no slave-ship—but the "Jemima,"
smuggling-cutter of Hythe.

"Shore ! shore !" exclaimed Barney, and he
looked with devouring eyes towards the beach.

"Ay, ay, sir," was the dogged reply of an old
tarpauling, "all in good time, your honour."

"Mayhap the gentleman never see'd Flushing,"
conjectured a second. "If so, we'll give him
passage free."

"My good fellows," cried Barney, whose extreme agitation rendered him insensible to the cold
irony of his captors, "my good fellows, I forgive
the joke—I—ha ! ha !—'twas a capital hoax—but
don't push it too far.   I must go ashore."

One of the crew approached him, and with a
confidential air, asked—"Can you swim ?"

"No—no—no !" cried Barney, scarcely repress-
ing his tears.

"What a pity !—for we can't spare you a boat.
Up with the anchor, lads."

"Gentlemen—I tell you I am looked for—I am
expected—I—I am going to be married !"

"Oh !" cried three or four, as though at once

won by the necessities of Barney, "he's going to
be married, lads—let's give him a wedding-suit."

Ere Barney could inquire into the liberal proposition, a bucket of tar was placed at his feet.
" Now, sir," asked one of the sailors, with forced
politeness, at the same time poising in his hand a
brush dropping the unsavory liquid—"now, sir,
which will you have on first, your waistcoat or your
breeches?" Barney opened his mouth, no doubt
to proclaim his preference, when the brush, maliciously directed, stopt the communication. Then
straightway, Barney grinning horribly the while,
was he daubed from head to heels. The clock struck
as the operation was finished.

" Ugh ! oh ! murder ! let me go ashore—let me
fly"—gasped the now water-proof Barney.

" Jack, the gentleman wants to fly ; where's his
wings ?"

With a noble sacrifice to the desires of the visitor,
the only feather-bed aboard was brought upon deck,
instantly unripped, and its contents carefully distributed about the person of Barney. As he picked
the feathers from his eyes and mouth, and blew out
his big cheeks, he looked a monstrous mixture of
the ape and penguin. " There—I declare," exclaimed one of his valets, " talk of a wedding !—
why you're drest for Neptune's daughter." The
boat was then brought alongside. Barnaby very

gladly took a seat in it, and four of the crew prepared to pull him ashore.   "I wonder," said one
of the men, "what's become of that fellow—Barnaby Palms I think they called him—who, when
he was turned from the firm of Nokes and Styles,
informed about that little matter of French lace?
I wonder what's become of him!"   Here Barnaby
might have been communicative; he said nothing,
but shook his feathers.   Having reached the shore,
the men insisted upon carrying Barney into the
churchyard——to the very spot where he was to
have met the false fair, from certain after circumstances shrewdly suspected to be the lawful wife of
one of the smugglers.

In a thought the conspirators had vanished, and
Barney was alone among the tombs.   Hearing the
sound of voices, and confused by the ludicrous
spectacle he presented, he ran blindly forward, was
tripped up by some osiers, and rolled headlong into
a grave, dug, as it would seem, on purpose, that
very morning.   As he lay stunned and confounded,
the bells rang out a merry peal, striking into Barney
a sense of his situation.   He rose upon his feet, and
with his hands grasping the edge of the grave he
lifted his head half way above the surface, and saw
—proceeding from the church—a blushing, new-
made bride, in the person of the late Mrs. Blond,
—and in her happy husband, the silkman from the

opposite shop.   Mrs. Blond had long reflected on
his secret offers, but the wisdom of Barney—his
fine delicate sense of feeling his way—had fixed her
for ever.   The silkman walked on, a bridegroom :
Barney stood where he was, a bachelor.   His rival
was bound for life : Barney was only tarred and
feathered !

CHAPTER IV.

In the foregoing chapters we have confined ourselves to two great disappointments of our hero,
who, however, as he felt his way through life, had
manifold small successes.   It is true that fortune,
when she promised most, had shown herself most
fickle ; yet had she rewarded Barney with a
thousand gifts.   Thus, ere he had completed his
three-and-fortieth year, Barney had " land and
beeves."   His miraculous sense of touch, like that
of Midas, had turned some of the dirtiest matters
into gold.   (Indeed, when we daily witness the
alchymy exercised by some folks, we think little
of the wonders of the long-eared king.)   It is
confessed, he had groped in dark corners for his
wealth—but then, how much higher his merit—
how much greater the discovery ?   It is only the

vulgar mind that thinks to win its fortune along the
broad highway of life, in clearest day; the nobler
genius, hugging itself in its supremacy, searches
pits and holes, with this sustaining creed—that
though the prize acquired be not really of half the
worth to that picked up in open light, it has to the
finder a double value, because obtained in secrecy
and gloom.

" A broken heart, Mr. Palms! you don't believe
in any such nonsense?"

In truth, Barney was not so weak; since he felt
himself a reasoning creature he had ever doubted
that much talked of phenomenon: moreover, a
recent visit to the museum at Surgeon's Hall had
confirmed him in his unbelief; he had seen, to the
best of his memory, no such preparation.   Hence,
he had used the words "a broken heart," as, we
trust, a pardonable figure of speech.   " To be sure
not, Mr. Fitch; to be sure not.   All I meant to
say was, that if Louisa"—

" You are a steady, sober man, Mr. Palms—
what is more, you have an excellent business,
Louisa wants a husband—you want a wife—I consent to the match—you don't object to it—then
what more need be said about the matter ?"

The speaker who was thus smoothing Barney's
walk to the church, was, in the course of events,
soon destined to go thither himself; certain it is,

he looked affianced to the undertaker. " A broken heart ! ha ! ha !" and the old, white-haired gentle-man crowed like a cock at the extravagance.

Barney smiled an instant approval of the old man's merriment, and then, looking becomingly grave, observed, " And—and your fortune, Mr. Fitch ?"

" Every penny yours—every penny, when—when I die," and Mr. Fitch straitened his back, and shook his head, and winked his eye, as though he had spoken of the Greek Kalends, or the millennium. Death himself—though about to strike—must have been tickled at the gay self-assurance of brave four-score.

" And the day,—the happy day, Mr. Fitch ?"

" Humph ! the day ? say Thursday, Barney—yes, Thursday. We'll keep the wedding at—at my friend Clay's house—the Fox-and-Goose at Stepney."

Now, Barney, since his affair with the widow Blond, was become less confident of his sorcery over the gentle sex ; and had thus, with the wisdom which haunted him through life, felt his way to the affec tions of Louisa, through the medium of her grand-father. Sure we are that Barney, in all he had said or looked at his bride, had never transgressed the bounds of the coldest drawn civility : the iciest nun had not complained of the warmth of Barney.

L 3

Louisa having no relative, no friend in the world, save her grandsire, was naturally enough, in the opinion of the venerable man—wholly and unreservedly at his disposal.   Having reared her from childhood, he looked upon her as so much live timber, to be carved into any image, after the fancy of the planter.   She might—indeed we must say she did—venture some remonstrance; but surely four-score better knew what was fitter for eighteen, than witless eighteen itself.   In a word, Louisa Fitch was to marry Barnaby Palms; the bride had received her orders from her rich grandfather—and Thursday was the day appointed.

At length, Barney approached the haven of his hopes.   He had felt his way to more than competence; he had now within a hair's breadth of his fingers a rich, a youthful, and not unhandsome bride; though in the main affairs of life, Barney shut his eyes to what is vulgarly called, and paid for, in some sort of coin—beauty.   Blind to outward bloom, he acknowledged virtue by the touch; and Louisa—on the death of her revered grandsire—was to have ten thousand pounds.   In the ears of Barney, the guineas were already ringing on the old man's tomb-stone!

Thursday came.   We will not dwell upon the emotions of the bride; such trifling—the more as it was unconsidered by our hero—accords not with the gravity of our theme—with the deep lesson that we hope to teach. Old Mr. Fitch and some half-dozen friends, all gaiety and smiles, were present: Barney was in his best, and Louisa was duly shrouded in white. The ceremony was concluded —despite the ominous spectres that even at the altar haunted the bridegroom. It might be the embarrassing novelty of his situation that deceived his senses, for, looking upward, he saw the wings of carved cherubims plumed with real feathers—and snuffing the air, he thought he scented the marine odour of tar. No matter; Barney was married. Placing the marble hand of his bride under his arm he quitted the church.

Up to this moment, old Mr. Fitch was gay and chirruping: whilst his benevolent tyranny was in course of execution, he was in the highest spirits. The knot, however, was no sooner tied, than— possibly from excess of joy—the old man turned ghastly pale. He was led from the church; but, ere he could gain the carriage at the gate, was compelled to rest himself; he sat upon a grave— and Barney approaching, looked at him, with an eye of anticipation. With some assistance, Mr. Fitch was placed in the coach; the party proceeded to the inn, and—the grandfather quickly rallying— there were high hopes of festive dinner. Vain are all earthly promises! Just as the first course was laid, the old man relapsed—was carried to bed—and, in three hours, was ready for the mattock and the spade. It was supposed that the extreme coldness of the church had quickened his end. We pass much woe and lamentation, to conclude our story.

Barney was the possessor of ten thousand pounds. Had he weakly consulted the wishes of Louisa, they had doubtless passed to another bridegroom: he had—he thanked his wisdom—felt his way through the grandfather!

It struck twelve as Barney sought his bridal couch. He had already one leg in bed, when a bright thought arrested him. Taking a candle, he withdrew from the chamber, to seek the room of the dead man. In good time, Barney had recollected the silly vanity of old Fitch, who was wont to carry in his pockets a thousand or two in bankpaper. This might be stolen; he, as heir, should instantly seize the property. As he became fully confirmed in this idea, a current of wind extinguished the candle. For a long time, Barney continued silently to feel his way; but the Fox-and-Goose was an old, old house—with corridor and passages, and winding staircases, and——

A shriek was heard, and no more!—

A coroner's inquest, sitting next day at the Fox-and-Goose, on the body of a gentleman discovered at the bottom of the stairs, returned a verdict of " Found dead."　This was of course in default of full evidence, otherwise the verdict would have run—" *Died of too much feeling his way.*"

Poor Barney ! he had smiled—nay, in his heart had chuckled—when he say old Fitch seated on a grave.　And now, had Barney " felt his way !"

TITUS TRUMPS;

THE MAN OF "MANY HOPES."

CHAPTER I.

It is recorded in the family archives of the Trumps, that at a very early age, our hero Titus gave striking promise of that faculty which, in his mature days, made him a proverb to all who knew him. A sheep-stealer of considerable celebrity—a luckless Jason—was about to pay the penalty of his unlawful love for other people's mutton; in hard, worldly phrase, was sentenced to be hanged. Many sheep had of late been missed, and the judge of the assize had, with considerable distress of mind, expressed his determination to make an example for the benefit of society. Gubbins was to be strangled, not for his proper crime alone, but for "an example" to society. Dame Trumps, the grandmother of little Titus, took the most laudable pains to impress upon the child a religious horror of the wickedness of Gubbins, dwelling very minutely on the awful ceremony to take place the

next morning; and marshalling to the fancy of the
bewildered infant, the sheriff, the parson, the javelin
men, the hangman, the constables, all the actors in
the social tragedy; Titus looking sadder and sadder
as the procession lengthened.   There was silence,
and the dame had renewed her darning, when little
Titus jumped from his stool at his grandam's feet,
and clapping his hands, leapt and laughed to the
astonishment of the old lady.

"You wicked child! what will become of you?
don't I tell you that to-morrow morning, the people
at the prison are ordered to take Gubbins out and
hang him—eh?" cried grandmother.

"Yes, I know—I know," said Titus, "only,
perhaps, grandmother," and the boy smiled and
rubbed his little hands, "perhaps"—

"Perhaps!" exclaimed Mrs. Trumps, "perhaps
what?"

"Perhaps they may forget it," said the boy,
and the hope had no sooner flashed upon him, than
it grew into a certainty.   This little story of the
nursery we had omitted, did it not, in an especial
manner, mark the development of that peculiarity
which clung to Titus to his last hour.   With Titus
there was neither past nor present; he lived in the
future.   Nothing about him was real; he dwelt in
a world of shadows: the tangible good was always

that *to come*.   His life had no yesterday, no to-day
—it was a life entirely made of to-morrows.

Whether the temperament of Titus be happy or
unfortunate—whether it was to him a fatal weakness, or a prosperous strength, the reader, if he
will attend the adventures of our " Man of Many
Hopes," may, for himself determine.

Titus Trumps, inheriting a small patrimony
from his deceased father, and having endowed himself with great hopes of an improved income from
a maternal maiden aunt, had never addressed himself to any calling.   A mere trade was vulgar, and
the more to be eschewed as he had assured himself
of the property of his sire's sister: she was a prudent, thrifty woman, and every day must add to her
wealth.   That the amount of her property was not
known, was, in the mind of Trumps, an assurance
of its immensity.   She dwelt in a small comfortable
cottage, where Titus was wont to be a frequent
visitor.   Indeed, his unchecked flow of spirits made
him a general favourite; and Miss Virginia Trumps
did not deserve the reproach, too frequently and
too hastily bestowed upon ungathered maidens.
She was a happy, equable soul, with a face for a
smile, nay, with lungs for laughter.   Titus sat one
day at tea with his aunt, when, to her surprise, he
advanced the following insinuation.

" Now, I dare say, aunt, you—you have some-where, another tea-pot besides that ?"

" To be sure, Tity," said Miss Trumps, " why, what put that in your head ?"

" I mean, aunt—ha ! ha !—perhaps, a rich, cu-rious tea-pot, eh ?" and Trumps rubbed his hands, and looked laughingly at the spinster.

" Well, I declare ! was there ever such a boy !"— and the old maid laughed in concert.

" I was sure you had, aunt—ha ! ha !—certain of it—a rich tea-pot, eh ? too rich for every day, eh ?"—and Titus twinkled his eyes, and rubbed his hands with glee.

" To be sure : every day, indeed ?—your dear uncle Robert, that was carried up the country by the black princess, and never heard of again"—

" Who knows !" interrupted Trumps, touched by his deceiver, hope—" who knows ? Perhaps, I've a cousin king somewhere—eh, who knows ?"

" Didn't he bring me a tea-pot from Canton ?" said Miss Trumps, unmindful of the possible honour accruing to her from a regal nephew.

" And you have hoarded it up,—you wouldn't take any money for it ?" cried Titus.

" Not its weight in gold," exclaimed Miss Trumps, with considerable emphasis ; and the heart of Titus leapt at the avowal.

The reader may, with the maiden aunt, feel some

surprise at the interest taken by Titus in tea-pots. Let us explain. Titus had only that morning read an account of the death of an old solitary woman, who, though passing as very poor among her neighbours, had left, with other hoarded wealth, a large tea-pot filled with guineas. Miss Trumps was about the age of the deceased woman—like her she lived alone—was very saving,—seldom stirred out, and was, indeed, in the opinion of Titus,—an opinion confirmed after a scrutinising view of his beloved aunt—the very woman to hoard guineas in a tea-pot. The significant manner with which his aunt declared the utensil to be worth its weight in gold, convinced Titus beyond all chilling doubt, that it was brim-full of that precious metal. In fact, the thing spoke for itself—indeed, she had owned it: the tea-pot was worth "its weight in gold !" Long before Titus had taken his leave, his hopes had conjured up the largest tea-pot ever manufactured in China, and had calculated the greatest number of guineas that could, by possibility, be laid in it.

Titus Trumps was in his two-and-twentieth year, when, full of hope, he sat in a London coach on his way to the metropolis. He had no friends, no acquaintance dwelling there, but he never doubted that he should immediately obtain those desirable advantages. He already saw himself in a circle of the most amiable, the most obliging people. How many men had walked to London with only a staff —had slept on the road by hay-stacks — had eaten cresses and dry bread, and had entered the capital of the world with blisters at their soles, and not a farthing in their pockets, and had afterwards become golden merchants ; yea, had, in their day, been aldermen and mayors, knights and baronets, to boot,—and dying, had left alms-houses for the helpless and the aged ! Leaning back in the coach, Titus with half-closed eyes, already saw himself at court — already felt the royal sword upon his shoulder—already beheld, as in a vision, his female pensioners in white caps and aprons—his old, old men, in decent grey ! Such were the hopes of Titus Trumps, when the coach suddenly stopt to change horses. A man ran from a neighbouring house to the dismounted coachman.

" Inside place, coachman ?" said the man.

" Full," said the laconic coachman. " One out."

"Oh ! she can't go out in this rain," said the man.—It poured a deluge.

" Stay behind, then," said the accommodating driver.

" But you don't know who she is"—here the stranger half-whispered confidentially to the coachman, Trumps distinctly hearing the important communication. " She's daughter of General Wolfe."

The coachman scratched his head at the intelligence, glanced inside the coach to assure himself that it was full, then cast his eye up at the box, and observed—" Wrap her up—plenty of coats."

At this instant the lady appeared, a damsel following her with a couple of fragile band-boxes. " Outside ! in such weather—impossible," cried the lady, on learning the proposal of the coachman.

" Sorry for it—time's up," said the driver, and he mounted the box.

"Stop—stop," cried Trumps, thrusting himself half out of the coach-window—and now smiling on the lady, and now looking from side to side for the coachman and guard, both of whom he requested, in a most peremptory manner, to attend to him.—" Stop—stop—here, guard—I'll get out —I'll"—and Trumps, opening the door, jumped from the coach. " Miss Wolfe can have my place," said Titus, bowing to the lady, greatly confused by the unexpected gallantry of the young and handsome passenger,—for Titus was a smart-looking fellow—the coachman and the guard exchanging looks of wonder, rather than admiration, at the generosity of the inside gentleman.

" Really—couldn't think of depriving the gentleman—in such dreadful weather, too,"—objected the young lady.

" Only a few drops—a passing shower," said the

hopeful Trumps, the rain pouring as from twenty thousand spouts.

"Better get in, Miss," said the guard, assisting the young lady, who, with the meekness of the sex, suffered herself to be overcome.

"A lovely girl, that," said Titus Trumps, when mounted beside the coachman, who was wet and dripping as an otter.

"Very fairish, sir," replied the driver. "A little wet, isn't it?" he then observed, with a malicious smile at the situation of Titus.

"I—I don't think it will last," answered the sanguine Trumps.

"No, sir; I shouldn't think it would go beyond the month," was the satirical comment. Then, after a pause—"Few gentlemen, sir, as would turn themselves inside out, this weather. Shouldn't wonder, sir, if the ladies give you a medal. It is wet, isn't it?" asked the coachman, a stream pouring from the rim of his hat between the neck and neckcloth of Titus.

"It *can't* last," said Trumps, suppressing a shiver. "A very beautiful girl—I may say, an angel."

"Everybody to their taste, sir. To be sure, if she isn't quite an angel at present, why, you know, it's her own fault if she isn't by-and-by. Very wet, sir?"

" It's going off," cried Trumps.

" Yes, sir ; you may say the tide's running very fast down,—better put that coat about your legs, sir," said the benevolent coachman.

" Thank you—thank you. No, it can't last long," said Titus, the rain falling in sheets.

" No, sir, at this rate I don't see where it's to come from.—I hope the lady 's comfortable."

" She lives in London ?" asked Trumps.

" I believe you, sir,—one of the best houses in it. After your civility, sir, I'm sure they'd like to see you there; poor thing ! she might have caught her death, for it *is* wet, sir—isn't it ?"

Trumps made no answer; his thoughts were far away from the querist—and his feelings were weather-proof. The daughter of General Wolfe ! He had resigned his place to the child of a hero—to the offspring of an immortal soldier ! He had always felt a mysterious respect for the profession of arms; and how strange that, as it might be said, in his first entry into life, accident should have cast him near the daughter of the great Wolfe ! There was, doubtless, patronage in the family. The lady had looked smilingly upon him ! If, now, he should be presented with a commission ; and, if ordered abroad on some delicate and dangerous service, he should be able to distinguish himself in the eyes of the world ; and if, returning, his brows bound with laurels, and his breast bearing a dozen orders, he should ask and win the lady for his wife! Or, if—for it was as well to consider the calamitous part of war—if he should be killed? Well he would die upon the bed of glory. No, there was gloom upon that picture, and he would not look on it. He might be slightly wounded, and would survive to receive the thanks of the army—of the parliament! —They made baronets, earls, marquises, dukes of prosperous heroes! He might be the father of a family, and his eldest son (the pledge of himself and the unsuspecting lady inside) might bear the royal train at the next coronation! How wise in him to have always spurned a trade! He might have been a grocer! He who would sit among the peers of England, and mend and make laws, might have vended barley-sugar—dealt in figs! That he should have been enabled to oblige Miss Wolfe! On what trivial things—such was the trite reflection of our traveller—hung the fate of man! And for twenty minutes, or more, Titus Trumps was a military duke, a conqueror, with at least one estate in six different countries, and with, perhaps, the office of commander-in-chief at home. Happy Titus Trumps! Quick and bountiful are the gifts of hope; and now, in her brightest blue, and with her sunniest looks, she leaned upon her anchor, and smiled graciously on Titus, who, though wet as a soaked sponge, was glowing in imaginary place.

The coach arrived late in London; Trumps hastened to descend, that he might hand the lady out. Quick as he was, he had been anticipated in that pleasing attention by a tall, sallow young man, sparkishly habited, who looked rather frowningly upon the advances of our hero.

"The gentleman had been so kind as to give up his place;" the tall young man bowed stiffly. "Dear heart!" added the lady, he was "very wet."

"Not at all——not in the least——perhaps, a little damp," replied the saturated Trumps. "He trusted, however, that Miss Wolfe"——

The tall young man bent his brows, the lady coloured, and Titus paused: ere he could again essay a speech, the fair damsel was lifted into a hackney-coach by the strange young gentleman, who followed and seated himself authoritatively beside her. If the reader have ever seen a tipstaff in a coach with his victim, he has seen, in the deportment of the functionary, the same cold consequence displayed by the companion of "Miss Wolfe." He sat, very like a bailiff or a brute of a husband. "Her brother, no doubt," thought Trumps, as the coach drove away: that the lady should be already

a wife, never suggested itself: though, had a fear
of that calamity possessed Titus, he would have
found comfort in the unhealthy complexion of her
yoke-fellow;—a man with such looks could not live
many months.   Trumps, foiled in his hopes of the
lady's single blessedness, would have sought comfort in her speedy widowhood.

CHAPTER II.

THE next morning, Trumps awoke haggard and
feverish. He had, in his dreams, been at Quebec—
had achieved the most heroic feats—had received
Miss Wolfe from the hands of her father—and had
been married by the chaplain of the garrison, the
troops forming in hollow square during the ceremony.   The marriage was no sooner solemnized,
than the dreamer heard the wild yell of the Indians
—the bride was torn from his arms—he had followed her through woods and swamps—and had at
last fallen into the hands of the savages.   Already,
the chief had flung him upon the earth—already,
the knife glittered in his eyes—already, the wild
man was about to add another scalp to his hundred, when Trumps, even dreaming, found hope in
the crisis; for he thought he wore a wig!   With
this exulting feeling, he awoke.   It was with some

satisfaction that he discovered his head upon a
goose-feather pillow—and on that head, the pride
of his heart, natural locks in luxuriant growth.
He ran his fingers through his curls, and felt himself a man again.

"Your name, sir, is "——

"Trumps—Titus Trumps," said our hero,
holding forth his hand to receive a letter brought
by the waiter, as Trumps seated himself for breakfast.

"Not for you, then, sir," said the man. "Beg
your pardon—gentleman in thirty-two," and the
servant quitted the room, to the disappointment of
Trumps, who, without any reasonable expectation
of the favour, saw in the missive a letter from his
aunt, and, looking inside it with the eyes of hope,
beheld there a bank-bill to a handsome amount.
"She certainly did not promise to write," thought
Trumps, buttering his roll; "but then there was
no knowing—she might." Trumps put the first
morsel in his mouth, then instantly jumped up, and
violently rang the bell. The waiter immediately
appeared.

"What might want, sir?" asked the man, looking
seriously at Titus, in whose face were strong marks
of disgust.

"Want! why, my man—this is—really—this is
very bad butter," said Trumps.

The waiter smiled, closed his hands, and with a slight, graceful bow, replied,—" Very bad, indeed, sir."

" And—and," Trumps stammered, confused by the acquiescence of the man—" and you don't call this tea? It's chopped birch—isn't it?"

Again the waiter smiled, closed his hands, bowed, and audibly answered,—" Chopped birch."

" Well! if ever I—and the milk—you don't call it milk—I—I call it water," said the astonished Trumps.

" Water, sir" observed Robert Straight, to the astonishment of the discontented guest.

" And this chop—phewgh !—you don't pretend to say it's eatable?" cried Trumps.

Robert Straight raised the accused article to his nose, then " took't away again," slightly lifted his shoulders, and said with some emphasis, — " Not eatable, sir."

Trumps felt himself defeated. He had condemned everything upon the table, and the waiter, having cheerfully acquiesced in his conviction, left him without words. It was useless to complain, where there was such unanimity of opinion. Titus looked about him for new matter of discontent, but found that he had exhausted every subject. Had Robert declared the butter to be sweet as new-blown hawthorn—the tea, from the private chest of the Emperor of China himself—the milk, the purest cream, and the chop but that morning from the living lamb, Trumps would have been pleased—gratified with the opposition of sentiment. It would have been some exercise for him to have contested the points ; but they were at once given up, quietly yielded by the enemy, and further words were but vain and useless flourishes. As nothing was disputed, nothing was to be said. Hence, Trumps ate the condemned breakfast in silent resignation, Robert Straight leaving him the full enjoyment of his undisputed opinion. (It would have been well, however, had Robert not always thus accommodated himself to the opinions of others—had he now and then ventured to demur, we think much remorse might have been spared him. Robert appeared a mild, peaceable man, and yet he had been accused by many of her conniving gossips, of the death of the wife of his bosom. " Ar'n't you a villain and a vagabond ?" Mrs. Straight would ask of her husband twenty times a day; and as often as she asked the question, so often would her impartial husband make answer and say,—" Both, my love; both." No woman could endure such treatment long : the poor creature died of a broken heart ; and it was roundly asserted, and seemingly with great truth, that she expired of the slow cruelty of her tyrannical helpmate.)

" You saw that lady who came last night by the coach ? " asked Trumps of Robert, summoned in due season to clear the table.

" Saw the lady, sir," said Robert.

" I mean Miss Wolfe."

" Oh ! Ha !—yes, Miss Wolfe," said the smiling Robert, whose creed it was to contradict nobody.

" She's very handsome; perhaps, very rich ?" remarked Trumps carelessly.

" Very handsome—very rich," cried Robert, to the satisfaction of Titus.

" People in your situation hear a great deal about high folks, eh ?" asked Trumps.

" Great deal," answered Robert.

" You know where that lady lives?" inquired Titus.

" Know where she lives," replied Robert.

" She is not engaged—I mean, there is no talk of ?"——

" Not engaged,—no talk," was the answer of Robert.

" And that young man, who—by the way, it was odd, that she should travel alone," said Titus.

" Odd, sir," responded Robert.

" And in a public coach, eh ?"

" Public coach, sir."

" Though your people of real dignity have no affectation," said Trumps.

"No affectation," answered Robert.

"It's only your mushrooms, who "——

"Only mushrooms, sir," replied Straight.

"Her father—ha!—a great man?"

"Very large, sir."

"But that young gentleman who was waiting for her? I suppose, her brother?" questioned Trumps, somewhat earnestly.

"Her brother," echoed Robert Straight; and if Trumps had supposed him to have been her father, —"her father" would have been the response of the accommodating Robert.

"You couldn't tell me where she lives?" asked Titus.

"Couldn't tell you where she lives, sir," chimed Straight.

"That's strange, eh?"

"Strange, sir;" and all this time, Robert was busily employed clearing the table, and when Trumps was about to put another question to that human echo, Straight had vanished.

"Not engaged! No—I was sure of that, quite sure," said the sanguine young gentleman, and he fell into a deep study, contemplating the necessary ways and means for the lawful possession of Miss Wolfe. "Waiter," cried Trumps, having at length decided upon the first step,—"waiter," and Robert, who was gliding across the floor, again

stood before Titus. " You perfectly recollect that
lady?"

" Perfectly: red ribands—beaver hat—silk gown,"
said Straight.

" Now, attend to me. I'll give you seven shillings,—you hear?"

" Seven shillings," replied the waiter very cor-
rectly.

" If you will procure for me the address of that
lady—and mind, not a word to anybody."

" Address, and not a word," answered Robert,
and departed to obtain the information; not that it
was at all necessary for him to quit the room for
the intelligence, as he was already in full possession
of it: but the pains he took seemed to enhance the
value of the knowledge to be conveyed, making it
better worth the offered price. " There, sir—the
address," said Robert, presenting the delighted
Trumps with a written card.

" I'll go this very morning," exclaimed Trumps.
" My bill."

" Don't you stay to-night, sir?" asked the
waiter.

" No—no: for my luggage, you can send it to
this address;" for, of course, thought Trumps,
they'll entertain me as their guest. " Humph—
ha!" said Titus, viewing himself in a glass, " must
brush up a little. A new loop in my hat—pshaw!

a new hat altogether—some new lace ruffles,—and,
egad ! this silver ring of grandfather's looks like a
lump of pewter on my finger—a little diamond
there won't be thrown away ; no, no, it doesn't
rain generals' daughters every day—I can afford
to lay out for an heiress ;" for in the flutter of his
hopes, Trumps had quite forgotten the " brother"
of the lady.   " Must dress to-day, if I'm a sloven
all my life," cried Trumps, still self-communing,
and he sallied into the street, determined to purchase the necessary decorations.   Titus had in his
purse little more than fifty guineas ; never before
had fifty guineas seemed such a trifle.   Elated with
the certainty of speedy fortune—for with Titus the
golden gift was no longer doubtful—he felt all the
carelessness, the indifference of a sultan towards the
petty cash about him.   Arithmetic seemed a science
suddenly unworthy of him—he might, in the fulness
of his wealth, snap his fingers at figures.   Such were
his exulting thoughts as he entered a shop, smitten
with the show of lace, with its cobweb meshes displayed to catch the flies without.   The bargain was
soon struck—the most expensive cravats and ruffles
ordered to the inn, a hat, furnished with a glittering
loop, and a cane, surmounted by a gold head, with
chasing worthy of a Cellini, speedily followed, and
Trumps thought himself equipped not for conquest
—for the victory was gained—but for a triumphal

entry. Thirty guineas yet remained to him, when he suddenly paused at the window of a jeweller. At all events, he would ask the price of a ring.

" The finest of fine waters," said Mr. Glitter, the tradesman, as he presented a diamond ring to Trumps, who looked down upon it, whilst a smile played about his lips, and his eyes melted at the bauble. The jeweller in a moment knew his man. " If the stone were only as big again, upon my honour, sir, I can't tell you what it would be worth —I may say, money couldn't buy it." Still Trumps gazed at the diamond. " There, sir ; look at the delicacy of the chasing. Ha ! I don't know what I'd give for a workman who could do the like ; the artist who did that, he's dead, poor man : any money is given for his work. Look at the stone any way, sir. Let a man travel through the centre of the earth, sir, and with that diamond on his finger, he'd want no light."

Trumps stood, his eyes fixed upon the stone. " I think 'tis too small for me," he ventured to observe.

" Try it, sir—try it—bless me !—well, you have a curiosity there,"—and Glitter raised his eyebrows and puckered his mouth, as he took up the silver seal-ring, laid down by Trumps.

" It was in our family," said Titus, a little abashed at the native vulgarity of the relic, brought

M 5

out in forcible contrast by the surrounding splendour. "Fits, I declare," said Trumps, placing the diamond ring on the finger, too long disgraced by the family treasure.

"Sir, I should be proud to sell you that ring, if I could afford it, at half price. As it is, I'll strike off five guineas."

Trumps looked at the ring, and with some anxiety, asked—"How much."

"As I said, sir," replied Glitter, "I'll let you have the ring cheaper than any gentleman I have ever clapped my eyes upon. And I'll tell you why, sir—you'll do especial credit to the ring. Now, there are some hands, that, upon my honour, sir, it goes to my heart to let my goods go upon ; hands ! did I say, sir,—lumps of flesh, with skin like sole-skin. It does I say go to my heart, to think of the pain and labour used to get the jewel from the mine—of the skill in cutting it—the taste and delicacy of setting a diamond as that is set—and after all, to be condemned to a hand, as red and as coarse as beef, sir ! Upon my honour, sir, I do feel—but what can we do in business ?—still I do feel that I am sometimes committing a sin in letting my goods go upon such fingers. May I never sell another stone, sir, if except his grace, the Duke of Marlborough—perhaps, for hands do run in families —perhaps, sir"—and Glitter placed his palms flatly against each other, and almost brought his forehead to the counter—"perhaps, I have the honour of addressing a branch of that distinguished house?"

" No," said Trumps, in a soft, low voice.

" I declare, sir, by your hand—and I am accounted a tolerable judge in such matters—I should have thought you a younger brother—or"—

" How much?" said Trumps, looking wistfully at the ring.

" Well, sir, as this is our first transaction—and I hope, sir, for the honour of your countenance for many years to come—I—I'll try and say five-and-thirty guineas," said the obliging Glitter.

The face of Trumps darkened at the sum, and with a melancholy look, he was about to draw the desired gem from his finger. Glitter observed the act, and suddenly raised his hands.

" But as I said—to you, sir—and in favour of your hand, for I should feel my goods recommended by such fingers—I will venture to say, thirty guineas."

" It's very cheap, no doubt—very cheap," said the prudent Trumps, " but I fear at present—I— I fear I can't afford it."

" Ha! ha! excuse my freedom, sir—I can't help laughing—not afford? Ha, sir! had I your wealth—well, well—I mean, the prospects that a

gentleman like you must have in a town like this—
pardon my freedom, sir,—the fortunes that many
lovely women would be proud to lay at your feet—
excuse my freedom, sir—but where merit is so
apparent—excuse my freedom"—

" Thirty guineas," repeated Trumps, and still
the ring remained upon his finger.

" As I'm an honest man, and a liveryman, sir,
I sold the fellow of it to the Marquis of——but I'll
not mention his name—for forty guineas. To be
sure, the marquis has a hand like Magog; though,
for all its size, it dips pretty deeply, sir—pretty
deeply, we know where"—and Glitter winked.

" I can't afford it," said Trumps, and he put his
thumb and finger to the ring and paused, as he
caught the supplicating looks of the jeweller.

" Don't, sir, don't—I cannot bear to see you
take it off in this shop. There—I'll say eight-and-
twenty; and after that, as I'm a Christian, sir, I
cannot speak again."

Trumps felt it would have been ungrateful in
him to have rejected such complacency. He had,
it was true, but thirty guineas. What of it? Could
he not raise money upon his ten cottages? Besides,
there were prospects, as the tradesman sagaciously
declared, beaming brightly on him ! The ring was
moreover a necessary—nay, an indispensable ornament to a gentleman; especially so, in the felicitous

circumstances in which Trumps found himself. It was a mute, yet delicate and brilliant avowal of gentility. A diamond like that was at once an introduction and a certificate. He had, it was true, only thirty guineas—only thirty from the fifty, his small income for the year—for the three hundred and sixty-five dinners required by the human animal in twelvemonths; with all the other small essentials demanded by a sense of comfort and propriety. For a moment, he paused; and then Miss Wolfe, leaning on a silver anchor, rose before him; and he plunged his hand into his pocket, and drew therefrom all his coined treasure. He paid for the diamond ring, placed the silver seal-ring of the family in the lightened purse, and was about to quit the shop, when a sense of new wants fell upon him. " Could Mr. Glitter recommend a pair of knee-buckles?"

" The prettiest things ever made; not fifty pair been sold yet—and those to the nobility only; they were as yet scarcely out of the House of Lords." Such was the character, such the history, of a pair of blue steel buckles, set with tolerable paste.

" The stones are not real?" asked Trumps.

" No, sir; although they have the advantage of appearance. They look real, but between our-selves—I deceive no customer, sir—between ourselves, they are not.   But then, sir, with that diamond on your finger, who would suspect your knees?"

"That's very true," said Titus.

"If a gentleman's hand is the real thing, his knees may very safely be sham," declared the jeweller.

"Then these are very cheap?" for Trumps thought, with a passing pang, of his reduced store.

"Dirt," said Glitter, "a little two guineas."

"For false stones?" asked Trumps.

"They look real, sir, and we must always pay for appearance.   Well, say thirty-five shillings.   I tell you what—'tis only worth so much old silver; I'll take thirty, and the old seal-ring for the lot."

Trumps paid the money, surrendered the bit of family silver, and returned to his inn to dress. The cravat, ruffles, hat, and stick had been sent before, and awaited him in his bed-room; while he himself was the happy and important bearer of the diamond ring, and the paste knee-buckles.

Gentle reader, Trumps is at his toilette dressing for the lady of his hopes—the daughter of General Wolfe.

CHAPTER III.

In about two hours, Titus, arrayed as for a court, descended from his room. The waiters stared from the passage, the chambermaids hung over the banisters to catch a view of his departing skirts. His hair bore testimony to the skill of the barber—his cravat flowed gracefully and voluminously—his ruffles drooped in bunches over his hands—he carried his gold-headed cane as it were potent as the caduceus—his little finger glowed with the diamond ring—and his knees throbbed with a sense of new buckles. His hat, with broad gold loop, sat like a diadem upon his brow.

" Your bill, sir," said Robert, at the same time presenting that social annoyance.

" Oh ! ha ! I have changed my mind," that is, Titus had changed his guineas—" I—I shall come back."

" Then, we're not to send your luggage, sir ?" asked the servant.

" Not to-day," replied Trumps, and stepping into the street, he turned to seek the abode of the daughter of General Wolfe. He had proceeded a very little way, when the eyes of the passengers convinced him that he was really too finely appointed to appear uncovered in the street—that an article so daintily set forth ought to be conveyed to its destination in a case. He therefore called a coach, and in sonorous tones, ordered the man to drive to —— square.

Many and hard were the blows of the knocker, moved by the sinewy hand of the coachman. The door of the desired house flew open, and a porter, with severe looks, questioned the manners of the disturber; " a hackney-coachman had no *right* to make such a noise ;" thus looked the porter, whose stern face relaxed somewhat on the appearance of Trumps, who quietly suffered himself to be charged treble the fare, the coachman jocosely declaring that " the knock was worth half the money."

" My Lord, shall I take your card in to Sir Jeremy ?" asked a footman.

" Certainly," and Titus put his hand into his pocket ; though for what we are ignorant ; for sure we are he had no card about him. Perhaps, he " hoped." Withdrawing his hand with nothing in it, he said, " Trumps, Mr. Titus Trumps." And the footman departed with the name of our hero to Sir Jeremy Sloth, whose custom it was to give audience to everybody who sought him ; possibly, in the belief that nobody having suffered one interview, would have courage left for a second.

Sir Jeremy Sloth was a baronet, and had moreover slept and voted in three parliaments. He knew very little of the constitution, but a great deal of heraldry. In his character of senator, he never gave his vote, but we believe after long and painful consideration ; and as he was wont to complain that no time was allowed between the last speech on a question, and the division that decided it, he had always made up his mind to his vote long before the question came on. This was what he called getting in advance of the public business. And yet if Sir Jeremy had any fault, it was that he was a little dilatory—that he complained of customs and usages long established, as little other than novel innovations. " Men, it was plain, were in a hurry to bring about the end of the world, or they wouldn't go on so fast ;" such was the cry of Sir Jeremy, when the broad-wheeled waggon gave place to the stage-coach. One incident will illustrate the constitution of Sir Jeremy. He was one day in company with a royal duke, when a sudden storm came on : our baronet stood at the window— the duke sat far in the room. " Quite a storm, Sir Jeremy," said the duke. " It is, indeed," said the baronet. " Bless my heart !" exclaimed Sir Jeremy, " may it please your Royal Highness, if not too great a trouble, to come a little this way to the window to look at this—flash of lightning !"

Titus Trumps stood before Sir Jeremy Sloth, a short, slim, dry little man, constantly at work upon his dignity, in order as he vainly thought to make the most of it. With many slow flourishes of the hand, Sir Jeremy waved Titus into a seat. There was a silence of two minutes, and for any movement of the baronet, the pause might have continued. Titus hoped Sir Jeremy would speak first: at length, our hero opened the sitting by modestly observing—" Sir Jeremy, my name is Trumps." The baronet acknowledged the intelligence by a grave inclination of the head. " My name is Trumps," repeated Titus.

" Tromp?" asked the baronet, in a voice that almost chilled even the blood of our sanguine friend,—" Tromp?"

" —umps," said Titus, emphatically correcting the termination.

" Pardon me," said Sir Jeremy, with a sickly smile, " I thought, possibly, a descendant of the famous Dutch Admiral."

Titus was evidently struck by the words of the baronet; it had never occurred to him before: he might be a descendant, and still be ignorant of the honourable fact.

" Not a descendant?" asked the baronet, looking grimly at the perplexed Titus.

" Really, Sir Jeremy, I—I cannot take it upon me to say—such liberties are taken with names, that"—

" Right, sir; very right,"—for Sir Jeremy was upon his favourite theme—" for my part, I know not if I would not as severely punish offences against names as against the person."

" A name, Sir Jeremy, is often the best part of a man," said Titus.

" Very often," replied the baronet, with emphasis. He then returned to the introductory declaration of his visitor. " Your name is Trumps? Well, sir, so far we understand each other."

" I—I arrived in London last night," proceeded Trumps, the baronet strangely enough unmoved by the intelligence. Trumps added with significance, bowing, and exhibiting his teeth with a smile,—" by the coach, Sir Jeremy."

" A romantic occurrence," said the sarcastic baronet. " Inside or out ?"

" Really, Sir Jeremy, I am proud to say—very proud to say,—out." And again Trumps smiled.

" Your name is Trumps—you came to town by the coach—and you are proud to say outside,"— slowly summed up Sir Jeremy.

" And I—I felt it my duty to pay my respects at this house, without loss of time. I hope the young lady is quite well ?" and Trumps smiled again.

" Do I understand, Mr. Trumps, that your visit
here is for the sole object of inquiring into the condition of the health of "——

" Exactly, Sir Jeremy—exactly," cried Titus,
impatient of the slow verbosity of the baronet. " I
feared she might have caught cold."

" You are not an apothecary, Mr. Trumps?"
asked Sir Jeremy, and every second he grew more
dignified.

" No, sir," replied Titus, with a gasp.

" Then, sir, may a strange and humble individual
like myself, venture to ask what you are?" drawled
Sir Jeremy.

Trumps was frozen by the unlooked-for chilliness
of the baronet, and, after some hesitation, replied,
essaying another smile,—" Nothing."

" Nothing!" echoed Sir Jeremy.

" That is," quickly rejoined Trumps—" a gentleman." Saying which, Trumps felt himself exhausted. He had expected to be welcomed, embraced by a delighted circle, and he sat in the
drawing-room of Sir Jeremy Sloth, as in a snow
house.

" And you are intimate with the young lady in
whose health you have shown so kind an interest;
is it not so, Mr. Trumps?" inquired the baronet."

" I—I may say, that I was happy in being able
to show some attention, which "——

" Which she accepted?" asked Sir Jeremy with unusual celerity.

" Which she did me the honour most graciously to accept," replied Trumps.

" Out of town, perhaps?" inquired the baronet.

" Precisely, Sir Jeremy—precisely," and Trumps tried to laugh.

Sir Jeremy stretched his hand towards the bell— drew it back—then rose, and addressing his visitor as if addressing " the House," the honourable baronet was understood by our hero to say,—" Mr. Titus Trumps, gentleman, may I solicit of you the courtesy of remaining in this apartment until my return?"

Trumps felt abashed at the ceremonious request of the baronet, and slightly colouring, replied— " Certainly."

Sir Jeremy Sloth walked leisurely as a ghost in armour from the room, and Titus, with all his constitutional sprightliness, felt somewhat melancholy. He heard footsteps, and he almost hoped that it was the footman come to twirl him into the street. And then, his eye fell upon his diamond ring, and he became assured of respectful consideration. The baronet had been cold, certainly; perhaps, however, it was the custom of the baronetage to be a little frigid.

The door opened, and showed Sir Jeremy Sloth

leading in a lady with as much grace as if about to commence a minuet. Trumps rose from his chair, and wished to smile.

"Emily," thus spoke Sir Jeremy Sloth to the lady, who betrayed some confusion as her eyes met the handsome face, and glanced at the goodly figure of our hero—"Emily, I presume I introduce you to an old acquaintance?"

"Papa!" The lady was neither very young nor very handsome: she was trembling on the verge of thirty—(bosom friends declared she had long since gone over),—and was thin as a mortified nun: indeed, she was one of those useful persons in this world of temptation, whose very looks preach abstinence. Still, it was either the surprise of the introduction to Titus, or his features, or form, or both or all these together, that sent a passing look of interest to the face of Miss Sloth: for a moment, she looked like an old picture revived. "Papa!" said Miss Emily Sloth, and fluttered and blushed.

"Mr. Trephonius Trumps"—began Sir Jeremy—

"Titus," was the brief correction of our hero.

"Mr. Titus Trumps," and Sir Jeremy bowed an acknowledgment of his error. Then, turning to the lady,—"Mr. Titus Trumps is, as he assures me, not an apothecary; yet has he bestowed upon us the favour of this visit for the express purpose of inquiring into the condition of your health."

INTRODUCTION OF TITUS TRUMPS TO "MISS WOLFE."

Vol. III. Page 262.

Published by Henry Colburn, Great Marlborough Street, 1838.

" I trust, Sir Jeremy—I"—poor Titus was confounded by the mistake—" I hope, that the young
lady is well,—but, I—the truth is, Sir Jeremy, that
is not the young lady, I—no, Sir Jeremy,—not
the young lady."

" I understood, sir, that you spoke of my
daughter, and being anxious to"——

" No, Sir Jeremy, no ;" Trumps endeavoured to
smile very blandly, " I meant, the daughter of the
—the late general."

" Late general ?" and Sir Jeremy slowly chewed
the words.

" Of the hero—the"—and then Trumps made a
last effort, and drawing himself up, said very distinctly—" the daughter of General Wolfe."

" General Wolfe, sir ? In my house ?—Were you
informed that such a lady lived here ?"

" Yes, sir; I understood at the inn, where we
put up"——

" Inn, sir ? What inn ?" asked the baronet
haughtily.

" The Flower-Pot," replied Titus with great
humility.

" And I am to understand, sir, that you came
from the—the Flower-Pot ?" and to the dismay of
Trumps, he thought he saw a contemptuous smile
on the face of Emily as her father spoke. " From"
—the baronet paused to leer at the smart clothes

of his visitor—"From the Flower-Pot? You look like it."

Titus was about to answer, when the baronet authoritatively held up his hand, and then proceeded to put poor Trumps to the question. "There is something in your air, your demeanour, Mr. Trumps, that demands from me immediate attention."

Trumps, astonished at the sudden civility of the baronet, pressed his hat between his hands, and bowed.

"Will you tell me from what place you come?"

"Cirencester," said Trumps, "last night."

"Cirencester," said Emily to herself, and, a second afterwards, rang the bell.

"And the lady, who"—the baronet was interrupted by the appearance of the footman, who crossed to Miss Emily, and took her commands—"and the lady"——repeated Sir Jeremy, as the servant left the room.

"The lady, sir, whom I thought your relative, was in the stage-coach."

"My relative—in—in a stage-coach!" cried Sir Jeremy: had Trumps said the pillory, the assertion had not been more offensive.

"Inside;" replied Trumps, "for it was very wet, Sir Jeremy, and it was my good fortune to see Miss Wolfe"——

" Miss Wolfe !" exclaimed the baronet.

" Yes, papa," said Miss Sloth, tittering, " I assure you, the daughter of"——

" That is the lady," cried Titus, as the door opened and he caught the face of his fair fellow-passenger, who coloured when she saw him, then curtsied respectfully to Miss Sloth, and then played with her apron-strings. The curtsey and the dress of the girl smote the heart of our hero.

" Young woman," said Sir Jeremy sternly, " do you know this person?" and the baronet pointed one finger at Titus as he would have pointed at a cur suspected of insanity.

" The gentleman came in the coach with me, Sir Jeremy, and it was very wet, and he was very kind," said the girl.

" Kind ! young woman, I am afraid you have given yourself a false character," cried the baronet.

" I, Sir Jeremy ! La ! Sir Jeremy ;" and the girl burst into tears.

" Pray, young woman, what do you know of General Wolfe ?" asked her master with a terrible frown.

" My father keeps it, that's all," sobbed the maiden.

" Keeps it !" cried Trumps and the baronet, Miss Sloth biting her lips to suppress her laughter.

" It *was* the Jackdaw and Pitcher, but—but "——

" But,—what? Speak!" called out Sir Jeremy.

" But Sergeant Flam said he'd recruit at the house, if father would alter the sign, so he had 'em painted out, and the General painted in. False character! I'm sure, Sir Jeremy, if that gentleman has said anything that a gentleman should be ashamed of saying,"——

" Permit me, Sir Jeremy—I—there is no blame to be attached to the young woman, I assure you," and Titus, utterly confounded, played with his hat, and breathed hard, and stared in the face of Sir Jeremy Sloth, and hoped that the floor would open. Sir Jeremy made no answer, when, at length, Trumps exclaimed, with energy—" It's my stupidity—I see it all,—my stupidity. Good morning, Sir Jeremy—altogether, my stupidity."

With this full and candid avowal, Titus Trumps vanished from the apartment, and made his way into the street.

" A pickpocket, no doubt," said Sir Jeremy Sloth. " The fellow has the look of a pickpocket —the—what! eh! gone? God bless me! Why didn't I send for a constable?"

CHAPTER IV.

" VERY odd — strange mistake," said Titus to himself, as he trod his way back to the Flower Pot. " Very odd : but Miss Sloth, though not a very, very lovely girl, looks amiable ; and she smiled and —General Wolfe ! Ha ! ha ! After all, if it even had been so, soldiers' daughters are generally no great prizes. Now, Sir Jeremy is very rich ; has the air of it—seems stiff and hard with gold. His daughter is, no doubt, an only child. Ha ! ha ! it was devilish odd—but good must come of it ; yes, something must be sure to turn up."

With these hopeful thoughts, Titus Trumps returned to the Flower Pot. " We didn't send your luggage, sir," said the waiter.

" Certainly not—I told you not to send," replied Titus, shocked for the moment at the recollection of his morning hopes. Trumps retired to his room : he had no sooner closed the door upon himself, than he felt his utter loneliness. He was about to assume his ordinary dress—to take off the suit donned for Miss Wolfe. How his heart sank as his fingers touched his knee-buckles ! He rose, and walked to and fro ; then went to his window— found himself unconsciously counting opposite rows

N 2

of tiles—coughed—whistled, and—sat down again. Intently brooding on the features and fortune of Miss Sloth, Titus heard not, for some time, the waiter's knuckles smiting the chamber-door.   At length, startled from the baronet's daughter, Trumps cried, " come in."

" Do you dine at home to-day, sir?" asked the waiter, with a simper.

" Dine—eh?—why, let me see," and Trumps unconsciously paused to consider if by so doing he should break an appointment—" yes—I think—to-day."   Whether duke, marquis, or earl might feast him on the morrow, Trumps knew not; but he had some small hopes.

" Alone?" asked the waiter.

" Eh? why"—the word came upon Titus like a snow-ball.   Alone—dine alone in—London!   He had looked to be welcomed to twenty boards.   He had, it was true, no acquaintance in the metropolis, yet, with an amiable readiness to make friends in any number, and at the shortest notice, it was hard upon him that he should chew in solitude.   " Yes —I think—alone," said Titus; quickly adding— " that is,—to-day."   New friends, like new flies, might swarm to-morrow.

Again, Titus thought to disrobe, when, on new consideration, he thought it best to remain in his state dress.   He might, after dinner, go to the play, and then and there something might happen. He quitted his room, and as he descended the stairs, observed, with some complacency, the attention he awakened in the household. The maids, with new eagerness, peeped out to look at him—the waiters whispered one another as he passed—the landlady and the landlady's daughter smiled very significantly, yet, as he thought, very graciously. A masculine face—as Trumps imagined, not altogether strange to him—looked suddenly from a corner, and was as suddenly withdrawn.

" When do you dine, sir?" asked Straight, the civilest of waiters, as Trumps seated himself.

" Can't I dine now?" questioned Titus.

" Now, sir," echoed Straight, and stood still and stared at Trumps.

" Have you nothing for dinner?" asked our hero.

" Nothing, sir," mechanically answered Robert; who then bethought himself—" beg pardon—anything," and went to an opposite corner of the room, where three persons sat with that peculiar seriousness in their faces, that betokens expectation of dinner. Robert bent to one of them—muttered a few syllables—jerked his head in the direction of Trumps, accompanying the motion with the words, " perfect gentleman—look at buckles." There was a short pause whilst the parties communed with one another, when Robert, with a backsliding bow, quitted the party, and returned to Trumps. "Can dine with party," said Robert, pointing to the triumvirate.

"Are they gentlemen?" asked Trumps.

"Gentlemen," cried the immoveable Robert.

"They don't look much of the gentlemen," said Titus.

"Don't look," said the laconic Straight.

"Merchants, probably?" was the supposition of Trumps.

"Merchants," replied Robert.

"Ha! and they are generally very simple in their dress," observed Trumps.

"Very simple," said Straight, and then, with an extraordinary prodigality of words, added—"goose for dinner."

"Either of them in the Turkey trade?" asked Trumps, the question, as we think, suggested to him by Robert's brief notice of goose.

"Turkey trade," pronounced the unconscious Robert, "with apple sauce."

Trumps would, we think, have continued the colloquy, had he not scented the odour of the coming bird. He rose as he snuffed the aroma, and advanced to the party. Making a most pains-taking bow, Titus Trumps observed that, "being a perfect stranger to the gentlemen, he felt particularly honoured at having been so readily admitted to their circle. It was an honour that even a prince need not hesitate to accept at the hands of English merchants."

The individuals thus courteously addressed, stared suspiciously at the visitor, and then, as he prepared himself to take a seat, looked at one another. Had Titus observed the faces and gestures of his new company, he would have doubtless thought it very strange that one English merchant should wink and thrust his tongue in his cheek——that the second merchant should purse up his mouth and twitch the elbow of the third commercial man of the British Isles——who should strangely enough acknowledge the action, by bending with the tip of his finger the tip of his nose.

" Bob, you've more goose?" asked one of the merchants, with gaping mouth, and looks of great anxiety.

" More goose," answered Robert, who for once replied to a question with a perfect comprehension of its import; for there *was* more goose.

" I do think, Mr. Chattels," said a second merchant, in a snuff-brown coat, with huge pockets, and a mustard-coloured shag waistcoat, " I do think a goose is the best thing as flies."

" A goose is the bird of paradise incog," answered

Chattels, with authority, and considerable emphasis on the last word.

"What's incog, Chattels?" asked the third merchant.

"Why, it was his lordship who called—you know Lord Maudle, him as I sold that 'Mother and Child' to"?—said Chattels to the second trader.

"I beg your pardon—but did the transaction take place in England—was his lordship in?——" Trumps was proceeding in his query.—

"At that time his lordship was in Indy," answered merchant Chattels.

"I apprehend," observed Trumps with great politeness; "yes—yes," he thought in silence — "blacks—slaves—but a strange bargain to speak of."

"I think I do know him," cried Mr. Hammer, the second merchant—"and I think, Mr. Chattels, considering all that passed in that affair, you might, before me at least, have held your tongue about that 'Mother and Child.'"

"Come, come," said Goings, the third and last merchant—"no old sores. In the way of business like ours, what's one 'Mother and Child' to squabble about?"

"I perceive," communed Trumps with himself— "all great slave-holders: a strange business, but,"

and he looked at his associates, with new charity—
" but, doubtless, very profitable."

" Was it his lordship as called the goose with
sage and onions, paradise incog?" asked Goings,
seeing his friend Hammer become moody at certain
recollections.   " Was it his lordship who?"———

" Damn his lordship, yes, and the goose too,"
cried Chattels, and with at least half the skeleton of
the bird upon his plate, he flung in another bone,
and called Bob " to take away."

" Gentlemen, on a day like this ought we to
quarrel?"   It was Mr. Goings who, on his legs,
looked about him as he put the question—" Quarrel,
—and before a stranger, too?"

" Never mind me—no ceremony before me,"
cried Trumps, with ill-timed suavity.

" When we have done so well to-day—when we
have hung together, as we always ought—and have
kept out all buyers, and have got things at our own
money—why, to quarrel after such a day's work as
this, what is it but flying in the face of providence?"
Thus spoke Mr. Goings.

" Well, I've done, Daniel," said Hammer—
" only, whenever I hear or think of that ' Mother
and Child,' it makes my blood *bile*.   I don't know
how it is, I'd a liking for the article.   But I've
done."

" Article," thought Titus—" how habits of com-

N 3

merce influence the language of a man !   A mother and child—an article !"

Titus Trumps, in his simplicity, thought his companions discoursed of live negroes—of breathing black flesh and blood : he looked upon them as vendors of real bones and muscles, when, in truth, they traded only in the painted likenesses of gods and goddesses, men, women, and children. They were not slave-merchants, they were only picture-brokers. The dinner they were met to consume, had been ordered to dignify the triumph of the day. They had scented a sale of valuable property at Bow, and had carried off, at their own penny, the choicest of the " articles."

CHAPTER V.

" C,ome sir,—what shall we say for you ?" asked Chattels, pushing the bottle towards Trumps.

" Gentlemen," replied our hero, filling—" here is security to property, at home and abroad," and Trumps thought that he had touched, with happy delicacy, on the human goods of the company assembled.

" Sir, you are a gentleman, and not a bit less— it's sentiment as shows the man," declared Hammer, waxing drunk. " The man as wants respect for property, would kill his father," and Hammer glared from under his eyebrows at the tranquil Chattels.

" Damn metaphysics," exclaimed the serious Goings, " let's be jolly. Come, gentlemen, I'll give you a toast that touches us all. May the *harts* flourish !" Now Goings had a peculiar interest in the toast, having, as he felt assured, picked up within the week a superb Corregio for one and sixpence.

" Mr. Goings," cried Chattels, hungry for knowledge—" what may be metaphysics ?"

" Why, this, sir," bellowed Hammer, clenching his raised fist, " metaphysics is the sacredness of property: metaphysics is the right every man has in any thing—even in a ' Mother and Child,' sir ; yes, a ' Mother and Child:'" saying which, Hammer laid his arms upon the table, and gazed like a pointer at Chattels.

Chattels was a philosopher ; for tranquilly, and in the blandest tones, he observed, " Thank you, Mr. Hammer, for the information."

" But, gentlemen, we have forgotten the toast,—" May the arts flourish !" interrupted Trumps.

" And every man keep his own ' Mother and Child,'" added the perturbed spirit of Hammer.

Luckily, at this critical moment, the waiter

entered the room, and approached the table—
" Person desired to see Mr. Trumps."

Trumps jumped up, crying—" Not from the
baronet's?" for hope was alive again, and would
speak.

" Baronet's," answered Robert.

" Oh! pray let the gentleman come in—make
no stranger of us—show him in, Bob," cried
Chattels, who, with his companions, felt a sudden
deference for Mr. Trumps.   " He's very young,
and may be a customer," was the disinterested
thought of Chattels, and perhaps not of him alone.

It was with great difficulty, that Trumps was
prevailed upon to remain.   But he sat in a corner,
and Chattels, with a smile, held him down.   Already, Titus saw a missive from Miss Sloth—
already, read the hour of assignation.   He thought
something would be sure to happen—yes, he knew
something would turn up.

Trumps had just assured himself of his good
fortune, when the messenger "from the baronet's"
entered.   Titus at once recognised in him the
young man who had spirited away " Miss Wolfe"
in the hackney-coach: he saw it—the man was of
the household; perhaps, the secretary of the baronet,
and bore a letter from Miss Sloth.   She might
have selected a more prudent person, for his face

was flushed with liquor, his cravat disordered, and he slid along the floor as though his soles were buttered.

" What! Frank—master Pink—glad to see you, " cried Chattels, and made way for the visitor, who was evidently no stranger to the merchants.

" Gentlemen, I'm your's," said Pink, with a hiccup, tumbling in a heap in a chair, and after peering round, fixing his eyes on Trumps, who smiled and nodded, whilst Pink stared and chuckled.

" And how—how is the excellent Sir Jeremy?" asked Goings.

" Well enough for an old 'un," answered Pink; then looking at Titus—" I believe your name is Trumps?"

" How imprudent!" thought Titus, " to send such a messenger;" then aloud,—" Yes, friend."

" Friend! Come—ha! ha!—well, that's easy."

" If you have any communication to make"— and Trumps rose.

" I have then, I can tell you," said Sir Jeremy Sloth's valet, for Pink was no less a functionary.

" This way, then"—and Titus tried to vacate his corner.

" Not a bit of it; all in good time, Mr. Trumps. The lady upon whose business, I"——

" Hush! for heaven's sake, sir—consider—deli-

cacy—pray be silent," and Trumps was in agony
for the reputation of the baronet's daughter.

— As for delicacy, Mr. Trumps, I hope I know
what that is, as well as any man—but I choose it
at its proper place and season.—Gentlemen," and
Mr. Pink prepared to drink to the company an
universal toast—"here's luck."

— Bravo!" cried Goings, "that's a toast after
my own heart—there's no politics, no party in it;
as a toast for saints and pickpockets."

— There's nothing like being prepared with a
general sentiment; for there's no knowing what
company a man may fall into," said the wise
lacquey. "what say ye, eh?" and he shook the
snoring merchant, Jacob Hammer.

— The greatest rogue unhanged, that Chattels,"
snarled the sleeping dealer.

— Ha! ha!" laughed the apologetic Chattels—
"he's only dreaming."

— Made away with ' Mother and Child'—sell his
father," growled Hammer.

— Wonderful, how true some people dream,"
said Pink, grinning at Chattels, who gulped his
wine.

— Now, now, sir—if you please"—and Trumps
made his way from the table, and touched the valet
on the shoulder.

" Wait for me in the street, and—and I'll join you," said Mr. Pink.

" In the street ! No, no ; in my room," urged the hopeful Trumps.

" Rather not, sir ; for its very important what I have to say to you—and—therefore—in the street," and the valet spoke like a man not to be denied.

Trumps quitted the room, and obediently sought the street. As he walked up and down, he began to calculate the expenses of running away with an heiress—the ready money required to incorporate the maiden flesh of his flesh. Let the worst happen, he had his diamond ring ; that would do something ; besides, there were his cottages ; and, more than all, there was his indulgent and mysteriously wealthy aunt. It was true, Miss Sloth might not be an heiress ; she might be dependent upon the baronet —he might prove inexorable. No matter ; " the first thing," said Titus to himself, " the first thing is to secure the girl. When—when I have married her, something will be sure to turn up."

Whilst Titus was treading the street, walking in an imaginary paradise, Chattels was pressing the wine upon Pink, with whose master the man of pictures had had many profitable dealings. " And how—how is the excellent Sir Jeremy ?"

" How does he like my ' Joseph and his Brethren'—ha !—he had it a bargain—how does he like it?" asked Goings.

" Liked it better than anything—gave it away," answered Pink.

" Gave it away—that beautiful picture !—gave away Joseph 'and his Brethren?'" exclaimed Goings.

" You don't know what a good man, Sir Jeremy is," drawled the valet, " gave it to the parish church of Farisee, just before the last election."

" What a sacrifice !" cried Goings.

" Not at all," replied the politic Pink, " for I've no manner of doubt that every one of the ' brethren' got Sir Jeremy ten plumpers. I've heard some of the members call the baronet Sir Benjamin—ha ! ha !—because he was the chosen of Joseph !"

" And my ' Leda and Swan'—that beautiful jewel —the baronet ha'n't given away that?" asked Chattels, with more than ordinary anxiety.

" Bless your heart, no—what do you take him for? You know he bought it because the lady's face was so like his dear grandmother's. Don't you remember?" asked the valet.

" I—I think I do " answered Chattels, for once taking his memory on trust.

" And he's so fond of it,—ha ! there's few such grandsons in these wicked times—he's so fond of it, that, would you believe it, Mr. Chattels, he's had the lady and the swan gloriously framed, and hung in his own bed-room? Ha! though I'm obliged to live by 'em, the nobility ar'n't what they used to be—few baronets would think of their grandmothers like Sir Jeremy. Ten o'clock—I must go to Mr. Trumps."

" Oh! what is he?" asked Chattels. " A man of wealth?"

" Great fool," replied the valet.—" I've a little matter of business with him, and so—good night, gentlemen — good—good night"—and Mr. Pink staggered along the room, clenching and opening his hands, and muttering, and smiling bitterly at his own fierce thoughts. He reeled into the street, and coming upon Titus, grappled his arm. Hooking himself upon our hero, he gave the word—" All right; march."

" But—but what have you to say to me?—or have you a letter,—or?"——

" All right—come along," cried the valet, becoming every moment more stupid. He rolled on, holding fast of Titus, who, after some minutes, recurred to the subject at his heart. Making a resolute stop, whilst the valet ineffectually tugged at his arm to pull him onward, Trumps thus addressed his companion. " My friend,"—said Titus.

" You be d——d," grunted Mr. Pink, but in so low a note that it escaped the ear of Trumps.

" My friend,—that there may be no mistake, let us understand each other. Do you come to me respecting a lady at the house of Sir Jeremy?"—

" I do," answered the valet quickly, and truly, he being the betrothed of the daughter of " the General Wolfe." Pink repeated—" I do."

" Do you bring a letter?"—inquired Titus with trepidation.

" By no means," replied Mr. Pink—" no letter in the business. Come along," and with sudden force, he pulled Trumps on; who, after a moment's reflection, suffered himself to be carried away, hoping that the valet had been charged to bring him to an interview with the dear expecting fair one. After a silence of some minutes, Trumps was resolved to end all doubt, by putting a plain question : " Did the lady desire you to bring me to her?"

" What—what lady?" asked the valet, and he suddenly stopt, and stared at Trumps.

" What lady? why,—hem !—Miss Sloth?"—answered Titus. The valet checked a violent desire to laugh,—chuckled—slapt his leg, as if welcoming a brilliant thought, then crowed out,—" Well, you are a lucky fellow !" Titus felt satisfied that all was right, and proceeded on, the valet still hanging on his arm, shaking as he staggered, with suppressed merriment.

" And where—where are we to meet ? At her father's house ?" Trumps ventured to inquire.

" You don't think that would be quite right, do you ?" asked Mr. Pink. " I say, sir—when you're married, won't you want a butler ?"

" No doubt—no doubt. But where are we to meet ?—it's getting very late," said Trumps.

" Not at all. Ladies of fashion never run away before midnight ; a minute sooner, would be very low," was the assurance of the valet. " Sir Jeremy is very rich, he can't live long."

" He shall be buried like a sultan," cried Trumps, with animation.

" Do you like shooting, sir ? Ha ! such sport at our country seat in Wilts—such a plenty of game, if afraid of fire-arms, you may kill with your walking-stick."

" But, my good friend, does the lady propose to go off to-night ?"—for even Trumps thought Miss Sloth a little precipitate.

" She told her maid—bless you, she's in the secret—she told General Wolfe's daughter—ha ! ha ! ha !" And here Mr. Pink gave himself up to mirth, and roared with laughter.

" Go on, there," cried a misanthropic watchman from a box. " Go on."

Pink had, generally, a proper respect for the authorities of the land ; but in the present instance, he was certainly deficient in the duties of a citizen; for, instead of complying with the desire of the officer of the peace, he turned and laughed defyingly in his teeth. The watchman was a choleric man; he huddled himself out of his box, and ran at the offender; but Pink, with the good fortune that is said ever to attend on drunkenness, escaped the hand of the watchman, at the same time, visiting the hat of that individual with a playful blow. The watchman, however, was not the man to take a jest in its true spirit, but with his hat over his eyes, furiously dealt his staff about him. That implement was manufactured of the choicest lance-wood, and coming in violent contact with the unsuspecting skull of Trumps, at the time hoping to mollify his reckless assailant, laid our hero flat upon the stones. The whirling rattle of the conqueror called a dozen watchmen to survey the fallen. Bleeding and almost senseless, Trumps was lifted up, the injured functionary rapidly enumerating the thousand insults that had been put upon him.

Trumps put his hand to his head and, the blood trickling through his fingers, benevolently gasped —" My good friend,—I—I—I only hope you mayn't be hanged for this."

" Hanged! Ha! ha! as if a watchman *could* go beyond manslaughter," observed one of the fraternity—" but Starlight," such was the name of the outraged officer—" didn't you say there was two ?"

" Yes,—but this was the rioter," answered Starlight, fixing his hand in the collar of Trumps. " The other's gone peaceably to bed : bring him along," and Titus, with the customary solemnity, was escorted to the watch-house.

Though Starlight was mistaken in the person of the offender, he was pretty correct in his intelligence of the purpose of the absent Mr. Pink. He had gone home to bed, perfectly satisfied with the situation in which he had left his innocent, yet too hopeful rival, for whose punishment he had sought the Flower Pot, where, to the infinite amusement of the whole household, he had, getting drunk the while, narrated the meeting of Titus that morning with the punctilious Sir Jeremy. Had he found Trumps obstinate or impatient in the matter of Miss Wolfe, her lover had determined to thrash him : finding him, however, full of hopes, he was content to leave him as he was.

CHAPTER VI.

THE appearance of Titus Trumps, pale, bruised and bleeding, was in itself sufficient to convince the constable of the night that our hero was some des-

perate offender.   No respectable man could appear
in such a place with a broken head.

"Now, watchman, what's this?" asked the judge
of the watch-house.

"Permit me, sir, to state that there was never
a more wanton,"——began Trumps.

"Silence," growled the constable, "let me hear
the watchman," and the obedient Trumps stood
silently sopping the blood from his skull with his
handkerchief, his cravat and ruffles being dabbled
with gore.

"I was calling the hour, Mr. Constable, and had
my eye upon my lanthorn, when this person," and
Starlight shook his head at Trumps, "came behind
me, and without saying a word, knocked me inhu-
manly on the crown of my hat.   And when I re-
monstrated with him, he called me a d——d old
glowworm, and said he'd kick the very light out of
me.   Saying which, sir, he lifts up his leg, to
assault the lanthorn ; when he loses his balance, and
falling on the corner of a stone, as you see, grazes
his eye."   Thus spoke Starlight, and rarely had
even a watchman shown greater powers of invention.

"What have you to say to this ?   Speak !" cried
the constable of the night.   "I see——not a word
in defence."

Trumps was tongue-tied, not with guilt, but

astonishment. Never mind, he thought—something
will come of it—something must turn up.   He
then, to the great indignation of the presiding constable, and the body of watchmen assembled, proceeded to state that every word uttered by Starlight
was a most flagrant and malicious lie.

" Yes—yes, of course; people in your situation,
—by the way, what's your name?   Trumps, eh?
Titus Trumps?   Ha! ha!   A very good name.
Pray, has Mr. Trumps turned up before?" asked
the constable, and the watchmen shouted at the
pleasantry.—When their humour had subsided,
each public guardian took a wary view of Titus,
but would not venture positively to assert that he
was a known offender.   " And pray, sir, what—
what are you?" asked the constable of Trumps.

" A—gentleman," replied Titus with vehemence.

" That's enough; you must find bail for the
assault—lock him up,"—said the constable.

" But, sir—I insist—I"—exclaimed Trumps
furiously.

" This way," cried a familiar of the watch-house,
and ere he was well aware of the motion, Titus
Trumps—who was at midnight to carry off the
daughter of Sir Jeremy Sloth—was abruptly transferred to a dark and noisome den: his heart sank
as the lock turned.

" Perhaps, however—perhaps, the servant had

fled to inform Miss Sloth of her lover's disaster, and
would return and obtain his release.   Oh! yes—
he was not to be left there all night; and at such
an eventful time—no, something would happen—
something must turn up."   Comforting himself with
this thought, Titus groped about his gaol for a seat.
Stooping and stretching his hand out, he became
suddenly, but not pleasantly, aware of the presence
of a fellow-prisoner, for in the darkness he obtru-
ded his fingers into the open mouth of the sleeping
captive, stretched at length on a bench.   "Hallo!"
exclaimed Titus, as he withdrew his fingers from
the mouth of his neighbour, who startled by their
sudden introduction, had almost made his teeth
meet in them.   "Ugh!" cried Trumps, and wrung
his wounded fingers in the dark.

"Want to steal my teeth?" asked the awakened
prisoner.

"Silence! there," roared a voice from without, and
a staff struck the iron-covered pannel.   "Silence!"

"I—I beg your pardon," said Titus to his
unseen companion.   "I hope, I hav'n't hurt you?"
and still Trumps wrung his fingers.

"Ha! sir," said the man, touched by the tones
and manner of Trumps, "I am sure you wouldn't
hurt anybody—much less a poor wretch like me.
Would you believe it, I hav'n't had a bit of meat
these six days?"

" I—I can easily believe it," said Trumps, tenderly pressing his fingers.

" What—what have you done?" asked the man, and with such apparent solicitude, that Trumps told him his whole story.   As he proceeded, he felt the stranger advance closer on the seat.

" But I—I shall soon be bailed," said Titus.

" I hope to the Lord, you may, sir !   Ha ! sir, you have friends," and the stranger sighed.

" But what misfortune has brought you to this wretched place ?" inquired Trumps.

" Ha ! sir—it's all for asking for a little of my own, sir," replied the prisoner.

" Dear me !   How. my good friend—how ?"

" I—I am the son of a lord," said the man, and he groaned.

" God bless me !" exclaimed Trumps, smitten with sudden interest for his companion. " Really?"

" Really, sir.—His own son—born, sir, through a wedding-ring—if, I had money to get my right. At present, sir, my uncle has the title and the estates.   Ha ! sir—when I think of Diddledum Park,—and see myself a little boy in scarlet coat and breeches trimmed with gold, running after the fallow deer, and my own mother walking with my own father, with a star at his breast and a garter round his leg,—when I remember all this, and think where I now am,"—and again the stranger groaned.

" And your uncle," asked the simple Titus, "does he possess ?"—

" All that should be mine.　And for only stopping him in the street this afternoon, and asking him how he could serve his own flesh in blood in such a manner, he directly cries ' stop thief,' when, without knowing what I did, I ran away.　I was caught, sir, when my cruel uncle—Oh ! I know all he wants is to send me to the plantations—said I'd picked his pocket of his amber-box.　But thank God ! sir—it wasn't true, sir ; no, sir—I defy him to prove it—for it wasn't found upon me.　I own, I was a little up, but who could help it.　I saw my uncle talking to General Bomby, a friend of my father's—ha ! sir, if this was a place for laughing in I could make you laugh to tell you, what when I was a boy I used to call the general—but, to make short, sir, I saw my uncle offer a pinch from my father's own box, and perhaps, I was a little rash"—

" In language, you mean ?" said Trumps.

" Nothing more, sir," said the wronged heir, " and then my uncle gets up a cry of ' stop thief,' and would you believe the wickedness of men,—but, sir, you're from the country, and don't know what men are in London,—would you believe, that in order to give a colour to the story, my barbarous relative flung my own dear father's amber box, gold mounted, with the arms of our family, into a filthy gutter? My poor mother! She's out of this wicked world : all I hope is, she doesn't know I'm here."

" And is this really true?" asked Titus, affected by the earnestness of the injured man.

" True as this watch-house," replied the captive, with great fervour. " Ha! if I had but a friend, I'd share my fortune with him, when——when I got it."

" I——I will be your friend," cried the compassionate Trumps. " I will see that justice is done you,"——Titus felt strong in hope. Yes——he would be the happy means of restoring a wronged heir to his right,——would obtain his lasting gratitude——he would secure, that best of all worldly goods, a real friend.

" And will you——will you stand by me?"——cried the captive. " Oh! give me your hand; let me, dear, kind, generous stranger, press the hand of a noble friend." Saying this, the man sidled close to Trumps, caught his right hand, pressed it, and, not satisfied with that, lavished even more attention on the left. Titus was overpowered.

At this moment, the lock of the prison-door was turned, and an official voice cried out,——" Titus Trumps——a lady wants you."

" Ha! Miss Sloth——I knew she'd come," cried Titus, and was about to rush from the dungeon. A sense of the misfortunes of the remaining captive made him pause. "Your name?" asked Titus hurriedly.

"Edgar—Edgar St. Evremond," answered the prisoner.

"Where—where shall I inquire for you?—speak," said Trumps. "Stay," he added. "My name is Trumps. Do you know the Flower Pot?"

"I shall get out to-morrow," said Edgar. "I'll be there," and the garish light flaring into the dungeon, the captive quickly turned away as if he loathed its beams.

"There, ma'am—is this the fellow?" Such was the question put by the constable of the night to a superbly dressed lady of a sacred age; that is,—of an age not to be touched upon.

"Oh, certainly not that gentleman,"—said the lady, and she curtsied and blushed, and then, as Trumps turned his head, and seeing the wound upon his temple, she exclaimed, almost with a shriek —"gracious heavens, sir! you are not hurt?"

"A very little," said Titus, with a smile of patience.

"Well, if he's not the thief,—you may go back again Mr. Trumps," cried the constable, and the dungeon-door was again unlocked.

"Thief!—thief!" roared Titus, and his honest indignation almost astounded the constable. "How dare you? What do you mean? I ask—how dare you ?"—and here Trumps trembled, and was speechless with rage.

" Why, the fact is this. This lady has been robbed at the playhouse by a good-looking fellow that sat next to her; and we—we paid the compliment to think it might be you. If so be, she doesn't identify you, why, you're all right."

" Many—many million pardons," said the lady. " I hope, sir, you will think me no party to—to the insult that"—and again the lady let her eyelids drop, put her hand to her bosom, and curtsied.

" Well, as you are not the gentleman wanted, Mr. Trumps, you had better—stop—there, you may sit down and warm yourself a little," and the constable directed the attention of Titus to an armchair in the chimney-corner. Titus did not reject the civility, and sat, meditating, seeing the face of Miss Sloth—who had *not* come—in the burning cinders, whilst the constable of the night prepared himself to receive from the lady—whose shoemaker he happened to be—a correct description of the play-house criminal.

Mrs. Sarah Anodyne gave, as the constable considered, a very hurried and imperfect account of the robber, and then, with feminine solicitude, sought to know the misfortunes of the very handsome gentleman in the chimney-corner. " What is the charge?" asked Mrs. Anodyne, in a low, anxious voice.

" Drunkenness and riotous conduct," answered
the constable, with the air of a man quite accustomed to the indiscretion.

" Is that all ?" exclaimed the lady ; and though
she doubtless rejoiced at the lightness of the offence,
she seemed to speak as one disappointed.

" Nearly murdered a watchman," continued the
constable.

"Nothing more ?" coldly observed Mrs. Anodyne.

" That's all we know at present," remarked the
watch-house Rhadamanthus, " but between you and
me, ma'am, I think a good many things will come out."

" He's very good-looking," said the lady, with a
side-long glance at the hopeful Titus.

" Shouldn't wonder if he turns up a tip-top
highwayman," was the opinion of the constable.

" Remarkably handsome," said Mrs. Anodyne.

" Shouldn't be surprised if he had a hand in
stopping the Derby mail."

" Extremely prepossessing," exclaimed the lady.

" The guard received a ball in the shoulder—
isn't expected to live."

" Oh ! a perfect gentleman"—concluded the
admiring female : then, turning quickly to the
constable, Mrs. Anodyne said with great earnestness, " My dear Mr. Pump—you must do me one
little favour—let the gentleman out."

" Do anything to oblige you, ma'am,—so if you
like to bail him,"—

" I ! a stranger !" exclaimed Mrs. Anodyne. " I mean"—so little does sympathizing woman reflect on the stern duty of a night constable—" I mean—let him slip."

" Couldn't ma'am—got a name in the parish to lose.   If, as I say, you like to be bail"—

" I ! Mr. Pump—bail a stranger ! He's evidently, a wild, thoughtless young man, and young men are too apt to misconstrue the humanity of women."

" Well, he seems to know nobody respectable," —said the constable.

" Dear young fellow !" involuntarily exclaimed Mrs. Anodyne.

" So I shall lock him up till the morning."

" Good night, Mr. Pump—good night; come, Frillwell," and Mrs. Anodyne hurriedly departed, accompanied by her matronly maid, who, we presume, in the double capacity of protector and companion, had attended her mistress to the theatre; and thence to give information of the robbery at the watch-house, where silent and motionless, she awaited her lady's further pleasure.

" Come, Mr. Titus Trumps, we can't let you roast there all night, like a chesnut," observed the night constable.

" You are sure nobody has inquired for me, Mr. Constable ?" asked Titus, and Pump shook his head and pointed to the door of the dungeon. " It's very odd—very odd, that nothing has yet turned up," and Trumps laid his hand to his bruised head.

The constable was about to command the return of the prisoner to his cell, when his eye caught the beckoning finger of the maid Frillwell, permitted by the suavity of a watchman to approach Mr. Pump, who gave an attentive ear to the whispers of the lady, and then impressed upon her as she was about to depart,—" Mind—good bail."

The purport of Mrs. Frillwell's speech we know not. We have, however, the pleasure to inform the reader, that Titus was suffered to brood at the fire over the probable advent of the baronet's daughter, and that scarcely a quarter of an hour had elapsed from the departure of Mrs. Frillwell, ere—the constable having first communed with a soft-spoken old lady—Trumps was told that a carriage was ready for him at the door.

" For me ?" exclaimed the delighted Trumps.

" Yes—lady has bailed you," said the night constable.

" What lady?   Was it"—Trumps was convinced it was Miss Sloth—" Was it"—

" The carriage waits, sir," said a footman, touching his hat with great humility to Trumps.

Titus paused for breath; the good fortune—though confidently expected—was, in its fullness, too much for him.   He then thought of his black eye; no matter—perhaps, in a few minutes, 'twould go off. Titus, bowing haughtily to the constable, quitted the watch-house.

" Buggins," wheezed a rheumatic, crooked watchman at the fire, leering contemptuously at the retiring figure of our hero, " Buggins,—see what it is to have a leg."

" Ha !" growled the watchman appealed to, " I only wish I was young and handsome, and had done a little bit o' murder."

Trumps mounted the carriage-steps as if ascending Jacob's ladder. The door was closed — the coachman cracked his whip—and away rolled our hopeful hero.

What is it—let us ask the reader—what is it that gives a peculiar charm, a new and subtle power to lutestring, rustling at dark midnight in the close confines of a carriage?—We humbly ask of sage experience to reveal the philosophy of the fascination; as for Titus Trumps, from head to foot, he trembled as he owned it.

And was Miss Sloth really in the carriage? Trumps was astounded—overcome by the benevolence of woman. He sat speechless and immoveable : again and again the lutestring rustled—when Titus seized an unresisting female hand, and with his own lips thanked his preserver.

Either the way was very short, or the horses the swiftest of their kind, for in about five minutes,

the carriage stopt.   The door was opened; the
footman briefly said, " sir, we're at home," and
Titus descended from the vehicle.   He gave his
hand to the lady, whose face and figure were closely
wrapt from the night air, and led her into the house.

" If—if she should have provided a parson,"
thought the sanguine Titus—" shall I—yes—I
ought—I will marry her."

Trumps was conducted into a very handsome
apartment, where an elegant supper was already
served.   Emotions of love, gratitude, hope, hunger,
possessed him.   He gave loose to his transports,
and caught the fair one in his arms,—" I must—must
gaze upon that lovely face—must "——

The lady, with silent dignity, revealed herself.
Trumps started back—" In heaven's name !" he
cried, " what are you ?"

Any man, if left breath sufficient, would have
put the same question : for when Trumps thought
to behold his amiable heiress, he saw a yellow,
painted old woman, grinning like a witch upon
him.   " Hag !" cried Trumps, with unusual fierce-
ness—" hag !—beldame ! what are you ?"

The woman folded her arms, and making a low
curtsey, said—" Your bail, Mr. Trumps."

Titus, smitten with a sense of his ingratitude,
laid his hand upon his heart, and bowed as to a
goddess.

CHAPTER VII.

TRUMPS left alone, eyed the supper: it was laid for two. "Yes—he saw it—Miss Sloth would come—it was plain enough—the old lady was her friend, and had acted by her direction. Miss Sloth *would* come!" And then `Titus approached the glass and looked at his still blackening eye. "Perhaps,—perhaps, however, she wouldn't see it."

Trumps surveyed the appointments of the room: they were very rich—every thing in the best taste: the pictures very beautiful. Perhaps they sinned a little on the side of subject; what then?—they only exhibited the extreme innocence of the mind of the possessor.

"I am very sorry, indeed, Mr. Trumps, to have kept you waiting," said the old woman, entering the room, "but I was compelled to arrange my dress a little before supper."

"And is the second cover for *her?*" thought Trumps, and he looked towards the table. "I believe, madam—that is, knowing that I owe my liberty to you, I believe I"——

"Not entirely to me, Mr. Trumps," said the old woman. "There is another lady,—but—you see, everybody is not a housekeeper."

" May I not know my preserver ?" asked Trumps.

" Never fear, Mr. Trumps; handsome young fellows like—dear heart ! well, I'd forgot—how is your eye ?"

" 'Twill go off by the morning," said Titus. ' Will the lady come here to-night ?"

" There, now — you men are so impatient ! I think,—not to-night. Well, well, she's a silly woman," said Mrs. Cagely, such being her name. " A silly woman ! she who might marry so well. She who"——

At this moment, the livery servant entered, and whispered to Mrs. Cagely. She suddenly put down her knife and fork. " Pray, sir," said the old lady, " continue your supper—some of my lodgers"——

" Lodgers !" cried Titus.

" That is, two or three gentlemen, unusually merry this evening,—I"——

" I beg your pardon, madam "——for Titus was resolved to be convinced,—" but do you know the family of Sir Jeremy Sloth ?"

" Hush !" quickly cried the hostess, " at this moment—down stairs," and Mrs. Cagely tripped from the room with the vivacity of sixteen.

" She is here, then !" exclaimed Trumps—" I knew it—was sure of it."

Titus had scarcely uttered the words, when, to his astonishment, they were loudly repeated by a

gentleman on the stairs——" She is here——I know it
—I'm sure of it!" cried a loud voice, and then
Titus heard a scuffling, with the denials and entreaties of Mrs. Cagely, together with threats and
masculine oaths.

" Can it be her father come hither in pursuit?"
thought Titus, and as the thought struck him, the
door was flung open, and three gentlemen apparently ripe from the tavern, reeled into the room,
followed by Mrs. Cagely.

" I know she's here——I'll swear it"——roared one
of the gentlemen, whilst the other two growled in
their throats, and shook their fists.

" If you'll believe me, dear Mr. Sloth," cried
Mrs. Cagely to the furious speaker, " dear Mr.
Sloth"——

" I see it"—thought Trumps, " her brother!"

" I tell you, Mother Cagely," cried young Sloth,
" I know she's here——and——I'll have her life."

" As I am an honest woman, Mr. Sloth"——

" I tell you what, Mrs. Cagely—no such protestations; if you must swear, respect our common
sense.   I know the girl's here," exclaimed young
Sloth with rising violence——" she's here, and my
honour's touched——I'll have her life."

Mrs. Cagely expressed herself again and again
ready to swear upon anything, that the lady sought
for was not in her house—that she knew nothing of

her, and further, that she wished to know nothing.
The contest had continued some time when Trumps
began to feel the insignificance of his situation: it
was unmanly in him, he at length considered, to
suffer the whole brunt of the fray to fall on the
venerable Mrs. Cagely.   At all events, he might
champion her against the violence of the gentlemen,
without compromising the name of his beloved
Emily.   So reasoning, he gathered himself up, and
addressed his hostess, almost shaken into tears by
the attack on her nerves.   " Mrs. Cagely," said
our hero, " will you allow me to speak to the gentlemen ?"

" Hear ! hear ! hear !" cried young Sloth, and
his friends.

" I believe, sir," said Titus with severe civility,
" you are the son of Sir Jeremy Sloth, baronet ?"

" Just as you please," answered the easy Sloth,
" if you'd prefer the great Mogul for my father, he
is quite at your service."

" May I then inquire, sir, why you take the
liberty, at this late hour of night"——Titus was
stopt short.

" Mother Cagely," said one of the gentlemen,
who had thrown himself upon a couch, " you
hav'n't an empty kilderkin that you could put your
friend in?—he could then preach to us through
the bung-hole."

" Pray, sir, what wages may Mrs. Cagely give you ? " asked young Sloth.

" Wages, sir ! " cried Trumps.

" Or are you one of those benevolent and eccentric persons, who champion such people gratis ? "

" Don't you know who he is, Sloth," cried the speaker on the sofa. " Don't you know him ? Why, it's Billy Skins the breeches-maker."

A man may sometimes parry the thrust of a wild bull better than a sarcasm. Titus Trumps felt himself that man. At first, too, he thought the gentleman might be mistaken—that, possibly, there might be a strong resemblance between himself and the breeches-maker.

" Ha ! egad, and so it is," exclaimed Sloth—" it is William Skins. And so your wife still beats you, eh, Billy ? Shocking black eye."

" Sir—Mr. Sloth—my name, sir, is Trumps."

" You don't mean it ? " asked young Sloth, with an affected look of wonder.

" Titus Trumps, sir—and since this lady has put herself under my protection"—and here Titus, pointing to Mrs. Cagely, was interrupted by a loud laugh from the three reprobates.

" She *has !* I'll tell your wife, Billy, 'pon my soul I will," cried Sloth, and his companions shouted, to the further confusion of Titus.

" Sir," exclaimed Titus to Sloth, " do you fight ? "

" Why, Skins, why ?" coolly inquired the baronet's son.

" Oh ! Mr. Trumps—not in my house—for the
love of heaven," exclaimed Mrs. Cagely, scenting
blood.

" Do you fight, sir ?" repeated Titus.

" Been out nine-and-fifty times, that's all, my
breeches-maker," answered young Sloth.

" I'm glad of it, sir," said Titus; " though, for
the present, permit me again to state that I am not
a breeches-maker."

" No ?"

" No, sir; yet sir, allow me to add, if I were a
breeches-maker"———

" Well, sir, if you were a breeches-maker ?"

" Seeing, sir, you have been called out so very
often, I should have felt myself particularly fortunate
in your custom."

Really generous minds are ever open to a joke.
A good jest is the touchstone that tries a good fellow.
Sloth and his companions burst into an applauding
shout of laughter.   The gallant on the sofa sprang
up, and clapping Titus on the shoulder, vowed he'd
swear by him for a gentleman and a jolly dog; and
the baronet's son—the victim who had received the
dangerous thrust—shook his assailant by the hand,
protesting that he had taken a sudden liking to
him.

It is stoutly insisted upon, especially by those who have been lucky themselves, that every man, no matter how low and wretched, has one golden offer in his life, if he will but accept it : no one, it is averred, is so neglected by fortune as not to have one chance, even, we presume, in a tin-mine. It is our faith that the dullest man—the merest clod—has his one joke, if he will but utter it. It is evident, that the supremacy of human nature consists in its capacity for jesting ; man acknowledges his common dignity in the jokes of mankind. To suppose, then, that there are benighted individuals whose brains have never throbbed with a jest—who have never felt that expansion of their nature attending the conception of a joke—is to lower them in the scale of created beings. It makes nothing against our position, that a man has never been known to utter a good thing ; like a lady with a loaded blunderbuss in her hand, he may have been afraid of it ; or, with enviable magnanimity, he may have refused to discharge his wit, thinking it dangerous to others in the explosion, and very dangerous indeed to himself in the recoil. We have met with men who, in moments of confidence, have averred that they always had their loaded small-arms about them, but loved their fellow-creatures and themselves too well, ever to pull a trigger. These philanthropists are very properly loud in their condemnation of less amiable men. For our part, we have a particular reverence towards those gentle spirits who " out-Herod Herod," and slay the witlings of their brain—simply because they may be troublesome to others—the moment they are conceived.

We have been so far tempted from the line of our narrative by the retort of Trumps upon young Sloth. It was the only instance recorded in his whole life of his having attempted such a feat: as he gave utterance to the reply, he felt suddenly upraised, elevated—he seemed to joke by inspiration. No one could be more surprised at the jest than Titus himself. Had a diamond, large as any in the crown, fallen from his mouth, he had not been more astonished : he did *not* think it had been in him. To continue our story.

Mrs. Cagely, seeing the agreeable turn of things, addressed young Sloth with renewed fervour : she protested upon every thing that was most dear to her in the next world, and upon every thing very particularly valuable to her in the present, that the lady he sought was not in the house; that she knew not her whereabout, or would, on the instant, be too proud and happy to confess it.

Young Sloth and his friends, mollified by the

humour of Trumps, affected to believe the declaration of Mrs. Cagely, and prepared themselves to depart.

" Perhaps, sir, unless you have more tender business on hand," said Sloth to Trumps, " you will favour us with your company to a bottle?—Stop—why should we go? Can't we pass the rest of the night here?"

" Impossible, gentlemen, on the present occasion: really, what do you take my house for?" asked the indignant hostess.

" Come, come, Mother Cagely—some burgundy. You drink burgundy, Mr. Trumps?" asked one of the gentlemen.

" Certainly — certainly," answered Titus, and then he thought " I have no money; no matter—something will turn up."

" Zounds! my dear Trumps," said young Sloth, and as Titus heard himself familiarly accosted by the baronet's son, his very marrow seemed in a glow —" that's an awkward rap"—and the speaker pointed to the bruise upon the temple and about the right eye of our hero.

" A scoundrel of a watchman," said Titus.

" A fight with a watchman! well, you are a lad of spirit,"—exclaimed Mr. Mims, the airiest of Sloth's companions.

" But—but I'll trounce him to-morrow," cried Trumps.

" Would you like to change your neckcloth and ruffles?"—they were dyed with blood—asked Mrs. Cagely.

" You couldn't oblige me ?" asked Trumps, making from the room, hoping that the offer was made by his hostess to get him quietly from the party, and thus to give him the glad opportunity of falling at the feet of Miss Sloth. " After all," thought Trumps, as he quitted the room, " how lucky that I should become so very intimate with her brother !"

" Where—where's the lady?" asked the anxious Titus, as he found himself outside the door, followed by Mrs. Cagely.

" She has sent word that she couldn't come to-night—will be sure to be here to-morrow," answered the hostess, and merely adding, " John will show you the room," turned away, we presume to attend to the multifarious duties of her hospitable homestead.

" Still, how very lucky that I should have met her brother," again thought Titus. " I have but to make him my friend—and he already seems very much taken with me—to marry Emily with her father's consent. I thought something would

happen—I felt sure that something would turn up."
Such were the hopes, such the self-complacency
of Trumps, whilst engaged at his toilette. Another
neckcloth, with ruffles of texture and web of even
superior fineness to his own—no doubt, thought
Titus, late property of the late husband of Mrs.
Cagely—replaced the blood-stained articles of our
hero, who again joined his new companions, and
was received by them with additional marks of
sudden friendship.

" Really, Mims," said young Sloth, as he crossed
to him, " a very decent lad—very."

" Very, but I think Arcadian," answered Mims
—" hasn't long left his oaten pipe and fleeces."

" Talking of fleeces," replied Sloth confidentially, " let's have cards." Then aloud to Trumps,
" What say you, Mr. Trumps? you play? Plague
on drink only! 'tisn't intellectual. You play?"

" A—a—little," answered Trumps. " I—I"—

" Oh, light work!—very light work! Button-
top stakes—merely button-tops"—said young Sloth.

" I have no cash about me, gentlemen," said
Trumps.

" No true gentleman ever has," answered Mims,
" but the honour of some men—and I am sure
Mr. Titus Trumps is one of them—is far preferable
to ready money."

Trumps gracefully acknowledged the compliment. "If—if" he thought, already forgetful of light stakes, "if I should win a thousand pounds!"

Titus knew nothing of cards—but, for a time, his luck was very great. He won and won, and as he won he quaffed the burgundy, and he seemed, like a young chick of fortune, to nestle warm beneath the wings of hope.

"Ha!" exclaimed Mims, as Trumps played the last card—"ha! I thought you held the best diamond.—What's the matter?"

"Nothing," said Trumps, with sudden paleness—"nothing." But Titus spoke not the truth: as Mims pronounced the word diamond, Trumps instinctively felt his left little finger—the ring was gone! "No matter—most likely took it off when I washed my hands—yes, I must have left it somewhere," concluded Titus—"it's sure to turn up,"—and the clock struck two.

CHAPTER VIII.

NINE o'clock, and the party still at cards. "There—there—it's becoming dissipation," cried young Sloth—"I'm quite—quite satisfied." And well he might be, for Trumps had lost to him and Mims all his first winnings, with the important addition of seven hundred pounds.

" I—I told you—Mr. Sloth," said Titus, his brain in a whirl with wine and a confused sense of his loss—" I told you I had no cash about me."

" Don't mention it—here's pen, ink, and paper; your acknowledgment, and the money any time in the course of to day or to-morrow."

" If something doesn't turn up," thought Trumps, with a pang, as he signed the necessary document—" if something doesn't turn up"—and he staggered from the table to a couch.

" Well! gentlemen," exclaimed Mrs. Cagely, as she bounced into the room—" if ever I suffer any such doings in my house again—drinking and playing all night! Had I known it, do you think I could have rested in my bed?"

" Come here, mother," said young Sloth, in an affectionate voice, to the matronly hostess—" come here. Now, tell me where that jade Maria is, and I'll give you fifty."

" May I never go to heaven, Mr. Sloth, if I know no more about her,"——

" I am sure she called here last night. Well—well—the baggage!—let me catch her! that's all," —and Sloth, Mims, and their quiet, nameless friend, having called a coach, quitted the open mansion of Mrs. Cagely.

" Mr. Trumps— Mr. Trumps,"—cried Mrs.

Cagely, shaking our hero, fallen asleep, on the couch.

"Sweet Emily," muttered Titus, in his heavy slumber.

"Curse Emily!" exclaimed the meek Mrs. Cagely. "Mr. Trumps——I wish Mrs. Anodyne had been further! I have enough to do with my own affairs—Mr. Trumps, I say"——

"Never mind your father," sighed the dreaming Titus.

"Mr. Trump——s," screamed Mrs. Cagely, in a high, prolonged note. Titus shook himself—stretched his legs—opened his eyes—and serenely asked, "What's the matter?"

"Matter! it's nearly ten o'clock, and you must go before the justice," replied the provident bail.

"I didn't leave a diamond ring upon the table, did I?" asked Trumps, and the question was answered by a clap of laughter on the part of Mrs. Cagely.

"Diamonds, forsooth! all your diamonds are on your knees, I take it," said the jocose hostess.

"Come, all's not gone," thought Titus, glancing at the paste in blue-steel, "I have my buckles."

"John, call a coach," ordered Mrs. Cagely, who was particularly assiduous in assisting Trumps to the door; and that the coachman might, by no possibility, drive to the wrong police office, the good woman ordered her footman to take his seat upon the box. "Mind, John, you know where," said Mrs. Cagely, as the coach drove off.

"How very good of her to send her servant!" thought Titus, who in a few minutes was conveyed to the hall of justice. John assisted Trumps to descend; and as he led the tipsy Titus to the door of the office, he muttered gratefully, "saved mistress's bail, however."

"I shall not be long, John," said Titus, and John, with a grin, touched his hat.

Ere Trumps entered the office, he turned again, and saw a carriage suddenly stop at the door. The door was opened, and, to his astonishment, Sir Jeremy Sloth discovered himself. But what was the surprise of Trumps when he beheld the gentle Emily herself in the vehicle! He kissed his hand to her, and the lady blushed and turned away her head. "How kind—how tender—how delightful her attention, to come herself, that she might hear without the least delay, the result of the proceedings!"

Sir Jeremy, without noticing Trumps, stalked into the office. Titus cast a burning glance at Emily, and followed, hoping speedily to dispatch the business, and then to return and carry off Miss Sloth. As Trumps proceeded down the passage, he caught the eye of the complaining watchman in the cause. "That's *him!*" said Starlight, pointing out the delinquent Titus to a companion—"that's him—but we'll teach him how to murder watchmen, for all his fine coat."

Trumps entered the office as the clerk called out the name of "Abraham Swag." The owner of that name was immediately put to the bar. Trumps immediately saw in the accused, his dungeon-friend "Edgar St. Evremond," the wronged heir, who had pressed both his hands with such genuine gratitude for service proffered. "I see it," said Titus to himself. "I see it—how delicate of him to hide his real name!"

The case was immediately gone into. General Bomby swore that he was in conversation with his friend Sir Jeremy Sloth, when the prisoner made a snatch at his gold-mounted amber box, and ran away. He was apprehended, but the box was found in the mud.

Sir Jeremy Sloth, in the most positive and careful manner, and at considerable length, corroborated the evidence of General Bomby.

The prisoner protested that he was very short-sighted—it was his family malady—that he ran against the general without seeing him, who set up a cry of "stop thief!" and that, without knowing what he did, he ran away. As for the box, he never saw it, as was proved by its not being found upon him.

" Why—why doesn't he speak of his wrongs?" thought Trumps—a confused recollection of Edgar's story dawning upon him.

" Very sorry, general, we can do nothing with this case. The property wasn't found upon the prisoner. Abraham Swag, you have had a very lucky escape : never let us see you here again," said the magistrate.

The prisoner bowed, and quitted the dock, taking no heed of the signs made to him by Titus Trumps, who was prevented following the lucky culprit, by the clerk calling—

" Titus Trumps." Titus was put into the place for delinquents, as Sir Jeremy was about to leave the court. The baronet paused near the offender, ascertained that he was really the person he suspected him to be, and then returned and whispered confidentially to the justice. After this, the baronet returned to his coach, and drove a morning round with Miss Sloth.

Starlight gave his evidence with considerable fluency; with the art of a master, painted his own enduring patience, and the savage brutality of the offender, Titus Trumps.

" Pray, have you ever been here before?" asked the magistrate.

" Never," said the muddled Titus.

" You have never been charged with entering

gentlemen's houses under suspicious circumstances, eh?" said the justice. "Does any body know him here?" Fortunately, no officer had any knowledge of the accused. "I suppose, watchman, he was drunk?"

"Your worship, beastly," said Starlight.

"You were not much hurt, watchman, by the assault of the prisoner?" asked the magistrate.

"Providence was upon me," answered Starlight.

"Notwithstanding, the watch must be protected. Titus Trumps, I shall fine you for drunkenness and riotous conduct, twenty shillings. And, now that you are sober, I expect that you will make an apology to that poor man;" but Starlight, with extraordinary magnanimity, expressed himself perfectly satisfied. "Titus Trumps, twenty shillings," said the magistrate.

Titus placed his hand in his empty breeches'-pocket, and found he had not twenty farthings: the shock sobered him.

"I—I must send for the money," said Trumps, confounded. "Oh!" there was hope still, "doubtless, Mrs. Cagely's footman had the money about him:" but to the astonishment of Titus, he discovered, on sending to seek him, that he and the coach were gone. "No matter—I—I must dispatch somebody to the Flower Pot."

"Very well," said an assistant of the office,

" any thing to accommodate, but till the money's paid, we must lock you up."

" Surely, something *must* happen," thought Titus, as he suffered himself to be led towards the strong-room.

" Ha ! what, Mr. Trumps ? Eh ! How's this ?" asked a person, who, to the joy of our hero, was one of the English merchants with whom he had dined the day before. " Don't you know me ? My name's Chattels."

" Very — very — very happy to see you," exclaimed Titus with the deepest sincerity.

" Why—what's that ? " asked the picture-dealer —" Eh? bless me! an awkward blow,"—and Chattels stared at the discoloured eye.

" 'Twill soon go off. I am almost ashamed to ask—but I last night fell into a little fray—the magistrate has convicted, and—the strangest thing in the world !—I really have not twenty shillings about me."

" Say no more, sir—the money's very much at your service," and Chattels produced the welcome guinea.

" I knew something would happen," thought Titus, as he paid the fine ; and generously gave the extra shilling to the poor-box. " What good luck was it brought you here ?"

" Luck ! That vagabond Hammer—it was after

you went—you heard something about the 'Mother and Child'—he's always flinging it in my teeth—well, one word brought another—and—and to make short of it, I'm come here to take out a warrant for him."

The reader must know, that in their professional dealings something had passed between Messrs. Hammer and Chattels, relative to a " Mother and Child" (an undoubted Guido), which, at least in the opinion of one of the parties, did not very favourably illustrate the honesty of Mr. Chattels. *Hinc*—the " warrant."

Chattels transacted his important business, and left the office with Trumps.   " How lucky that I met with you !" cried Titus.

" Ha ! Mr. Trumps, a real friend to a young man in a town like this—especially to a young man of property—for there are sharks, Mr. Trumps, believe me, sir—there are sharks"——

" I have some property," said Titus, and as he spoke, he stood stock-still, and scarcely suppressed a groan.   The thought of his loss to young Sloth fell upon him : his honour was at stake—the money must be raised.

" What's the matter, sir ?" asked Chattels.

" It will be impossible for me to pursue my suit with Miss Sloth until I have paid her brother," thought Titus.   " Mr. Chattels—as I said, I have some property: as a merchant—pardon the liberty I take with you—as a merchant, possibly you could put me in the way to realise—I have some houses"—

" Freehold ?" asked Chattels, smilingly.

" Freehold," answered Trumps.

" Say no more, sir—if my adviser, Tapetight, is satisfied with the title "—

" Thank you, sir—a thousand thanks," exclaimed Trumps, not waiting for more: " how lucky I met with you ! But so it is—I am certainly the most fortunate fellow alive. Whenever I am in difficulty, something is always sure to happen."

" We'll call to-night at the Flower Pot," said Chattels.

" To-night !" cried Trumps—" I must have the money to-day, Mr. Chattels. The fact is"—poor, simple Titus—" I am in desperate want of the money—my name will be dishonoured, unless the money be found to-day."

There is something, says Rochefoucauld, in the distresses of our friends, that is not altogether un-pleasing to us. Certain we are, that the expression of Mr. Chattel's countenance, as Trumps told his necessities, served to illustrate the truth of the Frenchman's maxim.

" Tut—tut, Mr. Trumps—you are very young in the world; the truth is, sir, no man as pays in the end, can be dishonoured.   We'll take a bit of dinner with you at the Flower Pot, at three," concluded Mr. Chattels, and shaking Trumps by the hand, hastily left him.

"The Flower Pot!"   The words immediately brought to the recollection of Titus the promise of Edgar St. Evremond.   Edgar—there was no doubting it—was gone to seek him at the Flower Pot. "Coach," called Titus, and he stept into the ready vehicle.   Put down at the desired inn, Trumps, with his hand to his black eye, commanded Robert to pay the coachman.   A moment Robert hesitated, paid the shilling, and followed Trumps up stairs.

" Mr. St. Evremond has not been here for me?" asked Titus, assured of an affirmative.

" Not been here," replied Robert.

" To be sure—there's been hardly time yet; but hark'ye, Robert—when he comes, let me immediately know; and Robert—I shall dine at home to-day, with—yes—for he will come—with three friends. Egad! how lucky. Mr. Chattels' lawyer may be the very man to assist poor St. Evremond. How fortunate! that things should so have turned up.   Mind—three o'clock, Robert.   What's the matter?" for Robert tarried.

" A woman, five minutes ago, brought little packet," said Robert.

" Where is it ?" exclaimed Trumps.

" There," and Robert pointed to the article on the dressing-table.

" Her picture, no doubt," concluded Trumps, as his eyes devoured the packet. " What *do* you want ?" for Robert lingered.

" Mistress wishes to know if you sleep at home to-night ? "

" Per—perhaps," answered Trumps, hoping the best, but not knowing where he might sleep.

The servant quitted the room, and Trumps, trembling all over, took up the packet. He sat down, holding it unopened in his hand. " Her picture, no doubt," repeated Titus; " and no doubt, set with brilliants."

Trumps broke the seal, and tearing away many covers, came at length to a most touching evidence of woman's tenderness. He gazed upon no painted beauties—but held a real good. He thought to gaze upon the eyes, mouth, the lovely nose and dimpled chin of a doating maiden, accompanied by a letter crammed with sweetest things; and he held a pot of ointment, encircled with a minute direction for its salutary application to a bruise.

" Very strange of her," said Trumps, " but very tender." A piece of paper bore these words. " Would Mr. Trumps think it too much trouble to look in at Mrs. Cagely's, this evening, at ten ?"

" I see it,"— Trumps always saw everything, and the clearer, for the utter darkness that enveloped it—" I see it: she observed my hurt from the carriage, and drove home that she might forward this;" and Titus gazed at the ointment. " How very tender! How lucky, too, that I received the blow—otherwise I hadn't known the delicacy of her affection !"

Titus took his late breakfast in his apartment; and, having amended his toilette, and anointed his eye, whose injuries were flung into shadow by a shade benevolently proffered by the daughter of the landlady, he descended to dine. Mr. Chattels, with his legal friend Tapetight, was punctual.

" Mr. St. Evremond not come ?" asked Titus.

" Not come," replied Robert.

" Very strange—but he *will* come. However, we'll not wait," and the party sat down to dinner.

We cannot for a certainty state what the intentions of Abraham Swag, alias Edgar St. Evremond, might have been had he remained perfectly himself; but this we know, when Trumps most expected him, he was most unfit to appear; being at the time far gone with several early friends in liquor, swallowed to commemorate the escape of Abraham from justice, and bought from the proceeds of a diamond ring, found under the strangest circumstances by the persecuted heir.

As for the negociation between our hero and Mr. Chattels for the sale of the property, the reader will, we think, feel inclined to believe that Mr. Tapetight was tolerably satisfied with the validity of the title, from the fact that his client at once advanced Mr. Trumps one hundred pounds—the remaining eight hundred to be paid on the signing of the deeds; with this proviso, that if, on inspection of the houses, Mr. Chattels should disapprove of the lot, the hundred pounds, for which Titus had given his bond, to be repaid.

Such was the bargain. Titus happily remembered that he had appointed that day or the next for the payment of his debt to young Sloth; and of course the gentleman would not expect it before the later time. Before then, he could obtain a further advance from Mr. Chattels—how very odd that he had turned out to be a picture-merchant!—and, at least, pay the greater part. Besides, before next day, many things might happen; yes, it was almost certain that something would turn up.

CHAPTER IX.

TWENTY minutes, at least, before the appointed hour of ten, Titus drove to the house of Mrs. Cagely, who received him with a sour and withered aspect. " Had Mr. Trumps," she asked with a contemptuous leer, " found his diamond ring?"

" No—but it's no matter, none in the least," replied Trumps airily.

" No—I don't suppose a gentleman like yourself can much miss it," observed the satirical hostess.

" It's very odd, though—very odd where I could have left it; no matter, some day 'twill turn up," said Titus. " And now, my dear Mrs. Cagely," and Trumps with more than his usual tenderness took the cold hand of the ungrateful woman—for she seemed to have wholly forgotten his politeness in the carriage,—" tell me if my charmer"—

" She'll be here at ten," drawled Mrs. Cagely.

" But young Sloth—I trust to-night, he'll not interrupt us?" said Titus. " It's clear she was frightened by him last night."

" He's out of town; and won't come back this week," replied Mrs. Cagely.

" How very lucky!" exclaimed Titus; and again he thought "how very lucky! He can't expect the money before he arrives, and by that time—how very lucky!"

" He's gone as I hear upon particular business— the marriage settlement of his sister."

" Marriage settlement!" repeated Titus, wonderingly. " Marriage settlement!"

" Yes—the match has been long talked about;

she's to marry a gentleman who was here last night."

"So I thought," observed Titus, and he stared vacantly at his informant.

"An old friend of his—Mr. Mims; that very pleasant gentleman," said Mrs. Cagely.

"Good God!" said Titus Trumps.

"What's the matter, sir? You hav'n't lost another diamond ring?" asked the malicious landlady.

"There must really be some mistake in this. Pray answer me, madam—for my peace, my happiness, my honour is involved in this affair. You say Miss Sloth is to marry Mr. Mims?"

"Joined in their very cradles," answered Mrs. Cagely, in a touching tone.

"Then—then—madam, can you inform me, who it is I came here to meet?"

Ere Mrs. Cagely could answer the impatient question of our hero, the footman announced "Mrs. Anodyne;" and the smiling widow swam into the room, and with her frank, bounteous heart melting in her eyes, made a captivating curtsey to Titus Trumps.

Titus drew back—recovered himself—then stammered, "I believe the lady I had the pleasure to meet in—in"—

"The watch-house," said Mrs. Anodyne, with

charming simplicity. "Ha!" she observed, looking archly at the black eye of our hero, "I knew how it would be."

"It's nothing," exclaimed Titus. "Nothing. 'Twill soon go off."

"I'll be bound for it," said Mrs. Anodyne with great vivacity, "or, my dear husband—may he rest, wherever he is!—spent forty years of his life to very little purpose."

Titus said nothing; but he could not conceive what connexion there could possibly be between his bruised eye and the forty years' labour of the late Mr. Anodyne.

"He was a physician, sir, of vast mind, but above the petty arts of practice. Strange, sir, as it may appear, he never kept his carriage."

"Content in his profession to be one of the infantry," observed Trumps.

Mrs. Anodyne smiled and said, "I was a baby when I married him. Wasn't I, Mrs. Cagely?"

"Quite a chick," answered that veracious woman, and folding her arms, she jutted from the room.

"He was more like a grandfather than a husband to me, Mr. Trumps," sighed Mrs. Anodyne. "But the goodness of his life was doubled at his death. Pardon this tedious tribute to his memory, sir; but when I look in your eye, I cannot but feel anew how much mankind are indebted to him."

" Perhaps," thought Trumps, " he attended my father—perhaps she's a bill against me as heir-at-law."

" On his death-bed, he called me to him. ' Adeliza,' he said, ' I have nothing to leave you.'   Ha, sir! that was a cruel hour, indeed."

" It must have been," assented the sympathizing Trumps.

" ' Nothing but this," '—and he gave me carefully sealed a paper. ' In that little packet is the produce of forty years' incessant study—take it, my Adeliza—take it, and heaven bless you with it.' And in that packet, sir, was a secret equal in worth to the mystery of the philosopher's stone."

" Of course, you administered ? " said Trumps.

" Alas, sir! even the alchemist might with all his wisdom perish in the street, wanting the money to set up his furnace. He may be able to turn lead to gold, but he must first buy the lead, sir."

" This is a remarkably sensible woman ! " thought Titus.

" I know not how it is that I have been induced to take this interest in a stranger ! I—you are from the country, sir ? "

" I am, madam," answered Titus, unnecessarily ; as Mrs. Frillington, the maid, had gathered his whole history from the good people at the Flower

Pot. "But, your husband's secret?" pressed Titus—"I don't dare to ask you what it is?"

"Ha! sir," replied Mrs. Anodyne, "you need not, for I am delighted to see you bear its magical effect about you."

"I,—Madam! Where?"

"Your eye, sir—your eye, Mr. Trumps;" and Mrs. Anodyne smiled with new sweetness on the good-looking Titus.

Our hero immediately perceived in the bounteous lady before him the donor of the ointment—immediately understood that that "sovereign remedy" for an outward bruise, was the golden fruit of forty years' study on the part of the late Dr. Anodyne. Titus put his hand to his heart, and bowed his silent thanks to the widow.

"I hope you were not detained long last night? I requested my good friend Mrs. Cagely—she's a charming woman, and has known me from a child —to fly to your release."

"Then it is to you, madam, I owe my deliverance last night from that den?"—asked the grateful Trumps.

"Never think of it, sir—never name it. And pray, sir, pardon what may have seemed a boldness unworthy of my sex; but fearing you were much hurt, and wishing to assure myself that the discovery of my late husband"—

" Where is the ointment to be had, madam ?" asked Titus, somewhat unceremoniously.

" It is not published," answered Mrs. Anodyne, with dignity.

" That's a great pity," said Trumps.

" I have often thought so," said the widow.

" So valuable a discovery," exclaimed Titus.

" A mine of wealth, sir," answered the lady.

" So useful to families," continued Trumps, " if it cures all bruises."

" To the whole civilised world, sir," replied the widow.

" And then such an honourable fortune might be obtained from it. Immense sums, I have heard, are made by lesser things."

" Sums, sir ! There's the Trittleton family— are you aware, sir, that that noble house owes its wealth, and consequently its rank to this simple occurrence,—its founder was the great originator of potted shrimps ? "

" Is it possible ?" asked Trumps.

" Look at their coach-pannel, sir ; they quarter them," said the widow hastily.

" What ! shrimps ?" exclaimed Trumps.

" Why, they choose to call them dolphins,"— said Mrs. Anodyne, with a tragic sneer.

" Well, I wouldn't be above the shrimp-sauce," cried Titus, with commendable humility.

" Why, sir, for what we can tell to the contrary, a coronet may be extracted from an anchovy,"— said the widow.

" May it, indeed ?"

" That is, in sauce—a coronet extracted from sauce.   Sir, it is very curious to look into the beginnings of people."

" And sometimes very disagreeable," rejoined Trumps.

" Would you believe it, sir,—I can point out a family, that has supplied one governor to a colony and three members to parliament, that owed all its original wealth to the introduction of cranberry tarts?   What say you to that, sir ?"

" Why, madam, there, curiously enough, you touch upon one of my tastes.   I think that noble family deserves all it gets," and Titus almost smacked his lips.   " But, why—why, madam, has Dr. Anodyne's"—

" I know what you are about to ask, sir.   Why has it not been given to the world ?   The truth is, a suit in Chancery, a suit, that *must* be decided in my favour, a suit involving many, many thousands"—

Suddenly the eyes of Trumps glowed with lambent fire towards Mrs. Anodyne, and he thought, " How lucky, that Mims marries Miss Sloth !"

" Although the money—it was left by my aunt—

is as nothing to what, with proper care, might be obtained from Dr. Anodyne's bequest."

"You wouldn't"—there was certainly a want of delicacy, both in the question and the manner of Titus—"you wouldn't sell it?"

"Not the whole of it," answered Mrs. Anodyne, with some coldness; and then relenting, she added, "but I should not object, if I approved of the person, to take a partner."

As Mrs. Anodyne rounded her small mouth with these words, Titus Trumps saw in it the type and promise of the wedding ring !

In half-an-hour Titus Trumps and Adeliza Anodyne mutually agreed to a partnership for life.

"I knew something would happen—I was certain something would turn up !" thought Trumps, as the reluctant widow promised to be his.

CHAPTER X.

"A ripe, handsome widow, a promising Chancery-suit, and a patent ointment ! Was ever man so lucky ? How fortunate that he had escaped Miss Sloth ! After all, it was very foolish in a man to marry out of his sphere—he was always looked upon by his wife's family as an interloper." These were the morning thoughts of Titus, lying late in bed at the Flower Pot. " To be sure—the patent was mortgaged for four hundred pounds; but then, luckily, it was in the hands of Mr. Chattels, a good-natured creature, who might be persuaded to do anything." (It certainly was a curious coincidence that the same Mr. Chattels, general dealer, who was about to advance money to our youth of many hopes, had some months since accommodated Mrs. Anodyne with the loan of certain sums, for the payment of which he had of late, in the words of the fair creditor, been "seriously rude.") Titus, however, was resolved, in so important a step as marriage, not to commit himself; no, he was determined to be particularly cautious; and the subjoined dialogue between him and Mr. Chattels, may, in some degree, illustrate the prudence of our hero.

" What do you think of—I believe you know the lady—what do you think of Mrs. Anodyne?" asked Titus of the dealer, who called at noon at the Flower Pot.

" Think of her ! Mr. Trumps, a charming woman—such sense—such spirits—everything that could make a man happy." This was the flattering opinion of Mr. Chattels; who, we may as well state, had had a recent opportunity of confirming it, having just quitted the lady, who possibly might have informed him of her approaching marriage with the youthful Titus.

"That's my opinion," said Titus. " Her husband, the doctor, was very old, eh ?—and very infirm ?"

"Very—but such a head, sir !   He left such a fortune behind him !"

" In land, or money ?" asked Titus, affecting the greatest ignorance.

" In better than anything—in an invention ; only, it's never been used," answered Chattels.

"You don't mean the ' Fortunatus Ointment,' eh ?"

" I offered Mrs. Anodyne five hundred pounds for only a share of it," said Chattels—" but women are obstinate, sir—she wouldn't take it."

" How very lucky," thought Titus.   " And you think it really—a—good thing ?"

" Wonderful.   There's Sackbut—he's clerk of Canaan Chapel—he and his wife fought so, the poor man used to lose half his Sundays—now, he's never seen with a spot upon him.   Folks think his wife's turned quite a lamb—bless you, that's not it— she's worse than ever.   Only poor Sackbut's taken this precaution—he's never without the ointment."

" I thought it wasn't to be purchased," observed Titus.

" No more it is," replied Chattels, " I gave it him."

" And then there's a Chancery suit, which Mrs. Anodyne must gain ?" said Trumps.

" In time," replied the dealer.

" I believe—you'll excuse the question—I believe Mrs. Anodyne is your debtor ?" asked Trumps.

" For a trifle," answered Chattels, " but we won't talk of that. I come now about your houses. You say, you want the money immediately ?"

" I hav'n't heard from young Sloth," thought Trumps—" to be sure, he'll be too busy with this marriage to think of the debt." And then aloud, " why, the truth is, Mr. Chattels, I am about to treat with Mrs. Anodyne for her patent."

" Patent !"

" The patent of the ' Fortunatus Ointment,'" said Trumps; for he thought he would keep his marriage a secret that he might make better terms with the dealer. " I believe the patent is mortgaged to you ?"—

" Yes—the—the prescription—it's all the same. That is, Mrs. Anodyne is under a heavy penalty to me, if she makes use of the secret. By-the-bye, if I had thought of it, I'd have sent you a pot : with a piece no bigger than a pea, your eye would have been quite well."

On this, Trumps began to doubt the instant efficacy of the salve; as he had fairly daubed his

wound with it, to little purpose. Again he thought
—" to be sure, my flesh is very difficult to heal—I
think there never was such flesh—very difficult,
indeed."

" I've advanced her four hundred pounds ; and,
I tell you what—you shall have the document for
three."

" You'll be able to get me that money on my
property ?" asked Trumps, musing.

" In a day or too," replied Chattels.

" Then it's a bargain," and Trumps shook the
dealer's hand. " How lucky!" thought Titus,
" thus I save a hundred."

Days pass on, and every day Titus pays his court
to the widow, who, for various delicate reasons, insists
that their approaching marriage should be kept a
perfect secret. Only one week had elapsed, ere the
happy Trumps was enabled to present Mrs. Anodyne with her bond redeemed from Chattels.
There never was so happy—so grateful a woman !

The next day, Trumps walked to the usual place
of appointment, to that sylvan haunt, Kensington
Gardens. Ere noon, punctual as time itself, Mrs.
Anodyne was wont to be there. For half-an-hour,
Titus lingered, his heart vainly jumping at the
approach of every petticoat. " I'm too early, no
doubt," thought Titus, and he walked solitarily for

another quarter of an hour. "She was always here at twelve—always—oh! I must be too early," saying which, Titus sauntered to the sun-dial. He saw by the shadow on the plate, that the time was a quarter to one. Any other less happy man would have been convinced that the widow had either forgotten, or was careless of her appointment. Not so Titus; for with his eye still upon the shadow he had hope—yes, even looking at the sun-dial, he involuntarily exclaimed—"Perhaps, it's too fast."

Trumps took his way to the house of the convenient Mrs. Cagely, who briefly informed him that Mrs. Anodyne had quitted London for some months; nay, more; that it was very uncertain whether she would ever return.

Titus was astounded at the intelligence. "A base, ungrateful, designing woman!" he cried, to the equable Mrs. Cagely. He was in a very fever of indignation, as he passed down the street; and then he stopt, and said exultingly to himself—"how very lucky I've secured the ointment."

Titus entered the public room of The Flower Pot; he was instantly addressed by Robert.

"Beg your pardon, sir, but gentleman—Mr. Mims—who's been often for you—he's been here."

"How lucky I was out!" thought Trumps.

" He's stuck something on the glass, sir."

Trumps walked to the mirror, and there saw . this pithy notice—

" This is to warn all gentlemen from playing with Titus Trumps, late of Cirencester, Gloucestershire, but now of the Flower Pot, London ; unless the said Titus Trumps first banks his stakes.

" J. S."

" Has anybody been here since this has been up?" asked Titus, who had turned as white as the paper. " Anybody, Robert?"

" One person, sir ;" answered Robert.

" And he—he looked towards the glass,—he" —stammered Titus.

" Looked towards glass," replied Straight.

Trumps bent his brows—bit his nail—then, suddenly brightening up, exclaimed " Never mind—perhaps—perhaps, he couldn't read."

At three that day, Mr. Chattels came to dine at the Flower Pot. He assured Titus, that, very much to his regret, he found it impossible to advance more than four hundred and fifty pounds upon the cottages : money never had been so scarce.

" All the better," thought Titus, when he found the dealer inexorable,—" all the better—I shall have the less to pay back. Very well, Mr. Chattels, four hundred and fifty."

" Of course, I include the picture I spoke of at

thirty—in time it will be worth a hundred," said Chattels.

" I'll send it to my aunt," determined Titus, " of course she'll return me something treble its worth. Very well."

" Well, then, Tapetight will call upon you to-morrow, and conclude the business."

" A fortunate escape for me, that Mrs. Anodyne," observed Titus.

" Ha! sir," replied Chattels—" I'd have been bound for that woman; but there's no trusting any of 'em. You leave the subject of the picture quite to me?"

" Quite: only let it be something handsome," answered Titus.

" Depend upon me, Mr. Trumps," said Chattels, and squeezing his customer's hand, the patron of the fine arts departed.

The next day Tapetight appeared with the necessary documents. Titus signed and held forth his hand for the balance: on which, Mr. Tapetight presented his bill of expenses, making Titus Trumps, Esq. his debtor to the amount of fifty pounds.

" Oh! yes, it's all perfectly right," said Tapetight, in his own pleasant way. " You see, one hundred advanced, three hundred the bond to Mrs. Anodyne"—

"I've secured the 'Fortunatus'" thought Trumps.

"That makes four hundred —thirty for a picture"—

"A parcel for you, sir, from Mr. Chattels," said the servant, presenting it.

"That's it, no doubt," said Tapetight. "Four hundred and thirty—and my bill seventy, leaves just a balance of fifty pounds. You'll find it quite right,—good morning," and the legal man departed.

"No matter—I've secured the ointment," repeated Trumps, as he inspected the parcel. "And here—here's the picture for auntey." For a minute, Titus stared at the likeness of a gentleman in a military dress, and looking at the back of the frame, to his astonishment, read—"Portrait of General Wolfe."

CHAPTER XI.

TITUS—he had made several handsome presents to Mrs. Anodyne—was left with about fifteen shillings in his pocket, a debtor to a lawyer, and the proprietor of the Flower Pot. "Never mind— something will happen. I have," he mused, "the prescription of 'the Fortunatus Ointment,' and something must turn up."

Mr. Tapetight sent a very polite letter, and the

keeper of the Flower Pot presented the bill. Titus was at his wit's end.

He sat, in a deep study of ways and means, when to the extreme astonishment of a gentleman in the coffee-room he jumped up exclaiming,—" I have it ! The tea-pot !"—

Yes, at that moment, the tea-pot—crammed with gold and bank paper—of Miss Virginia Trumps, beamed upon her hopeful nephew; who immediately called for pen, ink, and paper, and wrote a most eloquent letter to the virgin at Cirencester, stating that wealth and honour beyond description could be secured, if she could but be induced to advance only one-twentieth part of the riches contained in her tea-pot: in that valuable " tea-pot brought from Canton by uncle Robert, who had been carried up the country by a black princess, and never heard of again." Only one small handful of gold from that glorious vessel !

In sweet tranquillity Titus awaited the return of post. He received a letter in due season from his aunt. Good, kind old soul ! could she do less than meet his every wish?

Titus broke the seal, and read the letter, in which Miss Virginia Trumps in the briefest manner simply inquired of her nephew, " if he was only playing a joke—or if he was really mad ?"

" She doesn't mean it —no, she can't mean it,"

said Titus—"she'll write again; yes, or if not, something will happen."

And in this belief Titus was justified, for three days afterwards, he was in the Marshalsea, at the suit of Paul Tapetight, attorney-at-law.

"Hadn't you better look out for your bed?" asked a fellow-prisoner of Titus.

"You're very good—but—I shall not be here an hour—I've written to a friend—this is rather an unpleasant calamity—but something will be sure to turn up."

CHAPTER XII.

"Is there no letter to-day?" asked Titus for upwards of the thousandth time, having been three years in the gaol.

"Not to-day."

"Ha! there will be to-morrow. Oh, yes! sure to be something to-morrow."

For once, Titus was a true prophet. On the morrow, a letter, announcing the death of his aunt, with the bequest of her property to himself, enabled him again to breathe the free air, a free man.

Titus went to Gloucestershire, and married a thrifty soul, who suffered him to hope for the best, whilst she *did* for the best. Hence, Titus spent his days in competence and peace ; though, as a proof that his old failing still clung to him, it has been stated, that a neighbour once overheard him advise his little girl, whose canary had flown away, " to take the open cage into the garden—for, perhaps the bird would fly back again."

" Well, Titus, I never heard such a man as you," said Mrs. Trumps, the third cow having died— poisoned, as it was suspected, by some malicious villain—" don't I tell you the last cow is dead?"

" Never mind, my dear, I think the children are tired of milk. Besides, something will turn up. Why, my love, won't you always look at things on the bright side?"

" Bright side!" cried Mrs. Trumps, " but suppose they have no bright side?"

" Then, make one, my dear—make one," answered Titus.

" To *make* a bright side" is after all, not the worst philosophy, and such was ever the matured purpose of our last of men,—TITUS TRUMPS: THE MAN OF " MANY HOPES."

THE END.

PRINTED BY W. WILCOCKSON, ROLLS BUILDINGS, FETTER LANE.

CPSIA information can be obtained
at www.ICGtesting.com
Printed in the USA
BVHW071019150819
555975BV00015B/1174/P